"THE WAY OF RIGHTEOUSNESS program gives clear explanations of the Holy Scriptures. Listeners are now learning clearly about the Old and New Testament which is missing in their religious teachings. Though people like to listen to this program, they are hesitant to give responses for fear of threats. There are a few who are brave enough to tell us that they enjoyed these programs and have even asked for Bibles. In my region having a Bible is more dangerous than having a gun."
—PROGRAM PRODUCER IN KASHMIR, INDIA

"We sponsor the programs in Wolof on a local station three times a week. We get phone calls every time the broadcast airs and have many opportunities to explain the gospel. Even people in our own village, who are notoriously hard to reach, have their radios tuned to the program and are quick to tell us when the radio station doesn't put it on for some reason."
—MEDICAL WORKERS IN THE GAMBIA, WEST AFRICA

"We are seeing lasting fruit from THE WAY OF RIGHTEOUSNESS broadcasts. We receive calls from listeners in isolated areas. In Ghana, a group of 100 people have formed as a fellowship with 10 other cell groups. In Burkina Faso, 7 groups are listening to the radio programs and meeting together. In Ivory Coast, coffee and cocoa plantation workers are turning to Christ."
—TRANS WORLD RADIO MINISTRY DIRECTOR, WEST AFRICA

"I am listening and seeking the truth…."
—EGYPT

"This is so good! I am grateful. I've been listening for two months now…."
—MOROCCO

"By listening to the words of God our family members finally believe in the Lord Jesus after a long process. Praise God!"
—INDONESIA

"I am touched by how Jesus was crucified for our sins. His sacrifice is enough for us. We don't need to sacrifice animals."
—INDIA

"How can we be children of God? We are slaves of God! Your programs are messing up my brains. There are many things in [my faith] that I am not convinced of, so I am willing to understand what the Bible is all about."
—SAUDI ARABIA

Many Prophets.
One Plan.

THE WAY OF RIGHTEOUSNESS

Many Prophets.
One Plan.

100 Chronological Radio Programs
(from West Africa)

P. D. Bramsen

The WAY of RIGHTOUSNESS

by P. D. Bramsen

Copyright © 1998, 2020 ROCK International
This book is a revised version of the 1998 English book.
All new language translations will be translated from this 2020 version.

ISBN: 978-1-62041-010-3

ROCK International
Relief, Opportunity & Care for Kids • Resources Of Crucial Knowledge
www.rockintl.org • **www.king-of-glory.com**
P.O. Box 4766 Greenville, South Carolina 29608

Between 1992 and 1994, this radio series was first written and broadcast in the Wolof language of Senegal, West Africa. Today *The Way of Righteousness* (TWOR) is in scores of languages. To translate, record, or broadcast these 100 programs in a new language, please contact: **resources@rockintl.org**

Unless otherwise indicated, Bible quotations are from the *2016 World English Bible* (WEB), which is in the public domain. In this book, for the sake of TWOR's radio audience unfamiliar with God's Hebrew name *Yahweh* (used in this *WEB Version*), it has been replaced with the more familiar English term, **the LORD** (see page 202).

NOTE: All biblical scriptures in this book are in **bold** and/or indented. When greater clarity or an easier-to-understand English is needed, the *New International Version* or the *New Living Translation* are used and marked NIV or NLT.

Artwork: Dave C. Bramsen | Formatting: Kristen Golson; P.D. Bramsen

Published by:

EVERYDAY PUBLICATIONS INC.
310 Killaly Street West
Port Colborne, ON L3K 6A6
CANADA

T: 905-834-5552
E: books@everydaypublications.org
Web: www.everydaypublications.org
FB: www.facebook.com/E.P.I.Books

Printed in Canada

In the way of righteousness is life,
And in its pathway there is no death.

Prophet Solomon (Proverbs 12:28)

Contents

Part 1
The WAY of RIGHTEOUSNESS
According to
The Torah

Part 2
The WAY of RIGHTEOUSNESS
According to
The Psalms and the Prophets

Part 3
The WAY of RIGHTEOUSNESS
According to
The Gospel

Part 4
The WAY of RIGHTEOUSNESS
Summarized

The WAY of RIGHTEOUSNESS
Appendices

Preface to Revised Edition (2020)

In 1992 when I and my colleague Malick began to write and record this 100-program radio series, we only had in mind one language group: *the Wolof-speakers of Senegal (and The Gambia) of West Africa.* But God had even bigger plans, global plans. Today, for example, Trans World Radio (TWR), one of the world's largest radio/media ministries, reports: *THE WAY OF RIGHTEOUSNESS (TWOR) is a radio program that is expanding rapidly around the TWR world because of its proven ability to explain the Scriptures to Muslims. Airing across the regions, it generates great feedback from listeners including a remarkable number deciding to follow Jesus.*

Oral Learners

As you read (or translate) this 25-hour radio series, keep in mind that it was not written to be a book. This is an English translation of the Wolof radio series. Remember too that the art of speaking is different from the art of writing. In this story-telling journey through the Scriptures of the prophets, expect regular doses of repetition and review. While such redundancy may annoy some readers, oral learners love it and require it. Imagine if you were limited to one 15-minute class per week to hear *the words of eternal life* (John 6:68) and that you had no way to take notes. Would you want the teacher to repeat key concepts? Absolutely. *For precept must be upon precept, precept upon precept, line upon line, line upon line, here a little, there a little.* (Isaiah 28:10)

Extracted or Embedded

The Bible contains hundreds of stories (historical events) which all fit together to make one story – God's story and message of redemption. While many scholarly Bible teachers tend to skip over the stories (like those documented in Genesis) and seek only to present their embedded doctrines (like those explained in Romans), oral learners want to hear the biblical stories *and* their embedded truths about God, man, sin, and salvation. The stories provide context and clarity for the key doctrines about God's way of salvation.

Words or Thoughts

My wife and I have seven grandchildren. When the first was three years old, one day, seeing her daddy reading a book, she pointed to the page and asked, "Are those words?" Oral learners don't think in terms of individual words but in stories and streams of thoughts. It is in the Bible that we discover the words *and* thoughts of our Creator-Owner-Redeemer who says, *"For my thoughts are not your thoughts, neither are your ways my ways…. For as the heavens are higher than the earth, so are my ways higher than your ways and my thoughts than your thoughts."* (Isaiah 55:8-9)

Thinking God's Thoughts After Him

Johannes Kepler (1571-1630), who discovered the laws of planetary motion, believed that since everything was designed by an intelligent Creator, the laws of the universe had to follow a logical pattern. Reflecting on his many discoveries in math, astronomy, and physics, Kepler said, *"I was merely thinking God's thoughts after Him."*

My prayer to God is that this journey through the writings of His prophets may lead millions to do the same: to stop thinking man's invented thoughts and to start thinking God's revealed thoughts.

Recently, a listener in Saudi Arabia wrote: *How can we be children of God? We are slaves of God! Your programs are messing up my brains. There are many things in [my faith] that I am not convinced of, so I am willing to understand what the Bible is all about.*

May this chronological radio series continue to evoke a similar willingness in all who have not yet understood and believed *"all that the prophets have spoken!"* (Luke 24:25-27)

Paul D. Bramsen

South Carolina, 2020

Original Preface (1998)

Yoonu Njub Means *Way Of Righteousness*

The Way of Righteousness is an English translation of *Yoonu Njub*, a series of radio-programs originally written in the Wolof language for the Muslims of Senegal, West Africa. Beginning with the Torah of Moses, these one hundred 15-minute lessons take the listener on a journey through the Scriptures of the prophets to view God's unchanging purpose for mankind and to hear God's thrilling answer to the prophet Job's four-thousand-year-old question, *"How can a man be righteous before God?"* (Job 9:2)

Double Purpose

The reason for making the lessons available in English is twofold:
   1. to facilitate translation into other languages for broadcast worldwide;
   2. to promote reading by English-speaking Muslims and all who want to understand the stories and message of God's prophets.

The Very Religious Wolofs

The Wolof people, for whom this radio series was first produced, are the dominant ethnic group in Senegal, a West African nation on the southern edge of the Sahara. Wolofs are a proud, tall people, known for their wit and warmth, storytelling and hospitality, farming and fishing, elegant clothes and excellent cuisine. Patience and peace are primary cultural values.

More than 99% of Wolofs are Muslim. Wolof society turns around the religion of Islam, with traditional African beliefs mixed in. The widespread use of charms and amulets is one example of their allegiance to their ancestral religion. To Islamic and animistic practices, most Wolofs add the veneration of spiritual guides and intermediaries called *marabouts*, a common phenomenon in much of the Muslim world. As my Wolof language teacher told me, "To follow the requirements of Islam is good, but it does not provide assurance of salvation. The marabouts mediate for us and will help us get into paradise."

In short, most Wolofs are syncretists seeking to satisfy the requirements of Islam, animism, and maraboutism. Like the Athenians mentioned in Scripture, the Wolofs are *"in all things very religious."* (Acts 17:22) But being *religious* does not make one *righteous*. As Wolof NDiaye (a fictional character credited as the source of Wolof wisdom) says: *Even if a log soaks a long time in water it will never become a crocodile.*

Background Story

In 1981, my wife and I and our one-year-old boy, backed by the fervent prayers of the Lord's people, moved to Senegal. After spending a year in the capital city of Dakar, we settled in Saint Louis, a city near the border of the Islamic Republic of Mauritania. Six years, two languages (French and Wolof), two children, and many painful but profitable experiences later, we rejoiced to see one of our Wolof friends submit to God's way of righteousness. Since then, it has been our privilege to witness God's transforming work in the hearts and lives of several others who have declared their faith in the One about whom all the prophets wrote.

Scriptures in the Air

I look back to a scorching hot day on May 18, 1992 as the day that *The Way of Righteousness* radio-series was born. I, along with two of my Senegalese brothers, were in Louga, a large town in northern Senegal. We were seeking to reason with folks about the message of God's prophets, and distribute some illustrated booklets about the prophet Abraham and his sacrificial ram. After a while, some in the crowd began to tear up the literature and shout religious slogans. As we, with saddened hearts, watched them fling the shredded Scriptures into the air, a clear thought came into my mind,

"Is this really the best use of our time? Watching people tear up the Scriptures which they have not yet understood? What we need to do is to prepare a series of chronological lessons that clearly present the stories and message of God's prophets and broadcast them on the national radio station. Then people across the country can hear God's message of salvation and make an informed choice whether to accept it or reject it." I returned home that evening with this clear vision and with a settled confidence that God would somehow open the necessary doors.

Scriptures on the Air

Less than two months later, God opened the way for us to sign a two-year contract with Senegal's national radio station for a once-a-week 15-minute-program that would present *"the stories of the prophets according to the Bible."* It was during that two-year period that the radio-series *Yoonu Njub* came into existence.

Today these Wolof programs are being aired many times a week on various stations within Senegal. God has so worked that these lessons are also being translated and broadcast in the languages of other Muslim people around the world. *Great is our Lord, and mighty in power…His word runs very swiftly!* (Psalm 147:5,15)

Grateful Acknowledgments

I cannot claim originality for this series any more than one who arranges a bouquet can take credit for the fragrant aroma and exquisite beauty of the flowers. These lessons are a simple arrangement of the glorious word of God and a display of the One who is *altogether lovely.* (Song of Solomon 5:16)

I am deeply indebted to so many of God's servants for the creation of these programs. *Malick,* my beloved Wolof brother who was first to believe *all that the prophets have spoken* (Luke 24:25-27), and the voice of *Yoonu Njub,* has done a superb job of correcting and contributing ideas to the original hundred lessons written in the Wolof language. I could not have produced this series without him. I am also indebted to *Trevor McIlwain* of Australia, author of

Firm Foundations. In his excellent studies, Mr. McIlwain uses the chronological method of presenting God's good news. We have used and adapted many of McIlwain's outlines and illustrations.

Eric and Eithne of England and *Marilyn* of Hawaii diligently labored to translate the New Testament and much of the Old Testament into the Wolof language which made our task immeasurably easier. *Richard*, a colleague from Australia, is the one who got the proverbial ball rolling so that these Wolof lessons could begin to be translated into other languages. He translated, almost word for word, the series into English while studying Wolof and playing the audio cassettes of these lessons for the men and women of the village where he and his family live. Richard has been a tremendous encouragement, as have many others, such as my coworker, *Andreas* of Germany, and *Bill* of North Carolina, who helped expand the radio and cassette ministry in Senegal. *Russ and Nancy* in South Carolina proofread the English text and provided helpful critiques and suggestions. *Gerry* in Massachusetts also proofread the lessons despite intense physical pain which has been her companion for more than twenty years. In New Jersey, *Jani* skillfully moved the mouse to format the text into a book. My brother *Dave* did the cover artwork.

I reserve my final expression of heartfelt thanks for my favorite (and only!) wife, *Carol*, and our three faithful children, *Andy, Corrie and Nathan*, who have been a sweet support to me in this ongoing ministry. I could mention *scores of others* who have had a share in this project, but suffice it to say that, in the Lord's work, we do nothing by ourselves. We are workers together and eternally indebted to *the Author and Finisher of the Plan of Salvation* of whom these chronological lessons speak.

Paul D. Bramsen
Senegal, West Africa, 1998

The WAY of
RIGHTEOUSNESS
According to

The Torah

Some of the people studied in this section:

Adam	Isaac
Eve	Jacob
Cain	Joseph
Abel	Moses
Enoch	Aaron
Noah	Pharaoh
Abraham	Joshua
Lot	Ruth
Ishmael	

Part 1

"How can a man be righteous before God?"
The Prophet Job 9:2

Program 1
God Has Spoken

Introduction

Peace be with you, listening friends. We greet you in the name of God, the LORD of peace, who wants everyone to understand and submit to the way of righteousness that He has established and have true peace with Him forever. We are very happy that we can present to you your program, *The Way of Righteousness*. We call this radio program *The Way of Righteousness* because in it we plan to explore the writings of the prophets, which reveal how unrighteous people can become righteous before God.

Which way are you following, the way of righteousness or the way of unrighteousness? Do you want to know the way of righteousness that comes from God? The word of God says: **Blessed are those who hunger and thirst for righteousness, for they shall be filled.** (Matthew 5:6)

Perhaps there are those who think, "We already know the way of righteousness. We don't need to be concerned with the writings of the first prophets. What we know is good enough for us." If this is your attitude, listen to what the prophet of God, Solomon, wrote: **There is a way which seems right to a man, but in the end it leads to death.** (Proverbs 14:12)

In God's Book, in the section called *Psalms*,[1] the prophet David, father of Solomon, spoke much about our need to know the way of righteousness which God has established. He wrote: **There is no one righteous; no, not one. They have all turned away. They have together become unprofitable. There is no one who does good, no, not so much as one.** (Psalm 14:1,3; Romans 3:10,12) That is

---

1 Or: *Zabur*, the Qur'anic term for *the Psalms*

why David also wrote in the Psalms this prayer to the LORD: **Show me your ways…. Teach me your paths. Guide me in your truth, [and lead me by the hand].**[2] (Psalm 25:4-5)

If our Lord God does not guide us in the way of truth, we could never know His way of righteousness. We would be like a child lost in a big city or like a stray sheep in the desert. But the Scripture tells us that **God does not want anyone to perish… but wants all men to be saved and to come to a knowledge of the truth.** (2 Peter 3:9; 1 Timothy 2:4) Friends, nothing is more important than to know for sure that you are in the way of truth that leads to God.

In these *Way of Righteousness* programs we will study the Scriptures chronologically. We will follow the stories of God's prophets one by one from the beginning. God's book has a beginning and an end.[3] That is why we plan to explore the stories found in the Scriptures, beginning where God Himself begins – that is, at the very beginning.

We will learn many important things about God and the prophets. We will see that although many prophets wrote the Holy Scriptures, only one Author inspired the prophets: God. The scriptures of the prophets contain many stories, with one central message: the Good News about how people can be counted as righteous by God.

Therefore we ask you to listen attentively and faithfully to the program *The Way of Righteousness*. Wolof wisdom says: *Slowly, slowly* (and quietly) *one catches the monkey in the garden.* It also says: *A water pail will find the person who waits diligently at the well.* Similarly, God tells us in His word that **He is a rewarder of those who seek him.** (Hebrews 11:6)

To those who truly seek God, He promises, **"You shall seek me, and find me, when you search for me with all your heart."** (Jeremiah 29:13)

---

2 In this book: words in brackets [ ] generally reflect the way a verse was presented in Wolof.
3 Literally in Wolof: *a head and a tail*

Here on *The Way of Righteousness* programs we will increase our knowledge about God and His word. Do you know what God is like? Or where Satan came from? Do you know why God created man? Or how sin entered the beautiful world that God made? Have you ever read the amazing story about God's prophet, Noah, and the flood? Do you really know what the prophets of God wrote? Do you know why Abraham was called the Friend of God? Can you clearly explain to your friends or your children the message of the prophets?

Thousands of years ago, the prophet Job[4] asked the question, **"How can man be just with God?"** (Job 9:2) Do you know God's answer to Job's question? Do you know how you can be declared righteous by God? If you want to know God's response to this question and many others, we invite you to listen to the program *The Way of Righteousness*. Truly the word of God is deep, wonderful, alive and powerful. And something else: the word of God hides nothing. It reveals to us what man is really like. As the Scripture declares: **There is no creature that is hidden from his sight, but all things are naked and laid open before the eyes of him to whom we must give an account.** (Hebrews 4:13)

In the time left today there is an important truth that we must grasp. It is this: **God has spoken.** (Psalm 60:6) God, the Most High, has spoken. God has spoken to man (mankind) and God wants to speak to you. If you received a letter from a great king in a far-away land, would you read it? Would you consider what he had written to you in the letter? Would you pay attention to the words of the king? How much more ought we to pay attention when it is the Most High God who is speaking to us!

How has God spoken to man? The Holy Scripture tells us: **God, having in the past spoken to the fathers through the prophets at many times and in various ways.** (Hebrews 1:1) Yes, one of the main ways God has spoken to man is through the prophets. In the past God appointed certain men to proclaim His word and to write it down in books (scrolls). The word of God says:

---

4 Qur'anic/Arabic: *Ayyub*

perfectly-prepared rice and fish.[6] We all agree that rice and fish is delicious to eat and good for the body, but unless I eat it, it is of no benefit to me. I must eat it. In a similar way, I must partake of the word of God, which nourishes my heart, if I want benefit from it. In the Torah,[7] the prophet Moses wrote: **Man does not live by bread only, but man lives by every word that proceeds out of the LORD's mouth.** (Deuteronomy 8:3) And Jesus the Messiah said, **"Blessed are those who hunger and thirst after righteousness, for they shall be filled. "**(Matthew 5:6)

Do you hunger for the word of God? It is food, delicious food. It is not food that nourishes your body but food that nourishes your heart and soul.

So we say to you who fear God and revere His word: make a serious effort to follow regularly the program *The Way of Righteousness.* In this way you will increase your knowledge of what God said long ago through His prophets and learn how you can be made righteous before God the Holy One. **God has spoken** – and He wants to speak to you!

Before we leave you today, we must clarify one more thing. In our programs we will not rely on anything or anyone except that which is found in the writings of God's prophets. We who prepare these programs know nothing about God's Truth apart from what God has made known in the Scriptures. What the prophet John, the son of Zacharias, declared in the Gospel[8] is true: **A man can receive nothing unless it has been given him from heaven.** (John 3:27) We dare not rely on our own knowledge. We rely on God's word alone. Our desire is to make known what God has declared in His word through His prophets.

Do you know what God has said in the writings of the prophets? Are you among those who hunger and thirst for the word of God and for the righteousness that only He can provide? In His holy

---

6 *ceebu jën:* Senegal's national dish
7 Or: *Tawrat,* Qur'anic/Arabic term for the *Torah/Pentateuch*
8 Or: *Injil*

word, God has revealed Himself and His righteous way of salvation. We invite you to explore the Scriptures with us so that you might truly understand what God has said. The word of God tells us: **For whatever things were written before were written for our learning, that through perseverance and through encouragement of the Scriptures we might have hope.** (Romans 15:4)

May we all be certain of this one thing: God has spoken and He wants everyone to listen and live. Old and young, men and women, rich and poor, God is saying to every one of us: **Come to me with your ears wide open. Listen, and you will find life. I will make an everlasting covenant with you.** (Isaiah 55:3 NLT)

Friends, thank you for listening. In our next program, God willing, we will present our second lesson, entitled: *What is God Like?* If you have any questions about what you have heard today, we invite you to contact us....[9]
Email: **resources@rockintl.org**
Website: **www.king-of-glory.com**

May God bless you as you meditate on this great invitation from Him to you:

> **Come to me with your ears wide open.**
> **Listen, and you will find life.**
> (Isaiah 55:3 NLT)

---

9 In Wolof, each *Way of Righteousness* program concludes with contact information for listeners who have questions or comments. Sometimes a gift is offered to any who write, such as a scripture portion or a booklet (E.g. YOUR STORY www.king-of-glory.com). In this book version of the radio series, such closing information has been mostly removed.

Program 2

What Is God Like?

Genesis 1

Peace be with you, listening friends. We greet you in the name of God, the LORD of peace, who wants everyone to understand and submit to the way of righteousness that He has established and have true peace with Him forever. We are happy to be able to return today to present your program, *The Way of Righteousness*.[10]

In our first program, we talked about the writings of the prophets. We learned that there are many prophets who wrote the Holy Scriptures, but that there is only one Author. That One is God. In that first lesson we concluded with an important thought. It was this: **God has spoken.** God has spoken to mankind through the prophets, and He wants each of us to listen to Him. God wants to speak to us through the writings of the prophets. God never changes nor does His word. In every generation God has protected His word, which is why He says, **The Scripture can't be broken.** (John 10:35) **The world is passing away... but the Lord's word endures forever.** (1 John 2:17; 1 Peter 1:25)

Today we are going to move into the first section of the Holy Scriptures. It is called the Torah.[11] About 3500 years ago God planted this book in the mind of a man named Moses.[12] God told Moses what to write and Moses wrote it down. The Torah consists of five books, or five parts. The first part is known as Genesis.[13]

10 Note to translators: **This same opening greeting is used in all 100 radio programs.** But to save space and keep the story flowing, in this book – in programs 3-99 – this introduction has been removed. But it is an important element in each of TWOR's 100 programs.
11 *Tawrat*
12 Qur'an/Arabic: *Musa*
13 Literally in Wolof: *The Beginning*

There are fifty chapters in the book of Genesis. The first book is called Genesis because it tells us what happened in *the beginning*.

It is important for us to know the first book of the Torah very well because it is the foundation that God laid so that we might understand what He says in the other books of the prophets that follow. As we study this book we will deepen our knowledge of many important truths. We will learn about God and what He is like. We will read about the angels and Satan, the heavens and the earth, animals and man. We will see how sin and shame entered the world and brought with it great destruction and sorrow. However, we will also examine carefully the way of salvation which the Lord God planned and provided so that sinners can return to Him and have a wonderful relationship with Him.

In the first stories we will see the first people, the first sin, and the first murder. We will read about the first false religions, the first prophets, and the first nations. We will reflect on the stories of Adam and Eve, Cain and Abel, Noah and the flood, God's prophet Abraham and why he was called the friend of God. We will see Ishmael and Isaac, Esau and Jacob, and Joseph and his wicked brothers. The first book of the Torah contains all this and much more. And so, friends, we ask you to listen carefully, because the time has arrived for us to begin our journey together through the scriptures of the prophets.

In the first book of the Torah, chapter 1, verse 1, we read:
In the beginning God created the heavens and the earth.
(Genesis 1:1) This is where we must begin our lesson in the Holy Scriptures, because it is here that God Himself begins His Book.

Let us consider some of the implications of this verse. What existed before God created the heavens and the earth? What was there before the world existed? The Scriptures show us that nothing existed except God. That is why it says: **In the beginning ... God.** Everything that we can see and touch has a beginning. Long, long ago, there was a time when there was no sky or earth, no ocean or trees. In the beginning, before God created the heavens and the earth, there was no sun, no moon, no stars. In the beginning, there were no men or angels. There was a time when there was nothing as we know it today. Nothing except God.

That is why we read in the first verse of the first book of the Holy Scriptures: **In the beginning God created the heavens and the earth.** The Scriptures do not say: *In the beginning God and the angels* or *In the beginning God and men*. No. The Scripture tells us: **In the beginning God.** In the beginning, when nothing yet existed, before any angels or people existed, there was only One who was living. That One is God.

In our world some say, "I cannot see God; therefore there is no God." To those people who deny that God exists we would like to ask a few questions. Have you ever seen an atom? Or the oxygen you breathe? Have you ever seen the wind? You cannot see the wind, yet you know that the wind exists because you can see what it does. You can see the trees that move in the wind, but the wind itself no one can see. You cannot hold the wind in your hand, but you can feel its cooling breeze. That is how it is with God. We cannot see God because God is invisible to human eyes. However, we know that God exists because we see what God created. The Scripture says: **For since the creation of the world God's invisible qualities – his eternal power and divine nature – have been clearly seen, being understood from what has been made, so that people are without excuse.** (Romans 1:20 NIV)

Another thing we can learn from the first verse of the Torah is this: God has no beginning. God was not created in the beginning. He is the Lord of Eternity. Everything that we know and see here in our world had a beginning. But God had no beginning. He has no origin. He has no equal. Only He existed in the beginning. No one gave birth to Him. No one created Him, and He did not create Himself. That is why we read in the Holy Scriptures: **In the beginning God.** He alone has no beginning. He is the One who has always existed and lives forever. The LORD[14] is His name.

---

14 Literally in Wolof: *The Eternal One*

What He is like today, He was like yesterday. What He was yesterday, He will be forever. God never changes.

There is something else we can learn from the verse that says, **In the beginning God created the heavens and the earth.** It is this. God is great. God, who created everything, is greater than everything and everyone. He is the Lord of Creation. Truly, with our whole heart we can declare: "Allahu Akbar!" God is greater! He has no equal. He is greater than everything in the world – ocean, wind, sun and stars. He is wiser and more powerful than all spirits and people. He is worthy of glory forever. **Because he who built the house has more honor than the house** (Hebrews 3:3-4), so God is superior to everything, because He created everything. God is great. He lives by His own power. He doesn't depend on anything. He is not dependent on anyone. God is greater than everything. He needs nothing. He needs no one. He is the Great One.

We humans have many needs. Every day we must breathe and sleep, eat and drink. We need sun and rain, food and water, clothing and housing, father and mother, friends and money and so much more. How many are our needs! But the LORD, who created everything, needs nothing. He does not hunger. He does not thirst. He never gets tired. He does not need a body like we do. He has no limits. He has no end. He is the Eternal. The All-Powerful One.

Now, here is an important question. If God is not like us, what is He like? The Scripture responds to that question with a clear answer. It says: **God is spirit, and those who worship him must worship in spirit and truth.** (John 4:24) What is God like? God is spirit. Man is body and spirit, but God is only spirit. The Spirit of God has no limit. He is everywhere. We are limited by time, but God lives outside of time. God is above everything and everyone. He fills everything. He sees everything. Night and day are the same to Him. If you hide in your room, God is there and He sees you. God knows everything. He knows your thoughts and the intentions of your heart.

God is greater.

So what is God like? Perhaps we can summarize what we have studied today in this way: God is not like anyone. God is God and He has no equal. In future lessons of your program *The Way of Righteousness* we will increase our understanding of the character of God. In the Holy Scriptures, God has hundreds and hundreds of names and titles. He is *The LORD. The Most High. The Almighty. The Creator. The Author of Life. The Righteous Judge. The Holy One. The Compassionate One. The God of Love.* He is *the living and true God, the King of kings,* and *Lord of lords.*

In truth, God, who created the heavens and the earth in the beginning, is the Great One. Of Him the Scriptures say:

> [33]**Oh the depth of the riches** both of the wisdom and the knowledge of God! …[36] For of him, and through him, and to him are all things. To him be the glory forever! (Romans 11:33,36)

> [15]**Who is the blessed and only Ruler**, the King of kings, and Lord of lords. [16]He alone has immortality, dwelling in unapproachable light, whom no man has seen, nor can see: to whom be honor and eternal power. Amen. (1 Timothy 6:15-16)

In another chapter, the prophet Moses praises God in a beautiful song that says: **Great and marvelous are your works, Lord God, the Almighty! Righteous and true are your ways, you King of the nations. Who wouldn't fear you, Lord, and glorify your name? For you only are holy.** (Revelation 15:3-4)

God is infinitely great! That is what the first verse of God's word teaches us when it declares: **In the beginning God….**

And so friends, may we keep in our minds this truth that we have heard today: **In the beginning GOD.**

Only God the Creator existed in the beginning, and therefore, only God can reveal to us the truth about what happened in the beginning. Only God can reveal to us the truth about what will happen in the hereafter. And only God can reveal to us the truth about what He is like.

Yes, we know that some people say, "No one can know God or what will happen in the hereafter!" Nevertheless, the writings of the prophets tell us that we can know God and that we can know where we will spend eternity, for the word of God says:

> [13]**These things I have written to you** who believe in the name of the Son of God, that you may know that you have eternal life, and that you may [20]know him who is true, … the true God and eternal life. (1 John 5:13,20)

> [9]**"What no eye has seen, what no ear has heard**, and what no human mind has conceived" the things God has prepared for those who love him – [10]these are the things God has revealed to us by his Spirit. (1 Corinthians 2:9-10 NIV)

You who are listening to us today, do you know God personally? Or is He, for you, simply the great Creator who is far away and unknowable? Dear friends, God wants you to know Him and to live with Him forever. The scriptures of the prophets teach us how we can have a wonderful and close relationship with God. However, we must open our ears and our minds and our hearts to what God is saying to us. Listen to what God says in His holy word: **Look to me, and be saved, all the ends of the earth; for I am God, and there is no other.** (Isaiah 45:22)

Friends, this is where we must stop today. If you would like to listen to the audio version of this program, we invite you to visit: www.king-of-glory.com

Thank you for being with us today. In our next program, God willing, we will look into a fascinating topic: *Satan and the Angels*. Do you know the true story about where they come from?

God bless you as you consider this word from the Holy Scriptures:

> **God is spirit, and those who worship him must worship in spirit and truth.** (John 4:24)

Program 3

Satan and the Angels

Isaiah 14; Ezekiel 28

In our last program we talked about the very first verse in the Holy Scriptures, which says: **In the beginning God created the heavens and the earth.** (Genesis 1:1) We saw that everything has a beginning except God. In the beginning, when there was nothing, only One was living. That One was God – the true and living God! He alone existed in the beginning. He is the Lord of Eternity. God is great and has no equal. He has no beginning and no end. He has no needs. He is not limited. God is spirit and can be everywhere at once. He is above everything and everyone. He fills everything. He sees everything. He knows everything. He is unique. God is great! That is why the Scriptures say: **He alone has immortality, dwelling in unapproachable light, whom no man has seen, nor can see: to whom be honor and eternal power. Amen.** (1 Timothy 6:16)

Today we have come to our third lesson in the scriptures of the prophets. We intend to consider what God's word teaches about the angels and Satan. Do you know where angels come from? Or where Satan and demons come from? We could not know about such things if God had not told them to us. But God does tell us about them, in His word. Let us therefore carefully examine the Holy Scriptures, so that we might know the truth about the angels and Satan.

We remind you that in *The Way of Righteousness* programs we are doing a chronological[15] study of the stories and writings of the prophets, from beginning to end. That is why in the last broadcast

---

15 Literally in Wolof: we are *one by one-ing* the stories…

will make you free." (John 8:32) Do you know the truth that can free you from the terrible devices of Satan? Let us not forget: Satan is wiser than we are, but God is infinitely wiser than Satan. Satan is stronger than we are, but God is infinitely stronger than Satan. The devil and his demons are no match for God.

Do you know the word of Truth that can deliver you from Satan's power? Many people do not like to hear God's truth. Why do people refuse to listen to the truth? It is because the devil has deceived them. He incites them to believe what is not true. To be sure, the truth is not always pleasant to hear. As the proverb says: *Truth is a hot pepper.* But if you know the truth of God's word and believe it, you will be freed from Satan's power. God's truth can free people from Satan's lies. But you must know the truth and believe it.

Listen to what the word of God says:

> **Beloved, don't believe every spirit**, but test the spirits, whether they are of God, because many false prophets have gone out into the world. (1 John 4:1) [20] Don't despise [the words of the prophets]. [21]Test all things, and hold firmly that which is good. [22]Abstain from every form of evil. (1 Thessalonians 5:20-22)

Do you really know what the prophets of God have written? Do you understand the Word of Truth? Do you believe it in your heart?

Friends, thank you for listening. We invite you to join us in the next broadcast, when we study together: *How God made the world.*

We look forward to being with you next time. May God bless you as you consider the powerful promise in His word that says:

> **You will know the truth, and the truth will make you free.**
> (John 8:32)

How God Made the World

Genesis 1

L ast time we focused on what God's prophets have written about the angels and Satan. We learned that, in the beginning, God created millions of spirits, calling them angels. Among the angels was one who was more intelligent and more beautiful than the others. That angel's name was Lucifer. However, there came a day when Lucifer exalted himself in his heart and showed contempt for God by wanting to take God's place. A third of the angels chose to follow Lucifer in his sin. And so God, who cannot tolerate those who rebel against Him, expelled Lucifer and the evil angels from His holy presence. Lucifer's name was changed to *Satan*, meaning *adversary*. When God expelled Satan and his angels, He created for them the fires of hell, which will never be extinguished. One day God will throw Satan and all who follow him into that fire. But Satan has not yet been cast into hell. He is in the world, seeking to deceive whomever he can so that they too will perish.

Today is our fourth lesson in the writings of the prophets. In the first section of the Torah, called *Genesis*, in the first chapter, in the first two verses, we read: **In the beginning, God created the heavens and the earth. The earth was formless and empty. Darkness was on the surface of the deep and God's Spirit was hovering over the surface of the waters.** (Genesis 1:1-2)

In the beginning, when God first created the heavens and the earth, everything was formless and dark. But God planned to create humans, who would have the capacity to know Him, to love Him and to obey Him forever. But before He made the first man and woman, God planned to make a beautiful world where people could live in true prosperity.

Today then, we will see how God created and prepared the world for the people whom He planned to create.

What does the Scripture say about how God created the world? It says: **For in six days the LORD made heaven and earth, the sea, and all that is in them.** (Exodus 20:11) Now let us dig into the first chapter of the Torah to see what God created in those six days.

1. About the first day, the Scriptures say,

> [2]**And God's Spirit was hovering** over the surface of the waters.
> [3]God said, "Let there be light," and there was light. [4]God saw the light, and saw that it was good. God divided the light from the darkness. [5]God called the light "day", and the darkness he called "night". There was evening and there was morning, the first day. (Genesis 1:2-5)

What did God do on the first day of creation? He commanded light to pierce the darkness. Later the sun would shine on Earth, but not on Day One. God wants us to know that He is the Source of light. The Scripture says, **God is light; and in him is no darkness at all.** (1 John 1:5)

2. Concerning the second day of creation, the Scripture says,

> [6]**God said, "Let there be an expanse** in the middle of the waters, and let it divide the waters from the waters." [7]God made the expanse, and divided the waters which were under the expanse from the waters which were above the expanse; and it was so. [8]God called the expanse "sky". (Genesis 1:6-8)

On the second day God created what we call *the atmosphere* – the sky around the earth. The atmosphere surrounds the world and contains the air we breathe. That same atmosphere protects everything and everyone from the heat of the sun and many other calamities. Without this special sky that our Almighty God created on the second day we could not live on the earth.

3. On the third day God created the oceans, the dry land, and vegetation. Listen to what the Scripture says:

> [9]**God said, "Let the waters** under the sky be gathered together to one place, and let the dry land appear;" and it was so. [10]God called the dry land "earth", and the gathering together of the waters he called "seas". God saw that it was good.

> [11]**God said, "Let the earth yield grass,** herbs yielding seeds, and fruit trees bearing fruit after their kind, with their seeds in it, on the earth;" and it was so…. [12]And God saw that it was good. [13]There was evening and there was morning, a third day. (Genesis 1:9-13)

So we see that on the third day God, the Great Designer, created the oceans and the rivers, along with thousands of different types of trees and plants, each with its own fruit and seeds. What a delicious variety of foods God made: mangoes, bananas, coconuts, melons, tomatoes, cabbages, carrots, rice, millet, peanuts, and thousands of other kinds of food. And God said of all that He had created, "It is good."

Everything that God makes and does is good, wonderful and perfect. We have already seen that God cannot produce what is bad, because God is perfect and good.

Perhaps some of you are asking, "If God is good, then why is the world full of evil and strife? Why didn't my field produce well this year? Why is my child sick? If God is good, why does evil come forth from man?" Truly, these are important questions, and the Holy Scriptures give us satisfying answers, which we will hear in coming programs. For today though, let us simply keep in mind this important truth: God is good, and consequently everything that God created was good.

Let us take a moment to consider the generous goodness of God. We just heard how He created the trees on the third day. Do you know why God created the trees with their fruit? Did God need them? Did He create the trees full of lovely fruit to satisfy His own hunger? No. God the Creator is never hungry and needs nothing. Why, then, did God create the trees? The Scriptures inform us that God in His goodness created everything for humans, whom He planned to create on the sixth day.

Do you recognize the goodness of God? Can you taste a mango with its delicious flavor, or smell a flower with its lovely scent, and not thank God for His goodness? Can you see a tree and not thank the One who made it for you? Without trees, life would be horrible. Without trees, we would not have delicious fruit to eat, or shade in which to relax during the heat of the day, or leaves for tea and medicine. We would not have wood to burn, or timber to build a house, boat, or chair. Without trees, where would birds build their nests? Where would the animals of the forest live? Without trees, life on earth would be impossible. Trees remove carbon dioxide (CO_2) from the atmosphere and produce the oxygen (O_2) in the air we breathe. And trees are only one of the thousands of kinds of things that God made for us so that we can live and be happy. God wants us to recognize His goodness. That is why the prophet David wrote in the Psalms: **Taste and see that the LORD is good.** (Psalm 34:8)

4. On the fourth day,

> **God said, "Let there be lights** in the expanse of the sky to divide the day from the night; and let them be for signs to mark seasons, days, and years;" (Genesis 1:14)

God simply gave the order and the sun, the moon and the stars came into existence in the sky. God spoke another word and the earth began to orbit the sun. He spoke again and the moon began to orbit the earth.

What did God use to create everything in the world? What does the Scripture tell us? It says:

> **The universe has been framed by the word of God**, so that what is seen has not been made out of things which are visible. (Hebrews 11:3)

¹**In the beginning was the Word**, and the Word was with God, and the Word was God. ²The same was in the beginning with God. ³All things were made through him. Without him, nothing was made that has been made. (John 1:1-3)

We have already read that on the first day God simply spoke and said, "Let there be light," and there was light. On the second day God said, "Let there be an expanse" and there was an expanse. On the third day God spoke again and what He spoke came into existence, and so forth. Now, therefore, what did God use to create everything that is in the world? God used nothing except His word. All He did was speak, and what He spoke came to pass. God created everything by His word. And the Scripture tells us that not only did God create everything by His word, but that God also sustains everything (holds all things together) by His word. It is by the power of God's word that the moon and the stars stay in the sky in their appointed orbits. It is by the command of God that the sun rises and sets each day at its appointed times. Just think how terrible our lives would be if we did not know whether the sun would rise tomorrow or not. The Scriptures tell us that **God is faithful.**[18] (1 Corinthians 1:9) You can depend on Him. He never goes back on His word. He never changes. **The Lord's word endures forever.** (1 Peter 1:25)

5. On the fifth day, God, the Author of life, created thousands and thousands of kinds of fish and birds. The Scripture says:

²⁰**God said, "Let the waters abound** with living creatures, and let birds fly above the earth in the open expanse of the sky." ²¹God created the large sea creatures and every living creature that moves, with which the waters swarmed, after their kind, and every winged bird after its kind. God saw that it was good. ²²God blessed them, saying, "Be fruitful, and multiply, and fill the waters in the seas, and let birds multiply on the earth." ²³There was evening and there was morning, a fifth day. (Genesis 1:20-23)

---

18 In Wolof: *God keeps His covenants.*

6. On the sixth day, God created animals and man. Unfortunately, we do not have time today to explain this important event. But, God willing, in the next program, we will carefully examine what the Scriptures say about *how* God created the first man and *why* He created him.

Today we have considered the goodness of God. We have heard the prophet David say: **"Taste and see that the LORD is good!"** Friends, have you tasted, truly tasted, the goodness of God? Every day we taste and eat various foods that God has provided for us, but have we really tasted and recognized God's goodness? If you really want to taste the goodness of God you must listen to and believe the word of God. The Holy Scripture says: **Man shall not live by bread alone, but by every word that proceeds out of God's mouth.** (Deuteronomy 8:3; Matthew 4:4)

In our next lesson, we will discover that man not only has a body, but also a soul. Our souls must feed on the words of God. God's word is deliciously good and incomparably wonderful, but we must hunger for it. Does your soul hunger to know God and His eternal word as much as your stomach hungers for food? If you hunger for the word of God in this way, you will discover the truth that can give you perfect peace with God here on earth and an incorruptible inheritance in heaven above. We know that this is true because the word of God says: **Blessed are those who hunger and thirst for righteousness, for they shall be filled.** (Matthew 5:6)

Amen.

Thank you for your attention. We urge you to join us next time as we see *how God created the first man* and, even more importantly, *why He created him.*

May God bless you and your family as you remember and obey His wonderful invitation to you:

Taste and see that the LORD is good! (Psalm 34:8)

Why God Created Man

Genesis 1-2

I n our last program, we heard *how* God created the heavens, the earth, the oceans and all they contain. The LORD[19] made everything in six days just by speaking. We also saw *why* God created the world. He made it for the people whom He planned to create for His own glory. How good of God to create a beautiful and wonderful place where man could live in true prosperity!

Today we plan to examine the Scriptures to learn exactly *how* God created the first man. With God's help we will also seek to understand *why* He created man. In the Torah, in the book of Genesis, in the first chapter, in verse 26, the word of God says,

> [26]**God said, "Let us make man in our image**, after our likeness. Let them have dominion over the fish of the sea, and over the birds of the sky, and over the livestock, and over all the earth, and over every creeping thing that creeps on the earth." [27]God created man in his own image. In God's image he created him; male and female he created them. (Genesis 1:26-27)

We have before us a profound and awesome truth that everyone needs to understand: God created the first man and woman **in His own image**. Think of it: God made mankind to look and act, in many ways, like God Himself. Truly, humans are the most important creation among all the creatures that God made. Only humans were created in the image of God.

Now then, what does the Scripture mean when it says: "**God created man in His own image**"? In chapter 2, verse 7, we read:

---

19 God's name in Hebrew: *YHWH* meaning HE IS / I AM; in Wolof: *The Everlasting One*

The LORD God formed man from the dust of the ground, and breathed into his nostrils the breath of life; and man became a living soul. (Genesis 2:7)

When God created the first man, He created a body and then breathed His spirit into that body, and man became a living soul. God created man in two steps. Listen again to what the Scripture says: First, **the LORD God formed man from the dust of the ground.** Next, God **breathed into his nostrils the breath of life, and man became a living soul.**

From this Scripture we learn that when God created man, He first formed a body. Why did God make the body first? He made the body first because it would be the dwelling place into which He would place man's eternal soul. Do you know that your body is your house, the temporary tent in which the real *you* lives? That is what the Scriptures teach, saying: **The body we have on earth is like a tent.** (2 Corinthians 5:1 from Wolof) God created the human body for the soul to dwell in.

What did God use to create the first human body? He used dust (or soil) of the ground. Did you know that there are certain characteristics found in soil which are also found in the human body? With the knowledge we have today, we know that the dust of the earth is composed of about twenty primary chemicals. Scientists tell us that those same chemical substances are found in the human body. That is why the prophet David wrote in the Psalms: **The LORD…knows how we are made, he remembers that we are dust.** (Psalm 103:14)

Yes, the body is made of dust, but this does not mean that it is worthless. In the human body, there are more than seventy thousand-thousand-thousand-thousand (70 trillion) parts we call *cells*. And all those parts are woven together and designed to function in perfect harmony. The human body is a miracle. In our bodies God has placed the brain, heart, lungs, stomach, liver, intestines, bones, muscles, skin, eyes, ears, nose, mouth, and many, many other amazing parts. Every part "knows" its role. Only God could have created it. The prophet David also wrote, "**O LORD… I will give thanks to you, for I am fearfully and wonderfully made. Your works are wonderful. My soul knows that very well."** (Psalm 139:1,14)

Yes, the human body is an incredible wonder. Yet was it the body that God created in His own image? No, this cannot be, because God is spirit. God did not create the physical form of man in His own image. What then does the Scripture mean when it tells us that God created man in His own image? It means that God created the soul of man in His image.

We have already observed that when God first created the body of man from the dust of the earth, it was without life, like a corpse. Why did God first create man's body before He put the soul into it? Why did God, who is all powerful, not create man in one simple step, as He had done with the other creatures? Perhaps God did it in this way to teach us that man in himself has no power over life. Man cannot give himself life, and man cannot create anything that lives. God is the LORD of Life and in Him alone can life be found. Life does not come from man; it is a gift from God.

Again, the Scripture says: **The LORD God…breathed into his nostrils the breath of life, and man became a living soul.** The body that God had created began to live. Why was it alive? Because God, the LORD of Life, had breathed His Spirit into the corpse. The life that was in God was now in man. That is how man became a living being, composed of body, soul and spirit.

The *body* was merely the house, or tent, into which God breathed man's soul and spirit.

The *soul* was man's personal intellect, emotions, and will, which made it possible for man to think, feel, and choose.

The *spirit* connected man to God. While the body equipped man to connect with the visible world, the spirit equipped man to connect with the invisible God.

The LORD wanted humans to know Him. People would be God's special treasure.

Did you know that there are certain characteristics that are found in God which are also found in humans? Before we conclude today's lesson, we want to consider three characteristics, or attributes, found in God which are also found in people.

As we think about three features that we share with God, we will be able to understand better what the Scriptures mean when they say that **God created man in His own image.** The three features that God placed into the first man are:

> One: God gave man *a mind* (spirit), so he could know God.
> Two: God gave man *a heart* (emotions), so he could love God.
> Three: God gave man *a will*, so he could choose to obey God.

Just as God is the possessor of a mind, and a heart, and a will, so God placed in the soul of man a mind, a heart, and a will. Let us consider what this means.

1. First, God gave man a mind capable of knowing God and understanding God thoughts. God created man with such a powerful mind, because He planned for man to have close fellowship with Himself. When, later, we come to the story of the prophet Abraham, we will see that he was called *the friend of God*. Abraham knew God personally and had a close relationship with Him. However, Abraham is not the only one who has been offered the privilege of being God's friend. We, too, can be friends of God! God wants us to have close fellowship with Him. That is why He gave man a mind (spirit) that can harmonize with the mind (spirit) of God.

Perhaps we can clarify what we are saying with a question. What distinguishes a man from an animal? *The mind.* The human mind, man's spirit, is distinctly different from the mind of an animal. Why is it that animals cannot understand this radio program? Because they do not have the same kind of mind that we have. Listening friends, why are you able to understand our words today? Because you share the same kind of mind – a human mind. In a similar way, man's spirit is designed to harmonize (correspond, communicate, fellowship,) with God's Spirit.

Of course, in saying this, we must not think that our minds and the mind of God are equal in wisdom and knowledge. Never! The wisdom of God is infinitely deep, and His knowledge completely surpasses anything in man. What we need to understand is this: God has given to man a spirit that has the possibility of enjoying a meaningful relationship with God. The one true God does not want you to be like the animals, who cannot know Him. An animal has a brain but cannot think about God. An animal has a mouth, but it cannot thank God for the food that He provides for it each day. It has eyes, but it cannot appreciate the complexity and wonder of creation. It has ears, but it cannot listen to the word of God. However, humans, whom God created in His own image, can come to know the LORD God.

Yes, you who are listening today, you can know God! You can have a close relationship with your Creator if you will believe and receive the righteous way of salvation that He has established. In coming lessons we will clearly explain God's way of salvation, but what we must understand today is that God gave man a spirit capable of knowing Him.

2. God placed something else in the soul of man when He created him in His image: *a heart.* God gave man a heart so that he could love God. We are not talking about the heart that pumps blood but about what you feel in your soul, your emotions, and your thoughts. We are talking about the very intentions of your heart. God gave the first man the capacity to feel emotions that God Himself feels. God can love, hate, rejoice, and feel sorrow and compassion. That is why God placed within the soul of man a heart capable of feeling emotions such as love and hate. God wants man to love what God loves and hate what God hates. God wants us to love Him with all our heart. That is why He created man in His own image and gave him a heart.

3. There is something else that God gave to man, whom He created in His own image. He placed in the soul of man *a will.* God permits every person to choose his own path. God Himself has authority to choose whether He will do something or not. Thus, God created

humans with the right and responsibility to make important choices for themselves. God could have created man so that he would automatically do His will and not have any choice in the matter. However, God committed to man the responsibility to choose for himself whether to obey God. God did not want to create a mere machine, like a robot. God did not create humans to be like the sun that rises every day but has no choice in the matter. The sun fulfills the will of God every day, automatically. That is not how it is with man. Man is a special creation. God created us for Himself. God wants us to choose to love Him and worship Him. God gave to man a free will. Man must choose for himself whether to follow God or Satan, whether he will cherish the word of God or despise it.

God will not force anyone to believe His word. He will never force us to love Him and obey Him. Love is not love if it is coerced. God allows each of us to choose for ourselves which path we will follow. But, in the end, God will judge everyone who rejects His kingdom, because God created man for Himself.

We are here on earth for God. We are not here for ourselves or for money, or for anything or anyone else. God created us for Himself; for His pleasure and glory. God created us with the capacity to know Him, love Him, and obey Him forever. Yes, forever! The Eternal God has given to each of us an eternal soul. It is God's will that we have a deep and wonderful relationship with Him today, tomorrow, and throughout eternity. It is for this reason that **God created man in His own image**.

Thank you for listening. God willing, in our next program we will learn about *Adam and Eve and the garden of Paradise*.

We bid you farewell with this verse from the Scriptures that reminds us of God's intention for people:

> **The Lord our God, the Lord is one: you shall love the Lord your God with all your heart, and with all your soul, and with all your mind, and with all your strength!** (Mark 12:29-30)

Adam and Eve
and the Garden of Paradise

Genesis 2

We are continuing our study about what happened in the beginning. In today's lesson we will meet Adam and Eve and learn about their first day on earth. We have already read in the Torah that **in six days the LORD made heaven and earth, the sea, and all that is in them.** (Exodus 20:11) We also observed how God created the first man on the sixth day. God made man with a body, a soul, and a spirit. God formed the body of man from the dust of the earth and then He breathed into it an eternal soul and spirit. God created man in His own image. This means that God placed in man's soul a special mind (spirit), so that man could know God. He also gave man a heart (emotions) with which he could love God. And He gave man a will (choice) to choose for himself whether to obey God or to disobey God.

After God finished creating the first man, He had other things to do before He could rest from His work of creation. These works are what we want to learn about today. Let us continue in the Torah, in the second chapter of the book of Genesis. The Scripture says: **The LORD God planted a garden eastward, in Eden, and there he put the man whom he had formed.** (Genesis 2:8)

The Scripture tells us how God prepared a delightful garden for the man whom He had created. The garden was called *Eden*[20] or *the Garden of Paradise.* Some think that this garden in which God placed the first man was in heaven. However, the Scriptures tell us that it was located here on earth, in the east, in Eden, probably

---

20 Literally: *Delight*

where the country of Iraq is today. The writings of God's prophets never confuse the Garden of Paradise (Eden), which was on earth, with the heavenly Paradise, which is above, in the presence of God.

In the verses that follow, the Scripture says:

> [9]**Out of the ground the LORD God** made every tree to grow that is pleasant to the sight, and good for food, including the tree of life in the middle of the garden and the tree of the knowledge of good and evil. [10]A river went out of Eden to water the garden; and from there it was parted, and became the source of four rivers.... [15]The LORD God took the man, and put him into the garden of Eden to cultivate and keep it. (Genesis 2:9-10,15)

Thus we learn that God made for the first man, Adam, a lovely place where he could live in happiness. God placed him in a luscious garden full of trees that produced fruit beautiful to look at and delicious to eat. In this enchanting place everything was perfect and wonderful. Adam's senses were alive; his eyes took in the beauty, his ears took in the melody of birds singing in the trees, and his senses absorbed the fragrance of the flowers that permeated the garden. God gave Adam everything for his enjoyment. We also read how God in His goodness entrusted Adam with a satisfying task: to cultivate and care for the garden.

The most wonderful thing that took place in Eden was that God Himself would come to the garden in the cool of the evening so that He might walk and talk with the man whom He had created in His own image (See Genesis 3:8). Why did God visit man? It was because, as we have already learned, God created people to be His friends. God's intention was that He and humans might fellowship together, talk together, rejoice together, and spend eternity together with unified minds and hearts. Yes, God wanted humans to grow in a deep and wonderful relationship with Him forever.

Now there is something else we need to know about the garden where God placed the first man. In the middle of the garden, God planted two very important trees. One was called the tree of life and the other the tree of the knowledge of good and evil. God placed the tree of life in the garden to remind Adam that He intended for man to share in His eternal life. As for the tree of the knowledge of good and evil, God placed it in the middle of the garden to test Adam. Listen to what the Scripture says:

> ¹⁶**The LORD God commanded the man**, saying, "You may freely eat of every tree of the garden; ¹⁷but you shall not eat of the tree of the knowledge of good and evil; for in the day that you eat of it, you will surely die." (Genesis 2:16-17)

Why did God forbid Adam to eat from the tree of the knowledge of good and evil? Is God stingy? No, He is not stingy. In fact, one of His names is *the Generous One* (James 1:5 in Wolof). God told Adam, "You can eat of every tree except one." Was this a difficult command? No! God, in His grace, had given Adam everything he needed. He had not withheld from him any good thing. But God, in His perfect plan, placed before Adam a simple test, to give Adam the opportunity to show God that he loved Him enough to obey Him. As the Lord God says, **"If a man loves me, he will keep my word…. He who doesn't love me doesn't keep my words."** (John 14:23-24) God wanted to test Adam's love and loyalty – to see where his heart was. That is why He gave him this simple command. God did not create a robot. God created a man with a mind, a heart, and a free will so that he could choose for himself to love and obey God.

What was God's warning to Adam if he ate the fruit of the forbidden tree? God told him, **"You shall not eat of the tree of the knowledge of good and evil; for in the day that you eat of it, you will surely die."** Thus God informed Adam that disobedience to His command would produce death. God loved the man He had created so He warned him: *Adam, if you disobey me, you will die because my righteous law requires the death of the soul who sins.*

Perhaps someone is asking: What is sin? The Scriptures say: **Sin is lawlessness.** (1 John 3:4) **All unrighteousness is sin.** (1 John 5:17) **To him…who knows to do good, and doesn't do it, to him it is sin.** (James 4:17) Sin is going your **own way.** (Isaiah 53:6) Sin is anything that does not agree with the LORD God, who is holy. What will happen to those who sin against Him? As we just read, the word of the LORD says: **The soul who sins he shall die.** (Ezekiel 18:20). Another verse says: **The wages of sin is death.** (Romans 6:23)

And what is death? Some think that to die is to cease existing; everything is finished, and you no longer know anything. But if we rely on the Scriptures, we will see that this is not what death is. In the Hebrew language, in which the first part of the Scriptures were written, death signifies *separation*. Death is separation from life.

When God said to Adam, "**You shall not eat of the tree of the knowledge of good and evil; for in the day that you eat of it, you will surely die!**" (Genesis 2:16-17), this is what He was communicating: *Adam, if you eat from the tree which I have prohibited, in that day you will be separated from Me. If you disobey me, your close relationship with Me will be broken. I am holy and I cannot tolerate sin. I expelled Lucifer and his angels when they sinned, and I will expel you if you sin. Also, if you eat fruit from the forbidden tree, your body will begin to grow old and eventually it will die, which means that your soul will leave your body. And that is not all. If you disobey Me, not only will your body die, but your soul will go to the place I created for Satan and his angels. And there you will be forever separated from Me.*

Yes, sin produces three horrible separations. First, your *soul* (and *spirit*) is separated from God here on earth. That is, you have no relationship with God the Holy One because of the sin in your heart. Second, your soul will be separated from your *body* on the day you die. That is, your body will die and your soul will meet God for judgment. Third, your *spirit, soul and body* will be separated from God forever in the lake of fire.

Based on the authority of the word of God, what is death? In short, death is separation from God. Sin separates man from God, the Source of true life. God is holy and cannot coexist with sin. The soul that sins is like a tree branch that is cut off and cast away. What happens when a branch is no longer part of the tree? After a branch is cut off, is it alive? No, it is dead! The leaves do not instantly become dry, but they have begun to die. Similarly, if you have not received God's way of forgiveness of sin, you may think that you are alive but the scriptures of the prophets say that before God, you are **dead in transgressions and sins.** (Ephesians 2:1) **Your iniquities have separated you and your God; and your sins have hidden his face from you.** (Isaiah 59:2) You are **thrown out as a branch and … withered; and they gather them, throw them into the fire, and they are burned.** (John 15:6)

A branch that is no longer connected to the tree cannot produce fruit. That is how a sinner is before God. He cannot produce anything that is pleasing to God, because he has no relationship with God, who is *The True Tree*, the Source of true life. Sinners can only expect God's righteous judgment. However, in the writings of the prophets, God tells us how we can be made righteous before Him and know for sure that our sins are removed. It is this message of salvation that we will discover in coming lessons.

Before we close today, let's read the remainder of this chapter, which tells us how God created the first woman. Listen:

> [18]**The LORD God said, "It is not good for the man to be alone.** I will make him a helper comparable to him." … [21]The LORD God caused the man to fall into a deep sleep. As the man slept, he took one of his ribs, and closed up the flesh in its place. [22]The LORD God made a woman from the rib which he had taken from the man, and brought her to the man. [23]The man said, "This is now bone of my bones, and flesh of my flesh. She will be called 'woman,' because she was taken out of Man." [24]Therefore a man will leave his father and his mother, and will join with his wife, and they will be one flesh. [25]The man and his wife were both naked, and they were not ashamed. (Genesis 2:18, 21-25)

Yes, marriage was designed by God. God created one man and one woman so that they could love each other, share their lives together, and have a happy family that reflects and glorifies their Creator. God, who loved Adam and wanted him to be perfectly happy, gave him a most wonderful gift: *a wife.* God wanted

Adam to cherish his wife, provide for her, and love her as he loved himself. And best of all, God wanted both the man and the woman to enjoy a deep relationship with Himself – to know Him, love Him and obey Him forever. (See Ephesians 5)

Thus, God finished His work of creation. The Scripture says:

> [31]**God saw everything that he had made**, and, behold, it was very good. There was evening and there was morning, a sixth day. [1]The heavens, the earth, and all their vast array were finished. [2]On the seventh day God finished his work which he had done; and he rested on the seventh day from all his work which he had done. [3]God blessed the seventh day, and made it holy, because he rested in it from all his work of creation which he had done. (Genesis 1:31-2:3)

Why did God rest on the seventh day? Was it because He was tired? No, God is never tired! God rested because He had *finished* His work. Everything was perfect. Also, by creating our world in six days and resting on the seventh, God established the seven-day week, a work-rest cycle still practiced around the world.

Like a wise and loving father, the LORD God cared for the man and his wife. Each evening, He would come into the garden to walk and talk with them. They were happy and comfortable in His presence.

Imagine a perfect world with no sin and no shame; a world with no sadness, sickness, and death. Imagine a perfect couple in a growing relationship with their perfect Creator. That's how things were in the beginning.

What went wrong? Next time, God willing, we will learn *how sin and shame entered the world*. Meanwhile, God bless you as you ponder this declaration from His holy word:

> **The wages of sin is death,**
> **but the free gift of God is eternal life....**
> (Romans 6:23a)

How Sin Entered the World

Genesis 3

I n the past two studies, we learned how God created the first two people. The Scripture says: **God created man in his own image. In God's image he created him; male and female he created them.** (Genesis 1:27) Within the soul of the man and the woman God placed a spirit capable of knowing Him and a heart capable of loving Him. God also entrusted them with a will so that they could choose for themselves whether to obey Him or not. We also saw that before He formed the woman from the man's side, God placed the man in the Garden of Paradise, a delightful garden He had prepared on the earth in a place called Eden. God gave the first man, Adam, and the first woman, Eve, everything they needed to live in peace and happiness. God wanted people to get to know Him, love Him, and worship Him forever.

We saw that God, in keeping with His perfect plan, placed a simple test before the man whom He had created. In the middle of the garden, God planted the tree of the knowledge of good and evil and then commanded the man, saying, **"You may freely eat of every tree of the garden; but you shall not eat of the tree of the knowledge of good and evil; for in the day that you eat of it, you will surely die."** (Genesis 2:16-17)

Why did God test Adam in this way? God wanted to show the condition of Adam's heart. God did not test Adam to cause him to sin but to bless and strengthen him. The man whom God created had no defects and was without sin, but that does not mean he possessed a mature character or a deep, heart-felt love for God. So God placed a test before Adam, to test his love. If Adam stood the test and obeyed God, he would prove that he loved God in his heart. Also, if Adam stood the test and refused to sin, that test would strengthen him, because the Scripture says that **patience in times of trial produces character.** (Romans 5:4)

Today, then, we have come to the third chapter in the book of Genesis. This is the chapter which shows us how sin entered the world. If we are familiar with the teaching of this chapter, then we know why the heart of man is crooked and evil and why the world is full of sin and shame, suffering and death.

We have already seen that in the beginning Adam and Eve were in the Garden of Paradise, where they were perfectly satisfied and had everything for their enjoyment. The best thing of all was that the LORD God visited the garden each day, in the cool of the evening, so that He might talk with Adam and Eve, and they could learn from Him, their Creator and Friend. God visited them because He wanted to have a meaningful and wonderful relationship with them.

But the Scriptures tell us that someone else was also in the garden. Do you know who it was? It was Satan, God's adversary, the devil.

When God created the world and all that it contains, Satan was watching. When God gave Adam the commandment to not eat of the tree of the knowledge of good and evil, Satan was listening. And he did not stop at simply watching and listening; he was also weaving a plan to try to destroy God's wonderful works. Satan planned to tempt man, whom God had created, so that he would disobey God, commit sin, be separated from God, and perish. God, of course, knew everything that Satan was planning to do, but Adam and Eve knew nothing about it.

One day when Adam and Eve were standing near the forbidden tree, Satan came in the form of a serpent and began to speak with them. The Scripture says: **Now the serpent was more subtle than any animal of the field which the LORD God had made. He said to the woman, "Has God really said, 'You shall not eat of any tree of the garden'?"** (Genesis 3:1)

Let us pause here briefly. Why did Satan appear as a serpent? The Scripture gives us the answer when it says: **the serpent was more subtle than any animal … the LORD God had made.** Satan is the tempter, and therefore he presented himself as one who is wise. Satan did not come to Adam and Eve in the form of a huge red dragon saying, "Peace be upon you, Adam and Eve. I am the devil, the enemy of God! I have come today to tempt you to turn your back on God, the Lord of life, so that you might perish forever." Satan did not operate like that. So how did he appear to them? As a beautiful and wise creature. He chose to speak to them through a serpent because at that time, before sin entered the world, the serpent was the most clever of all the animals.

Satan is still like that. He is clever and crafty. He habitually presents what he has to offer as a good thing. The Scripture says: **Even Satan masquerades as an angel of light.** (2 Corinthians 11:14) Consequently, God warns us in His word, saying: **Beware of false prophets, who come to you in sheep's clothing, but inwardly are ravening wolves.** (Matthew 7:15)

Satan is a deceiver. That is why he appeared to Adam and Eve as a wise serpent. That is also why he preferred to talk with Eve, instead of with Adam himself, because he hoped that it would be easier to tempt Eve than Adam. Satan knew that God had given the commandment about the tree to Adam, before He created Eve. However, Eve also knew about God's commandment. The devil is highly intelligent, and he knew exactly what he wanted to achieve. Satan thought that if he could persuade the woman to eat of the tree of the knowledge of good and evil, perhaps Adam would follow her in disobeying God.

Thus, **the serpent said to the woman, "Has God really said, 'You shall not eat of any tree of the garden'?"** (Genesis 3:1) Did you hear what Satan said to Eve? He said, "Did God *really* say, 'You must not eat from *any* tree in the garden'?" Do you see what Satan was trying to do? He was attempting to plant doubt in the mind of Eve concerning the sure word of God. That is why he said, "Did God say…? Did God *really* say …?" Satan still uses this method.

He fights against the word of truth, because he knows that God's words have the power to disarm him and discredit his lies. The truth dispels lies, as light dispels darkness.

Now let us listen to the rest of the conversation between the woman and the devil. The Scripture says:

> [2]**The woman said to the serpent**, "We may eat fruit from the trees of the garden, [3]but not the fruit of the tree which is in the middle of the garden. God has said, 'You shall not eat of it. You shall not touch it, lest you die.'"

> [4]**The serpent said to the woman**, "You won't really die, [5]for God knows that in the day you eat it, your eyes will be opened, and you will be like God, knowing good and evil." (Genesis 3:2-5)

This is stunning! What did God say would happen to Adam and Eve if they ate of the forbidden tree? He said, **"You will surely die."** What did Satan say? He said: **"You won't really die."** Notice that Satan did not stop at merely casting doubt on God's word. He came right out and denied it. What do you think about this? Who was speaking the truth? God or Satan? The Holy Scriptures say that God is the True One and cannot lie. As for Satan, he does not hold to the truth, **because there is no truth in him. When he speaks a lie, he speaks on his own; for he is a liar, and the father of lies.** (John 8:44)

And we must also remember that Satan is not only a liar, he is a deceiver. He is crafty; he takes what is not true and mixes it with what is true. We can see that in what Satan said to Eve: "When you eat from this tree **your eyes will be opened, and you will be like God, knowing good and evil."** When Satan said, "You will be like God," that was a lie, because the one who sins is not like God, but like Satan. But when Satan said, "You will know good and evil," he was speaking the truth, because after Adam and Eve sinned, they came to know what evil is. However, Satan did not tell them of the bitterness that such knowledge would bring into their lives.

God said, "If you eat from the tree you will surely die." But Satan said, "If you eat of the tree you will not die." Satan is a liar. Telling lies is his native language. That is why when God said, **"You will die,"** Satan denied it, saying, **"You will not die."**

The moment had come for Adam and Eve to choose between the word of God and the word of Satan. The choice before them was simple: Would they believe the words of God or the words of Satan? Would they accept the truth or the lie? Would they follow the Lord of Light or the lord of darkness?

Let us read on to see the choice they made. The Scripture says:

> **When the woman saw** that the tree was good for food, and that it was a delight to the eyes, and that the tree was to be desired to make one wise, she took some of its fruit, and ate. Then she gave some to her husband with her, and he ate it, too. (Genesis 3:6)

Amazing! God created man in His own image so that man could know Him, love Him and obey Him forever. But what did man do? Did he love God enough to obey His command? No. He chose to disobey the God of love and to follow Satan, the enemy of both God and man.

Eve ate the forbidden fruit because she was deceived by Satan's tricks. Adam ate it because he deliberately chose to go his own way instead of God's way. Instead of submitting to their holy and loving Creator, mankind had surrendered to God's enemy. Our first parents had sinned.

What a sad day this was. Our ancestors, Adam and Eve, had turned their backs on the LORD their God, and their sin has affected us all.

The Wolof proverb describes the problem well:
An epidemic is not confined to the one from whom it originates.

And the word of God declares: **Sin entered into the world through one man, and death through sin; so death passed to all men, because all sinned.** (Romans 5:12)

Another proverb says: *The gazelle which jumps over (the underbrush) doesn't produce offspring that pierce through (it).*[21]

Like it or not, you and I and all mankind take after Adam. We are born sinners and must die, because we come from Adam. The first man who disobeyed God's commandment is our forefather and we are just like him.

Who among us can say that we have never disobeyed the commandments of God? Not a single one of us. So where did we inherit this nature in us that disobeys God's commandments? From Adam. Like a deadly contagious disease, the sin that was in Adam has spread to us all. Truly, *an epidemic is not confined to the one from whom it originates.* However, all hope is not lost, because the word of God also declares:

> [18]**So then as through one trespass**, all men were condemned; even so through one act of righteousness, all men were justified to life. [19]For as through the one man's disobedience many were made sinners, even so through the obedience of the one, many will be made righteous. (Romans 5:18-19)

Do you know who that *one righteous man* is? Two programs from now, we will begin to learn about God's plan to send into the world a Savior who would provide a righteous way of salvation by which lost, separated sinners could come back to God.

Friends, this has been your program, *The Way of Righteousness*. Next time, we plan to continue in Genesis chapter 3 to learn what happened after Adam and Eve strayed from God's righteous way and followed their own unrighteous way.

God bless you as you think on this foundational truth:

> **Sin entered into the world through one man, and death through sin; so death passed to all men, because all sinned.**
> (Romans 5:12)

---

21 Wolof proverb / English equivalents: *Like father, like son.* / *The apple doesn't fall far from the tree.*

Program 8

What Adam's Sin Produced

Genesis 3

I n our study in the Torah we learned that the LORD God created the first people in His own image. We also learned why God created them. God wanted them to love Him with all their minds, with all their hearts, and with all their strength, and to enjoy a close and deep and wonderful relationship with Him.

Thus, we saw how God placed before Adam a simple test, to see if he would love God enough to obey Him. Before God made the first woman, He had commanded the man: **"You may freely eat of every tree of the garden; but you shall not eat of the tree of the knowledge of good and evil; for in the day that you eat of it, you will surely die."** (Genesis 2:16-17) Thus, God tested Adam and warned him that the punishment for disobedience would be death, and separation from Him. God loved Adam and wanted him to enjoy fellowship with Him forever. But, as we heard in our last program, Adam and Eve listened to the devil and disobeyed God by eating fruit from the tree of the knowledge of good and evil.

Today then, we plan to continue our study in the Torah, in the third chapter of the book of Genesis, to see what happened after Adam sinned against God. In verse 7 of chapter 3 the Scripture says: **Their eyes were opened, and they both knew that they were naked. They sewed fig leaves together, and made coverings for themselves.** (Genesis 3:7)

What is the first thing that Adam and Eve did after they disobeyed God? They tried to hide their sin and cover their shame. We have already learned that before they ate from the tree of the knowledge of good and evil, **Adam and his wife were both**

naked, and they felt no shame. (Genesis 2:25 NIV) But now their thoughts about their bodies had changed. Now they felt guilty and ashamed before the Holy One who must judge them. In an attempt to hide their shame, they wove together leaves from a fig tree and tried to cover their naked bodies. However, the covering of leaves they put on their bodies did nothing to erase the guilt in their hearts. Next, the Scripture says: **They heard the LORD God's voice walking in the garden in the cool of the day, and the man and his wife hid themselves from the presence of the LORD God among the trees of the garden.** (Genesis 3:8)

How different things were for Adam and Eve after they sinned. Before they had disobeyed God they were happy whenever the LORD God came into the garden to walk and talk with them. But now when they heard Him approaching, they trembled with fear and shame and attempted to hide from God among the trees of the garden. Why was Adam afraid and hiding? That is not difficult to figure out. If someone is stealing from another's field, what will he do if he hears the voice of the owner of the field? He will try to hide. In the same way, Adam, who had taken what God had forbidden, was trying to hide. Adam knew very well that he had transgressed against God. That is why he and his wife felt ashamed.

Should Adam have been afraid after he had disobeyed God's command? Absolutely! Why? Because God had clearly said to him, **"In the day that you eat from the tree of the knowledge of good and evil, you will certainly die!"** Would God carry out His word? Would Adam really die? What do you think? Would God really punish the people He had created? Wolofs say that one should not answer a question with another question, but we can best answer this question with some questions. *What did the LORD do to Lucifer, that is, Satan, after he rejected God's rule over him? Did God acquit Satan and the angels who sinned?*

No, He did not acquit them. God expelled them from His holy presence. And not only that, He also created for them the eternal fire. Like Satan, Adam had rejected God's rule over him. Could God just say, "It's no big deal" and let Adam go free?

What did God do after Adam sinned? God went seeking for Adam, calling out to him, **"Where are you?"** Did Adam go looking for God? No, he did not. Instead, he tried to hide from God. Why did God call out to Adam? Did He not know where Adam was? God, who sees and knows everything, knew exactly where Adam was hiding. God called out to Adam because He wanted Adam to recognize and confess his sin. God still loved Adam even though Adam had disobeyed Him.

What did Adam reply when God asked, **"Where are you?"**

> ¹⁰**The man said, "I heard your voice** in the garden, and I was afraid, because I was naked; so I hid myself." ¹¹God said, "Who told you that you were naked? Have you eaten from the tree that I commanded you not to eat from?" ¹²[Adam] said, "The woman whom you gave to be with me, she gave me fruit from the tree, and I ate it." ¹³The LORD God said to the woman, "What have you done?" The woman said, "The serpent deceived me, and I ate." (Genesis 3:10-13)

Did you hear how Adam and Eve answered God? Each tried to blame someone else. Adam accused both God and Eve, saying: "It's not my fault. The woman you gave me – its her fault." As for Eve, she blamed the serpent, saying, "Don't blame me – the serpent deceived me." However, God, who knows the heart of man, knew that they were both guilty. God did not make them eat the fruit of the tree. Satan also did not make them eat it. Satan can tempt and deceive people, but he cannot force anyone to sin. Satan *deceived* the woman, but what she did was still sin before God. As for the man, the Scripture tells us that **Adam was not deceived** (1 Timothy 2:14). He chose to go his own way. Adam knew exactly what God had commanded, but he chose to stray from the way of righteousness and follow the way of unrighteousness. And he did not stop with disobeying God, but added sin to sin by trying to put the blame on others.

To this day, people still attempt to blame others for their transgressions, but God knows the truth. Through the Holy Scriptures God is speaking to people, saying: Where are you? Answer me! What have you done? Why do you refuse to believe and obey my word? Why do you despise my goodness? Why do you try to blame others for your own sin? **"As I live," says the Lord, "to me every knee will bow. Every tongue will confess to God." So then each one of us will give account of himself to God.** (Romans 14:11-12)

Now let us continue in the chapter to see how God judged the serpent, Satan, Eve and Adam. The Scripture says:

> [14]**The LORD God said to the serpent**, "Because you have done this, you are cursed above all livestock, and above every animal of the field. You shall go on your belly and you shall eat dust all the days of your life. [15]I will put hostility between you and the woman, and between your offspring and her offspring. He will bruise your head, and you will bruise his heel."

> [16]**To the woman he said**, "I will greatly multiply your pain in childbirth. You will bear children in pain. Your desire will be for your husband, and he will rule over you."

> [17]**To Adam he said**, "Because you have listened to your wife's voice, and have eaten from the tree, about which I commanded you, saying, 'You shall not eat of it,' the ground is cursed for your sake. You will eat from it with much labor all the days of your life. [18]It will yield thorns and thistles to you; and you will eat the herb of the field. [19]You will eat bread by the sweat of your face until you return to the ground, for you were taken out of it. For you are dust, and you shall return to dust." (Genesis 3:14-19)

Do you see what their sin produced? It produced sorrow and pain, thorns and thistles, toil and sweat, sickness and death. Yes, **the wages of sin is death.** (Romans 6:23)

What did God say would happen to Adam and Eve if they ate of the forbidden tree? He said, "In the day that you eat from it you will surely die." Were Adam and Eve buried on the day they ate it? No. But did they die on that day? Indeed they did. They died spiritually. On that very day, Adam and Eve died in their souls, because they no longer had a relationship with God.

As we already learned, death is separation from God. When Adam and Eve disobeyed God, they separated themselves from God, the Source of Life. When they chose to believe the devil and go along with him, they forfeited their friendship with God and lost their share in God's life. They had become God's enemies because they had sided with Satan, God's adversary. Their relationship with God had died. To illustrate, if you have an enemy and your friend takes sides with him, then is it not true that your friend has become your enemy? Your relationship with your friend has died. As we say: *Your friend's enemy is your enemy.*[22] In the same way, whoever obeys Satan is the enemy of God. Sin separates man from God.

Before we conclude today, there is something else we must understand and remember. We all are born into this world as those who are **dead in transgressions and sins** (Ephesians 2:1) and **alienated from the life of God.** (Ephesians 4:18) We may not like this, but that is what the word of God says.

The day that Adam disobeyed God he became a sinner. Adam, who sinned, is the father of the human race and the result of Adam's sin is that all of his descendants are born with a sin nature. A *rat only begets that which digs.*[23] Also, Adam's sin caused him to be separated from God. Adam, who rejected God's rule over him, is the father of all who live. The result is that all of Adam's descendants are born separated from God. As the proverb says: *An epidemic is not confined to the one from whom it originates.* This is exactly what the word of God teaches, when it says: **Sin entered into the world through one man, and death through sin; so death passed to all men, because all sinned.** (Romans 5:12)

Our forefather Adam, who separated himself from God, is like a branch cut from a tree. What happens if the branch is no longer united to the tree? It dries up. And what happens to the twigs

---

22 Wolof proverb
23 Wolof proverb

which are part of the branch that has been cut off? Are they alive? No, they are also dead, because they belong to the dry branch. In the same way, all the children of Adam are like the twigs of the branch that has been cut off. Because of his sin, Adam is like the dry branch, and we are one with him. The sin of our ancestor Adam has affected us all. We all share his character and condemnation.

The prophet David wrote in the Psalms: **Behold, I was born in iniquity. My mother conceived me in sin.** (Psalm 51:5) Sin is much like HIV/AIDS – a dreadful disease which has spread throughout the world. Once the virus enters a person's body, it will never leave. People who have AIDS can spread it to their children. HIV/AIDS is a killer for which humanity has no perfect cure. Sin is like that. It is a terrible calamity that has spread throughout the earth. Sin is a killer, causing people to perish forever, and in ourselves, we have no remedy for it.

However, we are praising God today with happy hearts, because God Himself has provided a remedy to save us from the penalty and power of sin. However, we must believe God's remedy and receive it.

God willing, in our next program, we will see how God gave Adam and Eve and all their descendants *a wonderful promise concerning a mighty Savior* who would come into the world to deliver sinners from sin, Satan and hell.

Thank you for listening.

God bless you as you think about these words spoken by the prophet David:

> **Behold, I was born in iniquity.**
> **My mother conceived me in sin.**
> (Psalm 51:5)

Program 9
The Wonderful Promise

Genesis 3

In our last two programs we've seen how Adam and Eve strayed from God's way by eating fruit from the tree of the knowledge of good and evil. Man, whom God had created in His own image, chose to follow Satan, the enemy of God. Before Adam and Eve sinned, they rejoiced whenever God came to the garden to talk with them, but now when they heard the voice of God, they were afraid and ashamed and tried to hide from God among the trees of the garden. But God pursued Adam and Eve, spoke with them, and told them of the curse their sin would bring into the world: sadness and suffering, thorns and thistles, sickness and death.

From that day to this day the shadow of death has hung over Adam's descendants. All of Adam's children are conceived in sin and born with a sin-bent nature. Whether we like it or not, we all share the character of our forefather, Adam. *A rat only begets that which digs.* It is because of Adam's sin that we are all born sinners. Truly, *an epidemic is not confined to the one from whom it originates.* And just as Adam's sin separated him from God, so our sin has separated us from God. That is what the Scriptures say:

> **Sin entered into the world through one man**, and death through sin; so death passed to all men, because all sinned. (Romans 5:12)
> All have sinned and fall short of the glory of God. (Romans 3:23)
> Your iniquities have separated you and your God, and your sins have hidden his face from you, so that he will not hear. (Isaiah 59:2)

This message is not pleasant to hear, but *truth is a hot pepper.* Adam's one sin separated the whole human race from God. On the day that he disobeyed God, Adam, and the human race yet to be born, left the kingdom of light and entered the kingdom of darkness. They no longer had a share in the kingdom of God. Because of their sin, their portion was with Satan, who had taken them as his captives and slaves. As those who had been created to bear God's image they could now no longer hope for anything in this life except slavery to sin and shame, and the fear of death – and in the hereafter, endless punishment in the eternal fire.

If the Scriptures ended here, we could only close the book and despair like someone lost at sea with no hope of rescue. If God had not opened a way of salvation for the children of Adam, we would be doomed forever. But blessed be the Lord our God, the scriptures of the prophets do not end with the story of Adam's sin and shame. The remainder of God's book is about His plan of salvation. That is why His word declares:

> **Where sin increased, grace increased all the more!** … Do not be afraid. I bring you good news that will cause great joy for all the people! … For the grace of God has appeared that offers salvation to all people! (Romans 5:20; Luke 2:10; Titus 2:11 NIV)

As we have already learned, God is holy and therefore must judge sinners. God is righteous and cannot overlook sin. He must judge evil. He must punish sin. The penalty for sin is death – eternal separation from God. God never changes and the penalty for sin never changes. However, today we will begin to learn how God, the Holy One, wove a plan to deliver sinners from the penalty of sin. We will see that God is not only *the Righteous One*, He is also *the Merciful One*. God, our Judge, had a plan to become our Savior!

Today we will see how that on the same day Adam and Eve sinned, God began to make known His wonderful plan to save sinners; to punish sin without punishing the sinner. Let us continue now in the Torah, in the book of Genesis, so that we might learn about this Good News. Let's read again, chapter 3, verse 15: God said to Satan, who was in the serpent, "**I will put hostility between you and the woman, and between your offspring and her offspring. He will bruise your head, and you will bruise his heel.**"

This difficult verse contains many profound and important truths, which God's prophets would later explain in detail. In short, God was beginning to make known His plan to bring into the world a Deliverer who would redeem the children of Adam from the dominion of Satan. This is the first verse that mentions the coming of the holy Redeemer.[24] In this verse let us consider four truths about the Savior God promised to send.

1. First, God was announcing that this Redeemer would be *the offspring of a woman.* All of us have a male and a female parent. However, the Redeemer who was to come would be born only of a woman, by the power of God. He would not have an earthly father. The Savior of sinners could not come from Adam because Adam's descendants are stained by sin. The Deliverer had to be without sin. He had to come from God, from heaven. Thus, the first thing we learn from this promise is that the Redeemer would be the offspring of a woman, but not the offspring of a man.

2. There is something else that God announced on the day that Adam and Eve sinned. Concerning the promised Redeemer, God said to Satan: *"You will bruise his heel."* That is how God began to announce that Satan would seek to destroy the Savior whom God would send down from heaven. In coming lessons we will see how the prophets foretold that Satan would incite men to persecute, torture and kill the Redeemer. A stricken Redeemer would be part of God's plan. In order to bring us back to God, the Savior of the world would have to shed His blood as a sacrifice for sin, the Righteous One dying for us, the unrighteous. He would willingly lay down His life to pay sin's penalty, death.

3. The third truth about the Redeemer was that God told Satan, who was in the serpent, *that He (the Redeemer) would bruise his (Satan's) head.* That was bad news for Satan, but good news for whoever wants to be delivered from the power of Satan, sin, death, and hell.

---

24 *Mediator, Intercessor, Go-between, Peacemaker, Getting-back-Man, One who pays a price to get something back*

4. Finally, God began to announce that there would be two lines of **offspring** (people) in the world: the people of Satan and the people of God.[25] The people of Satan would be all who refuse to believe God's righteous way of salvation. The people of God would be all who put their trust in the promised Redeemer.

And so, on the same day that Adam and Eve sinned, God began to announce His plan to redeem sinners. This was the first of many prophecies in which God would, little by little, make known His plan to rescue people from Satan, sin, and death. But to hide that plan from Satan and his followers, God put the prophecy in code.[26]

In coming programs, we will see how all of God's prophets announced the coming of this holy Savior who would free sinners from the grip of the devil. If what we have just explained is not yet clear in your mind, we want you to know that as we journey deeper into the Scriptures, God's message will become clear. Perhaps you've heard the proverb: *A water pail will find the person who waits diligently at the well.* Are you waiting at the "well" of Holy Scriptures? Good! The prophet Solomon wrote: **If you seek [God's truth] as silver, and search for her as for hidden treasures: then you will…find the knowledge of God.** (Proverbs 2:4-5)

Now then, let us finish our reading in the third chapter.

> [21]**The LORD God made garments of animal skins** for Adam and for his wife, and clothed them. [22]The LORD God said, "Behold, the man has become like one of us, knowing good and evil. Now, lest he reach out his hand, and also take of the tree of life, and eat, and live forever—" [23]Therefore the LORD God sent [Adam] out from the garden of Eden, to till the ground from which he was taken. [24]So he drove out the man; and he placed cherubim at the east of the garden of Eden, and a flaming sword which turned every way, to guard the way to the tree of life. (Genesis 3:21-24)

---

25 John 1:9-13; 8:42-47

26 1 Corinthians 2:7-8

Did you see what God did for Adam and Eve? The Scripture says: **The LORD God made garments of animal skins for Adam and for his wife and clothed them.** Do you remember what Adam and Eve did after they ate from the tree of the knowledge of good and evil? They wove together fig leaves and wrapped them around their waists in an attempt to hide their shame. Did God accept the clothes they had made for themselves, the coverings they made with leaves? No, He did not. Why did God not accept their coverings? Because God wanted to teach Adam and Eve that He is perfect and cannot accept the imperfect works of man. Concerning this, the Scripture says: **We have all become like one who is unclean, and all our righteousness is like a polluted garment.** (Isaiah 64:6) There is nothing that people can do to cover their sin and shame before God.

But God did something for man. God killed some animals, skinned them, and made clothes of skin for Adam and Eve. Yes, God made the first animal sacrifice. What a shocking sight for Adam and Eve as they watched the blood flow out of the animals that God had killed! Through the shed blood of animals, God wanted to teach Adam and Eve that **the wages of sin is death,** (Romans 6:23) and **apart from shedding of blood there is no [forgiveness].** (Hebrews 9:22) Adam and Eve should have been put to death for their sin, but the innocent animals had died in their place.

The penalty for sin must be paid. The penalty for sin is death. God can only pardon sins that have been paid for with a death-payment. A pure and innocent victim must die in the place of the guilty sinner. This is the only way God can forgive people of their sins without compromising His righteousness.[27] God established animal sacrifices to remind sinners that the penalty for sin is death. The animal sacrifice symbolized the holy Redeemer who would come into the world to shed His blood as a payment for sin. We will learn more about this later, but for now let us remember that God, in His justice and mercy, shed the blood of innocent animals in the place of Adam and Eve, who had sinned.

---

27 Literally in Wolof: *and still dwell in His righteousness*

And then, in His grace, God made for them beautiful garments from the skins and clothed them. The animal blood covered their sin. The animal skin robes covered their shame. Adam and Eve deserved to be put to death that day, but innocent animals had died in their place.

After this, God expelled Adam and Eve from the Garden of Paradise in Eden. He placed an angel holding a flaming, flashing sword to guard the way to the tree of life. Adam and Eve had chosen the way of death when they ate the fruit that God had forbidden. Only perfect people could live in God's perfect Garden of Paradise. Adam and Eve were no longer perfect. They had sinned and must grow old and die. We have already seen how God expelled Lucifer, that is, Satan, from the heavenly paradise because of his sin. And now we see that God expelled Adam and Eve from the earthly paradise because of their sin.

So dear friends, let us keep these two thoughts in mind. First, God is *the Righteous One*. He cannot tolerate sin. That is why He judged Adam and Eve and expelled them from the garden. Second, God is *the Merciful One*. Adam and Eve did not deserve God's forgiveness. They only deserved His wrath and judgment. But God does not want people to perish. That is why He put animals to death instead of Adam and Eve. And that is why He promised to send a Savior to earth who could deliver sinners from the darkness of the kingdom of Satan and transfer them into the light and glory of the kingdom of God.

Don't be deceived. God's *mercy* cannot ignore God's *righteousness*. These two characteristics of God must operate together. In future lessons, we will see more clearly how God can show mercy to sinners without contradicting His righteousness.

Thank you for listening. We invite you to join us for the next program called: *Cain and Abel: The Way of the Sacrifice.*

God bless you as you carefully consider what the Scripture says:

Where sin increased, [God's] grace increased all the more!
(Romans 5:20 NIV)

Cain and Abel:
The Way of Sacrifice

Genesis 4

L ast time, in our study in the Torah, we saw that after Adam and Eve sinned, God began to announce His plan to bring into the world One who would deliver the children of Adam from the power of Satan, sin, death, and hell. We also saw how God refused to accept the coverings of leaves Adam and Eve made for themselves. God wanted to teach them and us that sinners have no way to cover their shame and sin before the holy Judge who must expose and punish every sin. Only God can save sinners from His judgment. We saw how God Himself sacrificed some animals, made clothes of skin and put them on Adam and Eve. Innocent animals died in Adam and Eve's place. The animal blood covered their sin. The animal skin robes covered their shame. God Himself made the first blood sacrifice, which pointed to the Savior He promised to send into the world to save us from our sins. We also read how God announced that there would be two lines of people on earth: *those who refuse to believe God's plan* and *those who believe it.*

Today we will read about Adam and Eve's first two sons: Cain, who refused to believe God, and Abel, who believed God. As we saw, Adam and Eve were now living outside the Garden of Paradise (Eden). Because of their transgression, God had expelled them. Because of their sin, they could no longer live in the blessings of the Garden of Paradise. Their sin had spoiled their relationship with God. Yet God still loved them and cared for them.

Now then, let us read together from the Torah. In the fourth chapter of the book of Genesis, it is written:

> ¹**The man knew Eve his wife.** She conceived, and gave birth to Cain, and said, "I have gotten a man with the LORD's help." ²Again she gave birth, to Cain's brother Abel. Abel was a keeper of sheep, but Cain was a tiller of the ground. (Genesis 4:1-2)

We see that Adam and Eve bore two sons, Cain and Abel. Like their parents, they were sinners. The sin of Adam had spread to his children like a contagious disease. Cain and Abel were conceived in sin. Thus, the Scriptures tell us that Adam fathered sons **in his own likeness, after his image.** (Genesis 5:3) Like father, like son. Cain and Abel were born with a sinful nature.

The children grew physically and increased in knowledge. Cain became a farmer. He was a serious laborer and was not afraid of hard work. Abel was a shepherd. Both knew about God. They knew that God exists and that He is holy and hates sin. Both should have also known that to approach God, they needed to come by the way of the blood sacrifice which God had ordained.

There came a day in the lives of Cain and Abel when they both wanted to worship God and present to Him a sacrifice. Thus, the Scripture says:

> ³**As time passed, Cain brought an offering** to the LORD from the fruit of the ground. ⁴Abel also brought some of the firstborn of his flock and of its fat. The LORD respected Abel and his offering, ⁵but he didn't respect Cain and his offering. Cain was very angry, and the expression on his face fell. (Genesis 4:3-5)

Let us consider what happened. Two people wanted to worship God. Both presented sacrifices to God. But the Scripture says: **The LORD respected Abel and his offering, but he didn't respect Cain and his offering.** Why did God accept Abel's sacrifice and refuse Cain's sacrifice? What was the difference between those two sacrifices?

Truly, Cain's sacrifice and Abel's sacrifice were very different. Cain brought to God beautiful vegetables and delicious fruit. As for

Abel, he brought to God the blood of a lamb without blemish. God forgave Abel of his sins but did not forgive Cain of his sins.

Why did God forgive the sins of Abel, who shed the blood of a lamb, and did not forgive the sins of Cain, who presented vegetables and fruit? Was it because God does not like vegetables and fruit? No, that is not the reason. Why then did God judge Abel as righteous but leave Cain in his sin? Here is the reason:

Abel brought the sacrifice God required, but Cain brought something else. What was it that God required so that He could forgive their sins without compromising His righteousness? He required the blood – the life – of an unblemished animal. Abel believed God and brought a blood sacrifice. Thus, the Scripture says: **By faith, Abel offered to God a more excellent sacrifice than Cain, through which he had testimony given to him that he was righteous, God testifying with respect to his gifts.** (Hebrews 11:4) Abel submitted to God's plan, but Cain did not submit to it. Abel believed God but Cain did not.

What does it mean to believe God? To believe God is to have confidence in God to the point of obeying His word. To believe God is to accept what God says as true. If you say, "I believe in God," but you do not believe what God says in the Scriptures of His prophets, then you do not really believe Him. God and His word are one. If you believe God, you will believe and obey His word.

God accepted Abel because Abel believed His word and came with the blood of a lamb, as God required. God rejected Cain because Cain did not honestly believe the word of God. Cain claimed to believe God, but his actions denied it, because he did not bring a blood sacrifice for his sin, as God required.

Someone may be asking, "Why did God command animal sacrifices? Why did God say, **"Without the shedding of blood, there is no forgiveness of sin"**? Here is the reason: God's holy Law declares that the payment (wages, penalty) for sin is death. That is why blood had to be shed. God did not say, "Sin's penalty can be paid with fruits and vegetables." Nor did God say, "The payment for sin is praying and fasting and doing good works." No, what God, in His holiness, did say is: "The payment required for sin is *death*."

In the writings of the prophets God shows us that every person, every descendant of Adam, has sinned and that each sinner has a great debt before God, the Holy One. The sinner must die and then pay that debt of sin in hell forever. The debt of sin is huge, and you could never produce enough good works to cancel it before God. The penalty for sin is death and hell, which is why good works can never pay it off.

Let us try to illustrate this. Imagine that I owe a huge amount of money to a creditor and I go to him and say, "I know that I owe you a lot of money. However, I am totally broke, and cannot pay my debt with money, but I have another plan to pay you. Here's my plan: Every day this year, I will sweep the porch of your house. In this way I will work for you until I pay off my debt." How would the creditor respond to my proposition? Perhaps he would get angry, or perhaps he would laugh at me. But what is certain is that he would not accept my idea. Why would the creditor not accept my plan? Because even the best of my feeble efforts could never come close to paying the huge debt I owe.

Similarly, no one can pay off their debt of sin with good works. Only one thing can pay for sin: not money, not good works, but DEATH. The penalty for sin is death and judgment. Consequently, God could not cancel Cain's or Abel's debt of sin based on the works of their own hands. God's plan to cancel their debt of sin was through the blood of a sacrifice. The innocent must die in the place of the guilty.

Forgiveness of sin is not based on man's plan, but on God's plan. On the basis of the substitutionary sacrifice, God opened a door of forgiveness and salvation for the children of Adam. In the earliest generations of man, God decreed that every sinner must present an animal without blemish and slaughter it. The innocent animal would die as a substitute for the sinner. Because of the blood of such a sacrifice, God could be patient with Adam's descendants and cover their sins for a time. But the blood of animals could not cancel the debt of man's sin because the value of an animal is not equal to that of a man. That is why the Scriptures say that animal sacrifices were **a shadow of the good to come, not the very image of the things.… For it is impossible that the blood of bulls and goats [or lambs] should take away sins.** (Hebrews 10:1,4)

The most important thing to remember about animal sacrifices is that they were mere illustrations of the Savior who was to come into the world to pay the debt of sin for the descendants of Adam. This Savior whom God promised would die **for sins once, the righteous for the unrighteous, that he might bring you to God.** (1 Peter 3:18) As it is written in the Gospel: **All the prophets testify about [this Savior] that through his name everyone who believes in him will receive [forgiveness] of sins.** (Acts 10:43)

While God no longer requires animal sacrifices (because the promised Savior has come and shed His blood), in past generations God's plan of salvation required such sacrifices. But Cain ignored God's plan and came up with another way, a religion of his own making. Cain is the father of the first false religion. He brought to God the works of his own hands. He sacrificed to God that which he had cultivated, that is, the produce of the cursed earth. Did God accept such a bloodless sacrifice? No, He did not.

Abel, on the other hand, brought to God a lamb without blemish and slaughtered it so that the blood was shed. After that he burned it. Because of that sacrifice, Abel had a clear conscience before God. He knew that he himself deserved to die for his sin, but the innocent lamb had died in his place. In this way, Abel testified to his faith in the Redeemer who would come into the world to suffer and die in the place of sinners, to bear the punishment for their sin.

Today's story can be summarized with a question: *Why did God not accept Cain's sacrifice?* Was Cain a greater sinner than Abel? No, that's not the reason. They were both sinners. Both presented sacrifices to God. Cain was a religious person. On the surface, perhaps we could say that Cain's sacrifice was more respectable than Abel's sacrifice. Vegetables and fruits are beautiful, while a bloody, slaughtered lamb is not a pleasant sight. But sin is offensive to God and His holy law demands a death payment for sin, which is why the Scriptures teach that **apart from shedding of blood there is no [forgiveness of sin]**. (Hebrews 9:22) God refused Cain and his sacrifice because Cain did not respect God's holy nature and way of salvation.

No one can come to God, unless he comes by the righteous way that God has ordained. God's way is perfect and precise. It is like mathematics. If a teacher asks a student at school, "How much is two plus two?" there is only one correct answer. Two plus two equals four. The student who answers three is wrong. The one who says five is wrong. The person who says four and a half is also wrong. Two plus two can only equal four. That is the way it is with the righteous way of salvation that God has established. There is only one God and one way for sinners to be reconciled to God, the Holy One. It is the way of the absolutely perfect Sacrifice.

You who are listening today, do you know what the word of God says about the holy Sacrifice God has provided to permanently cancel your debt of sin? Do you know that God sent down to earth an almighty Savior so that you can be forgiven of your sins and have a pure heart before God? In coming lessons, we will be learning much about this Savior. Concerning Him, the Scripture says: **There is salvation in no one else, for there is no other name under heaven that is given among men, by which we must be saved!** (Acts 4:12)

Friends, this is where we must stop today. In the will of God, next time we will see what Cain did after God rejected his sacrifice.

God bless you as you take time to contemplate His basic law, which declares:

> **Apart from shedding of blood**
> **there is no [forgiveness].** (Hebrews 9:22)

Program 11

Unrepentant Cain

Genesis 4

I n our last program we learned about the first two sons of Adam and Eve, Cain and Abel. We saw how each of them wanted to worship God and present to Him a sacrifice. Cain took some crops he had cultivated and offered them to God. But Abel offered to God a lamb without blemish and slaughtered it as a sacrifice that covers sin. The Scripture declares that the LORD accepted Abel but did not accept Cain.

Why did God accept Abel but not Cain? Because God's way of righteousness demanded a blood sacrifice, a death-payment for sin. God judged Abel as righteous because he believed the word of God and brought the offering that God required. As for Cain, he attempted to approach God through his own efforts, which is why God did not accept him.

Today we plan to conclude our study about Cain and Abel. Do you know what happened after God refused Cain's sacrifice? Continuing in the book of Genesis, chapter 4, the Scripture says: **Cain was very angry, and the expression on his face fell.** (Genesis 4:5)

Why was Cain angry? This is not difficult to understand. To illustrate, if I do something bad and someone says to me, "You have done wrong. Change your ways and do what is right!" How might I respond to the one who rebuked me? Either I will humbly receive his words and change my ways or I will get angry with him and continue in my error.

God rebuked Cain so that he might realize that the works of his hands which he had presented as a sacrifice were worthless before his holy Creator. God wanted Cain to repent and to bring the sacrifice of a lamb without blemish, as Abel had done. God wanted to lead Cain in the right way, the way of forgiveness. But Cain, in his pride, refused to admit his transgression before God. Instead, he became angry and despondent. The Scripture continues:

> **The LORD said to Cain**, "Why are you angry? Why has the expression of your face fallen? [7]If you do well, won't it be lifted up? If you don't do well, sin crouches at the door. Its desire is for you, but you are to rule over it." (Genesis 4:6-7)

Why did God question Cain? He questioned him because He did not want Cain to perish. God wanted Cain to repent of his wrong thinking and wrong actions and follow the right way. God was warning Cain about a terrible enemy, which threatened to destroy him and his descendants. That enemy is called *Sin*.

What is sin? Sin is the problem of the world. It is our worst enemy. Sin is like a snake, full of deadly poison. It is like a little spark that can burn up a great forest. Sin is a torch with which Satan is burning up the world. The word of God says: **To him…who knows to do good, and doesn't do it, to him it is sin.** (James 4:17) **Sin is lawlessness…. He who sins is of the devil, for the devil has been sinning from the beginning.** (1 John 3:4,8) Sin is the force that moves in the members of our bodies and fights against what is true and good. Sin is anything that does not agree with the will of God. Sin is refusing to believe and obey the word of God. To go my own way is sin. (See Isaiah 53:6)

What will be the end of those who go their own way and refuse to believe God and obey Him? The Scripture says: **[They] will pay the penalty: eternal destruction from the face of the Lord and from the glory of his might.** (2 Thessalonians 1:9) Those who come by the way of salvation that God has decreed will be granted eternal life. But those who harden their hearts against the truth will face God's wrath and judgment. Still, the Scriptures declare that God does not want **anyone [to] perish, but that all should come to repentance.** (2 Peter 3:9) God did not want Cain to perish in his sin. What He wanted was for Cain to repent, forsake the way of unrighteousness that he had chosen, and choose the way of righteousness.

As we saw in the last program, the LORD God had revealed a plan by which sinners could be made righteous before Him. Abel believed in God's plan and slaughtered a spotless lamb as a sacrifice that would cover his sin. Abel believed what God said: **The [penalty for] sin is death, and apart from shedding of blood there is no [forgiveness of the sin debt].** (Romans 6:23; Hebrews 9:22)

Because of the shed blood of the lamb, Abel had a clear conscience before God. Abel knew that he was a guilty sinner deserving God's punishment, but he knew also that he had offered an innocent lamb, just as God required. The lamb which Abel sacrificed was an illustration of the Savior who was to come into the world to offer up His life as a sacrifice that would cancel man's debt of sin forever. As for Cain, he pretended to believe God, but his deeds denied it. Cain honored God with his mouth, but his heart was far from Him. The blood of a lamb is what God demanded, but Cain offered Him the works of his hands. Cain's worship was absolutely worthless before God because he did not accept God's way.

Let us read the next verse to see what Cain did after God rebuked him for his worthless sacrifice. The Scripture says: **Cain said to Abel, his brother, "Let us go into the field." While they were in the field, Cain rose up against Abel, his brother, and killed him.** (Genesis 4:8) What did Cain do? Did he repent? Did he believe God and bring Him the blood of a lamb as a sacrifice for sin? No, Cain added sin to sin by attacking his brother Abel and killing him.

Incredible! Cain, who refused to shed the blood of a lamb so that God could forgive him his sins, now shed the blood of his righteous brother. What do you think about this? Who placed into Cain's mind the idea to kill his brother? To whom was Cain listening? Cain was listening to Satan. The Scripture says that he killed his brother because Cain **belonged to the evil one.** (1 John 3:12 NIV). We have already seen how God announced that there would be two lines (groups) of people in the world, the people of God and the people of Satan. Abel belonged to God because he believed the word of God enough to obey it. Cain belonged to Satan because he did not believe the word of God.

And what did God say to Cain after he murdered his younger brother? The Scripture says:

> ⁹**The LORD said to Cain**, "Where is Abel, your brother?" He said, "I don't know. Am I my brother's keeper?" ¹⁰The LORD said, "What have you done? The voice of your brother's blood cries to me from the ground. ¹¹Now you are cursed because of the ground, which has opened its mouth to receive your brother's blood from your hand. ¹²From now on, when you till the ground, it won't yield its strength to you. You will be a fugitive and a wanderer in the earth." (Genesis 4:9-12)

In this way God punished Cain, saying, **"When you till the ground, it won't yield its strength to you."** Wolof wisdom says: *The cow may kick its calf but does not hate it.* Similarly, God did not punish Cain to condemn him, but to lead him to repent, submit to God's way, and receive forgiveness for his sins. Yet what did Cain do? Did he repent? No, he did not. The Scripture says: **Cain left the LORD's presence, and lived in the land of Nod….** (Genesis 4:16) Cain, who ignored the word of God, turned his back on God, shutting Him out of his life. It was not God who distanced Himself from Cain, but Cain who distanced himself from God.

Today, most of Adam's descendants resemble Cain, continuing in their own way and closing their hearts to God's voice. With their lips they say, "God is great!" but in their hearts they think, "God is far away. No one can know Him." However, the scriptures tell us that God **is not far from any one of us** since He is the One who **gives everyone life and breath and everything else.** (Acts 17:27,25 NIV) He is closer to us than our own heartbeat. God knows you personally and wants you to know Him personally too.²⁸ Why is it then that

---

28 Jeremiah 29:12-13; Romans 10:1-13;

most people do not come to know God? The Lord God Himself answers this question in the Scriptures, saying:

> **This is the judgment,** that the light has come into the world, and men loved the darkness rather than the light; for their works were evil. [20]For everyone who does evil hates the light, and doesn't come to the light, lest his works would be exposed. (John 3:19-20)

People do not know God because, like Cain, they have turned their backs on His word. In the Psalms, the prophet David wrote: **Your word [O LORD] is a lamp to my feet and a light for my path.** (Psalm 119:105) If you turn your back on the light of the word of God, you will remain in the darkness of your sin and shame – and you will never come to know God. He will seem far from you. Yet, God wants you to know that He is not far away. He is right behind you. He is at your side. He is right in front of you. God loves you and wants to have a close relationship with you. He wants to put His Holy Spirit in your heart. But you must not be like Cain who hardened his heart and refused to accept God's righteous way. God wanted Cain to repent. To this very day, God is commanding every person to repent and turn to Him and believe His word.

Do you know what it means *to repent*? It means *to change your thoughts*. To repent is to confess before God, *"I have been wrong in my thinking about the way of salvation that you have planned and provided."* To repent is to agree with God that you have no possible way to save yourself from His righteous judgment – and then to submit to His way of salvation.

Suppose you want to travel to a certain city. After getting on a bus, you realize you boarded the wrong bus. What do you do? You admit your error, get off that bus, and get on the right bus. That is what it means to repent.

To repent is to change your mind; to turn from what is false and submit to what is true. To repent before God does not mean that you must punish yourself for your sins. It does mean that you must see your sin as God sees it and accept His way of salvation.

To repent is to *turn from* your wrong thoughts, your sins, your idols and self-efforts and *turn to* God putting your faith in His way of salvation. That is true repentance. But Cain refused to change his thoughts and his ways. He did not repent. He chose to continue in his own way. He refused to submit to the way of forgiveness established by God. That is why the Scripture says that Cain perished in his way of unrighteousness, **for whom the blackest of darkness has been reserved forever.** (Jude 13)

Oh dear friends, may we not be like Cain! Let us pay attention to this solemn warning from God: **Unless you repent, you will all perish in the same way.** (Luke 13:3) God's judgment is sure and will fall upon all those who have never been cleansed from their sins.

Let there be no mistake about this: you will never become righteous before God based on your own good works. Like Cain, many people believe that they will escape God's judgment by attempting to follow the rules and regulations of their religion. But being religious does not make one righteous. God's word says:

> **By the works of the law, no flesh will be justified** in his sight… For we have all become like one who is unclean, and all our righteousness is like a polluted garment. (Romans 3:20; Prophet Isaiah 64:6)

> **For by grace you have been saved through faith**, and that not of yourselves; it is the gift of God, not of works, that no one would boast (Ephesians 2:8-9)

Thank you for listening. God willing, next time we will meet some of Adam's later descendants, including *God's prophet, Enoch*.

May the Lord bless you as you thoughtfully consider what you have heard today. The Scripture says:

> **[God] is patient with us, not wishing that anyone should perish, but that all should come to repentance…. But unless you repent, you will all perish in the same way.**
> (2 Peter 3:9; Luke 13:3)

The Prophet Enoch

Genesis 4-5

I n our last two programs we learned about Cain and Abel, the first two sons of Adam and Eve. We saw how each of them presented to God a sacrifice in order to worship Him. Abel believed God and brought the blood of a lamb but Cain tried to approach God through his own efforts. God accepted Abel's sacrifice but He rejected Cain's sacrifice. God called on Cain to repent but Cain just got angry and killed his brother Abel.

Today we plan to continue our study in the Torah in chapters 4 and 5 of the book of Genesis. The word of God tells us that Adam and Eve had **other sons and daughters.** (Genesis 5:4) However, among the descendants of Adam, God has made known to us the stories of just two family lines: the family line of Cain and the family line of Seth. Seth was one of Cain's younger brothers.

We will look first at Cain's family line. Cain chose a wife from among his relatives and they had children. However, just as *the gazelle which jumps over (the underbrush) doesn't produce offspring that pierce through (it)*, neither did Cain's offspring escape their father's way of acting and thinking. Like their father, they did not respect God's word. They had great knowledge and intelligence but they did not know God. They only valued earthly things. They built a city, made tools, flutes and harps and other beautiful things. One of those who descended from Cain was called Tubal-Cain. He too was ingenious and forged things out of bronze and iron. But beautiful handwork does not make a beautiful heart.

One of Cain's descendants, named Lamech, was in the seventh generation after Adam. Lamech walked in the footsteps of his ancestor Cain – except he was even worse. Lamech was the first to take two wives and, like Cain, he became a murderer. The Scriptures inform us that Lamech murdered two people and then boasted that he was more wicked than Cain. Like Cain and all his descendants, Lamech didn't care about the will of God. Lamech was selfish and loved money. He was proud and conceited. He was a lover of pleasure rather than a lover of God. Satan was his master, but he didn't realize it. Lamech was like this because he chose to follow the way of Cain. Let us keep the name of Lamech in our minds, because we will be coming back to him before we finish our lesson today.

Praise God, the Scripture does not stop with the story of Cain and his unrighteous descendants. It also tells us about the family line of Seth, saying that God gave Adam and Eve another son **instead of Abel, for Cain killed him.** (Genesis 4:25) His name was Seth. *Seth* means *chosen*. God chose Seth to replace Abel. Why did Seth need to replace Abel? Here is the answer. In the earthly Garden of Paradise, God had promised to send One into the world to defeat Satan and rescue the descendants of Adam from his power. That Savior could come through the family line of Abel, who believed God. However, Satan incited Cain to kill Abel. Satan wanted to hinder God's plan to send the Savior into the world. But God's wisdom is greater than Satan's devices. God had a marvelous plan to deliver the children of Adam from their sins and no one could hinder it, not even Satan. And so God, in keeping with His plan, gave Seth to Adam and Eve to replace Abel, whom Cain had killed. Thus, God's plan to send down the Redeemer continued to advance.

Seth was a true believer. Like Abel, his older brother, Seth chose the way of salvation established by God. Seth, like all of Adam's offspring, was born in sin. However, he believed what God had promised concerning the Savior who was to come and he manifested his faith by presenting to God the blood of a lamb as a sacrifice to cover sins. Another noteworthy thing about Seth was that he raised his children in the knowledge of the truth of God, which is why the Scripture says: **A son was also born to Seth, and… at that time men began to call on the LORD's name.** (Genesis 4:26)

And so we learn about these two family lines that came from Adam: the line of Cain and the line of Seth. Do you know what those two lines illustrate? They illustrate the two kinds of people that have been in the world since the time of Adam. In God's eyes, there are only two kinds of people on earth. He sees no distinction between those with black skin and those with white, nor between Wolof and Pulaar,[29] men and women, rich and poor. God is not prejudiced; nonetheless, He separates the people of the world into two distinct groups. What are these two groups of people? They are those who believe the word of God and those who do not believe it; those who know God and those who do not know Him; those who walk in the light and those who walk in darkness; those who are forgiven of their sins and those who are not forgiven. Everyone who believes God and chooses the way of righteousness which He has established will be saved and go to heaven, even as Seth and his family were saved. Whoever does not take God's way of righteousness will perish and go to hell, even as Cain and his family perished.

The Scriptures inform us that Adam lived until he was 930 years old and then he died. In those early times, men lived until they were extremely old – still, they died as all men die. Adam and Eve died just as God had said they would. When God created the first two people, it was not His will that they should die but that they should live. Why then did Adam and Eve die? Because they sinned against God – and sin produces separation from God, DEATH.

Now then, in the time remaining, we will look at the story of a man of God who was in the family line of Seth, who believed God. This man is Enoch, the prophet Enoch. Some know him as *Idris*.[30] In the fifth chapter of Genesis, we see the ancestry of Enoch. The Scripture tells us that Adam became the father of Seth; Seth became the father of Enosh; Enosh became the father of Kenan; Kenan became the father of Mahalalel; Mahalalel became the father of Jared; Jared became the father of Enoch. Thus, Enoch was the seventh generation after Adam in the line of Seth.

---

29 The two largest ethnic groups in Senegal
30 Qur'anic name for *Enoch*

Like all men, Enoch was a born sinner. However, when he was 65 years of age, Enoch repented, turned to the LORD God, and believed what He had promised concerning the Redeemer who was to come into the world to become the Perfect Sacrifice that takes away sin. Enoch showed his faith by offering to God the blood of an animal to cover his sin. Consequently, God credited Enoch's faith to Him as righteousness, forgave him of his sins, and purified his heart. Thus, the Scripture says: **Enoch walked with God for 300 years.** (Genesis 5:22)

Walking with God in Enoch's day was not easy, because it was a corrupt and wicked period, much like the present day. Most of those living in Enoch's time sought only after pleasure and lived lives of impurity. But Enoch knew that God had not created man to live in impurity, but in holiness. Therefore, Enoch did not allow covetousness to control him as it did his neighbors who did not know God. Like God Himself, Enoch loved righteousness and hated iniquity. People insulted him and persecuted him because of his righteous lifestyle, but Enoch didn't let it bother him because he knew that nothing is more important than to have peace with God.

God chose Enoch to be His servant and His prophet during that evil period. Like all the true prophets, Enoch testified about the Redeemer who was to come. He also announced that the Redeemer would one day return to punish all people who refuse to repent and believe in Him. Listen to the preaching of Enoch:

> [14]**"See, the Lord is coming with thousands** upon thousands of his holy ones [15]to judge everyone, and to convict all of them of all the ungodly acts they have committed in their ungodliness, and of all the defiant words ungodly sinners have spoken against him."** (Jude 14-15 NIV)

One more amazing thing that we need to know about the prophet Enoch is that he did not die. That's right. The word of God tells us that Enoch did not die. It says: **Enoch walked with God for 300 years … and he was not found, for God took him.** (Genesis 5:22,24)

Yes, God, in His power and His plan, translated Enoch directly to heaven, without making him pass through the door of death.

Why did God translate Enoch in that way? Through the life of Enoch, God wants to teach us what He thinks of those who truly trust Him and seek to please Him. The Scripture says:

> [5]**By faith, Enoch was taken away**, so that he wouldn't see death, and he was not found, because God translated him. For he has had testimony given to him that before his translation he had been well pleasing to God. [6]Without faith it is impossible to be well pleasing to him, for he who comes to God must believe that he exists, and that he is a rewarder of those who seek him. (Hebrews 11:5-6)

For three hundred years Enoch pleased God because he believed Him, loved Him and obeyed Him during a time in which most people didn't care about God's will and word. That is why one day God called his name, and instantly Enoch found Himself in Paradise, in the glory of God's house forever.

In Enoch's story, there is something very important God wants to show us. It is this: If you do not have faith in God as Enoch did, you will never please God. However, if you have faith in God and His plan like Enoch did, the LORD God will count you as righteous, and you will no longer fear death. You will know that God has conquered death for you, because if you listen to the word of God and believe it, then when your life on earth is over you will go to live in the presence of the Lord forever, just like Enoch. However, you must come to understand and believe what God has said about the righteous way of salvation He has provided for sinners.

To summarize this study we will make a few comparisons between the two descendants of Adam we have read about today: Lamech and Enoch.

Both Lamech and Enoch belonged to the seventh generation after Adam. Lamech descended through the line of Cain, and Enoch descended through the line of Seth. Lamech and Enoch lived in the same era, but they did not share the same interests. Their way of life was different, like night from day.

Lamech did not believe God and His word, but Enoch believed God and loved His word.

Lamech walked with Satan in impurity, whereas Enoch walked with God in holiness.

Lamech ignored the way of salvation decreed by God, while Enoch presented to God the blood of a slain lamb to cover his sins.

Lamech craved money, women, food, clothes and pleasure, whereas Enoch desired a life of close fellowship with the One who had given him life.

Lamech died in his sins and went down to hell, but God took Enoch up to be with Himself in heaven.

In closing, here is an important question: Are you most like Lamech or Enoch? Do you belong to the people of Cain and Lamech or to the people of Seth and Enoch? Does your life embrace the faith of Enoch, or are you going your own way like Lamech? God's word says: **Examine your own selves, whether you are in the faith… without faith [in God and His word] it is impossible to be well pleasing to [God].** (2 Corinthians 13:5; Hebrews 11:6)

Friends, this is where we must stop today. Next time, God willing, we will begin to look into the life of another prophet of God – *the prophet Noah*.

God bless you as you ponder this verse from His holy word:

> **Without faith it is impossible to be well pleasing to him, for he who comes to God must believe that he exists, and that he is a rewarder of those who seek him.**
>
> (Hebrews 11:6)

Program 13

The Prophet Noah:
God's Patience and Wrath

Genesis 6

U p to this point in our journey through the Holy Scriptures, we have seen that when God created the world, everything was good and perfect. But when our ancestor Adam disobeyed God, evil entered the world through him and spread to all men. Truly, *an epidemic is not confined to the one from whom it originates.* In our last program we learned about the two lines which came from Adam: the descendants of Cain and the descendants of Seth. The descendants of Cain did not believe God and His plan. However, among the descendants of Seth there were those who submitted to God's way of forgiveness, so God forgave them of their sins. One who came from Seth was named Enoch. Although most who lived in the time of Enoch followed Satan pursuing sin, Enoch walked with God in holiness.

Today we will begin to learn about another man who walked with God in a crooked and depraved era. This person is the prophet Noah,[31] Enoch's great-grandson. We have already learned that in early times people lived much longer than we do today. Do you know who lived to be the oldest man in the history of the world? It was Methuselah, the son of Enoch. He lived until he was 969 years old. Methuselah was the father of Lamech who was the father of Noah. This Lamech, Noah's father, is a different man from Lamech, the descendant of Cain whom we learned about last time. Noah belonged to the tenth generation after Adam. Noah was already 500 years old when he became the father of Shem, Ham, and Japheth.

---

31 Qur'anic/Arabic: *Nuh*

What we plan to study about Noah will be of great value to us because the days of Noah were similar to the times in which we live today. In the time of Noah, the world was filled to the brim with sin. The Scripture says:

> **The LORD saw that the wickedness of man** was great in the earth, and that every imagination of the thoughts of man's heart was continually only evil. (Genesis 6:5)

The hearts of the children of Adam were filled with evil thoughts, greed, deceit, lewdness, envy, slander, arrogance, strife, fighting, adultery, theft, murder, and folly.[32] Men were corrupting the world which God had created for them. Many had religion, but it was merely for show. Fleshly pleasure was their god, and their sins just kept piling up.

Listen to what the Scripture says in the Torah, the book of Genesis, chapter 6:

> ³**Then the LORD said**, "My Spirit will not strive with man forever, because he also is flesh; so his days will be one hundred twenty years." ⁵The LORD saw that the wickedness of man was great in the earth, and that every imagination of the thoughts of man's heart was continually only evil. ⁶The LORD was sorry that he had made man on the earth, and it grieved him in his heart. ⁷The LORD said, "I will destroy man whom I have created from the surface of the ground—man, along with animals, creeping things, and birds of the sky—for I am sorry that I have made them."(Genesis 6:3,5-7)

Thus we see how God purposed to wipe out the descendants of Adam from the earth because of their wickedness. However, we also see how God, in His mercy, would be patient with sinners to give them time to repent, so that they might not perish. But when that limit was reached, God would judge everyone who refused to repent and accept His way of righteousness.

---

32 List taken from Mark 7:21-22

What can we learn from this about the character of God? It is this: God is very patient, but His patience has a limit. He will speak and strive with man giving him every chance to repent, but not forever. That is why in the time of Noah God said, **"My Spirit will not strive with man forever...."** God planned to be patient with sinners for a time and then judge them if they refused to repent and turn to Him in faith. In this, we see two characteristics of God: His patience and His wrath. God is good and can be very patient; but He is also righteous and can get very angry.

Some think of God as one who hovers over them with a big stick, as one who is quick to get angry and takes pleasure in hitting and hurting people. But God is not like that. Others think that God is never angry and will merely forgive and forget their sins. "God is good! God is good!" is all they know. But God is not like that either.

The Holy Scriptures tell us the truth about the character of God. God is both good and righteous. He can be patient, and He can be angry. In His goodness and mercy He is patient with sinners, but He is angry when they sin against His righteousness and holiness. God is both a Savior and a Judge. The prophets wrote a great deal about the patience and wrath of God. Let us listen to some of their words.

The Scriptures say:

> [8]**But don't forget this one thing**... one day is with the Lord as a thousand years, and a thousand years as one day. [9]The Lord is not slow concerning his promise, as some count slowness; but he is patient with us, not wishing that anyone should perish, but that all should come to repentance. [10]But the day of the Lord will come as a thief. (2 Peter 3:8-10) [30]The Lord will judge his people. [31]It is a fearful thing to fall into the hands of the living God.... [25]See that you don't refuse Him who speaks...[26]for our God is a consuming fire. (Hebrews 10:30-31; 12:25,29)

In the Psalms it is written: **God is a righteous judge, yes, a God who has indignation every day [toward the sinner who] doesn't repent.** (Psalm 7:11-12)

In the Gospel it is written:

> [18]**For the wrath of God is revealed from heaven** against all ungodliness and unrighteousness of men who suppress the truth in unrighteousness… [2]the judgment of God…is according to truth. [You then,] [3]do you think…that you will escape the judgment of God? [4]Or do you despise the riches of his goodness, forbearance, and patience, not knowing that the goodness of God leads you to repentance? [5]But according to your hardness and unrepentant heart you are treasuring up for yourself wrath in the day of wrath, revelation, and of the righteous judgment of God; [6]who "will pay back to everyone according to their works". (Romans 1:18; 2:2-6)

The wrath of God is not like the wrath of man. Man can become very angry, but his anger will diminish little by little until he may even forget what made him angry in the first place. The anger of God is not like that. The passing of time does not diminish God's anger. God is a righteous Judge and He does not overlook sin. His anger does not diminish toward those who refuse to repent; instead, it increases. This is what we just finished reading in the Scriptures: **But according to your hardness and unrepentant heart you are treasuring up for yourself wrath in the day of wrath, revelation, and of the righteous judgment of God.**

The people of Noah's time were storing up for themselves the wrath of God. But there remained one man on earth who loved God with all his heart and believed God's word. That man was Noah. The Scripture says: **But Noah found favor** (grace) **in the LORD's eyes. Noah was a righteous man, blameless among the people of his time. Noah walked with God.** (Genesis 6:8-9)

Why did God show Noah His grace? Did Noah merit the grace of God? No! Grace which is merited is no longer grace. Grace means *undeserved favor*. Why did God extend His grace to Noah and not to the others? What does the Scripture say about that? It tells us that Noah believed God, while the others did not believe Him. Noah believed the word of God. He believed what God promised about the Redeemer who was to come into the world to rescue sinners. Like all of Adam's descendants, Noah had sin in him, but God counted Noah as a righteous person because he believed God and offered Him the blood of a sacrifice for his sin, as God had commanded. That is why the Scripture says: **Noah was a righteous man, blameless among the people of his time.** (Genesis 6:9)

One day God said to Noah:

> [13]**"I will bring an end to all flesh**, for the earth is filled with violence through them. Behold, I will destroy them and the earth. [14]Make an ark of gopher wood. You shall make rooms in the ark, and shall seal it inside and outside with pitch. [15]This is how you shall make it: [The ark is to be 150 meters long, 25 meters wide and 15 meters high.] [16]You shall make a roof in the ark…. You shall set the door of the ark in its side. You shall make it with lower, second, and third levels. [17]I, even I, will bring the flood of waters on this earth, to destroy all flesh having the breath of life from under the sky. Everything that is in the earth will die. [18]But I will establish my covenant with you. You shall come into the ark, you, your sons, your wife, and your sons' wives with you. [19]Of every living thing of all flesh, you shall bring two of every sort into the ark, to keep them alive with you. They shall be male and female…. [21]Take with you some of all food that is eaten, and gather it to yourself; and it will be for food for you, and for them. (Genesis 6:13-19,21)

Thus God told Noah how he planned to bring floodwaters on the earth to destroy everyone who refused to repent and believe the truth. God told Noah to build a massive ark (boat, ship) to escape the flood. The length of the ark had to be 150 meters; the length of one and a half football fields. It would be a refuge for Noah and his family and many animals and anyone else who would believe God's word. God ordered Noah to make many rooms on the inside of the ark, but only one door on the outside of the ark. Thus, God's message for the people of Noah's time was: Repent! Judgment is coming! Anyone who wishes to escape the judgment of the flood must pass through the door of the ark – or perish!

So Noah started to build the ark. It was a huge task. Noah and his three sons had to chop down hundreds and hundreds of large trees, cut them into planks, shape and nail them, and coat them with tar inside and out. Noah's wife and his son's wives also helped them in that hard work. And Noah probably hired others to help with this massive construction project. For a hundred years, day after day, God gave Noah the wisdom he needed to construct this massive place of refuge. But Noah did not limit his activity to building the ark. He also preached to the people of his day. Perhaps he said something like this: "Listen! The LORD has told me to warn you of His wrath! God's anger is boiling because of your sin. He has determined to bring a flood on the earth to destroy everyone who refuses to repent. But God has provided a way of escape. God, in His mercy, has ordered me to build an ark to be a refuge. Repent and believe God!" Thus Noah warned the people again and again, urging them to turn from the evil ways of their corrupt generation.

What do you think? Did the people of Noah's era believe the word which God announced to them through His prophet? We cannot reply now, because our time is gone. Next time, however, in the will of the Lord, we will continue with the story of the prophet Noah and see how God preserved everyone who believed His word, and how He judged those who did not believe His word, letting them drown in the waters of a great flood.

Thank you for listening. God bless you as you think about what we read today in the Scriptures:

> **The Lord is not slow concerning his promise, as some count slowness; but he is patient with us, not wishing that anyone should perish, but that all should come to repentance. But the [day of God's judgment] will come as a thief.**
> (2 Peter 3:9-10)

Noah and the Great Flood

Genesis 7

I n our last program we began to look at the solemn story of the prophet Noah, who was born ten generations after Adam. In a corrupt and depraved era, Noah walked with God. We saw how the LORD was grieved in His heart because of the sins of Adam's descendants. The Scripture says: **The LORD saw that the wickedness of man was great in the earth, and that every imagination of the thoughts of man's heart was continually only evil.** (Genesis 6:5) That is why God in His righteous wrath planned to wipe the unrepentant sinners from off the face of the earth. But God's grace was with Noah because Noah loved God and believed His word. So one day God told Noah that He was going to judge all mankind because the earth was filled with wickedness. God informed Noah of His plan to bring a great flood upon the earth that would destroy every living thing under the heavens. He told Noah to build a huge ark, that would be a refuge for him and his family.

For one hundred years, Noah and his family constructed the ark. But Noah did not limit his work to building the ark. He also preached to the people around him: *Repent of your sins then and return to God! God, the Righteous One, is going to judge the world!*

Did the people of Noah's time turn from their wrong thinking and wicked living and believe the word which God announced to them through His prophet? What do you think? Among the thousands and thousands of children of Adam who were upon the earth, how many of them repented, believed God and entered the ark? The Scriptures reply: **Only a few, that is, eight souls, were saved through water....** (1 Peter 3:20)

How many people believed God? Only eight: Noah and his wife, their three sons and their wives. All the others did not believe God's word. Some simply ignored Noah's preaching, while others mocked him. They thought he was crazy because of the ship he was building in a place where there was no water. The people may have mocked Noah like this: *Hey you guys! Come see this fellow who is building a huge boat out here in the wilderness! Noah must be insane! Floodwaters here in the desert? Impossible! Besides, God is good; He wouldn't destroy the people He has created. You're crazy, Noah!* But Noah ignored their insults because he believed what God had said. He went right on constructing the ark and preaching, saying, *Repent! God is going to judge the world in righteousness! Why do you refuse to believe the word of God? Why do you want to perish?*

Finally the day came when Noah and his family finished building the ark. In the last verse of the sixth chapter of the book of Genesis we read: **[Noah] did all that God commanded him.** (Genesis 6:22) The ark was ready. Everything was complete. It was time for Noah and his family to enter the ark. We can imagine Noah trying one more time to convince the people: *Listen to God! Repent and believe His word! The flood is soon to come! Enter the ark while there is still time! The door is open! Whoever passes through it will be saved. But if you refuse to enter, how will you escape the judgment of God?* Noah earnestly warned the people, but they would not listen.

Consequently, the Scripture says in chapter 7:

> [1]**The LORD said to Noah**, "Come with all of your household into the ark, for I have seen your righteousness before me in this generation. [2]You shall take seven pairs of every clean animal with you, the male and his female. Of the animals that are not clean, take two, the male and his female. [3]Also of the birds of the sky, seven and seven, male and female, to keep seed alive on the surface of all the earth. [4]In seven days, I will cause it to rain on the earth for forty days and forty nights. I will destroy every living thing that I have made from the surface of the ground." [5]Noah did everything that the LORD commanded him. (Genesis 7:1-5)

Why did Noah and his family enter the ark? Because they saw a cloudy sky? Because they smelled the coming rain? No. A clear sky is all they saw when they entered the ark. Why then did they go in? There is only one reason. They entered because they believed what God had said. Perhaps there were those outside who thought: *I also believe God, but I am not going to go inside that ark! I believe in God, but I cannot accept Noah's preaching!* What can we say about those people? We can say that they did not truly believe God, because they did not believe what God testified through His prophet. They refused to turn from their sins and they refused to accept the way of escape which God had provided for them through Noah. They may have honored God with their lips, but their hearts were far from Him. Thus, the Scripture says:

> [7]**Noah went into the ark** with his sons, his wife, and his sons' wives, because of the floodwaters. [8]Clean animals, unclean animals, birds, and everything that creeps on the ground [9]went by pairs to Noah into the ark, male and female, as God commanded Noah.... [16]Then the LORD shut him in.
> (Genesis 7:7-9,16)

Thus, God brought the pairs of animals, reptiles, insects, and birds. What a sight as they entered the ark, and settled into its thousands of compartments! And did you hear what God did after the animal pairs and Noah and his family entered the ark? The Scripture says: **The LORD shut them in.** The day of God's great wrath had come. God had been patient with the people of that generation for a long time, but now His patience had run out. Only His judgment remained. God had closed the door; and when God closes the door, no one can open it.

Thus, God brought the floodwaters on the earth just as He had promised. The sky began to darken; the wind began to blow. There were clouds and thunder and lightning and earthquakes. Now the children of Adam were trembling with fear. When everything was peaceful, it had been so easy for them to challenge God (and His prophet Noah) with insulting words and deeds. But now that the judgment of God had begun to descend upon them, their mouths were shut. The hour for them to face God's righteous judgment had arrived and there was no longer anywhere to hide.

> [11]**In the six hundredth year of Noah's life**, in the second month, on the seventeenth day of the month, on that day all the fountains of the great deep burst open, and the sky's windows opened. [12]It rained on the earth forty days and forty nights. (Genesis 7:11-12)

That is what happened.[33] From deep down under the earth, the vast reservoirs of water gushed up. Torrents of water fell from the sky. The rivers overflowed and the oceans rose, and surging into every town and village. Those who were not immediately swept away fled in terror, seeking higher ground. Those who had mocked Noah and rejected the word of God now knew that what God had said through His prophet Noah was the truth. But this knowledge was no longer of any benefit to them because the opportunity to repent was gone; the period of salvation was past. Perhaps some were calling to Noah, shouting out, *Noah! Noah! Open the door! Noah, help us! Save us! We believe you, Noah! You were right! We believe! We believe!* But it was too late. God had closed the door. The day of salvation was past. The day of judgment had come. Praying, weeping, beating on the door, even knowing the truth – nothing could change the mind of God. When God closes the door of salvation, no one can open it.

For forty days and nights there was a torrential downpour of rain and powerful flooding until all the mountains were covered. But the ark floated on top of the water. The Scripture says:

> [21]**All flesh died that moved on the earth**…. [23]Every living thing was destroyed that was on the surface of the ground, including man, livestock, creeping things, and birds of the sky. They were destroyed from the earth. Only Noah was left, and those who were with him in the ark. (Genesis 7:21,23)

---

33 For geological info relating to Genesis 7:11, search online the word *ringwoodite*. Due to this bluish, crystal-structured rock housed in earth's mantle, scientists estimate that there is 3 times more water under the earth than in all the world's oceans combined.

The global flood was the worst natural disaster in history. Except for eight souls sheltered in the ark, all humanity perished. A proud, unbelieving world learned the truth too late. Geological and fossil records affirm the biblical record. From the Sahara to the Himalayas, marine fossils can be unearthed in the world's great deserts and mountains.

Did God do what He had promised to do? Of course. Did He judge those sinners who refused to repent? He surely did. He judged everyone who was not in the ark, just as He had said He would do.

Dear friends, this is where we must stop today in the story of Noah. God willing, in our next program we will see what happened to Noah and his family in the ark. But before we bid you farewell today, there is a solemn lesson God wants to teach us through the judgment of the great flood. It is this: God has planned another day when He will judge the people of the world, and that coming Day of Judgment will be even more terrible than the judgment which came upon Noah's generation.

Listen to what one of God's prophets wrote about that coming day:

> [11]**I saw a great white throne**, and him who sat on it, from whose face the earth and the heaven fled away. There was found no place for them. [12]I saw the dead, the great and the small, standing before the throne, and they opened books. Another book was opened, which is the book of life. The dead were judged out of the things which were written in the books, according to their works…. [15]If anyone was not found written in the book of life, he was cast into the lake of fire. (Revelation 20:11-12,15)

Listening friend, are you confident as you contemplate that fearful judgment day? Is your name written in the book of eternal life? Have you passed through the door of salvation which God has opened? The word of God says: **Now is the acceptable time. Behold, now is the day of salvation.** (2 Corinthians 6:2)

Today, we have seen how God gave the people of Noah's day time to repent and be saved, but in the end, He shut the door of salvation.

All those who had refused to enter through the door of the ark faced God's fierce judgment.

Regarding that coming day when God will judge the world, the Scripture says: **For you yourselves know well that the day of the Lord comes like a thief in the night. For when they are saying, "Peace and safety," then sudden destruction will come on them, like birth pains on a pregnant woman. Then they will in no way escape.** (1 Thessalonians. 5:2-3) No one shall escape in that day, except those who have passed through the door of salvation which God has opened for the children of Adam.

Do you know about *The Door* the LORD God has opened for helpless sinners? Do you know the way of escape that He has provided for you? Who escaped the judgment of the flood in Noah's day? Only those who went through the door of the ark. Similarly, concerning Judgment Day, the Scriptures clearly show us that God has provided only one door of salvation for us – the children of Adam – with our sin and shame. Do you know about that door of salvation? Listen to these sure words spoken by the holy Messiah whom God sent from heaven to earth. He said: **"I am the Door; if anyone enters in by me, he will be saved."** (John 10:9) **"Most certainly I tell you, he who hears my word and believes him who sent me has eternal life, and doesn't come into judgment, but has passed out of death into life."** (John 5:24)

Friends, this is where we must stop today, but in future programs we will learn much more about this holy Savior who said, **"I am the Door; if anyone enters in by me, he will be saved."**

Thank you for listening. God willing, next time we will hear one more story about *the prophet Noah* and learn another crucial truth about the the true and living God.

May God give you insights into all we have considered today as you think on this weighty question found in His Book:

> **How will we escape if we neglect so great a salvation?**
> (Hebrews 2:3)

Program 15
Noah and the Faithfulness of God

Genesis 8-9

Today we plan to finish the story of God's prophet, Noah. First let us review what we learned in the past two programs from Noah and the great flood. In chapter 6 of the book of Genesis we saw that the wickedness of man was very great in the time of Noah; every inclination of the thoughts of man's heart was evil all the time. So God purposed to bring a flood upon the earth to wipe out all sinners who refused to *turn away from* their wicked ways and *turn to* the true and living God.

In that crooked and depraved generation, only one man pleased God. That man was Noah. Noah trusted God and loved Him. That is why God spoke to Noah one day and commanded him to build a great ark, which would be a refuge for him, his family and many animals – to bring them through the flood and preserve their lives. Noah spent a hundred years constructing the ark and exhorting the people to repent and believe the word of God. Yet no one paid attention to the preaching of Noah. No one really believed what Noah was telling them about the coming flood.

Nonetheless, a day came when the ark was ready. The hour for God to judge this evil world had arrived. God had been patient with scoffers for a long time, but now His patience had run out. Thus, the LORD told Noah to enter the ark with his family and take with him seven males and seven females of every kind of clean animal (animals fit for sacrifice), and two of each unclean animal, a male and a female. Noah and his family and the animals entered the ark as God had ordered. And the Scripture says: **Then the LORD shut him in.** (Genesis 7:16) God, who had opened the door of salvation for the children of Adam, was also the One who closed it.

The day of God's mercy was gone; the day for His fearsome wrath had arrived.

Then came the lightning, thunder and violent shaking of the earth. Heavy rains fell, causing a great flood. Everyone fled, seeking to go up into the mountains, but no one could escape from God's holy wrath. Those who had mocked Noah and rejected God's word now knew the truth. But now it was too late. The time of salvation was past. The time of judgment had come. And God Himself had shut the door.

For forty days and nights rain poured down from the sky and massive springs gushed up from the earth until even the mountains were covered. But the ark floated on top of the water. The Scripture says:

> [21]**All flesh died that moved on the earth**…. Every living thing was destroyed that was on the surface of the ground, including man, livestock, creeping things, and birds of the sky. [23]They were destroyed from the earth. Only Noah was left, and those who were with him in the ark. (Genesis 7:21,23)

Thus, the Scripture records that God carried out the punishment just as He had promised. Everyone outside the ark perished. God was faithful to keep His word.

What happened to those inside the ark? Did God forget Noah and his family? God, who feeds the birds of the air, and not one of them falls to the earth except that He wills it, did not forget them. Let us read what is written in the book of Genesis in chapter 8.

> [1]**God remembered Noah**, all the animals, and all the livestock that were with him in the ark; and God made a wind to pass over the earth. The waters subsided. …[4]The ark rested in the seventh month, on the seventeenth day of the month, on Ararat's mountains. (Genesis 8:1,4)

God remembered Noah and those who were with him inside the ark. He sent a mighty wind to blow over the earth to cause the waters to recede. God guided the ark so that it came to rest on Ararat, a massive mountain located in what is known today as eastern Turkey. After Noah and his family had been in the ark for one year and a week, much of the water which had covered the earth had dried up. Then God said to Noah, **"Go out of the ark, you, your wife, your sons, and your sons' wives with you."** (Genesis 8:16)

So Noah and his family went out of the ark, as did all the animals. When he had gone out he built an altar, took some of the clean animals and birds and offered them to the LORD on the altar as a burnt offering.

Did you hear what Noah did first after he left the ark? He sacrificed some innocent animals, burning them on an altar of stones he built, which symbolically suspended the sacrifice between heaven and earth, between God and man. God had not abolished His law which stated: **Apart from shedding of blood there is no [forgiveness of sin].** (Hebrews 9:22) While the great flood destroyed most of the sinners from off the face of the earth, it did not destroy the root of sin that remained in the hearts of the children of Adam. That is why Noah and his descendants still had to offer sacrifices for sin in order for them to have a restored relationship with God. These sacrifices that our ancestors slaughtered in early times symbolized (pictured) the Redeemer who was to come and shed His own blood to pay the debt of sin for Adam's descendants. That is why when Noah left the ark the first thing he did was to shed innocent animal blood, showing his children that the laws of God had not changed, that **the wages of sin is death** (Romans 6:23) and that **apart from shedding of blood there is no [forgiveness].** (Hebrews 9:22) Thus the Scripture says:

> [21]**The LORD smelled the pleasant aroma** (of the sacrifice)…. [1]God blessed Noah and his sons, and said to them, "Be fruitful, multiply, and replenish the earth…. [9]I establish my covenant with you, and with your offspring after you …. [11]All flesh will not be cut off any more by the waters of the flood. There will never again be a flood to destroy the earth…. [12]This is the token of the covenant which I make between me and you and

every living creature that is with you, for perpetual generations: [13]I set my rainbow in the cloud, and it will be a sign of a covenant between me and the earth. [14]When I bring a cloud over the earth, that the rainbow will be seen in the cloud, [15]I will remember my covenant, which is between me and you and every living creature of all flesh, and the waters will no more become a flood to destroy all flesh."
(Genesis 8:21; 9:1,9,11-15)

In these verses we have just read, there is a word which God repeated four times to Noah. Did you hear it? The word is *covenant*. In the word of God, a covenant is a special promise made by God to man. God is the Keeper of covenants. God is faithful, and He wants to show forth His faithfulness to the sons of Adam. That is why, in His goodness, He established a covenant with Noah and those who descended from Him, saying, "All flesh will not be cut off any more by the waters of the flood." That is what God promised. And He did not limit His promise to mere words, but He confirmed it by putting His rainbow in the clouds.

Did you know that the beautiful rainbow that we see sometimes in the clouds after it has rained is a sign which declares the faithfulness of God? Every time we see a rainbow, God wants to remind us of His faithfulness that endures from generation to generation. God put the rainbow in the clouds to confirm His covenant in which He promised that the waters will never again become a flood to destroy all life. Truly, God is the Keeper of covenants. He is faithful.

There are other significant events in Noah's life, but we do not have the time to mention them here. You and your family can read them however, in the Torah, the book of Genesis, chapter 9. You will see that after the flood, Noah lived another 350 years, and when he was very old, the faithful LORD whom Noah had trusted and obeyed, called him into His glorious presence.

In summary, perhaps we can conclude our talk about God's prophet Noah with a question or two. What was the difference between Noah and the people of his time? What is it that Noah did that pleased God? Noah believed the word of God. That is why he did not perish with the people of his generation. Listen to what God Himself says about Noah:

> **By faith, Noah**, being warned about things not yet seen, moved with godly fear, prepared an ark for the saving of his house, through which he condemned the world, and became heir of the righteousness which is according to faith. ... Without faith it is impossible to be well pleasing to [God]. (Hebrews 11:7, 6)

Before we bid you farewell today, there are two thoughts to keep in our minds. We just considered the first of these two thoughts. What made Noah pleasing to God? *His faith.* Noah believed God; he believed what God said. Noah had confidence in the LORD and obeyed His word even when all others around him rejected that word. It was Noah's faith that caused God to deliver him from the evil generation in which he lived. You who are listening to us today, do you truly believe what God has said? God's will for each of us is that we believe His word as Noah did.

The second thing we must remember from the story of Noah is even more important than Noah's faith. Do you know what it is? It is *God's faithfulness.* Why is God's faithfulness more important than Noah's faith? Because if God was not faithful to keep His covenants and promises, the faith that Noah had in Him would be of no benefit.

We all know what happens when we put our trust in someone who does not keep his promise. Suppose you have a friend who promises you: "Tomorrow I will bring you a sack of rice." You believe him; you have faith in him. What happens if he does not bring it? You will be disappointed – and perhaps hungry! The faith that you had in your friend was worthless. Why? Because your friend did not do what he had promised. You trusted someone who was unfaithful.

It is not like that with God.

The Scriptures say:

> **If we are faithless, he remains faithful**; for he can't deny himself. (2 Timothy 2:13) ²⁴For, all flesh is like grass, and all of man's glory like the flower in the grass. The grass withers, and its flower falls; ²⁵But the Lord's word endures forever.... ⁶He who believes in him will not be disappointed. (1 Peter 1:24-25; 2:6) [Yes!] God is faithful. (1 Corinthians 1:9)

He will do all that He has promised.

In the story of Noah we clearly see how God did everything that He promised. We read how God saved everyone who was inside the ark and judged everyone who was outside, just as He had said He would do. We also saw how God forgave Noah of his sins and declared him righteous because he offered up the blood of an animal as a sacrifice, just as God had told him to do. And we learned how God placed His rainbow in the clouds so that Noah and all people would not forget that **God is faithful.**

Friends, if you should forget everything we have considered today except one thing, remember this: **God is Faithful.** He cannot go back on His word. He does what He promises, even if it seems that He is slow in doing so. **God is faithful.... He who believes in him will not be disappointed.** (1 Corinthians 1:9; 1 Peter 2:6) Let us then believe Him and accept His word with humility. And may we benefit from the story of the prophet Noah and the global flood by imitating Noah who believed the word of God even when all the people around him refused to believe it.

This is where we must stop today. We thank you for listening. In our next lesson, God willing, we will see what became of Noah's descendants and learn how the many languages of the world came into existence at the *Tower of Babel.*

God bless you as you remember this faith-inspiring truth:

> **God is faithful.... and the one who trusts in him will never be put to shame."** (1 Corinthians 1:9; 1 Peter 2:6 NIV)

The Tower of Babel

Genesis 10-11

As you may remember, in our last program we concluded our study of God's prophet, Noah. We saw how God wiped out the children of Adam with a flood because of their wickedness. For a hundred years God gave sinners time to repent while Noah constructed the ark, which would be a refuge for those who believed the word of God. Still, none turned from their sin or believed the message of the Lord God, except Noah and his family. Thus, in the end, God, who is righteous and faithful, did just as He had promised. He wiped out everyone who had not passed through the door of the ark and He saved those few who did.

Today we will continue in the book of Genesis and learn what happened in the period following the time of Noah. In our talks about Noah, we learned that he had three sons, Shem, Ham, and Japheth. The Scriptures show us that it is from these three men that all the peoples of the world come. Shem was the father of the Jews and the Arabs. Most of the people of Africa and Asia are probably descendants of Ham. Europeans are descendants of Japheth.

If you would like to broaden your knowledge of the origin of the nations, you can study chapters 10 and 11 of the first book of the Torah. However, in our lesson today we have time only to explain one thing about the history of Noah's three sons, Shem, Ham, and Japheth. It is this: Shem was the one whom God chose to be in the ancestry of the Redeemer who would come into the world. That is why the Holy Scriptures only record the stories of the descendants of Shem. It is from his line that God provided for the world the prophets, the Scriptures, and the Savior of the world Himself.

All the peoples of the earth come from the three sons of Noah. You and I, all the people of Senegal, the people of Gambia, Mauritania[34] and all of Africa, as well as all the other peoples of the world – everyone living today is a descendant of Noah. Therefore we can say that we are here today because Noah believed God and made an ark to save his family; for when he saved his family from the flood, he saved you and me from extinction along with them.

God blessed Noah and his sons, saying to them, **"Be fruitful, multiply, and replenish the earth."** (Genesis 9:1) Thus, hundreds of years after the flood, once again there were multitudes of people dwelling upon the earth. And once again, the world began to be corrupted by sin. We have already seen that Noah and his sons were born sinners because they were descendants of Adam. When they entered the ark, their sinful nature, which they had received from Adam, went along with them. And when they went out of the ark, they went out with the root of sin still in their hearts. The flood did not change man's sinful condition. As the proverb says: *A rat only begets that which digs.* Therefore, all the people of the world continued to be born sinners, because they were all descendants of Noah, who was a descendant of Adam.

It is sad, but true, that a few hundred years after the great flood, most of Noah's descendants were no longer concerned about God and His will. They did not believe the word of God as did their ancestors Seth, Enoch, and Noah. They forgot God and did not thank Him for giving them life and breath and sunshine and rain and food. As for the rainbow that God had placed in the clouds to remind them of His faithfulness, most no longer even knew what it meant. Listen to what the word of God declares about them:

> [21]**Because knowing God**, they didn't glorify him as God, and didn't give thanks, but became vain in their reasoning, and their senseless heart was darkened. [22]Professing themselves to be wise, they became fools…. [25]Who exchanged the truth of God

---

34 The original Wolof TWOR radio series (*Yoonu Njub*), produced between 1992-1994, was broadcast primarily in Senegal and Gambia, and was also heard by many in Mauritania.

for a lie, and worshiped and served the creature rather than the Creator, who is blessed forever. Amen. (Romans 1:21-22,25)

Like Cain and his descendants, most of Noah's descendants chose to bury the truth and follow unrighteousness. They had religion, but it was a false religion because it did not follow the way of righteousness established by God. They did not listen to the true word of God. They were listening to Satan.

There was a man by the name of Nimrod, who descended from Noah's son, Ham. Nimrod was a great hunter who lived about five hundred years after the flood. His name means *rebel*. Nimrod was highly intelligent, but he did not know God. He ignored the word of God and followed the way of Satan, the way of Cain, and the way of the people of Noah's generation. Nimrod built several large cities and planned to build a great city in which all the people of the world could live together and be as one.

Let us read in chapter 11 of the book of Genesis to see what the Scriptures tell us about the great city which Nimrod and those with him planned to build. The Scripture says:

> ¹**The whole earth was of one language** and of one speech. ²As they traveled east, they found a plain in the land of Shinar, and they lived there. ³They said to one another, "Come, Let us make bricks, and burn them thoroughly." They had brick for stone, and they used tar for mortar. ⁴They said, "Come, Let us build ourselves a city, and a tower whose top reaches to the sky, and Let us make a name for ourselves, lest we be scattered abroad on the surface of the whole earth." (Genesis 11:1-4)

And so we learn how the sons of Adam planned to build a great city and a high tower that would reach to the heavens. Why did they want to build that high tower? Nimrod and those who agreed with him were seeking to make a name for themselves in the world. They planned to gather the people of the world into one place so that they would become powerful and not be scattered over the earth. However, what they planned to do did not please

God. God had told the children of Noah to spread out over the surface of the earth. God, who created man, knew what was best for the people of the world. However, most of Noah's descendants didn't care about the thoughts of God. They acted like they were more intelligent than God. Like Satan himself, their hearts were full of pride and rebellion against God. But the Scriptures say: **Whoever exalts himself will be humbled, and whoever humbles himself will be exalted.** (Matthew 23:12) And: **that which is exalted among men is an abomination in the sight of God.** (Luke 16:15)

To exalt man or to seek a great name for yourself is sin before God, because there is only one name worthy of praise and glory. That is the Name of the Lord God, who made heaven and earth. As the Scripture says: **But he who boasts, let him boast in the Lord. For it isn't he who [praises] himself who is approved, but whom the Lord [praises].** (2 Corinthians 10:17-18)

However, in the time of Nimrod most of the descendants of Adam had no respect for the Lord. They thought they didn't need God and His word; they did not need anyone to tell them anything. They were characterized by a spirit of independence and rebellion. To this day, that same attitude is found in the hearts of the children of Adam. We even see it in little children when they flip an arm[35] and say, "No, I won't!" And this same spirit is found all the more in adults. What is the cause of the strife found in the homes and nations of the world? It is nothing but this spirit of independence, which thinks, "I can take care of *myself*. I will follow the religion of *my* father (even if it contradicts the Scriptures of the prophets). *My* traditions are the best. *My* sect is right. *My* people are superior. *My* tribe is the smartest. *My* name is the most important. *My* things! *My* will! *My* works! *My* money! *My*! *My*!! *My*!!!"

That self-centered, self-seeking spirit of independence is why the world is full of quarrels, fights, and wars. But God hates such a spirit, for His name alone is worthy of glory. That is why He says in His word, **"I am the LORD. That is my name. I will not give my glory to another."** (Isaiah 42:8)

---

35 Wolof expression of stubborn refusal

But those who began to build the tower to reach to the heavens didn't care about God's glory. They sought only their own glory. Most didn't even know the name of their Creator. Certainly many people of that time were religious, but they had no relationship with God. They hoped to reach heaven in their own way. Think of it! Just five hundred years after the flood, people were once again going their own way and ignoring the Lord who gave them life and breath. They were like a horse that after it has been washed goes and rolls in the mud. (See 2 Peter 2:22) How foolish and wicked of man to want to live his life apart from God and His plan.

So what did God do? Did He ignore the people's plan to live apart from Him? Did He accept those who rebelled against Him? No, He did not. Listen to what God did. The Scripture says:

> [5]**The LORD came down to see the city and the tower**, which the children of men built. [6]The LORD said, "Behold, they are one people, and they all have one language, and this is what they begin to do. Now nothing will be withheld from them, which they intend to do. [7]Come, Let us go down, and there confuse their language, that they may not understand one another's speech." [8]So the LORD scattered them abroad from there on the surface of all the earth. They stopped building the city. [9]Therefore its name was called Babel, because there the LORD confused the language of all the earth. From there, the LORD scattered them abroad on the surface of all the earth. (Genesis 11:5-9)

That is how God upset the plans of Nimrod and the others who had begun to build a great city for their own glory. Until this time, everyone in the world spoke the same language. But on this day, God mixed up their language so that they could no longer understand each other. You will remember that God had commanded Noah's descendants **to replenish the earth,** (Genesis 9:1) to spread out all over the world. But Nimrod and his followers wanted to do things their own way and gather all the people of the world into one place. God defeated their intentions by giving them new languages. That is how He scattered them over the face of the whole earth. This is the reason we have hundreds of nations and thousands of languages in the world today.

God did a thorough job of mixing up the languages of the world! Think how many languages are spoken in this country alone. Oh, how great is our God! No one can go against Almighty God and prosper. *An egg should not wrestle with a rock!* Man tried to wrestle with God and lost.

Do you know the name of this city which man tried to build in rebellion against God? Yes, the name of the city is *Babel*. Babel means *confusion*. Life apart from God and His word is only confusion.

That is the story of the city of Babel and the people who tried to exalt their own name. Are we ever like the people of Babel? Do we ever exalt ourselves? God tells us that it is sin to do so. Listening friend, whose name are you seeking to exalt? Your own name? The name of a man, perhaps some marabout (religious leader)? Or are you seeking to exalt the Name of the Lord God and Him alone? Whose praise and approval are you seeking? The approval of man? Or are you seeking the approval of God? One thing is absolutely certain. The approval that comes from men will pass away, but the approval that comes from God will endure forever. God's word says: **All flesh is like grass, and all of man's glory like the flower in the grass. The grass withers, and its flower falls; but the Lord's word endures forever.** (1 Peter 1:24)

Listen to this word from the LORD Himself:

> [23]**"Don't let the wise man glory in his wisdom.** Don't let the mighty man glory in his might. Don't let the rich man glory in his riches. [24]But let him who glories glory in this, that he has understanding, and knows me, that I am the LORD who exercises loving kindness, justice, and righteousness in the earth, for I delight in these things," says the LORD. (Jeremiah 9:23-24)

God willing, in our next program, we will review everything that we have studied from the beginning until now. God bless you as you consider this word from His book:

> **For it is not the one who commends himself who is approved, but the one whom the Lord commends.** (2 Corinthians 10:18 NIV)

Review of The Beginning

Genesis 1-11

Today, with God's help, we plan to review and summarize what we have studied up to this point in the Torah of the prophet Moses. The Torah is the first section in the holy scriptures of the prophets. This section is very important because it is the foundation which God Himself has laid, by which we can test everything we hear so that we can know whether it comes from God or not. The Torah has five parts, or books. The first part we call *Genesis*. There are fifty chapters in the book of Genesis. In our chronological programs we have studied chapters 1 to 11.

Can you remember what is written in the first verse of God's book? Let us reread it. It says: **In the beginning God created the heavens and the earth.** (Genesis 1:1) God is the Lord of Eternity. In the beginning, when the world did not yet exist, only God existed. God is the Eternal Spirit who has no beginning. He lives outside of time. That is why the first verse of Scripture says: **In the beginning GOD.**

Next, we saw how God, before He created the world, created thousands and thousands of powerful spirits, calling them angels. Among the angels there was one who was wiser and more beautiful than all the others. That one was Lucifer, whom God appointed chief of the angels. But the Scriptures tell us that at some point Lucifer exalted himself and despised God in his heart, wanting to take God's place. A third of God's angels chose to take sides with Lucifer in his sin. That is why God, who cannot tolerate sin, expelled Lucifer and the evil angels. God changed Lucifer's name to *Satan*, which means *adversary*. After God expelled Satan and his angels, he created for them the fires of hell which are never extinguished. The Scriptures say that on the day of final judgment, God the Righteous One will throw Satan into that fire along with all who follow him.

Next, we read how the LORD created the heavens and the earth and everything they contain in six days, using nothing except His word. God created everything for humans whom He planned to create for His pleasure and glory. Humans are the most important creatures of all that God created, because they were created in the image of God. The LORD God wanted to have a deep and meaningful relationship with people. That is why He placed in the soul of man an intelligent *spirit* (mind) so that he could know God, He gave man a *heart* so that he could love God, and God endowed him with a *free will* so that he could choose for himself to obey God or to disobey Him.

In the second chapter of the Torah, we read that God planted a perfect garden somewhere in the Middle East, and placed in it the man, that is, *Adam*. God, in His goodness, gave Adam everything he would ever need for a life of perfect peace and happiness.

Also, on the day Adam was created, God said to him, **"You may freely eat of every tree of the garden; but you shall not eat of the tree of the knowledge of good and evil; for in the day that you eat of it, you will surely die."** (Genesis 2:16-17) From this we saw how God put a simple test before Adam. God wanted a meaningful relationship with the man whom He had created. That is why God tested him, giving him the authority to choose either to love Him enough to obey Him, or not to obey Him.

We also read that on the day that God created Adam, God gave him an incomparably wonderful gift: a wife. God created the woman from a rib which He took from Adam and then presented her to Adam. Later Adam named her *Eve*. She, too, was created in the image and likeness of God. In six days God completed His work of creation. The Scripture says: **God saw everything that he had made, and, behold, it was very good.** (Genesis 1:31)

On the seventh day God rested – that is, He ceased from His work of creation, and He rejoiced in all that He had made.

In the third chapter, we saw how sin came into our world. The Scriptures show us how that one day when Adam and Eve were near the tree which God had forbidden, Satan came as a crafty snake, saying,

> [1]**"Has God really said**, 'You shall not eat of any tree of the garden'?" [2]The woman said to the serpent, "We may eat fruit from the trees of the garden, [3]but not the fruit of the tree which is in the middle of the garden. God has said, 'You shall not eat of it. You shall not touch it, lest you die.'" [4]The serpent said to the woman, "You won't really die, [5]for God knows that in the day you eat it, your eyes will be opened, and you will be like God, knowing good and evil."(Genesis 3:1-5)

We saw from this how Satan contradicted the word of God. What had God told Adam about the consequences of eating of the tree which God had forbidden? He said, "You will die." And what did Satan say? He said, "You will not die." Whose word did Adam and Eve choose to believe and follow: the word of God or the word of Satan? Alas, the Scriptures record that Adam and Eve chose to believe the word of Satan and to eat the fruit of the tree which God had forbidden. Satan deceived Eve so that she transgressed. Adam deliberately chose to disobey God's command and to follow Satan. Thus, the Holy Scripture says: **Sin entered into the world through one man, and death through sin; and so death passed to all men, because all sinned.** (Romans 5:12)

Because of their sin, God expelled Adam and Eve from the earthly Garden of Paradise, just as He had said He would do. But before He put them out, God promised that one day He would send into the world a Savior who would provide for Adam's sin-ruined race a way of deliverance from their sin and shame, and from the power of Satan, death, and hell. To confirm that promise, and to display His justice, mercy, and grace, God slaughtered some animals and made clothes of the skins and put them on Adam and Eve. By means of those animal sacrifices, God was teaching Adam and Eve that **the wages of sin is death** (Romans 6:23) and that **apart from shedding of blood there is no [forgiveness of the sin debt].** (Hebrews 9:22)

In chapter 4 we read the story of Adam's first two children, Cain and Abel. We saw how Abel offered to God an innocent lamb, and slaughtered it as a sacrifice for sin - just as God had done for Abel's parents. But Cain tried to approach God in his own way, bringing what he had cultivated in the earth, which God had cursed. Thus, the Scripture says: **The LORD respected Abel and his offering, but he didn't respect Cain and his offering.** (Genesis 4:4-5) God called on Cain to give account so that he would repent and submit to God's way of righteousness, but Cain only got angry and murdered Abel, his younger brother.

Afterward, God gave Adam and Eve another child, named *Seth*. Seth, like Abel, believed God, honored God's holy law, and approached Him with the blood of a sacrifice. In this we learned about the two genealogies which came from Adam; that is, the line of Cain and the line of Seth. The descendants of Cain did not believe and submit to God. But among the descendants of Seth were those who trusted and followed the LORD God. One who descended from Seth was named *Enoch*. Enoch walked with God in a corrupt generation. Enoch had a great-grandson by the name of *Noah*.

In the days of Noah, God purposed to wipe out the children of Adam with a flood because of their wickedness. In that perverse time, only Noah believed God, which is why God told him to build a huge ark (massive boat, ship) as a refuge for him and his family and a pair of each animal kind, and any who would turn from their sins and believe the word of God. For a hundred years God patiently endured sinners while Noah constructed the ark. However, no one repented. No one believed God's message, except Noah and his family. Thus, in the end, God did all that He had promised. He judged every person who did not believe the truth. Everyone except Noah and his family perished in the global flood. Noah had three sons: Shem, Ham, and Japheth. All peoples of the world come from these three men. Sadly, most of their descendants quickly forgot God and His word.

In our previous lesson, we learned how Nimrod and those who went along with him planned to assemble all the people of the world in one location and build a great city with a high tower in rebellion against God. But God confused their language and scattered them throughout the earth. The city became known as Babel, which means *confusion*. That, in short, is what we have studied up to this point in the book of Genesis, in chapters 1 to 11.

How can we summarize what we have seen in these many stories? What does God want to teach us from what happened at the beginning of world history? There are many lessons to be learned, but today we have time to explain just two of them.

One lesson is that *Mankind is unrighteous.*

The other truth to be learned is that *God is righteous.*

In our studies, we have repeatedly seen the unrighteousness of man. We saw how it began in the (earthly) Garden of Paradise (Eden), when Adam ate the fruit of the tree which God had forbidden. We saw it again in Cain, Adam's firstborn son, who refused to follow the way of sacrifice which God had established. We observed this same unrighteousness in Cain's descendants, in the people of Noah's generation, and in those who tried to build the tower of Babel. In short, the story of the children of Adam is: Man is unrighteous. As it is written in the Scriptures: **[We] are all under sin....there is no one righteous, no, not one.... They have all turned away. They have together become unprofitable. There is no one who does good, no, not so much as one.** (Romans 3:9-10,12)

Just as we have seen the unrighteousness of man, so we have also seen the righteousness of God. The Scripture tells us that **God is light, and in him is no darkness at all.** (1 John 1:5) We witnessed God's righteousness when He expelled Lucifer from heaven because of his pride and rebellion. We saw it again when He expelled Adam and Eve from the garden because of their diso-bedience. God also revealed His righteousness by promising to send into the world a holy Redeemer who would pay the debt of sin for the children of Adam. And we learned of the holy character of God revealed in His law that states: **Apart from shedding of blood there is no [forgiveness].** (Hebrews 9:22) God displayed His righteousness when He accepted Abel because he approached

God with the blood of a lamb, but God rejected Cain who scorned God's way of forgiveness. Again, we saw God's righteous nature in the time of Noah, when, after giving man a hundred years to repent, God sent a mighty flood across the globe to wipe out all who refused to believe Him. And in our last program, we saw God reveal His righteousness when He confused the language of the people of the city of Babel who were rebelling against Him.

Yes, God is righteous and must judge people according to *His* standard of righteousness. Unrighteous sinners cannot approach Him on the basis of what they like to call *good deeds*. God must judge and condemn anything that is tainted by sin. The Scripture says: **Our God is a consuming fire… The Lord will judge his people. It is a fearful thing to fall into the hands of the living God.** (Hebrews 12:29; 10:30-31) And so we see that in the first eleven chapters of the Torah God has clearly made known to us the important truth concerning His absolute righteousness.

Does this mean that unrighteous man has no hope of being accepted by God? No, praise be to God, there is hope for sinners like you and me! God in His grace has revealed a way by which the unrighteous children of Adam can be made right before Him. Do you know the way of salvation which God has established for sinners? If you do not yet understand God's way of righteousness, we invite you to join us in the upcoming programs as we study about the prophet Abraham, who was called *the friend of God*. In the amazing story of Abraham we will see more of God's plan by which unrighteous people can be made righteous in His sight.

Thank you for listening. May God bless you as you think about all we have studied today. God's word says:

> **For whatever things were written before were written for our learning, that through perseverance and through encouragement of the Scriptures we might have hope.**
> (Romans 15:4)

Program 18

Why God Called Abraham

Genesis 11-12

In past lessons we have been learning about God and His way of righteousness. We have seen Adam and Eve, Cain and Abel, Seth and Enoch, Noah and the people of his generation, and Nimrod and the tower of Babel. Only a few of our ancestors followed God and His way of righteousness; most followed Satan and his way of unrighteousness.

Today we have come to the story of a man whose name is well known in the word of God, and who had an important place in God's plan to redeem the children of Adam. The Scripture refers to this man as *the friend of God*[36] and *the father of all who believe*. Do you know who it is? It is God's prophet *Abraham.*[37] The Holy Scriptures have much to say about Abraham. His name appears in the writings of the prophets over 300 times. Therefore, God willing, today and in coming lessons, we will search the Scriptures to discover what they teach about this *friend of God*. Today we intend to look into the beginning of the story of Abraham to discover how and why God called him.

Before we begin, you should know that at first Abraham's name was not Abraham, but *Abram*. Two lessons from now we will learn why God changed Abram's name to Abraham. Today, however, let us just keep in mind that Abraham was first called Abram.

In chapter 11 of the book of Genesis we learn that Abram belonged to the descendants of Shem. Do you remember Shem, Ham, and Japheth? They were the three sons of Noah. Between Shem and

---

36 Arabic: *Khalilu Allah*
37 Arabic: *Ibrahim*

Abram there were ten generations, just as there were ten generations between Adam and Noah. So the Scripture says: **Terah became the father of Abram, Nahor, and Haran. Haran became the father of Lot.** (Genesis 11:27) Lot was the son of Abram's older brother. Lot's father had died.[38] Abram's wife's name was Sarai. Now **Sarai was barren. She had no child.** (Genesis 11:30) Abram and Sarai had the same father but not the same mother.

Abram lived in a city named Ur, which was located in the country of Chaldea, known today as Iraq. This city was not far from where Nimrod tried to build the city of Babel with its tall tower. The people of the land worshiped idols. Like all of Adam's offspring, Abram was born in the darkness of sin. Abram's father did not know the true God and neither did Abram.

But the Scriptures tell us that one day the LORD God appeared to Abram and spoke to him. It is helpful to know that in early times, sometimes God spoke directly with people, because they did not yet have the writings of the prophets. Today God speaks to people through the Holy Scriptures. While God still sometimes reaches out to individuals through visions and dreams, it is important to understand that everything we need to know about God's way of righteousness is found in God's book. When we listen to and meditate on the Holy Scriptures, we are hearing the voice of God.

Let us now listen to what God said to Abram. In chapter 12 verse 1, we read: **Now the LORD said to Abram, "Leave your country, and your relatives, and your father's house, and go to the land that I will show you."** (Genesis 12:1)

Did you hear what God commanded Abram? He told Abram to leave his father's house, bid farewell to his relatives, leave his country, and move to a country to which God would lead him. To man's way of thinking, what God asked Abram to do was extremely difficult, but God had wonderful plans for him. Let us now read again this verse and the two verses which follow, to know why God called Abram to leave his home and move to another land.

---

38 In Wolof culture that would make Abram Lot's functional father.

¹**Now the LORD said to Abram**, "Leave your country, and your relatives, and your father's house, and go to the land that I will show you. ²I will make of you a great nation. I will bless you and make your name great. You will be a blessing. ³I will bless those who bless you, and I will curse him who treats you with contempt. All the families of the earth will be blessed through you." (Genesis 12:1-3)

Why did God command Abram to move to another country? This is why: God planned to make of Abram a new nation, from which would come the prophets, the Scriptures, and the Savior of the world. That is why God promised Abram saying, "**I will make of you a great nation… and you will be a blessing… [and] all the families of the earth will be blessed through you.**"

Here is a great truth. Do you understand it? God chose Abram to become the father of the ancestors through whom the promised Redeemer would be born into the human family. This Redeemer was destined to be the Savior for all the peoples of the world, so that whoever believes in Him might be saved from the dominion of Satan, sin and death, and from the eternal fire. Thus, we see that when God called Abram, He was moving forward with His plan to send to earth the Savior of sinners. Abram himself was not the Savior of the world, but he was to become the father of a nation from which the promised Savior would come.

That is the promise (or *covenant*) that God made to Abram – on the condition that he would leave his homeland and go to the place which God would show him. Did Abram obey God? What do you think? The word of God tells us:

⁴**So Abram went, as the LORD had told him** … Abram was seventy-five years old when he departed from Haran. ⁵Abram took Sarai his wife, Lot his brother's son, all their possessions that they had gathered, and the people whom they had acquired in Haran, and they went to go into the land of Canaan. They entered into the land of Canaan. (Genesis 12:4-5)

Why did Abram obey God and turn his back on his father's home and religion? There could be only one reason. Abram trusted God. Abram did not know where he was going, but he believed the word of the LORD, which told him, "Move out! If you move, I will greatly bless you." Abram had confidence in God and left his country as the LORD God had commanded him. In His faithfulness, God led Abram to the land of Canaan, which today is called Palestine, or Israel. Next, the Scripture says: **Abram passed through the land.... At that time, Canaanites were in the land. The LORD appeared to Abram and said, "I will give this land to your offspring."** (Genesis 12:6-7)

Thus we learn that God, who had promised to make Abram the father of a new nation, also promised him a new land in which to live and establish this nation. That is what God meant when He appeared to Abram and promised him, **"I will give this land to your offspring."**

We see something here that surpasses human wisdom. There were people living throughout the land of Canaan. How could Abram and his descendants possess it? Abram was seventy-five years old. His wife was sixty-five and childless. Could such an elderly couple have children and descendants to fill the land and rule over it? How could this happen?

Let us try to illustrate what God promised Abram. Think of an elderly man who has no children and comes from a far-off land to visit Senegal.[39] He comes with his elderly wife, who has never been able to conceive. When they arrive, someone says to them, "One day you and your descendants will possess the whole land of Senegal!" The old man laughs and says, "You are very funny! My descendants are going to possess the land? I do not even have any descendants! I am an old man; I have no children, and my wife is unable to conceive – and you say to me that my descendants are going to multiply and possess Senegal? Are you ill?"

---

39 In this book a number of illustrations are presented in the Senegalese context, since it was for the Wolof people of Senegal, West Africa that this radio series was originally produced.

Perhaps this illustration seems a little absurd; nonetheless, this is the kind of promise God made to Abram – to a man who was old and childless, with a wife who could not conceive. Now listen to what God promised Abram in chapter 13. He said:

> [15]**"For I will give all the land which you see** to you and to your offspring forever. [16]I will make your offspring as the dust of the earth, so that if a man can count the dust of the earth, then your offspring may also be counted. [17]Arise, walk through the land in its length and in its width; for I will give it to you." (Genesis 13:15-17)

Did God do what He promised? Did He make of Abram a great nation? Did He give the land of Palestine to Abram's descendants? He surely did. In future lessons we will see that Abram became the father of the Hebrew nation, to whom God gave the land that today is often referred to as *the Holy Land*. Next, the Scripture says:

> [7]**[Abram] built an altar there to the LORD**, who had appeared to him. [8]He left from there to go to the mountain on the east of Bethel and pitched his tent.... There he built an altar to the LORD and called on the LORD's name. (Genesis 12:7-8)

What was the first thing that Abram did upon arriving in the new country which God had promised to give him? He slaughtered an animal and burned it on an altar he had constructed, suspending the sacrifice for sin between heaven and earth, between God and man. Just as Abel, Seth, Enoch and Noah had done, in the same way Abram offered up animal sacrifices to God. Why did Abram do this? He did it because God had not cancelled His law which states: **Apart from shedding of blood, there is no [forgiveness of the sin debt].** (Hebrews 9:22) Abram, like all of Adam's offspring, was a sinner. The only reason God could overlook Abram's sins was because he believed God and brought to Him the blood of a sacrifice, which symbolized the holy Redeemer who was to come into the world to suffer and die in the place of sinners.

Our time is about up. What we have studied today is so very important and must not be forgotten. Do you understand now why God called Abram to turn his back on his father's house and move to another country? Yes, God intended to make of Abram a new nation, which would be a door of blessing for all peoples of the earth. What God planned to do with Abram was part of the wonderful plan that He announced in the Garden of Paradise on the day our ancestors Adam and Eve sinned. Do you remember how God had promised One who would come into the world to deliver the children of Adam from the power of Satan? Two thousand years later, in the time of Abram, God had not forgotten His promise.

And so today we have seen how God, in His faithfulness, called Abram so that he might become the father of a nation through which the promised Savior would come into the world. That is why God promised Abram saying,

> [2]**"I will make of you a great nation.** I will bless you and make your name great. You will be a blessing. [3]I will bless those who bless you, and I will curse him who treats you with contempt. All the families of the earth will be blessed through you." (Genesis 12:2-3)

Have you grasped today's lesson? Allow us to pose a couple of questions which summarize what we have studied today.

First: *Why did God call Abram to leave his home and go to a new land?* Because God planned to make of Abram a new nation. Second: *Why did God want to make of Abram a new nation?* Because it was through this nation from which God would provide for the world the prophets, the Holy Scriptures and at last, the Redeemer Himself. And so we see that when God called Abram, He was moving forward with His plan to bless you and me, our families, communities, and every nation, tribe, people and language.

Friends, we must stop here today. In our next lesson, God willing, we will learn why Abram was called *the friend of God....* God bless you as you meditate on God's promise to Abram:

> **I will make of you a great nation...you will be a blessing....**
> **All the families of the earth will be blessed through you.**
> (Genesis 12:2-3)

Program 19

Abraham God's Friend

Genesis 13-15

Are you ready to discover some more powerful truths from the life of the prophet Abraham? Last time we learned that, at first, his name was not Abraham, but *Abram*. We also learned that he was born in the country of Chaldea, which today is called Iraq. The people of that land bowed down to idols. But in the middle of all the idolatry, one day the LORD God appeared to Abram and told him to leave his father's house and to move to a country which the LORD God would show him.

Do you remember why God commanded Abram to move to another country? It was because God planned to make of Abram a new nation from which would come the prophets of God, the Holy Scriptures, and finally the Savior of the world Himself. Thus, we discovered that when God called Abram, He was moving forward with His plan to bring into the world the promised Redeemer. That is why God said to Abram, **"You will be a blessing…. All the families of the earth will be blessed through you."** (Genesis 12:2-3)

Thus, we saw that Abram obeyed God and left his city, not even knowing where God would lead him. When Abram left his father's house, he was seventy-five years old. Abram took with him Sarai, his wife, and Lot, the son of his older brother, along with his flocks of sheep and goats, herds of cattle, and many servants. They headed in the direction of Canaan. Canaan is the land which today is known as Palestine or Israel.

When Abram arrived in Canaan, the LORD appeared to him again and said, **"I will give this land to your offspring."** (Genesis 12:7) This is how God, who promised to make Abram the father of a new nation, also promised to give him a new land for his offspring to dwell in. Incredible! Abram and his wife were elderly and did not have any children. How then could they have descendants who would fill the land? We will soon see God's answer to this.

Now, let us continue in the story of Abram. We are studying in the Torah, in the book of Genesis, chapter 13. In this chapter we will see what happened between Abram and his nephew Lot. The Scripture says:

> ²**Abram was very rich in livestock**, in silver, and in gold. ³He went on his journeys from the South as far as Bethel, to the place where his tent had been at the beginning, between Bethel and Ai, ⁴to the place of the altar, which he had made there at the first. There Abram called on the LORD's name. ⁵Lot also, who went with Abram, had flocks, herds, and tents. ⁶The land was not able to bear them, that they might live together; for their possessions were so great that they couldn't live together. ⁷There was strife between the herdsmen of Abram's livestock and the herdsmen of Lot's livestock….
>
> ⁸**Abram said to Lot**, "Please, let there be no strife between you and me, and between your herdsmen and my herdsmen; for we are relatives. ⁹Isn't the whole land before you? Please separate yourself from me. If you go to the left hand, then I will go to the right. Or if you go to the right hand, then I will go to the left."
>
> ¹⁰**Lot lifted up his eyes**, and saw all the plain of the Jordan, that it was well-watered everywhere, before the LORD destroyed Sodom and Gomorrah, like the garden of the LORD, like the land of Egypt, as you go to Zoar. ¹¹So Lot chose the Plain of the Jordan for himself. Lot traveled east, and they separated themselves from one other.
>
> ¹²**Abram lived in the land of Canaan**, and Lot lived in the cities of the plain, and moved his tent as far as Sodom. ¹³Now the men of Sodom were exceedingly wicked and sinners against the LORD. (Genesis 13:2-13)

What do you think of Lot's choice? Lot chose the verdant fields, and left his uncle Abram with the drier ones. But the portion which Lot chose was in the region of Sodom, a city filled with wickedness.

Lot chose his own will, while Abram chose God's will. Two studies from now, Lord willing, we will see what happened to Lot, who followed his own desires. In the end Lot lost everything: his riches, his wife, his family, his happiness, and his testimony. As for Abram, who left everything in the hands of the Lord his God, he was greatly blessed by God.

How can we profit from the story of Lot and Abram? Perhaps by asking ourselves a simple question. Which of the two am I most like? Lot or Abram? Am I seeking after the things of the world, like Lot? Or the things of eternity, like Abram? Like those two men, each of us must also choose between our own will and God's will. The one who is wise will choose God's will. The Scriptures say:

> **For what does it profit a man, to gain the whole world**, and forfeit his life? (Mark 8:36) ¹⁵Don't love the world or the things that are in the world... ¹⁷[because] the world is passing away with its lusts, but he who does God's will remains forever. (1 John 2:15,17)

What is it that you want more than anything else? The things of the earth which are passing away or things of God which will last forever and ever?

Now let's continue with the story of Abram:

> ¹⁴**The LORD said to Abram**, after Lot was separated from him, "Now, lift up your eyes, and look from the place where you are, northward and southward and eastward and westward, ¹⁵for I will give all the land which you see to you and to your offspring forever. ¹⁶I will make your offspring as the dust of the earth, so that if a man can count the dust of the earth, then your offspring may also be counted. ¹⁷Arise, walk through the land in its length and in its width; for I will give it to you." ¹⁸Abram moved his tent, and came and lived by the oaks of Mamre, which are in Hebron, and built an altar there to the LORD. (Genesis 13:14-18)

¹**After these things the word of the LORD came to Abram** in a vision, saying, "Don't be afraid, Abram. I am your shield, your exceedingly great reward." ²Abram said, "Sovereign Lord, what will you give me, since I go childless, and he who will inherit my estate is Eliezer of Damascus?" ³Abram said, "Behold, you have given no children to me: and, behold, one born in my house is my heir." ⁴Behold, the LORD's word came to him, saying, "This man will not be your heir, but he who will come out of your own body will be your heir." ⁵The LORD brought him outside, and said, "Look now toward the sky, and count the stars, if you are able to count them." He said to Abram, "So your offspring will be." ⁶He believed in the LORD, who credited it to him for righteousness. (Genesis 15:1-6)

Think how hard it must have been for Abram to believe this promise. He and his wife were elderly and had no child. Yet God continued to make promises to Abram concerning a great people that would issue from him. How could this be? How could Abram become the father of a great nation? There is only one answer: The one true God is the One who can do all things. God is great! Nothing is impossible for Him. What He promises He performs.

What about Abram? Did he believe the LORD, who had promised something that seemed impossible? Let's listen again to the Scripture. It says: [**Abram**] **believed in the LORD, who credited it to him for righteousness.** What a wonderful thing God had promised Abram, something which, humanly speaking, could not happen. And how did Abram respond? He believed what God had promised him. And what did God do? God judged Abram as one who is righteous, because of his faith in the LORD and His plan.

This truth ought to thrill the hearts of those who want God to judge them as righteous. Why did God declare Abram as one who is righteous? Was Abram a perfectly holy righteous person in himself? No. In our next lesson we will see that Abram had a sinner's nature, like every descendant of Adam, like you and me. Why then did God judge Abram as righteous? God counted Abram as one who is righteous, because Abram believed what

God said. That is why the Scripture says: **He believed the LORD, and the LORD counted him as righteous because of his faith.** (Genesis 15:6 NLT)

What does it mean to believe God? As we know, the scriptures of the prophets were written in the Hebrew language. In Hebrew, the word for *believe* is *aman*, from which we get our word *amen*. When you say, "Amen" you are simply saying, "Yes, it is true" or "Yes, I agree." This is what it means to believe. When God made a promise to Abram, Abram's heart response was: "Amen. Yes. It is true. I believe your words." Based on that simple "Amen" to the word of the LORD, God declared Abram as righteous.

How about you? Do you want God to count you as one who is righteous, as He counted Abram righteous? Then you must trust the LORD God as Abram trusted Him. You must believe what God says, even if it is not easy. You must accept the true word of God, even if your relatives or your friends do not believe it. God wants to clothe you in His righteousness and give you the right to live in His holy presence forever, but you must trust Him and His way of salvation. The Holy Scriptures say:

> **Without faith it is impossible to be well pleasing to him**…. (Hebrews 11:6) [8]For by grace you have been saved through faith, and that not of yourselves; it is the gift of God, [9]not of works, that no one would boast. (Ephesians 2:8-9)

> [1]**What then will we say that Abraham**, our forefather, has found according to the flesh? [2]For if Abraham was justified by works, he has something to boast about, but not toward God. [3]For what does the Scripture say? "Abraham believed God, and it was accounted to him for righteousness." (Romans 4:1-3)

It was because Abram believed what God said that the LORD credited to Abram the gift of perfect righteousness. And the most wonderful thing in all of this is that the Scriptures go on to say:

> [23]**Now it was not written** that it was accounted to him for his sake alone, [24]but for our sake also, to whom it will be

accounted, who believe in him who raised Jesus, our Lord, from the dead, [25]who was delivered up for our trespasses, and was raised for our justification. (Romans 4:23-25)

God made him who had no sin to be sin for us, so that in him we might become the righteousness of God. (2 Corinthians 5:21)

How about you? Do you really believe God? We are not asking if you believe that God exists, or if you believe that God is one. The Scriptures speak of that kind of faith, saying: **You believe that God is one. You do well. The demons also believe, and shudder.** (James 2:19) Satan himself knows that there is only one God. Believing that there is one God will not cause God to forgive your sins and declare you as one who is righteous. What God wants is for you to believe His word and submit to it. God wants to speak to you through the writings of the prophets. He wants you to know and to believe the good news of salvation which shows how you can be made forever righteous before God, the Holy One.

Dear friend, has God clothed you with His righteousness? Or are you merely wearing the clothes of religion? Are you listening to the trustworthy word of God or to the unreliable words of men? Do you know what the Holy Scriptures declare about the way of righteousness established by God? Have you believed it?

As for Abram, he believed the word of God, even though it meant bidding farewell to his relatives and his father's religion. And that is precisely why he was called *the friend of God*. That is what the Scriptures tell us. **"Abraham believed God, and it was credited to him as righteousness," and he was called God's friend.** (James 2:23) How about you? Are you a friend of God?

This is where we must stop today. We thank you for listening and invite you to join us next time for the story of *Abram and Ishmael*.

God bless you as you think on this powerful verse from His word:

"Abraham believed God, and it was credited to him as righteousness," and he was called God's friend. (James 2:23 NIV)

Program 20

Abraham and Ishmael

Genesis 16, 17

Two lessons ago in our study in the Holy Scriptures we began to explore the story of the prophet Abraham. At the first, his name was Abram. But in our program today we will discover why God changed his name to Abraham. The first part of today's lesson is a sad story which unveils something that Abram did which was not pleasing to God. Some people think that God's prophets never sinned, but the Holy Scriptures declare:

> **For there is no distinction, for all have sinned**, and fall short of the glory of God; (Romans 3:22-23) If we say that we haven't sinned, we make [God] a liar, and his word is not in us. (1 John 1:10)

We have already seen how Adam's sin spread to all people – young and old, men and women, pagan and prophet. Only one Person was not stained by the sin of Adam. That One is the holy Redeemer whom God sent to earth to pay the penalty for sin in our place . He was not stained by sin, because He came from above, from the holy presence of God. He came into the human family but did not originate from it.

In our last two lessons we saw how God promised to make of Abram the father of a great nation, from which the Redeemer would arise. Both Abram and his wife were elderly and had no children, yet that did not cause Abram to doubt the word of God. Today, though, we will see that ten years after God first promised to give Abram descendants, Abram tried to help God fulfill His promise, and we will see how what Abram did in his impatience produced many problems.

Now then, let us continue in the Torah to see how Abram and Sarai arranged things in an effort to beget the son that God had promised. In chapter 16 of the book of Genesis, we read:

> [1]**Now Sarai, Abram's wife, bore him no children.** She had a servant, an Egyptian, whose name was Hagar. [2]Sarai said to Abram, "See now, the LORD has restrained me from bearing. Please go in to my servant. It may be that I will obtain children by her." Abram listened to the voice of Sarai. [3]Sarai, Abram's wife, took Hagar the Egyptian, her servant, after Abram had lived ten years in the land of Canaan, and gave her to Abram her husband to be his wife. [4]He went in to Hagar, and she conceived. When she saw that she had conceived, her mistress was despised in her eyes. [5]Sarai said to Abram, "This wrong is your fault. I gave my servant into your bosom, and when she saw that she had conceived, she despised me. May the LORD judge between me and you." [6]But Abram said to Sarai, "Behold, your maid is in your hand. Do to her whatever is good in your eyes." Sarai dealt harshly with her, and she fled from her face. (Genesis 16:1-6)

And so we see how Abram's sin produced bitterness and conflict in his household. Sarai was jealous because Hagar was pregnant. Hagar, in fear of Sarai's mistreatment, ran away from her.

Next, the Scripture says:

> [7]**The LORD's angel found her** by a fountain of water in the wilderness.... [8]He said, "Hagar, Sarai's servant, where did you come from? Where are you going?" She said, "I am fleeing from the face of my mistress Sarai." [9]The LORD's angel said to her, "Return to your mistress, and submit yourself under her hands." [10]The LORD's angel said to her, "I will greatly multiply your offspring, that they will not be counted for multitude." [11]The LORD's angel said to her, "Behold, you are with child, and will bear a son. You shall call his name Ishmael, because the LORD has heard your affliction. [12]He will be like a wild donkey among men. His hand will be against every man, and every man's hand against him. He will live opposed to all of his brothers." (Genesis 16:7-12)

The LORD showed His love and care for Hagar that day in a sweet and special way. So **she called the name of the LORD who spoke to her, "You are a God who sees," for she said, "Have I even stayed alive after seeing him?"** (Genesis 16:13) Then Hagar returned to Sarai her mistress, as the angel of the LORD had commanded her.

> [15]**Hagar bore a son for Abram.** Abram called the name of his son, whom Hagar bore, Ishmael. [16]Abram was eighty-six years old when Hagar bore Ishmael to Abram. (Genesis 16:15-16)

That is how Ishmael was born, who became the father of the Arab race. As we will see, God cared for Ishmael and had a plan for him, but Ishmael was not the son that God had promised to Abram. God's wonderful plan to make a new nation of Abram had not changed. God is not in a hurry as was Abram. God always does what He promises, even if it seems to us that He is slow.

For thirteen years after the birth of Ishmael God remained silent, saying nothing to Abram. But one day God spoke again to him. Let us read in chapter 17 and hear the announcement God made to Abram after those long years of silence. The Scripture says:

> [1]**When Abram was ninety-nine years old,** the LORD appeared to Abram and said to him, "I am God Almighty. Walk before me and be blameless. [2]I will make my covenant between me and you, and will multiply you exceedingly." [3]Abram fell on his face. God talked with him, saying, [4]"As for me, behold, my covenant is with you. You will be the father of a multitude of nations. [5]Your name will no more be called Abram, but your name will be Abraham; for I have made you the father of a multitude of nations. [6]I will make you exceedingly fruitful, and I will make nations of you. Kings will come out of you. [7]I will establish my covenant between me and you and your offspring after you throughout their generations for an everlasting covenant, to be a God to you and to your offspring after you. [8]I will give to you, and to your offspring after you, the land where you are traveling, all the land of Canaan, for an everlasting possession. I will be their God."

⁹**God said to Abraham**, "As for you, you shall keep my covenant, you and your offspring after you throughout their generations. ¹⁰This is my covenant, which you shall keep, between me and you and your offspring after you. Every male among you shall be circumcised. ¹¹You shall be circumcised in the flesh of your foreskin. It will be a token of the covenant between me and you. ¹²He who is eight days old shall be circumcised among you, every male throughout your generations.…"

¹⁵**God said to Abraham**, "As for Sarai your wife, you shall not call her name Sarai, but her name shall be Sarah. ¹⁶I will bless her, and moreover I will give you a son by her. Yes, I will bless her, and she will be a mother of nations. Kings of peoples will come from her." ¹⁷Then Abraham fell on his face, and laughed, and said in his heart, "Will a child be born to him who is one hundred years old? Will Sarah, who is ninety years old, give birth?" ¹⁸Abraham said to God, "Oh that Ishmael might live before you!" ¹⁹God said, "No, but Sarah, your wife, will bear you a son. You shall call his name Isaac. I will establish my covenant with him for an everlasting covenant for his offspring after him.

²⁰**As for Ishmael**, I have heard you. Behold, I have blessed him, and will make him fruitful, and will multiply him exceedingly. He will become the father of twelve princes, and I will make him a great nation. ²¹But I will establish my covenant with Isaac, whom Sarah will bear to you at this set time next year."
(Genesis 17:1-12,15-21)

That is the record of how Abram listened to the counsel of his wife by going to bed with Hagar her servant. What Abram did was wrong. Ishmael, the son born to Abram and Hagar, was not part of the plan of God to create a new nation to bring blessing to all the nations of the world. But the unfaithfulness of men cannot thwart the faithfulness of God.

Thus, as we just read, when Abram was 99 years old, God reappeared to him to confirm the promise He had made to him so long ago. So the LORD said, "**I am God Almighty.…You will be the father of a** multitude of nations. Your name will no more be called Abram, but your name will be Abraham; for I have made you the father of a multitude of nations." In keeping with His plan of salvation, God changed Abram's name to *Abraham*, which means *the father of many*. God also changed Sarai's name to *Sarah*, which means *princess*.

Think of it. Here is an old couple who have never had a child of their own: Abram and Sarai. And now God is giving them new names in order to announce what is to take place. A very old Abram is renamed *Abraham*, *the father of many*, and his very old wife Sarai is called *Sarah*, meaning *princess*. Yes, God was going to give Abraham and Sarah a son, and from that son, a nation. Through that nation many kings and prophets would arise, and finally the Savior of the world. Truly, the LORD is great and worthy of praise forever. God did not forget what He had promised to Abraham long before.

So what did Abraham do after God confirmed His promise to give him a child in his old age? The Scripture says: **Then Abraham fell on his face, and laughed, and said in his heart, "Will a child be born to him who is one hundred years old? Will Sarah, who is ninety years old, give birth?"** (Genesis 17:17) Abraham laughed! But he did not laugh because of unbelief, but because of his joy in God's promise.

That is why the Scripture says:

> [18]**Besides hope, Abraham in hope believed**, to the end that he might become a father of many nations, according to that which had been spoken, "So will your offspring be." [19]Without being weakened in faith, he didn't consider his own body, already having been worn out, (he being about a hundred years old), and the deadness of Sarah's womb. [20]Yet, looking to the promise of God, he didn't waver through unbelief, but grew strong through faith, giving glory to God, [21]and being fully assured that what he had promised, he was also able to perform. (Romans 4:18-21)

Nevertheless, Abraham wanted to know what would happen to Ishmael, the child of his servant, Hagar. God replied,

20As for Ishmael, I have heard you. Behold, I have blessed him, and will make him fruitful, and will multiply him exceedingly. He will become the father of twelve princes, and I will make him a great nation.

21But I will establish my covenant with Isaac, whom Sarah will bear to you at this set time next year.... 19God said, "No, but Sarah, your wife, will bear you a son. You shall call his name Isaac. I will establish my covenant with him for an everlasting covenant for his offspring after him. (Genesis 17:20-21,19)

In this way God confirmed His purpose to provide for all people the prophets, the Scriptures, and the Savior of the world Himself through the descendants of Isaac.

In the next lesson, God willing, we will learn *what happened to Lot* (Abraham's nephew in Sodom), and we will witness *the birth of the son of the promise – Isaac.*[40]

Truly, God is faithful. All that He promises He fulfills. Nothing is difficult for Him. Listen to these beautiful verses from the Gospel[41]:

33Oh the depth of the riches both of the wisdom and the knowledge of God! How unsearchable are his judgments, and his ways past tracing out! 34For who has known the mind of the Lord? Or who has been his counselor? 35Or who has first given to him, and it will be repaid to him again? 36For of him, and through him, and to him are all things. To him be the glory for ever! Amen. (Romans 11:33-36)

Thank you for listening.

May God bless you as you consider this powerful statement from the Holy Scriptures:

If we are faithless, he remains faithful;
for he can't deny himself. (2 Timothy 2:13)

---

40 Arabic: *Ishaq*
41 *Injil* Arabic for *Good News*. While this term is most often used to refer uniquely to the gospel record, it is also used to refer to the entire New Testament.

Abraham: Sodom's Ruin and Isaac's Birth

Genesis 18-21

In our reading in the Torah we have seen how God promised to make Abraham the father of a new nation that would become a channel of eternal blessing to the world. But at this point in the story, Abraham and his wife Sarah, who were both very old, had not yet had the son from whom that new nation would come.

As we begin today's program we will first hear from three men who came to visit Abraham. As you will see, these three men were more than mere humans. Two of them were angels and the other was the LORD God Himself. All three appeared in human form to deliver their messages and carry out their missions. Yes, the same Lord who walked and talked with Adam and Eve in the Garden, also made personal visits to Abraham, *the Friend of God*.

We are reading from the book of Genesis, chapter 18:

> ¹**The LORD appeared to him** by the oaks of Mamre, as he sat in the tent door in the heat of the day. ²He lifted up his eyes and looked, and saw that three men stood near him. When he saw them, he ran to meet them from the tent door, and bowed himself to the earth, ³and said, "My lord, if now I have found favor in your sight, please don't go away from your servant. ⁴Now let a little water be fetched, wash your feet, and rest yourselves under the tree. ⁵I will get a piece of bread so you can refresh your heart. After that you may go your way, now that you have come to your servant." They said, "Very well, do as you have said."

⁶**Abraham…**⁸took butter, milk, and the calf which he had dressed, and set it before them. He stood by them under the tree, and they ate. ⁹They asked him, "Where is Sarah, your wife?" He said, "There, in the tent." ¹⁰He said, "I will certainly return to you at about this time next year; and behold, Sarah your wife will have a son." Sarah heard in the tent door, which was behind him. ¹¹Now Abraham and Sarah were old, well advanced in age. Sarah had passed the age of childbearing. ¹²Sarah laughed within herself, saying, "After I have grown old will I have pleasure, my lord being old also?" ¹³The LORD said to Abraham, "Why did Sarah laugh, saying, 'Will I really bear a child when I am old?' ¹⁴ Is anything too hard for the LORD?…"

²⁰**The LORD said, "Because the cry of Sodom** and Gomorrah is great, and because their sin is very grievous, ²¹I will go down now, and see whether their deeds are as bad as the reports which have come to me. If not, I will know." ²²The men turned from there, and went toward Sodom, but Abraham stood yet before the LORD.

²³**Abraham came near, and said**, "Will you consume the righteous with the wicked? ²⁴What if there are fifty righteous within the city? Will you consume and not spare the place for the fifty righteous who are in it? ²⁵May it be far from you to do things like that, to kill the righteous with the wicked, so that the righteous should be like the wicked. May that be far from you. Shouldn't the Judge of all the earth do right?" ²⁶The LORD said, "If I find in Sodom fifty righteous within the city, then I will spare the whole place for their sake." ²⁷Abraham answered, "See now, I have taken it on myself to speak to the Lord, although I am dust and ashes. ²⁸What if there will lack five of the fifty righteous? Will you destroy all the city for lack of five?" He said, "I will not destroy it if I find forty-five there." ²⁹He spoke to him yet again, and said, "What if there are forty found there?" He said, "I will not do it for the forty's sake." ³⁰He said, "Oh don't let the Lord be angry, and I will speak. What if there are thirty found there?" He said, "I will not do it if I find

thirty there." ³¹He said, "See now, I have taken it on myself to speak to the Lord. What if there are twenty found there?" He said, "I will not destroy it for the twenty's sake." ³² He said, "Oh don't let the Lord be angry, and I will speak just once more. What if ten are found there?" He said, "I will not destroy it for the ten's sake." ³³The LORD went his way as soon as he had finished communing with Abraham, and Abraham returned to his place. (Genesis 18:1-6,8-14,20-33)

¹**The two angels came to Sodom at evening.** Lot sat in the gate of Sodom. Lot saw them, and rose up to meet them. He bowed himself with his face to the earth, ²and he said, "See now, my lords, please come into your servant's house, stay all night, wash your feet, and you can rise up early, and go on your way." They said, "No, but we will stay in the street all night." ³He urged them greatly, and they came in with him, and entered into his house. He made them a feast, and baked unleavened bread, and they ate. ⁴But before they lay down, the men of the city, the men of Sodom, surrounded the house, both young and old, all the people from every quarter. ⁵They called to Lot, and said to him, "Where are the men who came in to you this night? Bring them out to us, that we may have sex with them." (Genesis 19:1-5)

These men of Sodom were homosexuals.

⁶**Lot went out to them through the door**, and shut the door after himself. ⁷He said, "Please, my brothers, don't act so wickedly. ⁸don't do anything to these men, because they have come under the shadow of my roof." ⁹They said, "Stand back!" Then they said, "This one fellow came in to live as a foreigner, and he appoints himself a judge. Now we will deal worse with you than with them!" They pressed hard on the man Lot, and came near to break the door. ¹⁰But the men reached out their hand, and brought Lot into the house to them, and shut the door. ¹¹They struck the men who were at the door of the house with blindness, both small and great, so that they wearied themselves to find the door.

¹²**The men said to Lot**, "Do you have anybody else here? Sons-in-law, your sons, your daughters, and whomever you have in the city, bring them out of the place: ¹³for we will destroy this place, because the outcry against them has grown so great before the LORD that the LORD has sent us to destroy it." ¹⁴Lot went out, and spoke to his sons-in-law, who were pledged to marry his daughters, and said, "Get up! Get out of this place, for the LORD will destroy the city!" But he seemed to his sons-in-law to be joking.

¹⁵**When the morning came**, then the angels hurried Lot, saying, "Get up! Take your wife and your two daughters who are here, lest you be consumed in the iniquity of the city." ¹⁶But he lingered; and the men grabbed his hand, his wife's hand, and his two daughters' hands, the LORD being merciful to him; and they took him out, and set him outside of the city. ¹⁷It came to pass, when they had taken them out, that he said, "Escape for your life! Don't look behind you, and don't stay anywhere in the plain. Escape to the mountains, lest you be consumed!"

²⁴**Then the LORD rained on Sodom** and on Gomorrah sulfur and fire from the LORD out of the sky. ²⁵He overthrew those cities, all the plain, all the inhabitants of the cities, and that which grew on the ground. ²⁶But Lot's wife looked back from behind him, and she became a pillar of salt.

²⁷**Abraham went up early in the morning** to the place where he had stood before the LORD. ²⁸He looked toward Sodom and Gomorrah, and toward all the land of the plain, and saw that the smoke of the land went up as the smoke of a furnace. ²⁹When God destroyed the cities of the plain, God remembered Abraham, and sent Lot out of the middle of the overthrow, when he overthrew the cities in which Lot lived. (Genesis 19:6-17, 24-29)

That is the solemn story of how God judged the people of Sodom and Gomorrah with brimstone and fire from the sky. Today the ruins of Sodom lie under the Dead (Salt) Sea in Palestine (Israel). To pursue sin is never a wise choice. God is serious about judging sin.

In the time we have left today, we want to learn about some of the events surrounding the birth of the son whom God gave to Abraham and Sarah in their old age, just as He had promised.

> [1]**The LORD visited Sarah as he had said**, and the LORD did to Sarah as he had spoken. [2]Sarah conceived, and bore Abraham a son in his old age, at the set time of which God had spoken to him. [3]Abraham called his son who was born to him, whom Sarah bore to him, Isaac. [4]Abraham circumcised his son, Isaac, when he was eight days old, as God had commanded him. [5]Abraham was one hundred years old when his son, Isaac, was born to him. [6]Sarah said, "God has made me laugh. Everyone who hears will laugh with me." [7]She said, "Who would have said to Abraham that Sarah would nurse children? For I have borne him a son in his old age."

> [8]**[Isaac] grew and was weaned.** Abraham made a great feast on the day that Isaac was weaned. [9]Sarah saw the son of Hagar the Egyptian, whom she had borne to Abraham, mocking. [10]Therefore she said to Abraham, "Cast out this servant and her son! For the son of this servant will not be heir with my son, Isaac." [11]The thing was very grievous in Abraham's sight on account of his son. [12]God said to Abraham, "Don't let it be grievous in your sight because of the boy, and because of your servant. In all that Sarah says to you, listen to her voice. For your offspring will be named through Isaac. [13]I will also make a nation of the son of the servant, because he is your child." [14]Abraham rose up early in the morning, and took bread and a container of water, and gave it to Hagar, putting it on her shoulder; and gave her the child, and sent her away. She departed, and wandered in the wilderness of Beersheba. (Genesis 21:1-14)

Ishmael's departure was painful for Abraham, but it had to be, since God had revealed to him that the new nation through which **"all the families of the earth will be blessed"** (Genesis 12:3) would come from Isaac's family line, not Ishmael's. Ishmael, who was about fifteen years old when Isaac was weaned, made fun of his (half) brother and failed to appreciate God's plan to make of Isaac a great nation which would become a channel of blessing for all peoples on earth. He had no clue that it was from that new nation that the prophets, the Holy Scriptures, and the promised Savior would come.

So what happened to Ishmael? Hagar and Ishmael were sent away, but the LORD was good to them, too. The Scripture says:

> [20]**God was with the boy, and he grew.** He lived in the wilderness, and…became an archer. [21]He lived in the wilderness of Paran. His mother got a wife for him out of the land of Egypt. (Genesis 21:20-21)

Ishmael became the father of the mighty Arab race, which God has blessed in so many ways. But the LORD revealed to Abraham that there would be an intense rivalry between Ishmael's and Isaac's offspring, which is true to this day. The good news is that God loves all people in every nation – and that includes you and your family. He invites all to turn to Him in repentance and faith, and enjoy a close relationship with Him for time and for eternity, just like Abraham, *the Friend of God*.

Friends, our time is gone. But, once again, we have seen how the God of Abraham is the faithful and holy God who keeps His promises, both to save and to judge. That is why He rescued Abraham's nephew Lot before raining fire down on the people of Sodom and Gomorrah for their sin – as He said He would do. And that is why He gave Abraham and Sarah a son in their old age – just as He had promised twenty-five years earlier.

Thank you for your attention. We urge you to join us next time to look into the most painful and well-known event in the life of the prophet Abraham. It is the story of *Abraham's Great Sacrifice*, an event many celebrate without understanding what it means.

We close with this warning from God to us to learn from the stories of Abraham, Lot, and Sodom and Gomorrah:

> **Now all these things happened to them by way of example, and they were written for our admonition….** (1 Corinthians 10:11)

Program 22

Abraham's Sacrifice

Genesis 22

I n our studies in the Torah, we have explored many wonderful and insightful stories about God's prophet Abraham. Today we come to the best-known event from the life of Abraham: the true story behind a feast celebrated annually throughout the Muslim world: *Eid al-Adha* or *Tabaski*,[42] *the Festival of the Sacrifice.*

In our last lesson we learned how God gave Abraham and Sarah a child in their old age, thus fulfilling what God had promised long before. Their son's name was Isaac. God had promised Abraham that through Isaac He would bring forth a new nation that would bless every nation on earth. We also learned how Ishmael and his mother, Hagar, left Abraham's household, and moved to Egypt. And so, where today's story begins, only Isaac, the one born according to God's promise, remained at home.

One day God told Abraham to do a shocking and difficult thing. In the Torah, the book of Genesis, chapter 22, the Scripture says:

> ¹**After these things, God tested Abraham,** and said to him, "Abraham!" He said, "Here I am." ²He said, "Now take your son, your only son, Isaac, whom you love, and go into the land of Moriah. Offer him there as a burnt offering on one of the mountains which I will tell you of." (Genesis 22:1-2)

What!? What was God asking of Abraham? He was commanding Abraham to take his beloved son to a far-away mountain, and offer him as a burnt sacrifice! How could this be? Abraham had waited

---

42 *Tabaski*: a familiar term in West Africa. Verb: *to sacrifice a sheep on the feast day;*
Noun: Muslim festival *Eid al-Adha* commemorating Abraham's sacrifice (Qur'an 37:100-107).

for twenty-five long years to have the son which God had promised him, and now God was telling him to slay his son as a sacrifice! How did Abraham answer God? Did he argue with the words of God because they were difficult to accept? The Scripture says:

> ³**Abraham rose early in the morning**, and saddled his donkey; and took two of his young men with him, and Isaac his son. He split the wood for the burnt offering, and rose up, and went to the place of which God had told him. (Genesis 22:3)

For three days, Abraham and his son and two servants walked and walked, heading toward the mountain where God told Abraham to go. Abraham's heart was ready to break as he neared that fearful place where he would slay his beloved son and cremate him. Of course we who are reading the story today know that God was only testing Abraham's faith, but Abraham didn't know that. What God had asked of him was a terrible and painful trial.

> ⁴**On the third day Abraham lifted up his eyes**, and saw the place far off. ⁵Abraham said to his young men, "Stay here with the donkey. The boy and I will go over there. We will worship, and come back to you." ⁶Abraham took the wood of the burnt offering and laid it on Isaac his son. He took in his hand the fire and the knife. They both went together. ⁷Isaac spoke to Abraham his father, and said, "My father?" He said, "Here I am, my son." He said, "Here is the fire and the wood, but where is the lamb for a burnt offering?" ⁸Abraham said, "God will provide himself the lamb for a burnt offering, my son." So they both went together.

> ⁹**They came to the place** which God had told him of. Abraham built the altar there, and laid the wood in order, bound Isaac his son, and laid him on the altar, on the wood. ¹⁰Abraham stretched out his hand, and took the knife to kill his son.

> ¹¹**The LORD's angel called to him out of the sky**, and said, "Abraham, Abraham!" He said, "Here I am." ¹²He said, "Don't lay your hand on the boy or do anything to him. For now I know

that you fear God, since you have not withheld your son, your only son, from me." [13]Abraham lifted up his eyes, and looked, and saw that behind him was a ram caught in the thicket by his horns. Abraham went and took the ram, and offered him up for a burnt offering instead of his son. [1]

[4]**Abraham called the name of that place** "The LORD Will Provide". As it is said to this day, "On the LORD's mountain, it will be provided." (Genesis 22:4-14)

The story of Abraham's sacrifice has three sides: *a historical side, a symbolic side* and *a prophetic side*. To understand the full meaning of Abraham's sacrifice, we need to understand three things: first, what took place; second, what the sacrifice symbolized; and third, what the prophet Abraham foretold about a future event.

Regarding *the historical side*, we just read how God tested Abraham's faith and saved his son from death by providing a ram to die in Isaac's place. This happened about 4000 years ago in the place where Jerusalem is located today. That, in short, is the historical side of the story of Abraham's sacrifice.

Concerning *the symbolic side* of the story, God's word tells us that we are all like Abraham's son. God, in His justice, condemned Abraham's son to death. We, too, are all condemned sinners and deserve God's judgment. But God, in His grace, saved Abraham's son from death. Similarly, God, in His grace, has provided a way of escape for us. What is that way of redemption? The story of Abraham's sacrifice teaches us that it is the way of the perfect Sacrifice provided by God Himself.

In today's story, we saw that God provided a ram to die in the place of Abraham's son. Since only the horns of the sheep were caught in the thicket the sheep's skin was not torn. If the sheep had a single flaw, it could not have replaced Abraham's son on the altar. But the sacrifice which God provided was a perfect sheep, without blemish. In our study in the first chapters of the Torah, we learned about the way of salvation established by God. After Adam and

Eve sinned, God decreed that, since the penalty for sin is death, forgiveness of sin required a death payment. Sinners who wanted to have their sins forgiven were required to take an animal without blemish, slay it, and present it to God as a burnt offering. The innocent animal had to die in the place of the guilty person. This was how God could forgive sins without compromising His justice.

Something else to remember is this: The Scriptures say that a sacrificial animal was just a symbol of what God really required. A slain animal was merely **a shadow of the good to come, not the very image of the things.... For it is impossible that the blood of bulls and goats should take away sins.** (Hebrews 10:1,4) The blood of animals cannot pay for sin because animals and humans are not of equal value. The ram which replaced Abraham's son on the altar merely illustrated the perfect Sacrifice God planned to provide for the sin of the world. In short, that is what Abraham's sacrificial sheep symbolized. It pointed to the Savior whom God promised to send into the world to save sinners from His righteous judgment.

Concerning *the prophetic side* of the story, do you remember what Abraham said to his son as they were climbing the mountain? He told him: **"God will provide himself the lamb for a burnt offering."** And do you remember what Abraham announced after he had slain the ram, and burned it in place of his son? He called the place of sacrifice: **The LORD Will Provide.** And the prophet Moses, who wrote the Torah, adds: **As it is said to this day, "On the LORD's mountain, it will be provided."** What was the reason for this? Why did the prophet Abraham say, **"The LORD will provide"**? Why did he not say, "Praise be to God! The LORD has provided a sacrifice"? Friends, this is a question of tremendous importance, because the answer to it contains the Good News of God, which each of us must understand and believe if we want to be delivered from God's righteous judgment.

Why did Abraham call the place, **the LORD will provide**? Here is why. Abraham was announcing an event that was to yet take place on those same mountains where the ram had replaced his son on the altar. In short, Abraham was declaring: "I praise God, because He has provided a ram to replace my son on the altar. However, I am telling you that one day, on this same mountain, God will provide another sacrifice which will be infinitely greater than the ram which saved my son today from the knife and the fire. Yes, the Sacrifice which God will provide will have the power to save the children of Adam from the punishment of eternal death in the fire which never goes out. God will send down a holy Redeemer who will die as a sacrifice, the innocent for the guilty, so that whoever believes in Him will not perish." This is God's Good News for all people which Abraham announced when he said, **"God will provide himself the lamb for a burnt offering, my son."**

Before we conclude the story of Abraham's sacrifice today, each of us needs to know that about two thousand years after Abraham prophesied that God would provide His own Sacrifice for sinners, the LORD God fulfilled Abraham's prophecy. We cannot say much about it today, but those of you who know the Gospel, know the story of the Messiah-Savior. You know that He was born of a virgin woman who belonged to the family line of Abraham and Isaac, just as God had promised. This Redeemer who was to die in the place of sinners had no earthly father. He came from heaven, and thus, did not inherit Adam's sinful nature. He had no sin; He had no blemish. That is why He was worthy to die as the perfect Sacrifice; as a substitute for the sinful children of Adam.

That Savior's name is **Jesus**. The name *Jesus* means *The LORD saves*. Some call Jesus *Isa*.[43] Later, when we come to the Gospel Writings[44] we will read about the prophet John[45] whom God sent to prepare the way before Jesus the Messiah. When John saw Jesus coming toward him, he said, **"Behold, the Lamb of God, who takes away the sin of the world!"** (John 1:29) Why did the prophet John call Jesus *the Lamb of God*? It was because Jesus was born to be the Sacrifice which does more than just cover sin. The blood of Jesus takes away sin. The ram that died for Abraham's son saved him from physical death, but Jesus the

---

43 See Lesson 61 for more on this.
44 *Injil*
45 Qur'anic/Arabic: *Yahya*

Lamb of God came to die for the world to save all who trust in Him from eternal death. Jesus is the perfect and final Sacrifice of whom Abraham prophesied when he said, **"God will provide himself the lamb for a burnt offering, my son."**

In the Gospel we will read how Jesus the Messiah willingly delivered Himself up to his enemies, and how they nailed Him to a Roman cross. Jesus the Redeemer, whom God provided, fulfilled the prophetic and the symbolic meaning of Abraham's sacrificed sheep. That is why, just before Jesus died, He cried out, **"It is finished!"**[46] (John 19:30) And three days later, God confirmed His satisfaction with the Redeemer's sacrifice by raising Him from the dead.

Jesus is the One who perfectly fulfilled the meaning of Abraham's sacrifice. Just as the ram died in the place of Abraham's son, so Jesus the Messiah died in our place. And did you know that the location where Jesus died in the place of sinners was on the same mountain range where Abraham slaughtered the ram in place of his son? Do you know the location of those two sacrifices? Yes, it is Jerusalem.

Dear friends, whoever you are, wherever you are, God commands you to turn from your wrong ideas and futile works, and to place your hope completely in the perfect and final Sacrifice that He Himself has provided. For the Scripture says that Jesus the Messiah **himself bore our sins in his body on the tree, that we, having died to sins, might live to righteousness. You were healed by his wounds.** (1 Peter 2:24)

Today we saw that Abraham's son accepted the sacrifice which God provided for him to die in his place. How about you? Have you accepted the Sacrifice that God has provided for you?

God bless you as you carefully consider the deeper meaning of Abraham's words from Mount Moriah when he said,

> **"God will provide himself the lamb."** and:
> **"On the LORD's mountain, it will be provided."** (Genesis 22:8,14)

---

46 Wolof: *All is complete; absolutely perfect; nothing change or add!*

Program 23
Esau and Jacob:
The Temporal and the Eternal

Genesis 25

In our last program, we looked into the story of Abraham's sacrifice. The Gospel gives us an interesting summary of this important story when it says:

> [17]**By faith, Abraham, being tested**, offered up Isaac. Yes, he who had gladly received the promises was offering up his one and only son, [who was born according to God's promise], [18]to whom it was said, "Your offspring will be accounted as from Isaac," [19]concluding that God is able to raise up even from the dead. Figuratively speaking, he also did receive him back from the dead. (Hebrews 11:17-19)

Our last five lessons have been taken up with stories from the life of the prophet Abraham. There are many more stories in the Torah about Abraham, but, unfortunately, we do not have time to read them all. However, before we leave Abraham and go on to the stories of his descendants, there is something that God said to Abraham that we should know about. One day God told Abraham:

> [13]**Know for sure that your offspring** will live as foreigners in a land that is not theirs, and will serve them. They will afflict them four hundred years. [14]I will also judge that nation, whom they will serve. Afterward they will come out with great wealth. (Genesis 15:13-14)

With those words God was announcing that the descendants of Abraham would become slaves in the land of Egypt. God also promised that after four hundred years He would deliver them from the dominion of the people of Egypt. Four lessons from now, in the will of God, we will begin to see how these precise prophecies were fulfilled, just as God told Abraham.

Then, in chapter 25, the Scripture says:

> ⁷**These are the days of the years of Abraham's life** which he lived: one hundred seventy-five years. ⁸Abraham gave up his spirit, and died at a good old age, an old man, and full of years, and was gathered to his people. ⁹Isaac and Ishmael, his sons, buried him in the cave of Machpelah, in the field of Ephron, …which is near Mamre, ¹⁰the field which Abraham purchased from the children of Heth. Abraham was buried there with Sarah, his wife. (Genesis 25:7-10)

Thus, Abraham, the friend of God, entered the presence of the LORD, whom he knew and loved. How then can we conclude and summarize our study about the prophet of God, Abraham? Perhaps with two questions and their answers.

The first question is: *Why did God tell Abraham to move and go to another country?* Answer: Because God planned to make of Abraham a new nation through which the promised Redeemer would come into the world.

The second question is: *Why did God declare Abraham as one who is righteous and accept him into His holy presence forever?* Answer: Because Abraham believed what God promised. Abraham was saved by faith in God's promises and not by his own works. This is what the Scripture declares when it says: **"Abraham believed God, and it was credited to him as righteousness," and he was called God's friend.** (James 2:23 NIV)

In chapter 25 in the book of Genesis, the Scripture continues with the story of Isaac and his twin sons.

> ¹⁹**This is the history of the generations of Isaac**, Abraham's son. Abraham became the father of Isaac. ²⁰Isaac was forty years old when he took Rebekah, the daughter of Bethuel the

Syrian of Paddan Aram, the sister of Laban the Syrian, to be his wife. [21]Isaac entreated the LORD for his wife, because she was barren. The LORD was entreated by him, and Rebekah his wife conceived. [22]The children struggled together within her. She said, "If it is like this, why do I live?" She went to inquire of the LORD. [23]The LORD said to her, "Two nations are in your womb. Two peoples will be separated from your body. The one people will be stronger than the other people. The elder will serve the younger."

[24]**When her days to be delivered were fulfilled**, behold, there were twins in her womb. [25]The first came out red all over, like a hairy garment. They named him Esau. [26]After that, his brother came out, and his hand had hold on Esau's heel. He was named Jacob. Isaac was sixty years old when she bore them. [27]The boys grew. Esau was a skillful hunter, a man of the field. Jacob was a quiet man, living in tents. (Genesis 25:19-27)

Thus, we see that Isaac and Rebecca had twins, Esau and Jacob.[47] They were twins, but that does not mean they were the same. As Esau grew up, he set his affections only on the things of the world, which are temporary, but Jacob valued the things of God, which last forever. Esau did not care about the promises God had made to Abraham, his grandfather, and to his father Isaac about the new nation to come from them. But Jacob did care about God's promises.

Esau was the firstborn. Therefore, humanly speaking, he was the one who should have received the inheritance of the firstborn and become the father of the great nation which God had promised to his grandfather, Abraham, and to his father, Isaac. However, even before the twins were born, God told Rebecca, their mother, **"the elder will serve the younger."** (Genesis 25:23) God, in His foreknowledge, was announcing that the inheritance of the firstborn and the descendants of the new nation would come through Jacob and not through Esau. As for Jacob, he should have waited for God, leaving all in the hands of the One who had the power to

---

47 Qur'anic/Arabic: *Ya'qub*

give him the inheritance in His appointed time. But Jacob did not wait for God. Let us read on to see how Jacob acted in order to take the inheritance from Esau, his older brother.

The Scripture says:

> [29] **Jacob boiled stew.** Esau came in from the field, and he was famished. [30] Esau said to Jacob, "Please feed me with some of that red stew, for I am famished."… [31] Jacob said, "First, sell me your birthright." [32] Esau said, "Behold, I am about to die. What good is the birthright to me?" [33] Jacob said, "Swear to me first." He swore to him. He sold his birthright to Jacob. [34] Jacob gave Esau bread and lentil stew. He ate and drank, rose up, and went his way. So Esau despised his birthright. (Genesis 25:29-34)

Do you understand what Esau did? He exchanged his inheritance as the firstborn son for a little bit of food. Imagine a very rich man who has two sons. The man has fields and houses, and riches and lots of money. The firstborn is the one who should inherit most of his wealth. However one day, the elder comes in from the bush and sees his younger brother cooking fish and rice beside the path. The firstborn says to his younger brother. "I am starved; give me some of that rice to eat!" But the brother replies, "I will not give it to you, but I will sell it to you." The elder asks, "How much will you sell it to me for?" The younger brother says, "Your rights of inheritance as the firstborn." The elder replies, "Sold! I am hungry enough to die. Of what use is my birthright to me?" So the elder swears to hand over to his younger brother his whole inheritance. Then the firstborn sits down, eats and drinks, gets up and goes on his way without a thought about what he has lost.

What can we say about this firstborn who exchanged fields and houses, and riches and authority for one bowl of rice and fish? We can say just one thing: *How foolish!* Yet that is what Esau did. And the things Esau despised were infinitely more valuable than the riches of the world, because what Esau despised was the right to be a part of the new nation through which the Savior of the world would come. What does God want to teach us today through the story of Esau and Jacob? God wants to warn us not to follow in the footsteps of Esau by trading the riches of eternity for the pleasures of the world, which are passing away. The word of the Lord says:

> **For what will it profit a man** if he gains the whole world and forfeits his life? Or what will a man give in exchange for his life? (Matthew 16:26) Looking carefully lest there be any man who falls short of the grace of God…or profane person, like Esau, who sold his birthright for one meal. (Hebrews 12:15-16)

Esau missed out on the grace of God because he did not value the things of God. By telling us his story, God is warning us, saying: Do not walk in the footsteps of Esau. Do not despise the eternal blessings I want to give to you.

How about you? Do you want God's blessings? God loves you and wants to bless you greatly, but you must give Him first place in your life. You must value the word of God more than food and money. Then you will begin to understand what the Scriptures mean when they say: **"No eye has seen, no ear has heard, and no mind has imagined what God has prepared for those who love him."** (1 Corinthians 2:9 NLT)

God wants to bless us greatly. He wants to forgive all our sins, change our wicked hearts, purify us and fill us with His love, joy, peace and assurance. And these blessings are only part of the inheritance God gives to all who trusts Him. However, you must seek the things of eternity with all of your heart. He who does not passionately want God's eternal blessings will never receive them. As we sometimes hear: *Whoever wants honey must brave the bees.*[48]

Do you want to receive God's blessings? Then you must seek to understand what God has promised in His word. Do you know His wonderful promises, which surpass human understanding? Do you cherish them? Or are you merely seeking after the things of the world? The word of God shows us that there are two kinds of people in the world: Those who value most the temporal things

---

48 Wolof proverb

of earth, and those who value most the things that last forever. Which kind of person are you? Listen to what is written in the Psalms, in the first chapter:

> ¹**Blessed is the man** who doesn't walk in the counsel of the wicked, nor stand on the path of sinners, nor sit in the seat of scoffers; ²but his delight is in the LORD's law. On his law he meditates day and night. ³He will be like a tree planted by the streams of water, that produces its fruit in its season, whose leaf also does not wither. Whatever he does shall prosper. ⁴The wicked are not so, but are like the chaff which the wind drives away. ⁵Therefore the wicked shall not stand in the judgment, nor sinners in the congregation of the righteous. ⁶For the LORD knows the way of the righteous, but the way of the wicked shall perish. (Psalm 1:1-6)

How about you? In which way are you walking? Are you walking in the way of those who treasure God's promises? Or are you like Esau, who traded the promises of God for the passing things of the world? The word of God warns us, saying:

> **For what will it profit a man** if he gains the whole world and forfeits his life? Or what will a man give in exchange for his life? (Matthew 16:26) Don't work for the food which perishes, but for the food which remains to eternal life, which the [Redeemer] will give to you. For God…has sealed him. (John 6:27) While we don't look at the things which are seen, but at the things which are not seen. For the things which are seen are temporal, but the things which are not seen are eternal. (2 Corinthians 4:18)

Dear listeners, this is where we must stop today. Next time, in the will of God, we will continue in the Torah with the story of Jacob.

God bless you as you carefully consider this warning from Him:

> **Looking carefully lest there be any man who falls short of the grace of God…or profane person, like Esau, who sold his birthright for one meal.** (Hebrews 12:15-16)

Program 24

Jacob Becomes Israel

Genesis 28-32

I n our last program we read about the twins Isaac begot, that is, Esau and Jacob. Esau despised the promises which God made to his grandfather, Abraham, and exchanged his firstborn inheritance for a bowl of food. As for Jacob, he valued God's promises. But this does not mean that Jacob was without faults. Jacob's very name means *deceiver*. Today then, we plan to continue in the Torah and see how God changed *Jacob-the-deceiver* into *Jacob-the-man-of-God*.

Jacob was a real trickster – a deceiver. The Scriptures, which do not hide the shortcomings of the prophets, record for us how Jacob deceived his older brother Esau twice in order to take his birthright from him. It was for this reason that Esau, in his anger, purposed to kill his younger brother. Consequently, their mother, Rebecca, called Jacob in secret and advised him to flee to his maternal uncle Laban, who lived in Haran, and to stay there until his brother's anger subsided.

Now, let us read in the book of Genesis, chapter 28, to see what happened after Jacob left his father Isaac's house and headed for his uncle Laban's house.

The Scripture says:

> [10]**Jacob went out from Beersheba**, and went toward Haran. [Haran was the country in which Abraham lived before he moved to Canaan.] [11][Jacob] came to a certain place, and stayed there all night, because the sun had set. He took one of the stones of the place, and put it under his head, and lay down in that place to sleep.

¹²**He dreamed and saw a stairway** set upon the earth, and its top reached to heaven. Behold, the angels of God were ascending and descending on it. ¹³Behold, the LORD stood above it, and said, "I am the LORD, the God of Abraham your father, and the God of Isaac. I will give the land you lie on to you and to your offspring. ¹⁴Your offspring will be as the dust of the earth, and you will spread abroad to the west, and to the east, and to the north, and to the south. In you and in your offspring, all the families of the earth will be blessed. ¹⁵Behold, I am with you, and will keep you, wherever you go, and will bring you again into this land. For I will not leave you until I have done that which I have spoken of to you…."

¹⁶**Jacob awakened out of his sleep**, and he said, "Surely the LORD is in this place, and I didn't know it." ¹⁷He was afraid, and said, "How awesome this place is! This is none other than God's house, and this is the gate of heaven." ¹⁸Jacob rose up early in the morning, and took the stone that he had put under his head, and set it up for a pillar, and poured oil on its top. ¹⁹He called the name of that place Bethel [which means *the house of God*]. (Genesis 28:10-19)

So we see how God appeared to Jacob in a dream and promised to him the same thing He had promised his grandfather Abraham and his father Isaac: that is, to make of his offspring a great nation to bless all peoples on earth. Thus, the birthright Jacob stole from his older brother was given to him by God in the end. Jacob did not deserve to become the father of the new nation which would bring the Redeemer into the world. But the LORD is a God of mercy and grace who gives good things to those who trust Him.

What did Jacob see in his dream? The Scripture says that he **saw a stairway set upon the earth, and its top reached to heaven. Behold, the angels of God were ascending and descending on it.** The ladder Jacob saw was an unusual one, a very tall ladder, reaching from earth to heaven and entering into the very presence of God.

Through the dream of the tall ladder, God was showing Jacob that He wanted to have a wonderful and close relationship with him. God also wanted to show him that the Savior who was to come into the world would be like that ladder which went between heaven and earth – the one true Mediator between God and man.

To this day, many think that a person can climb up and enter Paradise based on his own good works. But God's word tells us that there is only one ladder between God and man, and that ladder does not come from man, but from God. We, the children of Adam, in our own strength have no means to climb up and enter the presence of God. This is because of our sin and our total lack of strength to please God the Holy One. But God, who is full of mercy, because of His great love for people, has provided a way of salvation for Adam's descendants.

We can understand, then, that the ladder which Jacob saw in his dream symbolized the Mediator whom God had promised to send into the world to save sinners. The Mediator is like the ladder which Jacob saw between heaven and earth. That is what the Scriptures teach when they say: **For there is one God, and one mediator between God and men, the man Christ Jesus, who gave himself as a ransom for all…[so] that whoever believes in him should not perish, but have eternal life.** (1 Timothy 2:5-6; John 3:16) God's word is clear on this matter: No one comes to God except through the holy Mediator that God sent down from heaven.

Now, let us see what happened after Jacob arrived at his maternal uncle's house. God's word says that **whatever a man sows, that he will also reap.** (Galatians 6:7) We have already heard how Jacob deceived his older brother. Now we will see how Jacob's uncle deceives him. His uncle's name was Laban and he was a crafty man.

We are reading in chapter 29 of Genesis. The Scripture says:

> [14]**Laban said to [Jacob]**, "Surely you are my bone and my flesh." Jacob stayed with him for a month. [15]Laban said to Jacob, "Because you are my relative, should you therefore serve me for nothing? Tell me, what will your wages be?" [16]Laban had two daughters. The name of the elder was Leah, and the name of the younger was Rachel.

¹⁷**Leah's eyes were weak**, but Rachel was beautiful in form and attractive. ¹⁸Jacob loved Rachel. He said, "I will serve you seven years for Rachel, your younger daughter." ¹⁹Laban said, "It is better that I give her to you, than that I should give her to another man. Stay with me." ²⁰Jacob served seven years for Rachel. They seemed to him but a few days, for the love he had for her. ²¹Jacob said to Laban, "Give me my wife, for my days are fulfilled, that I may go in to her." ²²Laban gathered together all the men of the place, and made a feast. ²³In the evening, he took Leah his daughter, and brought her to Jacob. He went in to her....

²⁵**In the morning, behold, it was Leah!** He said to Laban, "What is this you have done to me? Didn't I serve with you for Rachel? Why then have you deceived me?" ²⁶Laban said, "It is not done so in our place, to give the younger before the firstborn. ²⁷Fulfill the week of this one, and we will give you the other also for the service which you will serve with me for seven more years." ²⁸Jacob did so, and fulfilled her week. He gave him Rachel his daughter as wife.... ³⁰He went in also to Rachel, and he loved also Rachel more than Leah, and served with him seven more years. (Genesis 29:14-23,25-28,30)

That is how Laban deceived his nephew Jacob. What happened was not a good thing, but you can be sure that God had His hand upon the things happening in the life of Jacob and would make them turn out for Jacob's good. Eventually, Jacob became the father of twelve sons. Jacob lived in his uncle's house for twenty years. During those twenty years, God, in His love, allowed Jacob to pass through some very painful trials so that He might discipline him and purify his faith, just as fire purifies gold.

A day came when God appeared again to Jacob and said, **"Return to the land of your fathers, and to your relatives, and I will be with you."** (Genesis 31:3) So Jacob arose, packed up and moved out, both he and his family. They headed in the direction of Canaan, the land which God had promised to give to Abraham, Isaac, Jacob, and their descendants. As Jacob and his family were on the way to Canaan, the LORD appeared to Jacob in a very special way and changed Jacob's name. We are reading in chapter 32.

> [24] **Jacob was left alone**, and wrestled with a man there until the breaking of the day. [25]When he saw that he didn't prevail against him, the man touched the hollow of his thigh, and the hollow of Jacob's thigh was strained as he wrestled. [26]The man said, "Let me go, for the day breaks." Jacob said, "I won't let you go unless you bless me." [27]He said to him, "What is your name?" He said, "Jacob". [28]He said, "Your name will no longer be called Jacob, but Israel; for you have fought with God and with men, and have prevailed." [29]Jacob asked him, "Please tell me your name." He said, "Why is it that you ask what my name is?" So he blessed him there. [30]Jacob called the name of the place Peniel; [which means *Face of God*] for he said, "I have seen God face to face, and my life is preserved." (Genesis 32:24-30)

This is amazing story is full of important lessons. We see God appearing to Jacob as a man and wrestling with him. Why did He wrestle with Jacob? Because God wanted Jacob to recognize his weakness before Him. God wanted Jacob to know that all true strength and wisdom comes from God alone. God had wonderful plans for Jacob, but God's best blessings can only come to those who know that they cannot please God in their own strength.

Jacob was beginning to realize that, in himself, he had no strength before the LORD God. On that night, God gave Jacob a new name, that is, *Israel*. Jacob means *one who deceives*. But Israel means *one who reigns with God*. Israel would be the name of the new nation God promised to bring forth from the descendants of Abraham, Isaac, and Jacob. It is from the twelve sons of Jacob that the nation of Israel arose. And it is through the people of Israel that the Redeemer came into the world.

Someone might ask: Why did God choose a deceiver like Jacob and make him the father of the nation which would bring the promised Savior into the world? Listen to the answer from the Scriptures:

27But God chose the foolish things of the world that he might put to shame those who are wise. God chose the weak things of the world that he might put to shame the things that are strong. **28**God chose the lowly things of the world, and the things that are despised, and the things that don't exist, that he might bring to nothing the things that exist, **29**that no flesh should boast before God. (1 Corinthians 1:27-29)

Jacob was a deceiver. He was a sinner. In his own strength, there was no way that he could save himself from God's judgment and make himself acceptable to God. There was nothing good in him except this: Jacob believed God. Jacob treasured God's promises. Receiving God's blessings was more important to Jacob than anything else in the world. That is why God made Himself known to Jacob and blessed him. God, in His eternal purposes, changed the heart of Jacob, *the deceiver*, into Israel, *the man of God*.

How about you? Have you, like Jacob, recognized your inability to save yourself? Or are you boasting in your own strength and your own supposed good deeds? Listen to what God says about this:

There is no distinction … for all have sinned and fall short of the glory of God. (Romans 3:22-23) God resists the proud, but gives grace to the humble. Humble yourselves therefore under the mighty hand of God, that he may exalt you in due time. (1 Peter 5:5-6) Blessed are the poor in spirit,[49] for theirs is the kingdom of heaven. (Matthew 5:3)

Thank you for listening. In our next study, God willing, we will begin to look at *the amazing story of Joseph, one of Jacob's twelve sons*.

May the Lord bless you, your family, and your community. We leave you with this word from the Scriptures of the prophets:

Yet the LORD longs to be gracious to you; therefore he will rise up to show you compassion. For the LORD is a God of justice. Blessed are all who wait for him! (Isaiah 30:18 NIV)

---

49 In Wolof, *poor in spirit* is translated: *you who know your lack of strength to please God*

Program 25

Joseph's Humiliation

Genesis 37-39

In our last lesson we learned about the prophet of God, Jacob, Abraham's grandson and we saw how God gave Jacob a new name: Israel. Jacob means *deceiver*, but Israel means *one who reigns with God*. Now Jacob had two names: Jacob and Israel. Israel is also the name of the new nation which God had promised to make from the descendants of Abraham, Isaac, and Jacob. Jacob had twelve sons. From these twelve sons arose the people of Israel, the nation through which the Redeemer would come.

Do you know the names of the twelve sons of Jacob? They are Reuben, Simeon, Levi, Judah, Zebulun, Issachar, Dan, Gad, Asher, Naphtali, Joseph and Benjamin. Today we begin the story about the sons of Jacob, especially the one named Joseph, the eleventh son. Now let us get into the captivating story of Joseph. We are reading in the Torah, the book of Genesis, in chapter 37:

> ²**This is the history of the generations of Jacob.** Joseph, being seventeen years old, was feeding the flock with his brothers…. Joseph brought an evil report of them to their father. ³Now Israel loved Joseph more than all his children, because he was the son of his old age, and he made him a tunic of many colors. ⁴His brothers saw that their father loved him more than all his brothers, and they hated him, and couldn't speak peaceably to him.
>
> ⁵**Joseph dreamed a dream**, and he told it to his brothers, and they hated him all the more. ⁶He said to them, "Please hear this dream which I have dreamed: ⁷for behold, we were binding sheaves in the field, and behold, my sheaf arose and also stood

upright; and behold, your sheaves came around, and bowed down to my sheaf." [8]His brothers asked him, "Will you indeed reign over us? Will you indeed have dominion over us?" They hated him all the more for his dreams and for his words. [9]He dreamed yet another dream, and told it to his brothers, and said, "Behold, I have dreamed yet another dream: and behold, the sun and the moon and eleven stars bowed down to me." [10]He told it to his father and to his brothers. His father rebuked him, and said to him, "What is this dream that you have dreamed? Will I and your mother and your brothers indeed come to bow ourselves down to the earth before you?" [11]His brothers envied him, but his father kept this saying in mind.

[12]**His brothers went to feed their father's flock** in Shechem. [13]Israel said to Joseph, "Aren't your brothers feeding the flock in Shechem? Come, and I will send you to them." He said to him, "Here I am." [14]He said to him, "Go now, see whether it is well with your brothers, and well with the flock; and bring me word again." So he sent him out of the valley of Hebron, and he came to Shechem.

[17]**Joseph went after his brothers**, and found them in Dothan. [18]They saw him afar off, and before he came near to them, they conspired against him to kill him. [19]They said to one another, "Behold, this dreamer comes. [20]Come now therefore, and Let's kill him, and cast him into one of the pits, and we will say, 'An evil animal has devoured him.' We will see what will become of his dreams." [21]Reuben heard it, and delivered him out of their hand, and said, "Let's not take his life." [22]Reuben said to them, "Shed no blood. Throw him into this pit that is in the wilderness, but lay no hand on him"—that he might deliver him out of their hand, to restore him to his father.

[23]**When Joseph came to his brothers**, they stripped Joseph of his tunic, the tunic of many colors that was on him; [24]and they took him, and threw him into the pit. The pit was empty. There was no water in it. [25]They sat down to eat bread, and they lifted up their eyes and looked, and saw a caravan of Ishmaelites was

coming from Gilead, with their camels bearing spices and balm and myrrh, going to carry it down to Egypt. [26]Judah said to his brothers, "What profit is it if we kill our brother and conceal his blood? [27]Come, and let's sell him to the Ishmaelites, and not let our hand be on him; for he is our brother, our flesh." His brothers listened to him. [28]Midianites who were merchants passed by, and they drew and lifted up Joseph out of the pit, and sold Joseph to the Ishmaelites for twenty pieces of silver. The merchants brought Joseph into Egypt.

[29]**Reuben returned to the pit**, and saw that Joseph wasn't in the pit; and he tore his clothes. [30]He returned to his brothers, and said, "The child is no more; and I, where will I go?" [31]They took Joseph's tunic, and killed a male goat, and dipped the tunic in the blood. [32]They took the tunic of many colors, and they brought it to their father, and said, "We have found this. Examine it, now, and see if it is your son's tunic or not." [33]He recognized it, and said, "It is my son's tunic. An evil animal has devoured him. Joseph is without doubt torn in pieces." [34]Jacob tore his clothes, and put sackcloth on his waist, and mourned for his son many days. [35]All his sons and all his daughters rose up to comfort him, but he refused to be comforted. He said, "For I will go down to Sheol to my son, mourning." His father wept for him. (Genesis 37:2-14,17-35)

[1]**Joseph was brought down to Egypt.** Potiphar, an officer of Pharaoh's, the captain of the guard, an Egyptian, bought him from the hand of the Ishmaelites that had brought him down there. [2]The LORD was with Joseph, and he was a prosperous man. He was in the house of his master the Egyptian. [3]His master saw that the LORD was with him, and that the LORD made all that he did prosper in his hand. [4]Joseph found favor in his sight. He ministered to him, and Potiphar made him overseer over his house, and all that he had he put into his hand. [5]From the time that he made him overseer in his house, and over all that he had, the LORD blessed the Egyptian's house for Joseph's sake. The LORD's blessing was on all that he had, in the house and in the field. [6]He left all that he had in Joseph's

hand. He didn't concern himself with anything, except for the food which he ate.

Joseph was well-built and handsome. [7]After these things, his master's wife set her eyes on Joseph; and she said, "Lie with me." [8]But he refused, and said to his master's wife, "Behold, my master doesn't know what is with me in the house, and he has put all that he has into my hand. [9]No one is greater in this house than I am, and he has not kept back anything from me but you, because you are his wife. How then can I do this great wickedness, and sin against God?" [10]As she spoke to Joseph day by day, he didn't listen to her, to lie by her, or to be with her.

[11]**About this time, he went into the house** to do his work, and there were none of the men of the house inside. [12]She caught him by his garment, saying, "Lie with me!" He left his garment in her hand, and ran outside. [13]When she saw that he had left his garment in her hand, and had run outside, [14]she called to the men of her house, and spoke to them, saying, "Behold, he has brought a Hebrew in to us to mock us. He came in to me to lie with me, and I cried with a loud voice. [15]When he heard that I lifted up my voice and cried, he left his garment by me, and ran outside."

[16]**She laid up his garment by her**, until his master came home. [17]She spoke to him according to these words, saying, "The Hebrew servant, whom you have brought to us, came in to me to mock me, [18]and as I lifted up my voice and cried, he left his garment by me, and ran outside." [19]When his master heard the words of his wife, which she spoke to him, saying, "This is what your servant did to me," his wrath was kindled. [20]Joseph's master took him, and put him into the prison, the place where the king's prisoners were bound, and he was there in custody. [21]But the LORD was with Joseph, and showed kindness to him, and gave him favor in the sight of the keeper of the prison. [22]The keeper of the prison committed to Joseph's hand all the prisoners who were in the prison. Whatever they did there, he was responsible for it. [23]The keeper of the prison didn't look

after anything that was under his hand, because the LORD was with him; and that which he did, the LORD made it prosper. (Genesis 39:1-23)

This is just the beginning of the story of Joseph, the son of Jacob.

We can summarize what we have seen today with this statement: *Joseph loved righteousness and hated wickedness.* He would rather suffer in prison than enjoy the passing pleasures of sin. That was why, when the wife of his master invited him to lie with her and commit adultery, Joseph refused, answering her, **"How then can I do this great wickedness, and sin against God?"**

Joseph understood that sin is a bad thing. He knew that serving God and serving sin do not go together. Joseph had presented his heart to God. That is why he loved righteousness and hated wickedness. Like his great-grandfather, Abraham, Joseph also believed what God had promised concerning the Savior who was to come to earth to suffer and die for the sins of Adam's descendants. God judged Joseph to be righteous because Joseph believed the word of God. Because of his faith, God cleansed Joseph's heart and filled it with the desire and the power to overcome sin, and to live righteously in an evil world.

God walked with Joseph because Joseph walked with God. Joseph could not enjoy sin, because his heart belonged to God. The one who believes and worships the LORD God from the heart will love what God loves and hate what God hates. That is what the Scripture declares when it says:

> **No one can serve two masters**, for either he will hate the one and love the other, or else he will be devoted to one and despise the other. (Matthew 6:24) For what fellowship do righteousness and iniquity have? Or what fellowship does light have with darkness? (2 Corinthians 6:14)

> **God is light, and in him is no darkness at all.** If we say that we have fellowship with him and walk in the darkness, we lie, and don't tell the truth. (1 John 1:5-6)

Those who truly belong to God believe the word of God and seek to obey it. But those who do not belong to God are controlled by sin. They may have an outward form of religion, but sin still controls their thoughts, the intentions of their hearts, their words and their deeds. They may intend to overcome sin, but they are unable to do so, because sin is stronger than they are. They do not have in their hearts the power of God's Holy Spirit, whom God gives to all those who believe His word and accept the righteous way of salvation which He has provided.

You who are listening today, has God renewed your heart by His Holy Spirit? Have you believed the Good News about the One who has the power to cleanse your heart from sin? Or are you still living under the dominion of sin? The Scripture says:

> [11]**For the grace of God has appeared** that offers salvation to all people. [12]It teaches us to say "No" to ungodliness and worldly passions, and to live self-controlled, upright and godly lives in this present age…. (Titus 2:11-12 NIV)

It is important to understand that such righteous living is only possible because of **our great God and Savior, Jesus Christ, who gave himself for us, that he might redeem us from all iniquity, and purify for himself a people for his own possession, zealous for good works.** (Titus 2:13-14)

In our next study we plan to continue with the story of Joseph and hear *how he got out of prison and became the supreme ruler over the land of Egypt.*

God bless you as you meditate upon this foundational truth from the Holy Scriptures:

> **God is light, and in him is no darkness at all. If we say that we have fellowship with him and walk in the darkness, we lie, and don't tell the truth.** (1 John 1:5-6)

Program 26
Joseph's Exaltation

Genesis 40-42

In our last lesson we began to learn about Joseph, who was the eleventh of Jacob's twelve sons. We read how Joseph dreamed that his brothers would one day bow down to him. His brothers did not believe him, but today we will see how God fulfilled Joseph's dream by causing his brothers to come and bow down before him.

As we learned, Joseph's older brothers hated and persecuted him because of his dreams. In their jealousy and anger they even went so far as to sell him as a slave to traveling merchants who were descendants of Ishmael. The Ishmaelites took Joseph to Egypt and sold him to an official of Pharaoh, king of Egypt. As for Joseph, he was a faithful servant and honest in his work, because he walked with God.

Joseph was also very handsome, which caused the wife of his master to lust after him, wanting to lie with him. But Joseph told her, **"How then can I do this great wickedness, and sin against God?"** (Genesis 39:9) When Joseph refused to commit adultery with her, the woman spoke against him and had him locked up. Joseph preferred to be put in prison rather than to enjoy the fleeting pleasures of sin. God was first in Joseph's life. For two years Joseph remained in the dungeon, but God had not forgotten him.

Now then, let us continue in the Torah and see how God changed Joseph's circumstances. We are reading in the book of Genesis, chapter 41, where we learn that after Joseph had been in prison for two full years, Pharaoh, the king of Egypt, had a dream:

¹**He stood by the river.** ²Behold, seven cattle came up out of the river. They were sleek and fat, and they fed in the marsh grass. ³Behold, seven other cattle came up after them out of the river, ugly and thin, and stood by the other cattle on the brink of the river. ⁴The ugly and thin cattle ate up the seven sleek and fat cattle. So Pharaoh awoke. ⁵He slept and dreamed a second time; and behold, seven heads of grain came up on one stalk, healthy and good. ⁶Behold, seven heads of grain, thin and blasted with the east wind, sprung up after them. ⁷The thin heads of grain swallowed up the seven healthy and full ears. Pharaoh awoke, and behold, it was a dream.

⁸**In the morning, his spirit was troubled**, and he sent and called for all of Egypt's magicians and wise men. Pharaoh told them his dreams, but there was no one who could interpret them to Pharaoh.

⁹**Then the chief cup bearer** spoke to Pharaoh, saying, "I remember my faults today. ¹⁰Pharaoh was angry with his servants, and put me in custody in the house of the captain of the guard, with the chief baker. ¹¹We dreamed a dream in one night, he and I. Each man dreamed according to the interpretation of his dream. ¹²There was with us there a young man, a Hebrew, servant to the captain of the guard, and we told him, and he interpreted to us our dreams. He interpreted to each man according to his dream. ¹³As he interpreted to us, so it was. He restored me to my office, and he hanged him."

¹⁴**Then Pharaoh sent and called Joseph**, and they brought him hastily out of the dungeon. He shaved himself, changed his clothing, and came in to Pharaoh. ¹⁵Pharaoh said to Joseph, "I have dreamed a dream, and there is no one who can interpret it. I have heard it said of you, that when you hear a dream you can interpret it." ¹⁶Joseph answered Pharaoh, saying, "It isn't in me. God will give Pharaoh an answer of peace." (Genesis 41:1-16)

So Pharaoh related his dream to Joseph and then said:

24"**I told it to the magicians**, but there was no one who could explain it to me." 25Joseph said to Pharaoh, "The dream of Pharaoh is one. What God is about to do he has declared to Pharaoh. 26The seven good cattle are seven years; and the seven good heads of grain are seven years. The dream is one. 27The seven thin and ugly cattle that came up after them are seven years, and also the seven empty heads of grain blasted with the east wind; they will be seven years of famine. 28That is the thing which I have spoken to Pharaoh. God has shown Pharaoh what he is about to do. 29Behold, seven years of great plenty throughout all the land of Egypt are coming. 30Seven years of famine will arise after them, and all the plenty will be forgotten in the land of Egypt. The famine will consume the land, 31and the plenty will not be known in the land by reason of that famine which follows; for it will be very grievous. 32The dream was doubled to Pharaoh, because the thing is established by God, and God will shortly bring it to pass. 33"Now therefore let Pharaoh look for a discreet and wise man, and set him over the land of Egypt. 34Let Pharaoh do this, and let him appoint overseers over the land, and take up the fifth part of the land of Egypt's produce in the seven plenteous years. 35Let them gather all the food of these good years that come, and store grain under the hand of Pharaoh for food in the cities, and let them keep it. 36The food will be to supply the land against the seven years of famine, which will be in the land of Egypt; so that the land will not perish through the famine."

37**The thing was good** in the eyes of Pharaoh, and in the eyes of all his servants. 38Pharaoh said to his servants, "Can we find such a one as this, a man in whom is the Spirit of God?" 39Pharaoh said to Joseph, "Because God has shown you all of this, there is no one so discreet and wise as you. 40You shall be over my house. All my people will be ruled according to your word. Only in the throne I will be greater than you."

41**Pharaoh said to Joseph,** "Behold, I have set you over all the land of Egypt." 42Pharaoh took off his signet ring from his hand,

and put it on Joseph's hand, and arrayed him in robes of fine linen, and put a gold chain about his neck. ⁴³He made him ride in the second chariot which he had. They cried before him, "Bow the knee!" He set him over all the land of Egypt. ⁴⁴Pharaoh said to Joseph, "I am Pharaoh. Without you, no man shall lift up his hand or his foot in all the land of Egypt."

⁴⁵**Pharaoh called Joseph's name Zaphenath-Paneah** [meaning "Preserver of Life"]….Joseph went out over the land of Egypt. ⁴⁶Joseph was thirty years old when he stood before Pharaoh king of Egypt. Joseph went out from the presence of Pharaoh, and went throughout all the land of Egypt. ⁴⁷In the seven plenteous years the earth produced abundantly. ⁴⁸He gathered up all the food of the seven years which were in the land of Egypt, and laid up the food in the cities. He stored food in each city from the fields around that city. ⁴⁹Joseph laid up grain as the sand of the sea, very much, until he stopped counting, for it was without number.…

⁵³**The seven years of plenty**, that were in the land of Egypt, came to an end. ⁵⁴The seven years of famine began to come, just as Joseph had said. There was famine in all lands, but in all the land of Egypt there was bread. ⁵⁵When all the land of Egypt was famished, the people cried to Pharaoh for bread, and Pharaoh said to all the Egyptians, "Go to Joseph. What he says to you, do." ⁵⁶The famine was over all the surface of the earth. Joseph opened all the store houses, and sold to the Egyptians. The famine was severe in the land of Egypt. ⁵⁷All countries came into Egypt, to Joseph, to buy grain, because the famine was severe in all the earth. (Genesis 41:24-49,53-57)

¹**Now Jacob** [the father of Joseph and his brothers] saw that there was grain in Egypt, and Jacob said to his sons, "Why do you look at one another?" ²He said, "Behold, I have heard that there is grain in Egypt. Go down there, and buy for us from there, so that we may live, and not die." ³Joseph's ten brothers went down to buy grain from Egypt. ⁴But Jacob didn't send Benjamin, Joseph's brother, with his brothers; for he said, "Lest perhaps

harm happen to him." [5]The sons of Israel came to buy among those who came, for the famine was in the land of Canaan.

[6]**Joseph was the governor over the land.** It was he who sold to all the people of the land. Joseph's brothers came, and bowed themselves down to him with their faces to the earth. [7]Joseph saw his brothers, and he recognized them, but acted like a stranger to them, and spoke roughly with them. He said to them, "Where did you come from?" They said, "From the land of Canaan, to buy food." [8]Joseph recognized his brothers, but they didn't recognize him. [9]Joseph remembered the dreams which he dreamed about them. (Genesis 42:1-9)

Do you see what happened? We see Joseph's older brothers bowing down before their younger brother, just as Joseph had dreamed more than twenty years earlier. This Joseph, whom they had hated, denied, and wanted to kill – they were now bowing before him! Joseph immediately recognized his brothers, but they did not recognize him, because they had not seen him for twenty years. In our next lesson, God willing, we will finish this emotional story and see how Joseph made himself known to his brothers.

But what about today's story? What does God want to teach us through Joseph and his brothers? God wants to make known to us that what happened between Joseph and his brothers is an illustration of what would happen between the Savior of the world and the descendants of Adam. Friends, if we remember only one thing from today's program, let it be this: *Joseph's life was a shadow, a picture, of the Savior whom God had promised to send to earth.* Amazingly, there are at least a hundred events and elements in Joseph's story which are similar to the story of the Messiah who came to earth 1800 years after the time of Joseph. Obviously, we do not have time on this program to mention all hundred comparisons, but we will mention three.

First, *we saw how Joseph's older brothers rejected him* and his dreams. They hated him, insulted him and even sold him. The same things happened to the Savior whom God sent into the world. The people of the world rejected both the Savior and His message – insulting Him, persecuting Him, selling Him, and even nailing Him to a cross.

The second picture is this: At first, people despised, ignored, mistreated, and imprisoned Joseph. Yet in God's chosen time the king of Egypt appointed Joseph as the supreme ruler over the land, declaring to all who wanted to be saved from hunger and death: *Go to Joseph, the preserver of life!* In the same way, the LORD God says: *If you want to be saved from eternal death then go to the Savior whom I have appointed!* He is The Preserver of Life who says, **"I am the bread of life. Whoever comes to me will not be hungry…. Most certainly, I tell you, he who believes in me has eternal life."** (John 6:35,47)

The third comparison between Joseph and the Redeemer is a solemn one. *In the end, Joseph's brothers submitted to his authority.* They had no choice but to prostrate themselves before the brother they had denied and dishonored. In the same way, the word of God declares that the Savior of the world, whom so many deny and dishonor to this very day, will one day return to judge the world in righteousness. In that day all the people of the world will bow before Him; all will know that He is the One appointed by God to be the Savior or the Judge of all.

Listening friend, how about you? Have you submitted yourself to the Savior whom God has appointed to save you from eternal judgment? Or will you wait until it is too late – when you will be forced to bow before Him?

In our next program we will hear *the rest of Joseph's story.*

May God bless you and give you insight in all you have heard today. We leave you with this word from His book:

> **We have the more sure word of prophecy; and you do well that you heed it, as to a lamp shining in a dark place, until the day dawns, and the morning star arises in your hearts.** (2 Peter 1:19)

Program 27

Joseph: The Rest of the Story

Genesis 42-50

I n the past two programs we have been reading about Joseph, the son of Jacob. Today we plan to hear the rest of his story, which will bring us to the end of the first section of the Torah.

As we saw, Jacob, Abraham's grandson, had twelve sons. Joseph was the eleventh son. They lived in Canaan, the land which God had promised to give to the descendants of Abraham, Isaac, and Jacob. When Joseph was a young man he dreamed that his older brothers would one day bow down before him. But his brothers despised him and his dreams, and sold him as a slave into the land of Egypt. But God delivered Joseph from his troubles and gave him the wisdom to interpret the dream of Pharaoh, king of Egypt. Thus, Joseph predicted the severe seven-year famine which was to take place throughout the land. Pharaoh, impressed with Joseph's wisdom, appointed him supreme ruler over the land of Egypt. After the seven years of plenty, the famine which Joseph had predicted came upon Egypt and upon the land of Canaan. But in the land of Egypt there was grain stored up in abundance because of the grace and wisdom God had given Joseph.

When Jacob heard that Egypt had grain[50] he sent Joseph's ten older brothers to go buy some. But he did not send with them Benjamin, Joseph's younger brother, for fear that some harm would come to him. Thus, the ten older brothers arrived in Egypt and bowed down to Joseph fulfilling what he had dreamed long before. Joseph recognized his brothers, but they did not recognize him. In their minds, Joseph was long dead.

---

50 In Wolof: *millet*, Senegal's staple food

Today we will see how Joseph made himself known to his brothers. Joseph did not immediately reveal himself to his brothers, because he wanted first to test them to know whether their wicked, deceitful hearts had changed. **Joseph saw his brothers, and he recognized them, but acted like a stranger to them, and spoke roughly with them. He said to them, "Where did you come from?" They said, "From the land of Canaan, to buy food."** (Genesis 42:7)

Joseph asked them many questions, accused them of being spies and locked them in prison. Joseph wanted to help them think about their lives and the condition of their hearts before God. Three days later Joseph allowed them to depart, but he kept one of them in prison, telling the others to return to Egypt with their younger brother Benjamin, their father's [lastborn son].

After many months the older brothers returned to Egypt to buy more grain, bringing Benjamin with them. When they arrived they prostrated themselves before Joseph the ruler of the land, but they still did not recognize him. Joseph brought them into his house, which caused them to be greatly afraid. He then put on a great feast for them, arranging their seats around the table in the order of their ages, from the eldest to the youngest. Benjamin received five times more food than the others. Joseph was testing his brothers to see if they would be jealous of Benjamin, as they had been jealous of him. None of them showed any jealousy toward their younger brother.

After the feast, Joseph ordered a servant to fill their sacks with grain and to hide his special silver cup in Benjamin's sack. After Joseph's brothers had left, Joseph sent his chief steward to pursue them and to accuse them of stealing. When the chief steward caught up with them, he said, **"Why have you rewarded evil for good? Isn't this that from which my lord drinks?"** (Genesis 44:4-5) They replied, "We did not take it. Let the one with whom you find the cup die and we ourselves will become your slaves." The chief steward replied, "Whoever is found to have the cup will become my slave, but the rest of you may go on your way."

The chief steward searched all the sacks, beginning with the eldest and ending with the sack of the youngest. And the cup was found in Benjamin's sack. At this, Joseph's older brothers tore their clothes, and returned to the city, and threw themselves to the ground before Joseph. Joseph then said to them, "What have you done? Did you think you could deceive me?" Judah, the fourth son of Jacob, said to him, **"What will we tell my lord? What will we speak? How will we clear ourselves? God has found out the iniquity of your servants. Behold, we are my lord's slaves, both we and he also in whose hand the cup is found."** But Joseph replied, **"…The man in whose hand the cup is found, he will be my slave; but as for you, go up in peace to your father."** (Genesis 44:16-17)

Then Judah came near to Joseph and told him of the anguish which his father had in letting Benjamin accompany them to Egypt. After this, Judah pleaded with Joseph to have mercy on them and to allow Benjamin to return home to his father. Judah also asked that he, Judah, become Joseph's slave instead of Benjamin. When Joseph saw the distress which the brothers felt because of their past sins, and the pity they had for their father and their younger brother, Joseph knew that the wicked hearts of his older brothers had truly changed.

The time had come for Joseph to make himself known to his brothers. The Scripture says:

> [1]**Then Joseph couldn't control himself** before all those who stood before him, and he called out, "Cause everyone to go out from me!" No one else stood with him, while Joseph made himself known to his brothers. [2]He wept aloud. The Egyptians heard, and the house of Pharaoh heard. [3]Joseph said to his brothers, "I am Joseph! Does my father still live?" His brothers couldn't answer him; for they were terrified at his presence.

> [4]**Joseph said to his brothers,** "Come near to me, please." They came near. He said, "I am Joseph, your brother, whom you sold into Egypt. [5]Now don't be grieved, nor angry with yourselves, that you sold me here, for God sent me before you to preserve

life. ⁶For these two years the famine has been in the land, and there are yet five years, in which there will be no plowing and no harvest. ⁷God sent me before you to preserve for you a remnant in the earth, and to save you alive by a great deliverance. ⁸So now it wasn't you who sent me here, but God, and he has made me a father to Pharaoh, lord of all his house, and ruler over all the land of Egypt. ⁹Hurry, and go up to my father, and tell him, 'This is what your son Joseph says, "God has made me lord of all Egypt. Come down to me. Don't wait. ¹⁰You shall dwell in the land of Goshen, and you will be near to me, you, your children, your children's children, your flocks, your herds, and all that you have. ¹¹There I will provide for you; for there are yet five years of famine; lest you come to poverty, you, and your household, and all that you have."' ¹²Behold, your eyes see, and the eyes of my brother Benjamin, that it is my mouth that speaks to you. ¹³You shall tell my father of all my glory in Egypt, and of all that you have seen. You shall hurry and bring my father down here."

¹⁴**He fell on his brother Benjamin's neck and wept**, and Benjamin wept on his neck. ¹⁵He kissed all his brothers, and wept on them. After that his brothers talked with him.
(Genesis 45:1-15)

And so Joseph's brothers prepared to return to their father's house. Joseph gave them carts, as Pharaoh had commanded, and he also gave them provisions for their journey.

²⁵**They went up out of Egypt,** and came into the land of Canaan, to Jacob their father. ²⁶They told him, saying, "Joseph is still alive, and he is ruler over all the land of Egypt." His heart fainted, for he didn't believe them. ²⁷They told him all the words of Joseph, which he had said to them. When he saw the wagons which Joseph had sent to carry him, the spirit of Jacob, their father, revived. ²⁸Israel said, "It is enough. Joseph my son is still alive. I will go and see him before I die."
(Genesis 45:25-28)

After this, the Scriptures tell how Jacob and his family moved from Canaan to Egypt. On the journey, Jacob offered a sacrifice, and there God spoke to him again, saying,

> ³**"I am God, the God of your father.** Don't be afraid to go down into Egypt, for there I will make of you a great nation. ⁴I will go down with you into Egypt. I will also surely bring you up again. Joseph's hand will close your eyes." (Genesis 46:3-4)

And so Jacob and his family arrived in Egypt. How happy Jacob was to see his beloved son Joseph after so many years! And Jacob, who is also called *Israel*, settled in Egypt, he and his family, in the region of Goshen. Jacob lived in Egypt for seventeen years. When he was 147 years old, Jacob, the father of the tribes of Israel, died, and went to be with the LORD his God. Joseph and his brothers and all the people of Egypt mourned for him for seventy days. Jacob's sons buried their father in the land of Canaan, in the tomb of Abraham, his grandfather.

In chapter 50, the final chapter in the book of Genesis we read:

> ¹⁵**When Joseph's brothers saw** that their father was dead, they said, "It may be that Joseph will hate us, and will fully pay us back for all the evil which we did to him."… ¹⁹[When Joseph later heard his brother's thoughts, he] said to them, "Don't be afraid, for am I in the place of God? ²⁰As for you, you meant evil against me, but God meant it for good, to save many people alive, as is happening today. ²¹Now therefore don't be afraid. I will provide for you and your little ones." He comforted them, and spoke kindly to them. ²²Joseph lived in Egypt, he, and his father's house. Joseph lived one hundred ten years.… ²⁴Joseph said to his brothers, "I am dying, but God will surely visit you, and bring you up out of this land to the land which he swore to Abraham, to Isaac, and to Jacob." ²⁵Joseph took an oath from the children of Israel, saying, "God will surely visit you, and you shall carry up my bones from here." ²⁶So Joseph died, being one hundred ten years old, and they embalmed him, and he was put in a coffin in Egypt. (Genesis 50:15,19-22,24-26)

That is how the book of Genesis ends. **So Joseph died…and… was put in a coffin in Egypt.** This book, which began with the story of God creating life, ends with a story of death. Because of Adam's sin, death has come to all men. Even a good man like Joseph, who bore the title *Preserver of Life,* had to die, because he too was a descendant of Adam with the root of sin in his heart.

Joseph, with the help of God, was able to preserve the people of Egypt and his family from starving to death, but, ultimately, he could not preserve them from death itself. Yet we can praise God with joyful hearts,[51] because in the book of Genesis we also read about God's promise to send us the mighty Savior who would conquer death itself. Death is a result of sin.

The Savior God promised to send would rescue Adam's descendants from the penalty of sin and from the root of sin. The penalty of sin is death and eternal separation from God. The root of sin is in the heart of man. The Savior whom God sent came to defeat Satan, sin, death, and hell and to send His Spirit into the hearts of all who trust in Him.

You who are listening today, do you know this glorious Savior who has defeated the devil and demons, sin and shame, death and hell, and offers eternal life to all who believe in Him? Of this Redeemer, the prophet Zacharias said, **"Praise be to the Lord, the God of Israel, because he has come to his people and redeemed them. … (as he said through his holy prophets of long ago)."** (Luke 1:68,70 NIV)

In our next program, God willing, we will begin the second book of the Torah, called *Exodus.*

God bless you as you consider this verse of Holy Scripture which summarizes the book of Genesis:

> **Where sin abounded, [God's] grace abounded more exceedingly.** (Romans 5:20)

---

51 Literally in Wolof: *cold heart*, which in a hot-climate culture means *a very happy heart!*

Program 28
Review of the First Book of the Torah

Genesis 1-Exodus 1

We are still studying in the Torah, written by the prophet Moses. As you may remember, the Torah is the first part in the writings of the prophets and is divided into five sections, or books. The first book is called *Genesis.*[52] In our last broadcast, we completed our studies in Genesis. Today, God willing, we will begin the second book of the Torah, which is called *The Exodus*, or *The Going Out*, because it contains the amazing account of how God freed the descendants of Israel from 400 years of slavery in Egypt.

Before we get into the book of Exodus, let us review what we have studied in the first section of the Torah. It is crucial that we have a thorough knowledge of the book of Genesis because it is the foundation that God has laid for us so that we might understand and believe all that is written in the other books of the prophets which follow.

Do you remember the first verse of the book of Genesis? It tell us: **In the beginning God created the heavens and the earth.** (Genesis 1:1) This is important. **In the beginning, God.** Before there were angels, people, planets, or stars, only the LORD God existed.

Next, we learned how God, by the power of His eternal word and His Holy Spirit, created millions of holy angels. God created the angels so that they might know Him, serve Him, and praise Him forever. Among the angels was one with superior wisdom and beauty. That one was Lucifer, the chief of the angels. But the Scriptures tell us that Lucifer became conceited and despised

---

52 Literally in Wolof: *The Beginning*

God in his heart. Lucifer and many other angels began to weave a plan to overthrow the LORD God. But no one can overthrow Him. And God will not tolerate those who rebel against Him.[53] Consequently, God expelled Lucifer and his evil angels and changed Lucifer's name to *Satan*, which means *adversary*. And after God expelled Satan and his angels He created for them the fires of hell. The Scriptures say that on the Day of Judgment, God, the Righteous One, will throw Satan into that everlasting fire along with all who follow him.

Next we learned how in six days the LORD made a beautiful, amazing planet for the people whom He planned to create. Man[54] is the greatest of all the creatures God made, because man was created in the image of His Creator. God wanted to have a deep and wonderful relationship with the male and female humans He had created to glorify and enjoy Him forever. That is why He placed in the soul of humans a mind capable of knowing God, a heart capable of loving God, and a free will capable of choosing to obey God.

Next we saw how God placed a test before the man and the woman whom He had created. God warned Adam, saying, **"You may freely eat of every tree of the garden; but you shall not eat of the tree of the knowledge of good and evil; for in the day that you eat of it, you will surely die."** (Genesis 2:16-17) To sin against God would result in humans being separated from Him forever.

And so we saw how our ancestors, Adam and Eve, chose to follow Satan by eating from the forbidden tree, which is why the word of God says: **Therefore as sin entered into the world through one man, and death through sin; so death passed to all men, because all sinned.** (Romans 5:12) How true it is that *an epidemic is not confined to the one from whom it originates.*[55] Because of Adam's sin we are all sinners. Because of Adam's sin we all deserve to die and face God's judgment.

---

53 Literally: *refuse His rule*
54 Neuter: *a human*
55 This Wolof proverb illustrates the reality of our inherited sin nature.

Next we learned how God expelled Adam and Eve from the earthly Garden of Paradise because of their sin. But before He expelled them, God announced how He planned to send into the world a Redeemer (to save the children of Adam from the power of Satan and from the penalty of sin). God, in His wonderful design, had a plan to rescue sinners. His plan was to send to earth a perfect Man who would not be contaminated by the sin of Adam. He would be the offspring of a woman. He would have a human mother, but no human father. This righteous man would show people what God is like and then He would willingly shed His blood to pay the debt of sin for Adam's descendants. In this way, God could forgive people of their sins without compromising His justice. Truly, this first prophecy about the coming Redeemer was a wonderful promise that gave sinful humanity a glimmer of hope.

Next we saw how God confirmed that promise by sacrificing some animals and making for Adam and Eve clothes from the skins. God was teaching Adam and Eve that **the wages of sin is death** and that **apart from shedding of blood there is no [forgiveness of sin].** (Romans 6:23; Hebrews 9:22)

After that, we learned about Adam's first two sons, Cain and Abel. We saw how Abel offered to God an innocent lamb and slaughtered it, thus symbolizing the Redeemer who was to come to suffer and die in the place of sinners. As for Cain, he tried to approach God through his own efforts, offering to God what he had cultivated in the cursed ground. But his offering had no blood, no death-payment for sin. Consequently, **the Lord accepted Abel, but He did not accept Cain.** Why did God not accept the sacrifice of Cain? Because God's law did not say that "the payment for sin is good works." Rather, it stated: **the wages of sin is death** and **apart from shedding of blood there is no [forgiveness].** God urged Cain to repent and accept God's way of righteousness, but Cain just got angry and killed his younger brother Abel.

Most of Adam's descendants followed in the footsteps of Cain, so that by the time of the prophet Noah, the Scripture says: **The Lord saw that the wickedness of man was great in the earth,**

and that every imagination of the thoughts of man's heart was continually only evil. (Genesis 6:5)

Because of man's wicked heart, God purposed to send a worldwide flood to wipe out rebellious sinners. In that corrupt time, only Noah and his family believed God, which was why God told him to build a spacious ark (boat), which would be a refuge for all who entered it. God was patient with sinners for a long time while Noah was constructing the ark, but no one repented and entered the ark except Noah and his wife and their three sons, Shem, Ham, and Japheth, and their wives. Eight souls in all.

The prophet Abraham descended from Shem. We read how God commanded Abraham to leave his father's house and go to the land of Canaan. God planned to make of Abraham a new nation through which He would provide the prophets, the Scriptures, and the promised Savior. That is why God said to Abraham, **"You will be a [door of] blessing.… All the families of the earth will be blessed through you."** (Genesis 12:2-3)

We also heard how Abraham became the father of Isaac in his old age, just as God had promised. Isaac became the father of Jacob, and Jacob, whom God renamed Israel, had twelve sons, and from those twelve sons came the nation of Israel.

In the last three programs, we heard the amazing story of the twelve sons of Jacob, focusing mainly on Joseph, the eleventh son. Joseph's older brothers hated him and sold him as a slave, but God loved him and made him the supreme ruler over Egypt. In time, a famine fell over the land of Egypt and the land of Canaan, causing great misery, so that Jacob and his sons had nothing left to eat. When Jacob heard that there was food in Egypt, he sent his sons there to buy grain. We then saw how Joseph made himself known to his brothers, forgave them, and arranged for his father and brothers and their families to move from Canaan to Egypt.

Thus, at the end of the book of Genesis, we learned that the children of Israel were no longer in Canaan, which God had promised to give to Abraham, but in Egypt. All this happened to fulfill what God had told Abraham long beforehand, saying:

> ¹³**Know for sure that your offspring** will live as foreigners in a land that is not theirs, and will serve them. They will afflict them four hundred years. ¹⁴I will also judge that nation, whom they will serve. Afterward they will come out with great wealth. (Genesis 15:13-14)

God Himself had his hand on all that happened to the children of Israel. Why did God allow Abraham's great-grandchildren, the Israelites, to settle in Egypt, when He had promised them the land of Canaan? Because God intended to display His glory and His power through what would happen to the Israelites in the land of Egypt. God planned to deliver the children of Israel by His awesome power, so that everyone might know that He is the King of kings and Lord of lords, the Almighty.

Now, listening friends, in the few minutes that we have left today, let us read from the first chapter of the book of Exodus:

> ⁶**Joseph died, as did all his brothers**, and all that generation. ⁷The children of Israel were fruitful, and increased abundantly, and multiplied, and grew exceedingly mighty; and the land was filled with them. ⁸Now there arose a new king over Egypt, who didn't know Joseph. ⁹He said to his people, "Behold, the people of the children of Israel are more and mightier than we. ¹⁰Come, let's deal wisely with them, lest they multiply, and it happen that when any war breaks out, they also join themselves to our enemies and fight against us, and escape out of the land."

> ¹¹**Therefore they set taskmasters over them** to afflict them with their burdens. They built storage cities for Pharaoh: Pithom and Raamses. ¹²But the more they afflicted them, the more they multiplied and the more they spread out. They started to dread the children of Israel. ¹³The Egyptians ruthlessly made the children of Israel serve, ¹⁴and they made

their lives bitter with hard service in mortar and in brick, and in all kinds of service in the field, all their service, in which they ruthlessly made them serve.

¹⁵**The king of Egypt spoke to the Hebrew midwives**, of whom the name of the one was Shiphrah, and the name of the other Puah, ¹⁶and he said, "When you perform the duty of a midwife to the Hebrew women, and see them on the birth stool, if it is a son, then you shall kill him; but if it is a daughter, then she shall live." ¹⁷But the midwives feared God, and didn't do what the king of Egypt commanded them, but saved the baby boys alive. ¹⁸The king of Egypt called for the midwives, and said to them, "Why have you done this thing and saved the boys alive?" ¹⁹The midwives said to Pharaoh, "Because the Hebrew women aren't like the Egyptian women; for they are vigorous and give birth before the midwife comes to them."

²⁰**God dealt well with the midwives**, and the people multiplied, and grew very mighty. ²¹Because the midwives feared God, he gave them families. ²²Pharaoh commanded all his people, saying, "You shall cast every son who is born into the river, and every daughter you shall save alive." (Exodus 1:6-22)

This is where the first chapter of the book of Exodus ends. In the next broadcast we plan to go deeper into this extraordinary story and see how God raised up a deliverer to rescue the descendants of Jacob-Israel from 400 years of slavery in Egypt and from the cruel hand of Pharaoh, the king. Do you know the name of this deliverer? Yes, it is Moses – God's prophet Moses.

Thank you for listening.

God bless you as you consider this reminder from His book:

Such things were written in the Scriptures long ago to teach us. And the Scriptures give us hope and encouragement as we wait patiently for God's promises to be fulfilled.
(Romans 15:4 NLT)

Program 29

The Prophet Moses

Exodus 1-2

There are five books in the Torah, all written by the prophet Moses. In our last program we completed our journey through the book of Genesis and crossed over into the book of *Exodus*. Our prayer to God is that He will instruct our minds and our hearts as we continue our journey in the Scriptures.

Last time we noticed that the second book of the Torah begins where the first book ends. We saw how the descendants of Abraham, Isaac, and Jacob, that is, the Israelites, settled in Egypt, far from the land of Canaan that God had promised to give them.

The book of Exodus begins with these words:

> [1]**Now these are the names of the sons of Israel**, who came into Egypt (every man and his household came with Jacob): [2]Reuben, Simeon, Levi, and Judah, [3]Issachar, Zebulun, and Benjamin, [4]Dan and Naphtali, Gad and Asher. [5]All the souls who came out of Jacob's body were seventy souls, and Joseph was in Egypt already. [6]Joseph died, as did all his brothers, and all that generation. [7]The children of Israel were fruitful, and increased abundantly, and multiplied, and grew exceedingly mighty; and the land was filled with them.
>
> [8]**Now there arose a new king over Egypt**, who didn't know Joseph. [9]He said to his people, "Behold, the people of the children of Israel are more and mightier than we. [10]Come, let's deal wisely with them, lest they multiply, and it happen that when any war breaks out, they also join themselves to our enemies and fight against us, and escape out of the land." [11]Therefore they set

taskmasters over them to afflict them with their burdens. They built storage cities for Pharaoh: Pithom and Raamses. [12]But the more they afflicted them, the more they multiplied and the more they spread out. They started to dread the children of Israel. [13]The Egyptians ruthlessly made the children of Israel serve, [14]and they made their lives bitter with hard service in mortar and in brick, and in all kinds of service in the field, all their service, in which they ruthlessly made them serve. (Exodus 1:1-14)

Let us pause here. More than three hundred years had passed since the death of Joseph. Another Pharaoh was reigning over Egypt, a king who had forgotten all that Joseph had done for the people of Egypt. This Pharaoh oppressed Israel, making them his slaves. How hard he made them work! Perhaps the Israelites thought that God had forgotten what He had promised their ancestor Abraham about making them into a great nation. But God had not forgotten a thing. God was, in fact, in the process of fulfilling what He had promised so long ago.

Truly, God is faithful. He keeps His covenants. What God promises to do, He will do, even if man thinks He is slow. God was the One who conceived the plan to create a new nation from which the prophets and the Redeemer would come, and nothing would hinder the accomplishment of His plan.

We remember that when God first revealed His plan to create that special nation, He started with an elderly couple, Abraham and Sarah. When Abraham was one hundred years old, he begot Isaac; Isaac begot Jacob; and Jacob begot twelve sons, who produced the tribes of Israel. When they moved to the land of Egypt, they were seventy people. But now, after some three hundred years, they had become a great multitude of two or three million people. Did God do what He had promised long ago? Was God forming Abraham's descendants into a new and vast nation? Yes, He was. God is faithful. He keeps His word.

In today's reading we see how Pharaoh oppressed the tribes of Israel, making them his slaves. However, every time Pharaoh tried to dominate and diminish the tribes of Israel, God would cause them to flourish and multiply. And so Pharaoh gave this command to all his people: **"Cast every son who is born into the river."** (Exodus 1:22) What do you think about this? Who was leading Pharaoh in this wicked plan? Satan, that's who. Why did Satan want to oppress and destroy the people of Israel? Because Satan knew that God had promised to send into the world a Redeemer who would deliver Adam's offspring from the power of sin and death. It seems that Satan also knew that this promised Redeemer would come forth from the nation of Israel. That is the reason Satan incited Pharaoh to persecute the people of Israel and tried to wipe them out by having all their baby boys thrown into the Nile river.

But God, who is infinitely stronger than Satan, planned to use a man from within the tribes of Israel to deliver His chosen people from the hand of Pharaoh. Do you know the name of this hero? Yes, it is the renowned prophet of God, Moses.[56] But Moses' parents, Amram and Jochebed, were also heroes because **they were not afraid of the king's commandment.** (Hebrews 11:23; Exodus 6:20)

The Scripture says:

> [1]**A man of the house of Levi** [the third son of Jacob] went and took a daughter of Levi as his wife. [2]The woman conceived and bore a son. When she saw that he was a fine child, she hid him three months. [3]When she could no longer hide him, she took a papyrus basket for him, and coated it with tar and with pitch. She put the child in it, and laid it in the reeds by the river's bank. [4]His sister stood far off, to see what would be done to him.

> [5]**Pharaoh's daughter came down to bathe at the river.** Her maidens walked along by the riverside. She saw the basket among the reeds, and sent her servant to get it. [6]She opened it, and saw the child, and behold, the baby cried. She had compassion on him, and said, "This is one of the Hebrews' children."[The Egyptians called the people of Israel *Hebrews*.] [7]Then [Miriam, the sister of the baby, who had been hiding

---

56 Arabic: *Musa*

among the reeds] said to Pharaoh's daughter, "Should I go and call a nurse for you from the Hebrew women, that she may nurse the child for you?" ⁸Pharaoh's daughter said to her, "Go." The young woman went and called the child's mother. ⁹Pharaoh's daughter said to her, "Take this child away, and nurse him for me, and I will give you your wages." The woman took the child, and nursed it. ¹⁰The child grew, and she brought him to Pharaoh's daughter, and he became her son. She named him Moses, and said, "Because I drew him out of the water." (Exodus 2:1-10)

Do you see the hand of God in this? While other boy babies were being killed, baby Moses was being nourished by his own mother and protected by Pharaoh, the wicked king himself. God had His hand on all that was happening. He planned to use Moses to deliver the children of Israel from their slavery. How deep is the wisdom of God, far surpassing the wisdom of Satan or man! Do you know where Moses grew up after he was weaned? Yes, he grew up in the house of Pharaoh, who, as you know, was oppressing the people of Israel. Yet God intended to use Moses to deliver the Israelites from the hand of Pharaoh. In His plan, God chose to use the daughter of the cruel king to protect Moses. God knew that the king's house would be the safest and best place for Moses. God knew that there were many things Moses needed to learn and understand so that he would be properly prepared to lead the children of Israel. The Scripture says: **Moses was instructed in all the wisdom of the Egyptians. He was mighty in his words and works.** (Acts 7:22) But Moses still had much to learn.

His story continues:

¹¹**In those days, when Moses had grown up**, he went out to his brothers and saw their burdens. He saw an Egyptian striking a Hebrew, one of his brothers. ¹²He looked this way and that way, and when he saw that there was no one, he killed the Egyptian, and hid him in the sand. ¹³He went out the second day, and behold, two men of the Hebrews were fighting with each other. He said to him who did the wrong, "Why do you strike your fellow?" ¹⁴He said, "Who made you

a prince and a judge over us? Do you plan to kill me, as you killed the Egyptian?" Moses was afraid, and said, "Surely this thing is known." [15]Now when Pharaoh heard this thing, he sought to kill Moses. But Moses fled from the face of Pharaoh, and lived in the land of Midian.... (Exodus 2:11-15)

At first Moses tried to deliver the children of Israel by his own wisdom and power. But that is not how God wanted it done. God wanted to use Moses as an instrument to liberate the children of Israel but their deliverance was not to come from Moses, but from God. Moses, in himself, was only a man with no power to free the people of Israel from the hand of Pharaoh unless God gave it to him.

Thus, the Scriptures tell us that for forty years Moses lived out in the desert, in the land of Midian. God had many important lessons to teach Moses in that hot, dry wilderness. There is a verse in the word of God which says: **He who is faithful in a very little is faithful also in much. He who is dishonest in a very little is also dishonest in much.** (Luke 16:10) Before God could commit to Moses the weighty task of shepherding the people of Israel, Moses first needed to show himself faithful in smaller tasks. Thus, the Scriptures relate to us that there in a land far from Egypt Moses became a shepherd, got married and had two children. For forty years Moses was a faithful shepherd. There in the wilderness, while Moses was shepherding his father-in-law's flock, God was preparing Moses for the day when he would shepherd the nation of Israel. God had amazing plans for Moses and for His people Israel.

Next, the Scripture says:

> [23]**In the course of those many days**, the king of Egypt died, and the children of Israel sighed because of the bondage, and they cried, and their cry came up to God because of the bondage. [24]God heard their groaning, and God remembered his covenant with Abraham, with Isaac, and with Jacob. [25]God saw the children of Israel, and God was concerned about them. (Exodus 2:23-25)

For 400 years the children of Israel remained slaves in Egypt where they suffered great oppression. But God had not forgotten them.

God planned to deliver the people of Israel from their slavery. We might ask: Why did God plan to free the children of Israel from the hand of Pharaoh? Was it because they were better than others? No, like the people of Egypt, like all people, the Israelites were sinners. Why then did God have such special plans for them? Because of His mercy and faithfulness. Let us read again the last verse.

> **God heard their groaning**, and God remembered his covenant with Abraham, with Isaac, and with Jacob. [25]God saw the children of Israel, and God was concerned about them. (Exodus 2:24-25)

God remembered His covenant with Abraham, when He promised:

> [2]**I will make of you a great nation**…. [3]All the families of the earth will be blessed through you. (Genesis 12:2-3)

> [13]**Know for sure that your offspring** will live as foreigners in a land that is not theirs, and will serve them. They will afflict them four hundred years. [14]I will also judge that nation, whom they will serve. Afterward they will come out with great wealth;" (Genesis 15:13-14)

In coming programs as we observe God protecting this nation, it is helpful to remember that whenever He protected Israel, He was protecting His plans to bless you and me since it was from that nation that the prophets, the Scriptures, and the Redeemer came.

Next time, Lord willing, we will see *how God appeared to Moses* in a very unusual way and called him to go to Egypt to deliver the Israelites from their slavery, just as He had promised Abraham long beforehand. Thank you for listening.

God bless you. We bid you farewell with this word from the Psalms:

> **Give thanks to the LORD, call on his name. Make his doings known among the peoples…. He has remembered his covenant forever, the word which he commanded to a thousand generations, the covenant which he made with Abraham, his oath to Isaac.** (Psalm 105:1,8-9)

Moses Meets God

Exodus 3-4

In our last lesson, we saw how Pharaoh, the king of Egypt, oppressed Abraham's descendants by making them his slaves and working them ruthlessly. We also read that **the more they afflicted them, the more they multiplied and the more they spread out. [The Egyptians] started to dread the children of Israel.** (Exodus 1:12) So Pharaoh issued a decree that every infant boy born to the Israelites be thrown into the Nile River to die.

But God's plans would not be thwarted. One day the daughter of Pharaoh discovered an Israelite baby floating in a basket in the river. She had pity on him and adopted him as her son, naming him *Moses*. Baby Moses grew up in the house of Pharaoh, the very one who sought to destroy the people of Israel. God planned to use Moses to deliver His people from the hand of the wicked king. When Moses was forty years old he ran from Pharaoh, who wanted to kill him. For forty years Moses lived in the wilderness, where he took a wife, had children, and tended his father-in-law's flock.

Now let us continue reading to see how God revealed Himself to Moses in order to send him back to Pharaoh to lead the Israelites out of Egypt. We are reading in the book of Exodus, chapter 3:

> ¹**Now Moses was keeping the flock of Jethro**, his father-in-law, ...and he led the flock to the back of the wilderness, and came to God's mountain, to [Sinai]. ²The Lord's angel appeared to him in a flame of fire out of the middle of a bush. He looked, and behold, the bush burned with fire, and the bush was not consumed. ³Moses said, "I will go now, and see this great sight, why the bush is not burned."

⁴**When the LORD saw** that he came over to see, God called to him out of the middle of the bush, and said, "Moses! Moses!" He said, "Here I am." ⁵He said, "Don't come close. Take off your sandals, for the place you are standing on is holy ground." ⁶Moreover he said, "I am the God of your father, the God of Abraham, the God of Isaac, and the God of Jacob." Moses hid his face because he was afraid to look at God.

⁷**The LORD said**, "I have surely seen the affliction of my people who are in Egypt, and have heard their cry because of their taskmasters, for I know their sorrows. ⁸I have come down to deliver them out of the hand of the Egyptians, and to bring them up out of that land to a good and large land, to a land flowing with milk and honey; to the place of the Canaanite... ⁹Now, behold, the cry of the children of Israel has come to me. Moreover I have seen the oppression with which the Egyptians oppress them. ¹⁰Come now therefore, and I will send you to Pharaoh, that you may bring my people, the children of Israel, out of Egypt."

¹¹**Moses said to God**, "Who am I, that I should go to Pharaoh, and that I should bring the children of Israel out of Egypt?" ¹²He said, "Certainly I will be with you. This will be the token to you, that I have sent you: when you have brought the people out of Egypt, you shall serve God on this mountain." ¹³Moses said to God, "Behold, when I come to the children of Israel, and tell them, 'The God of your fathers has sent me to you,' and they ask me, 'What is his name?' what should I tell them?" ¹

⁴**God said to Moses, "I AM WHO I AM,"** and he said, "You shall tell the children of Israel this: 'I AM has sent me to you.'" ¹⁵God said moreover to Moses, "You shall tell the children of Israel this, 'The LORD, the God of your fathers, the God of Abraham, the God of Isaac, and the God of Jacob, has sent me to you.' This is my name forever, and this is my memorial to all generations." (Exodus 3:1-15)

There are at least four things we can learn about God's character from what He told Moses from the burning bush on Mount Sinai.

1. First, we learn that *God is holy*. When Moses saw the flames of the burning bush he drew near to investigate and he heard the voice of God calling out to him. Moses trembled with fear and did not dare to look. Why was Moses afraid? Because he was standing in the presence of God, the Holy One. God declared His holiness by saying to Moses: **"Don't come close. Take off your sandals, for the place you are standing on is holy ground!"**

Truly, God, who appeared to Moses in the fiery flames, is holy. God wants everyone to recognize His holiness. Concerning the angels who stand in the presence of God, the Scripture says: **They have no rest day and night, saying, "Holy, holy, holy is the Lord God, the Almighty, who was and who is and who is to come!"** (Revelation 4:8) The angels recognize the holiness of God. You who are listening today, do you recognize God's holiness?

Let us think a little about what this means. As we have already seen in previous lessons, the holiness of God caused Him to expel Adam and Eve from the Garden of Paradise after they had sinned. The holiness of God caused Him to reject Cain's sacrifice. It was also God's holiness that caused Him to wipe out the people of Noah's day with a flood. In the period that followed, God mixed up the language of the world, scattering the people of Babel, those who were trying to rebel against God. And in Abraham's time, the holiness of God caused Him to rain fire from the sky on the people of Sodom, who were taking pleasure in wickedness.

Tragically, to this day most people do not respect the holiness of God. They do not comprehend who God is. They have not recognized His absolute purity. We see this in the way people practice sin and take pleasure in it. We also see how little importance people attach to the holiness of God when they wear religion like a cloak but do not examine the Holy Scriptures in order to understand God's truth. Many habitually use God's name in insincere expressions. They invoke the name of God in vain by saying, "Bi ism Allah" (Arabic: *In the name of God*), or "Insha'a Allah" (*If God wills it*) when the will of God is the farthest thing from their minds. We see people's failure to understand the holiness of God as they seek to establish their own righteousness before God and refuse His righteous way of salvation. Some think that they can make themselves pure before God by prolonged fasting, repetitious praying, or ceremonies of washing and ablutions. But, as we clearly see in the writings of the prophets, such outward actions do not satisfy God, the Holy One who requires that a person be pure on the inside. Dear friends, God is holy! That is why He said to Moses, **"Don't come close. Take off your sandals, for the place you are standing on is holy ground."**

2. Next, based on what God said to Moses from the burning bush, we discover that God is not only the Holy One, but He is also *the Faithful One.*[57] Did you notice what God first said to Moses? He said, **"I am the God of your father, the God of Abraham, the God of Isaac, and the God of Jacob."** (Exodus 3:6) These words should bring joy to the heart of anyone who wants to approach God and enjoy a close relationship with Him. God, the Holy One, is the One who established a covenant with Abraham, Isaac, and Jacob. God is the Faithful One. Even after hundreds of years He had not forgotten all that He had promised to Abraham, Isaac, Jacob, and their descendants.

What about you? Do you appreciate the faithfulness of God? Do you enjoy a relationship with the holy and faithful God who spoke to Abraham, Isaac, and Jacob? This is a crucial question for anyone who wants to enjoy the peace of God in this life and in the life to come. We are not asking if you have a religion – since following the rules of religion cannot make you righteous before God. What we are asking is: Do you have a right relationship with God? Have you understood and believed God's way of redemption? Do you see that observing a religion and having a relationship with the LORD Himself are two different things? Today there are thousands of religions in the world. For example, experts tell us that in the country of Brazil alone, there are more than 4000 religions and sects. Four thousand religions? Are there four thousand gods? Or four thousand ways that lead to God? No. The Scripture says that **there is one God, and one mediator between God and men.** (1 Timothy 2:5)

---

57 Literally: *the One who keeps His covenants*

Why then are there thousands of religions and thousands of different sects in the world today? It is because most of Adam's descendants have ignored the foundation of truth that God established with Abraham, Isaac, and Jacob. They do not know about the promises which God made to Abraham and his descendants concerning the Mediator who was to come into the world to deliver the children of Adam from the penalty and power of sin. They do not know the story and message of the holy God who never changes. They do not know the Faithful One.

3. When the LORD appeared to Moses in the fire that blazed in the bush, God manifested another characteristic. Mercy. God is not only the Holy One and the Faithful One, but He is also *the Merciful One*. That is why God said to Moses:

> **⁷The LORD said, "I have surely seen the affliction** of my people who are in Egypt, and have heard their cry because of their taskmasters, for I know their sorrows. ⁸I have come down to deliver them out of the hand of the Egyptians, and to bring them up out of that land to a good and large land…." (Exodus 3:7-8)

Why did God plan to liberate the people of Israel and lead them into a good land? Did the Israelites deserve God's mercy? Were they better than other nations? No, they were not. Why then did God purpose to deliver them and bless them so? Because of His faithfulness and His mercy. **God heard their groaning, and God remembered his covenant with Abraham, with Isaac, and with Jacob. God saw the children of Israel, and [had mercy on] them.** (Exodus 2:24-25) Yes, God is the Merciful One.

4. Finally, there is one more aspect of God that we can observe in the story of the burning bush. *God has a personal Name*. We heard Moses ask God what His name is. Can the nature of the eternal God be described in a single name? This God who is so great and holy, faithful and merciful; this God whom man cannot see with his eyes; this God who created everything, sees everything, knows everything, and can do anything – What is His name? Some think God's name is simply *God* (*Allah*). Truly, God is God. However, *God*

is not His name. God is who He is. I am a man, but *Man* is not my name. Each of us has a name by which we are known. What is God's name? What answer did God give to Moses? God replied,

> [14]**"I AM WHO I AM,"** and he said, "You shall tell the children of Israel this: 'I AM has sent me to you.'" [15]God said moreover to Moses, "You shall tell the children of Israel this, 'the LORD, the God of your fathers, the God of Abraham, the God of Isaac, and the God of Jacob, has sent me to you.' This is my name forever." (Exodus 3:14-15)

What is the name of God that describes His eternal nature? Did you hear it? His name is **the LORD**. In Hebrew, that name is **YaHWeH**.[58] It means **HE IS** or **I AM**. In the Holy Scriptures, the prophets ascribe to God hundreds of names and titles, but the name *Yahweh* is used more than any other – about 6,500 times. God is the LORD, the Eternal I AM, the One who was, who is, who will exist forever. He has no beginning. He has no end. He has no limits. He has no equal. He is the One who exists by His own power. What He was yesterday and is today, He will be forever. He never changes. *The LORD* is His Name!

Listening friend, do you know the LORD? Do you recognize His holiness? Are you rejoicing in His faithfulness? Have you received His mercy? Have you entered into a close relationship with the God of Abraham, Isaac, and Jacob? Do you know the LORD who spoke to Moses from the burning bush?

God willing, next time we will continue *the story of Moses and see how God sent him to Pharaoh.*

As we bid you farewell, we invite you to think deeply on what God has revealed in the Scriptures of His prophets about His own name:

> **I AM WHO I AM… I am the LORD… This is my name forever. And everyone who calls on the name of the LORD will be saved!** (Exodus 3:14-15; 6:2; Joel 2:32 NIV)

---

58 English translation the LORD is from the Hebrew YHWH. In Wolof, the name is translated: *Aji Sax Ji*, meaning *The Eternal (Enduring) One.*

Program 31

Pharaoh: Who Is the Lord?

Exodus 4-7

Today we are continuing in the second book of the Torah, which tells the story of God's prophet, Moses, and the people of Israel in Egypt. In past programs we saw how Pharaoh, king of Egypt, persecuted the Israelites, making them his slaves. But amid all the suffering, God had a plan to overturn the evil that Pharaoh was doing. God planned to use Moses, a man from among the children of Israel, to deliver His people from the hand of Pharaoh.

We learned that Moses was educated in all the knowledge of Egypt, and that when he was forty years old he attempted to deliver his people by his own methods. Moses' efforts, however, produced only problems, forcing him to flee from Pharaoh and hide in the wilderness. Moses had to learn that in himself he had no power to deliver the people of Israel unless God gave it to him. Moses spent forty years in the wilderness raising a family and caring for his father-in-law's flock.

When Moses was eighty years old, God appeared to him on a mountain called Sinai, in the flames of a burning bush. The bush was on fire, but it did not burn up. When Moses saw it he was amazed. As he drew near to investigate, he heard the voice of God saying, **"I am the God of your father, the God of Abraham, the God of Isaac, and the God of Jacob."** (Exodus 3:6) Moses trembled with fear and did not dare to look. Then God said, **"Take off your sandals, for the place you are standing on is holy ground. I have surely seen the affliction of my people who are in Egypt, and have heard their cry because of their taskmasters.… I have come down to deliver them.… Come now therefore, and I will send you to Pharaoh."**

204 | Part 1: The WAY of RIGHTEOUSNESS according to the Torah

Now let us continue reading to see how God concluded His talk with Moses and sent him to the king of Egypt. In chapter 3 we heard how God promised to be with Moses, to give him wisdom and authority before Pharaoh and the people of Egypt. But Moses didn't want to go. In chapter 4 we read:

> ¹**Moses answered,** "But, behold, they will not believe me, nor listen to my voice; for they will say, 'The LORD has not appeared to you.'" ²The LORD said to him, "What is that in your hand?" He said, "A rod." ³He said, "Throw it on the ground." He threw it on the ground, and it became a snake; and Moses ran away from it. ⁴The LORD said to Moses, "Stretch out your hand, and take it by the tail." He stretched out his hand, and took hold of it, and it became a rod in his hand. ⁵"This is so that they may believe that the LORD, the God of their fathers, the God of Abraham, the God of Isaac, and the God of Jacob, has appeared to you."
>
> ¹⁰**Moses said to the LORD,** "O Lord, I am not eloquent, neither before now, nor since you have spoken to your servant; for I am slow of speech, and of a slow tongue." ¹¹The LORD said to him, "Who made man's mouth? Or who makes one mute, or deaf, or seeing, or blind? Isn't it I, the LORD? ¹²Now therefore go, and I will be with your mouth, and teach you what you shall speak." ¹³Moses said, "Oh, Lord, please send someone else." ¹⁴The LORD's anger burned against Moses, and he said, "What about Aaron, your brother, the Levite? I know that he can speak well. Also, behold, he is coming out to meet you. When he sees you, he will be glad in his heart. ¹⁵You shall speak to him, and put the words in his mouth. I will be with your mouth, and with his mouth, and will teach you what you shall do…. ¹⁷You shall take this rod in your hand, with which you shall do the signs."
>
> ¹⁸**Moses went and returned** to Jethro his father-in-law, and said to him, "Please let me go and return to my brothers who are in Egypt, and see whether they are still alive." Jethro said to Moses, "Go in peace."

¹⁹**The LORD said to Moses in Midian**, "Go, return into Egypt; for all the men who sought your life are dead." ²⁰Moses took his wife and his sons, and set them on a donkey, and he returned to the land of Egypt. Moses took God's rod in his hand. ²¹The LORD said to Moses, "When you go back into Egypt, see that you do before Pharaoh all the wonders which I have put in your hand.... ²²You shall tell Pharaoh, 'The LORD says, Israel is my son, my firstborn, ²³and I have said to you, "Let my son go, that he may serve me;" and you have refused to let him go. Behold, I will kill your firstborn son.'"

²⁷**The LORD said to Aaron**, "Go into the wilderness to meet Moses." He went, and met him on God's mountain, and kissed him. ²⁸Moses told Aaron all the LORD's words with which he had sent him, and all the signs with which he had instructed him. ²⁹Moses and Aaron went and gathered together all the elders of the children of Israel. ³⁰Aaron spoke all the words which the LORD had spoken to Moses, and did the signs in the sight of the people. ³¹The people believed, and when they heard that the LORD had visited the children of Israel, and that he had seen their affliction, then they bowed their heads and worshiped. (Exodus 4:1-5,10-15,17-23,27-31)

¹**Afterward Moses and Aaron came**, and said to Pharaoh, "This is what the LORD, the God of Israel, says, 'Let my people go, that they may hold a feast to me in the wilderness.'" ²Pharaoh said, "Who is the LORD, that I should listen to his voice to let Israel go? I don't know the LORD, and moreover I will not let Israel go." (Exodus 5:1-2)

Let us stop here briefly. We see how God spoke to Pharaoh through the mouth of Moses and Aaron.⁵⁹ Did Pharaoh believe the word of God? No, he did not. Did you hear how he answered Moses and Aaron? He said, **"Who is the LORD, that I should listen to his voice to let Israel go? I don't know the LORD and moreover I will not let Israel go."**

Pharaoh did not know the LORD. Pharaoh and all the people of Egypt had religion, but they did not have a relationship with the

---

59 Arabic: *Harun*

one true God. They only cared about following the religion of their ancestors. They did not care about knowing the LORD, the God of Abraham, Isaac, and Jacob. Pharaoh and the Egyptians put their confidence in their customs, their idols, their fetishes and their religious leaders, but they did not believe in the LORD and His plan.

In chapter 6 we read:

> ¹**The LORD said to Moses**, "Now you shall see what I will do to Pharaoh, for by a strong hand he shall let them go, and by a strong hand he shall drive them out of his land." ²God spoke to Moses, and said to him, "I am the LORD. ³I appeared to Abraham, to Isaac, and to Jacob, as God Almighty; but by my name the LORDI was not known to them. ⁴I have also established my covenant with them, to give them the land of Canaan, the land of their travels, in which they lived as aliens. ⁵Moreover I have heard the groaning of the children of Israel, whom the Egyptians keep in bondage, and I have remembered my covenant. ⁶Therefore tell the children of Israel, 'I am the LORD, and I will bring you out from under the burdens of the Egyptians, and I will rid you out of their bondage, and I will redeem you with an outstretched arm, and with great judgments. ⁷I will take you to myself for a people. I will be your God; and you shall know that I am the LORD your God, who brings you out from under the burdens of the Egyptians. ⁸I will bring you into the land which I swore to give to Abraham, to Isaac, and to Jacob; and I will give it to you for a heritage: I am the LORD.'" (Exodus 6:1-8)

> ⁴"**But Pharaoh will not listen to you**, so I will lay my hand on Egypt, and bring out my armies, my people the children of Israel, out of the land of Egypt by great judgments. ⁵The Egyptians shall know that I am the LORD when I stretch out my hand on Egypt, and bring the children of Israel out from among them." ⁶Moses and Aaron did so. As the LORD commanded them, so they did. ⁷Moses was eighty years old, and Aaron eighty-three years old, when they spoke to Pharaoh. (Exodus 7:4-7)

From this we learn that the Lord planned to judge Pharaoh and the people of Egypt with awesome displays of His power. God, in His righteousness, purposed to punish the Egyptians for the hundreds of years of suffering which they had brought on the descendants of Abraham. Also, through the miracles that God planned to perform by the hand of Moses, the Lord wanted to display His glory and power. In this way He would show the people of Egypt and the whole world that the LORD who spoke to Abraham, Isaac, Jacob, and Moses is the living and true God.

As we have already learned, God is the Merciful One and does not want anyone to perish but wants everyone to repent and to know and receive the truth. That was why He planned to perform miracles that would confirm the message He spoke through Moses. The LORD wanted everyone to know beyond any doubt that the God who was speaking through Moses is the one true God.

We need to remember that there were hundreds of idols in Egypt which the Egyptians considered gods. But God wanted them to know that there is only one true God. He wanted them to know that the one true God is the God who established His covenant with Abraham, Isaac, and Jacob – promising to make of them a nation through which God would provide the prophets, the Scriptures, and the Savior of the world Himself.

However, Pharaoh was not interested in knowing the one true God. That is why when God sought to speak to Pharaoh through His prophets, Moses and Aaron, Pharaoh answered them, saying, **"Who is the LORD, that I should listen to his voice to let Israel go? I don't know the LORD, and moreover I will not let Israel go."** (Exodus 5:2)

Pharaoh spoke the truth when he said that he did not know the LORD. He did not know the God who had established an eternal covenant with Abraham, Isaac, and Jacob. Pharaoh had religion, but he did not have a relationship with God. Pharaoh's heart was hard. His mind was closed. And so he ignored the message from God to him through Moses and Aaron.

To this very day, most people in the world follow the way of Pharaoh. They talk about God, but they pay no attention to the word of the LORD. Consequently, they do not know God. They know some things *about* God, but they do not know God *Himself*. They have a religion handed down to them by their parents, but they do not have a personal relationship with the living God who revealed Himself to Moses.

How about you? Do you know the LORD? Do you understand and believe what He has revealed in the writings of His prophets? Do you know the Savior about whom the prophets wrote, the Messiah who, as the Scripture says, **suffered for sins once, the righteous for the unrighteous, that he might bring you to God**? (1 Peter 3:18) Do you believe in Him? Do you love Him with all your heart? Do you want to obey Him? Or are you, like Pharaoh, just following the religion of your ancestors?

Oh dear friends, may not even one of us be like Pharaoh, who refused to listen to and believe the message of the Eternal God! Listen to this warning from God's word: **See to it, brothers and sisters, that none of you has a sinful, unbelieving heart that turns away from the living God.** (Hebrews 3:12 NIV) Today, if you hear his voice, do not harden your hearts like Pharaoh, who said, "Who is the LORD, that I should obey him?"

Thank you for listening.

God willing, in our next study we will continue this captivating story and see how God brought upon Pharaoh and the Egyptians ten plagues so that they might know that He is the LORD.

May the LORD God bless you as you heed this solemn warning from His holy word:

> **Today, if you will hear his voice, don't harden your hearts.**
>
> (Hebrews 3:15)

Program 32

The Plagues

Exodus 7-10

An egg should not wrestle with a rock. This Wolof proverb summarizes what we will study today in the Scriptures. What happens when an egg and a rock collide? The egg breaks, but the rock remains unchanged. Today we will see what happened when Pharaoh, king of Egypt, tried to fight against the LORD God, of whom the prophet Moses writes: **"[He is] the Rock, his work is perfect, for all his ways are just."** (Deuteronomy 32:4)

Last time, we saw God send Moses and Aaron to Pharaoh to free the people of Israel from their slavery in Egypt. They said to Pharaoh:

> [1]**"This is what the LORD, the God of Israel, says,** 'Let my people go, that they may hold a feast to me in the wilderness.'" [2]Pharaoh said, "Who is the LORD, that I should listen to his voice to let Israel go? I don't know the LORD, and moreover I will not let Israel go." (Exodus 5:1-2)

In brief, God determined to free the people of Israel, whereas Pharaoh was determined to keep them as his slaves. But *an egg should not wrestle with a rock.*[60] Let us now return to the second part of the Torah, the book of Exodus, chapter 7, to see how Pharaoh tried to fight with God. The Scripture says:

> [10]**Moses and Aaron went in to Pharaoh**, and they did so, as the LORD had commanded. Aaron cast down his rod before Pharaoh and before his servants, and it became a serpent. [11]Then Pharaoh also called for the wise men and the sorcerers. They also, the magicians of Egypt, did the same thing with their enchantments.

---

60 Wrestling is the traditional, national sport of Senegal

> [12]For they each cast down their rods, and they became serpents;
> but Aaron's rod swallowed up their rods. (Exodus 7:10-12)

Notice the start of what we might call a wrestling match between Pharaoh and the LORD. On one side we see Pharaoh with his wise men and sorcerers; on the other side we see Moses and Aaron. After Aaron's staff was changed into a snake, Pharaoh's sorcerers[61] imitated the miracle with their incantations. **For they each cast down their rods, and they became serpents; but Aaron's rod swallowed up their rods.**

What can we say about all this? We know that the wonders which Moses and Aaron performed came from God. However, Pharaoh's marabouts also performed wonders. From where did they get their power? Did they get it from God? No. God does not fight against Himself. So where did their power come from? Pharaoh's marabouts relied on the art of deception and on a power that comes from Satan.

The Holy Scriptures show us that Satan is very crafty and loves to deceive people; he is also very powerful and can perform miracles. However, what is certain is that God is infinitely more powerful than Satan, as we see when Aaron's staff swallowed the staffs of Pharaoh's sorcerers. However, this did not cause Pharaoh to repent and to listen to the word of God. Next the Scripture says:

> [14]**The LORD said to Moses**, "Pharaoh's heart is stubborn. He refuses to let the people go. [15]Go to Pharaoh in the morning. Behold, he is going out to the water. You shall stand by the river's bank to meet him. You shall take the rod which was turned to a serpent in your hand. [16]You shall tell him, 'The LORD, the God of the Hebrews, has sent me to you, saying, "Let my people go, that they may serve me in the wilderness. Behold, until now you haven't listened." [17]The LORD says, "In this you shall know that I am the LORD. Behold: I will strike with the rod that is in my hand on the waters which are in the river, and they shall be turned to blood...."

---

61 Literally in Wolof: marabouts, spiritual guides

[20]**Moses and Aaron did so**, as the LORD commanded; and he lifted up the rod, and struck the waters that were in the river, in the sight of Pharaoh, and in the sight of his servants; and all the waters that were in the river were turned to blood. [21]The fish that were in the river died. The river became foul. The Egyptians couldn't drink water from the river. The blood was throughout all the land of Egypt. [22]The magicians of Egypt did the same thing with their enchantments. So Pharaoh's heart was hardened, and he didn't listen to them, as the LORD had spoken. [23]Pharaoh turned and went into his house, and he didn't even take this to heart. [24]All the Egyptians dug around the river for water to drink; for they couldn't drink the river water. [25]Seven days were fulfilled, after the LORD had struck the river. (Exodus 7:14-17,20-25)

[1]**The LORD spoke to Moses**, "Go in to Pharaoh, and tell him, 'This is what the LORD says, "Let my people go, that they may serve me. [2]If you refuse to let them go, behold, I will plague all your borders with frogs. [3]The river will swarm with frogs, which will go up and come into your house, and into your bedroom, and on your bed, and into the house of your servants, and on your people, and into your ovens, and into your kneading troughs. (Exodus 8:1-3)

But Pharaoh ignored God's warnings from the prophet Moses.

[5]**Then the LORD said to Moses**, "Tell Aaron, 'Stretch out your hand with your rod over the rivers, over the streams, and over the pools, and cause frogs to come up on the land of Egypt.'" [6]Aaron stretched out his hand over the waters of Egypt; and the frogs came up, and covered the land of Egypt. [7]The magicians did the same thing with their enchantments, and brought up frogs on the land of Egypt. [8]Then Pharaoh called for Moses and Aaron, and said, "Entreat the LORD, that he take away the frogs from me and from my people; and I will let the people go, that they may sacrifice to the LORD."

[12][**Then**] **Moses cried to the LORD** concerning the frogs which he had brought on Pharaoh.… The frogs died.…

¹⁴They gathered them together in heaps, and the land stank. ¹⁵But when Pharaoh saw that there was a respite, he hardened his heart, and didn't listen to them, as the LORD had spoken.

¹⁶**The LORD said to Moses**, "Tell Aaron, 'Stretch out your rod, and strike the dust of the earth, that it may become lice throughout all the land of Egypt.'" ¹⁷They did so; and Aaron stretched out his hand with his rod, and struck the dust of the earth, and there were lice on man, and on animal; all the dust of the earth became lice throughout all the land of Egypt. ¹⁸The magicians tried with their enchantments to produce lice, but they couldn't. There were lice on man, and on animal. ¹⁹Then the magicians said to Pharaoh, "This is God's finger;" but Pharaoh's heart was hardened, and he didn't listen to them, as the LORD had spoken. (Exodus 8:5-8,12,14-19)

Did you see what happened with the sorcerers, Pharaoh's marabouts? We have already seen how they had a certain power, which they received from Satan. That is why they managed through their secret arts to imitate God's power and change a little water into blood and make frogs appear – as if the Egyptians needed more blood in their water and frogs in their beds! But their power was limited. Pharaoh's sorcerers were unable to remove the plagues which Almighty God had brought down upon the land of Egypt. After Aaron struck the ground with his staff and the dust became gnats, the sorcerers performed their secret arts, trying to change the dust into gnats, but they could not. They had to admit to Pharaoh, **"This is God's finger!"**

Certainly Satan has power and can give to man certain powers, but those powers will never exceed the limits that God has fixed. God alone is the All-Powerful One. Only He can do all things. He alone is the One without limitations. Pharaoh's marabouts were beginning to learn about the unlimited greatness of God, but Pharaoh still refused to submit to God. Pharaoh continued to harden his heart and imagine that he could wrestle with the LORD God of Israel and win.

The Scriptures go on to record how God brought upon Pharaoh and upon the land of Egypt seven more plagues by the hands of Moses and Aaron. Unfortunately, we do not have time to read about each plague. We can only name them.

The fourth plague consisted of **swarms of flies** which filled the land, even the people's houses, causing much destruction. In the fifth plague a terrible **sickness fell on the livestock** and many died. However, not one died among the herds of the children of Israel. Nevertheless, Pharaoh hardened his heart and refused to let the people of Israel go. Next, terrible **boils broke out on men and animals**. The Scripture says that **The magicians couldn't stand before Moses because of the boils; for the boils were on the magicians and on all the Egyptians.** (Exodus 9:11) In the seventh plague a terrible **hail and lightning storm** of proportions never before seen in Egypt, destroyed all the fields. After that was over, the land was filled with **locusts**, which ate whatever the hailstorm had left. This was the eighth plague.

In the ninth plague, God said to Moses, **"Stretch out your hand toward the sky, that there may be darkness over the land of Egypt, even darkness which may be felt."** (Exodus 10:21) For three days no one could see anything. But in the district where the children of Israel lived, there was light. Not one plague broke out on them. Yet all of this did not cause Pharaoh to repent and let the people of Israel go. The Scripture tells us that **Pharaoh said to him, "Get away from me! Be careful to see my face no more; for in the day you see my face you shall die!"** (Exodus 10:28)

There is one more plague that God brought down on Pharaoh and the Egyptians, but we will wait until next time to look at it, because our time is almost gone.

How can we summarize what we have heard today? Perhaps like this: Pharaoh tried to fight against the LORD God. Did Pharaoh and his marabouts overcome the Almighty One? Could they overpower Him? No. No one can grapple with God and overpower Him. An egg does not fight with a rock and win.

What can we learn from what we have read today? The Scripture says: **Now all these things happened to them by way of example, and they were written for our admonition.** (1 Corinthians 10:11) God wants to warn us. God wants us to take a good look at our own lives and attitudes and to heed His warnings.

You who are listening today, are you paying attention to the true word of God? Are you obeying it? Or, are you, like Pharaoh, fighting God? Let your own heart answer. Are you submitted to the word of God? This does not mean, are you submitted to the customs of your ancestors and their religion, but rather, have you received with humility the word of the LORD? Or are you attempting to fight with Him?

An egg should not wrestle with a rock. Man is like a fragile egg and the word of God is like a massive rock. The Scripture says: **All flesh is like grass, and all of man's glory like the flower in the grass. The grass withers, and its flower falls; but the Lord's word endures forever.** (1 Peter 1:24-25)

The word of the Eternal God is a solid Rock and everyone who builds his life upon this Rock has placed his life on a solid foundation. However, if you refuse to build your life on that Rock, one day the Rock of the word of God will fall on you and crush you. An egg cannot fight with a rock and win. Neither can man contend with God's eternal word and escape punishment.

This is where we must stop. Thank you for listening. God willing, in our next study we will hear about *the blood of the Passover Lamb*, which broke Pharaoh's grip and caused him to let the children of Israel to leave Egypt.

God bless you as you think about what the prophet Moses wrote in the Torah, saying:

> **He is the Rock, his works are perfect, and all his ways are just. A faithful God who does no wrong, upright and just is he.**
>
> (Deuteronomy 32:4 NIV)

Program 33

The Passover Lamb

Exodus 11-12

Our reading from the Torah in the last program was about when Pharaoh, king of Egypt, tried to fight with God. The LORD purposed to deliver the people of Israel from their slavery in Egypt, but Pharaoh was determined to keep them as his slaves. But *an egg should not wrestle with a rock*. No one can fight with God and win. The LORD brought upon Egypt nine terrible plagues and king Pharaoh lost nine times in a row. Yet he still refused to release the Hebrew slaves.

Today we will see how God brought upon Egypt a tenth and final plague, so that Pharaoh would release the people of Israel. After the ninth plague, Pharaoh had told Moses and Aaron, **"Get away from me! Be careful to see my face no more; for in the day you see my face you shall die!"** (Exodus 10:28) Here is how God Himself answered the king, through the mouth of Moses.

⁴**Moses said [to Pharaoh],** "This is what the LORD says: 'About midnight I will go out into the middle of Egypt, ⁵and all the firstborn in the land of Egypt shall die, from the firstborn of Pharaoh who sits on his throne, even to the firstborn of the female servant who is behind the mill, and all the firstborn of livestock. ⁶There will be a great cry throughout all the land of Egypt, such as there has not been, nor will be any more. ⁷But against any of the children of Israel a dog won't even bark or move its tongue, against man or animal, that you may know that the LORD makes a distinction between the Egyptians and Israel. ⁸All these servants of yours will come down to me, and bow down themselves to me, saying, "Get out, with all the

people who follow you;" and after that I will go out.'" He went
out from Pharaoh in hot anger. (Exodus 11:4-8)

Yes, God planned to bring a tenth plague upon the land of Egypt
which was to be worse than the other nine plagues that had already
happened. God announced the impending death of every firstborn
son in Egypt. What a terrible plague! And what would happen to
the firstborn of the Israelites? Would they die along with those of
the Egyptians? They did not deserve to escape God's judgment,
because they too were sinners, like all the people of Egypt. But God,
who is faithful and merciful, designed a plan to protect the people
of Israel from that plague as He had from the others.

Let us continue in chapter 12 to hear what God told Moses to tell
the Israelites to do for their firstborn to escape death.

> [1]**The LORD spoke to Moses and Aaron**…, [3]"Speak to all the
> congregation of Israel, saying, 'On the tenth day of this month,
> they shall take to them every man a lamb, according to their
> fathers' houses, a lamb for a household;… [5]Your lamb shall
> be without defect, a male a year old. You shall take it from the
> sheep or from the goats. [6]You shall keep it until the fourteenth
> day of the same month; and the whole assembly of the congre-
> gation of Israel shall kill it at evening. [7]They shall take some of
> the blood, and put it on the two door posts and on the lintel, on
> the houses in which they shall eat it. [8]They shall eat the meat in
> that night, roasted with fire, with unleavened bread. They shall
> eat it with bitter herbs. [9]Don't eat it raw, nor boiled at all with
> water, but roasted with fire; with its head, its legs and its inner
> parts.… [46]It must be eaten in one house. You shall not carry any
> of the meat outside of the house. Do not break any of its bones."
> (Exodus 12:1,3,5-9,46)

[11]"**It shall be, when the LORD brings you into the land** of the
Canaanite, as he swore to you and to your fathers, and will give
it you, [12]that you shall set apart to the LORD all that opens the
womb, and every firstborn that comes from an animal which you
have. The males shall be the LORD's. [13]Every firstborn of a donkey

you shall redeem with a lamb; and if you will not redeem it, then you shall break its neck; and you shall redeem all the firstborn of man among your sons. (Exodus 13:11-13)

Let us pause here. Do you see the plan that God decreed to save the firstborn sons of Israel from death and redeem the people of Israel from their bondage of slavery in Egypt? It was an amazing plan, a plan which, to man's way of thinking, was utterly ridiculous. He purposed to redeem them with *the blood of a lamb* – the blood of a lamb without blemish – blood with which they would stain the doorframes of their houses. Only the blood of the lamb could save their firstborn from death.

After the LORD had finished speaking to Moses and Aaron, they assembled all the elders of Israel, telling them what God had said about the blood of the lamb. When the elders of Israel heard how God planned to save their firstborns from death, they prostrated themselves and worshiped the LORD. And the elders and all the people of Israel did exactly as God had commanded Moses.

> [29]**At midnight, the LORD struck all the firstborn** in the land of Egypt, from the firstborn of Pharaoh who sat on his throne to the firstborn of the captive who was in the dungeon, and all the firstborn of livestock. [30]Pharaoh rose up in the night, he, and all his servants, and all the Egyptians; and there was a great cry in Egypt, for there was not a house where there was not one dead. (Exodus 12:29-30)

Did you hear what happened on that dreadful night? Did the LORD judge the nation of Egypt as He said He would? Yes He did. At midnight the angel of destruction passed through the land of Egypt, striking all the firstborn, from the firstborn of king Pharaoh to the firstborn of those in prison. On that night, great mourning and wailing echoed throughout Egypt, because there was not one Egyptian house without someone dead!

But what happened in the houses of the Israelites? Did God spare their firstborn from the plague of death? What do you think?

God had promised them, saying, **"When I see the blood, I will pass over you."** The people of Israel had stained the doors of their houses with the blood of a lamb that each household had sacrificed, just as God had commanded them. Consequently, none of their firstborn died. But in the houses of the Egyptians every firstborn died because they did not take part in God's way of deliverance by the blood of a lamb.

Next the Scripture tells us:

> [31]**He called for Moses and Aaron by night**, and said, "Rise up, get out from among my people, both you and the children of Israel; and go, serve the LORD, as you have said! [32]…and bless me also!" [33]The Egyptians were urgent with the people, to send them out of the land in haste, for they said, "We are all dead men." (Exodus 12:31-33)

Finally, Pharaoh had no choice but to give in and let the Israelites go. We have already seen how at first Pharaoh said to Moses and Aaron, **"Who is the LORD, that I should listen to his voice to let Israel go? I don't know the LORD, and moreover I will not let Israel go."** But, in the end, Pharaoh and all the Egyptians were forced to admit that the God of Israel is the one true God, more powerful than their idols, fetishes, and marabouts. *An egg must not wrestle with a rock.* No one can fight with God and win.

On that night the Israelites made their exodus from Egypt and left with much wealth which the LORD had moved the Egyptian people to give them (a kind of back pay for their years as slaves).

> [35]**The children of Israel** did according to the word of Moses; and they asked of the Egyptians jewels of silver, and jewels of gold, and clothing. [36]The LORD gave the people favor in the sight of the Egyptians, so that they let them have what they asked. They plundered the Egyptians.… [40]Now the time that the children of Israel lived in Egypt was 430 years. (Exodus 12:35-36,40)

All this took place to fulfill what God had promised Abraham hundreds of years earlier, saying,

¹³**He said to Abram**, "Know for sure that your offspring will live as foreigners in a land that is not theirs, and will serve them. They will afflict them four hundred years. ¹⁴I will also judge that nation, whom they will serve. Afterward they will come out with great wealth." (Genesis 15:13-14)

This historical event is like a deep and wide ocean full of hidden treasures. There is so much that we could say about it. Obviously, we do not have time to explain all the truths contained in the Passover. But there is one very important truth which we must retain in our minds. It is God's promise to the Israelites: **"When I see the blood I will pass over you."**

Why did the firstborns of Israel not die along with the Egyptian firstborns? They did not die because God had provided a way of salvation by the blood of a lamb. God promised that the firstborn would be saved from death in every house where the doorframe was stained with the blood of a lamb. But in every home where the blood had not been applied, the firstborn died.

Listening friends, here is an important question for you. In thinking of all the Egyptian and Hebrew homes on that solemn night: *How many households witnessed a death?* Think carefully before you answer.

The correct answer is: *Every household witnessed a death.* Yes, every household. *Either the firstborn died or a lamb died.* No exceptions.

Imagine a firstborn son in one of the Hebrew homes asking his father that night, "Papa, why did our innocent lamb have to die?" The father replies, "My son, as you know, God had condemned every firstborn son in the land without exception. Because of our sins, we all deserved God's judgment. But in His mercy, the LORD told us that if we sacrificed a lamb without defect and put the blood on the top and side of our doorframes, then the plague of death would not strike you. Just as our forefather Abraham sacrificed the ram in his son's place, so tonight we sacrificed the lamb in your place. Our faithful God who promised, 'when I see the blood, I will pass over you' has kept His word!"

Friends, before God, all of Adam's descendants are like the firstborn sons of the people of Egypt and Israel. God's holy law condemns each of us to die and face God's righteous judgment. The penalty for sin is eternal condemnation, shut out **from the face of the Lord.** (2 Thessalonians 1:9)

What then must we do to be saved? How can God save sinners from the penalty of their sins without compromising His righteousness? We cannot take it very far today, but what we need to understand is this: The lambs which the Israelites sacrificed to escape the plague of death symbolized the Redeemer who was to come and pour out his blood to take on Himself the punishment that our sins require. That Redeemer is Jesus the Messiah of whom the prophet John declared, **"Behold! the Lamb of God, who takes away the sin of the world!"** (John 1:29)

Concerning that Lamb of God, the Scripture says: Jesus the Messiah **suffered for sins once, the righteous for the unrighteous, that he might bring you to God … For indeed Christ, our Passover, has been sacrificed in our place.** (1 Peter 3:18; 1 Corinthians 5:7)

The blood of the lamb, which the Israelites applied to their doors, pictured the blood which Jesus the Lamb of God shed on the cross some 1500 years later, so **that whoever believes in him should not perish, but have eternal life.** (John 3:16)

How about you? On the Day of Judgment, will God's terrible judgment pass over you? Or will it fall on you as it did on those who had not applied the blood of the lamb to their doorframes?

In our next program, God willing, we will continue with the story of the Israelites and see *how God opened a path of escape through the middle of the sea.*

Meanwhile, God bless you as you consider the deeper meaning of His promise to His ancient people:

When I see the blood, I will pass over you. (Exodus 12:13)

Program 34
A Path Through the Sea

Exodus 13-15

In our last lesson we saw how God delivered the people of Israel from their bondage by slaying the firstborn sons of the Egyptians. But He saved the firstborn sons of the Israelites through the blood of the lamb, which they put on the doorframes of their homes. God Himself had promised them, saying, **"The blood shall be to you for a token on the houses where you are. When I see the blood, I will pass over you."** (Exodus 12:13)

We also saw how on that night all the tribes of Israel made their exodus (went out) from Egypt. That night of the Passover was a night of great joy for them. Imagine the scene. For hundreds of years the rulers of Egypt had mistreated them and oppressed them with hard work to the point where there was no happiness left in their lives. But now, now they were free!

On that night of the Passover the LORD God delivered them. Their chains of slavery were broken and now God Himself was guiding them through the wilderness with the plan to organize them into a nation and then take them back to the land of Canaan, the land which today is known as Palestine or Israel. That was the land which God had sworn long beforehand to give to the descendants of Abraham, Isaac, and Jacob. Canaan was the land where, four hundred years earlier, Jacob and his sons had lived before they moved to Egypt where Joseph had become the supreme ruler.

Today we will read the historical account of how God delivered the children of Israel from the armies of Pharaoh. Here is the story from the Torah, recorded by the prophet Moses:

³⁷**The children of Israel traveled** from Rameses to Succoth, about six hundred thousand on foot who were men, in addition to children. ³⁸A mixed multitude went up also with them, with flocks, herds, and even very much livestock. (Exodus 12:37-38)

¹⁹**Moses took the bones of Joseph with him**, for he had made the children of Israel swear, saying, "God will surely visit you, and you shall carry up my bones away from here with you."… ²¹The LORD went before them by day in a pillar of cloud, to lead them on their way, and by night in a pillar of fire, to give them light, that they might go by day and by night: ²²the pillar of cloud by day, and the pillar of fire by night, didn't depart from before the people. (Exodus 13:19,21-22)

¹**The LORD spoke to Moses saying**, ²"Speak to the children of Israel, that they turn back and encamp… by the [Red] sea. ³Pharaoh will say of the children of Israel, 'They are entangled in the land. The wilderness has shut them in.' ⁴I will harden Pharaoh's heart, and he will follow after them; and I will get honor over Pharaoh, and over all his armies; and the Egyptians shall know that I am the LORD." They did so.

⁵**The king of Egypt was told that the people had fled**; and the heart of Pharaoh and of his servants was changed toward the people, and they said, "What is this we have done, that we have let Israel go from serving us?" ⁶He prepared his chariot, and took his army with him; ⁷and he took six hundred chosen chariots, and all the chariots of Egypt, with captains over all of them.

⁹**The Egyptians pursued them.** All the horses and chariots of Pharaoh, his horsemen, and his army overtook them encamping by the sea, beside Pihahiroth, before Baal Zephon. ¹⁰When Pharaoh came near, the children of Israel lifted up their eyes, and behold, the Egyptians were marching after them; and they were very afraid. The children of Israel cried out to the LORD. ¹¹They said to Moses, "Because there were no graves in Egypt, have you taken us away to die in the wilderness? Why have you treated us this way, to bring us out of Egypt? ¹²Isn't this the word that we

spoke to you in Egypt, saying, 'Leave us alone, that we may serve the Egyptians?' For it would have been better for us to serve the Egyptians than to die in the wilderness." (Exodus 14:1-7,9-12)

What were the people of Israel saying? Why were they not trusting the LORD? Could not the God who had delivered them from the bondage of slavery again deliver them from Pharaoh's troops? Of course He could, but the Israelites did not think about this because they were so terrified. The sea was in front of them. Mountains were on their right and on their left. Behind them, Pharaoh's troops were advancing to recapture them or even kill them. What should they do? What could they do? How could they be saved?

The Scriptures tell us:

> [13]**Moses said to the people**, "Don't be afraid. Stand still, and see the salvation of the LORD, which he will work for you today; for you will never again see the Egyptians whom you have seen today. [14]The LORD will fight for you, and you shall be still." [15]The LORD said to Moses, "Why do you cry to me? Speak to the children of Israel, that they go forward. [16]Lift up your rod, and stretch out your hand over the sea and divide it. Then the children of Israel shall go into the middle of the sea on dry ground. [17]Behold, I myself will harden the hearts of the Egyptians, and they will go in after them. I will get myself honor over Pharaoh, and over all his armies, over his chariots, and over his horsemen. [18]The Egyptians shall know that I am the LORD...."

> [19]**The angel of God**, who went before the camp of Israel, moved and went behind them; and the pillar of cloud moved from before them, and stood behind them. [20]It came between the camp of Egypt and the camp of Israel. There was the cloud and the darkness, yet it gave light by night. One didn't come near the other all night.

> [21]**Moses stretched out his hand over the sea**, and the LORD caused the sea to go back by a strong east wind all night, and made the sea dry land, and the waters were divided. [22]The

children of Israel went into the middle of the sea on the dry ground; and the waters were a wall to them on their right hand and on their left. [23]The Egyptians pursued, and went in after them into the middle of the sea: all of Pharaoh's horses, his chariots, and his horsemen. [24]In the morning watch, the LORD looked out on the Egyptian army through the pillar of fire and of cloud, and confused the Egyptian army. [25]He took off their chariot wheels, and they drove them heavily; so that the Egyptians said, "Let's flee from the face of Israel, for the LORD fights for them against the Egyptians!"

[26]**The LORD said to Moses**, "Stretch out your hand over the sea, that the waters may come again on the Egyptians, on their chariots, and on their horsemen." [27]Moses stretched out his hand over the sea, and the sea returned to its strength when the morning appeared; and the Egyptians fled against it. The LORD overthrew the Egyptians in the middle of the sea. [28]The waters returned, and covered the chariots and the horsemen, even all Pharaoh's army that went in after them into the sea. There remained not so much as one of them. [29]But the children of Israel walked on dry land in the middle of the sea, and the waters were a wall to them on their right hand and on their left.

[30]**Thus the LORD saved Israel that day** out of the hand of the Egyptians; and Israel saw the Egyptians dead on the seashore. [31]Israel saw the great work which the LORD did to the Egyptians, and the people feared the LORD ; and they believed in the LORD and in his servant Moses. (Exodus 14:13-31)

Then Moses and the Israelites sang this song to the LORD: **"I will sing to the LORD, for he has triumphed gloriously.... The LORD is my strength and song; He has become my salvation."** (Exodus 15:1-2) That is how they began to sing and thank God for the great deliverance He had accomplished for them. Miriam, the sister of Aaron and Moses, took a tambourine, and all the women followed her, beating tambourines and singing and dancing. Miriam struck up this song: **Sing to the LORD for He has triumphed gloriously. He has thrown the horse and his rider into the sea.** (Exodus 15:21)

And so dear friends, that is the historical record[62] about when God opened a path through the Red Sea for the people of Israel.

How then can we conclude our lesson today? Perhaps with this question: *Who could save the Israelites from Pharaoh's troops?* Could they save themselves? The sea was in front of them. The mountains were on their right and left. And Pharaoh's troops were behind them. Could the children of Israel save themselves? Could they cause the sea to dry up? Or level the mountains? Or battle Pharaoh's troops? No, they could not. Who then could save them? God alone! Only the LORD God could deliver them. That is why Moses told them, **"Don't be afraid. Stand still, and see the salvation of the LORD, which he will work for you today."** Only God could save them. And He did. That is why, after they had arrived on the other side of the sea, they sang, **"The LORD is my strength and song; He has become my salvation."**

The LORD Himself was their salvation. The only thing the Israelites could do to be saved from Pharaoh's troops was to follow the path God had opened for them in the midst of the sea, and then praise Him on the other side for delivering them from certain death.

Dear friends, God wants us to understand that we are like the children of Israel. Like them, we have no hope of escaping the disaster that will soon befall us unless God delivers us. Perhaps the sea is not before us, but death and hell await us. Perhaps the mountains are not at our sides, but the holiness of God fences us in and condemns us. Pharaoh and his troops are not behind us, but Satan and our sins are upon us and threaten to destroy us forever.

Who can rescue us from God's righteous judgment? Who can save the sinner from the fire that never goes out? Who can free man from the power of Satan? Who can deliver us from our sin and shame? Who can get us to the other side of the sea of sin and into God's holy heaven? God alone. Only God can save us. Man has no possibility of saving himself nor of saving another person.

---

62 For geological information/evidence for the Red Sea crossing, see endnote #4 in the *KING of GLORY Illustrated Study Guide*. www.king-of-glory.com

This is what the Scriptures declare:

> [8]**For by grace you have been saved through faith**, and that not of yourselves; it is the gift of God, [9]not of works, that no one would boast. (Ephesians 2:8-9)

The path of salvation which God has opened for the children of Adam through the sea of sin and death and judgment is not based upon what we can do in our own strength, nor is it based on following the requirements of a religion. God says that it is **not of works, that no one would boast.**

What then is the way of salvation God has provided for helpless sinners like you and me? The Redeemer who came from heaven to shed His blood for our sins and conquer death *is* The Way. He alone can free us from slavery to Satan and sin, and rescue us from death and judgment. Of Him, the Scriptures say: **There is salvation in no one else, for there is no other name under heaven that is given among men, by which we must be saved!** (Acts 4:12)

Yes, God has opened a way for you and me through the sea of condemnation and judgment to the place of forgiveness and eternal life. Concerning this way of salvation, Jesus the Messiah who God sent into the world said,

> **"I am the way**, the truth, and the life. No one comes to the Father, except through me. (John 14:6) Most certainly I tell you, he who hears my word and believes him who sent me has eternal life, and doesn't come into judgment, but has passed out of death into life." (John 5:24)

Dear friend, have you crossed over from death to life?

Thank you for listening. Next time, Lord willing, we will see *how God fed the Israelites in the desert.*

God bless you as you reflect on Moses' message to the Israelites:

> **Don't be afraid. Stand still, and see the salvation of the LORD, which he will work for you today.** (Exodus 14:13)

Food in the Desert

Exodus 16-17

In our last lesson, we saw how God rescued the people of Israel from the hand of Pharaoh and his chariots and troops. When the Israelites came to the shore of the Red Sea they had no possible means of escaping from Pharaoh's army. Then we heard how the LORD pushed back the waters for them so that they could walk through the middle of the sea on dry ground. But when Pharaoh's troops tried to cross, they were drowned. This was how the Lord God saved Israel from the hand of Pharaoh and his army. And when the Israelites saw the awesome power of the LORD they feared Him and sang to Him, **"I will sing to the LORD, because He is my Salvation!"** (Exodus 15:1-2)

At this point in the story, the Israelites were journeying through the desert between Egypt and Canaan. Canaan is the country which God had promised to give to their forefather Abraham and his descendants. Today we are going to see how God fed the Israelites in the desert. The LORD God Himself went before them, guiding them through the hostile desert with a pillar of cloud to provide shade during the day, and with a pillar of fire to provide light at night. One thing is sure, if God had not guided them and cared for them, they would have perished in the desert.

Did the Israelites trust God or did they worry about what they would eat and what they would drink? Surely they should have trusted the LORD God, who had done so many wonderful things for them. He had freed them from their bondage of slavery by means of the ten plagues. He had delivered their firstborn from death, by means of the blood of the lamb. He had opened a dry path through the middle of the sea. He had destroyed their enemies. And now He was going before them in a cloud to lead them back to the land of Canaan, as He had promised their forefather Abraham. What do you think? Did the people of Israel have confidence in their great God? With all this evidence of His power and His care for them, did they believe that God could do what He had promised? We find the answer in chapter 16 of the book of Exodus in the Torah of Moses. The Scripture says:

> ¹**They took their journey from Elim,** and all the congregation of the children of Israel came to the wilderness of Sin, which is between Elim and Sinai, on the fifteenth day of the second month after their departing out of the land of Egypt. ²The whole congregation of the children of Israel murmured against Moses and against Aaron in the wilderness; ³and the children of Israel said to them, "We wish that we had died by the LORD's hand in the land of Egypt, when we sat by the meat pots, when we ate our fill of bread, for you have brought us out into this wilderness to kill this whole assembly with hunger." (Exodus 16:1-3)

So, did the tribes of Israel have confidence in the LORD their God? No, they did not. Instead of thanking Him for His faithful and loving care, they were grumbling against Him and His prophet Moses. Listen to how God answered them.

> ¹¹**The LORD spoke to Moses,** saying, ¹²"I have heard the murmurings of the children of Israel. Speak to them, saying, 'At evening you shall eat meat, and in the morning you shall be filled with bread. Then you will know that I am the LORD your God.'" ⁴Then the LORD said to Moses, "Behold, I will rain bread from the sky for you, and the people shall go out and gather a day's portion every day, that I may test them, whether they will walk in my law or not."

> ¹³In the evening, quail came up and covered the camp; and in the morning the dew lay around the camp. ¹⁴When the dew that lay had gone, behold, on the surface of the wilderness was a small round thing, small as the frost on the ground. ¹⁵When the children of Israel saw it, they said to one another, "What is it?" For

they didn't know what it was. Moses said to them, "It is the bread which the LORD has given you to eat…." [31]The house of Israel called its name "Manna", and it was like coriander seed, white; and its taste was like wafers with honey. (Exodus 16:11-12,4,13-15,31)

That is how God fed this huge multitude in the desert until the day they came to the border of the land of Canaan. Where did their food come from? It came from heaven. In the evening, quail meat, and in the morning a bread called *manna*. The Scripture says: **When the dew fell on the camp in the night, the manna fell on it.** (Numbers 11:9) **When the dew that lay had gone, behold, on the surface of the wilderness was a small round thing, small as the frost on the ground and its taste was like wafers with honey.** (Exodus 16:14,31) Their daily food came from the LORD their God. Did the Israelites deserve this food from heaven? Certainly not. They didn't deserve anything except God's judgment for their unbelief and ungratefulness.

Now let's continue in the Torah to see what happened some days later when the people ran out of water. We are reading in chapter 17:

[1]**All the congregation of the children of Israel traveled…** starting according to the LORD's commandment, and encamped in Rephidim; but there was no water for the people to drink. [2]Therefore the people quarreled with Moses, and said, "Give us water to drink." Moses said to them, "Why do you quarrel with me? Why do you test the LORD?" [3]The people were thirsty for water there; so the people murmured against Moses, and said, "Why have you brought us up out of Egypt, to kill us, our children, and our livestock with thirst?"

[4]**Moses cried to the LORD**, saying, "What shall I do with these people? They are almost ready to stone me." [5]The LORD said to Moses, "Walk on before the people, and take the elders of Israel with you, and take the rod in your hand with which you struck the Nile, and go. [6]Behold, I will stand before you there on the rock in Horeb. You shall strike the rock, and water will come out of it, that the people may drink." Moses did so in the sight of the elders of Israel. (Exodus 17:1-6)

Moses did as God commanded, and God met the people's need. Moses struck the massive rock and the LORD split it open **and waters gushed out. They ran as a river in the dry places** (Psalm 105:41) and all the people drank, they and their children and their herds.

Let us stop here and think a little about the story we are reading today. After all that God had done for the Israelites, did they have faith in Him? Were their hearts full of praise and thankfulness because of all that He had done for them? No, they were not. They did not trust God. They did not thank and praise Him. Instead they complained and spoke against the LORD who had already delivered them and protected them from so many, many dangers.

What did God do? The LORD God, in His patience, faithfulness, goodness, mercy and grace, gave them food and water in the desert. Did the people of Israel deserve God's mercy and grace? No, they did not. They only deserved God's judgment. Why did God show them such kindness? Because God is merciful and faithful. That is why He provided food and water for the Israelites even though they were ungrateful sinners. If salvation from hunger and thirst depended on the goodness and faithfulness of the people themselves, they would have perished in the desert.

It is important to understand this. God did not protect them and provide for them simply because of His goodness, but also because of His faithfulness to the covenant He had made with Abraham hundreds of years earlier.

Do you remember the two big promises the LORD had made to Abraham? First, God had told him: **"I will make of you a great nation."** (Genesis 12:2) God kept His word. Abraham had Isaac, Isaac had Jacob, and Jacob had twelve sons whose families became the twelve tribes of Israel. And now here they were – around three million people in the desert with God Himself guiding them back to the land He had promised to give to Abraham and his descendants!

God had also promised Abraham: **"All the families of the earth will be blessed through you."** (Genesis 12:3)

God kept that part of His promise too. By working with this new nation, God has demonstrated for all people on earth what He is like and how sinners can come to Him. When God protected the children of Israel, He was protecting His plans to bless you and me, for, as we have heard many times, it was from this nation that the prophets, the Holy Scriptures, and the promised Savior came.

Yes, God is faithful. God is love. The tribes of Israel did not deserve His protection and care. Yet even when they disobeyed God and spoke against Him, God gave them delicious food from heaven and fresh water from the rock.

Perhaps someone asks: *Of what value to us are all these stories about the children of Israel?* The word of God answers this question: **Now all these things happened to them by way of example, and they were written for our admonition… to the intent we should not lust after evil things, as they also lusted.** (1 Corinthians 10:11,6)

God wants us to learn from the nation of Israel. Here is one lesson from today's story. We ask you: *What did the Israelites have to do so they would not perish in the desert?* They simply had to drink the water and gather and eat the food[63] that God sent to them. From where did their deliverance come? Did it come from their own efforts? No, their deliverance came from the LORD. Apart from Him they were helpless to save themselves from hunger, starvation, and death.

The Holy Scriptures show us that we are all sinners like the people of Israel and when it comes to saving ourselves we too are helpless. Perhaps we are not walking through a dry desert as were the Israelites, but the shadow of death still hangs over us as it hung over them.

The word of God is clear: All who refuse to receive the means of salvation that the LORD has provided will die in their sin and end up in the eternal fire.

These are horrific thoughts. Die in sin! Come into judgment! End up in the place called Hell, forever separated from the LORD God!

---

63 Or: *bread*. In Wolof the word for bread is translated as: *food* or *sustenance*.

The good news, however, is that no one needs to die in their sin. Even as God gave the Israelites food and water so that they could live and not die of hunger and thirst in the desert, so God has provided for us the spiritual food and drink we need for a life of peace and joy for today and for all eternity.

What is the food that gives eternal life? Can we buy food in the market that can give us the power to live forever in God's presence? No, this kind of food cannot be found in the market. Well then, where and what is this Food, this Bread, that gives eternal life?

About 1500 years after God fed the Israelites in the desert with the bread from heaven, God sent down the Redeemer, the Savior of the world. He is the Food which God has provided to save us from sin and death, judgment and hell. Let us listen to what the Redeemer Himself said when He was on earth. He said,

> [47]**"Most certainly, I tell you**, he who believes in me has eternal life. [48]I am the bread [food, sustenance] of life. [49]Your fathers ate the manna in the wilderness and they died. [50]This is the bread which comes down out of heaven, that anyone may eat of it and not die. [51]I am the living bread which came down out of heaven.... [35]Whoever comes to me will not be hungry, and whoever believes in me will never be thirsty. (John 6:47-51,35)

Dear friends, this is where we must stop today. God willing, in our next program, we will see how God gave to His people *the Ten Commandments*.

God bless you as you feed on these wonderful words of life from the Messiah Himself:

> **I am the bread of life. Whoever comes to me will not be hungry, and whoever believes in me will never be thirsty.** (John 6:35)

Program 36
Fiery Mount Sinai

Exodus 19-20

I n our last lesson we saw how God cared for the tribes of Israel
in the barren desert, giving them water from the rock and
food from the sky so that they would not perish. We saw also
how the Israelites provoked God time after time because of their
lack of belief and their lack of thankfulness.

Today we will see how God appeared to the people of Israel in the
desert and gave them His holy law. We are reading in the Torah,
the book of Exodus, chapter 19. It begins like this: **In the third
month after the children of Israel had gone out of the land of
Egypt, on that same day they came into the wilderness of Sinai.**
(Exodus 19:1) Where were Moses and the Israelites now in their
journey through the desert? They had come to Mount Sinai. Do
you remember where Moses was when God first called him and
spoke to him from the bush which was on fire but didn't burn up?
It was on that same mountain of Sinai. God had told Moses:

> [7]**"I have surely seen the affliction of my people** who are in
> Egypt. … [8]I have come down to deliver them…. [10]Come now
> therefore, and I will send you to Pharaoh…. [12]Certainly I will
> be with you. This will be the token to you, that I have sent you:
> when you have brought the people out of Egypt, you shall
> serve God on this mountain." (Exodus 3:7-8,10,12)

Did God do for Moses what He had promised? We have seen
that He did. Where is Moses in our reading today? He and the
multitude of about three million people are at the base of Mount
Sinai, just as God had promised Moses when He spoke to him
from the burning bush.

Now let us see how God appeared again to Moses and spoke to the people of Israel at Mount Sinai. The Scripture says:

> [3]**Moses went up to God,** and the LORD called to him out of the mountain, saying, "This is what you shall tell the house of Jacob, and tell the children of Israel: [4]'You have seen what I did to the Egyptians, and how I bore you on eagles' wings, and brought you to myself. [5]Now therefore, if you will indeed obey my voice and keep my covenant, then you shall be my own possession from among all peoples; for all the earth is mine; [6]and you shall be to me a kingdom of priests and a holy nation.'These are the words which you shall speak to the children of Israel."

> [7]Moses came and called for the elders of the people, and set before them all these words which the LORD commanded him. [8]All the people answered together, and said, "All that the LORD has spoken we will do." Moses reported the words of the people to the LORD. (Exodus 19:3-8)

Did you hear how the Israelites answered God? They said, **"All that the LORD has spoken we will do."** Was what they said true? Could they keep all the commandments of God? God knew that the Israelites could not do everything that He commanded. What God really wanted was for them to recognize their inability to please Him, admit their sinful condition before Him, and believe the Good News about the Redeemer who was to come to earth to redeem sinners. God had forgiven the sins of their ancestors Abraham, Isaac, and Jacob based on their faith in God's promises. He wanted to do the same for them.

God's way of salvation has always been by faith alone in God and His righteous way of salvation. The Scripture says: **Now that no man is justified by the law before God is evident, for, "The righteous will live by faith."** (Galatians 3:11; Habakkuk 2:4)

Up to this point the people of Israel had imagined that they could achieve righteousness before God by their own efforts. How foolish of them! They had forgotten how many times they had offended God. They did not yet realize just how great their sin was before Him. In their thoughts, sin was not such a serious affair, but in the sight of God, who must judge them, sin is a terrible affair. God is holy and perfect; He cannot accept any works that are less than perfect, but the Israelites had not yet recognized this. That is why they said (presumptuously), **"All that the LORD has spoken we will do."** Nevertheless, God had a plan to show them that they could not (and would not) do "all that the LORD has said."

Now then, let us continue in the Scriptures to see how God came down on Mount Sinai, and gave ten commandments to the tribes of Israel.

The Scripture says:

> [10]**The LORD said to Moses,** "Go to the people [and tell them that in three days] [11]the LORD will come down in the sight of all the people on Mount Sinai. [12]You shall set bounds to the people all around, saying, 'Be careful that you don't go up onto the mountain, or touch its border. Whoever touches the mountain shall be surely put to death. [13]No hand shall touch him, but he shall surely be stoned or shot through; whether it is animal or man, he shall not live.'"

> [16]**On the third day, when it was morning,** there were thunders and lightnings, and a thick cloud on the mountain, and the sound of an exceedingly loud trumpet; and all the people who were in the camp trembled. [17]Moses led the people out of the camp to meet God; and they stood at the lower part of the mountain. [18]All of Mount Sinai smoked, because the LORD descended on it in fire; and its smoke ascended like the smoke of a furnace, and the whole mountain quaked greatly. [19]When the sound of the trumpet grew louder and louder…. [20]The LORD came down on Mount Sinai….(Exodus 19:10-13,16-20)

> [1]**God spoke all these words:** [2]"I am the LORD your God, who brought you out of the land of Egypt, out of the house of bondage.

1. **You shall have no other gods before me.**

2. **You shall not make for yourselves an idol… for I [am] the LORD your God.**

3. **You shall not misuse the name of the LORD your God, for the LORD will not hold him guiltless who misuses his name.**

4. **Remember the Sabbath day to keep it holy.**

5. **Honor your father and your mother.**

6. **You shall not murder.**

7. **You shall not commit adultery.**

8. **You shall not steal.**

9. **You shall not give false testimony against your neighbor.**

10. **You shall not covet your neighbor's house. You shall not covet your neighbor's wife, nor his male servant nor his female servant, nor his ox, nor his donkey, nor anything that is your neighbor's.**

[18]**All the people perceived the thunderings**, the lightnings, the sound of the trumpet, and the mountain smoking. When the people saw it, they trembled, and stayed at a distance. [19]They said to Moses, "Speak with us yourself, and we will listen; but don't let God speak with us, lest we die."

[20]**Moses said to the people**, "Don't be afraid, for God has come to test you, and that his fear may be before you, that you won't sin." [21]The people stayed at a distance…. (Exodus 20:1-5,7-8,12-21)

God willing, in the next program we will talk about each of the Ten Commandments which God gave to the Israelites on Mount Sinai. But before we bid you farewell today, there is something that God wants to teach us through what we have just read. It is this: the LORD God is perfectly pure and holy and, unless He provides for us a way to approach Him, we have a deadly serious problem since, in ourselves, we are not pure and holy! The Scripture declares that **all flesh is like grass** (1 Peter 1:24) and that **our God is a consuming fire.** (Hebrews 12:29) We all know what happens to grass if it is in the path of a wildfire. Will it survive the fire? No! Neither can a sinner survive in the presence of the holy LORD God!

At the beginning of our lesson today, we heard the Israelites tell Moses, **"All that the LORD has spoken we will do."** They said that because they had not yet recognized the holiness of God. They somehow thought that they could please God through their own efforts. But after God appeared to them on Mount Sinai, their thoughts changed drastically. When they experienced the thunder, the lightning, the mountain erupting with fire and smoke, and heard the voice of the LORD echoing out to them with ten holy commandments, **they trembled, and stayed at a distance. They said to Moses, "Speak with us yourself, and we will listen; but don't let God speak with us, lest we die."** (Exodus 20:18-19)

The people were beginning to recognize the holiness of God and their inability to approach Him. At the base of Mount Sinai they became aware of the truth of Scripture: **All flesh is like grass, and our God is a consuming fire.** (1 Peter 1:24; Hebrews 12:29) In the presence of God the Holy One, the Israelites began to understand that they could not honestly say, "No problem; everything the LORD has said we will do!" Instead, they now sensed their own unholiness and their inability to keep God's perfect law. They felt like dry grass in the path of a wildfire.

How about you? Do you recognize the holiness of God? Do you realize that your heart and your best efforts are unrighteous in God's eyes? Or are you like the Israelites, thinking, "No problem! I will do everything God requires. I will draw near to God with my good deeds." Truly, such thoughts do not agree with God's thoughts. Can those who are filthy and stained with sin dwell with the One who is pure and holy? Certainly not. Can God approve anything that is half good and half evil? No, He cannot and He will not. God demands perfection. Do you realize this? Or are you hoping that, on the Day of Judgment, what you consider to be "good deeds" will somehow wipe out your evil deeds? If that were so, then God would not be a righteous judge.

What would you think of a judge who tells a murderer, "You are guilty of murder, but because of the good deeds you have done in the past, I won't sentence you. You won't be punished. You may go free." What would we say about a judge who did that? We would declare him to be an unjust judge.

Friends, God is the righteous Judge. He cannot overlook sin. The LORD, who must judge the world, demands that our sins be punished with death and eternal separation from Him. Our "good works" cannot cancel our debt of sin. The Scripture says: **All of us have become like one who is unclean, and all our righteous acts are like filthy rags; we all shrivel up like a leaf, and like the wind our sins sweep us away.** (Isaiah 64:6 NIV) God is like a consuming fire and the "good works" of the sons of Adam are like dry grass. In our own righteousness we will not survive the flames of God's holy judgment.

Did the Israelites dare get close to the fire of God which had descended on Mount Sinai? Did they try to climb up the mountain to where God was? Did they even dare to approach the mountain, which quaked and rumbled with thunder and lightning; the mountain which billowed up smoke like smoke from a furnace? No, they did not approach it. The Scripture says that **they trembled** with fear. But that fear was a good thing. The prophet Solomon wrote: **The fear of the LORD is the beginning of knowledge.** (Proverbs 1:7)

Friends, thank you for listening. Next time, we hope *to talk about each of the Ten Commandments* which God gave the Israelites there on the mountain of Sinai.

May God bless you and as you think on this word of hope from the One who has provided the solution for our sin problem:

> **The product of sin is death but the gift of God is eternal life in our Lord Jesus the Messiah.** (Romans 6:23 Aramaic Bible in Plain English)

Ten Holy Commandments

Exodus 20

I n our last lesson we saw how the mountain of Sinai was billowing with smoke because the LORD God had descended upon it in fire, thunder, and lightning to give ten commands to the children of Israel. God warned the Israelites not to touch the mountain where He was lest they die. God was teaching them just how holy He is.

Today we want to look at each of the Ten Commandments and compare them with our lives, to know how we stand before God, the Holy One. We are reading in the Torah, the book of Exodus, chapter 20. After God descended on Mount Sinai in the midst of the fire and smoke, He spoke these words: **"I am the LORD your God, who brought you out of the land of Egypt, out of the house of bondage."** (Exodus 20:1-2)

1. For the first commandment, the LORD said: **"You shall have no other gods before me."** (Exodus 20:3) God wanted the people to understand that He alone must be their God. He will not share His glory with another. God, the Creator, is the only One we must worship. What we see in this country and throughout the world is quite another thing. People exalt other men to a place of which God alone is worthy. Only His name is holy and awesome. He alone deserves our total devotion and confidence. Yet when people have a problem or face an obstacle, their first thought is not to turn to God and pray to Him who created everything and can do anything. Instead, they put their hope in other human beings like themselves and give to them the place that belongs to God alone. Those who do that have another god before the one true God. To have another god is sin.

2. In the second commandment, God said: **"You shall not make for yourselves an idol… you shall not bow yourself down to them, nor serve them, for I, the LORD your God, am a jealous God."** (Exodus 20:4-5) In this commandment, God tells us to keep ourselves from idols. Idols are not limited to sculptured images which are worshiped in certain locations or in the niches of houses. An idol is anything that comes between us and God. For some people, football is their god, because football is more important to them than God. For others, television or the internet comes between them and God. They don't care about looking into the word of God to understand it; they don't have time for anything except watching television and the internet. Then there are others who, as you know, wear amulets, implying that God Himself is not enough for them. For still others, it is their wealth that replaces God. God doesn't have first place in their lives; money does. They will even get involved with things that are not pleasing to God in order to get more money. For such people their god is money. Anything which replaces the one true God is an idol.

3. In the third commandment, the LORD God said: **"You shall not misuse the name of the LORD your God, for the LORD will not hold him guiltless who misuses His name."** (Exodus 20:7) If you claim to be submitted to the one true God, but are not seeking to know Him and obey His word, then you are misusing His holy name. God does not want us to misuse His name. Yet almost every day you can hear someone making a promise to his neighbor, saying, "*Insh'a Allah* [Arabic: If God wills it], I will do this or that, or I will go to such and such a place," while, in his heart he has no intention of doing it. The will of God is the farthest thing from his mind. He only uses the name of God to make his neighbor believe his lies. That is sin. Others say, "*Bilaay* [Arabic: By God], I did not do such and such," when they know perfectly well that they did that very thing. Someone else says, "*God knows* that I did not do this or that," but they are only lying. People who do these things are misusing the name of God. The word of God says: **"But let your 'Yes' be 'Yes' and your 'No' be 'No.' Whatever is more than these is of the evil one."** (Matthew 5:37)

4. In the fourth commandment, God spoke to the children of Israel saying: **"Remember the Sabbath day to keep it holy. You shall labor six days, and do all your work… for in six days the LORD made heaven and earth, the sea, and all that is in them, and rested the seventh day."** (Exodus 20:8-10) In this we see that God wanted the children of Israel to rest every seventh day to honor Him.

5. In the fifth commandment which God gave, He said: **"Honor your father and your mother, that your days may be long in the land which the LORD your God gives you."** (Exodus 20:12) Here we can see that our parents are very special and worthy of honor, and that we should give them the respect that they deserve. But this is not what we see in today's generation. We see children who talk back to their parents, turn their noses up at them and go their way. They do not honor their parents. This is not the way of living that we learn from the fifth commandment. The will of God for children is that they love their parents, honor them, and obey them in everything that pleases God and agrees with His will.

6. In the sixth commandment, God said: **"You shall not murder."** (Exodus 20:13) Here God tells us that anyone who kills a man sins against God, because God is the One who gives to every person his life and soul. To murder a man is to hate God, because God made mankind in His own image. The word of God also shows us that murder is not limited to killing a person, since the Scripture says: **"Whoever hates his brother is a murderer."** (1 John 3:15) What many ignore is that God does not merely judge a person according to what he has done, but also according to what he wants to do; that is, according to his intentions. Since God looks at the heart, hatred and murder are equal in His sight.

7. In the seventh commandment, the LORD said: **"You shall not commit adultery."** (Exodus 20:14) Marriage is a precious gift from the LORD. God knows what is best for us, which is why, it is His will that a man limit himself to his wife and refuse to have a single lustful desire for any other woman. God's word says that **husbands also ought to love their own wives as their own bodies** (Ephesians 5:28) and that **whoever divorces his wife, except for sexual immorality,**

and marries another, commits adultery. (Matthew 19:9) When people disobey God's law and do what is forbidden to them, they often receive in their bodies the consequences of their acts. That is why many deadly diseases fall on those who have sexual relations outside the limits of marriage decreed by God. But we need to understand too that adultery is not limited to what we do with our bodies; it also includes what we do in our minds. The Scripture says: **Everyone who gazes at a woman to lust after her has committed adultery with her already in his heart.** (Matthew 5:28)

8. In the eighth commandment, God said: **"You shall not steal."** (Exodus 20:15) If you have ever taken something that is not yours or cheated on an exam, you have broken this law. Stealing has many sides to it. For example, if your employer commits to you a job, and he pays you to do that job, and he believes that you are working when in reality you are just wasting time, then you are stealing. Yes, you have stolen from your employer's profits. And what is the punishment for stealing and for every other sin? It is to die and be cast into the fire of hell, which is never extinguished.

9. The ninth commandment says: **"You shall not give false testimony against your neighbor."** (Exodus 20:16) The LORD God is the God of truth and has nothing to do with lies. Man thinks it is permissible to tell little lies to avoid problems and keep peace. But with the God of Truth there are no little lies. The LORD God says that everyone who lies takes on the character of Satan, **for he is a liar and the father of lies.** (John 8:44) Satan lied to our ancestors, Adam and Eve, and he continues to deceive people with his lies. Whoever gives false testimony is like Satan.

10. In the tenth commandment the LORD says: **"You shall not covet your neighbor's house. You shall not covet your neighbor's wife, nor his male servant, nor his female servant, nor his ox, nor his donkey, nor anything that is your neighbor's."** (Exodus 20:17) This commandment shows us clearly that God knows just how crooked and wicked the heart of man is. Covetousness and greed are found in the hearts of the children of Adam. Our wicked hearts cause us to lust after another man's wife or to

set our eyes on something that someone else has which we do not have. This is sin, because God's word says: **For we brought nothing into the world, and we certainly can't carry anything out. But having food and clothing, we will be content with that.** (1 Timothy 6:7-8) This last commandment tells us it is wrong even to want to have what belongs to someone else. God sees the sin in our hearts.

These are the Ten Commandments which God entrusted to Moses and to the children of Israel.

How should we conclude our lesson today? Perhaps with a question which each of us must answer: Have I – I myself – obeyed every one of these ten commands? You may already know that when the holy Redeemer came from heaven to earth, He summarized the Ten Commandments in two points. He said:

> 1) **Love the LORD your God with all your heart**, with all your soul, and with all your mind and,
> 2) **Love your neighbor as yourself.** The whole Law and the Prophets depend on these two commandments.
> (Matthew 22:37,39-40)

If you want to examine yourself to know whether you have perfectly kept the Ten Commandments which God gave to Moses, you can ask yourself these questions: First: What is my relationship with God like? *Do I love God with all my heart?* Second: What are my relationships with people like? *Do I love my neighbor as I love myself?*

What is your relationship *with God*? Let your heart answer honestly. Do you love God with your whole mind? Do you love him with all your heart? Does the LORD and His word always have first place in your life?

How about your relationship *with people*? Do you love your neighbor as you love yourself? Do you put others before yourself in everything? Do you care for your fellow man as you care for yourself? Do you love your enemies? Do you do for others everything that you would like them to do for you?

If you cannot answer "yes" to all these questions, know that, before God, you are a transgressor. By your own efforts, you cannot hope for anything except the damnation of God's righteous judgment. The Scripture says: **But for the cowardly, unbelieving, sinners, abominable, murderers, sexually immoral, sorcerers, idolaters, and all liars, their part is in the lake that burns with fire and sulfur, which is the second death.** (Revelation 21:8)

God is holy and cannot tolerate anything that is unholy. God is perfect and cannot accept any works which are imperfect. That is why He said: **Cursed is he who doesn't uphold the words of this law by doing them** (Deuteronomy 27:26) and: **Whoever keeps the whole law, and yet stumbles in one point, he has become guilty of all.** (James 2:10)

Merely trying to keep the Ten Commandments will not cause anyone to be **justified in [the sight of God].... For all have sinned and fall short of the glory of God.** (Romans 3:20,23)

Yes, dear friends, the word of God is clear: **All have sinned** and **all who rely on observing the law are under a curse.** (Galatians 3:10 NIV)

Perhaps someone asks, *"Well then, why did God give these Ten Commandments to us if none of us can keep them?"* This is a very important question and, in the will of the Lord, in our next program we will hear how God answers it.

May God bless you and reveal to you the foundational truth contained in this statement from His book:

> **Whoever keeps the whole law, and yet stumbles in one point, he has become guilty of all.** (James 2:10)

Purpose of the Commandments

Exodus 20

I n our last two programs we saw how God descended on Mount Sinai in fire, thunder and lightning to deliver ten holy commandments to the tribes of Israel. In the first commandment God said: **You shall have no other gods before me.** In the second: **You shall not make for yourselves an idol.** Third: **You shall not misuse the name of the LORD your God.** Fourth: **Remember the Sabbath day to keep it holy.** Fifth: **Honor your father and your mother.** Sixth: **You shall not murder.** Seventh: **You shall not commit adultery.** Eighth: **You shall not steal.** Ninth: **You shall not lie.** Tenth: **You shall not covet.**

These are the Ten Commandments which God sent down to Moses and the new nation of Israel. God promised His people that they would be blessed above all other nations if they obeyed His laws, but that they would be cursed if they disobeyed them. Moses passed on to them these words from God:

> ²⁶**Behold, I set before you today a blessing and a curse:** ²⁷the blessing, if you listen to the commandments of the LORD your God, which I command you today; ²⁸and the curse, if you do not listen to the commandments of the LORD your God, but turn away out of the way which I command you today, to go after other gods which you have not known. (Deuteronomy 11:26-28)

How could the commands of God bring a curse? We already heard the response of the people when they first learned that God was going to give them His laws. They had answered, **"All that the LORD has spoken we will do"** But God knew that on their own they could not do everything He required. The Israelites had not yet understood that God demands perfect righteousness. Through these ten commands God wanted to reveal to the tribes of Israel His holiness and their inability to live up to His holy laws. The Israelites were like religious people today who think that God simply wants them to try to do good, and then on Judgment Day, if their good works outweigh their bad works, God will say to them: *Welcome to Paradise! Come and dwell with me forever!* Those who think like this are mistaken and do not know the Scriptures or the holiness of God. God is the righteous Judge who must judge sin.

Here's a question. How many sins did our ancestor Adam commit before God expelled him from the Garden of Paradise? Just one. One sin and Adam was no longer perfect before God. One sin and he could no longer dwell with God. One sin and he had to die. One sin and he earned for himself a place in the eternal fire.

Yes, God is holy and does not take sin lightly. That is why His word says: **For whoever keeps the whole law, and yet stumbles in one point, he has become guilty of all.** (James 2:10)

Now, if this is what the holiness of God is like, what we want to know is: *Why did God give the Ten Commandments to the Israelites when He knew that they could not keep them?* Listen to God's answer: **No one will be declared righteous in God's sight by the works of the law; rather, through the law we become conscious of our sin.** (Romans 3:20 NIV) So what is the purpose of the Ten Commandments? To remove sin? *No,* says God, *the purpose of the commandments is to make you **conscious** of [your] sin.*

Is this clear? Why did God give His ten holy commandments to Moses and the children of Israel? Did He give them those commands so that by keeping them they could earn the right to live forever in the presence of God? No, that cannot be, because God says: **For whoever keeps the whole law, and yet stumbles in one point, he has become guilty of all.** (James 2:10) Can the children of Adam perfectly obey God in all that He has commanded? Can anyone draw pure, clean water from a dirty, polluted water pot? That, of course, is impossible.

The Holy Scriptures tell us that the purpose of the commandments is *to reveal our sin*. God did not give the commandments to save us from judgment. He gave them to show us that we are condemned sinners and that *we need a Savior*. Is this clear in your mind?

The Ten Commandments are somewhat like an X-ray machine at the hospital. If I am sick and I do not know what is wrong with me, perhaps the doctor will examine me by taking some X-rays. What is the purpose of an X-ray image? It has one purpose: *to reveal* what is wrong inside my body. In a similar way, the holy law which God entrusted to Moses is like a hospital X-ray machine. Its purpose is to reveal what is wrong: the sin that is in my heart and soul. How can the Ten Commandments reveal the sin that is in me? They reveal my sin in this way: If I compare my conduct with God's holy law, I will see how far I am from God – in my thoughts, my words, and my deeds. When I look at God's law and then I look at myself, I know that I have sinned against God and sinned against man and that I cannot be admitted into the pure and uncontaminated presence of my holy Creator.

Just as the hospital X-ray machine is useful for showing what is not right in a person's body, so the Ten Commandments are useful for showing what is not right in a person's heart. And just as the X-ray cannot cure the one who is sick, so the Ten Commandments cannot cure my heart, which is full of sin. In order for that to happen, I must go back to the Great Physician, that is, to the LORD God. He alone has a way to save me from the death and condemnation that await me because of the sin that is inside me.

Perhaps someone says, "Wait a minute! I'm a good person; I am not like others who steal, cheat, and commit adultery." If that is your attitude, clearly you have not yet understood God's holiness. What you need to know is that on the Day of Judgment, God will not compare you with your sinful neighbor. He will compare you with His holy and perfect standard, which states: **For whoever keeps the whole law, and yet stumbles in one point, he has become guilty of all.** (James 2:10) The God who says: **"You shall not commit adultery"** also says, **"You shall not lie."** If you have not committed adultery, but have told a lie, then you have transgressed the whole law and can never live with God in Paradise, because the Scripture says: **There will in no way enter into it anything profane, or one who causes an abomination or a lie, but only those who are written in the Lamb's book of life.** (Revelation 21:27) What is certain is that we can never please God through our own efforts. That is what the word of God declares:

> **For we have all become like one who is unclean**, and all our righteousness is like a polluted garment. (Isaiah 64:6)

> [10]**There is no one righteous; no, not one.** [12]They have all turned away. There is no one who does good, no, not so much as one. [22]For there is no distinction, [23]for all have sinned, and fall short of the glory of God. (Romans 3:10,12,22-23)

Now if that is what we are like before the One who must judge us, how can we escape His punishment? What must we do to be saved? Are we without hope? If salvation depended on our own efforts we would be hopeless. But thanks be to God, He has designed a plan to rescue the children of Adam from the penalty of sin. He has a way to punish sin without punishing the sinner.

Let us now continue in the book of Exodus, chapter 20, and see the way God provided for the children of Israel to be saved from the curse which His holy law brought. Here is what happened after God gave the Israelites the Ten Commandments:

> [18]**All the people perceived the thunderings**, the lightnings, the sound of the trumpet, and the mountain smoking. When the people saw it, they trembled, and stayed at a distance.… [21]Moses came near to the thick darkness where God was. [22]the LORD said to Moses, "This is what you shall tell the children of Israel: 'You yourselves have seen that I have talked with you from heaven.…

> [24]**You shall make an altar of earth for me**, and shall sacrifice on it your burnt offerings and your peace offerings, your sheep and your cattle. In every place where I record my name I will come to you and I will bless you.'" (Exodus 20:18,21-22,24)

And so, early in the morning, Moses built an altar at the base of Mount Sinai as God had commanded. The altar would suspend the sacrifice between heaven and earth, between God and man. Next, Moses sent some young men to offer animal sacrifices as burnt offerings, collect the blood in bowls, and burn the flesh on the altar. Then Moses took the blood and sprinkled it on the altar, on the book in which he had written the Ten Commandments, and on the crowd, and then told them, **"This is the blood of the covenant which the LORD has made with you."** (Exodus 24:4-7) Later, God further explained to Moses why these sacrifices were necessary, saying: **For the life of the flesh is in the blood. I have given it to you on the altar to make atonement for your souls; for it is the blood that makes atonement by reason of the life.** (Leviticus 17:11)

What was the reason for all of this? God wanted to remind the Israelites of what He had taught their ancestors Adam, Abel, Noah, Abraham, Isaac, and Jacob, that the penalty for sin is death and **apart from shedding of blood there is no [forgiveness of the sin debt].** (Hebrews 9:22) Everyone who wished to approach God had to approach Him on the basis of the substitutionary sacrifice.

God's holy law states that the penalty for even the smallest of sins is death and eternal condemnation, far from God and His great glory. And since the children of Israel could not keep His holy commandments, they had to bring to God a sacrifice without blemish, so that the innocent victim could replace the offender, the one who was guilty. This is how God punished sin without punishing the sinner. But as we have already learned, animal sacrifices could not remove sin, they could only cover man's sin until God sent the holy Redeemer into the world. That Redeemer would willingly offer Himself as the true and final Sacrifice for sin.

How glad we are today to know that this Savior has come and has paid for our sins once for all. Do you know His name? It is *Jesus*. His name means *the LORD saves*. Jesus the Messiah had no earthly father. One of His titles is *The Word of God*. He came from heaven. He did not inherit the sin nature found in Adam's descendants. Jesus perfectly obeyed the Ten Commandments and fulfilled

God's righteous requirements. Because He was without sin, He was qualified to give His life as the Lamb of God to pay the sin debt of the world. If you will believe in the Redeemer's perfect sacrifice, God will declare you righteous. The Scripture says: **God made him who had no sin to be [the sin offering] for us, so that in him we might become the righteousness of God. … that whoever believes in him should not perish, but have eternal life.** (2 Corinthians 5:21; John 3:16 NIV)

So as we conclude today, once more, we ask the question: *What is one of the main purposes of the Ten Commandments?* It is this: the Ten Commandments show me that I am a sinner in need of a Savior. Listen to this word from the Gospel:

> [10]**For as many as are of the works of the law** are under a curse. For it is written, "Cursed is everyone who doesn't continue in all things that are written in the book of the law, to do them." [11]Now that no man is justified by the law before God is evident, for, "The righteous will live by faith." [12]The law is not of faith, but, "The man who does them will live by them." [13] [Jesus the Messiah] redeemed us from the curse of the law, having become a curse for us.… (Galatians 3:10-13)

> [5]**For there is one God, and one mediator** between God and men, the man Christ Jesus, [6]who gave himself as a ransom for all. (1 Timothy 2:5-6)

Thank you for listening.

Next time we will hear the sad story about *how the people of Israel were breaking God's laws* while Moses was up on the mountain with God receiving those laws.

May God bless you and give you insight into this elementary truth:

No one will be declared righteous in God's sight by the works of the law; rather, through the law we become conscious of our sin. (Romans 3:20 NIV)

Program 39

Broken Commandments

Exodus 32

In our last three programs we saw how God spoke with the people of Israel from amid the fire, smoke, thunder and lightning that enveloped the summit of Mount Sinai from where He boomed forth His ten holy commandments. We also heard God command Moses to make an altar at the base of Sinai and offer innocent animals as sin offerings.

Why did God require those animal sacrifices? He required them because He is holy, and His righteous law demanded a death payment for sin. Since the Israelites could not keep God's laws, they had to approach God with burnt offerings for sin in which a healthy, blemish-free animal died in the place of the guilty person. The animal forfeited its life so the sinner would not have to be put to death.

Our lesson today is called: *Broken Commandments*. At this point in the story of the prophet Moses and the tribes of Israel, they are still camping in front of Mount Sinai in the desert. Let us now return to the Torah to see what happened after God announced the Ten Commandments from Mount Sinai. We are reading in the book of Exodus, chapter 24:

> [12]**The LORD said to Moses**, "Come up to me on the mountain, and stay here, and I will give you the stone tablets with the law and the commands that I have written, that you may teach them." [13]Moses rose up with Joshua, his servant, and Moses went up onto God's Mountain. [14]He said to the elders, "Wait here for us, until we come again to you. Behold, Aaron and Hur are with you. Whoever is involved in a dispute can go to them."

> [15]**Moses went up on the mountain**, and the cloud covered the mountain. [16]The LORD's glory settled on Mount Sinai, and the cloud covered it six days. The seventh day he called to Moses out of the middle of the cloud.
>
> [17]**The appearance of the LORD's glory** was like devouring fire on the top of the mountain in the eyes of the children of Israel. [18]Moses entered into the middle of the cloud, and went up on the mountain; and Moses was on the mountain forty days and forty nights. (Exodus 24:12-18)

In the next study, Lord willing, we will learn about some of what God told Moses on Mount Sinai during that forty-day period. But today we are going to see what the Israelites did in the camp at the base of the mountain as they were waiting for Moses to return. We all know that waiting patiently for God is not easy. It is much easier to ignore God's Word and go our own way. This is what the people of Israel did. God wants to warn us through this shocking story. In chapter 32, we read:

> [1]**When the people saw that Moses delayed** coming down from the mountain, the people gathered themselves together to Aaron, and said to him, "Come, make us gods, which shall go before us; for as for this Moses, the man who brought us up out of the land of Egypt, we don't know what has become of him." [2]Aaron said to them, "Take off the golden rings, which are in the ears of your wives, of your sons, and of your daughters, and bring them to me." [3]All the people took off the golden rings which were in their ears, and brought them to Aaron. [4]He received what they handed him, fashioned it with an engraving tool, and made it a molded calf. Then they said, "These are your gods, Israel, which brought you up out of the land of Egypt." (Exodus 32:1-4)

Do you see what the Israelites were doing? Not many days after they had said, "All that the LORD has spoken we will do" we see them breaking the first and second commandments which God had just given them. God had commanded them, "You shall have no other gods before me"; and "You shall not make for yourself an idol." But what did the Israelites do? They turned their backs on God and made for themselves an idol in the shape of a calf, like the idols they had seen in Egypt.

Why did the Israelites so quickly turn their backs on the LORD their God? Perhaps because they wanted a god that didn't require perfect righteousness; a god they could see and touch; a god of their own making. They were like people today who choose to ignore the word of God and choose instead to follow men and their traditions. Following a man, whom the eye can see, is easier than following God, whom no one can see.

Let us now see what happened after the Israelites made the golden calf. The Scripture says:

> ⁵**When Aaron saw this**, he built an altar before it; and Aaron made a proclamation, and said, "Tomorrow shall be a feast to the LORD." ⁶They rose up early on the next day, and offered burnt offerings, and brought peace offerings; and the people sat down to eat and to drink, and rose up to play. (Exodus 32:5-6)

Did you hear what Aaron did and said? The Scripture tells us that **he built an altar before [the calf], and said, "Tomorrow shall be a feast to the LORD."** Was that the truth? Could the Israelites worship the LORD at such an altar? Definitely not. God had no part in the worship festival that they were organizing. Now they had not only broken the first and second commandments, but also the third commandment which says: **You shall not misuse the name of the LORD your God.**

"God the LORD! God, God, God!" was in their mouths, but their hearts were far from Him. Their worship was in vain. Their prayers were nothing more than a lot of meaningless bowing down, which only angered the LORD. The Scripture continues:

> ⁷**The LORD spoke to Moses**, "Go, get down; for your people, who you brought up out of the land of Egypt, have corrupted themselves! ⁸They have turned away quickly out of the way which I commanded them. They have made themselves a

molded calf, and have worshiped it, and have sacrificed to it, and said, 'These are your gods, Israel, which brought you up out of the land of Egypt.'" ⁹The LORD said to Moses, "I have seen these people, and behold, they are a stiff-necked people. ¹⁰Now therefore leave me alone, that my wrath may burn hot against them, and that I may consume them; and I will make of you a great nation."

¹¹**Moses begged the LORD his God**, and said, "LORD, why does your wrath burn hot against your people, that you have brought out of the land of Egypt with great power and with a mighty hand? ¹²Why should the Egyptians talk, saying, 'He brought them out for evil, to kill them in the mountains, and to consume them from the surface of the earth?' Turn from your fierce wrath, and turn away from this evil against your people. ¹³Remember Abraham, Isaac, and Israel, your servants, to whom you swore by your own self, and said to them, 'I will multiply your offspring as the stars of the sky, and all this land that I have spoken of I will give to your offspring, and they shall inherit it forever.'" ¹⁴So the LORD turned away from the evil which he said he would do to his people. ¹⁵Moses turned, and went down from the mountain, with the two tablets of the covenant in his hand; tablets that were written on both their sides. They were written on one side and on the other. ¹⁶The tablets were the work of God, and the writing was the writing of God, engraved on the tablets. ¹⁷When Joshua [who accompanied Moses] heard the noise of the people as they shouted, he said to Moses, "There is the noise of war in the camp." ¹⁸He said, "It isn't the voice of those who shout for victory. It is not the voice of those who cry for being overcome; but the noise of those who sing that I hear."

¹⁹**As soon as he came near to the camp**, he saw the calf and the dancing. Then Moses' anger grew hot, and he threw the tablets out of his hands, and broke them beneath the mountain. ²⁰He took the calf which they had made, and burned it with fire, ground it to powder, and scattered it on the water, and made the children of Israel drink it. ²¹Moses said to Aaron, "What did these

people do to you, that you have brought a great sin on them?" [22]Aaron said, "Don't let the anger of my lord grow hot. You know the people, that they are set on evil. [23]For they said to me, 'Make us gods, which shall go before us. As for this Moses, the man who brought us up out of the land of Egypt, we don't know what has become of him.' [24]I said to them, 'Whoever has any gold, let them take it off.' So they gave it to me; and I threw it into the fire, and out came this calf." [25]When Moses saw that the people were out of control, (for Aaron had let them lose control, causing derision among their enemies), [26]then Moses stood in the gate of the camp, and said, "Whoever is on the LORD's side, come to me!" All the sons of Levi gathered themselves together to him.

[27]**He said to them, "The LORD, the God of Israel, says,** 'Every man put his sword on his thigh, and go back and forth from gate to gate throughout the camp, and every man kill his brother, and every man his companion, and every man his neighbor.'" [28]The sons of Levi did according to the word of Moses. About three thousand men fell of the people that day. [35]The LORD struck the people, because of what they did with the calf, which Aaron made. (Exodus 32:7-28,35)

After this, the LORD told Moses to chisel out two stone tablets to replace the ones which he had broken. On these the LORD rewrote the ten commandments which the children of Israel had broken. What a great sin the Israelites committed! They had broken God's holy law. The evil heart of man had shown itself again. Despite all the LORD had done for the people of Israel, we see how quickly they had turned away from the one true God and His truth. They chose to follow another way, a religion of their own making. The name of God was on their lips, but their hearts were far from Him.

What does God want to teach us through this shocking story? God wants us to think about where we are in our relationship with Him. Perhaps there are those who are thinking: "I am not like the Israelites. I have never turned my back on God and worshiped an idol." You who think this way, are you positively sure that you have never worshiped an idol? Idolatry is not limited to sculptured images that people worship. An idol is anything which comes between us and God. An idol can be money, food, clothes, sex, sports, television, self, another person, fame, power, traditions, ancestors, fetishes, amulets, or a hundred other things! For some, their religious obligations are their idols; they put more importance on reciting prayers and fasting than on seeking God's truth and submitting to Him and His holy word. Anything that replaces God and His truth is an idol.

Who is your God? Who do you worship? the LORD God? or an idol? Is the name of the LORD merely on your lips or do really know Him and love Him? There is something that distinguishes those who truly worship God from those who worship idols. It is the Word of God. What is your attitude towards what God has revealed in the Scriptures of His prophets? Do you know those Scriptures? Have you submitted to them? Or are you like the Israelites? Of some of them, God said: **"These people draw near to me with their mouth, and honor me with their lips; but their heart is far from me. And in vain do they worship me, teaching as doctrine rules made by men."** (Matthew 15:8-9)

Concerning the story we have heard today, the Scripture says:

> [1]**Now I would not have you ignorant, brothers**, that our fathers were all under the cloud, and all passed through the sea…. [5]However… God was not well pleased, for they were overthrown in the wilderness. [6]Now these things were our examples, to the intent we should not lust after evil things, as they also lusted. [7]Don't be idolaters, as some of them were.

> [11]**Now all these things happened to them** by way of example, and they were written for our admonition…. [14]Therefore, my beloved, flee from idolatry. (1 Corinthians 10:1,5-7,11,14)

Next time, God willing, we will hear about *a very special tent* the LORD God asked the sinful people of Israel to make so that He could live among them and so that they could approach Him.

God bless you as you reflect on this warning from His word:

Little children, keep yourselves from idols. (1 John 5:21)

Program 40

The Tent of Meeting

Exodus 24-40, Leviticus 16

I n the last program, we saw how the Israelites turned away
from the LORD their God who had redeemed them from
their slavery in Egypt. While Moses was receiving God's laws
on Mount Sinai, the Israelites made a calf of gold and worshiped
it! About 3000 people died as a result of their idolatry. Today we
will hear a much happier story. But we must pay close attention
because the story is filled with deep meaning. We are going to
hear how God told Moses and the Israelites to make a special tent
so that He could live among them and so they could learn how to
approach Him, meet with Him, and worship Him. God's design was
that this tent be the center around which His people would camp
as they made their way from Egypt to Canaan.

Reading again in the book of Exodus, chapter 24, the Scripture says:

> [16]**The LORD's glory settled on Mount Sinai**, and the cloud
> covered it six days. The seventh day he called to Moses out of
> the middle of the cloud. [17]The appearance of the LORD's glory
> was like devouring fire on the top of the mountain in the eyes
> of the children of Israel. [18]Moses entered into the middle of the
> cloud, and went up on the mountain; and Moses was on the
> mountain forty days and forty nights. (Exodus 24:16-18)

> [1]**The LORD spoke to Moses, saying**, [2]"Speak to the children of
> Israel, that they take an offering for me. From everyone whose
> heart makes him willing you shall take my offering. [3]This is the
> offering which you shall take from them: gold, silver, bronze,
> [4]blue, purple, scarlet, fine linen, goats' hair, [5]rams' skins dyed
> red, sea cow hides, acacia wood, [6]oil for the light, spices for

the anointing oil and for the sweet incense, [7]onyx stones, and stones to be set for the ephod and for the breastplate.

[8]Let them make me a sanctuary, that I may dwell among them. [9]According to all that I show you, the pattern of the tabernacle, and the pattern of all of its furniture, even so you shall make it. (Exodus 25:1-9)

What God told Moses is absolutely amazing. The LORD God planned to dwell among the Israelites, among those who had sinned against Him so many, many times! Why would God, who is infinitely great and holy, want to live with such sinners? Why would God, who is Spirit and has need of nothing, want a relationship with descendants of Adam, who had turned away from Him? As we have already seen, God created humans in His own image because He wanted to have fellowship with them. Man's sin broke that fellowship, but God established a righteous way by which sinners could come back to Him.

By means of the unique tent (tabernacle) and detailed laws, God planned to illustrate how Adam's descendants can draw near to Him. And as we have already learned, because God is holy, sinners cannot approach Him in just any way. For this reason, God commanded the Israelites to make a tent like no others so that He could be in their midst in a way worthy of His holiness and glory. Also, by means of this tabernacle, God planned to teach future generations many important lessons about what He is like and about the Savior He planned to send into the world.

Before we examine what God told Moses concerning the dwelling place which the Israelites were to build for Him, we must first understand that God did not tell them to build it because He needed a place to live. God, the Most High, who created the world and everything in it, does not live in houses made by men. In the writings of the prophets, the LORD Himself declares: **"Heaven is my throne, and the earth is my footstool. What kind of house will you build to me? Where will I rest? For my hand has made all these things...."** (Isaiah 66:1-2; Acts 7:48-49)

Why then, did God command the Israelites to make a sanctuary for Him? As we have already said, God wanted to teach the Israelites and all the peoples of the world that He wants to have fellowship with them. God also wanted to put before them a picture of the righteous way by which people can be forgiven of their sin debt and have the right to live forever with God in heaven.

Thus, God commanded Moses and the Israelites to make for Him a special tent so that He could dwell in their midst. But that tent of meeting was not to be like any ordinary tent. The Scriptures contain fifty chapters which describe how the work of the tent of meeting was to be done. They are profound chapters and we do not have time to explore them all; we can only attempt to summarize a few of the most important things.

The first thing you need to know about this tent of meeting is that God told Moses that it must have two rooms.

The first room was called **the Holy Place**. There were three things in that room: a gold table on which they burned incense each day, an oil lamp, and a table on which special bread was presented before God in worship. No one could enter that room except the priests. The priests were those whom God had chosen from the descendants of Aaron to kill the animals as sacrifices to cover sin.

The second room of the tent was **the Holiest Place** (Holy of Holies). It was called the Holiest Place because once the tent was finished God came down and filled that room with His glory. The Holiest Place illustrated heaven (Paradise) where God dwells. That special room belonged to God alone.

The tent of meeting was one tent, but a beautiful **veil**, a heavy curtain, divided the tent into two rooms. This veil shut man out from the glorious presence of the infinitely holy God. To one and all, the veil declared: KEEP OUT or DIE! No one was to enter that Holiest Place except the High Priest who could only enter once a year. And to enter into it he had to bring with him the blood of a sacrifice for his own sins and for the sins of the people.

Inside the Holiest Place, God commanded Moses to place a chest made of acacia wood overlaid with pure gold. That chest was called the **ark of the covenant**. Inside the ark of the covenant they were to keep the two tablets of stone on which the Ten Commandments were written. Above the ark they placed a lid of gold with two special angels. The ark pictured God's throne in heaven. Once each year, the High Priest had to sprinkle the blood of a goat on the ark so that God could forgive the Israelites their sins. That is why God called this lid the atonement cover, or **mercy seat**.[64]

After that, God taught Moses how they must make a large, white curtain to serve as a high wall around the tent of meeting and the **courtyard**. In the curtain surrounding the tent, they were to make **one door** (entrance), so that no one could approach the tent of meeting without passing through the one door. Inside the courtyard, in front of the entrance, God commanded Moses and the Israelites to place an **altar made of bronze**. Everyone who passed through the door of the courtyard had to come to the bronze altar. God wanted to teach the Israelites and all of Adam's descendants that the way of the blood sacrifice was the only way that they could have a relationship with God.

Everyone who wanted to enter the courtyard of God's dwelling place had to enter with an **animal sacrifice** as an atonement for sin. What does *atonement*[65] mean? It has to do with paying the required ransom price so that sins can be covered, cleansed, and forgiven. By requiring a blood sacrifice, God was teaching the Israelites that no one can ever approach Him except on the basis of a death-payment for sin. That is why God told Moses: **For the life of the flesh is in the blood. I have given it to you on the altar to make atonement for your souls; for it is the blood that makes atonement by reason of the life.** (Leviticus 17:11)

Those who wanted to worship God had to first offer an animal sacrifice for the forgiveness of their sins. The worshiper had to bring a bull, a sheep, or a bird into the courtyard of the tent of

---

64 Literally in Wolof: *the means, instrument or place of forgiveness*
65 *Atonement* in Wolof is expressed as: *the means by which sins can be paid for*

meeting. In front of the altar, worshipers would place their hands on the head of the sacrifice they had brought, confess to God that they were sinners who deserved to die for their sins. Next, the priest would slay the animal. After that, the priest would take the blood of the sacrifice, sprinkle it on the altar and on the ground around the altar, and then burn the sacrifice on the altar. In this way God could forgive (cover) the guilty persons' sins, because the innocent animal had died in their place. The Israelites had to repeat these sacrifices over and over.

But animal sacrifices could not satisfy God's holiness forever. They were temporary illustrations of the Redeemer who was to come and die in the place of sinners so that God could permanently erase man's debt of sin without compromising His righteousness.

To illustrate what the Redeemer would do for sinners, God set aside one day a year when the High Priest would enter the second room, the Holiest Place, of the tent of meeting. That day was called *The Day of Atonement.*[66] On that one day and only on that day, once each year in October, the High Priest had the authority from God to enter the Holiest Place and sprinkle blood on the atonement cover of the ark of the covenant. He could never enter the Holiest Place without bringing the blood of spotless animals to cover His own sins and the sins of the people. In this way God was anticipating the day when the Redeemer would shed His blood so that God could forgive sinners and welcome them into His presence forever.

Ah, fellow listeners, there is so much more that we would like to say, but our time is almost gone. But before we bid you farewell, there is something else which you should understand about the tent of meeting. In the last chapter of the book of Exodus, we read:

> [42]**According to all that the LORD commanded Moses**, so the children of Israel did all the work. [43]Moses saw all the work, and behold, they had done it as the LORD had commanded. They had done so; and Moses blessed them.... [34]Then the cloud covered the tent of meeting, and the LORD's glory filled

---

66 Literally in Wolof: *the Day when God covered sins*

the tabernacle. ³⁵Moses wasn't able to enter into the tent of meeting, because the cloud stayed on it, and the LORD's glory filled the tabernacle. (Exodus 39:42-43; 40:34-35)

Once the tent of meeting was finished, the blazing glory of God descended on it and filled the Holiest Place, shining forth with a brightness surpassing the light of the sun! All of this pointed to the promised Savior who would come from heaven to dwell among the children of Adam. The tent of meeting, and everything connected with it, pictured HIM. As it is written in the holy Gospel:

In the beginning was the Word, and the Word was with God, and the Word was God. … The Word became flesh, and lived among us. We saw his glory… full of grace and truth. (John 1:1,14)

²¹**You shall name him Jesus**, for it is he who shall save his people from their sins. ²²Now all this has happened that it might be fulfilled which was spoken by the Lord through the prophet, saying, ²³"Behold, the virgin shall be with child, and shall give birth to a son. They shall call his name Immanuel," which is, being interpreted, "God with us."(Matthew 1:21-23)

Behold, the Lamb of God who takes away the sin of the world! (John 1:29)

Jesus the Messiah fulfilled everything symbolized in the tent of meeting. He is the Holy One who came from heaven to dwell in the tent of a human body. He is also the One who shed His blood as the Lamb of God to make it possible for us to enjoy a close relationship with the LORD God for time and for eternity.

May God bless you as you ponder these two verses, one from the Torah and one from the Gospel:

Let them make me a sanctuary, that I may dwell among them.

Behold, the virgin shall be with child, and shall give birth to a son. They shall call his name Immanuel, which is, being interpreted, "God with us." (Exodus 25:8; Matthew 1:23)

The Israelites' Unbelief

Numbers 13-14

We continue to explore the Torah. As we have learned, the Torah is the first part of the writings of the prophets and contains five sections, or books. In the first book, called *Genesis*, we learned how sin entered the world, bringing with it suffering, death, and condemnation. We also saw that God had a plan to save Adam and his descendants from the penalty of sin, the eternal fire of hell. We learned how God promised to send a Redeemer to die for sinners so that God could forgive sinners without compromising His own righteousness. The book of Genesis also informed us how God chose Abraham and promised to make of him a great nation, the nation through which the prophets and the Savior of the world would come.

In the second book of the Torah, that is, *Exodus*, we saw how God delivered Abraham's descendants, the Israelites, from hundreds of years of slavery in the land of Egypt. With Moses as their leader, God led the tribes of Israel out of Egypt and into the wilderness, bringing them to Mount Sinai, where He gave them His laws and taught them the way of blood sacrifice by which He would temporarily cover their sins.

In the last program we saw how God commanded Moses and the Israelites to build for Him a beautiful and special tent so that He could dwell in their midst. Once everything was ready, **the cloud covered the tent of meeting, and the LORD's glory filled the tabernacle.** (Exodus 40:34) God was showing the Israelites how He wanted to have a close relationship with them, but that no one could approach Him except by means of the blood of a sacrifice offered on the altar of the tent of meeting. The tent of meeting and its animal sacrifices were mere shadows and illustrations of the Redeemer who was to come from heaven, dwell on earth, and shed His blood as a sacrifice to take away sin.

In the third section of the Torah, called *Leviticus*,[67] God inspired Moses to write the laws that explain in detail how the Israelites were to present to God sacrifices which covered sin and expressed thanksgiving, praise and worship to God. This book is profound, and we do not have time to look at all it contains. If you study it for yourself, you will notice two words which appear about 200 times. These two words summarize the message of the entire book. The two words are: *HOLY* – and – *BLOOD*. Why do these two words appear repeatedly in this book? Because one of the most important messages a person can ever grasp is that **the LORD God is holy**, (Leviticus 11:45 NIV) and that **it is the blood that makes atonement by reason of the life.** (Leviticus 17:11) The value of the third book of the Torah was to teach the Israelites how a person corrupted and stained with sin, could approach God who is pure and holy. God showed clearly that no one could approach Him except by the blood of a sin offering, a sacrifice which foreshadowed the holy Redeemer who would come into the world and die in the place of sinners.

Let us cross over now into the fourth section of the Torah of Moses, called *Numbers*. In this book we learn that the Israelites lived at the base of Mount Sinai for one year. During that year, God taught them what a holy nation should look like. He also inspired Moses to write much of the Torah from which we are reading today.

But God did not intend for the His nation to stay in the wilderness forever. That is why one day He told Moses to have them to pack up, move out, and continue onward to the abundant land He had promised them, the land of Canaan. On the day they were to depart from Sinai, the cloud of the glory of God, which covered the tent of meeting, arose and began to move out in front of them. This is how the LORD made His presence felt and led them, with the cloud during day and with the pillar of fire at night.

---

67 Literally: *The laws of the tribe of Levi*

Thus, the Israelites followed the cloud until they arrived at the border of Canaan, the land God had promised to Abraham and his descendants hundreds of years earlier. God did not forget any of His promises. Because of God's faithfulness and power, the Israelites had arrived at the border of the land of Canaan, which today we call Palestine or Israel.

But Canaan was filled with inhabitants. The people of Canaan were many and mighty. How then could the Israelites possess it? There was only one way: God would give them the land. Nothing is too hard for God. God promised Abraham: **"I will give this land to your offspring."** (Genesis 12:7) God planned to decimate the people of Canaan and turn the land over to the descendants of Abraham. It is important to understand that the sins of the people of Canaan were very great. They were guilty of gross immoralities, even sacrificing their children to their false gods. God had been very patient with the people of Canaan, but they continued in their sinful and shameful ways. Consequently, God planned to give their land to the tribes of Israel.

Now then, let us read in the fourth section of the Torah to see what happened when the Israelites arrived at the border of the land of Canaan. In chapter 13 of Numbers we read:

> [1]**The LORD spoke to Moses, saying,** [2]"Send men, that they may spy out the land of Canaan, which I give to the children of Israel. Of every tribe of their fathers, you shall send a man, every one a prince among them." [3]Moses sent them from the wilderness of Paran according to the commandment of the LORD.... [21]So they went up, and spied out the land....
>
> [25]**They returned from spying out the land** at the end of forty days. [26]They went and came to Moses, to Aaron, and to all the congregation of the children of Israel, to the wilderness of Paran, to Kadesh; and brought back word to them and to all the congregation. They showed them the fruit of the land. [27]They told him, and said, "We came to the land where you sent us. Surely it flows with milk and honey, and this is its fruit.

²⁸However, the people who dwell in the land are strong, and the cities are fortified and very large. Moreover, we saw the children of [giants called] Anak there.

³⁰**Caleb [one of the men who had explored the land]** stilled the people before Moses, and said, "Let's go up at once, and possess it; for we are well able to overcome it!" ³¹But the men who went up with him said, "We aren't able to go up against the people; for they are stronger than we." ³²They brought up an evil report of the land which they had spied out to the children of Israel, saying, "The land, through which we have gone to spy it out, is a land that eats up its inhabitants; and all the people who we saw in it are men of great stature. ³³There we saw the Nephilim [giants]…. We were in our own sight as grasshoppers, and so we were in their sight." (Numbers 13:1-3,21,25-28,30-33)

¹**All the congregation lifted up their voice**, and cried; and the people wept that night. ²All the children of Israel murmured against Moses and against Aaron. The whole congregation said to them, "We wish that we had died in the land of Egypt, or that we had died in this wilderness! ³Why does the LORD bring us to this land, to fall by the sword? Our wives and our little ones will be captured or killed! Wouldn't it be better for us to return into Egypt?" ⁴They said to one another, "Let's choose a leader, and let's return into Egypt."

⁵**Then Moses and Aaron fell on their faces** before all the assembly of the congregation of the children of Israel. ⁶Joshua the son of Nun and Caleb the son of Jephunneh, who were of those who spied out the land, tore their clothes. ⁷They spoke to all the congregation of the children of Israel, saying, "The land, which we passed through to spy it out, is an exceedingly good land. ⁸If the LORD delights in us, then he will bring us into this land, and give it to us: a land which flows with milk and honey. ⁹Only don't rebel against the LORD, neither fear the people of the land; for they are bread for us. Their defense is removed from over them, and the LORD is with us. Don't fear them!"

¹⁰**But all the congregation threatened to stone them** with stones. The LORD's glory appeared in the tent of meeting to all the children of Israel. ¹¹The LORD said to Moses, "How long will this people despise me? How long will they not believe in me, for all the signs which I have worked among them? (Numbers 14:1-11)

Let us pause here. Do you hear how Israel transgressed and offended God? Do you see their unbelief? Do you notice how they accused God of going back on His word? Yes, on that day, the Israelites sinned greatly because they did not believe God's promise to give them the land of Canaan. They did not believe the promises God had made to Abraham, Isaac, Jacob, Joseph, and Moses. They were like so many today who say, "We believe in God and the prophets," but do not really believe God, nor do they believe the prophets because they do not believe what God has revealed through His prophets in the Holy Scriptures. Unbelief is a terrible, deadly sin before God.

Enough said. Let us continue the story.

²⁶**The LORD spoke to Moses and to Aaron, saying,** ²⁷"How long shall I bear with this evil congregation that complain against me? I have heard the complaints of the children of Israel, which they complain against me. ²⁸Tell them, 'As I live, says the LORD, surely as you have spoken in my ears, so I will do to you. ²⁹Your dead bodies shall fall in this wilderness; and all who were counted of you, according to your whole number, from twenty years old and upward, who have complained against me, ³⁰surely you shall not come into the land concerning which I swore that I would make you dwell therein, except Caleb the son of Jephunneh, and Joshua the son of Nun. ³¹But I will bring in your little ones that you said should be captured or killed, and they shall know the land which you have rejected. ³²But as for you, your dead bodies shall fall in this wilderness….' ³⁵I, the LORD, have spoken. I will surely do this to all this evil congregation who are gathered together against me. In this wilderness they shall be consumed, and there they shall die."

> ³⁶**The men whom Moses sent to spy out the land**, who
> returned and made all the congregation to murmur against
> him by bringing up an evil report against the land, ³⁷even those
> men who brought up an evil report of the land, died by the
> plague before the LORD. ³⁸But Joshua… and Caleb… remained
> alive of those men who went to spy out the land [because they
> believed the word of the LORD]. (Numbers 14:26-32,35-38)

Thus we see how the Israelites refused to believe the LORD even
though He had redeemed them from the hand of Pharaoh and
brought them to the border of the land of Canaan. What did God do
with those who refused to believe His word? He condemned them to
die in the wilderness. Why did this generation of Israelites not enter the
land of Canaan? Because they would not believe the word of the LORD.

Friends, refusing to believe God's word is a wicked thing with tragic
consequences. Whoever despises and treats with indifference what
God declares in His holy word is calling God a liar and can have no
part in His eternal kingdom. It is not God's will that anyone perish
in unbelief. God wants all to believe the Good News about the
righteous way of salvation that He Himself has established. But
each and every person must choose for themselves. All who refuse
to believe God's word will perish. Listen to this warning from the
Holy Spirit of God through the prophets:

> ⁷**Therefore, even as the Holy Spirit says**, "Today if you will hear
> his voice, ⁸don't harden your hearts, as in the rebellion, in the day
> of the trial in the wilderness.…" ¹²Beware, brothers, lest perhaps
> there might be in any one of you an evil heart of unbelief, in
> falling away from the living God. (Hebrews 3:7-8,12; Psalm 95:7-11)

Next time, Lord willing, we will see how *all who had refused to
believe God perished in the desert.* May God bless you, your family,
and your community as you heed this warning from His book:

> **Beware… lest perhaps there might be in any one of you
> an evil heart of unbelief, in falling away from the living God.**
> (Hebrews 3:12)

Program 42

The Bronze Snake

Numbers 20-21

Last time, in the fourth section of the Torah, the book of Numbers, we saw how the Israelites arrived at the border of Canaan, the land God had promised to Abraham, Isaac, Jacob and their descendants. God planned to drive out the strong and powerful nations who lived in the land, and to turn it over to His people. But most of the people were afraid of the giants and did not believe God's promise to give them the land of Canaan. And so we saw how God punished the Israelites for their unbelief, telling them:

> ³⁰**Surely you shall not come into the land** concerning which I swore that I would make you dwell therein, except Caleb the son of Jephunneh, and Joshua the son of Nun. ³¹But I will bring in your little ones that you said should be captured or killed, and they shall know the land which you have rejected. ³²But as for you, your dead bodies shall fall in this wilderness. (Numbers 14:30-32)

God wanted to abundantly bless His people, but He could not bless them because they did not trust Him. And so God condemned them to wander in the desert for forty long years, until all those over twenty years old died.

Now let us continue in the book of Numbers to see what happened at the end of those forty years. In chapter 20, we read:

> ¹**The children of Israel, even the whole congregation**, came into the wilderness of Zin in the first month. The people stayed in Kadesh [where they had first refused to believe God and enter the land of Canaan which He had promised to them] Miriam (the elder sister of Moses) died there, and was buried there.

> ²**There was no water for the congregation**; and they assembled themselves together against Moses and against Aaron. ³The people quarreled with Moses, and spoke, saying, "We wish that we had died when our brothers died before the LORD! ⁴Why have you brought the LORD's assembly into this wilderness, that we should die there, we and our animals? ⁵Why have you made us to come up out of Egypt, to bring us in to this evil place? It is no place of seed, or of figs, or of vines, or of pomegranates; neither is there any water to drink." (Numbers 20:1-5)

Did you hear the Israelites? After all God had done for them and their fathers, were their hearts filled with thankfulness? No! They were doing just as their fathers had done. They were grumbling. Yes, they were weary of life in the desert, but it was because of their history of unbelief that they were where they were. True, they did not have water. Why then did they not pray to God? The One who had cared for them for forty years in the parched wilderness – could He not again give them water to drink? God wanted to supply all their needs, but they had not yet learned to fully trust Him. Now let us read on:

> ⁶**Moses and Aaron went from the presence** of the assembly to the door of the tent of meeting, and fell on their faces. The LORD's glory appeared to them. ⁷The LORD spoke to Moses, saying, ⁸"Take the rod, and assemble the congregation, you, and Aaron your brother, and speak to the rock before their eyes, that it pour out its water. You shall bring water to them out of the rock; so you shall give the congregation and their livestock drink." ⁹Moses took the rod from before the LORD, as he commanded him. ¹⁰Moses and Aaron gathered the assembly together before the rock, and he said to them, "Hear now, you rebels! Shall we bring water out of this rock for you?" ¹¹Moses lifted up his hand, and struck the rock with his rod twice, and water came out abundantly. The congregation and their livestock drank. ¹²The LORD said to Moses and Aaron, "Because you didn't believe in me, to sanctify me in the eyes of the children of Israel, therefore you shall not bring this assembly into the land which I have given them." (Numbers 20:6-12)

Did you grasp what happened? What did God command Moses to do to provide water for the multitude. God said, **"Speak to the rock."** Did Moses obey God by speaking to the rock? No, in his anger Moses struck it twice with his staff. This did not prevent God, in His goodness, from causing a river of water to gush forth from the rock, but what Moses did displeased God. That is why He told Moses, **"Because you didn't believe in me, to sanctify me in the eyes of the children of Israel, therefore you shall not bring this assembly into the land which I have given them."** (Numbers 20:12)

Perhaps in our thinking, the punishment that God imposed on Moses was too severe. However, we must remember that God requires faith in His word and obedience to His word. God never condones anything that goes against His word – even if it comes from a prophet like Moses.

God does not show favoritism. Moses was a great prophet, but he was a human like all of us. Therefore he was also a sinner like all of Adam's offspring. Even the prophet of God, Moses, could not save himself by his good works. Like all of Adam's descendants he had defects and did not fulfill all that is righteous. The prophet Moses, like all the Israelites, had to come to God by the way of salvation which He had established, by the way of the blood sacrifice. Through this act of disobedience by Moses God wants to remind us that we too are sinners. **All have sinned and fall short of the glory of God.** (Romans 3:23) No one is righteous; no one – except the holy Redeemer who came to earth to save us from our sin and shame.

Continuing the story of the Israelites, at the end of chapter 20, we learn that Aaron, Moses' older brother, died on the mountain called Hor, and that the community of Israel mourned for him there for thirty days. Then, in chapter 21, the Scripture says:

> [4]**They traveled from Mount Hor** by the way to the Red Sea.... The soul of the people was very discouraged because of the journey. [5]The people spoke against God and against Moses: "Why have you brought us up out of Egypt to die in the

wilderness? For there is no bread, there is no water, and our soul loathes this disgusting food!"

⁶**The LORD sent venomous snakes among the people,** and they bit the people. Many people of Israel died. ⁷The people came to Moses, and said, "We have sinned, because we have spoken against the LORD and against you. Pray to the LORD, that he take away the serpents from us." Moses prayed for the people. ⁸The LORD said to Moses, "Make a venomous snake, and set it on a pole. It shall happen that everyone who is bitten, when he sees it, shall live." ⁹Moses made a serpent of bronze, and set it on the pole. If a serpent had bitten any man, when he looked at the serpent of bronze, he lived. (Numbers 21:4-9)

This is an amazing story. Why did God send venomous snakes among the Israelites? He sent the snakes because of their sin. We heard how they spoke against the LORD and Moses and despised the food which God sent down to them. That is why God sent venomous snakes to bite them, causing many to die.

What could the Israelites do to be saved from the deadly venom of the snakes? Could they save themselves from death? Could they heal themselves of the deadly poison? They could not. What could they do then? They could cry out to God. And that is what they did. We saw how the Israelites repented and went to Moses, saying to him, "We have sinned. We have transgressed against you and against God. Pray to the LORD for us that He might have mercy on us and take away these snakes."

Did God take away the snakes from them? He did something better than that! God told Moses to make a snake out of bronze and raise it up on a pole so that **when [anyone who was bitten] looked at the serpent of bronze, he lived.** (Numbers 21:9) This was God's remedy. If a snake bit someone, all that person had to do was to look at the bronze snake hung on the pole and that person would be healed. This was the way of deliverance that God planned and offered.

Look and live.

God promised to heal whoever looked at the bronze snake which Moses suspended on the pole. And what happened to those who did not look? They died a painful death. But whoever believed God and looked at the bronze snake was delivered from death because God had promised them, saying, **"When [anyone who was bitten] looked at the serpent of bronze, he lived."**

Truly, this is a fascinating story, but it is more than fascinating. It was recorded to instruct us. God wants to show us that we all are like the Israelites. We too are sinners and have offended God in our thoughts, in our words and in our deeds. Satan is like the venomous snake. Sin is like the poison that was killing them. Satan has bitten all of the offspring of Adam and the poison of sin would cause every one of us to perish forever unless God had provided a remedy. The penalty of sin is to perish in the eternal fire and in ourselves we have no means of escape. But, praise God, because just as He had a plan to save the people of Israel from the poison of the snakes, so also He has a plan to save Adam's race from the poison of sin.

Listening friends, do you know what God has done to save you from the curse that sin has brought? Listen to what the holy Redeemer declared 1500 years after Moses raised up the bronze snake in the wilderness. Jesus the Messiah said:

> **"As Moses lifted up the serpent in the wilderness,** even so must the Son of Man [the Redeemer of the world] be lifted up, [15]that whoever believes in him should not perish, but have eternal life."** (John 3:14-15)

From this verse in the holy Gospel, we learn that the bronze snake which Moses raised up in the desert was an illustration (shadow, picture, symbol) of the promised Redeemer who came to be lifted up on a cross to shed His blood to **bring to nothing him who had the power of death, that is, the devil.** (Hebrews 2:14) The serpent on the pole pictures what the Messiah came to do: **Defeat Satan, sin, and death.**

Oh, how thrilling this message is! As we will discover in future programs, through the death and resurrection of the Redeemer, God has opened for the children of Adam a door of eternal life, peace and joy. What God wants is for you to admit that you cannot save yourself from the power of sin and death, and believe in your heart what God has testified concerning the Savior who died on the cross to pay for your debt of sin. God still says, *"Look and Live."* Look to the Redeemer and you will not perish. Believe on Him and God will heal you from the poison of sin and give you the gift of righteousness and eternal life.

Young and old, men and women, rich and poor, God is saying to you: *"Look and live!"* Look to the mighty Redeemer whom God has sent and you will be saved. But God is also saying: "If you do not look (whether because of denying or delaying), if you do not believe in the Savior who has provided the cure for the venom of sin, then **you will die in your sins."** (John 8:24)

God's righteous law declares that whoever does not accept the remedy that He has provided will perish. God has no other remedy by which the children of Adam can be cured from the poison of sin. Have you looked to the Savior, the holy Redeemer about whom all the prophets wrote? He will cleanse you and give you eternal life if you will look to Him and believe.

Listen once again to what the Scripture says:

> **As Moses lifted up the serpent in the wilderness,** even so must the Son of Man [the Redeemer of the world] be lifted up, that whoever believes in him should not perish, but have eternal life.
> (John 3:14-15)

Our time is up today. Thank you for listening. Next time, God willing, we will consider *the final words of the prophet Moses* and conclude our study in the holy Torah.

God bless you as you ponder this promise from the Lord God:

> **Look to me, and be saved, all the ends of the earth;
> for I am God, and there is no other.** (Isaiah 45:22)

Moses' Final Message

Deuteronomy

O ver the past forty-two lessons, we have been looking into the first book of the Holy Scriptures, the Torah.[68] As you know, it is God who implanted His words in the mind of the prophet Moses, inspiring him to write them down. Approximately 3500 years have passed since Moses wrote the Torah, yet it is still of immeasurable value to us today. The Torah is the foundation that God Himself laid by which we can test everything we hear and discern whether it comes from God or not. The teaching contained in the Torah is pure truth. Any teaching that contradicts it is false. All of God's truth is in perfect harmony with what is written in the Torah. There is one thing that Almighty God cannot do. Do you know what that is? It is that God cannot contradict Himself. In the Torah, Moses penned these words:

> **God is not a man, that he should lie**, nor a son of man, that he should repent. Has he said, and he won't do it? Or has he spoken, and he won't make it good? (Numbers 23:19)

Through our study in the Torah of Moses, God has revealed to us many profound mysteries. Today we plan to conclude our journey through the holy Torah. But before we look at the final chapters, let us review what we have seen from the first day to today.

In the first section of the Torah, the book of *Genesis*, we saw how God created the first man in His own image. God wanted to have a wonderful and meaningful relationship with humans. That is why He placed in the soul of man a mind (spirit) so that he might know God, gave him a heart so that he could love God and entrusted

---

68 Or: *Tawrat*, Qur'anic/Arabic term for the *Torah/Pentateuch*

to him a will so that he could choose for himself whether to obey God or to disobey Him.

In the third chapter, we saw how the first man, Adam, chose to obey Satan and eat from the one tree that God had prohibited. Thus, the Scripture says: **Sin entered into the world through one man, and death through sin; so death passed to all men, because all sinned.** (Romans 5:12) The penalty of sin is death and eternal separation from God.

We saw too how God expelled Adam and Eve from the Garden of Paradise because of their sin. But before He put them out, God announced that He planned one day to send a Redeemer into the world to open a door of salvation for Adam's offspring; to free those who believe from the power of Satan and the penalty of sin.

We also learned how God called Abraham, promising to make of him a new nation – from which the prophets, the Scriptures, and the Redeemer would come. In time, Abraham begot Isaac, Isaac begot Jacob, and Jacob begot twelve sons. Later God changed Jacob's name to Israel. The twelve sons of Israel formed the new nation which God had promised Abraham. The ten[69] older sons sold their younger brother Joseph as a slave who was taken to Egypt. But what **a man sows, that he will also reap.** (Galatians 6:7) Consequently, all the children of Israel became slaves in Egypt. But God did not forget the promise He made to Abraham and his descendants. In the book of *Exodus* we saw how God fulfilled His promises by preparing and sending Moses to free the Israelites from the misery of slavery.

In studying the story of Moses we heard the amazing account about how God delivered the multitude of Israel from the oppression of Pharaoh and the people of Egypt. We also heard how God protected and cared for them in the desert and brought them to the border of Canaan, the land which He had promised to their forefather Abraham long before. But most of the Israelites were afraid of the giants of Canaan and did not trust God to do for them what He had promised.

---

69 Technically, *nine sons*, since Reuben was absent when his brothers sold Joseph. (Gen. 37:29)

Because of their unbelief, the Israelites wandered around in the desert for forty years, until all the older generation who had not believed God died.

Now then, the time has come to complete our journey in the Torah. Remember, the Israelites were in the desert because God was chastening them for their unbelief. Every one of those more than twenty years old who had refused to believe what God had promised about the land of Canaan had died. Not one remained. Now their children were at the border of Canaan. After forty long years in the desert, the children of Israel were now eager to get settled in the land their parents had failed to claim.

Our study today is from the fifth section of the Torah, the book of *Deuteronomy.*[70] In this final section Moses reviews God's holy law and teaches it to the tribes of Israel. This wonderful book contains the final message that Moses preached to the people to prepare them to enter the land which God had promised to give to them. We do not have time to read Moses' entire sermon today, but we can summarize Moses' message in these few words:

   "Do not forget!" (Deuteronomy 4:9,23; 6:12; 8:1,11, etc. NIV)

In brief, Moses said something like this to the Israelites: *Be careful not to forget that you were slaves in Egypt. Do not forget all that God did for you on the way between Egypt and the new land which you are about to enter. Do not forget how you sinned against the LORD your God. Do not forget how the LORD judged your parents because of their unbelief, which is why their corpses remain in the desert. Do not forget that God was good to your parents, but that they were hardheaded and refused to believe Him. Do not forget!*

Today, when you hear the voice of God, do not harden your hearts, as your parents did in the wilderness. Will you be like your ancestors, who refused to believe the word of God? Or will you believe the LORD your God? If you refuse to believe the word of God as your ancestors did, God will punish you as He punished them. Do not forget!

---

70 Literally: *Second Law*

God, who is faithful will bring you into this wonderful land, which He promised to give your ancestors. But do not forget the LORD your God who, for 40 years, **humbled you, causing you to hunger and then feeding you with manna, which neither you nor your ancestors had known, to teach you that man does not live on bread alone but on every word that comes from the mouth of the LORD.** (Deuteronomy 8:3 NIV) **Do not forget!**

After Moses had finished his sermon, the LORD said to Moses:

> [49]**"Go up into this mountain** of Abarim… that is across from Jericho; and see the land of Canaan, which I give to the children of Israel for a possession. [50]Die on the mountain where you go up… [51]because you trespassed against me among the children of Israel… in the wilderness… because you didn't uphold my holiness among the children of Israel. [52]For you shall see the land from a distance; but you shall not go there into the land which I give the children of Israel."
> (Deuteronomy 32:49-52)

> [1]**Moses went up from the plains of Moab to Mount Nebo…** The LORD showed him all the land… [2]all the land of Judah, to the Western Sea.… [4]The LORD said to him, "This is the land which I swore to Abraham, to Isaac, and to Jacob, saying, 'I will give it to your offspring.' I have caused you to see it with your eyes, but you shall not go over there." [5]So Moses the servant of the LORD died there in the land of Moab, according to the LORD's word. [6]He buried him in… Moab… but no man knows where his tomb is to this day. [7]Moses was one hundred twenty years old when he died. His eye was not dim, nor his strength gone. [8]The children of Israel wept for Moses in the plains of Moab thirty days, until the days of weeping in the mourning for Moses were ended.

> [9]**Joshua [who replaced Moses as the new leader]…** was full of the spirit of wisdom, for Moses had laid his hands on him. The children of Israel listened to him, and did as the LORD commanded Moses.

[10]Since then, there has not arisen a prophet in Israel like Moses, whom the LORD knew face to face, [11]in all the signs and the wonders which the LORD sent him to do in the land of Egypt, to Pharaoh, and to all his servants, and to all his land, [12]and in all the mighty hand, and in all the awesome deeds, which Moses did in the sight of all Israel. Amen. (Deuteronomy 34:1-2,4-12)

So dear friends, this is where the Torah concludes. Everything written in the Torah is recorded so that we might gain knowledge, knowledge that will lead us to faith in the LORD God and His way of salvation. Truly Moses was a great prophet who knew the LORD God face to face. He performed miraculous signs from God. By the hand of Moses, God delivered the Israelites from the oppression of Pharaoh. Also by his hand God has given us the Torah, the foundation of all that God has revealed through His prophets in the Holy Scriptures. Everyone should know what the prophet Moses wrote. Whoever does not know the Torah of Moses will be mistaken in much and is in danger of perishing in the way of un-righteousness. We must not forget that the Torah is the foundation which God Himself laid, the foundation upon which God, through all the other prophets, would build the rest of His holy book.

In Deuteronomy, chapter 18, Moses told the Israelites that God planned to raise up another, greater prophet, who would speak directly for God. Listen to what Moses told the people of Israel:

[15]"**Your God will raise up to you a prophet** from among you, of your brothers, like me. You shall listen to him. [16]This is according to all that you desired of the LORD your God in Horeb (Mount Sinai) in the day of the assembly, saying, 'Let me not hear again the LORD my God's voice, neither let me see this great fire any more, that I not die.' [17]The LORD said to me, 'They have well said that which they have spoken. [18]I will raise them up a prophet from among their brothers, like you. I will put my words in his mouth, and he shall speak to them all that I shall command him. [19]It shall happen, that whoever will not listen to my words which he shall speak in my name, I will require it of him.'" (Deuteronomy 18:15-19)

By this declaration from Moses, God was announcing the coming of another prophet who would come forth from the Hebrew nation, a man who would speak forth the word of God in all fullness and purity, a prophet who would be a Mediator between God and man. Do you know who that Prophet was? Do you know which Prophet spoke with even greater authority than Moses? Do you know which Prophet displayed works which were greater than the miracles performed by Moses? Yes, this Prophet of whom Moses spoke is the righteous Messiah, who was born of a Jewish virgin. Concerning Him, Moses issued to the nation of Israel an early warning from God: **"You shall listen to him.... Whoever will not listen to my words which he shall speak in my name, I will require it of him."** (Deuteronomy 18:15,19)

Friends, this is where our study of the Torah must end. How can we conclude our journey in this vast and deep and lofty book? Let us finish with what Moses himself proclaimed to the nation on the day he died. He declared:

> [1]**Listen, you heavens, and I will speak**; hear, you earth, the words of my mouth. ... [3]I will proclaim the name of the LORD. Oh, praise the greatness of our God! [4]He is the Rock, his works are perfect, and all his ways are just. A faithful God who does no wrong, upright and just is he. (Deuteronomy 32:1,3-4 NIV)

With those mighty words from God through the mouth of Moses we bid you farewell. Next time, we plan to look into the next holy book, the book of Joshua, to see *how God brought the Israelites into the land flowing with milk and honey* just as He had promised.

May God, who alone is worthy of glory and majesty forever, bless you as you think on this word from the prophet Moses:

> **Man does not live on bread alone but on every word that comes from the mouth of the LORD.** (Deuteronomy 8:3 NIV)

Program 44

Joshua and the Land of Canaan

Joshua

In our last program we concluded our study of the first part of the writings of the prophets, the Torah of Moses. In those Scriptures we learned how sin entered the world and brought with it a curse, but we also heard how the LORD God promised to send to earth a Savior who would redeem the children of Adam from the curse which sin had brought. To move forward with His plan, God called Abraham to leave his father's house, religion, and country and move to the faraway land of Canaan. God planned to make of Abraham a new nation through which the Redeemer would enter the world. Today we will see how the LORD fulfilled what He had promised hundreds of years earlier to Abraham, when He told him:

> "**I will give to you, and to your offspring after you**, the land where you are traveling, all the land of Canaan, for an everlasting possession. I will be their God." (Genesis 17:8)

Last time, in the final chapter of the Torah we heard how Moses died on the mountain overlooking Canaan. After the death of Moses, his assistant Joshua became the new leader.[71] Joshua was designated by God to replace Moses. We have seen Joshua several times already. The distinguishing characteristic of Joshua was that he believed all that God promised, even when most of the Israelites did not believe. Joshua was one of the two spies who believed God when the Israelites first arrived at the border of the land of Canaan. The Israelites were ready to throw stones and kill him, simply because he encouraged them to believe the LORD and possess the land of Canaan. Today we will see that this same Joshua whom the

---

71 Literally in Wolof: *inherited the burden*

Israelites had rejected forty years earlier was the very one whom God chose to be their leader to take them into Canaan.

The book of *Joshua*, which we are reading today, is found in the Holy Scriptures, between the Torah and the Psalms. The book of Joshua recounts how, against all odds, the LORD God went before His people to deliver into their hands the land of Canaan, one city at a time.

At this point in our study the Israelites did not yet have a country of their own. They were still wanderers in the desert, and the land of Canaan in which they were to live was full of giants who were mighty warriors. But the Almighty God planned to decimate the inhabitants of Canaan because of their many repulsive sins, and entrust that abundant land to the Israelites.

Now let us see how Joshua and the Israelites entered the land, conquered and possessed it. In the first chapter, the Scripture says:

> [1]**Now after the death of Moses** the servant of the LORD, the LORD spoke to Joshua the son of Nun, Moses' servant, saying, [2]"Moses my servant is dead. Now therefore arise, go across this Jordan, you and all these people, to the land which I am giving to them, even to the children of Israel. [3]I have given you every place that the sole of your foot will tread on, as I told Moses. [4]From the wilderness and this Lebanon even to the great river, the river Euphrates, all the land of the Hittites, and to the great sea toward the going down of the sun, shall be your border. [5]No man will be able to stand before you all the days of your life. As I was with Moses, so I will be with you. I will not fail you nor forsake you.
>
> [6]"**Be strong and courageous**; for you shall cause this people to inherit the land which I swore to their fathers to give them.… [9]Haven't I commanded you? Be strong and courageous. Don't be afraid. Don't be dismayed, for the LORD your God is with you wherever you go." [10]Then Joshua commanded the officers of the people, saying, [11]"Pass through the middle of the camp, and

command the people, saying, 'Prepare food; for within three days you are to pass over this Jordan, to go in to possess the land which the LORD your God gives you to possess.'" (Joshua 1:1-6,9-11)

After this, the Scriptures tell how Joshua sent two spies, saying to them, "Go and look over the land, especially Jericho." The two spies went and investigated the city of Jericho and the tall, massive walls that surrounded it. At night the two spies hid in Jericho, seeking to hide in the house of a prostitute named Rahab. But some people of Jericho saw the Israeli spies enter Rahab's house. They informed the king, telling him, "Some of the Israelites are in the city to spy." The king sent soldiers to the house to arrest them, but Rahab had hidden them on the roof. After the soldiers left Rahab went up to the roof and told the two spies:

> [9]**She said to the men, "I know that the LORD** has given you the land, and that the fear of you has fallen upon us, and that all the inhabitants of the land melt away before you. [10]For we have heard how the LORD dried up the water of the Red Sea before you, when you came out of Egypt; and what you did to the two kings of the Amorites, who were beyond the Jordan, to Sihon and to Og, whom you utterly destroyed. [11]As soon as we had heard it, our hearts melted, and there wasn't any more spirit in any man, because of you: for the LORD your God, he is God in heaven above, and on earth beneath." (Joshua 2:9-11)

Rahab then asked the spies to protect her and her family when they conquered Jericho. The two spies promised her full protection for all those who were gathered in her house.

In chapter three, the Scriptures recount how the people of Israel needed to cross the Jordan River to enter the land of Canaan, but the river was deep and wide. How could a multitude of two or three million cross it? That, of course, would not be a problem, because the LORD God Almighty, who had opened a path for them through the Red Sea, had not changed. God again opened a path for the Israelites, this time through the Jordan River, so that they passed between the waters on dry ground. All the Israelites crossed the river, arriving in front of the great city of Jericho. The people of Jericho had closed the gates of the city so that no one could enter the city and no one could leave. In chapter five, the Scripture continues:

> [13]**When Joshua was by Jericho**, he lifted up his eyes and looked, and behold, a man stood in front of him with his sword drawn in his hand. Joshua went to him and said to him, "Are you for us, or for our enemies?" [14]He said, "No; but I have come now as commander of the LORD's army." Joshua fell on his face to the earth, and worshiped, and asked him, "What does my lord say to his servant?" [15]The [commander] of the LORD's army said to Joshua, "Take off your sandals, for the place on which you stand is holy." Joshua did so. (Joshua 5:13-15)

Friends, do you know who was talking with Joshua? It was the LORD Himself. We have already seen how God appeared to Abraham as a man and spoke with him and how He appeared to Moses in the flames of a fire in a bush. And now we see God appearing to Joshua as a mighty commander bearing a sword. The LORD God told Joshua:

> [2]**The LORD said to Joshua**, "Behold, I have given Jericho into your hand, with its king and the mighty men of valor. [3]All of your men of war shall march around the city, going around the city once. You shall do this six days. [4]Seven priests shall bear seven trumpets of rams' horns before the ark. On the seventh day, you shall march around the city seven times, and the priests shall blow the trumpets. [5]It shall be that when they make a long blast with the ram's horn, and when you hear the sound of the trumpet, all the people shall shout with a great shout; then the city wall will fall down flat, and the people shall go up, every man straight in front of him." (Joshua 6:2-5)

Then the LORD finished speaking to Joshua and left. Joshua immediately went to the Israelites and told them everything the LORD had commanded him. Then Joshua ordered them to take the ark of the covenant and march around the city once. But he told them, **"You shall not shout nor let your voice be heard, neither shall any word proceed out of your mouth until the day I tell you to shout. Then you shall shout."** (Joshua 6:10) After they had marched around the city one time they went back to the camp and spent the night there. On the second day they marched around the city once and returned to camp. This is what they did for the first six days.

But on the seventh day they went out at daybreak and marched around the city seven times. After they had circled the city the seventh time, the priests sounded the trumpet blast. Then Joshua commanded the multitude, **"Shout! for the LORD has given you the city!"** (Joshua 6:16)

When the Israelites heard the trumpet sound, they shouted a great shout, and the walls around the city collapsed – those mighty fortifications became heaps of rubble on the ground. The men of Israel then entered the city, every man going straight in. That is how Joshua and the Israelites conquered the first city in the land of Canaan. On that day all the people of Jericho died except Rahab and her family, just as the two spies had promised her. The house of Rahab did not collapse, because she had turned from her idols to trust in the LORD God of Israel.

Why were Joshua and the Israelites able to conquer that heavily fortified city and enter the land which God had promised them? They conquered it because they believed the word of God. God is with those who trust in Him. Why did Rahab and her family not die with the people of Jericho when the city fell? She survived because she did not stop at merely being amazed by God's power; she trusted Him to save her and her family from the destruction and death that came upon her city. The Scripture says:

> [30]**By faith, the walls of Jericho fell down**, after they had been encircled for seven days. [31]By faith, Rahab the prostitute didn't perish with those who were disobedient.… [6]Without faith it is impossible to be well pleasing to him, for he who comes to God must believe that he exists, and that he is a rewarder of those who seek him. (Hebrews 11:30-31,6)

We wish we could tell more of the stories contained in the Book of Joshua, but time does not allow us to do so. In summary, you should know that this book describes in detail how God was with Joshua and the Israelites, and how He delivered to them the land of Canaan, city by city, region by region, just as He had promised, which is why the Scripture says: **So the LORD gave to Israel all the land.... The LORD gave them rest all around.... The LORD delivered all their enemies into their hand.** (Joshua 21:43-44)

Friends, did God fulfill what He had promised Abraham and his descendants long beforehand? Did God give the land of Canaan to the Israelites as He said He would? Yes, He did. God is faithful to keep His covenants. Everything He promises, He will do, even if man thinks He is slow in doing so. The LORD God longed to be gracious to the children of Israel and give them the plentiful land of Canaan, but He was waiting for them to trust Him. The Israelites wasted many years before they began to accept what God had promised to give them. A whole generation of the Israelites failed to inherit the blessings of the land of Canaan because they did not believe the promises of God.

How about you? Do you believe God? We are not asking you if you believe in the existence of God or in the oneness of God. The devil himself knows that God exists and that God is One. The question you must answer today is: Do you trust His word with all your heart? Do you believe God Himself? Do you love Him?

Listening friend, God loves you and wants to bless you beyond what you can imagine, but you must believe and receive His righteous way of salvation.

Join us next time for *the sweet story of Ruth*, another woman from a pagan society who, like Rahab, chose to follow the one true God.

God bless you as you consider this word from Him:

> **"No eye has seen, no ear has heard, and no mind has imagined what God has prepared for those who love him."**
> (1 Corinthians 2:9 NLT)

Program 45

Judges and Ruth

Judges & Ruth

I n our last program we saw how Joshua, the servant of Moses, led the Israelites into Canaan and how the LORD God went before them to expel their enemies and give them possession **of that land to a good and large land, to a land flowing with milk and honey** (Exodus 3:8) just as He had promised to do.

Today we plan to look briefly into the two holy books which come after the book of Joshua: *Judges* and *Ruth*. These two books record events that took place between the time of Joshua and the time of the prophet King David.

Before we look into the book of Judges let's listen to Joshua's final message before he died. In the last chapter of the book named for him, Joshua met with the elders of Israel to warn them and to encourage them to love and obey the LORD, who had freed them from slavery and brought them into the abundant land in which they now lived. In His final speech to them, Joshua said:

> [15]**"If it seems evil to you to serve the LORD**, choose today whom you will serve; whether the gods which your fathers served that were beyond the River, or the gods of the Amorites, in whose land you dwell; but as for me and my house, we will serve the LORD." [16]The people answered, "Far be it from us that we should forsake the LORD, to serve other gods; [18]Therefore we also will serve the LORD; for he is our God." (Joshua 24:15,16,18)

That's what the people said. Now let's look at what they actually did. In Judges, chapter 2, the Scripture says:

> **⁷The people served the LORD** all the days of Joshua, and all the days of the elders who outlived Joshua, who had seen all the great work of the LORD that he had worked for Israel. ⁸Joshua… died, being one hundred ten years old. ⁹They buried him… in the hill country of Ephraim.
>
> ¹⁰**After that whole generation** had been gathered to their fathers, another generation grew up, who knew neither the LORD nor what he had done for Israel. ¹¹The children of Israel did that which was evil in the LORD's sight, and served the Baals. ¹²They abandoned the LORD, the God of their fathers, who brought them out of the land of Egypt, and followed other gods, of the gods of the peoples who were around them, and bowed themselves down to them; and they provoked the LORD to anger. ¹³They abandoned the LORD, and served Baal.
>
> (Judges 2:7-13)

Thus the Israelites began to forget the LORD their God, turn their backs on Him, and follow the religions of the nations around them, who did not know the one true God and did not have His word. They worshiped Baal, a false god which the people of Canaan believed to be God. They made for themselves images which were representations of Baal and they worshiped the images. Deceived by Satan, most Israelites ignored the Laws of Moses and no longer offered animal sacrifices on the altar to cover their sin. Instead of following God's righteous way, they followed the ways of those around them. They broke the first of the Ten Commandments, which states:

> ³**You shall have no other gods before me**…⁵for I, the LORD your God, am a jealous God, visiting the iniquity of the fathers on the children, on the third and on the fourth generation of those who hate me, ⁶and showing loving kindness to thousands of those who love me and keep my commandments. (Exodus 20:3,5-6)

The Israelites' choice to turn away from the true and living God produced disastrous consequences. Continuing in chapter 2 of the book of Judges, the Scripture says:

[11]**The children of Israel did that which was evil** in the LORD's sight, and served the Baals.… [14]The LORD's anger burned against Israel, and he delivered them into the hands of raiders who plundered them. He sold them into the hands of their enemies all around, so that they could no longer stand before their enemies.

[15]**Wherever they went out**, the LORD's hand was against them for evil, as the LORD had spoken, and as the LORD had sworn to them; and they were very distressed. (Judges 2:11,14-15)

The book of Judges records story after story about how the Israelites forsook the LORD to follow other gods. Again and again they hardened their hearts and rebelled against the One who had made them into a nation. That is why God handed them over to their enemies not only to punish them but also to help them acknowledge their sin and repent. Whenever the Israelites truly repented of their evil ways, God raised up for them judges (deliverers) to save them from their oppressors. We would love to tell you the stories of deliverers like Gideon who with just 300 men conquered an army of 135,000 warriors; or about Samson who single-handedly defeated 1,000 soldiers – but time does not allow us to do so.

In summary, the book of Judges shows us that each time the Israelites strayed from God and His word, the LORD punished them so that they would turn from their sin and return to Him. When they repented, God would raise up a powerful leader to rescue them from their enemies. And then they would eventually forget God again and go their own way. That is the cycle of rebellion and deliverance recorded in the book of Judges.

Time after time the Israelites transgressed against God, but could their unfaithfulness hinder God's plan? No, it could not. Of course God punished those who sinned, but He preserved the nation of Israel as a whole because God would fulfill the promise He made to Abraham long beforehand when He told him, **"All the families of the earth will be blessed through you."** (Genesis 12:3)

Nothing could hinder God's wonderful design: not the sin of the Israelites, not Pharaoh, not the slave drivers in Egypt, not the people of Canaan, not a false religion like that of Baal, not even Satan himself. Nothing could hinder God's plan to send down the Messiah through the nation of Israel; the Redeemer who would **save His people from their sins.** (Matthew 1:21)

In the time we have left today, we want to take a brief look into the book that follows the book of Judges. It is the book of *Ruth*. The story of Ruth is a marvelous one. It is like a lovely flower growing in the midst of a smelly garbage dump, because it tells the story of a beautiful young woman who chose to follow the LORD God in the midst of a crooked and depraved generation.

We do not have time to tell Ruth's full story, which is the captivating and complex account of God at work in a young lady's life at a hard time in history. But we can at least introduce you to her.

Ruth was a young widow who did not belong to the nation of Israel. She lived in the land of Moab, which was situated south of the land of Israel. The people of Moab were idolaters who despised both the God of Israel and the Israelites. Ruth belonged to the nation of Moab, but she had heard the stories about the God of Israel and the awesome miracles He had performed in delivering the people of Israel from their slavery in Egypt. Also, she had learned many of the truths which the prophet Moses had written in the Torah. Ruth believed in the LORD with all her heart and accepted His word and way of righteousness.

But Ruth lived in Moab among idolaters. Ruth's parents were idolaters, and Ruth was born into their religion, but now she no longer believed the religion of her father. The God of Israel was the One in whom Ruth had put her trust. Ruth had a choice to make, and it was not easy. Should Ruth remain in her father's house, continue in her father's religion and marry a man who did not know the one true God? Or should she turn her back on her father's house and religion in order to follow the true and living God? That was the difficult choice Ruth had to make.

Before we find out which path Ruth chose, you should also know that Ruth had a sister-in-law named Orpah who was also a widow. Like Ruth, Orpah also knew about the God of Israel. She also had to choose between continuing in the religion of her father or following the LORD God of Abraham, Isaac, and Jacob.

Which path did Ruth and Orpah choose? Orpah chose the easier path; that is, to remain in her father's house and marry a man who shared her father's religion. But Ruth chose the difficult path, which involved moving to the land of Israel. Ruth knew that she could not mix worshiping the one true God with worshiping the idols of Moab. Ruth was willing to be misunderstood by her family and friends in order to follow the LORD. As the (Wolof)proverb says, *Whoever wants honey must brave the bees.*

Through circumstances arranged by the LORD, Ruth ended up leaving her people, and moving to Israel, to a small town called Bethlehem.

There was a man in Bethlehem whose name was Boaz. Boaz was the son of Rahab, the woman from Jericho who protected the spies of Israel and escaped the destruction and death which came upon her city (as we saw in the last program). Her son Boaz was a kind man who loved the LORD and treasured His word. Boaz was a wealthy landowner in Bethlehem with fields of grain, but he did not yet have a wife.

The Scriptures tell how Ruth, who now lived in the town of Bethlehem, had the habit of going out early every morning to go to the fields to glean (gather) the ears of barley[72] that the harvesters missed or dropped. Ruth was a poor peasant, and according to the law that God gave Moses for the Israelites, the poor were allowed to glean in this way so that they might not go hungry. The Scripture says: **She went, and came and gleaned in the field after the reapers; and she happened to come to the portion of the field belonging to Boaz.** (Ruth 2:3)

---

72 Wolof: *millet*

Boaz noticed Ruth gleaning in his field. In time, he saw the beauty of her character and her love for God. Boaz was a righteous man and he recognized that Ruth was a virtuous woman. Can you guess what happened? It isn't too hard to figure out. Yes, Boaz and Ruth got married. Ruth had put God first in her life and God blessed her for it.

The book of Ruth concludes by telling us that Boaz and Ruth had a son named Obed. Obed became the father of Jesse, and Jesse became the father of David who became the greatest king in the history of Israel and the prophet who wrote many of the Psalms. And it was from David's family line (a thousand years later) that the promised Savior, Jesus, Son of Mary, was born.

As with the story of Rahab, Ruth provides us with another wonderful example of God's love and acceptance of all who seek Him with an honest heart. Like Rahab, Ruth was from a pagan nation. While many Israelites turned away from the LORD their God to follow the religions of the surrounding nations, Ruth chose to turn her back on the religion of her people in order to follow the LORD God of Israel who had led her to Bethlehem, marry Boaz and become the great-grandmother of King David. In all this, we see the hand of God arranging the details of His plan to bring into the world the Redeemer – in His time and His way – because it was from the descendants of King David and in the town of Bethlehem that the Savior of the world would be born.

This is where we must stop. Next time, God willing, we will begin to look at *the life of a prophet and king, named David*.

May God bless you as you think on Joshua's final words to the people of Israel:

> **Choose today whom you will serve….**
> **As for me and my house, we will serve the LORD.**
> (Joshua 24:15)

The WAY of
RIGHTEOUSNESS
According to

The Psalms
and the Prophets

Some of the people studied in this section:

Samuel	Jonah
Saul	Isaiah
David	Jeremiah
Goliath	Daniel
Bathsheba	Zechariah
Solomon	Malachi
Elijah	

Part 2

"Do you believe the prophets?"
Acts 26:27

Program 46

Samuel, Saul, and David

1 Samuel 1-16; Psalm 23

I n our last program, we saw that the time following the death of Joshua was a corrupt period in the history of the nation of Israel. But even during that dark time we observed the light of the goodness and faithfulness of God. And the LORD had not forgotten His promise to Abraham and his descendants regarding the Redeemer who would be born of a woman who belonged to the nation of Israel.

We saw how God was at work in the life of a woman named Ruth. Ruth was not an Israelite, but she believed in the God of Israel with all her heart. And while many Israelites turned from the LORD their God to follow the idolatrous religions of the surrounding nations, Ruth chose to turn from the religion of her parents to align herself with the God who communicated with Abraham and his descendants. Ruth moved to the land of Israel and settled in the town of Bethlehem where she married Boaz, the son of Rahab. Boaz and Ruth had a son named Obed and Obed begot Jesse, the father of the prophet David. God's plan to redeem the children of Adam from their sins was moving ahead, because it was through the descendants of David that the Redeemer would enter the world. And it was in Bethlehem, David's hometown, that the Savior would be born.

In coming lessons we will hear how God's prophets wrote about these future events and then how the Redeemer fulfilled them hundreds of years later.

Only God can write history before it happens.

David[73] is prominent in the Holy Scriptures. His name appears more than one thousand times. What do you know about David? Perhaps you know that he was the young man who defeated Goliath the giant with nothing but a sling and stone. You probably also know that David was Israel's most famous king and the prophet who wrote many Psalms.[74] If you know these things, that is good, but your knowledge of David should not end there.

If we know that the prophet David was a great king but do not know what made him great, what good is such knowledge to us? Or if we know that God inspired David to write part of the Scriptures but do not know the message he communicated, of what use is that to us?

Friends, if you want to increase your knowledge about the prophet David and hear some of the wonderful and powerful words that he wrote in the Psalms, then we invite you to join us for today's study and for the next five programs.

Do you know the name of the prophet of God who came before David? It is the prophet *Samuel*. God chose Samuel to turn the people of Israel back to the LORD at a time when their hearts were far from God. Today we will read from the first book of Samuel. This holy book is important among the writings of the prophets because it contains valuable stories from the life of Samuel and from the first three kings of Israel: Saul, David, and Solomon.

As we have seen, God gave the Israelites leaders like Moses, Joshua, and Samuel to guide and judge them, but the LORD God, who had delivered them from their bonds of slavery in Egypt, was their rightful King. God, who commanded them to make a special tent so that He could place His glory in their midst, wanted to be their Ruler. They were to obey and follow Him alone. But most of the Israelites were not content to have just the LORD as their King. They wanted to be like the nations around them who had another human, a son of Adam to reign over them as their king.

---

73 Arabic: *Dawud*
74 Qur'anic name: *Zabur*

In chapter 8 of the first book of Samuel, the Scripture says:

> ⁴**Then all the elders of Israel** gathered themselves together
> and came to Samuel to Ramah. ⁵They said to him, "Behold, you
> are old, and your sons don't walk in your ways. Now make us a
> king to judge us like all the nations." ⁶But the thing displeased
> Samuel when they said, "Give us a king to judge us." Samuel
> prayed to the LORD. ⁷The LORD said to Samuel, "Listen to the
> voice of the people in all that they tell you; for they have not
> rejected you, but they have rejected me as the king over them.
> ⁸According to all the works which they have done since the day
> that I brought them up out of Egypt even to this day, in that
> they have forsaken me and served other gods, so they also do
> to you. ⁹Now therefore, listen to their voice. However, you shall
> protest solemnly to them, and shall show them the way of the
> king who will reign over them." (1 Samuel 8:4-9)

We might wonder why God told Samuel to give the people what
they wanted and to appoint a king for them. God did not want
the Israelites to have another king besides Him, but since they
had rejected God's reign, God would let them have their way. He
would not rule over them by force.

Thus, the prophet Samuel appointed a king for the Israelites; a man
by the name of *Saul*. The Scripture says: **Then Samuel took the vial
of oil and poured it on his head.** (1 Samuel 10:1) That is what the
Israelites did whenever they appointed someone to a special work
of leadership. They poured oil on the head of the prophet, priest,
or king to set him apart. After Samuel poured oil on Saul's head,
he said to all the people, **"Do you see him whom the LORD has
chosen, that there is no one like him among all the people?" All
the people shouted and said, "Long live the king!"** (1 Samuel 10:24)

At first, the Israelites rejoiced greatly in their king, Saul. He was
strong and brave, young and handsome, and taller than any of
the other children of Israel. By outward appearances, Saul should
have been an excellent king. But God does not evaluate things as
man does. Man looks at the outward appearance, but God looks

at the heart. King Saul started out well, but in time he became proud, jealous, and self-sufficient. Saul honored God with his lips, but his heart was far from Him. Saul did not respect and obey the word of God. He did what he wanted to do instead of what God wanted him to do. That is why the Scripture tells us that some years after Saul was appointed king,

> [10] **Then the LORD's word came to Samuel**, saying, [11]"It grieves me that I have set up Saul to be king, for he has turned back from following me, and has not performed my commandments." Samuel was angry; and he cried to the LORD all night. [12]Samuel rose early to meet Saul in the morning.... [13]Samuel came to Saul; and Saul said to him, "You are blessed by the LORD! I have performed the commandment of the LORD."
>
> [22]**Samuel said**, "Has the LORD as great delight in burnt offerings and sacrifices, as in obeying the LORD's voice? Behold, to obey is better than sacrifice, and to listen than the fat of rams. [23]For rebellion is as the sin of witchcraft, and stubbornness is as [bad as worshiping idols]. Because you have rejected the LORD's word, he has also rejected you from being king."
> (1 Samuel 15:10-13,22-23)

That is how Samuel told Saul that the kingdom would be taken from him and given to another. In the next chapter, we read:

> [1]**The LORD said to Samuel**, "How long will you mourn for Saul, since I have rejected him from being king over Israel? Fill your horn with oil, and go. I will send you to Jesse the Bethlehemite, for I have provided a king for myself among his sons." [2]Samuel said, "How can I go? If Saul hears it, he will kill me." The LORD said, "Take a heifer with you, and say, I have come to sacrifice to the LORD. [3]Call Jesse to the sacrifice, and I will show you what you shall do. You shall anoint to me him whom I name to you." [4]Samuel did that which the LORD spoke, and came to Bethlehem. The elders of the city came to meet him trembling, and said, "Do you come peaceably?" [5]He said, "Peaceably; I have come to sacrifice to the LORD. Sanctify yourselves, and

come with me to the sacrifice." He sanctified Jesse and his sons, and called them to the sacrifice.

⁶**When they had come**, he looked at Eliab, and said, "Surely the LORD's anointed is before him." ⁷But the LORD said to Samuel, "Don't look on his face, or on the height of his stature, because I have rejected him; for I don't see as man sees. For man looks at the outward appearance, but the LORD looks at the heart."

⁸**Then Jesse called Abinadab**, and made him pass before Samuel. He said, "The LORD has not chosen this one, either." ⁹Then Jesse made Shammah to pass by. He said, "The LORD has not chosen this one, either." ¹⁰Jesse made seven of his sons to pass before Samuel. Samuel said to Jesse, "The LORD has not chosen these." ¹¹Samuel said to Jesse, "Are all your children here?" He said, "There remains yet the youngest. Behold, he is keeping the sheep." Samuel said to Jesse, "Send and get him, for we will not sit down until he comes here." ¹²He sent, and brought him in. Now he was ruddy, with a handsome face and good appearance. The LORD said, "Arise! Anoint him, for this is he." ¹³Then Samuel took the horn of oil and anointed him in the middle of his brothers. Then the LORD's Spirit came mightily on David from that day forward. (1 Samuel 16:1-13)

That is how God appointed David to be the king of Israel after Saul. But David did not become the king that day. David was only a youth, and the time which God appointed for him to reign as king had not yet come. In fact, David would have to wait ten years before he would sit on the throne of Israel.

So David returned to the fields of Bethlehem to tend and guard his father's flocks. David was a faithful and brave shepherd boy. He feared nothing because he knew that the LORD his God was always with him. For example, one day, as David was tending his father's flock, a lion snatched up one of the sheep. David **went after it, struck it and rescued the sheep from its mouth. When [the lion] turned on [David, he] seized it by its hair, struck it and killed it.** (1 Samuel 17:35)

David was not only a good shepherd; he could also sing and play the harp. The Spirit of God inspired David to compose many songs of praise, prayers in times of distress, and prophecies about the promised Messiah, and to write them in the book of the Psalms. Oh, how David loved the LORD God and His word!

The book of Psalms contain 150 songs. David wrote about half of them. We would like to conclude today's program by reading David's best-known song, Psalm 23. In this psalm, David writes about his relationship with God. He compares himself to a sheep and speaks of the LORD as his good and faithful Shepherd.

Imagine young David in the fields, walking among his father's sheep, strumming his harp and singing this song to the LORD:

> ¹**The LORD is my shepherd: I shall lack nothing.** ²He makes me lie down in green pastures. He leads me beside still waters. ³He restores my soul. He guides me in the paths of righteousness for his name's sake.
>
> ⁴**Even though I walk through the valley** of the shadow of death, I will fear no evil, for you are with me. Your rod and your staff, they comfort me. ⁵You prepare a table before me in the presence of my enemies. You anoint my head with oil. My cup runs over.
>
> ⁶**Surely goodness and loving kindness** shall follow me all the days of my life, and I will dwell in The LORD's house forever. (Psalm 23:1-6) Amen!

In the next program, we plan to hear the story of the contest between *young David and the giant Goliath*.

God bless you as you think about what God told Samuel:

> **"[The LORD doesn't] see as man sees. For man looks at the outward appearance, but the LORD looks at the heart."**
> (1 Samuel 16:7)

Program 47

David and Goliath

1 Samuel 17; Psalm 27

I n the last program we began to look at the prophet David. Listen to what God testified concerning him: **"I have found David the son of Jesse, a man after my heart, who will do all my will."** (Acts 13:22) We saw how the prophet Samuel went to Bethlehem and anointed David to be the next king of Israel because the first king, Saul, did not obey the LORD's commands. But David was still a youth, and the time God had appointed for him to receive the kingdom had not yet arrived. So David returned to the fields to tend his father's flocks.

Today we will read the story that shows how God was with David because David had a heart to please the LORD his God. Our lesson is called *David and Goliath*. We will be reading from the first book of Samuel, chapter 17. The Scripture says:

> ¹**Now the Philistines** [who were the relentless enemies of Israel] gathered together their armies to battle…. ²Saul and the men of Israel were gathered together, and encamped in the valley of Elah, and set the battle in array against the Philistines. ³The Philistines stood on the mountain on the one side, and Israel stood on the mountain on the other side: and there was a valley between them.

> ⁴**A champion out of the camp of the Philistines** named Goliath of Gath, whose height was over three meters went out. ⁵He had a helmet of bronze on his head, and he wore a coat of mail; and the weight of the coat was 60 kilos of bronze. ⁶He had bronze shin armor on his legs and a bronze javelin between his shoulders. ⁷The staff of his spear was like a weaver's beam; and his spear's head weighed seven kilos. His shield bearer went before him.

⁸**He stood and cried to the armies of Israel**, and said to them, "Why have you come out to set your battle in array? Am I not a Philistine, and you servants to Saul? Choose a man for yourselves, and let him come down to me. ⁹If he is able to fight with me and kill me, then will we be your servants; but if I prevail against him and kill him, then you will be our servants and serve us." ¹⁰The Philistine said, "I defy the armies of Israel today! Give me a man, that we may fight together!" ¹¹When Saul and all Israel heard those words of the Philistine, they were dismayed and greatly afraid. (1 Samuel 17:1-11)

As Goliath was taunting Israel, over in Bethlehem, 20 kilometers away, David was tending his father's flocks, and meditating on the word of God. But David had three older brothers who were soldiers with Israel's army. One day David's father came to him and said,

¹⁷**"Now take for your brothers** a [sack] of this parched grain and these ten loaves, and carry them quickly to the camp to your brothers; ¹⁸and bring these ten cheeses to the captain of their thousand; and see how your brothers are doing, and bring back news." ¹⁹Now Saul, and they, and all the men of Israel were in the valley of Elah, fighting with the Philistines. ²⁰David rose up early in the morning and left the sheep with a keeper, and took the provisions and went, as Jesse had commanded him. He came to the place of the wagons as the army which was going out to the fight shouted for the battle. (1 Samuel 17:17-20)

While David was speaking with his older brothers, Goliath stepped out from his lines facing the soldiers of Israel and threatened them as he had been doing for the past forty days. When the Israeli soldiers saw him, they ran from him in fear.

²⁶**David spoke to the men who stood by him,** saying, "What shall be done to the man who kills this Philistine and takes away the reproach from Israel? For who is this uncircumcised Philistine, that he should defy the armies of the living God?"

The soldiers answered David,

²⁵**"The king will give great riches to the man who kills him**, and will give him his daughter, and will make his father's house tax-free in Israel." ... ²⁸Eliab his oldest brother heard when [David] spoke to the men; and Eliab's anger burned against David, and he said, "Why have you come down? With whom have you left those few sheep in the wilderness? I know your pride and the evil of your heart; for you have come down that you might see the battle." (1 Samuel 17:26,25,28)

But a soldier who heard David's courageous words went and reported them to Saul. So Saul sent for David.

³²**David said to Saul**, "Let no man's heart fail because of him. Your servant will go and fight with this Philistine."

³³**Saul said to David**, "You are not able to go against this Philistine to fight with him; for you are but a youth, and he a man of war from his youth."

³⁴**David said to Saul**, "Your servant was keeping his father's sheep; and when a lion or a bear came and took a lamb out of the flock, ³⁵I went out after him, struck him, and rescued it out of his mouth. When he arose against me, I caught him by his beard, struck him, and killed him. ³⁶Your servant struck both the lion and the bear. This uncircumcised Philistine shall be as one of them, since he has defied the armies of the living God." ³⁷David said, "The LORD, who delivered me out of the paw of the lion and out of the paw of the bear, will deliver me out of the hand of this Philistine." Saul said to David, "Go! The LORD will be with you." ³⁸Saul dressed David with his clothing. He put a helmet of bronze on his head, and he clad him with a coat of mail. ³⁹David strapped his sword on his clothing and he tried to move, for he had not tested it. David said to Saul, "I can't go with these, for I have not tested them." Then David took them off.

⁴⁰**He took his staff in his hand**, and chose for himself five smooth stones out of the brook, and put them in the pouch of his shepherd's bag which he had. His sling was in his hand;

and he came near to the Philistine. [41]The Philistine walked and came near to David; and the man who bore the shield went before him. [42]When the Philistine looked around and saw David, he disdained him; for he was but a youth, and ruddy, and had a good looking face. [43]The Philistine said to David, "Am I a dog, that you come to me with sticks?" The Philistine cursed David by his gods. [44]The Philistine said to David, "Come to me, and I will give your flesh to the birds of the sky and to the animals of the field."

[45]**Then David said to the Philistine**, "You come to me with a sword, with a spear, and with a javelin; but I come to you in the name of the LORD of Armies, the God of the armies of Israel, whom you have defied. [46]Today, the LORD will deliver you into my hand. I will strike you and take your head from off you. I will give the dead bodies of the army of the Philistines today to the birds of the sky and to the wild animals of the earth, that all the earth may know that there is a God in Israel, [47]and that all this assembly may know that the LORD doesn't save with sword and spear; for the battle is the LORD's, and he will give you into our hand."

[48]**When the Philistine arose**, and walked and came near to meet David, David hurried and ran toward the army to meet the Philistine. [49]David put his hand in his bag, took a stone and slung it, and struck the Philistine in his forehead. The stone sank into his forehead, and he fell on his face to the earth. [50]So David prevailed over the Philistine with a sling and with a stone, and struck the Philistine and killed him; but there was no sword David's hand. [51]Then David ran, stood over the Philistine, took his sword, drew it out of its sheath, killed him, and cut off his head with it. When the Philistines saw that their champion was dead, they fled. [52]The men of Israel and of Judah arose and shouted, and pursued the Philistines as far as Gai and to the gates of Ekron. (1 Samuel 17:32-52)

This is how young David saved his nation from their enemies with a sling, a stone, and a solid faith in the LORD God. This story of David and Goliath contains many important lessons.

We saw how Saul and the Israeli soldiers feared Goliath greatly. None of them dared to fight him, but David was not afraid of the giant; he knocked him to the ground and killed him. Why were Saul and his soldiers afraid of the giant, but David was not afraid of him? What was the difference between David and the Israeli soldiers? We can summarize the difference between them like this: David was not afraid of the giant because he had confidence in the LORD God. But Saul and his soldiers did not have confidence in God. That is why they were afraid of the giant.

Saul and his soldiers saw the powerful giant. David saw Almighty God. Saul and the Israeli soldiers had a form of religion, but that did not give them a true relationship with the LORD God. Belonging to a religion does not cause you to belong to God.

Saul and his soldiers knew very well that God exists and that God is one and that He is great and powerful. But that knowledge alone could not save them from Goliath. But David had a genuine relationship with God. David knew the LORD and enjoyed His presence day and night. And David believed the promises of God written in the scriptures of the previous prophets. That is why David was not afraid of Goliath.

You who are listening today, who are you most like? David? or Saul and his soldiers? Do you know God personally? Do you know the promises of the one true God? Does His word fill your heart with peace and joy? Or are you merely trying to fulfill your religious obligations? Do you have a solid and happy relationship with the living God? Or do you just have a bone-dry religion?

Listen to what the prophet David wrote in the Psalms about the relationship he had with God. He said:

> [1]**The LORD is my shepherd**, I shall lack nothing.... [4]Even though I walk through the valley of the shadow of death, I will fear no evil, for you are with me....[6]Surely goodness and loving kindness shall follow me all the days of my life, and I will dwell in the LORD's house forever. (Psalm 23:1,4,6)

How about you? Do you enjoy a relationship with God as David did? Do you know the LORD as your Shepherd? Do you love Him? Are you certain that you will dwell in His house forever? David had such confidence because he knew the promises of God. And he didn't just know them in his head; he believed them in his heart.

David had a genuine faith. His faith was not based on the unreliable words of men. His faith was based on the sure words of the LORD God who never abandons His people. Listen to what David wrote in the Psalms:

> ¹**The LORD is my light and my salvation.** Whom shall I fear? The LORD is the strength of my life. Of whom shall I be afraid?… ³Though an army should encamp against me, my heart shall not fear. Though war should rise against me, even then I will be confident. ⁴One thing I have asked of the LORD, that I will seek after: that I may dwell in the LORD's house all the days of my life,   to see the LORD's beauty, and to inquire in his temple.… ⁷Hear, O LORD, when I cry with my voice. Have mercy also on me, and answer me. ⁸When you said, "Seek my face," my heart said to you, "I will seek your face, LORD." (Psalm 27:1,3-4,7-8)

> ¹**I love you, O LORD, my strength.** ²The LORD is my rock, my fortress, and my deliverer; my God, my rock, in whom I take refuge; my shield, and the horn of my salvation, my high tower.… ²⁹For by you, I advance through a troop. By my God, I leap over a wall. ³⁰As for God, his way is perfect. The LORD's word is tried. He is a shield to all those who take refuge in him. (Psalm 18:1-2,29-30)

Thank you for listening. In our next lesson, Lord willing, we will continue with the story of David and see how he began to reign as king over the nation of Israel.

God bless you. We bid you farewell with this word in the Psalms, written by the sheperd David in the Psalms:

> **Oh taste and see that the LORD is good. Blessed is the man who takes refuge in him!** (Psalm 34:8)

King David and God's Promise

1 Samuel 18 - 2 Samuel 7

Today we are continuing our study about the prophet David. Two lessons ago we saw how God chose young David to be the second king of Israel, though he did not begin to reign the day God appointed him. God rejected Saul, the first king, because he was not committed to doing God's will. On the other hand, God testified of David, **"I have found David the son of Jesse, a man after my heart, who will do all my will."** (Acts 13:22)

In the last program we saw David kill the giant Goliath, defeating him with a sling and a stone and a solid faith in the living God. Now let us continue in the first book of Samuel:

> ⁶**When David returned from the slaughter** of [Goliath] the Philistine, the women came out of all the cities of Israel, singing and dancing, to meet king Saul with tambourines, with joy, and with instruments of music. ⁷The women sang to one another as they played, and said, "Saul has slain his thousands, and David his ten thousands." ⁸Saul was very angry, and this saying displeased him. He said, "They have creditd David with ten thousands, and they have only credited me with thousands. What can he have more but the kingdom?" ⁹Saul watched David from that day and forward. (1 Samuel 18:6-9)

The Israelites dearly loved David. But the more they loved him, the more Saul hated him. Jealousy filled Saul's heart and controlled him so that all he could think of was what he must do to get rid of David. Consequently, David fled and hid in the desert, together with four hundred men of Israel who were loyal to him. Saul and his soldiers hunted for David and his men. Saul did everything in his power to catch David and kill him, but he could not do so because the LORD was with David. Still, Saul caused David a lot of distress. For eight long years, David and his men had to run and hide from an angry King Saul.

But the jealousy and anger that Saul displayed toward David did not cause David to hate him. Why didn't David hate Saul who was trying to kill him? He could not hate Saul, because David walked with the LORD God who is love. The Scripture says:

> [7]**Beloved, let's love one another**, for love is of God; and everyone who loves has been born of God, and knows God. [8]He who doesn't love doesn't know God, for God is love.… [19]We love him, because he first loved us. [20]If a man says, "I love God," and hates his brother, he is a liar; for he who doesn't love his brother whom he has seen, how can he love God whom he has not seen? (1 John 4:7-8,19-20)

We don't have time to read all that happened between Saul and David, but here's one of the stories that reveal David's heart of love and humility. One day some of Saul's men came to him and said:

> [1]**"Behold, David is in the wilderness of En Gedi."** [2]Then Saul took three thousand chosen men out of all Israel, and went to seek David and his men on the rocks of the wild goats. [3]He came to the sheep pens by the way, where there was a cave; and Saul went in to relieve himself. Now David and his men were staying in the innermost parts of the cave.
>
> [4]**David's men said to him**, "Behold, the day of which the LORD said to you, 'I will deliver your enemy into your hand, and you shall do to him as it shall seem good to you.'" Then David arose, and cut off the skirt of Saul's robe secretly. [5]Afterward, David's heart struck him, because he had cut off Saul's skirt. [6]He said to his men, "The LORD forbid that I should do this thing to my lord, the LORD's anointed, to stretch out my hand against him, since he is the LORD's anointed." [7]So David checked his men with these words, and didn't allow them to rise against Saul. Saul rose up out of the cave, and went on his way.

⁸**David also arose afterward**, and went out of the cave, and cried after Saul, saying, "My lord the king!" When Saul looked behind him, David bowed with his face to the earth, and showed respect. ⁹David said to Saul, "Why do you listen to men's words, saying, 'David seeks to harm you?' ¹⁰Behold, today your eyes have seen how the LORD had delivered you today into my hand in the cave. Some urged me to kill you; but I spared you; and I said, I will not stretch out my hand against my lord; for he is the LORD's anointed. ¹¹Moreover, my father, behold, yes, see the skirt of your robe in my hand; for in that I cut off the skirt of your robe, and didn't kill you, know and see that there is neither evil nor disobedience in my hand, and I have not sinned against you, though you hunt for my life to take it. ¹²May the LORD judge between me and you, and may the LORD avenge me of you; but my hand will not be on you. ¹³As the proverb of the ancients says, 'Out of the wicked comes wickedness;' but my hand will not be on you.

¹⁶**It came to pass, when David had finished speaking** these words to Saul, that Saul said, "Is that your voice, my son David?" Saul lifted up his voice, and wept. ¹⁷He said to David, "You are more righteous than I; for you have done good to me, whereas I have done evil to you. ¹⁸You have declared today how you have dealt well with me, because when the LORD had delivered me up into your hand, you didn't kill me. ¹⁹For if a man finds his enemy, will he let him go away unharmed? Therefore may the LORD reward you good for that which you have done to me today. ²⁰Now, I know that you will surely be king, and that the kingdom of Israel will be established in your hand. (1 Samuel 24:1-13,16-20)

After that, Saul returned home, but it wasn't long before jealousy took hold of his heart again and incited him to go back into the desert to resume his hunt for David. Driven by jealousy, Saul did this for eight years. Yet, each time, God rescued David from Saul.

In the end, Saul reaped the evil he had sown. The Scripture says:

> [1]**Now the Philistines fought against Israel**; and the men of Israel fled from before the Philistines, and fell down slain on Mount Gilboa. [2]The Philistines overtook Saul and his sons; and the Philistines killed Jonathan, Abinadab, and Malchishua, the sons of Saul. [3]The battle went hard against Saul, and the archers overtook him; and he was greatly distressed by reason of the archers. [4]Then Saul said to his armor bearer, "Draw your sword, and thrust me through with it, lest these uncircumcised come and thrust me through, and abuse me!" But his armor bearer would not; for he was terrified. Therefore Saul took his sword, and fell on it. (1 Samuel 31:1-4)

In the chapters that follow, the Scriptures relate how God turned over the kingdom of Israel to David. King David was a just ruler who loved righteousness and hated iniquity. David loved the LORD God with his whole heart. The word of God and the glory of God occupied first place in David's thoughts. Therefore, when David began to rule over Israel the first thing he wanted to do was to bring the tent of meeting and the ark of the covenant to Jerusalem. Jerusalem had become the capital of Israel, which is why David wanted to set up the tent of worship and the altar of sacrifice there.

After David moved the tent to Jerusalem, he began to make plans to build a beautiful temple to honor the name of the LORD. David wanted to build a temple in which the ark of the covenant could be placed and where sinners could come to worship God with sacrifices that cover sin. But the LORD told David that he would not be the one to build a house for God, but that God would give *him* a house, that is, a posterity that would endure forever. The LORD said to David:

> [12]**When your days are fulfilled**, and you sleep with your fathers, I will set up your offspring after you, who will proceed out of your body, and I will establish his kingdom. [13]He will build a house for my name, and I will establish the throne of his kingdom forever. [14]I will be his father, and he will be my son.… [16]Your house and your kingdom will be made sure forever before you. Your throne will be established forever. (2 Samuel 7:12-14,16)

Do you understand the covenant (agreement) God established with King David on that day? God promised that David would have a royal family line, a kingdom and a dynasty that would never end.

What? How could King David have an eternal kingdom? How could David, a mere man, have a government that would last forever? Here is the answer: God promised that one of David's descendants would establish an everlasting government. A man would be born into David's royal family line with the authority to reign in heaven and on earth forever. He would be called the Prince of Peace and King of Glory. Hundreds of years after David's time, and 700 years before this Prince was born, the prophet Isaiah penned these words:

> [6]**For a child is born to us.** A son is given to us; and the government will be on his shoulders. His name will be called Wonderful Counselor, Mighty God, Everlasting Father, Prince of Peace. [7]Of the increase of his government and of peace there shall be no end, on David's throne, and on his kingdom, to establish it, and to uphold it with justice and with right-eousness from that time on, even forever. The zeal of the LORD Almighty will perform this. (Isaiah 9:6-7)

Do you know who, among the descendants of David, has been given the authority to rule forever? Do you know who will judge the world on the Day of Judgment and reign throughout eternity? Yes, it is the promised Messiah who was born of a virgin, a virgin who was a descendant of King David. Concerning this Messiah-King, the Scripture says: **God also highly exalted him, and gave to him the name which is above every name.** (Philippians 2:9)

So how did David react when he heard God's amazing plan to send the promised Redeemer through his family line? The Scripture says:

> [18]**Then David the king went in,** and sat before the LORD; and he said, "Who am I, Sovereign LORD, and what is my house, that you have brought me this far? [19]This was yet a small thing in your eyes, Sovereign LORD; but you have spoken also of your servant's house for a great while to come; and this among men,

Sovereign LORD! ...²²Therefore you are great, LORD God. For there is no one like you, neither is there any God besides you, according to all that we have heard with our ears.... ²⁸Now, O Sovereign LORD, you are God, and your words are truth, and you have promised this good thing to your servant. ²⁹Now therefore let it please you to bless the house of your servant, that it may continue forever before you; for you, Sovereign LORD, have spoken it. Let the house of your servant be blessed forever with your blessing." (2 Samuel 7:18-19,22,28-29)

That is how David thanked the LORD for His promise to send the Savior-King through his descendants. And all who know the Holy Scriptures know that God has already fulfilled this promise. For the Gospel informs us that a thousand years after David's time, God sent an angel to some shepherds who were tending their flocks in the same fields of Bethlehem where David had tended his father's flock. And the angel of the LORD said to the shepherds:

¹⁰"**Don't be afraid, for behold, I bring you good news** of great joy which will be to all the people. ¹¹For there is born to you today, in David's city, a Savior, who is Christ the Lord" (Luke 2:10-11)

Yes, the King whom God promised to send through David's posterity has been born! At present He is back up in heaven awaiting that terrible and glorious day when He will return to judge the world in righteousness. In that day it will be said,

The kingdom of the world has become the kingdom of our Lord, and of his Christ. He will reign forever and ever!! (Revelation 11:15)

We must stop here for today. Thank you for listening. Next time, we plan to continue the story of King David and hear of an event that will make your ears tingle.

God bless you. We leave you with this word from the Holy Scriptures that remind us how David was able to love his enemy.

He who doesn't love doesn't know God, for God is love. We love him because He first loved us. (1 John 4:8,19)

David and Bathsheba

2 Samuel 11-12; Psalms 51, 32

In our last program, we saw how the prophet David ascended to the throne of Israel. David was a just and compassionate king who cherished the word of God and had a heart to do the will of God. Today, however, we are going to read something about David that is not pleasant to hear. King David did something that was abominable in God's sight.

Here is something we should understand. The Holy Scriptures do not conceal the sins of the prophets. If the writings of the prophets were merely a human book, surely an effort would have been made to hide, ignore, or make excuses for their sins and mistakes. But the true Scriptures tell us the truth. So in our study today, if you find yourself asking, "Why is such an awful story found in the Holy Scriptures?" The Scripture itself answers your question, saying: **Everything that was written in the past was written to teach us** (Romans 15:4 NIV) **and as warnings for us.** (1 Corinthians 10:11 NIV) God does not hide the sins of His people because God is holy and wants to teach us valuable lessons to help us to not fall into the same pit of sin. We can learn a lot from bad examples. Today we will learn, first from King David's bad example, and then from his good example.

Now let us return to the second book of Samuel to learn from David's fall. In chapter 11 we read:

> [1] … **At the time when kings go out [to battle]**, David sent Joab, and his servants with him, and all Israel; and they destroyed the children of Ammon, and besieged Rabbah. But David stayed at Jerusalem. [2]At evening, David arose from his bed and walked on the roof of the king's house. From the roof, he saw a

woman bathing, and the woman was very beautiful to look at. [3]David sent and inquired after the woman. One said, "Isn't this Bathsheba,… Uriah the Hittite's wife?" [4]David sent messengers, and took her; and she came in to him, and he lay with her… and she returned to her house. [5]The woman conceived; and she sent and told David, and said, "I am with child." (2 Samuel 11:1-5)

Next, the Scriptures describe how David tried to cover up his sin. When he heard that Bathsheba was pregnant, he sent word to Joab, the leader of his army, and ordered him to send to him Uriah, Bathsheba's husband, a mighty man in Israel's army.

[7]**When Uriah had come to him**, David asked him how Joab did, and how the people fared, and how the war prospered. [8]David said to Uriah, "Go down to your house and wash your feet." Uriah departed out of the king's house, and a gift from the king was sent after him. [9]But Uriah slept at the door of the king's house with all the servants of his lord, and didn't go down to his house. [10]When they had told David, saying, "Uriah didn't go down to his house," David said to Uriah, "Haven't you come from a journey? Why didn't you go down to your house?" [11]Uriah said to David, "The ark, Israel, and Judah, are staying in tents; and my lord Joab and the servants of my lord, are encamped in the open field. Shall I then go into my house to eat and to drink, and to lie with my wife? As you live, and as your soul lives, I will not do this thing!" [12]David said to Uriah, "Stay here today also, and tomorrow I will let you depart." So Uriah stayed in Jerusalem that day, and the next….

[14]**In the morning, David wrote a letter to Joab**, and sent it by the hand of Uriah. [15]He wrote in the letter, saying, "Send Uriah to the forefront of the hottest battle, and retreat from him, that he may be struck, and die." [16]When Joab kept watch on the city, he assigned Uriah to the place where he knew that valiant men were. [17]The men of the city went out, and fought with Joab. Some of the people fell, even of David's servants; and Uriah the Hittite died also. [18]Then Joab sent and told David all the things concerning the war [with the news:]…

²¹"Your servant Uriah the Hittite is also dead."…²⁶When Uriah's wife heard that Uriah her husband was dead, she mourned for her husband. ²⁷When the mourning was past, David sent and took her home to his house, and she became his wife, and bore him a son. But the thing that David had done displeased the LORD. (2 Samuel 11:7-12,14-18,21,26-27)

So the LORD sent to the king a prophet by the name of Nathan. Here was Nathan's message from God to David:

¹**"There were two men in a certain town**, one rich and the other poor. ²The rich man had a very large number of sheep and cattle, ³but the poor man had nothing except one little ewe lamb that he had bought. He raised it, and it grew up with him and his children. It shared his food, drank from his cup and even slept in his arms. It was like a daughter to him. ⁴Now a traveler came to the rich man, but the rich man refrained from taking one of his own sheep or cattle to prepare a meal for the traveler who had come to him. Instead, he took the ewe lamb that belonged to the poor man and prepared it for the one who had come to him." ⁵[When David heard this story, he] burned with anger against the man and said to Nathan, "As surely as the LORD lives, the man who did this deserves to die! ⁶He must pay for that lamb four times over, because he did such a thing and had no pity."

⁷**Nathan said to David, "You are the man.** This is what the LORD, the God of Israel, says:'I anointed you king over Israel, and I delivered you out of the hand of Saul. ⁸I… gave you the house of Israel and of Judah; and if that would have been too little, I would have added to you many more such things. ⁹Why have you despised the LORD's word, to do that which is evil in his sight? You have struck Uriah the Hittite with the sword, and have taken his wife to be your wife, and have slain him with the sword of the children of Ammon. ¹⁰Now therefore the sword will never depart from your house, because you have despised me, and have taken Uriah the Hittite's wife to be your wife.' ¹¹This is what the LORD says:'Behold, I will raise up evil against you out

of your own house; and I will take your wives before your eyes, and give them to your neighbor, and he will lie with your wives in the sight of this sun. ¹²For you did this secretly, but I will do this thing before all Israel, and before the sun.'"

¹³**David said to Nathan**, "I have sinned against the LORD." Nathan said to David, "The LORD also has put away your sin. You will not die. ¹⁴However, because by this deed you have given great occasion to the LORD's enemies to blaspheme, the child also who is born to you will surely die." (2 Samuel 12:1-14)

In the chapters that follow, the Scriptures show us that as a result of David's sins of covetousness, adultery, murder, lies, and so on, he would reap horrific trouble and tragedies within his family. Yes, God forgives sins but He doesn't wipe out the consequences. Yet because David knew God, he would face each of those consequences knowing that the LORD would not abandon him. As the Scriptures say: **Where sin abounded, [God's] grace abounded more exceedingly.** (Romans 5:20) In the time remaining today, we want to see how God could extend to David His forgiveness and grace.

Did you hear how David responded when Nathan said to him, "You are the man"? (God's prophet Nathan had great courage to say such a thing to the great King of Israel.) How did David respond?

Did he lock Nathan in prison, or have him executed, as many kings would have done? No, he did not do that. Did David try to justify his sins by saying, "God willed it," or "God is good, perhaps He will erase my evil deeds because of my good deeds"? Did David answer Nathan like that? No, he did not. Then how did David respond? He said, **"I have sinned against the LORD."**

To see into David's heart, we must read the confession he made to God after Nathan rebuked him for his sin with Bathsheba. Here is part of his confession, recorded in Psalm 51:

¹**Have mercy on me, God**, according to your loving kindness. According to the multitude of your tender mercies, blot out

my transgressions. [2]Wash me thoroughly from my iniquity. Cleanse me from my sin.

[3]**For I know my transgressions.** My sin is constantly before me. [4]Against you, and you only, I have sinned, and done that which is evil in your sight, so you may be proved right when you speak, and justified when you judge. [5]Behold, I was born in iniquity. My mother conceived me in sin. [6]Behold, you desire truth in the inward parts. You teach me wisdom in the inmost place. [7]Purify me with hyssop, and I will be clean. Wash me, and I will be whiter than snow. …[10]Create in me a clean heart, O God. Renew a right spirit within me. [11]Don't throw me from your presence, and don't take your Holy Spirit from me. [12]Restore to me the joy of your salvation. Uphold me with a willing spirit. … [17]The sacrifices of God are a broken spirit. O God, you will not despise a broken and contrite heart. (Psalm 51:1-7,10,17)

This was David's prayer of confession to God and God alone. He mourned greatly because of his sin; his heart was broken and crushed before God. King David was not like those who have religion but continue in sin every day. Truly, David had fallen into a pit of sin, but he could not live in it because he loved God who hates sin. Oh, how David hated the sins he had committed!

After David had repented, what did God say to him through the prophet Nathan? Did Nathan tell him, "Go, do some good works and God will erase your sins"? No, Nathan told him, **"The LORD also has put away your sin. You will not die."**

After this, David wrote another Psalm, describing the blessedness of the man whom God has forgiven, apart from his own works, saying: **Blessed is he whose disobedience is forgiven, whose sin is covered. Blessed is the man to whom the LORD doesn't impute iniquity, in whose spirit there is no deceit.** (Psalm 32:1-2) God forgave David and declared him righteous. That did not mean that God revoked the tragedies David's sin produced. It did mean that on the Day of Judgment, God would not remember David's sins. He had erased them all from His book.

How could God do that? How could God erase all of David's sins and yet remain a righteous judge? Did God simply ignore all the evil which David had done? Of course not. God is a righteous judge. He cannot merely close His eyes to the sins of the children of Adam. Well then, how did God forgive David without God compromising His righteous requirements?

Do you remember what David prayed to God after he grieved over his sin? He prayed, **Wash me thoroughly from my iniquity.... Purify me with hyssop, and I will be clean. Wash me, and I will be whiter than snow.** (Psalm 51:2,7) God had commanded the Israelites to use a branch of the hyssop plant to sprinkle the blood of the sacrifices on and around the altar. The sprinkled blood illustrated the cleansing that the Redeemer's shed blood would provide to pay off the sin debt of the world. God could forgive David's sins, because of the holy Redeemer who would endure for King David and for you and for me the punishment that our sin deserves. David was saying, "LORD, have mercy on me, a sinner! Wash me in the blood of the holy Redeemer and I shall be clean!"

Did God, in His grace, forgive David all his sins? Did God cleanse David's heart and judge him as righteous? Yes. Yes! On what basis did God do this? God forgave David because he confessed his sinful condition before the holy LORD God and believed what God had promised concerning the Redeemer who would come and bear the punishment for sin.

In our next two programs we plan to look into the holy book of Psalms to see what the prophet David prophesied about the Redeemer, who would bear our punishment so that God could forgive us our sins forever.

May God bless you as you think on King David's joyful declaration:

> **Blessed is the one whose transgressions are forgiven, whose sins are covered. Blessed is the one whose sin the Lord does not count against them and in whose spirit is no deceit.**
> (Psalm 32:1-2 NIV)

Program 50

The Prophet David and the Messiah

Psalms 1-2

I n the past four programs we have been reading about the prophet King David. We have seen that he was a *shepherd, musician, singer, song writer, student of God's word, warrior, king,* and *prophet*. And in our last program, we saw that, like all of Adam's offspring, King David was also a *sinner*. Tempted by his own desires, David fell into the deep pit of sin, but he did not stay in it. David had a heart to please the LORD. David received God's forgiveness because he was broken over his sin and knew that God had covered his sins with the blood of a lamb until such time as the Messiah, *The* Lamb of God, would come to pay off the sin debt of the world.

Today we plan to meditate on the wonderful book found in the middle of the Holy Scriptures. Do you know its name? Yes, it is the *Psalms*.[75] The book of the Psalms has 150 songs.[76] Over hundreds of years, God inspired several men to write the Psalms. Those writers included Moses, Solomon, Asaph, Korah's sons, and, of course, David who wrote about half of the psalms. Today we want to consider the first two psalms.

Psalm 1 reveals two kinds of people: *Those who walk in the way of righteousness* and *those who walk in the way of unrighteousness*. Let's listen to the first Psalm:

> [1]**Blessed is the man** who doesn't walk in the counsel of the wicked, nor stand on the path of sinners, nor sit in the seat of scoffers; [2]but his delight is in the LORD's law. On his law he meditates day and night. [3]He will be like a tree planted by the

75 Qur'anic name: Zabur
76 psalms, hymns, songs of praise and worship

streams of water, that produces its fruit in its season, whose leaf also does not wither. Whatever he does shall prosper. ⁴The wicked are not so, but are like the chaff which the wind drives away.

⁵**Therefore the wicked shall not stand** in the judgment, nor sinners in the congregation of the righteous. ⁶For the LORD knows the way of the righteous, but the way of the wicked shall perish. (Psalm 1:1-6)

Did you notice the two choices? You can choose to be blessed, or you can choose to perish. Everyone wants to be blessed. No one wants to perish. God wants you to be blessed, but you must walk in the way of blessing which He has established. And what is that way of blessing? This psalm summarizes it in two thoughts:
First: *Do not follow those who mock the true word of God.*
Second: *Take time to think on God's word so that you can understand, believe, and submit to His righteous way of salvation.*

If you delight in His word and meditate constantly on it, you will be **like a tree planted by the streams of water**; your life will yield good **fruit** such as love, joy, and peace. But if you do not love the LORD and His word, you will be **like the chaff which the wind drives away.**

Now let us read the second Psalm. Here God inspired King David to write about the coming Messiah-King. Let us listen carefully to this serious message. The prophet David wrote:

¹**Why do the nations rage**, and the peoples plot a vain thing? ²The kings of the earth take a stand, and the rulers take counsel together, against the LORD, and against his Anointed, (the Messiah) saying, ³"Let's break their bonds apart, and cast their cords from us."

⁴**He who sits in the heavens will laugh.** The Lord will have them in derision. ⁵Then he will speak to them in his anger, and terrify them in his wrath: ⁶ "Yet I have set my King on my holy hill of Zion." ⁷I will tell of the decree: the LORD said to me, "You are my son. Today I have become your father. ⁸Ask of me, and I will give the nations for your inheritance, the uttermost parts

of the earth for your possession. [9]You shall break them with a rod of iron. You shall dash them in pieces like a potter's vessel."

[10]**Now therefore be wise, you kings.** Be instructed, you judges of the earth. [11]Serve the LORD with fear, and rejoice with trembling. [12]Give sincere homage to the Son, lest he be angry, and you perish on the way, for his wrath will soon be kindled. Blessed are all those who take refuge in him. (Psalm 2:1-12)

In this prophecy, God unveils three wonderful titles of the Savior who was to come to earth to provide salvation for all who put their trust in Him. The Redeemer's three titles are: **the Messiah, the King**, and **the Son**. Let's think about these three titles.

First, we see that God calls the Redeemer **the Messiah**, a Hebrew word meaning the *One whom God has appointed*.[77] By calling the promised Savior the *Messiah*, God was announcing to the children of Adam that He is the One whom God Himself has chosen to be the Savior and Judge of the world. We also see in the first three verses that most people will reject God's Chosen One.

[1]**Why do the nations rage**, and the peoples plot a vain thing? [2]The kings of the earth take a stand, and the rulers take counsel together, against the LORD, and against his Anointed, saying, [3]"Let's break their bonds apart, and cast their cords from us." (Psalm 2:1-3)

Why would people reject the Messiah sent by God? They would reject Him because He is the only perfect person ever to be born, and the Scripture tells us that **everyone who does evil hates the light, and will not come into the light for fear that their deeds will be exposed.** (John 3:20 NIV) In these verses, God was foretelling how the nations of the world would seek to kill the Savior and Judge of the world. But God sees and knows and even uses the schemes of wicked men. That is why the psalm says: **He who sits in the heavens will laugh. The Lord will have them in derision.** (Psalm 2:4)

---

77 Hebrew word *Messiah* means: *Anointed One,* or *Selected One.* Greek equivalent of this word is: *Christ.* Arabic word for Messiah: *Almasih*

And so, the first name that God uses for the Redeemer in this psalm is **the Messiah**. You might be interested to know that the Hebrew word *Messiah* has the same meaning as the Greek word *Christ*. Both mean *the One whom God has appointed.*

The second title is **the King**. The Messiah is also *the King*. With that title God wants everyone to know that, in His own time, the Messiah will be the Judge and Ruler of the world. On the great Day of Judgment everyone will bow before Him because He is the One whom God has appointed to be the King-Judge. Like it or not, the Messiah-King will be either your Savior or your Judge – because He is *the King* whom God has appointed to rule and reign forever.

The third title used in this psalm for the Messiah is **the Son**. This is a title we must consider very carefully. Many people reject the term *Son of God* because they have never understood it. But just because we don't understand something does not mean it isn't true. God's word warns us that the Holy Scriptures contain **some things that are hard to understand, which the ignorant and unsettled twist… to their own destruction.** (2 Peter 3:16)

Ignorance is a terrible thing, especially when it concerns the holy Redeemer whom God sent to earth to buy sinners back and rescue them from Satan, sin, death, and hell. A Wolof proverb says: *Before you know it, ignorance will kill you.* Let us keep that thought in mind as we think through this second psalm.

Let us read verse 7 again where we heard the Messiah say:
I will tell of the decree: the LORD said to me, "You are my son. Today I have become your father." (Psalm 2:7)

Did you hear what the LORD said to the Messiah? He said, **"You are my Son… I have become your Father."** Do you know why God called the Messiah *His Son*? Do you know what this name means? We hope that you know what the name does *not* mean. It does not mean that God married a wife and begat a son. Such a thought is blasphemy. God is spirit and He does not beget children as a man begets a son.

So then, why did God say to the Messiah, **"You are my Son"**? The LORD God Himself has told us why. We do not have time to go very deep into this subject today, but we would like to give you three reasons from Scripture why God called the Messiah *His Son*.

First, God called the Messiah *His Son* because the Messiah *came from above*; from heaven. The Messiah did not have an earthly father. As a human, He came through the family line of King David, born of a young virgin who was a descendant of King David. On His mother's side, the Messiah was the son of Mary, but on His Father's side, He was the *Son of God*. The same Word by which God created the world, the same Voice which thundered from fiery Mount Sinai is the only perfect child ever to be born.

The Scripture says:

> [1]**In the beginning was the Word**, and the Word was with God, and the Word was God. The same was in the beginning with God. [14]The Word became flesh, and lived among us. We saw his glory, such glory as of the one and only Son of the Father, full of grace and truth. (John 1:1-2,14)

That is why God could say to Him, **"You are my Son. Today I have become your Father."**

God also called the Messiah *His Son* because God and the Messiah share the same *holy character*. Like Father, like Son. The promised Redeemer had to be pure and holy even as God is pure and holy. The Messiah was not like the descendants of Adam, who are stained with sin. As we have seen, even the greatest of the prophets had sin natures. But the Messiah could not sin. He always did the will of God. He was the perfect man. The Scriptures says that He is the one who is **holy, guiltless, undefiled, separated from sinners, and made higher than the heavens.** (Hebrews 7:26) That is why God calls Him *His Son*.

Finally, you should know that God called the Messiah *His Son* to distinguish Him from all the other prophets.

Abraham was called *the friend of God*. Moses was called *the man of God*. David was called *a man after God's own heart*. But the Messiah is called *the Word of God*. That is why, when that *Word* became flesh, God joyfully said of Him, **"You are my Son. Today I have become your Father!"**

You who are listening today, do you know this Messiah-King whom God calls *His Son*? God wants us to know Him, listen to Him, and believe in Him. Let's read again King David's conclusion:

> [10]**Therefore, you kings, be wise**; be warned, you rulers of the earth. [11]Serve the LORD with fear and rejoice with trembling. [12]Kiss the Son, lest he be angry and you be destroyed in your way, for his wrath can flare up in a moment. Blessed are all who take refuge in him. (Psalm 2:10-12 NIV)

"Kiss the Son" means *Honor Him!* Listen to what Jesus the Messiah said one day to a religious crowd that mocked Him because He was calling God His Father. Jesus told them:

> [22]**"For the Father judges no one**, but he has given all judgment to the Son, [23]that all may honor the Son, even as they honor the Father. He who doesn't honor the Son doesn't honor the Father who sent him.

> [24]**"Most certainly I tell you, he who hears my word** and believes him who sent me has eternal life, and doesn't come into judgment, but has passed out of death into life (John 5:22-24)

Do you honor the Son?

Thank you for listening. We invite you to join in next time as we think our way through another profound psalm written by the prophet David.

God bless you as you give serious thought to what King David wrote:

> **Kiss the Son.... Blessed are all who take refuge in him.**
> (Psalm 2:11-12 NIV)

Program 51

More from the Psalms

Psalm 22

L ast time we examined the first two chapters in the book of Psalms. It would be great if we had the time on our broadcast to read and discuss every chapter, but since the book of Psalms contains one hundred and fifty chapters, that will not be possible.

But before we close this book we want to look into one more psalm that God put into the mind of David: *Psalm 22*. This chapter is very important, because it predicts how the Messiah would suffer and die to pay the debt of sin for all the children of Adam. In this chapter, David, who lived a thousand years before the Messiah came, prophesied some thirty events which would take place on the day that the Messiah was to die. When we read the Gospel (*Injil*) which contains the story of the Messiah, we will see that everything took place precisely as God's prophet, David, had predicted. This is why we can be certain that David's words did not come from his own mind, but from the mind of God. Only God can predict the future with perfect accuracy.

Now let us listen to what the prophet David wrote in the twenty-second Psalm where he recorded the thoughts which would be in the mind of the Messiah on the day that He would suffer and die for the sins of the world. Listen.

> [1]**My God, my God, why have you forsaken me?** Why are you so far from helping me, and from the words of my groaning? … [3]But you are holy, you who inhabit the praises of Israel. … [6]But I am a worm, and no man; a reproach of men, and despised by the people. … [14]I am poured out like water. All my bones are

out of joint. My heart is like wax. It is melted within me. [15]My strength is dried up like a potsherd. My tongue sticks to the roof of my mouth. You have brought me into the dust of death. [16]...A company of evildoers have enclosed me. They have pierced my hands and feet. (Psalm 22:1,3,6,14-16)

Let us pause here briefly. Did you grasp what the prophet David wrote about the Messiah? A thousand years before the Messiah came into the world, David had written: **A company of evildoers have enclosed me. They have pierced my hands and feet.**

With these words David foretold that the sons of Adam would pierce the hands and feet of the Messiah by nailing Him to a cross. Why did the prophet David write in the Psalms that evil men would pierce the Messiah's hands and feet? Why should the Messiah die such a painful and shameful death? Why would God allow men to murder the holy Redeemer whom He sent?

The word of God gives us the answer. It was necessary for the Redeemer to suffer such pain and shame and to die such an excruciating death in order to take our place and bear for us the punishment that our sin requires. Since the payment of sin is death and eternal punishment in hell, it was necessary that the Messiah taste the separation and horror of hell which we deserve because of our sin. The LORD God out of His great love and grace planned to send the Redeemer, who was unstained by sin, so that He, of His own free will, might **taste of death for everyone.** (Hebrews 2:9) In this way God could open for the children of Adam a way of forgiveness from sin and a door to eternal life, without compromising His justice. The Messiah would pay the penalty for our sins. His sufferings and death are the reason that God can pardon sin and declare as righteous who believe in Him.

What the prophet David wrote concerning the Messiah's death is truly amazing. Think of it: A thousand years before the Messiah was born, David wrote in detail how the Redeemer would suffer upon a cross to which He would be nailed. Perhaps what we need to understand and remember is this: The Romans are the ones who established the method of execution called *crucifixion* – the most horrific (state-sponsored) method of execution ever devised. To add public shame to excruciating pain, the Roman soldiers stripped victims naked before driving nails through their hands and feet, into a cross or tree.

When David wrote about this in the Psalms, the nation of Rome (Roman Empire) did not yet exist. Yet God inspired His prophet to write about the Messiah's death on a cross long before it happened so that we might know that His suffering and death on a Roman cross was God's plan to save us from our sin and shame, and from Satan, death, and eternal hell.

The truth in this chapter is perfectly clear, and we should pay attention to it. However, not everyone accepts this message from God. To this day, some contradict what God's prophet David wrote in the Psalms concerning the Messiah's death on the cross. They say, "God would never allow the Messiah to die such a shameful and painful death." Those who say this are ignorant of the scriptures of the prophets and of God's plan to rescue sinners. Dear listening friends, be careful not to ignore God's way of salvation. Wolof wisdom says: *Before you know it, ignorance will kill you.* And God's word says: **The message of the cross is foolish to those who are headed for destruction! But we who are being saved know it is the very power of God.** (1 Corinthians 1:18 NLT)

Now let us go deeper into what the prophet David wrote about the circumstances of the Messiah's sufferings. David wrote this prayer that would be in the mind and heart of our Savior as He hung on the cross for our sins:

> [7]**All those who see me mock me.** They insult me with their lips. They shake their heads, saying, [8]"He trusts in the LORD. Let him deliver him. Let him rescue him, since he delights in him." … [14]I am poured out like water. All my bones are out of joint. My heart is like wax. It is melted within me. [15]My strength is dried up like a potsherd. My tongue sticks to the roof of my mouth. You have brought me into the dust of death. [16]For

dogs have surrounded me. A company of evildoers have enclosed me. They have pierced my hands and feet. [17]I can count all of my bones. They look and stare at me. [18]They divide my garments among them. They cast lots for my clothing. (Psalm 22:1,7-8,14-18)

With these words, David was predicting that after men nailed our Redeemer to the cross, they would insult Him, mock Him, stare at Him and gamble among themselves for his clothes. This is exactly what happened a thousand years after David wrote it. Listen to what is written in the Gospel:

> [35]**When they had crucified him**, they divided his clothing among them, casting lots, [36]and they sat and watched him there.…[39]Those who passed by blasphemed him, wagging their heads [40]and saying, "…If you are the Son of God, come down from the cross"

> [41]**Likewise the chief priests also mocking** with the scribes, the Pharisees, and the elders, said, [42]"He saved others, but he can't save himself. If he is the King of Israel, let him come down from the cross now, and we will believe in him. [43]He trusts in God. Let God deliver him now, if he wants him; for he said, 'I am the Son of God.'" (Matthew 27:35-36,39-43)

Thus the Gospel confirms the fulfilment of what David wrote.

We also heard today how David had foretold that the Messiah would thirst and suffer greatly in His body and in the depths of His soul and spirit. That is why the Messiah says in the first verse, **"My God, my God, why have you forsaken me?"**

Why did the Messiah cry out on the cross, **"My God, my God, why have you forsaken me?"** Because, as it also says in Psalm 22, God **is holy** (Psalm 22:3) and cannot tolerate sin. As the past, present, and future sins of the world were loaded onto the Messiah, God in heaven had to look away because, as the Scripture says: **[His] eyes are too pure to look on evil.** (Habakkuk 1:13 NIV) The Scripture also says that **God made [the Messiah] who had no sin to be [the sin** offering] for us, so that in him we might become the righteous-ness of God. (2 Corinthians 5:21 NIV)

And, God be praised, there is something else the prophet David predicted in the Psalms – some very good news! In the sixteenth chapter, David wrote down the thoughts and words of the Messiah, saying: You [God] will not leave my soul in Sheol neither will you allow your holy one to see corruption. You will show me the path of life. (Psalm 16:10-11) In this way, David predicted that God would raise the Messiah from the grave and open a door to eternal life for all who trust in Him. The Gospel tells us that [Jesus the Messiah] died for our sins according to the Scriptures, that he was buried, that he was raised on the third day according to the Scriptures. (1 Corinthians 15:3-4 NIV)

In those same Scriptures, David also foretold that after the Lord rose from the dead, He would ascend back up to heaven, and sit at God's right hand, until He returns to judge the people of the earth. That is what David wrote in the Psalms, chapter 110, saying: The LORD says to my Lord: "Sit at my right hand, until I make your enemies a footstool for your feet." (Psalm 110:1)

At the end of chapter 22, the prophet David writes:

> [27]All the ends of the earth shall remember and turn to the LORD. All the relatives of the nations shall worship before you…. [30]Posterity shall serve him. Future generations shall be told about the Lord. [31]They shall come and shall declare his righteousness to a people that shall be born, for he has done it. (Psalm 22:27,30-31)

Don't miss the concluding words: He has done it. What would the Messiah do? He would die in the place of sinners. He would fulfill all that God had promised Adam and Eve about the Redeemer who would provide a righteous way of forgiveness for them and their descendants. The Messiah would die, as the Scripture says, once for [our] sins, the righteous for the unrighteous, to bring [us] to God. (1 Peter 3:18)

Through His death on the cross, He would fulfill and abolish the symbolic animal sacrifices which God required from sinners in earlier times. Like the ram that died in the place of Abraham's son, *Jesus the Lamb of God* would die in the place of sinners as the final and perfect Sacrifice for sin.

This is God's good news to you: The Messiah died in *your* place. Place *your* faith in Him and you will be saved from eternal judgment. The door of salvation is wide open to all who believe it. That is why, just before Jesus the Messiah died, He cried out, **"It is finished!"** (John 19:30) Yes, **HE has done it!** (Psalm 22:31) And God confirmed His acceptance of the Messiah's perfect sacrifice by raising Him from the dead on the third day. We will see this in detail when we study the Gospel record (*Injil*).

Meanwhile, may we remember this: One thousand years before the birth of Jesus Christ, the prophet David predicted that wicked men would **pierce His hands and feet.** The Messiah chose to suffer in this way because He loves *you* and wants *you* to be with Him forever. Jesus said:

> [11]**"I am the good shepherd.** The good shepherd lays down his life for the sheep.... [17]I lay down my life, that I may take it again. [18]No one takes it away from me, but I lay it down by myself. I have power to lay it down, and I have power to take it again. I received this commandment from my Father." (John 10:11,17-18)

Dear friend, have you ever thanked the LORD God for the Good Shepherd who choose to lay down His life for you?

May God make clear to you everything we have read today. God willing, in our next program, we will move forward in the writings of the prophets to learn from King David's son, Solomon.

May God bless you and instruct your mind and heart as you think about what the prophet David wrote 1000 years before the Messiah came into the world to die on a Roman cross for our sins:

They have pierced my hands and feet. (Psalm 22:16)

Program 52

The Prophet Solomon

1 Kings 2-10; Psalm 72

I f God appeared to you one night and said, "Ask for whatever you want, and I will give it to you," what would you choose? A long life? Great riches? Fame? Or something else? One day God appeared to Solomon, the son of David, in a dream and said to him, "Ask for whatever you want me to give you." Do you know what Solomon chose? We will hear his answer shortly.

In the past six lessons we have been looking into the story of the prophet of God, David. We have read some of the songs he wrote in the book of Psalms. In our last lesson we saw how David prophesied that the sons of Adam would kill the Messiah by piercing His hands and His feet. David also foretold that God would raise the Messiah from the dead. Today we plan to leave the story of David and move on to the story of his son, Solomon.[78]

In the first book of Kings, chapter 2, the Holy Scripture says:

> [1]**Now the days of David came near that he should die**; and he commanded Solomon his son, saying, [2]"I am going the way of all the earth. You be strong therefore, and show yourself a man; [3]and keep the instruction of the LORD your God, to walk in his ways … [as] written in the law of Moses, that you may prosper in all that you do, and wherever you turn yourself."
>
> [10]**David slept with his fathers**, and was buried in David's city. [11]The days that David reigned over Israel were forty years…. [12]Solomon sat on David his father's throne; and his kingdom was firmly established. (1 Kings 2:1-3,10-12)

[3]**Solomon loved the LORD**, walking in the statutes of David his father …[5]The LORD appeared to Solomon in a dream by night; and God said, "Ask for what I should give you." [6]Solomon said, "…[7]Now, the LORD my God, you have made your servant king instead of David my father. I am just a little child. I don't know how to go out or come in… [9]Give your servant therefore an understanding heart to judge your people, that I may discern between good and evil; for who is able to judge this great people of yours?" [10]This request pleased the Lord, that Solomon had asked this thing.

[11]**God said to him**, "Because you have asked this thing, and have not asked for yourself long life, nor have you asked for riches for yourself, nor have you asked for the life of your enemies, but have asked for yourself understanding to discern justice; [12]behold, I have done according to your word. Behold, I have given you a wise and understanding heart; so that there has been no one like you before you, and after you none will arise like you. [13]I have also given you that which you have not asked, both riches and honor, so that there will not be any among the kings like you for all your days. [14]If you will walk in my ways, to keep my statutes and my commandments, as your father David walked, then I will lengthen your days." [15]Solomon awoke; and behold, it was a dream. Then he came to Jerusalem, and stood before the ark of The LORD's covenant, and offered up burnt offerings, offered peace offerings, and made a feast for all his servants.

[16]**Then two women who were prostitutes** came to the king, and stood before him. [17]The one woman said, "Oh, my lord, I and this woman dwell in one house. I delivered a child with her in the house. [18]The third day after I delivered, this woman delivered also. We were together. There was no stranger with us in the house, just us two in the house. [19]This woman's child died in the night, because she lay on it. [20]She arose at midnight, and took my son from beside me, while your servant slept, and laid it in her bosom, and laid her dead child in my bosom.

²¹When I rose in the morning to nurse my child, behold, it was dead; but when I had looked at it in the morning, behold, it was not my son, whom I bore." ²²The other woman said, "No; but the living one is my son, and the dead one is your son." The first one said, "No; but the dead one is your son, and the living one is my son." They argued like this before the king.

²³**Then [King Solomon] said**, "One says, 'This is my son who lives, and your son is the dead;' and the other says, 'No; but your son is the dead one, and my son is the living one.'" ²⁴The king said, "Get me a sword." So they brought a sword before the king. ²⁵The king said, "Divide the living child in two, and give half to the one, and half to the other."

²⁶**Then the woman whose the living child** was spoke to the king, for her heart yearned over her son, and she said, "Oh, my lord, give her the living child, and in no way kill him!" But the other said, "He shall be neither mine nor yours. Divide him." ²⁷Then the king answered, "Give her the living child, and definitely do not kill him. She is his mother." ²⁸All Israel heard of the judgment which the king had judged; and they feared the king; for they saw that the wisdom of God was in him, to do justice. (1 Kings 3:3,5-7,9-28)

²⁹**God gave Solomon abundant wisdom** and understanding, and very great understanding, even as the sand that is on the seashore. ³⁰Solomon's wisdom excelled the wisdom of all the children of the east and all the wisdom of Egypt. ³¹For he was wiser than all men;... and his fame was in all the nations all around. ³²He spoke three thousand proverbs; and his songs numbered one thousand five. ... ³⁴People of all nations came to hear the wisdom of Solomon, sent by all kings of the earth, who had heard of his wisdom. (1 Kings 4:29-32,34)

Next, the Scriptures record that at that time there was a queen, the queen of Sheba, who had heard of the profound wisdom and great majesty of Solomon. So the queen made plans to go to Jerusalem to visit Solomon, to know whether or not what she had heard about him was the truth. This queen lived in a land far from

Jerusalem, in the land of Sheba, which lies south of Saudi Arabia. The country of Sheba is known today as Yemen. Between that country and Jerusalem is a distance of about 2,000 kilometers. But that great distance over the hostile desert did not discourage the queen of Sheba from traveling to visit Solomon. The Scripture says:

> ¹**When the queen of Sheba heard** of the fame of Solomon concerning the LORD's name, she came to test him with hard questions. ²She came to Jerusalem with a very great caravan, with camels that bore spices, very much gold, and precious stones; and when she had come to Solomon, she talked with him about all that was in her heart. ³Solomon answered all her questions. There wasn't anything hidden from the king which he didn't tell her. ⁴When the queen of Sheba had seen all the wisdom of Solomon, the house that he had built, ⁵the food of his table, the sitting of his servants, the attendance of his officials, their clothing, his cup bearers, and his ascent by which he went up to the LORD's house; there was no more spirit in her.

> ⁶**She said to the king**, "It was a true report that I heard in my own land of your acts, and of your wisdom. ⁷However I didn't believe the words until I came and my eyes had seen it. Behold, not even half was told me! Your wisdom and prosperity exceed the fame which I heard. ⁸Happy are your men, happy are these your servants, who stand continually before you, who hear your wisdom. ⁹Blessed is the LORD your God, who delighted in you, to set you on the throne of Israel. Because the LORD loved Israel forever, therefore he made you king, to do justice and righteousness." (1 Kings 10:1-9)

This is where we must stop today in the story of King Solomon, but did you know that 900 years after the time of Solomon, the Messiah spoke about the queen of Sheba? Jesus the Messiah said, **"The Queen of the South will rise up in the judgment with this generation and will condemn it, for she came from the ends of the earth to hear the wisdom of Solomon; and behold, someone greater than Solomon is here."** (Matthew 12:42)

Did you hear what the Messiah said? He said that the queen of Sheba's investigation of the glory and wisdom of Solomon would condemn all those who refuse to investigate the glory and wisdom of the Messiah. The queen of Sheba did everything in her power to see the glory of Solomon and listen to his wisdom. She even traveled 4,000 kilometers, round trip, to know if what she had heard was true.

There is an important lesson for us here. The Messiah, who came from heaven, far exceeds Solomon in glory, in wisdom, in knowledge and in power, yet most of the children of Adam do not recognize His glory, nor are they willing to investigate the matter to know the truth. That is why the Messiah said: **"The Queen of the South will rise up in the judgment with this generation and will condemn it, for she came from the ends of the earth to hear the wisdom of Solomon; and behold, someone greater than Solomon is here."** (Matthew 12:42)

Dear friends, do you recognize the glory of the holy Messiah whom God sent? Or do you put Him on the same level as the prophets? Do you remember what the title *Messiah* means? Yes, it means *the One whom God has appointed.* The Messiah is the One whom God chose to be the Savior and Judge of the world. Yet, to this very day, most people ignore Him. They do not know who He is because they have never searched for Him in the writings of the prophets.

Our time is almost up, but before we bid you farewell, we want to mention that King Solomon wrote three wonderful and profound books which are a part of the Holy Scriptures. Those books are: *Proverbs, Ecclesiastes,*[79] and *the Song of Songs.* Like his father David, Solomon wrote some of the psalms. To conclude today's program, we would like to read part of the seventy-second psalm, which the prophet Solomon wrote. In this song, Solomon predicts that the Messiah will return to earth one day to judge mankind. Listen to what King Solomon prophesied about the perfect King, who surpassed him in wisdom and glory. Solomon wrote:

> [2]**He will judge your people with righteousness**, and your poor with justice.… [8]He shall have dominion also from sea to sea…

---

79 Literally: *the Preacher*

to the ends of the earth. [9]Those who dwell in the wilderness shall bow before him. His enemies shall lick the dust. [10]...The kings of Sheba and Seba [in Arabia] shall offer gifts. [11]Yes, all kings shall fall down before him. All nations shall serve him. ... [15]They shall live!

[17]**His name endures forever.** His name continues as long as the sun. Men shall be blessed by him. All nations will call him blessed. [18]Praise be to the LORD God, the God of Israel, who alone does marvelous deeds. [19]Blessed be his glorious name forever! Let the whole earth be filled with his glory! Amen and amen. (Psalm 72:2,8-11,15,17-19)

This is how King Solomon foretold that one day all the people of the earth will submit to the Messiah, the King of kings and the Judge of the world. Of course, what God wants is for each of us to submit to Him today, while we are free to choose.

How about you? Are you truly submitted to the LORD God? Do you recognize the glory and authority of the Messiah whom He has sent and will send back to judge the world in righteousness? Or do you place Jesus the Messiah on the same level as the prophets?

Whether people believe it or not, Jesus the Messiah is the One about whom all the prophets wrote. The Scripture says: **All the prophets testify about him, that through his name everyone who believes in him will receive [forgiveness] of sins.** (Acts 10:43)

Do you believe the prophets? (Acts 26:27)

Thank you for listening. God willing, next time, we will learn about the prophet Elijah who called down fire from heaven.

God bless you as you ponder this word spoken by the Messiah when He was on earth:

Someone greater than Solomon is here. (Matthew 12:42)

Program 53
The Prophet Elijah

1 Kings 6-18

I n the last lesson, we studied the story of Solomon, son of the prophet David. We saw how God gave Solomon great wisdom and discernment. In the time of King Solomon, Jerusalem was the most beautiful city in the world. But of all the buildings Solomon built in Jerusalem, nothing surpassed the beauty of the Temple of the LORD. King Solomon designed the Temple to replace the tent of meeting, the special tent of worship, that God had directed Moses and the Israelites to make in the wilderness, so that the LORD God could dwell among them.

King Solomon employed two hundred thousand workers for seven years to build this beautiful place of worship. Today one can still see in Jerusalem the great stones of part of the foundation of the temple. When the temple was finished, the priests sacrificed thousands of sheep and bulls to symbolize the Redeemer who would come and shed His blood for sinners. This is how they consecrated (offered, devoted) to God the temple that they had built for His name. After they had offered those animals and burnt them on the bronze altar of the temple, the priests carried the ark of the covenant, which had been in the tent of meeting, and placed it in the Holiest Place (Holy of Holies) of the new temple. When the priests left the Holiest Place, immediately the glory of the LORD filled the room. Just as the glory of God had filled the tent of meeting which Moses and the Israelites had made in the wilderness, so the glory of God filled the Temple that Solomon built in Jerusalem.

Concerning the rest of King Solomon's life, the Scriptures tell us that the latter part of his reign was not like the beginning. Listen to what is written in the first book of Kings, chapter 11. Again we notice that the holy word of God does not ignore or hide the sins of the prophets. The Scripture says:

> [1]**Now king Solomon loved many foreign women**…. [4]When Solomon was old, his wives turned away his heart after other gods; and his heart was not perfect with the LORD his God, as the heart of David his father was. (1 Kings 11:1,4)

Then Solomon built on the hills east of Jerusalem high places for all of his foreign wives, to burn incense and offer sacrifices to their gods. God was angry with Solomon, because he had turned his back on the word of God. So the LORD said to Solomon:

> [11]**"Because this is done by you**, and you have not kept my covenant and my statutes, which I have commanded you, I will surely tear the kingdom from you, and will give it to your servant. [12]Nevertheless, I will not do it in your days, for David your father's sake; but I will tear it out of your son's hand. [13]However I will not tear away all the kingdom; but I will give one tribe to your son, for David my servant's sake, and for Jerusalem's sake which I have chosen." (1 Kings 11:11-13)

The Scriptures tell us that after Solomon died there was fighting and strife within the nation of Israel. The twelve tribes of Israel, which came from the family of Jacob, split in two, just as God had told Solomon. They were no longer one nation; they became two nations, *Israel* and *Judah*. The ten tribes of Israel in the north of the land formed the kingdom of Israel. The tribe of Judah, joined by the little tribe of Benjamin, formed Judah's southern kingdom. Judah was the tribe of King David and the lineage through which the Messiah would be born. The people of Judah would eventually become known as *Jews*.

Israel and Judah had many kings and most of them turned their backs on the LORD and followed the religions of the nations around them. Among all the kings of Israel, one was more evil and wicked than the others. Do you know who it was? It was King Ahab. Ahab was the eighth king after Solomon.

The Scripture says: **Ahab the son of Omri did that which was evil in the LORD's sight above all that were before him.** (1 Kings 16:30) King Ahab married Jezebel, an evil woman who hated the LORD. Driven by the queen, King Ahab built in Israel a temple to the name of Baal. (Baal was a false god to which the people of Canaan bowed down.) Thus Ahab angered the LORD by leading the Israelites to follow an empty, false religion in submission to its false prophets.

However, at that same time, there was a prophet in Israel who walked with the LORD God. His name was *Elijah*. One day God sent Elijah to King Ahab. Elijah said to Ahab, **"As the LORD, the God of Israel, lives, before whom I stand, there shall not be dew nor rain these years, but according to my word."** (1 Kings 17:1)

And just as the prophet Elijah had predicted, for three and a half years no rain fell on the land of Israel. The famine became severe throughout the country. In chapter 18, the Scripture says:

> [1]**After many days, the LORD's word came to Elijah**, in the third year, saying, "Go, show yourself to Ahab; and I will send rain on the earth." [2]Elijah went to show himself to Ahab.... [17]When Ahab saw Elijah, Ahab said to him, "Is that you, you troubler of Israel?" [18]He answered, "I have not troubled Israel; but you, and your father's house, in that you have forsaken the LORD's commandments, and you have followed the Baals. [19]Now therefore send, and gather to me all Israel to Mount Carmel, and four hundred fifty of the prophets of Baal, and four hundred of the prophets of the Asherah, who eat at Jezebel's table."

> [20]**So Ahab sent to all the children of Israel**, and gathered the prophets together to Mount Carmel. [21]Elijah came near to all the people, and said, "How long will you waver between the two sides? If the LORD is God, follow him; but if Baal, then follow him." The people didn't say a word.

²²**Then Elijah said to the people**, "I, even I only, am left as a prophet of the LORD; but Baal's prophets are four hundred fifty men. ²³Let them therefore give us two bulls; and let them choose one bull for themselves, and cut it in pieces, and lay it on the wood, and put no fire under; and I will dress the other bull, and lay it on the wood, and put no fire under it. ²⁴You call on the name of your god, and I will call on the LORD's name. The God who answers by fire, let him be God." All the people answered, "What you say is good."

²⁵**Elijah said to the prophets of Baal**, "Choose one bull for yourselves, and dress it first; for you are many; and call on the name of your god, but put no fire under it." ²⁶They took the bull which was given them, and they dressed it, and called on the name of Baal from morning even until noon, saying, "Baal, hear us!" But there was no voice, and nobody answered. They leaped about the altar which was made. ²⁷At noon, Elijah mocked them, and said, "Cry aloud; for he is a god. Either he is deep in thought, or he has gone somewhere, or he is on a journey, or perhaps he sleeps and must be awakened." ²⁸They cried aloud, and cut themselves in their way with knives and lances, until the blood gushed out on them. ²⁹When midday was past, they prophesied until the time of the evening offering; but there was no voice, no answer, and nobody paid attention.

³⁰**Elijah said to all the people**, "Come near to me!"; and all the people came near to him. He repaired the LORD's altar that had been thrown down. ³¹Elijah took twelve stones, according to the number of the tribes of the sons of Jacob, to whom the LORD's word came, saying, "Israel shall be your name." ³²With the stones he built an altar in the LORD's name. He made a trench around the altar, large enough to contain [about 17 liters] of seed. ³³He put the wood in order, and cut the bull in pieces, and laid it on the wood. He said, "Fill four jars with water, and pour it on the burnt offering, and on the wood."

³⁴**He said, "Do it a second time;"** and they did it the second time. He said, "Do it a third time;" and they did it the third time.

³⁵The water ran around the altar; and he also filled the trench with water.

³⁶**At the time of the evening offering**, Elijah the prophet came near, and said, "The LORD, the God of Abraham, of Isaac, and of Israel, let it be known today that you are God in Israel, and that I am your servant, and that I have done all these things at your word. ³⁷Hear me, LORD, hear me, that this people may know that you, the LORD, are God, and that you have turned their heart back again."

³⁸**Then the LORD's fire fell**, and consumed the burnt offering, the wood, the stones, and the dust, and licked up the water that was in the trench. ³⁹When all the people saw it, they fell on their faces. They said, "The LORD, he is God! The LORD, he is God!"

⁴⁰**Elijah said to them**, "Seize the prophets of Baal! Don't let one of them escape!" They seized them; and Elijah brought them down to the brook Kishon, and killed them there. ⁴¹Elijah said to Ahab, "Get up, eat and drink; for there is the sound of abundance of rain." ⁴²So Ahab went up to eat and to drink. Elijah went up to the top of Carmel; and he bowed himself down on the earth, and put his face between his knees.... ⁴⁵In a little while, the sky grew black with clouds and wind, and there was a great rain. (1 Kings 18:1-2,17-42,45)

Did you hear the question the prophet Elijah put before the people of Israel? Before he challenged the four hundred and fifty false prophets of Baal, Elijah asked the people, **"How long will you waver between the two sides? If the LORD is God, follow him; but if Baal, then follow him."** (1 Kings 18:21)

At first, the Israelites gave no response, but when they saw how the LORD answered the prayer of Elijah in raining fire down from heaven upon his altar, the whole crowd fell down prostrate and cried, **"The LORD, he is God! The LORD, he is God!"**

That is how in a single day God's prophet Elijah publicly exposed and discredited the false prophets of Baal and turned the hearts of the Israelites back to the LORD their God.

Why did God answer Elijah's prayer? Because Elijah loved the LORD and believed His word and because God wanted His people to turn back to Him. *Why did God ignore the prayer of the prophets of Baal?* Because they ignored God's word and followed their own religious traditions. They were zealous in observing their rituals, but they did not serve the living God – therefore all their religious zeal was utterly worthless. They were like the men in the proverb:

Ten men dig a deep hole, ten men fill it – there's lots of dust, but no hole.

Similarly, the false prophets of Baal had plenty of religion; they made a lot of noise with their prayers and sacrifices, but it was all in vain because it was not founded upon the word of the Living God. *Lots of dust, but no hole.*

On that momentous day, Elijah challenged the Israelites to make a choice. Who will you follow? The LORD God and His way of eternal life? Or man's religion with its empty rituals? **"How long will you waver between the two sides?"** How long will you waver between the truth of God and the lying traditions of men?

The Holy Scripture says: **No one can serve two masters, for either he will hate the one and love the other, or else he will be devoted to one and despise the other.** (Matthew 6:24) You cannot mix serving the LORD God and serving an empty religion.

Dear friends, thank you for listening. Next time we plan to hear the story of *a prophet who spent three days inside a huge fish.* Do you know the name of this prophet?

We bid you farewell with the prophet Elijah's question:

How long will you waver between the two sides?
If the LORD is God, follow him; but if Baal, then follow him.
(1 Kings 18:21)

The Prophet Jonah

Jonah

I n our last program, we looked into the story of God's prophet, Elijah. The power of the Spirit of God was upon Elijah. He prayed to God that it would not rain and there was no rain in Israel for three and a half years. Also, Elijah confronted the prophets of Baal, exposing their false religion before all the Israelites. In this way God used the prophet Elijah to turn the hearts of many Israelites back to the LORD their God.

Today in our continuing journey through the Scriptures of the prophets we want to hear the story of another prophet, who lived some time after Elijah. His name is Jonah.[80]

We are reading in the book of Jonah, the first chapter:

> **¹Now the LORD's word came to Jonah** the son of Amittai, saying, ²"Arise, go to Nineveh, that great city, and preach against it, for their wickedness has come up before me." (Jonah 1:1-2)

Do you understand what the LORD commanded Jonah to do? God told him to go and warn the people of the city of Nineveh to turn from their evil ways or else He would destroy them. Nineveh was the capital of the nation of Assyria, and the people of Assyria were a wicked people who wanted to destroy the Israelites.

Why did the LORD God want to send Jonah to those foreigners who despised and hated the Israelites? Did God also care about Israel's enemies? Yes, He did. God was about to judge the people of Nineveh because their sins had reached to heaven. But God

---

80 Arabic: *Yunus*

takes no pleasure in destroying sinners. God wants everyone to repent, believe His word, have their minds and hearts transformed and be saved. That is why the LORD commanded Jonah to go to the people of Nineveh and warn them so that they too could repent of their sin, turn to God, and be saved.

But Jonah did not want to go and warn his enemies. He did not want to be a prophet to the city of Nineveh. God wanted the people of Nineveh to repent so that He could have mercy on them, but Jonah wanted God to punish them. So Jonah refused his assignment and tried to run away from the LORD God.

Where could Jonah flee to get away from the presence of God? Let us continue the story to see what Jonah did. The Scripture says:

> ³**But Jonah rose up to flee to Tarshish** [that is, a place very far from Nineveh] from the presence of the LORD. He went down to Joppa, and found a ship going to Tarshish; so he paid its fare, and went down into it, to go with them to Tarshish from the presence of the LORD. ⁴But the LORD sent out a great wind on the sea, and there was a mighty storm on the sea, so that the ship was likely to break up. ⁵Then the mariners were afraid, and every man cried to his god. They threw the cargo that was in the ship into the sea to lighten the ship. But Jonah had gone down into the innermost parts of the ship, and he was laying down, and was fast asleep. ⁶So the ship master came to him, and said to him, "What do you mean, sleeper? Arise, call on your God! Maybe your God will notice us, so that we won't perish." ⁷They all said to each other, "Come! Let's cast lots, that we may know who is responsible for this evil that is on us." So they cast lots, and the lot fell on Jonah.

> ⁸**Then they asked him**, "Tell us, please, for whose cause this evil is on us. What is your occupation? Where do you come from? What is your country? Of what people are you?" ⁹He said to them, "I am a Hebrew, and I fear the LORD, the God of heaven, who has made the sea and the dry land." ¹⁰Then the men were exceedingly afraid, and said to him, "What have

you done?" For the men knew that he was fleeing from the presence of the LORD, because he had told them. ¹¹Then they said to him, "What shall we do to you, that the sea may be calm to us?" For the sea grew more and more stormy. ¹²He said to them, "Take me up, and throw me into the sea. Then the sea will be calm for you; for I know that because of me this great storm is on you." ¹³Nevertheless the men rowed hard to get them back to the land; but they could not, for the sea grew more and more stormy against them.

¹⁴**Therefore they cried to the LORD**, and said, "We beg you, LORD, we beg you, don't let us die for this man's life, and don't lay on us innocent blood; for you, the LORD, have done as it pleased you." ¹⁵So they took up Jonah, and threw him into the sea; and the sea ceased its raging. ¹⁶Then the men feared the LORD exceedingly; and they offered a sacrifice to the LORD, and made vows. ¹⁷The LORD prepared a huge fish to swallow up Jonah, and Jonah was in the belly of the fish three days and three nights. (Jonah 1:3-17)

Let us pause here. Up to this point, we see how God pursued Jonah, His fleeing prophet. Jonah could run, but he could not escape the hand of God. Why did God pursue him? It was because He loved Jonah and wanted to teach him some important lessons. He wanted Jonah's heart to be more like God's heart. He also wanted Jonah to deliver His message of repentance and hope to the people of Nineveh. That is why God prepared a huge fish to swallow him but not kill him.

Poor Jonah – because of his disobedience he now found himself in the belly of a huge fish! What could he do to save himself? Nothing. Nothing except call out to the LORD God. Only God could save him.

For three days, God watched over Jonah inside the sea creature. During that time Jonah did a lot of praying. On the third day, he submitted his will to God's will, and said, **"I will pay that which I have vowed. Salvation belongs to the LORD."** (Jonah 2:9) The moment Jonah said, **"Salvation belongs to the LORD,"** the LORD spoke to the fish, and it vomited out Jonah on the dry land. (Jonah 2:9-10)

In next chapter we read:

> ¹**The LORD's word came to Jonah** the second time, saying,
> ²"Arise, go to Nineveh, that great city, and preach to it the
> message that I give you." ³So Jonah arose, and went to
> Nineveh, according to the LORD's word. Now Nineveh was
> an exceedingly great city, three days' journey across. ⁴Jonah
> began to enter into the city a day's journey, and he cried out,
> and said, "In forty days, Nineveh will be overthrown!"
>
> ⁵**The people of Nineveh believed God**; and they proclaimed
> a fast, and put on sackcloth, from their greatest even to their
> least. ⁶The news reached the king of Nineveh, and he arose
> from his throne, and took off his royal robe, covered himself
> with sackcloth, and sat in ashes. ⁷He made a proclamation and
> published through Nineveh by the decree of the king and his
> nobles, saying, "Let neither man nor animal, herd nor flock, taste
> anything; let them not feed, nor drink water; ⁸but let them be
> covered with sackcloth, both man and animal, and let them cry
> mightily to God. Yes, let them turn everyone from his evil way,
> and from the violence that is in his hands. ⁹Who knows whether
> God will not turn and relent, and turn away from his fierce anger,
> so that we might not perish?" ¹⁰God saw their works, that they
> turned from their evil way. God relented of the disaster which he
> said he would do to them, and he didn't do it. (Jonah 3:1-10)

So God had mercy on the people of Nineveh, because they
believed the word which He sent to them through His servant
Jonah. With broken hearts, the Ninevites repented of their wicked
ways and turned to the LORD.

But Jonah was not happy that God showed mercy to the people of
Nineveh. The Scripture says:

> ¹**But it displeased Jonah exceedingly**, and he was angry. ²He
> prayed to the LORD, and said, "Please, the LORD, wasn't this what
> I said when I was still in my own country? Therefore I hurried
> to flee to Tarshish, for I knew that you are a gracious God, and

merciful, slow to anger, and abundant in loving kindness, and you relent of doing harm. ³Therefore now, LORD, take, I beg you, my life from me; for it is better for me to die than to live."

⁴**The LORD said, "Is it right for you to be angry?"** ⁵Then Jonah went out of the city, and sat on the east side of the city, and there made himself a booth, and sat under it in the shade, until he might see what would become of the city. ⁶The LORD God prepared a vine, and made it to come up over Jonah, that it might be a shade over his head, to deliver him from his discomfort. So Jonah was exceedingly glad because of the vine.

⁷**But God prepared a worm at dawn the next day**, and it chewed on the vine, so that it withered. ⁸When the sun arose, God prepared a sultry east wind; and the sun beat on Jonah's head, so that he fainted, and requested for himself that he might die, and said, "It is better for me to die than to live." ⁹God said to Jonah, "Is it right for you to be angry about the vine?" He said, "I am right to be angry, even to death." ¹⁰The LORD said, "You have been concerned for the vine, for which you have not labored, neither made it grow; which came up in a night, and perished in a night. ¹¹Shouldn't I be concerned for Nineveh, that great city, in which are more than one hundred twenty thousand persons who can't discern between their right hand and their left hand; and also much livestock?" (Jonah 4:1-11)

That is how the book of Jonah ends.

Listening friends, there is much to be learned about the nature of God and the nature of man from the story of the prophet Jonah. One thing we learn is that God is no respecter of persons.[81] Jonah showed favoritism, but God did not. God's heart was so very different from Jonah's heart. Jonah's heart was full of favoritism, but God's heart is full of compassion for all people. Jonah loved his own people and hated his enemies, but God loved the people of Israel and the people of Nineveh. Jonah wanted the people of Nineveh to perish because they were enemies of Israel, but God wanted them to repent and turn to Him and be saved.

---

81 Literally: God does not show one-sidedness, favoritism

God does not show favoritism. Whoever you are, whatever you are like, God loves you. He hates your sin and rebellion, but He loves *you*. God loves the people of the world and wants everyone to repent and to believe His message of salvation. To repent means to change your mind; to turn from what is false and submit to what is true. To repent is to stop going your own way and to follow God's way.

Some people think that God has arbitrarily chosen some to burn in hell and others to bask in Paradise. While it is true that many people will die in their sins and face God's righteous wrath, it is wicked to think that God wants people to end up in hell.

The Holy Scriptures says: **[God] desires all people to be saved and come to full knowledge of the truth.** (1 Timothy 2:4) Another verse says: **The Lord… is patient with us, not wishing that anyone should perish, but that all should come to repentance.** (2 Peter 3:9)

But the Scripture says that, in the end, the holy LORD God will judge those who refuse **to love the truth and so be saved. … [and] that all will be condemned who have not believed the truth but have delighted in [unrighteousness].** (2 Thessalonians 2:10,12 NIV) This is the word of the LORD.

Yes, God is good and merciful and has provided a way of forgiveness for every person. But God is also holy and must judge every soul who does not accept His righteous way of salvation. As it is written: **[God] desires all people to be saved.** (1 Timothy 2:4) **Unless you repent, you will all perish in the same way.** (Luke 13:3)

In the next program, God willing, we will learn from the prophet Isaiah who wrote down many amazing prophecies about the Redeemer who was to come into the world to save sinners.

God bless you as you remember these two lessons that He wanted to teach His unfaithful prophet, Jonah:

> One: **Salvation belongs to the LORD.** (Jonah 2:9)
> Two: **God doesn't show favoritism.** (Acts 10:34)

The Prophet Isaiah

Isaiah

L ast time we studied the story of the prophet Jonah who tried to run away from the LORD. Jonah did not want to take God's message of repentance and forgiveness to his enemies as the LORD had told him to do. But trying to run from the presence of God is like trying to run from your shadow. God pursued Jonah and arranged to have him swallowed by a great fish. Jonah repented, was rescued, and reluctantly fullfilled his mission in the end.

Today we plan to read about a prophet who came after the time of Jonah and whose name is well known in the Holy Scriptures. This is the prophet *Isaiah*, who lived seven hundred years before the Messiah was born. Isaiah was a priest who worked in the temple which Solomon had built in Jerusalem. Every morning and every evening Isaiah and the other priests had to sacrifice a lamb on the altar. These sacrifices symbolized the Messiah who would shed His blood for the sin of the world. Here is what happened to Isaiah one day when he was offering a sacrifice in the temple. In the book of Isaiah, chapter 6, he wrote:

> ¹**In the year that king Uzziah died**, I saw the Lord sitting on a throne, high and lifted up; and his train filled the temple. ²Above him stood the seraphim. Each one had six wings. With two he covered his face. With two he covered his feet. With two he flew. ³One called to another, and said, "Holy, holy, holy, is the LORD of Armies! The whole earth is full of his glory!"

> ⁴**The foundations of the thresholds shook** at the voice of him who called, and the house was filled with smoke. ⁵Then I said, "Woe is me! For I am undone, because I am a man of unclean

lips, and I dwell among a people of unclean lips: for my eyes have seen the King, the LORD of Armies!" [6]Then one of the seraphim flew to me, having a live coal in his hand, which he had taken with the tongs from off the altar. [7]He touched my mouth with it, and said, "Behold, this has touched your lips; and your iniquity is taken away, and your sin forgiven." [8]I heard the Lord's voice, saying, "Whom shall I send, and who will go for us?" Then I said, "Here I am. Send me!" (Isaiah 6:1-8)

This is how the Lord revealed His glory and His holiness to Isaiah and called him to announce His message to the Israelites, that is, the Jews. God also led Isaiah to write God's message in a book for the benefit of generations to come. The book of Isaiah is lengthy and profound, but today we can summarize Isaiah's main message in two big thoughts.

First, Isaiah told the Jews *the bad news* about their sin and the punishment that they deserved. Second, Isaiah presented to them *the good news* about the holy Messiah who was to come into the world to bear the punishment for their sin.

To repeat, the message of the prophet Isaiah is: 1.) the bad news about sin and its penalty; and 2.) the good news about the promised Savior who would pay the penalty of sin for sinners.

Let us first read a little about the bad news God communicated to Isaiah so that he might announce it to the Jews and to anyone who had ears to hear. Isaiah wrote:

[2]**Hear, heavens, and listen, earth; for the LORD has spoken:** "I have nourished and brought up children and they have rebelled against me. [3]The ox knows his owner, and the donkey his master's crib; but Israel doesn't know. My people don't consider." [4]Ah sinful nation, a people loaded with iniquity, offspring of evildoers, children who deal corruptly! They have forsaken the LORD. They have despised the Holy One of Israel. They are estranged and backward. … [13]Bring no more vain offerings. Incense is an abomination to me. New moons, Sabbaths, and convocations: I can't stand evil assemblies. [14]My soul hates your New Moons and your appointed feasts.

They are a burden to me. I am weary of bearing them. [15]When you spread out your hands, I will hide my eyes from you. Yes, when you make many prayers, I will not hear. (Isaiah 1:2-4,13-15)

That is how the LORD rebuked the people of Israel for their hypocrisy. He summarized their sin with these words: **The Lord said, "Because this people draws near with their mouth and honors me with their lips, but they have removed their heart far from me, and their fear of me is a commandment of men which has been taught."** (Matthew 15:8; Isaiah 29:13)

After Isaiah rebuked the people for their stubbornness and sinfulness, he began to tell them God's good news, which has the power to purify the hearts of all who believe it. Let us listen to some prophecies God revealed to his prophet about the Messiah who was to come. The prophet Isaiah wrote:

"Come now, and let's reason together," says the LORD: "Though your sins are as scarlet, they shall be as white as snow. Though they are red like crimson, they shall be as wool." (Isaiah 1:18)

[1]**Comfort, comfort my people, says your God.** ... [3]The voice of one who calls out, "Prepare the way of the LORD in the wilderness! Make a level highway in the desert for our God. [4]Every valley shall be exalted, and every mountain and hill shall be made low. The uneven shall be made level, and the rough places a plain. [5]The LORD's glory shall be revealed, and all flesh shall see it together; for the mouth of the LORD has spoken it." ... [9]You who tell good news to Zion, go up on a high mountain. You who tell good news to Jerusalem, lift up your voice with strength! Lift it up! Don't be afraid! Say to the cities of Judah, "Behold, your God!" (Isaiah 40:1,3-5,9)

Therefore the Lord himself will give you a sign. Behold, the virgin will conceive, and bear a son, and shall call his name Immanuel," which is, being interpreted, "God with us." (Isaiah 7:14; Matthew 1:23)

The LORD was revealing a great mystery through the prophet Isaiah. God planned to send His Spirit into the womb of a virgin (a woman who had never been intimate with a man). This is how the sinless, holy Messiah would be born into the world.

As you know, the Messiah had no earthly father. Before He was born, He was in heaven, because He is **the Word who was with God in the beginning.** (John 1:1-5,14 NIV) He is also the One Isaiah saw in his vision of **the Lord seated on a throne, high and lifted up.** (Isaiah 6:1; John 12:41) According to Isaiah's prophecy, the Messiah would be **God with us** on earth – in a human body. God, who is Spirit, planned to place His Spirit and Word into the womb of a virgin and to be born into the world as a baby. That is what Isaiah was foretelling when he wrote: **The virgin will conceive, and bear a son, and shall call his name Immanuel – which is, being interpreted, *God with us.*** (Isaiah 7:14)

Isaiah writes much about the coming of the Messiah, what He would be like and what He would do. For example, he wrote:

> ²**The people who walked in darkness** have seen a great light. The light has shined on those who lived in the land of the shadow of death. … ⁶For a child is born to us. A son is given to us; and the government will be on his shoulders. His name will be called Wonderful Counselor, Mighty God, Everlasting Father, Prince of Peace. (Isaiah 9:2,6)

> ⁵**Then the eyes of the blind will be opened**, and the ears of the deaf will be unstopped. ⁶Then the lame man will leap like a deer, and the tongue of the mute will sing; for waters will break out in the wilderness, and streams in the desert. (Isaiah 35:5-6)

In these verses, Isaiah foretold that the Messiah would bring God's holiness and compassion and power to earth. He also prophesied that the Messiah would do mighty works like no one had ever done so that people could recognize that He was the promised Messiah about whom all the prophets wrote. Isaiah announced that the Savior would be called: **Wonderful Counselor, Mighty God, Everlasting Father, Prince of Peace.** (Isaiah 9:6) The prophet Isaiah did not do like people today who want to put the Messiah on the same level as the prophets. Isaiah recognized the infinite glory of the One who was to come from heaven to earth.

One of the most amazing chapters in all of Scripture is Isaiah, chapter 53. In it the prophet foretold how the Messiah would suffer and die **like a lamb led to the slaughter** to bear the punishment for our sins. Here now is what God revealed to His prophet Isaiah 700 years before the Messiah was born:

> [1]**Who has believed our message?** To whom has the LORD's arm been revealed? [2]For he [that is, the Messiah] grew up before him as a tender plant, and as a root out of dry ground. He has no good looks or majesty. When we see him, there is no beauty that we should desire him. [3]He was despised and rejected by men, a man of suffering and acquainted with disease. He was despised as one from whom men hide their face; and we didn't respect him. [4]Surely he has borne our sickness and carried our suffering; yet we considered him plagued, struck by God, and afflicted.

> [5]**But he was pierced for our transgressions.** He was crushed for our iniquities. The punishment that brought our peace was on him; and by his wounds we are healed.

> [6]**All we like sheep have gone astray.** Everyone has turned to his own way; and the LORD has laid on him the iniquity of us all. [7]He was oppressed, yet when he was afflicted he didn't open his mouth. As a lamb that is led to the slaughter, and as a sheep that before its shearers is silent, so he didn't open his mouth. [8]He was taken away by oppression and judgment. As for his generation, who considered that he was cut off out of the land of the living and stricken for the disobedience of my people?

> [9]**They made his grave with the wicked, and with a rich man** in his death, although he had done no violence, nor was any deceit in his mouth. [10]Yet it pleased the LORD to bruise him. He has caused him to suffer. When you make his soul an offering for sin, he will see his offspring. He will prolong his days

and the LORD's pleasure will prosper in his hand. [11]After the suffering of his soul, he will see the light [of life] and be satisfied. My righteous servant will justify many by the knowledge of himself; and he will bear their iniquities. [12]Therefore I will give him a portion with the great. He will divide the plunder with the strong; because he poured out his soul to death and was counted with the transgressors; yet he bore the sins of many and made intercession for the transgressors. (Isaiah 53:1-12)

That is what Isaiah wrote about the Messiah who would shed His blood for us so that God could forgive our sin without compromising His righteousness. In summarizing God's message to the world, Isaiah wrote: **He was pierced for our transgressions. He was crushed for our iniquities…. All we like sheep have gone astray. Everyone has turned to his own way; and the LORD has laid on him the iniquity of us all.** (Isaiah 53:5-6)

It is important that we understand the good news *and* the bad news. *The bad news* is that we are all helpless sinners with no way to get ourselves to God. That is why the prophet Isaiah wrote: **ALL we like sheep have gone astray. Everyone has turned to his own way.**

The good news is that God has a plan so that sinners like you and me can come to Him. About this, Isaiah wrote: **HE was pierced for our transgressions. He was crushed for our iniquities… and the LORD has laid on him the iniquity of us ALL.** (Isaiah 53:5-6)

Isaiah also wrote: **Who has believed our message? To whom has the LORD's arm been revealed?** (Isaiah 53:1) Dear friend, have you believed the message of the prophets? Do you believe in your heart that Jesus the Messiah is **the LORD's arm** to save you from judgment and bring you to God?

We leave you today with this invitation to you from the LORD God:

> **"Come now, let's settle this," says the LORD. "Though your sins are like scarlet, I will make them as white as snow. Though they are red like crimson, I will make them as white as wool."**
> (Isaiah 1:18 NLT)

Program 56
The Prophet Jeremiah

Jeremiah

In the last program, we heard from the prophet Isaiah who wrote much about the coming Messiah. Seven hundred years before the Messiah's birth, God revealed to Isaiah that the Savior of sinners would come from the presence of God, be born of a virgin, live a perfectly holy life, and do great miracles. Isaiah also prophesied that the Messiah would suffer and shed His blood like a sacrificed lamb to take the punishment for our sins. And once His sacrifice was completed, He would be buried in the tomb of a rich man, come back to life, and justify all who believe in Him.

Today we plan to study another great prophet of God: Jeremiah. Jeremiah lived about a hundred years after the prophet Isaiah. As we have seen, Israel was no longer a unified nation. It had become two kingdoms: Israel and Judah. In Jeremiah's day, the kingdom of Israel, which was to the north, was destroyed. God delivered the people of Israel into the hands of their enemies because they did not repent of their ways and believe the message of the prophets. Of the two nations of the people of Israel, only Judah remained. Judah was the nation to the south; its capital was Jerusalem, where the temple that Solomon had built was located. As we have already learned, Judah was the tribe through which God had promised to bring the Messiah into the world.

Jeremiah was a Jew. He was born in a small town just five kilometers from Jerusalem, where his father served as a priest in the temple. In that time, most of the Jews in Jerusalem were still religious, following the traditions of their ancestors, but they did not heed the word of the LORD God. Jeremiah, however, was a man who cherished the word of God and obeyed it.

Now let us hear how God called Jeremiah to be His prophet. In chapter 1 of the book that bears his name, Jeremiah wrote:

> **⁴Now the LORD's word came to me**, saying, ⁵"Before I formed you in the womb, I knew you. Before you were born, I sanctified you. I have appointed you a prophet to the nations." ⁶Then I said, "Ah, Sovereign Lord! Behold, I don't know how to speak; for I am a child." ⁷But the LORD said to me, "Don't say, 'I am a child;' for you must go to whomever I send you, and you must say whatever I command you. ⁸Don't be afraid because of them, for I am with you to rescue you," says the LORD. ⁹Then the LORD stretched out his hand, and touched my mouth.
>
> **Then the LORD said to me**, "Behold, I have put my words in your mouth. ¹⁰Behold, I have today set you over the nations and over the kingdoms, to uproot and to tear down, to destroy and to overthrow, to build and to plant." (Jeremiah 1:4-10)

That is how God called Jeremiah to be His prophet. God appointed him to go to his fellow Jews and tell them that God would judge them if they did not repent of their sin and turn back to the LORD and His word. Jeremiah's task was heavy and difficult because the Jews did not want anyone to tell them that their religious works did not please God. But the prophet Jeremiah was not a man-pleaser; and so, for twenty-four years, he preached in Jerusalem and throughout the land of Judah, saying: "God wants me to warn you that if you do not repent of your sins and obey the word of the LORD, God will allow the army of the nation of Babylon to come, enter Jerusalem, destroy and burn both the city and the temple. And they will take you as captives to a faraway land." That is the message Jeremiah proclaimed to the Jews living in Judah.

Let us read a few excerpts from the writings of Jeremiah where he warned his fellow Jews. In chapter 7, we read:

> **¹The word that came to Jeremiah from the LORD**, saying, ²"Stand in the gate of the LORD's house, and proclaim this word there, and say, 'Hear the LORD's word, all you of Judah,

who enter in at these gates to worship the LORD.'" ³The LORD of Armies, the God of Israel says, "Amend your ways and your doings, and I will cause you to dwell in this place. ⁴Don't trust in lying words, saying, 'The LORD's temple, The LORD's temple, [God will never judge us because the temple of the LORD is here.]' ⁵I For if you thoroughly amend your ways and your doings, if you thoroughly execute justice between a man and his neighbor; ⁶if you don't oppress the foreigner, the fatherless, and the widow, and don't shed innocent blood in this place, and don't walk after other gods to your own hurt; ⁷then I will cause you to dwell in this place, in the land that I gave to your fathers, from of old even forever more. ⁸Behold, you trust in lying words that can't profit. ⁹Will you steal, murder, commit adultery, swear falsely,…and walk after other gods that you have not known, ¹⁰then come and stand before me in this house, which is called by my name, and say, 'We are delivered,' that you may do all these abominations?" (Jeremiah 7:1-10)

In this way Jeremiah rebuked the Jews who pretended to know God but denied Him by their actions. In chapter 17, Jeremiah adds:

> ⁵The LORD says: "Cursed is the man who trusts in man, relies on strength of flesh, and whose heart departs from the LORD…." ⁹The heart [of man] is deceitful above all things and it is exceedingly corrupt. Who can know it? ¹⁰"I, the LORD, search the mind. I try the heart, even to give every man according to his ways, according to the fruit of his doings." (Jeremiah 17:5,9-10)

Jeremiah further warned the people of Judah that if they did not repent and return to the LORD, the armies of Babylon would destroy the city of Jerusalem and its temple, and they would become slaves in Babylon.

What do you think about this? Do you think the people of Judah respected the word which the LORD had spoken to them through the mouth of Jeremiah? Most of them did not. Not even the priests (who offered sacrifices in the temple) believed the words of Jeremiah. In fact, when the priests heard what he said, they arrested him, whipped him, and put his feet in chains for the day. The priests could not believe that God would allow their enemies, the Babylonians, to enter Jerusalem and destroy the city and the temple that Solomon had built. In their thinking, this could never happen! They were angry with Jeremiah because he predicted the destruction of Jerusalem and wrote God's words in a book.

Not only did the people and the priests refuse to accept the words of God's prophet, Jeremiah, the king of Judah also rejected them. When the king read the book (scroll) which Jeremiah had written, he cut it up with a knife and threw it into the firepot so that the entire book was consumed. That is what the king of Judah did. He did not repent of his sin, and he did not accept the word of the LORD. Yes, the king burned the book of Jeremiah, but he could not change God's decree. God simply directed Jeremiah to rewrite all His words in another book.

If you study the book of Jeremiah, you will see how the king and priests and people of Judah greatly persecuted him, imprisoning him often. Once they put him into a deep, muddy pit, but God came to his rescue, sending to him an African man to pull him out.

Something important to consider is that although most of the Jews refused to listen to the prophet Jeremiah, this does not mean that they were not listening to anyone. They were listening to men who called themselves prophets – but they were false prophets. The Scriptures tell us about many men who made themselves out to be prophets of God, but who were, in reality, hypocrites and deceivers, because their messages did not come from God. Consequently, while Jeremiah was proclaiming God's judgment which was to befall Jerusalem, the false prophets were speaking to the people of Judah, saying, "No, no! The disaster Jeremiah is predicting will not happen. Babylon cannot destroy Jerusalem. No one can destroy the temple of God. You will not see disaster. You will only have peace, nothing but Peace!"[82]

---

82 One Wolof proverb says: *Peace is everything.* In Wolof greetings, a standard reply to "How are you doing?" is, "Nothing but peace." Another proverb says: *A lie that heals is better than the truth that hurts.* That was the thinking of the false prophets in Jeremiah's time.

But Jeremiah spoke to all the Jews saying,

> [16]**The LORD of Armies says, "Don't listen to the words** of the prophets who prophesy to you. They teach you vanity. They speak a vision of their own heart, and not out of the mouth of the LORD. … [21]I didn't send these prophets, yet they ran. I didn't speak to them, yet they prophesied. [22]But if they had stood in my council, then they would have caused my people to hear my words, and would have turned them from their evil way, and from the evil of their doings. (Jeremiah 23:16,21-22)

That is how Jeremiah warned the Jews to beware of the words of those who preached falsehood. Sadly, most of the people of Judah did not heed the warning of God's prophet, Jeremiah. Instead they believed the words of the false prophets. Nevertheless, in the end, after it was too late, the king, the priests, the people, and the false prophets found out who had proclaimed the true word of God. They found out because everything that Jeremiah had announced concerning the destruction of Jerusalem came to pass. God's word always comes true.

Listen to what the Scripture says:

> [4]**In the ninth year of [Zedekiah, King of Judah's] reign** … Nebuchadnezzar king of Babylon came, he and all his army, against Jerusalem, and encamped against it; and they built forts against it round about. [5]So the city was besieged…. [6]In the fourth month, in the ninth day of the month, the famine was severe in the city, so that there was no bread for the people of the land. [7]Then a breach was made in the city… [and Nebuchadnezzar's soldiers captured the king of Judah]…. [9]Then they took the king, and carried him up to the king of Babylon… and he pronounced judgment on him. [10]The king of Babylon killed the sons of [the king of Judah] before his eyes…. [11]He put out the eyes of Zedekiah; and the king of Babylon bound him in fetters, and carried him to Babylon…. [13][Then Nebuchadnezzar, king of Babylon and his soldiers] burned the LORD's house, and the king's house; and all the houses of

Jerusalem, even every great house, he burned with fire. [14]...
[and] broke down all the walls of Jerusalem all around. [15]Then
Nebuzaradan the captain of the guard carried away captive of
the poorest of the people, and the residue of the people who
were left in the city, and those who fell away, who fell to the
king of Babylon, and the residue of the multitude. [16]But Nebuzaradan the captain of the guard left of the poorest of the land
to be vineyard keepers and farmers. [27]...So Judah was carried
away captive out of his land. (Jeremiah 52:4-7,9-11,13-16,27)

From this we can see how God fulfilled everything that He had
predicted through the mouth of Jeremiah, His prophet. Now all
the Jews knew that the words of Jeremiah had been the words
of truth, but this knowledge was of little benefit to them because
they were now captives in the hands of the Babylonian soldiers.

How should we conclude our lesson today? Perhaps we can finish
with this thought: In the Day of Judgment every descendant of
Adam will finally know what is true and what is false. But God wants
you to discern what is true and what is false now – because on
Judgment Day it will do you no good to know the truth which you
disdained during your lifetime on earth. On the Day of Judgment
it will be too late to repent, because you will have perished in your
sins. That is why the word of God says: **Now is the acceptable time.
Behold, now is the day of salvation.** (2 Corinthians 6:2) **Beloved, don't
believe every spirit, but test the spirits, whether they are of God,
because many false prophets have gone out into the world.**
(1 John 4:1)

In the next lesson, we will see what happened to the Jews who
were carried away to Babylon.

God bless you as you consider this sure promise from the LORD,
penned by the prophet Jeremiah:

> **You shall seek me, and find me,
> when you search for me with all your heart.**
> (Jeremiah 29:13)

The Prophet Daniel

Daniel 1, 6

I n the last program we examined the book of Jeremiah. The prophet Jeremiah lived some six hundred years before the coming of the Messiah. Jeremiah warned his fellow Jews, telling them that if they did not repent of their sins and turn back to God, the army of Babylon would destroy the city of Jerusalem and take them captive. Tragically, most of the Jews listened to the false prophets who contradicted Jeremiah's message from God. Consequently, the Babylonian army came, destroyed Jerusalem, and carried the Jews far away to Babylon. Everything happened exactly as God had predicted through the mouth of Jeremiah, His prophet.

But the destruction of Jerusalem did not mean that God had abandoned the Jews, the people He had chosen long beforehand. God would not forget the covenant that He had made with Abraham, Isaac, and Jacob when He said to them, "**All the families of the earth will be blessed through you.**" (Genesis 12:3) God had not forgotten His plan to send the Redeemer into the world through the nation which descended from Abraham. And so the Scriptures relate how God took care of the Jews in Babylon for seventy years until He brought them back to Jerusalem, just as He had promised. We will go into that story on our next program.

Today we plan to read about a young Jewish man who was one of the captives taken to Babylon. That young man is Daniel, another faithful prophet of God. The name Daniel means *God is my judge*, and that was Daniel's testimony in short. Daniel feared no one except Almighty God before whom every person must give an account one day. Daniel was not concerned about what men thought of him; only God's thoughts mattered to him.

God was Daniel's judge. Daniel believed what the prophet Solomon had written long before: **The fear of man proves to be a snare, but whoever puts his trust in the LORD is kept safe.** (Proverbs 29:25)

God inspired Daniel to write an exceedingly profound book. The book of Daniel contains many revelations which the human mind could not invent. Only God knows what will happen in the future. Yet the prophet Daniel wrote about the history of many nations of the world – and he wrote their history hundreds of years before those nations existed. For example, Daniel wrote how the kingdoms of Persia and Greece and Rome would come into existence and what their kings would do. Also, like so many of God's prophets, Daniel wrote about the first coming and the second coming of the Savior and Judge of the world. Daniel prophesied that at the Messiah's first coming He would be **cut off** (Daniel 9:26), that is, killed as a sacrifice for sin, but when the Messiah returns to earth He will judge the world in righteousness. Listen to the vision of the prophet Daniel about the Messiah's second coming:

> [9]**I watched until thrones were placed**, and one who was ancient of days sat. His clothing was white as snow, and the hair of his head like pure wool. His throne was fiery flames, and its wheels burning fire. [10]A fiery stream issued and came out from before him. Thousands of thousands ministered to him. Ten thousand times ten thousand stood before him. The judgment was set. The books were opened.
>
> [13]**I saw in the night visions**, and behold, there came with the clouds of the sky one like a son of man, and he came even to the ancient of days, and they brought him near before him. [14]Dominion was given him, and glory, and a kingdom, that all the peoples, nations, and languages should serve him. His dominion is an everlasting dominion, which will not pass away, and his kingdom one that which will not be destroyed. (Daniel 7:9-10,13-14)

Since time doesn't allow us to delve into the many other profound prophecies of Daniel, let's just focus on the story of Daniel himself.

In the first chapter of Daniel's book, we see that Nebuchadnezzar, King of Babylon, selected some of the Jewish young men in order to train them for service in his government. He chose those who were the most handsome and intelligent, with an aptitude for every kind of learning, such as mastering the difficult alphabet and language of Babylon. Daniel was one of those chosen by the king.

On the very first day of his schooling in Babylon Daniel faced a dilemma. The great King of Babylon had decided that the young men who were part of his school must drink the best wine and eat the best food. But this wine and food had been offered to idols. Could Daniel participate in the worship of idols? Absolutely not. Why not? Because Daniel feared God. Daniel preferred death to doing something that was not pleasing to God, his Lord. So the Scripture says: **But Daniel resolved [in his heart] not to defile himself with the royal food and wine, and he asked the chief official for permission not to defile himself this way.** (Daniel 1:8 NIV)

God rescued Daniel from that dilemma, blessed him, and gave him deep knowledge and wisdom. The Scripture says: **In every matter of wisdom and understanding about which the king questioned them, he found them ten times better than all the magicians and enchanters in his whole kingdom.** (Daniel 1:20 NIV) For seventy years Daniel worked for four different kings, and God was with him.

We have time to read one story from the life of Daniel – a story that shows how Daniel feared no one but God alone. We will see how he was different from the other officials who worked for the King. They were the kind of men who habitually twisted the truth and received bribes, because the fear of God was far from their hearts. But Daniel refused all unrighteousness and falsehood because the fear of God filled his heart. He preferred to be thrown into a den of lions rather than to displease the Lord his God.

Where our story begins, Daniel is now an old man serving under his fourth king. The kingdom of Babylon had ceased to exist because the Medes and the Persians had conquered it and divided it in two, just as the prophet Daniel had prophesied.

In chapter six, the Scripture says:

> ¹**It pleased Darius [the King]** to set over the kingdom one hundred twenty local governors, who should be throughout the whole kingdom; ²and over them three presidents, of whom Daniel was one; that these local governors might give account to them, and that the king should suffer no loss. ³Then this Daniel was distinguished above the presidents and the local governors, because an excellent spirit was in him; and the king thought to set him over the whole realm. ⁴Then the presidents and the local governors sought to find occasion against Daniel as touching the kingdom; but they could find no occasion or fault, because he was faithful. There wasn't any error or fault found in him.
>
> ⁵**Then these men said,** "We won't find any occasion against this Daniel, unless we find it against him concerning the law of his God." ⁶Then these presidents and local governors assembled together to the king, and said this to him, "King Darius, live forever! ⁷All the presidents of the kingdom, the deputies and the local governors, the counselors and the governors, have consulted together to establish a royal statute, and to make a strong decree, that whoever asks a petition of any god or man for thirty days, except of you, O king, he shall be cast into the den of lions. ⁸Now, O king, establish the decree, and sign the writing, that it not be changed, according to the law of the Medes and Persians, which doesn't alter." ⁹Therefore king Darius signed the writing and the decree.
>
> ¹⁰**When Daniel knew that the writing was signed**, he went into his house (now his windows were open in his room toward Jerusalem) and he kneeled on his knees three times a day, and prayed, and gave thanks before his God, as he did before. ¹¹Then these men assembled together, and found Daniel making petition and supplication before his God. ¹²Then they came near, and spoke before the king concerning the king's decree: "Haven't you signed a decree that every man who makes a petition to any god or man within thirty days, except to you, O king, shall be cast into the den of lions?" The king

answered, "This thing is true, according to the law of the Medes and Persians, which doesn't alter." [13]Then they answered and said before the king, "That Daniel, who is of the children of the captivity of Judah, doesn't respect you, O king, nor the decree that you have signed, but makes his petition three times a day."

[14]**Then the king, when he heard these words**, was very displeased, and set his heart on Daniel to deliver him; and he labored until the going down of the sun to rescue him. [15]Then these men assembled together to the king, and said to the king, "Know, O king, that it is a law of the Medes and Persians, that no decree nor statute which the king establishes may be changed." [16]Then the king commanded, and they brought Daniel, and cast him into the den of lions. The king spoke and said to Daniel, "Your God whom you serve continually, he will deliver you." [17]A stone was brought, and laid on the mouth of the den; and the king sealed it with his own signet, and with the signet of his lords; that nothing might be changed concerning Daniel. [18]Then the king went to his palace, and passed the night fasting. No musical instruments were brought before him; and his sleep fled from him.

[19]**Then the king arose very early in the morning**, and went in haste to the den of lions. [20]When he came near to the den to Daniel, he cried with a troubled voice. The king spoke and said to Daniel, "Daniel, servant of the living God, is your God, whom you serve continually, able to deliver you from the lions?" [21]Then Daniel said to the king, "O king, live forever! [22]My God has sent his angel, and has shut the lions' mouths, and they have not hurt me; because as before him innocence was found in me; and also before you, O king, I have done no harm." [23]Then the king was exceedingly glad, and commanded that they should take Daniel up out of the den. So Daniel was taken up out of the den, and no kind of harm was found on him, because he had trusted in his God. [24]The king commanded, and they brought those men who had accused Daniel, and they cast them into the den of lions, them, their children, and their wives; and the lions mauled them, and broke all their bones in pieces, before they came to the bottom of the den.

²⁵**Then king Darius wrote to all the peoples**, nations, and languages, who dwell in all the earth: "Peace be multiplied to you. ²⁶I make a decree that in all the dominion of my kingdom men tremble and fear before the God of Daniel; for he is the living God, and steadfast forever. His kingdom is that which will not be destroyed. His dominion will be even to the end. ²⁷He delivers and rescues. He works signs and wonders in heaven and in earth, who has delivered Daniel from the power of the lions." (Daniel 6:1-27)

Did you hear what the heathen king said after he saw how God had saved Daniel from the lions? He said, **"I make a decree that in all the dominion of my kingdom men tremble and fear before the God of Daniel; for he is the living God!"**

Listening friends, *do you fear the God of Daniel?* Perhaps you ask, "Who is the God of Daniel?" The God of Daniel is the God of Abraham, Isaac, and Jacob. The God of Daniel is the God of the prophets Moses and David. The God of Daniel is the God who gave us the Holy Scriptures and promised to send to earth a Redeemer to save us from a power stronger than the power of lions. He came to save us from the power of Satan, sin, death, and hell. The God of Daniel is God – the One True God.

Do you *fear the God of Daniel?* We are not asking whether you fear your family and friends and their thoughts, or whether you fear your ancestors and their customs, or your marabouts and their demands. The question is: Do you fear God? Do you want to please the LORD God and obey His holy word? Daniel chose to be thrown to the lions rather than displease the LORD his God. How about you? Do you fear God? Do you hate unrighteousness as Daniel hated it? Do you cherish the word of God as Daniel cherished it?

In our next lesson, we plan to look at some amazing prophecies written by Zechariah, a prophet who came after Daniel.

God bless you as you meditate on this foundational truth:

The fear of man proves to be a snare, but whoever puts his trust in the LORD is kept safe. (Proverbs 29:25)

Program 58
The Prophet Zechariah

Zechariah

Two programs ago, we heard how the prophet Jeremiah, warned his fellow Jews that if they did not heed the word of the LORD, God would allow the soldiers of Babylon to come in, destroy their country, and carry them far away. Most of the Jews paid no attention to Jeremiah's warnings. Consequently, the army of Babylon came from the east, destroyed Jerusalem, destroyed the temple and took the Jews captives, transporting them to Babylon, just as the prophet Jeremiah had predicted. And so, the Jewish people were dispersed, because they refused to believe and obey the word of God's prophets.

But could the Jews' unfaithfulness frustrate the faithfulness of God? No. Listen to what the prophet Jeremiah told the Jews, who were now captives in Babylon because of their sins. He said to them:

> [4]**The LORD Almighty, the God of Israel**, says to all the captives whom I have caused to be carried away captive from Jerusalem to Babylon:… [10]"After seventy years are accomplished for Babylon, I will visit you and perform my good word toward you, in causing you to return to [Jerusalem]. [11]For I know the thoughts that I think toward you… thoughts of peace, and not of evil, to give you hope and a future." (Jeremiah 29:4,10-11)

With this declaration the prophet Jeremiah was informing the Jews that even if they had forgotten God, God had not forgotten them. After seventy years, God planned to bring them back to the land of their ancestors. That is what Jeremiah told the Jews who were captives in Babylon. Truly, God is faithful.[83] God had not forgotten

---

83 Literally: *the keeper of covenants*

that He had promised to bless all the nations of the world through the descendants of Abraham, Isaac, and Israel. God had not forgotten that He purposed to entrust His truth to the Israelites so that they might pass it on to all the descendants of Adam. In our study we have seen how God chose His prophets from among the Jews, inspiring them to proclaim His holy word and write it down for the people of future generations. We know how God placed the Torah in the mind of Moses and many psalms in the heart of David. We have seen similarly how God inspired other Jews like Joshua, Samuel, Solomon, Isaiah, Jeremiah, and Daniel to write the word of God. We have observed how all the Writings of God's prophets announce the wonderful plan of God to send forth the Savior of the world through the nation of Israel.

Today we will see how God brought the Jews back to the land of Judah where the Messiah was to be born, thus moving forward with His plan to bring the Redeemer into the world. We will learn how the Jews returned to Jerusalem after seventy years of captivity, just as Jeremiah, God's prophet, had predicted.

As we begin reading, let us remember that the land of Babylon was now called Persia, because Persia had conquered Babylon. In the book of Ezra, chapter 1, the Scripture says:

> ¹**Now in the first year of Cyrus king of Persia,** that the LORD's word by Jeremiah's mouth might be accomplished, the LORD stirred up the spirit of Cyrus king of Persia, so that he made a proclamation throughout all his kingdom, and put it also in writing, saying, ²"Cyrus king of Persia says, 'The LORD, the God of heaven, has given me all the kingdoms of the earth; and he has commanded me to build him a house in Jerusalem, which is in Judah. ³Whoever there is among you of all his people, may his God be with him, and let him go up to Jerusalem, which is in Judah, and build the house of the LORD, the God of Israel….' ⁵Then the heads of fathers' households of Judah and Benjamin, the priests, and the Levites, all whose spirit God had stirred to go up rose up to build the LORD's house which is in Jerusalem. ⁶All those who were around them strengthened their hands

with vessels of silver, with gold, with goods, with animals, and with precious things, in addition to all that was willingly offered. [7]Also Cyrus the king brought out the vessels of the LORD's house, which Nebuchadnezzar had brought out of Jerusalem, and had put in the house of his gods. (Ezra 1:1-3,5-7)

Did God fulfill what He had promised long beforehand through the mouth of Jeremiah, His prophet? Of course He did. We have already seen how God allowed the king of Babylon to destroy Jerusalem and break down the temple of God – precisely as Jeremiah had prophesied. And now we see how Cyrus, the king of Persia, commanded any Jews who so desired, to return to their land and rebuild the temple and the city of Jerusalem – again just as the prophet Jeremiah had prophesied.

Truly, the LORD is the King of kings. He is the One who controls the times and the seasons. All that He declares will happen. And as King Solomon wrote: **The king's heart is like a stream of water directed by the LORD; he guides it wherever he pleases.** (Proverbs 21:1 NLT)

Next, the Scriptures describe how a group of Jews left the land of Persia and traveled back to the land of Judah and the city of Jerusalem. A Jew named *Zerubbabel* was their leader. When they came to Jerusalem they were greatly troubled because the whole city was destroyed and the temple of the LORD which Solomon had built was in ruins. Nothing was left but ashes and broken pieces of stone.

The Scriptures then relate how these Jews first had a meeting in the place where the temple of the LORD had been. There they rebuilt the altar and sacrificed some animals. Together they thanked and praised the LORD for protecting them in Babylon and Persia for seventy years and for bringing them back to their homeland. God was with those Jews to help them and strengthen them so that, amid great opposition, after many years of courageous work they rebuilt the temple of the LORD, the city of Jerusalem, and the walls that surrounded it. These compelling stories are recorded in the books of *Ezra* and *Nehemiah*.

Perhaps some of you are asking: *What relevance does the story of the return of the Jews to Jerusalem have for us?* The return of the Jews to their land is important for all of us because it was in that land of Judah, the southern part of Palestine, that the Messiah would be born. It was necessary that the Jews return to the land of Judah so that the Redeemer of the world – your Redeemer, my Redeemer – could be born there.

At the time of the Jews' return to Jerusalem, God sent with them a prophet by the name of *Zechariah*. This Zechariah is different from *Zacharias*,[84] the father of the prophet John.[85] God sent Zechariah to strengthen the Jews' faith in God and His promises. Zechariah had an important message to deliver. The time appointed by God to send down the Messiah was drawing closer. Only five hundred years remained before the Redeemer would come into the world.

Let us examine some of the words that God placed into the mind of Zechariah. In the book of Zechariah, chapter 1, the Scripture says:

> [1]**In the eighth month, in the second year of Darius**, the LORD's word came to Zechariah the son of Berechiah, the son of Iddo, the prophet, saying, [2]"The LORD was very displeased with your fathers. ... [4]Don't you be like your fathers, to whom the former prophets proclaimed, saying: The LORD Almighty says, 'Return now from your evil ways, and from your evil doings;' but they didn't hear, nor listen to me, says the LORD. [5]Your fathers, where are they? And the prophets, do they live forever? [6]But my words and my decrees, which I commanded my servants the prophets, didn't they overtake your fathers? (Zechariah 1:1-2,4-6)

Did you hear the warning the prophet Zechariah gave to the Jews? He said to them, **"The LORD was very displeased with your fathers! Don't be like your fathers!"** Why was God angry with their fathers? It was because they did not heed the words of the prophets that He had sent to them. That was why they became captives in Babylon. Their fathers were religious, but God was not

---

84 Qur'anic/Arabic: *Zakariya* (*Zacharias* is the Greek equivalent of the Hebrew name, *Zechariah*.)
85 Qur'anic/Arabic: *Yahya*

happy with them because they ignored the words of the prophets. The Jews of that time were like people of today who say, "Of course we believe all the prophets." But it is obvious that they do not really believe the prophets, because they do not believe and follow what God has revealed through His prophets in the Holy Scriptures. They have a religion, but they do not have a personal relationship with the LORD God Himself. That is what most of the Jewish ancestors were like. They did not appreciate the words of the prophets. They honored God with their lips, but they did not receive His word into their hearts. So God sent His servant Zechariah to them, to warn them not to follow the example of their ancestors who had "God, God, God" on their lips but ignored the word which God had sent to them through His prophets.

After Zechariah warned the Jews, he began to speak of the Redeemer who was to come to earth. We do not have time today to read everything that the prophet Zechariah wrote about the Messiah, but here are a few excerpts. In the book of Zechariah, chapter 9, Zechariah prophesied that the Messiah would enter Jerusalem, riding on a donkey. He said: **Rejoice greatly, daughter of Zion! Shout, daughter of Jerusalem! Behold, your King comes to you! He is righteous, and having salvation; lowly, and riding on a donkey, even on a colt, the foal of a donkey.** (Zechariah 9:9)

In chapter 11, Zechariah penned another remarkable prophecy. We do not have time to explain it in detail, but one event Zechariah predicted was that the Messiah would be sold for thirty pieces of silver. The prophet wrote: **I said to them, "If you think it best, give me my wages; and if not, keep them." So they weighed for my wages thirty pieces of silver…. I took the thirty pieces of silver, and threw them… in the LORD's house.** (Zechariah 11:12-13)

In chapter 12, Zechariah foretold that the Messiah would be pierced and killed. The prophet wrote these words of the LORD:

> **I will pour on David's house**, and on the inhabitants of Jerusalem, the spirit of grace and of supplication; and they will look to me whom they have pierced; and they shall mourn for

him, as one mourns for his only son, and will grieve bitterly for him, as one grieves for his firstborn.... One will say to him, 'What are these wounds [in your hands]?' Then he will answer, 'Those with which I was wounded in the house of my friends.'" (Zechariah 12:10; 13:6)

Thus, Zechariah wrote of the Messiah's wounds. We will see the fulfilment of this in the Gospel, how the Messiah's fellow Jews persuaded the Romans to crucify Him, nailing His hands and feet to a cross and piercing His side with a spear. What the prophet Zechariah wrote is in perfect harmony with what the prophet David foretold hundreds of years earlier in the Psalms, when he wrote: **They have pierced my hands and feet.** (Psalm 22:16)

Friends, God wants us to know that the sufferings and death of the Messiah on the cross is the central part of His plan to save the children of Adam from the penalty of sin, that the righteous Messiah would shed His blood for the unrighteous. That is the message of God's prophets. Is this clear? Do you understand what Zechariah foretold five hundred years before the Messiah was born? Do you truly believe the message of the prophets – that the Messiah would suffer and die and, as the first to rise from the dead, proclaim forgiveness of sins and peace with God for all who believe? Do you believe the prophets? Or are you like those who honored God's prophets with their lips, but did not believe their message? The Scriptures say:

> **Don't despise prophecies.** (1 Thessalonians 5:20) We have the word of the prophets made more certain, and you will do well to pay attention to it, as to a light shining in a dark place, until the day dawns and the morning star rises in your hearts. (2 Peter 1:19) Do you *believe* the prophets? (Acts 26:27)

God willing, in our next program we will hear from the prophet Malachi who wrote the last book of the Old Testament. God bless you as you answer this crucial question from the word of God:

> **Do *you* believe the prophets?** (Acts 26:27)

The Message of the Prophets Summarized

Malachi

For a long time now we have been studying the first section of the Scriptures. This section, called *the First Covenant,* also known as *the Old Testament,* contains the Torah, the Psalms, and the other writings of the prophets. God used more than thirty prophets over a period of 1500 years to write the First Covenant.

Today we will complete our journey through the first section of God's book. But before we look at the final chapters of the First Covenant, we want to talk a little about what we have been hearing from the first day until now. We can summarize the central message of all the prophets in three big thoughts:

> One: *God is holy and must judge every sin.*
> Two: *The children of Adam are born in sin and face God's judgment.*
> Three: *God promised to send to earth a holy Redeemer who would bear the punishment of sin for the children of Adam.*

To repeat, here again are the 3 big truths preached by the prophets:

> First: *God is holy and cannot overlook sin.*
> Second: *Man is unholy, corrupted by sin, and has no way to save himself from the penalty of sin.*
> Third: *God has a plan to save sinners from judgment.*

Have you grasped these truths? Have these truths grasped you? Do you recognize God's blazing holiness? Do you understand how serious your sins are in the eyes of the One who must judge you? Do you know that God has a plan to cleanse you from your sins?

Indeed, God is holy, and man is unholy. We have seen those two truths often in our study of the Holy Scriptures. The holiness of God was the reason He created the unquenchable fire for Satan and all who follow him. The holiness of God was the reason He expelled Adam and Eve from the garden of Paradise on the day that they ate of the forbidden tree. The holiness of God was the reason the LORD God commanded the sons of Adam to sacrifice animals as burnt offerings to cover sin. His holiness was also the reason He did not accept Cain's offering. Because God is holy He destroyed sinners in Noah's time with a flood of water and rained fire on the people of Sodom in Abraham's time. The holiness of God is the reason **he has appointed a day in which he will judge the world in righteousness by the man whom he has ordained.** (Acts 17:31)

Listen to what God's prophets wrote about the holiness of God and the unholiness of man:

> **Aren't you from everlasting, O LORD my God?** … You who have purer eyes than to see evil, and who cannot look on perversity. (Habakkuk 1:12-13) For we have all become like one who is unclean, and all our righteousness is like a polluted garment. (Isaiah 64:6)

If God is so holy and man is so unclean, who then can be saved? How can we be saved from the eternal fire? How can the children of Adam live forever in the presence of the God who is pure and holy? The response to that question is the third point in the message of the prophets. After the prophets preached that God is holy and that the children of Adam are unholy, they declared that God Himself had a plan to cleanse the children of Adam from their sin.

The most important message of the book of the First Covenant (Old Testament) is that God promised to send into the world a righteous Redeemer who would suffer and die in the place of the unrighteous children of Adam, to redeem all those who believe in Him. This was and is God's plan to save sinners. Only through the Redeemer's shed blood can God forgive sin and reconcile sinners to Himself without compromising His holiness.

To advance His plan to send down the Savior, God called Abraham to make of him a new nation, from whom the prophets of God and the Messiah would come. God spoke to Abraham, saying, **"You will be a blessing … [and] all the families of the earth will be blessed through you."** (Genesis 12:2-3) So Abraham begot Isaac in his old age, and Isaac begot Jacob, and Jacob begot twelve sons who produced the tribes of Israel. Thus, we learned that when God called Abraham, He was advancing His plan to send the Savior to earth, because it was from the lineage of Abraham, through the nation of Israel, that the Messiah was to be born.

Next we saw the children of Israel leave Canaan and settle in Egypt, where they became slaves of Pharaoh. But God did not forget Abraham's offspring, the Israelites. God called Moses to free the Israelites and lead them to the land which God had promised to their ancestor Abraham long before. God also used the prophet Moses to give us the book called the Torah, which is the foundation of everything God has made known since then.

After the time of Moses, we saw how God sent many prophets to the Israelites, but most did not heed their words. Still, the unfaithfulness of the Israelites did not thwart God's plans. And so we saw how God chose David to be king of Israel and the lineage through which the Messiah would be born. David would also write half of the powerful and profound songs and prayers found in the book of Psalms. The prophet David wrote a lot about the Messiah. He foretold how the children of Adam would persecute Him and pierce His hands and His feet. But David also prophesied that after the Messiah had shed His blood as a sacrifice that washes away sin, He would conquer death and rise from the grave.

But it was not only the prophets Moses and David who wrote about the Messiah. All of God's prophets announced His coming. For example, the prophet Isaiah foretold that the Messiah would be born in a way that no human had ever been born. Isaiah wrote: **The virgin will conceive, and bear a son, and shall call his name Immanuel (which means, *God with us*).** (Isaiah 7:14; Matthew 1:23)

There was another prophet who lived in the same time as Isaiah. His name was Micah. God revealed to Micah in which town the Messiah would be born. In the book of Micah, chapter 5, we read:

> **But you, Bethlehem Ephrathah**, being small among the clans of Judah, out of you one will come out to me that is to be ruler in Israel; whose goings out are from of old, from ancient times." (Micah 5:2)

With this prophecy Micah was foretelling that the Messiah would be born in **Bethlehem**, the hometown of King David. But why did he call it **Bethlehem Ephrathah**? Why not just **Bethlehem**? Because in the Jews' homeland there were two towns named Bethlehem. One was in Judah in the south; the other was in the north. The Bethlehem in Judah was also known as **Ephrathah**. So Micah's prophecy made it clear in which Bethlehem the Messiah-King from heaven was to be born.

How carefully God prepared for the arrival of the Savior of the world! The writings of the prophets contain hundreds of references about the coming Messiah. Perhaps you are asking: *Why did God place into the minds of the prophets all these thoughts about the Messiah before He came into the world?*

God inspired the prophets to write much about the Messiah before He came, so that when He came and fulfilled all that the prophets had written, we might know beyond any doubt that He and He alone is the Savior whom the LORD God chose and sent.

God does not want anyone to deceive you. He wants you to know who the Messiah the Savior of sinners is so that you can believe in Him and follow Him and be saved from your sins. That is one of the reasons He gave us this wonderful, reliable Book called the First Covenant (Old Testament) – so that we might distinguish truth from error.

To finish our journey through the first part of the Holy Scriptures, we need to read from the book of Malachi, the final book in the First Covenant. The words of the prophet Malachi are important for us because they are the final words God gave to the children of Adam before the Messiah came to earth. Less than four hundred years remained before the Redeemer would be born.

Let's listen to what the LORD says in the final chapter:

> [1]**"Behold, I send my messenger**, and he will prepare the way before me; and the Lord, whom you seek, will suddenly come to his temple; and the messenger of the covenant, whom you desire, behold, he comes!" says the LORD Almighty.… [6]"For I, the LORD, don't change.… [2]But to you who fear my name shall the sun of righteousness arise with healing in [his] wings."
> (Malachi 3:1,6; 4:2)

Thus the prophet Malachi prophesied that God would send a prophet before the Messiah to prepare His way. Do you know who that prophet was? In our next lesson, we will meet him. The one who prepared the way before the Messiah was the prophet John.

Malachi also wrote: **The LORD Almighty says: "The messenger of the covenant, whom you desire, behold, he comes.… I, the LORD, don't change."** (Malachi 3:1,6) About two hundred years earlier, the prophet Jeremiah had prophesied:

> [31]**"Behold, the days come," says the LORD**, "that I will make a new covenant with the house of Israel, and with the house of Judah: [32]not according to the covenant that I made with their fathers in the day that I took them by the hand to bring them out of the land of Egypt; which covenant of mine they broke, although I was a husband to them," says the LORD.

> [33]**"But this is the covenant that I will make** with the house of Israel after those days," says the LORD: "I will put my law in their inward parts, and I will write it in their heart.… [34]I will forgive their iniquity, and I will remember their sin no more."
> (Jeremiah 31:31-34)

With these words, God was announcing that the Messiah would establish with His people a New Covenant that would fulfill the symbols, promises, and conditions of the First Covenant. For thousands of years God had required the sacrifice of animals so that He might forgive the sins of Adam's descendants. Animal sacrifices were an important part of the First Covenant which God gave to mankind through His prophets. But the Messiah would bring into the world a new agreement, the New Covenant, which would fulfill the symbolism of all the animal sacrifices and the He would set aside the First Covenant.

The Messiah would not come to abolish the words of the prophets, but to accomplish them. That is why the prophet Malachi calls Him *the Sun of Righteousness.*

How would the Messiah be like the sun? The prophets were like the moon or a candle diffusing rays of light in a dark world. But the Messiah would be like the rising sun, driving out the darkness of our sin and shame, and opening a permanent door of salvation for all who trust in Him. Who needs the light of the moon or a candle once the sun has arisen? The Messiah is the Sun of Righteousness. In our next lesson, we will hear Zacharias, the father of the prophet John, say:

> [78]**Because of the tender mercy of our God...**[79] [the rising sun will] shine on those who sit in darkness and the shadow of death; to guide our feet into the way of peace." (Luke 1:78-79)

Friends, we have come to the end of our journey though the books of the First Covenant. Next time, God willing, we will begin the section that follows it and fulfills it: **the New Covenant**, the book of the Gospel (*Injil*). It is in the Gospel that we discover how the Messiah fulfilled the words of the prophets.

God will bless you as you heed this word from Him:

> **You must pay close attention to what [the prophets] wrote, for their words are like a lamp shining in a dark place, until the Day dawns, and Christ the Morning Star shines in your hearts.** (2 Peter 1:19 NLT)

The WAY of
RIGHTEOUSNESS
According to

The Gospel

Jesus asked His disciples,
"Who do the crowds say that I am?"
They replied, "Some say...one of the prophets..."
"But what about you? Who do you say that I am?"
Gospel according to Luke 9:18-20

Part 3

"What do you think about the Messiah?"
Gospel according to Matthew 22:42

Program 60

The Prophet John

Luke 1

I n our previous program, we completed our journey through the first section of the Holy Scriptures, containing the Torah (*Tawrat*), the Psalms (*Zabur*) and the Prophets. That first section is the First Covenant, known as *the Old Testament. Testament* means covenant, agreement, or contract. Today we will begin our study in the second division of God's word, the New Covenant, more commonly known as *the New Testament.*

Six hundred years before God inspired the New Testament Scriptures, He told His prophet Jeremiah to write: **"The days are coming," declares the Lord, "when I will make a new covenant."** (Jeremiah 31:31) Why did God plan to establish a new agreement with people? One reason is that His first way of forgiveness which required the shed blood of animals to cover sin was only symbolic and temporary. The New Covenant would bring in God's permanent and final provision by which He could forgive sin and declare sinners righteous.

Some people criticize Holy Scripture because it has an Old and a New Testament. They think that New Testament means that someone has attempted to nullify and replace the original writings of the prophets with another book. But the New Testament does not nullify what the prophets wrote rather, it confirms their writings. The New Covenant records how God fulfilled the promises and prophecies and symbols of the First Covenant.

In the First Covenant the prophets had announced: The Messiah *will* come. He *will* come! But the New Covenant informs us: The

Messiah *has* come. The Messiah, of whom all the prophets spoke and wrote, *has* come!

Yes, we should thank God with joyful hearts that the Holy Scriptures have an Old and a New Testament, because in those two parts we discover that what God's prophets foretold long beforehand, God has fulfilled. As the seed of the baobab[86] grows up into a mighty baobab tree, in a similar way the Old Testament comes to maturity in the New Testament.

The New Testament contains the Gospel. In the Arabic language it is called the *Injil*. Both words mean Good News. Truly, the message of the Gospel is extremely good news, because it tells how the Messiah accomplished what the prophets had foretold. He Himself is the way of righteousness by which helpless sinners can have peace with the holy LORD God forever!

The Messiah did not write the Book of the Gospel (*Injil*). Just as God used many men to write the books of the First Covenant, so He used several others to write the books of the New Covenant. The New Testament contains four gospel books. Why four? Why not just one? In the Torah, God told Moses: **A matter must be established by the testimony of two or three witnesses.** (Deuteronomy 19:15 NIV) To confirm the testimony, God used four men to write down the Messiah's story. Those four men are *Matthew, Mark, Luke*, and *John*. God wanted to communicate to us a message which would be beyond doubt and worthy of full confidence.

Just as a table with four legs is more stable than a table with one leg, so four witnesses are more reliable than one witness. God employed four witnesses so that we might know that everything written in the Book of the Gospel about the Messiah is absolutely true.

Just as God placed His words in the minds of the prophets, so He guided these four men who lived in the same era as the Messiah to write what they had seen and heard concerning the Savior of the world.

---

86 A common, amazing, useful tree in West Africa; Senegal's national symbol

God inspired a total of eight men to write the New Testament. The letters of the apostles, Paul, Peter, James, Jude and John are also part of the Gospel Writings. All they wrote is in perfect harmony.

Do you know in which language God's servants wrote the holy Gospel? It was Greek. We, of course, will be reading it in *English*[87] since most of us do not understand Greek! We thank God that He put it into the hearts of scholars to translate the Gospel from Greek into our heart language, as well as into the languages of other nations around the world.

Sometimes we hear those who try to discredit the book of the Gospel saying, "No one can trust it. It has been tampered with. It contains errors and contradictions." Friends, the one who fights with the Gospel is fighting with God who inspired it.

An egg should not wrestle with a rock.

The Holy Scriptures are worthy of our full confidence and obedience. Just as the word of God is perfect in the Torah and the Psalms, so it is also perfect in the Gospel. God is great and has preserved His Truth for all who seek Him with all their heart. No one can actually alter the living and enduring word of God. That is what the Lord Himself declares in the Gospel when He says: **Heaven and earth will pass away, but my words will not pass away.** (Matthew 24:35)

And so the moment has arrived for us to begin our journey through the book of the Gospel. In our last program, we heard about the prophet Malachi who lived four hundred years before the Messiah. During those four hundred years between Malachi and Messiah, God did not send any more prophets to write the word of God. Why do you think that was? He sent no more revelation because the Old Testament Scriptures were complete. God had said everything He wanted to say through prophets and symbols. He was now awaiting the appointed time when He would send the promised Savior into the world to establish the New Testament.

---

87 The original 100 programs were written and recorded in the Wolof language of Senegal.

We have already seen how the prophets Isaiah and Malachi foretold God's plan to send a prophet to announce the Messiah's arrival. That prophet was *John, the son of Zacharias*.[88] Zacharias was a priest who served God and the people by offering animal sacrifices on the altar of the temple in Jerusalem.

Now let us open the Gospel (*Injil*) and hear what Luke wrote about the prophet John's birth. Dr. Luke was a physician and a careful historian who lived at the time when the Messiah walked on earth. In chapter 1 of his book Luke writes:

> [5]**There was in the days of Herod, the king of Judea**, a certain priest named Zacharias, of the priestly division of Abijah. He had a wife of the daughters of Aaron, and her name was Elizabeth. [6]They were both righteous before God, walking blamelessly in all the commandments and ordinances of the Lord. [7]But they had no child, because Elizabeth was barren, and they both were well advanced in years. [8]Now while [Zacharias] executed the priest's office before God.... [10]The whole multitude of the people were praying outside at the hour of incense. [11]An angel of the Lord appeared to him, standing on the right side of the altar of incense. [12]Zacharias was troubled when he saw him, and fear fell upon him.

> [13]**But the angel said to him**, "Don't be afraid, Zacharias, because your request has been heard. Your wife, Elizabeth, will bear you a son, and you shall call his name John. [14]You will have joy and gladness, and many will rejoice at his birth. [15]For he will be great in the sight of the Lord, and he will drink no wine nor strong drink. He will be filled with the Holy Spirit, even from his mother's womb. [16]He will turn many of the children of Israel to the Lord their God. [17]He will go before him in the spirit and power of Elijah, 'to turn the hearts of the fathers to the children, and the disobedient to the wisdom of the just; to prepare a people prepared for the Lord." [18]Zacharias said to the angel, "How can I be sure of this? For I am an old man, and my wife is well advanced in years."

---

88 Arabic: *Yahya / Zakariya*

¹⁹**The angel answered him, "I am Gabriel**, who stands in the presence of God. I was sent to speak to you and to bring you this good news. ²⁰Behold, you will be silent and not able to speak until the day that these things will happen, because you didn't believe my words, which will be fulfilled in their proper time."

²¹**The people were waiting for Zacharias**, and they marveled that he delayed in the temple. ²²When he came out, he could not speak to them. They perceived that he had seen a vision in the temple. He continued making signs to them, and remained mute. ²³When the days of his service were fulfilled, he departed to his house. ²⁴After these days Elizabeth his wife conceived… saying, ²⁵"Thus has the Lord done to me in the days in which he looked at me, to take away my reproach among men." (Luke 1:5-8,10-25)

That is how God sent the angel Gabriel to Zacharias to announce to him that Elizabeth his wife would have a son. This son would become the prophet privileged to prepare the way before the Messiah. At the end of the first chapter, the Scripture says:

⁵⁷**Now the time that Elizabeth should give birth** was fulfilled, and she gave birth to a son. ⁵⁸Her neighbors and her relatives heard that the Lord had magnified his mercy toward her, and they rejoiced with her. ⁵⁹On the eighth day, they came to circumcise the child; and they would have called him Zacharias, after the name of his father. ⁶⁰His mother answered, "Not so; but he will be called John." ⁶¹They said to her, "There is no one among your relatives who is called by this name."

⁶²**They made signs to his father**, what he would have him called. ⁶³He asked for a writing tablet, and wrote, "His name is John." They all marveled. ⁶⁴His mouth was opened immediately and his tongue freed, and he spoke, blessing God. ⁶⁵Fear came on all who lived around them, and all these sayings were talked about throughout all the hill country of Judea. ⁶⁶All who heard them laid them up in their heart, saying, "What then will this child be?" The hand of the Lord was with him.

67His father Zacharias was filled with the Holy Spirit, and prophesied, saying, 68"Blessed be the Lord, the God of Israel, for he has visited and redeemed his people; 69and has raised up a horn of salvation (an Almighty Savior) for us in the house of his servant David 70(as he spoke by the mouth of his holy prophets [long ago]), 71salvation from our enemies and from the hand of all who hate us; 72to show mercy toward our fathers, to remember his holy covenant, 73the oath which he swore to Abraham our father, 74to grant to us that we, being delivered out of the hand of our enemies, should serve him without fear, 75in holiness and righteousness before him all the days of our life.

After Zacharias said this, he turned toward baby John, and said,

76And you, child, will be called a prophet of the Most High; for you will go before the face of the Lord to prepare his ways, 77to give knowledge of salvation to his people by the remission of their sins, 78because of the tender mercy of our God, by which the dawn from on high will visit us, 79to shine on those who sit in darkness and the shadow of death; to guide our feet into the way of peace." (Luke 1:57-79)

With those words, Zacharias praised God for the birth of John, which meant that the time had arrived for the long-awaited Redeemer to be born. John, the son of Zacharias, was the special-prophet whom God had chosen to announce the Messiah's arrival and prepare the people to recognize and receive Him.

We urge you to tune in next time as we hear how *God again sent down His angel Gabriel, this time to a virgin named Mary.*

God bless you as you meditate on these words of Zacharias:

68"Blessed be the Lord … for he has visited and redeemed his people; 69and has raised up [an Almighty Savior] for us in the house of his servant David (as he spoke by the mouth of his holy prophets [long ago]). (Luke 1:68-70)

Program 61

The Announcement

Luke 1; Matthew 1

Over the past sixty lessons, we have been studying the Scriptures of the First Covenant; that is, the Torah (*Tawrat*) of Moses, the Psalms (*Zabur*) of David, and the writings of the other ancient prophets. Last time, we began to study the New Covenant, that is, the *Injil*, an Arabic word meaning *Good News*. Truly, the message of the Gospel (*Injil*) is very good news for all who believe it, because it tells us how God sent to earth a mighty Savior, just as He promised through His prophets.

Before we begin our study in the Gospel, it would be good for us to remember why God planned to send a Savior to the descendants of Adam. Do you remember what happened the day Adam and Eve disobeyed God? In our study of the Torah we saw how Adam's disobedience led the human race away from the kingdom of God and into the kingdom of Satan. Adam's sin is the reason every one of us is born in crookedness. Just as *a rat only begets that which digs*, in the same way Adam and his offspring can only beget children that sin. Sinners produce sinners, and our sin condemns us so that we have no possible way of making ourselves right before the One who must judge us.

But praise God, the scriptures of the prophets do not end with the story of Adam's transgression. As we have already seen, on the same day that Adam and Eve sinned, God began to make known His wonderful plan to send into the world a Redeemer who could deliver the descendants of Adam from the dominion of Satan and sin. On that dark day when sin entered the world, God announced that this holy Redeemer would be born exclusively of a woman. (Genesis 3:15; Galatians 4:4) The Messiah, who was to shed His blood as the perfect Sacrifice for sinners, could not come from a father tainted with sin. He had to be perfect and holy even as God is perfect and holy. That is why the prophet Isaiah (who lived 700 years before the Messiah came) wrote: **The virgin will conceive, and bear a son, and shall call his name Immanuel – which is, being interpreted, *"God with us."*** (Isaiah 7:14; Matthew 1:23)

Let us now return to the book of the Gospel to see how God fulfilled what He promised concerning this perfect and holy Redeemer who was to be born of a virgin – a woman who had never been intimate with a man. In our last lesson, we saw how God's angel, Gabriel, appeared to an elderly Jew named Zacharias. Gabriel told Zacharias that he and his wife would have a son by the name of John, who was to prepare the way before the Redeemer.

To hear the story of Gabriel's visit to Mary, we are reading from Gospel of Luke, chapter 1:

> [26]**[When Elizabeth, the mother of John**, was] in the sixth month, the angel Gabriel was sent from God to a city of Galilee named Nazareth, [27]to a virgin pledged to be married to a man whose name was Joseph, of David's house. The virgin's name was Mary. [28]Having come in, the angel said to her, "Rejoice, you highly favored one! The Lord is with you. Blessed are you among women!" [29]But when she saw him, she was greatly troubled at the saying, and considered what kind of salutation this might be. [30]The angel said to her, "Don't be afraid, Mary, for you have found favor with God. [31]Behold, you will conceive in your womb and give birth to a son, and shall name him 'Jesus.' [32]He will be great and will be called the Son of the Most High. The Lord God will give him the throne of his father David, [33]and he will reign over the house of Jacob forever. There will be no end to his kingdom."
>
> [34]**"Mary said to the angel**, "How can this be, seeing I am a virgin?" [35]The angel answered her, "The Holy Spirit will come on you, and the power of the Most High will overshadow you. Therefore also the holy one who is born from you will be called the Son of God. [36]Behold, Elizabeth your relative also has conceived a son in her old age; and this is the sixth month with her who was called

barren. [37]For nothing spoken by God is impossible." [38]Mary said, "Behold, the servant of the Lord; let it be done to me according to your word." Then the angel departed from her. (Luke 1:26-38)

Let's pause here and talk a little about what happened when God's angel, Gabriel, appeared to Mary. Mary was a young woman who esteemed the word of God. Although she was promised in marriage to Joseph, they were not yet living together. Both Joseph and Mary were descendants of King David. You will remember that God's prophets not only foretold that the Messiah would be born of a virgin, but also that He would belong to the family line of King David.

So that no one misunderstands, there is something else you should know about Mary. It is this: Mary was a descendant of Adam. Like all of us, she was born with a sin nature. It is necessary that we say this, because some people worship Mary and pray to her. This is idolatry. Certainly Mary is worthy of honor since she was the woman through whom God brought the Messiah into the world. But this favor that God bestowed upon her does not make her worthy of worship because the Scripture says: **Worship the Lord your God, and ... serve him only.** (Matthew 4:10)

In the text we just read, Gabriel visited Mary and told her that she was the virgin through whom God intended to bring the Savior of sinners into the world. Gabriel also told Mary the name of the Child that she was to bear, saying, **"You are to give him the name Jesus."** The name *Jesus* means *the LORD saves*.[89] However, there was another name by which Gabriel referred to the Messiah. Did you hear it? He called Him **the Son of the Most High**. Like it or not, that is what Gabriel said. We have already read in the Psalms of David where God calls the Messiah *His Son*. Now we hear God's angel Gabriel also calling the Messiah **the Son of God.**

Friends, we know that some of you who hear the term *Son of God* may be thinking, "That's impossible! *Astaghfirullah!*[90] But as the

---

89 *Jesus* is a transliteration of the Greek form of the Hebrew *Yeshua* (alternative form of *Yehoshua - Joshua*), meaning *the LORD saves; rescues; delivers*. The Qur'an calls Jesus *Isa*.
90 Islamic maxim expressing: *May God forgive me/you (for uttering such blasphemy)*

(Wolof) proverb says: *Before you slap the shepherd on the mouth, you should find out what he is whistling about.* Similarly, before you denounce the name *Son of God* you should seek to learn what the term *Son of God* means.

In the Holy Scriptures, the Messiah is called *God's Son* more than 120 times. We, then, who believe the writings of the prophets cannot deny that God calls the Messiah *His Son*. What we want to know is *why* God calls Jesus His Son.

First, we need to know what the name *Son of God* does *not* mean. It does not mean that God took a wife and fathered a son. Such thoughts are blasphemy. The LORD God is the Highest One and does not produce children as a man produces them. That must be perfectly clear in our minds. We do not have time today to explain all that the name *Son of God* means, but let us be perfectly clear about what it does not mean. It does not mean that God took a wife and begot a son. This should not be difficult to understand.

For example, if you were born and raised in Senegal, and you travel outside the country, people may call you *"a son of Senegal,"* but that does not mean that Senegal took a wife and fathered a son. It simply means that you come from Senegal, your place of origin. That is how it is with Jesus the Messiah. God calls Him *His Son* because He came from God. The Messiah came from heaven. Before He was born He was with God; He was in God. He is the *Ruh Allah*,[91] the Spirit from God, and the *Kalimat*,[92] the Word, which was with God in the beginning. The Scripture says:

> [1]**In the beginning was the Word**, and the Word was with God, and the Word was God. [2]The same was in the beginning with God. [3]All things were made through him. Without him, nothing was made that has been made.… [14]The Word became flesh, and lived among us. (John 1:1-3,14)

---

91 *Ruh Allah* is Arabic for *Spirit/Soul of God*; like the Hebrew *Ruah*. This is a Qur'anic title for Jesus. The Bible reveals Jesus as God's *Eternal Spirit Son*, the second Spirit (Person, Entity) in the One true God who is a complex tri-unity. Genesis 1:1-3,26: God, His Spirit, and His Word. For more on this, see chapter 9 in ONE GOD ONE MESSAGE. www.king-of-glory.com
92 *Kalimat Allah*: Arabic for *the Word of God*, a title given to Messiah in the Bible and Qur'an.

Yes, the Messiah is the Word of God which came from heaven to be born as a man. We all know that the Messiah had no earthly father. So if He did not have an earthly father, then where did He come from? *Whose Son is He?* Listen again to what Gabriel told Mary. He said to her, **"The Holy Spirit will come on you, and the power of the Most High will overshadow you. [That is why] the holy one who is born from you will be called the Son of God."** (Luke 1:35)

Perhaps you have heard some say, *"Oh yes, we know that Jesus had no earthly father, but Jesus' birth of a virgin isn't so important. God merely wanted to show His power. God created Adam without father or mother. Next, He created Eve with only a father, that is, He formed her from the rib He took from Adam. Then to display His power further, God created a man using only a woman. That is the only reason Jesus was born without an earthly father."*

Dear friends, it is true that God is the Almighty One and nothing is impossible for Him. But concerning Jesus' birth of a virgin, you must know that the reason for it was infinitely more important than merely to display God's power! Do not let anyone deceive you. There is a very, very important reason that Jesus was born of a virgin thousands of years after God created Adam and Eve. Do you know the reason? The Holy Scripture tells us that Jesus the Messiah **came into the world to save sinners.** (1 Timothy 1:15) Jesus was born into the world to redeem the lost, sinful, contaminated, condemned descendants of Adam – therefore He could not originate from a man tainted with sin. As we have already seen, according to God's plan the Messiah had to shed His blood as a sacrifice to pay for sin. To be the Perfect Sacrifice, the Redeemer had to be without a single sin or fault, like the healthy, innocent sheep sacrificed yearly at the Feast of Sacrifice (*Eid al-Adha*).

God wants us to understand that the Messiah and the descendants of Adam are very different. We are sons of Adam, but Jesus is the Son of God. We, as children of Adam, are like the dirty earth because of our sin, but Jesus is like the rain that comes from heaven. He is pure and holy, just as God is pure and holy. That is why God is not ashamed to call Him *His Son.*

We hope these few thoughts are helpful in clarifying why the Messiah had to be born of a virgin and what the name *Son of God* means and does not mean.

We just heard Mary's story, but what about her fiancé Joseph? Several months after Mary became pregnant by the power of the Spirit of God, God sent His angel to Joseph. We will read from the Gospel of Matthew, chapter 1:

> [18]**Now the birth of Jesus Christ was like this:** After his mother, Mary, was engaged to Joseph, before they came together, she was found pregnant by the Holy Spirit. [19]Joseph, her husband, being a righteous man, and not willing to make her a public example, intended to put her away secretly.
>
> [20]**But when he thought about these things**, behold, an angel of the Lord appeared to him in a dream, saying, "Joseph, son of David, don't be afraid to take to yourself Mary as your wife, for that which is conceived in her is of the Holy Spirit. [21]She shall give birth to a son. You shall name him Jesus, for it is he who shall save his people from their sins." [22]Now all this has happened that it might be fulfilled which was spoken by the Lord through the prophet, saying, [23]"Behold, the virgin shall be with child, and shall give birth to a son. They shall call his name Immanuel," which is, being interpreted, "God with us."
>
> [24]**Joseph arose from his sleep**, and did as the angel of the Lord commanded him, and took his wife to himself; [25]and didn't know her sexually until she had given birth to her firstborn son. He named him Jesus. (Matthew 1:18-25)

We must stop here, but God willing, next time we will continue in the Gospel to hear the wonderful story of the Savior's birth.

God bless you as you ponder what the angel told Joseph:

> **You shall name him Jesus, for it is he who shall save his people from their sins.** (Matthew 1:21)

Program 62

The Messiah Is Born

Luke 2; Matthew 2

In the last lesson, in our study in the holy Gospel (Injil) we saw how God sent His angel Gabriel to the land of Israel, to the city of Nazareth, to a virgin named Mary. The angel told Mary that she would become pregnant by the power of the Spirit of God, give birth to a son, and name Him *Jesus*. Jesus means *the LORD saves.*

Do you remember the promise God made on the day that Adam ate the forbidden fruit? God had announced that the **Offspring of a woman** (Genesis 3:15) would crush the Serpent's head. That promised Offspring was now in the womb of a virgin girl and was about to make His entrance! Our program today is called *The Messiah is Born*.

At that time in history, the emperor of Rome, Caesar Augustus, was ruling over many countries, including the land of the Jews. But the Roman empire would not hinder God's plan to send the Redeemer into the world. In fact, God planned to use the Romans to fulfill the words of the prophets and the very plan of God.

Do you remember what the prophet Micah had written 700 years earlier about the Messiah's birth? Micah had written that the Messiah-King would be born in Bethlehem, the ancient hometown of King David. But there was a problem. Mary and Joseph lived in Nazareth, 150 kilometers to the north. How would the Scriptures be fulfilled? How would the Messiah be born in Bethlehem?

Ah, friends, as you know, nothing is too hard for the LORD God. He is God and is in perfect control. He knows everything that is going to happen. The Scriptures tell us that as the time drew near for

Mary to give birth, the great emperor of Rome issued a decree for every man and woman to go to the city of his ancestors to register there to pay a tax. This meant that Joseph and Mary would have to go to Bethlehem, to the city of King David, because they belonged to the descendants of David. Now let us return to the Gospel of Luke, chapter 2, and hear how Jesus the Messiah was born in Bethlehem, just as the prophets had announced it.

The Scripture says:

> ¹**Now in those days, a decree went out** from Caesar Augustus that all the world should be enrolled.... ³All went to enroll themselves, everyone to his own city. ⁴Joseph also went up from Galilee, out of the city of Nazareth, into Judea, to David's city, which is called Bethlehem, because he was of the house and family of David; ⁵to enroll himself with Mary, who was pledged to be married to him as wife, being pregnant.

> ⁶**While they were there,** the day had come for her to give birth. ⁷She gave birth to her firstborn son. She wrapped him in bands of cloth, and laid him in a feeding trough, because there was no room for them in the inn. (Luke 2:1,3-7)

We must pause here. Did you notice the circumstances in which the Messiah was born? He was born as a peasant, in very lowly circumstances. He was born in an animal stable because the inn in Bethlehem was full. The One who was to be the Savior and the Judge of the world was born in a smelly stable! Perhaps some are thinking: "This is incredible. If Jesus is the Savior of the world and the Lord of glory who will judge all the children of Adam, why was He not born in a palace, with great glory, so that everyone might know that He is the King of kings and the Lord of lords?"

Friends, we must remember that God's thoughts are different from our thoughts, and the glory of God is different from the glory of the world. Surely, the birth of Jesus was accompanied by great glory, but most of the children of Adam did not recognize it because God's glory and the world's glory are so different.

To illustrate, perhaps you have seen rich people who live in large and beautiful houses, wearing expensive clothes and living a life of luxury with servants attending to their every desire. That is the glory of the world. But God's glory is different from the world's glory. That is why the Messiah, who came from the presence of God, was not born in comfort and luxury. He was not like many rich people who do not understand the misery and hardships of the poor. No. The One whom God sent to rescue the children of Adam from the power of Satan and sin was born in lowly circumstances, yes, even in a stable. Now no one can say that the Messiah came only to save the wealthy, or that He doesn't understand the feelings of the poor. God wants everyone to know that the Redeemer came into the world to deliver whoever believes in Him – old and young, men and women, rich and poor, free and slave. As the Scripture says: **For you know the grace of our Lord Jesus Christ, that though he was rich, yet for your sakes he became poor, that you through his poverty might become rich.** (2 Corinthians 8:9)

Christ is the Greek word for the Hebrew word *Messiah*, meaning *the Anointed One*, or *the One Appointed by God*. Jesus Christ is the only one who ever chose to be born; and He chose to be born as a poor man. Perhaps one reason Jesus was born in a stable is to remind us that He is *the Lamb of God*. Many lambs are born in stables. A few lessons from now, we'll learn more about Jesus' title as *the Lamb of God*.

Now let us continue the story of the Messiah's birth in Bethlehem. The Scripture says:

> [8]**There were shepherds in the same country** staying in the field, and keeping watch by night over their flock. [9]Behold, an angel of the Lord stood by them, and the glory of the Lord shone around them, and they were terrified. [10]The angel said to them, "Don't be afraid, for behold, I bring you good news of great joy which will be to all the people. [11]For there is born to you today, in David's city, a Savior, who is Christ the Lord. [12]This is the sign to you: you will find a baby wrapped in strips of cloth, lying in a feeding trough."

¹³**Suddenly, there was with the angel** a multitude of the heavenly army praising God, and saying, ¹⁴"Glory to God in the highest, on earth peace, good will toward men."

¹⁵**When the angels went away** from them into the sky, the shepherds said to one another, "Let's go to Bethlehem, now, and see this thing that has happened, which the Lord has made known to us." ¹⁶They came with haste, and found both Mary and Joseph, and the baby was lying in the feeding trough.

¹⁷**When they saw it**, they publicized widely the saying which was spoken to them about this child. ¹⁸All who heard it wondered at the things which were spoken to them by the shepherds…. ²⁰The shepherds returned, glorifying and praising God for all the things that they had heard and seen, just as it was told them. (Luke 2:8-18,20)

Who were the first people God chose to hear the good news about the Messiah's birth? Did God give that most important news to the Roman emperor, the wealthy, or the religious leaders? No, God first announced the news of the Messiah's birth to peasants, humble shepherds who were waiting for Him to come. How thrilled the shepherds were to see the baby Jesus! What an awesome privilege! They were the first to see the One all the prophets had written about, the Messiah, the Savior of the world, the Eternal word of God wrapped in the tiny body of a baby!

Continuing in the Gospel, let us see what happened some time after Jesus was born. We have just heard how God proclaimed the birth of Jesus to some peasants by His angels who appeared in the sky. Now we are going to hear how God announced the Messiah's birth to some Magi[93] by an unusual star which appeared in the sky. We are reading from the Gospel of Matthew, chapter 2.

¹**Now when Jesus was born in Bethlehem of Judea** in the days of King Herod, behold, wise men from the east came to Jerusalem, saying, ²"Where is he who is born King of the Jews?

---

93 Or: *wisemen*; in Wolof: *masters of knowledge*

> For we saw his star in the east, and have come to worship him."
> ³When King Herod heard it, he was troubled, and all Jerusalem
> with him. ⁴Gathering together all the chief priests and scribes
> of the people, he asked them where the Christ would be born.
> ⁵They said to him, "In Bethlehem of Judea, for this is written
> through the prophet, ⁶'You Bethlehem, land of Judah, are
> in no way least among the princes of Judah; for out of you
> shall come a governor who shall shepherd my people, Israel.'"
> ⁷Then Herod secretly called the wise men, and learned from
> them exactly what time the star appeared. ⁸He sent them to
> Bethlehem, and said, "Go and search diligently for the young
> child. When you have found him, bring me word, so that I also
> may come and worship him." (Matthew 2:1-8)

But King Herod did not plan to worship the child; he planned to
kill Him. He did not want anyone to be king except himself.

> ⁹**[The wise men,] having heard the king**, went their way;
> and behold, the star, which they saw in the east, went before
> them until it came and stood over where the young child
> was. ¹⁰When they saw the star, they rejoiced with exceedingly
> great joy. ¹¹They came into the house and saw the young child
> with Mary, his mother, and they fell down and worshiped him.
> Opening their treasures, they offered to him gifts: gold, frank-
> incense, and myrrh. ¹²Being warned in a dream not to return
> to Herod, they went back to their own country another way.
> (Matthew 2:9-12)

Herod wanted to murder the Messiah-King. The people of
Jerusalem ignored Him. But the Magi, who crossed a scorching
desert to find Him, worshiped Him and gave Him gifts fit for
a king: gold, incense, and myrrh, which is a costly spice for
embalming the dead. Why the embalming spice? Did these
wisemen know that Jesus had been born to die?

What do you think about the birth of the Messiah-King? One
thing we can all agree on is that the birth of Jesus is unequaled in

the history of the world. Among all the prophets and kings and peoples of the earth, no one has ever been born like Jesus.

We have seen that the Messiah was born of a virgin by the power of God, just as the prophets of God and the angel Gabriel had foretold it. We have heard that Jesus was born in the town of Bethlehem, just as the prophet Micah had announced it some 700 years earlier. We saw how God sent His angel and a glorious radiance from heaven to some shepherds to tell them: **"I bring you good news of great joy which will be to all the people. For there is born to you today, in David's city, a Savior, who is Christ the Lord."** Then we saw how a multitude of angels appeared with the first angel, praising God and saying, **"Glory to God in the highest, on earth peace, good will toward men."** We also saw that God placed a great star in the sky to announce to some Magi who lived in a faraway land that the Messiah-King had been born.

No man has ever been born like this man. Jesus' birth is unique. We cannot compare Him with others. Jesus was more than a prophet. He is the One of whom all the prophets wrote. He is the Lord from heaven.

Friends, if Jesus were simply a prophet among many prophets, then why did God's prophets write about him hundreds of years before He was born? And why did the angels come down from heaven to celebrate His birth? If Jesus were merely a prophet among the prophets, then why did God place a great star in the sky to proclaim His birth? And for what reason was He born of a virgin? May you carefully consider these important questions.

Thank you for listening. In the next lesson, God willing, we will see *how Jesus the Messiah began His ministry on earth.*

God bless you as you ponder the angel's message to the shepherds:

> **Don't be afraid, for behold, I bring you good news of great joy which will be to all the people. For there is born to you today, in David's city, a Savior, who is Christ the Lord!**
> (Luke 2:10-11)

Program 63
The Holy Son

Luke 2; Matthew 3-4

Last time we heard the story of the Messiah's birth. No one has ever been born as Jesus was. Conceived of a virgin, He was born in the town of Bethlehem, exactly as prophesied. On the night of His birth, God sent a multitude of angels to poor shepherds who were spending the night in the fields of Bethlehem. An angel said to them, **"I bring you good news of great joy which will be to all the people. For there is born to you today, in David's city, a Savior, who is Christ the Lord!"** (Luke 2:10-11)

The book of the Gospel informs us that after the birth of Jesus, Joseph and Mary had four sons and some daughters. The child Jesus grew up with his younger siblings in a crowded house in northern Palestine, in the town of Nazareth. As you know, Joseph did not beget Jesus, but in the eyes of men, Jesus was the son of Joseph. Since Joseph was a carpenter, Jesus also worked as a carpenter while He lived at home. He was accustomed to hard work. The Scripture says: **And Jesus increased in wisdom and stature, and in favor with God and men.** (Luke 2:52)

Like all children, Jesus ate and slept, played and studied. But there was something about Him that made Him different from other children. Do you know what it was? The Scripture tells us: **[He] didn't sin, neither was deceit found in his mouth.** (1 Peter 2:22) He never said to anyone, "Forgive my faults,"[94] because He never wronged anyone. He could not commit sin, because there was no root of sin in Him. He had a holy nature. Evil was not a part of Him. He did only what pleased God. He had

---

94 Wolof: formula for asking forgiveness, especially on certain feast days

a physical body like ours, but He did not have an evil nature like ours. That is what the Scriptures declare when they say:

> **For we don't have a high priest** (mediator, spiritual leader) who can't be touched with the feeling of our infirmities, but one who has been in all points tempted like we are, yet without sin. (Hebrews 4:15)

Jesus did not have a wife, a house, or worldly riches. But He had a mission: to do the will of His Father in heaven who sent Him and to finish His work. When Jesus was thirty years old, one day He said goodbye to His family in Nazareth and headed down to the Jordan River, where the prophet John was preaching and baptizing the people in water.

Do you remember John (*Yahya*)? He was born six months before Jesus. John was the prophet God chose to prepare the hearts of people so that they might repent and welcome the Messiah sent from heaven. Listen to what is written in the Gospel about the prophet John and how he prepared the way before the Messiah. In the Gospel of Matthew, chapter 3, the Scripture says:

> ¹**In those days, John the Baptizer came**, preaching in the wilderness of Judea, saying, ²"Repent, for the kingdom of Heaven is at hand!" ³For this is he who was spoken of by Isaiah the prophet, saying, "The voice of one crying in the wilderness, make the way of the Lord ready! Make his paths straight!" ⁴Now John himself wore clothing made of camel's hair with a leather belt around his waist. His food was locusts and wild honey. ⁵Then people from Jerusalem, all of Judea, and all the region around the Jordan went out to him. ⁶They were baptized by him in the Jordan, confessing their sins. (Matthew 3:1-6)

Did you hear John's message? In brief, John preached: "Repent and prepare to meet the holy Messiah who has come to you from heaven!" Those who confessed their sins before God were baptized by John in the river. This is why the prophet John became known as *John the Baptizer*.

Being baptized in water could not wash away the people's sins, but by being baptized they showed their faith in the Messiah who had come to cleanse them from sin, heal them of their shame, and clothe them in His righteousness.

Some of those who responded to John so that he might baptize them belonged to the two most famous Jewish sects, the Sadducees and the Pharisees. The *Sadducees* were the wealthiest Jews and had influence in the Roman government. They liked to appear religious, but in their hearts they did not care about the writings of the prophets. The *Pharisees* were the religious experts who were zealous in praying, fasting, giving alms and paying tithes. Still, their worship was worthless, because they were trying to become righteous before God by their own efforts. Also, the Pharisees mixed their own traditions with the true word of God. Consequently, their worship of God had become nothing more than a flashy show combined with contempt for those who did not belong to their group. In short, the Pharisees and the Sadducees honored God with their lips, but their hearts were far from Him.

Now then, let us continue reading and hear how John rebuked these religious experts for their hypocrisy. The Scripture says:

> [7]**But when [John] saw many of the Pharisees** and Sadducees coming for his baptism, he said to them, "You offspring of vipers, who warned you to flee from the wrath to come? [8]Therefore produce fruit worthy of repentance! [9]Don't think to yourselves, 'We have Abraham for our father,' for I tell you that God is able to raise up children to Abraham from these stones. [10]Even now the ax lies at the root of the trees. Therefore every tree that doesn't produce good fruit is cut down, and cast into the fire. [11]"I indeed baptize you in water for repentance, but he who comes after me is mightier than I, whose sandals I am not worthy to carry. He will baptize you in the Holy Spirit. [12]His winnowing fork is in his hand, and he will thoroughly cleanse his threshing floor. He will gather his wheat into the barn, but the chaff he will burn up with unquenchable fire."

> [13]**Then Jesus came from Galilee to the Jordan to John**, to be baptized by him. [14]But John would have hindered him, saying, "I need to be baptized by you, and you come to me?" [15]But Jesus, answering, said to him, "Allow it now, for this is the fitting way for us to fulfill all righteousness." Then he allowed him. (Matthew 3:7-15)

We see that John baptized the Lord Jesus in the Jordan River. Some might ask, "Why did Jesus, who was without sin, ask the prophet John to baptize Him?" It is true that the Lord Jesus did not need to repent of anything, because He had never committed sin. Why then did Jesus come to John so that John might baptize Him as he was baptizing sinners? What did Jesus say about this? He said to John, **"Allow it now; for this is the fitting way for us to fulfill all righteousness."** By being baptized, Jesus not only put before us an example to follow, but He also showed us that He came to live as one of us and to die for us. At the end of the chapter, the Scripture says:

> [16]**Jesus, when he was baptized**, went up directly from the water: and behold, the heavens were opened to him. He saw the Spirit of God descending as a dove, and coming on him. [17]Behold, a voice out of the heavens said, "This is my beloved Son, with whom I am well pleased." (Matthew 3:16-17)

Whose voice thundered from the sky? Yes, it was the voice of God the Father. And what did He say? He said of Jesus, **"This is my beloved Son, with whom I am well pleased."** We have already heard the prophet David and the angel Gabriel calling the Messiah **"God's Son."** Now we hear God Himself calling Jesus **"my Son, whom I love."** Why did God call Jesus His Son? As we have already seen, Jesus the Messiah is **the Son of God** because He came from God, but there is another reason. God delighted to call Jesus His Son because He reflected God's nature.

All humans descended from Adam have been born with a nature stained by sin, but Jesus didn't come from Adam. Jesus came into the human family, but He did not originate from it. The

Messiah took on a physical form like ours but He did not take on our sinful nature. He had a perfect, holy nature. That is why God, the Holy One, took pleasure in Jesus as a father takes pleasure in an obedient, faithful son. It is sometimes said that the son is the shadow of the father. Whoever sees the son knows what his father is like. Likewise whoever knows Jesus knows what God is like, because Jesus is the Word who came from God to display God's character. The Scripture says: **The Word became flesh, and lived among us.… No one has seen God at any time. The one and only Son, who is in the bosom of the Father, has declared him.** (John 1:14,18) Jesus is the holy Son. That is why God was not ashamed to say from heaven: **"This is my beloved Son, with whom I am well pleased!"**

In the remaining time today we will read what Jesus did after He was baptized:

> [1]**Then Jesus was led up by the Spirit** into the wilderness to be tempted by the devil. [2]When he had fasted forty days and forty nights, he was hungry afterward. [3]The tempter [that is Satan] came and said to him, "If you are the Son of God, command that these stones become bread." [4]But he answered, "It is written, 'Man shall not live by bread alone, but by every word that proceeds out of God's mouth.'"

> [5]**Then the devil took him** into the holy city. He set him on the pinnacle of the temple, [6]and said to him, "If you are the Son of God, throw yourself down, for it is written, 'He will command his angels concerning you,' and, 'On their hands they will bear you up.'…" [7]Jesus said to him, "Again, it is written, 'You shall not test the Lord, your God.'"

> [8]**Again, the devil took him** to an exceedingly high mountain, and showed him all the kingdoms of the world and their glory. [9]He said to him, "I will give you all of these things, if you will fall down and worship me." [10]Then Jesus said to him, "Get behind me, Satan! For it is written, 'You shall worship the Lord your God, and you shall serve him only.'" [11]Then the devil left him, and behold, angels came and served him. (Matthew 4:1-11)

Three times Satan tried to entice Jesus to obey him and sin. All three times Jesus answered the devil by quoting the word of God. As Satan had tempted Adam and Eve to sin in the earthly Garden of Paradise (Eden), so also he tempted the Lord Jesus to sin in the wilderness. But Jesus did not sin.

Why did the devil tempt Jesus? Because he knew that Jesus was the Redeemer who had come from heaven to earth to save the children of Adam from his dominion. Satan knew that if Jesus were to commit a single sin, He could not save the children of Adam from the dominion of sin. Thus Satan harassed Jesus, attempting to deceive Him. But Jesus did not fall into the devil's trap.

Yes, Satan overcame and corrupted our ancestors, Adam and Eve, but he could not overcome the holy Son of God. The Lord Jesus could not sin because God cannot sin. Like Father, like Son. Jesus was the Word of God in a human body. God sent Him into the world to deliver the children of Adam from the power of Satan and the penalty of sin. Only the Lord Jesus can deliver us from Satan and sin, because only He overcame Satan and sin. That is why the Scripture says of the Messiah:

> 26**For such a high priest was fitting for us:** holy, guiltless, undefiled, separated from sinners, and made higher than the heavens; 27[the Lord Jesus] doesn't need, like those high priests, to offer up sacrifices daily, first for his own sins, and then for the sins of the people. For he did this once for all, when he offered up himself. (Hebrews 7:26-27)

Thank you for listening.

May the LORD give you insight into all this. We invite you to join us next time for a program called *The Lamb of God*.

We leave you with this verse from the Holy Scripture:

> **[Jesus Christ] was revealed to take away our sins, and in him is no sin.** (1 John 3:5)

Program 64

The Lamb of God

John 1, 3

In the past two programs, we saw that Jesus the Messiah was unique in His birth and in His character (nature). Regarding *His birth*, Jesus was unique. He had no earthly father. By being born of a virgin woman He came into the human race, but He did not originate from the human race. Regarding *His character*, Jesus was perfectly holy. Because He came from God and not from Adam, He had a body like ours, but He did not have our sin nature.

Today we plan to continue in the Gospel (*Injil*) and hear what the prophet John (*Yahya*) testified about Jesus. John was the prophet whom God sent to prepare the way before the Messiah.

In the Gospel of John,[95] chapter 1, we read:

> [19]**This is John's testimony**, when the Jews sent priests and Levites from Jerusalem to ask him, "Who are you?" [20]He declared, and didn't deny, but he declared, "I am not the Christ [the Messiah]." … [22]They said therefore to him, "Who are you? Give us an answer to take back to those who sent us. What do you say about yourself?" [23]He said, "I am the voice of one crying in the wilderness, 'Make straight the way of the Lord.'" … [26]John answered them, "I baptize in water, but among you stands one whom you don't know. [27]He is the one who comes after me, who is preferred before me, whose sandal strap I'm not worthy to loosen." [28]These things were done in Bethany beyond the Jordan, where John was baptizing.

---

²⁹**The next day, he saw Jesus coming to him**, and said, "Behold, the Lamb of God, who takes away the sin of the world! ³⁰This is he of whom I said, 'After me comes a man who is preferred before me, for he was before me.' (John 1:19-20,22-23,26-30)

Let us pause here and think about the testimony of the prophet John. Did you hear how he referred to the Messiah? Let us listen again to the Scripture. It says: [**John**] **saw Jesus coming to him, and said, "Behold, the Lamb of God, who takes away the sin of the world!"** We have already read how the prophets of God called the Messiah by many names such as the Redeemer, the Savior, the King, the Lord, the word of God and the Son of God. Now we hear Him being called **the Lamb of God.**

Why did John call Jesus *the Lamb of God*? Was Jesus a lamb? No, Jesus was not an actual lamb, just as we who are Senegalese are not actual lions, although we sometimes call ourselves such. ⁹⁶All of us know clearly that this is only a manner of speech, because we would like to have the strength and courage of a lion. But why did the prophet John call Jesus the Lamb of God? How was the Messiah like a lamb? Why did John point to Jesus, and say to his disciples, **"Behold, the Lamb of God, who takes away the sin of the world"**?

To understand what the title *Lamb of God* means, we should remember what God decreed after Adam and Eve had sinned. God decreed that the payment for sin is death and hell and that if the blood of a spotless sacrifice is not shed, there could be no forgiveness of sin. Then we read how Adam and Eve's second son, Abel, believed God, slaughtered a lamb and offered it to God on an altar as a sacrifice to cover his sin. When God saw the blood of the lamb, He canceled the punishment for Abel's sin, and judged him as righteous because an innocent lamb had died in his place. But God also made it known that the blood of a lamb was only a temporary solution. A lamb could not be accepted as a sufficient payment for sin forever, because the value of a lamb

---

96 Senegal's mascot is the lion.

is not equal to the value of a man, woman, or child. The lamb was only a shadow of the holy Redeemer who was to come into the world and shed His blood to deliver sinners from God's righteous judgment. Because of who Jesus was (the Eternal Word and Son of God), He was qualified to pay off the sin debt of the world.

Seven hundred years before the birth of Jesus, the prophet Isaiah wrote that the Messiah would be **as a lamb that is led to the slaughter** as a sacrifice to take away our sins. (Isaiah 53:7) Thus, between the time of Abel and the time of the Messiah, all who believed God respected and participated in the sacrifices of lambs. Noah, Abraham, Moses, David, the other prophets, and all who believed in God and His plan, had the habit of sacrificing spotless lambs to cover sin. These sacrifices pointed to a time when God would send down very His own Lamb who would come to take away sin.

That is why, dear friends, when the prophet John saw Jesus coming toward him, he pointed to Him and said to his disciples, **"Behold, the Lamb of God, who takes away the sin of the world!"** This is how John made known to his disciples that this Jesus who was standing before them was the Messiah, the Lamb which God had sent down from heaven to become the Perfect Sacrifice. Jesus is the holy sacrifice who came into the world to die in the place of the children of Adam so that God can forgive us of our sins forever.

After this, the Scripture says:

> [35]**Again, the next day, John was standing** with two of his disciples, [36]and he looked at Jesus as he walked, and said, "Behold, the Lamb of God!" [37]The two disciples heard him speak, and they followed Jesus. [38]Jesus turned and saw them following, and said to them, "What are you looking for?" They said to him, "Rabbi" (which is to say, being interpreted, *Teacher*), "where are you staying?" [39]He said to them, "Come, and see." They came and saw where he was staying, and they stayed with him that day. It was about the tenth hour. [40]One of the two who heard John and followed him was Andrew,

Simon Peter's brother. [41]He first found his own brother, Simon, and said to him, "We have found the Messiah!" … [42]He brought him to Jesus. Jesus looked at him, and said, "You are Simon the son of Jonah. You shall be called Cephas" (which is by interpretation, Peter [that is, *Rock*]).

[43]**On the next day, he was determined to go** out into Galilee, and he found Philip. Jesus said to him, "Follow me." [44]Now Philip was from Bethsaida, of the city of Andrew and Peter. [45]Philip found Nathanael, and said to him, "We have found him, of whom Moses in the law, and the prophets, wrote: Jesus of Nazareth, the son of Joseph." [46]Nathanael said to him, "Can any good thing come out of Nazareth?" Philip said to him, "Come and see." (John 1:35-46)

Thus, the disciples of God's prophet John began to follow Jesus. Why did John's disciples leave him to follow the Lord Jesus? It was because they believed what John had told them when he said that Jesus was the Messiah and the Lamb of God about whom the prophets wrote. That is why Andrew (who had been John's disciple), when he recognized that Jesus was the Messiah, went to find his brother Simon Peter and said to him, **"We have found the Messiah!"** And when another disciple, Philip, recognized who Jesus was, he too was overjoyed and told his friend Nathanael, **"We have found him, of whom Moses in the law, and the prophets, wrote: Jesus of Nazareth!"**

Andrew and Peter, Philip and Nathanael all rejoiced greatly when they saw Jesus, because they knew that for thousands of years the prophets had been predicting the coming of the Messiah. And now they were seeing Him with their own eyes. Praise God! The mighty Redeemer of whom all of the prophets wrote was in their midst! At last, the Messiah had come! These four disciples of John began to follow Jesus, becoming His first disciples. Next, the Scripture says:

[21]**Going on from there, [Jesus] saw two other brothers**, James the son of Zebedee, and John his brother, in the boat with

Zebedee their father, mending their nets. … [¹⁹He said to them, "Come after me, and I will make you fishers for men."] ²²They immediately left the boat and their father, and followed him.

²³**Jesus went about in all Galilee**, teaching in their synagogues, preaching the Good News of the kingdom, and healing every disease and every sickness among the people. ²⁴The report about him went out into all Syria. They brought to him all who were sick, afflicted with various diseases and torments, possessed with demons, epileptics, and paralytics; and he healed them. ²⁵Great multitudes from Galilee, Decapolis, Jerusalem, Judea, and from beyond the Jordan followed him. (Matthew 4:21,19,22-25)

In the next lesson, we plan to read more about how Jesus taught the crowds and worked great miracles. But in the remaining time today, we want to see what happened to the prophet John. As he proclaimed that Jesus was the Messiah about whom all the prophets wrote, John's disciples began to leave him in order to follow Jesus the Messiah. Did that please John? We can hear the answer in the Gospel of John, chapter 3.

²⁶**[Some people] came to John** and said to him, "Rabbi, he who was with you beyond the Jordan, to whom you have testified, behold, he baptizes, and everyone is coming to him." ²⁷John answered, "A man can receive nothing unless it has been given him from heaven. ²⁸You yourselves testify that I said, 'I am not the Christ,' but, 'I have been sent before him.' ²⁹He who has the bride is the bridegroom; but the friend of the bridegroom, who stands and hears him, rejoices greatly because of the bridegroom's voice. This, my joy, therefore is made full. ³⁰He must increase, but I must decrease. (John 3:26-30)

What do you think about this? John expressed great joy when his disciples left him to follow the Messiah. John's joy was complete because he had accomplished his mission; he had prepared the way before the Messiah. Like a true prophet of God, John's desire was to lead people to the Savior. That's why John said, "**He must** increase, but I must decrease." How different the prophet John was from so many religious leaders today. A true spiritual leader will always point you to the Lord Jesus, because Jesus is the only One who can get you into the holy presence of God in Paradise. John knew that there were many prophets of God, but only one Savior. The prophet John said: **One who believes in the Son (Jesus the Messiah) has eternal life, but one who disobeys the Son won't see life, but the wrath of God remains on him.** (John 3:36)

Concerning the end of John's life, the Scripture says:

> [18]**With many other exhortations he preached good news** [about the Messiah] to the people. [19]But... Herod the tetrarch, [was] reproved by [John for marrying Herodias, his brother's wife, and] for all the evil things which Herod had done. (Luke 3:18-19)

John rebuked King Herod for his sin, but instead of repenting of his sin, the king got angry and gave orders to have John arrested, bound, imprisoned, and, eventually, beheaded. And John found himself, as the Scripture puts it, **absent from the body, and...at home with the Lord.** (2 Corinthians 5:8)

Jesus told His disciples that the prophet John was greater than all the prophets who came before him. What made John so great? Because He pointed people to Jesus the Messiah. While the previous prophets proclaimed "*The Messiah will come,*" John preached "*The Messiah is here! Believe in Him. Follow Him.*"

In the will of God, in our next program, we will discover why Jesus is called *the Great Physician*.

May God give you insight into what we have studied today, especially into what the prophet John said of Jesus:

> **"Behold, the Lamb of God, who takes away the sin of the world!"** (John 1:29)

Program 65

The Great Healer

Mark 1-2

As most of you know, in our journey through the Holy Scriptures we are now studying in the Gospel (*Injil*). This is the holy book which relates the Good News about the Messiah who came into the world to free the children of Adam from the dominion of Satan and sin. In our last program we read that Jesus the Messiah began to visit the towns, teaching the multitudes and healing every disease and sickness among the people. His name became famous throughout the land.

Today we continue the narrative about Jesus the Messiah, to hear more of His teachings and see more of His works. In the Gospel of Mark, chapter 1, we read:

> ²¹[**Jesus and his disciples**] went into [the city of] Capernaum, and immediately on the Sabbath day he entered into the synagogue and taught. ²²They were astonished at his teaching, for he taught them as having authority, and not as the scribes. ²³Immediately there was in their synagogue a man with an unclean spirit, and he cried out, ²⁴saying, "Ha! What do we have to do with you, Jesus, you Nazarene? Have you come to destroy us? I know you who you are: the Holy One of God!" ²⁵Jesus rebuked him, saying, "Be quiet, and come out of him!" ²⁶The unclean spirit, convulsing him and crying with a loud voice, came out of him. ²⁷They were all amazed, so that they questioned among themselves, saying, "What is this? A new teaching? For with authority he commands even the unclean spirits, and they obey him!" ²⁸The report of him went out immediately everywhere into all the region of Galilee and its surrounding area. (Mark 1:21-28)

The teachings of Jesus were very different from the teachings of the religious teachers. All who were listening to Jesus in the synagogue (special building for worship and instruction in the Scriptures) were amazed at His words because He taught them with an authority which their teachers of the law did not have.

You know about the teachers of the law. They were supposed to explain the Torah (*Tawrat*), the Psalms (*Zabur*) and the other books of the prophets. However, most of them could not correctly explain the writings of the prophets because they did not really understand them. They knew all about their religious duties and the traditions of their ancestors but they did not know the word of the LORD. These religious "experts" honored God with their lips but did not love His word. So when Jesus (who had never studied in their schools of religious training) entered their synagogue and began to explain the Scriptures with authority and clarity, these teachers were greatly embarrassed. To add to their humiliation, the people in the synagogue were totally amazed by Jesus' words and works and were asking each other, *"Who is this? Where does He get this new teaching? How can He teach with such authority? He even commands evil spirits, and they obey Him. We have never seen anything like this. No one has ever taught like this man. No one has ever done such things as He."*

Truly, from the day that Adam sinned until the day that Jesus began to do miracles, people had never seen anyone so powerful. But now they were seeing One who with a single word could make Satan and his demons flee. Only the Messiah who came from heaven could do that. Did you hear what the demon-possessed man said to Jesus? He cried out saying, **"What do we have to do with you, Jesus, you Nazarene? Have you come to destroy us? I know you who you are: the Holy One of God!"** (Mark 1:24) The demons knew well where Jesus had come from and who He was. But most of the people did not know who Jesus really was. Satan and his evil angels greatly feared the Lord Jesus because they knew with certainty that He was the Word by which God had created the heavens and the earth in the beginning. They knew that Jesus was the Holy One who had the authority to throw them into the eternal fire. That is why they trembled with fear at the name of Jesus.

Now then, let us continue in chapter 1. The Scripture says:

> ²⁹[**After Jesus and His disciples**] had come out of the synagogue, they came into the house of Simon [Peter] and Andrew, with James and John. ³⁰Now Simon's wife's mother lay sick with a fever, and immediately they told him about her. ³¹He came and took her by the hand and raised her up. The fever left her immediately, and she served them. ³²At evening, when the sun had set, they brought to him all who were sick and those who were possessed by demons. ³³All the city was gathered together at the door. ³⁴He healed many who were sick with various diseases and cast out many demons. He didn't allow the demons to speak, because they knew him.
>
> ³⁵**Early in the morning, while it was still dark**, he rose up and went out, and departed into a deserted place, and prayed there. ³⁶Simon and those who were with him searched for him. ³⁷They found him and told him, "Everyone is looking for you." ³⁸He said to them, "Let's go elsewhere into the next towns, that I may preach there also, because I came out for this reason." ³⁹He went into their synagogues throughout all Galilee, preaching and casting out demons. ⁴⁰A leper came to him, begging him, kneeling down to him, and saying to him, "If you want to, you can make me clean." ⁴¹Being moved with compassion, he stretched out his hand, and touched him, and said to him, "I want to. Be made clean." ⁴²When he had said this, immediately the leprosy departed from him and he was made clean. (Mark 1:29-42)

So we see that Jesus healed people of every disease and sickness, showing compassion to the children of Adam because they were weary and helpless, like sheep without a shepherd. But there was another reason for the many great miracles that Jesus did. Jesus healed every kind of disease and drove out demons to provide proof so that people could know that He was the Messiah whom God had promised so long ago through His prophets. For instance, we have already read that the prophet Isaiah, hundreds of years before Jesus was even born, wrote that when the Messiah comes, **Then the eyes of the blind will be opened, and the ears of the deaf will be unstopped. Then the lame man will leap like a deer, and the tongue of the mute will sing.** (Isaiah 35:5-6) With these words the prophet Isaiah announced that the Messiah would do miracles that no one had ever done. We have already read how God gave Moses and Elijah the ability to do great miracles, but the miracles which those two prophets did were few compared to the ones which the Messiah did. Also, Moses and Elijah did not have any power of their own to perform miracles, but Jesus the Messiah overflowed with the power of God because He Himself was the Word of God through whom the world was created.

Continuing in the Gospel of Mark, chapter 2, the Scripture says:

> [1]**When he entered again into Capernaum** after some days, it was heard that he was at home. [2]Immediately many were gathered together, so that there was no more room, not even around the door; and he spoke the word to them. [3]Four people came, carrying a paralytic to him. [4]When they could not come near to him for the crowd, they removed the roof where he was. When they had broken it up, they let down the mat that the paralytic was lying on. [5]Jesus, seeing their faith, said to the paralytic, "Son, your sins are forgiven you."
>
> [6]**But there were some of the scribes** (teachers of the law of Moses) sitting there and reasoning in their hearts, [7]"Why does this man speak blasphemies like that? Who can forgive sins but God alone?" [8]Immediately Jesus, perceiving in his spirit that they so reasoned within themselves, said to them, "Why do you reason these things in your hearts? [9]Which is easier, to tell the paralytic, 'Your sins are forgiven;' or to say, 'Arise, and take up your bed, and walk?' [10]But that you may know that the Son of Man [that is, the Messiah] has authority on earth to forgive sins"—he said to the paralytic— [11]"I tell you, arise, take up your mat, and go to your house." [12]He arose, and immediately took up the mat and went out in front of them all, so that

they were all amazed and glorified God, saying, "We never saw anything like this!" (Mark 2:1-12)

In this narrative, we see that the power of Jesus was not limited to healing a person's sick body, but He also had the power to heal a person's sinful heart. Jesus, who is the Great Physician, knew that the most critical problem the lame man had was not his impotent legs, but the sin that was in his heart. That is why Jesus first said to him, **"Son, your sins are forgiven you."**

What were the teachers of the law thinking when Jesus said this? They were saying to themselves, "Jesus is blaspheming! No one can forgive sins but God alone." Their thoughts were partly true and partly false. It is true that no one can forgive sins except God alone. However, when the teachers of the law thought that Jesus was blaspheming God, they were mistaken, because they did not comprehend that Jesus was the Mediator whom God had sent down to make sinners right with God. Jesus was the Word of God, so that when He said, "Your sins are forgiven," it was God Himself saying it. The Lord Jesus was the Voice of God on earth. And not only that, Jesus is also the One who was born to give His life as the perfect Sacrifice which takes away sin forever. As a father grants his son the authority to work for him and to speak for him, so God the Father in heaven gave Jesus the authority to forgive sins on earth. But the teachers of the law did not believe this.

We only have a little time left. Therefore, let us read on a little farther in the verses that follow.

> **As Jesus passed by** from [the house where he had healed the paralytic], he saw a man called Matthew sitting at the tax collection office. He said to him, "Follow me." He got up and followed him (Matthew 9:9) [15]He was reclining at the table in [Matthew's] house, and many tax collectors and sinners sat down with Jesus and his disciples, for there were many, and they followed him. [16]The scribes and the Pharisees, when they saw that he was eating with the sinners and tax collectors, said to his disciples, "Why is it that he eats and drinks with tax collectors and sinners?" [17]When Jesus

heard it, he said to them, "Those who are healthy have no need for a physician, but those who are sick. I came not to call the righteous, but sinners to repentance." (Mark 2:15-17)

With those words, Jesus, the Great Physician, wanted to show the teachers of the law that they were sick before God because of their sin. But these religious teachers did not recognize their sin. In fact, they were criticizing Jesus because He was eating with tax collectors and those who were known as "sinners." However, to be with sinners and to save them from their sin was the very reason for which Jesus was born.

How about you? Do you realize that you were born with a terrible disease called sin? The sin within you is why you must die and come before the judgment of God the Holy One. But praise God, there is One who can heal you of the sin in your heart! Do you know who that One is? Yes, it is Jesus the Messiah – the One who was without sin; the One who came into the world to save the children of Adam from their sin and shame. But before the Lord Jesus can cure your heart of sin, you must first recognize that you are sick – sick with sin. Only those who know they are sick will go to the doctor. Likewise, only those who know they are sinners will turn to Jesus, the Savior of sinners. Jesus did not come for those who imagine that they are righteous, but for those who know that they are sinners. That is why He said to the teachers of the law, **"Those who are healthy have no need for a physician, but those who are sick. I came not to call the righteous, but sinners to repentance."** (Mark 2:17)

Friends, this is where we must stop today. In our next program, in the will of God, we will continue in the Gospel and hear some wonderful and profound words which came from the mouth of Jesus, the Healer of sinners.

God bless you as you ponder Jesus' words to the religious teachers:

> **Those who are healthy have no need for a physician, but those who are sick. I came not to call the righteous, but sinners to repentance.** (Mark 2:17)

Program 66

The Great Teacher

Matthew 5-7

I n the last program, we saw that Jesus the Messiah was visiting the towns in Palestine, teaching the multitudes, healing the sick, and driving out demons. People were amazed and asked each other, **"What is this? A new teaching? For with authority he commands even the unclean spirits, and they obey him!"** (Mark 1:27)

Today we plan to continue in the book of the Gospel and hear the wonderful words which came from the mouth of the Lord Jesus one day when He was on a mountainside with His disciples and a great crowd. We do not have time to read everything that Jesus taught His disciples on that day, but anyone who wants to can read the entire message in the Gospel of Matthew, chapter 5 to chapter 7. So friends, wherever you are right now, we invite you to listen to *The Sermon on the Mount* – a sermon the Lord Jesus preached about two thousand years ago. The Scripture says:

¹**Seeing the multitudes, [Jesus]** went up onto the mountain. When he had sat down, his disciples came to him. ²He opened his mouth and taught them, saying,

³"**Blessed are the poor in spirit**, for theirs is the kingdom of Heaven. ⁴Blessed are those who mourn, for they shall be comforted. ⁵Blessed are the gentle, for they shall inherit the earth. ⁶Blessed are those who hunger and thirst for righteousness, for they shall be filled. ⁷Blessed are the merciful, for they shall obtain mercy. ⁸Blessed are the pure in heart, for they shall see God. ⁹Blessed are the peacemakers, for they shall be called children of God. ¹⁰Blessed are those who have been persecuted for righteousness' sake, for theirs is the kingdom

of Heaven. [11]Blessed are you when people reproach you, persecute you, and say all kinds of evil against you falsely, for my sake. [12]Rejoice, and be exceedingly glad, for great is your reward in heaven. For that is how they persecuted the prophets who were before you.

[17]"**Don't think that I came to destroy the law** or the prophets. I didn't come to destroy, but to fulfill. [18]For most certainly, I tell you, until heaven and earth pass away, not even one smallest letter or one tiny pen stroke shall in any way pass away from the law, until all things are accomplished. [19]Therefore, whoever shall break one of these least commandments and teach others to do so, shall be called least in the kingdom of Heaven; but whoever shall do and teach them shall be called great in the kingdom of Heaven. [20]For I tell you that unless your righteousness exceeds that of the scribes and Pharisees, there is no way you will enter into the kingdom of Heaven.

[21]"**You have heard that it was said to the ancient ones**, 'You shall not murder;' and 'Whoever murders will be in danger of the judgment.' [22]But I tell you that everyone who is angry with his brother without a cause will be in danger of the judgment…. [27]You have heard that it was said, 'You shall not commit adultery;' [28]but I tell you that everyone who gazes at a woman to lust after her has committed adultery with her already in his heart…. [33]Again you have heard that it was said to the ancient ones, 'You shall not make false vows, but shall perform to the Lord your vows,' [34]but I tell you, don't swear at all: neither by heaven, for it is the throne of God; [35]nor by the earth, for it is the footstool of his feet…. [37]But let your 'Yes' be 'Yes' and your 'No' be 'No.' Whatever is more than these is of the evil one.

[38]**You have heard that it was said**, 'An eye for an eye, and a tooth for a tooth.' [39]But I tell you, don't resist him who is evil; but whoever strikes you on your right cheek, turn to him the other also. [40]If anyone sues you to take away your coat, let him have your cloak also. [41]Whoever compels you to go one mile, go with him two.…

⁴³**You have heard that it was said**, 'You shall love your neighbor and hate your enemy.' ⁴⁴But I tell you, love your enemies, bless those who curse you, do good to those who hate you, and pray for those who mistreat you and persecute you, ⁴⁵that you may be children of your Father who is in heaven. For he makes his sun to rise on the evil and the good, and sends rain on the just and the unjust. ⁴⁶For if you love those who love you, what reward do you have? Don't even the tax collectors do the same? ⁴⁷If you only greet your friends, what more do you do than others? Don't even the tax collectors do the same? ⁴⁸Therefore you shall be perfect, just as your Father in heaven is perfect. (Matthew 5:1-12,17-22,27-28,33-35,37-41,43-48)

¹**"Be careful that you don't do your charitable giving** before men, to be seen by them, or else you have no reward from your Father who is in heaven. ²Therefore, when you do merciful deeds, don't sound a trumpet before yourself, as the hypocrites do in the synagogues and in the streets, that they may get glory from men. Most certainly I tell you, they have received their reward. ³But when you do merciful deeds, don't let your left hand know what your right hand does, ⁴so that your merciful deeds may be in secret, then your Father who sees in secret will reward you openly.

⁵**"When you pray, you shall not be as the hypocrites**, for they love to stand and pray in the synagogues and in the corners of the streets, that they may be seen by men. Most certainly, I tell you, they have received their reward. ⁶But you, when you pray, enter into your inner room, and having shut your door, pray to your Father who is in secret; and your Father who sees in secret will reward you openly. ⁷In praying, don't use vain repetitions as the Gentiles do; for they think that they will be heard for their much speaking. ⁸Therefore don't be like them, for your Father knows what things you need before you ask him.

⁹**"Pray like this: 'Our Father in heaven**, may your name be kept holy. ¹⁰Let your kingdom come. Let your will be done on earth as it is in heaven. ¹¹Give us today our daily bread. ¹²Forgive us

our debts, as we also forgive our debtors. [13]Bring us not into temptation, but deliver us from the evil one. For yours is the kingdom, the power, and the glory forever. Amen.'

[16]**"Moreover when you fast**, don't be like the hypocrites, with sad faces. For they disfigure their faces that they may be seen by men to be fasting. Most certainly I tell you, they have received their reward. [17]But you, when you fast, anoint your head and wash your face, [18]so that you are not seen by men to be fasting, but by your Father who is in secret; and your Father, who sees in secret, will reward you.

[19]**"Don't lay up treasures for yourselves on the earth**, where moth and rust consume, and where thieves break through and steal; [20]but lay up for yourselves treasures in heaven, where neither moth nor rust consume, and where thieves don't break through and steal; [21]for where your treasure is, there your heart will be also.

[22]**"The lamp of the body is the eye.** If therefore your eye is sound, your whole body will be full of light. [23]But if your eye is evil, your whole body will be full of darkness. If therefore the light that is in you is darkness, how great is the darkness! [24]No one can serve two masters, for either he will hate the one and love the other, or else he will be devoted to one and despise the other. You can't serve both God and Mammon.

[25]**"Therefore I tell you, don't be anxious for your life:** what you will eat, or what you will drink; nor yet for your body, what you will wear. Isn't life more than food, and the body more than clothing? [26]See the birds of the sky, that they don't sow, neither do they reap, nor gather into barns. Your heavenly Father feeds them. Aren't you of much more value than they? [27]Which of you by being anxious, can add one moment to his lifespan?

[28]**"Why are you anxious about clothing?** Consider the lilies of the field, how they grow. They don't toil, neither do they spin, [29]yet I tell you that even Solomon in all his glory was not

dressed like one of these. [30]But if God so clothes the grass of the field, which today exists and tomorrow is thrown into the oven, won't he much more clothe you, you of little faith? [31]Therefore don't be anxious, saying, 'What will we eat?', 'What will we drink?' or, 'With what will we be clothed?' [32]For the Gentiles seek after all these things; for your heavenly Father knows that you need all these things. [33]But seek first God's kingdom and his righteousness; and all these things will be given to you as well. (Matthew 6:1-13,16-33)

[1]**"Don't judge, so that you won't be judged.** [2]For with whatever judgment you judge, you will be judged; and with whatever measure you measure, it will be measured to you. [3]Why do you see the speck that is in your brother's eye, but don't consider the beam that is in your own eye? [4]Or how will you tell your brother, 'Let me remove the speck from your eye,' and behold, the beam is in your own eye? [5]You hypocrite! First remove the beam out of your own eye, and then you can see clearly to remove the speck out of your brother's eye.... [12]Therefore, whatever you desire for men to do to you, you shall also do to them; for this is the law and the prophets.

[7]**"Ask, and it will be given you. Seek, and you will find.** Knock, and it will be opened for you. [8]For everyone who asks receives. He who seeks finds. To him who knocks it will be opened.

[13]**"Enter in by the narrow gate**; for the gate is wide and the way is broad that leads to destruction, and there are many who enter in by it. [14]How narrow is the gate, and restricted is the way that leads to life! Few are those who find it.

[15]**"Beware of false prophets**, who come to you in sheep's clothing, but inwardly are ravening wolves. [16]By their fruits you will know them. Do you gather grapes from thorns or figs from thistles? [17]Even so, every good tree produces good fruit, but the corrupt tree produces evil fruit. [18]A good tree can't produce evil fruit, neither can a corrupt tree produce good fruit. [19]Every tree

that doesn't grow good fruit is cut down and thrown into the fire. [20]Therefore by their fruits you will know them.

[21]**"Not everyone who says to me**, 'Lord, Lord,' will enter into the kingdom of Heaven, but he who does the will of my Father who is in heaven. [22]Many will tell me in that day, 'Lord, Lord, didn't we prophesy in your name, in your name cast out demons, and in your name do many mighty works?' [23]Then I will tell them, 'I never knew you. Depart from me, you who work iniquity.'

[24]**"Everyone therefore who hears these words of mine** and does them, I will liken him to a wise man who built his house on a rock. [25]The rain came down, the floods came, and the winds blew and beat on that house; and it didn't fall, for it was founded on the rock. [26]Everyone who hears these words of mine and doesn't do them will be like a foolish man who built his house on the sand. [27]The rain came down, the floods came, and the winds blew and beat on that house; and it fell—and its fall was great."

[28]**When Jesus had finished saying these things**, the multitudes were astonished at his teaching, [29]for he taught them with authority, and not like the scribes. (Matthew 7:1-5,12,7-8,13-29)

Friends, we must stop here today, because our time is up. We hope that you will join us next time to consider together *many more profound and wonderful words of Jesus*, the Teacher from heaven.

May God give you understanding in what you have heard today. We leave you with this powerful word spoken by the Lord Jesus on the mountain:

But seek first God's kingdom and his righteousness; and all these things will be given to you as well.
(Matthew 6:33)

You Must Be Born Again

John 3

In our study in the holy Gospel (*Injil*), we have seen that Jesus the Messiah was unique in His birth, in His character, and in His works. And in our last program, we recognized that Jesus was unique in His teaching. Never has there been another who has spoken such clear and profound words as He. Those who heard Him were astonished, because He taught them with an authority which their priests (*marabouts*) and teachers of the law (*imams*) did not have. A few words from the mouth of Jesus were of greater value than a multitude of words from their religious leaders. Because of this, most of the leaders of the Jews were not pleased with Jesus. Not only did He teach things that contradicted their traditions, but He also exposed their hypocrisy before everyone.

In our last lesson we heard the sermon that Jesus taught while up on a mountain with His disciples and crowds of His followers. His sermon can be summarized in a few words. **"Do not be as the hypocrites."** (Matthew 6:5) Hypocrisy is repulsive to God and destructive to man. That is why Jesus warned the people against it. You know what it means to be a hypocrite. If someone pretends to have a character trait which is not consistent with what is in his heart, he is a hypocrite. Jesus said that a hypocrite is like a whitewashed tomb: beautiful on the outside but full of uncleanness on the inside. (Matthew 23:27)

No one can deceive God. The word of God says: **All things are naked and laid open before the eyes of him to whom we must give an account.** (Hebrews 4:13) Jesus, who knew the heart of man, saw the hypocrisy which was in the religious leaders, the Pharisees and the teachers of the law. On the outside they were zealous in praying, fasting, and giving alms, but in their hearts they really did not love God and His word. Consequently, all their "righteous" deeds and rituals were worthless. That is why Jesus taught His disciples these things about praying:

> **When you pray, you shall not be as the hypocrites**, for they love to stand and pray in the synagogues and in the corners of the streets, that they may be seen by men. Most certainly, I tell you, they have received their reward. (Matthew 6:5) Therefore, when you do merciful deeds, don't sound a trumpet before yourself, as the hypocrites do in the synagogues and in the streets, that they may get glory from men. Most certainly I tell you, they have received their reward. (Matthew 6:2) Moreover when you fast, don't be like the hypocrites, with sad faces. For they disfigure their faces that they may be seen by men to be fasting. Most certainly I tell you, they have received their reward. (Matthew 6:16)

> **You shall not be as the hypocrites.** For I tell you that unless your righteousness exceeds that of the scribes and Pharisees, there is no way you will enter into the kingdom of Heaven. (Matthew 6:5; 5:20) Blessed are the poor in spirit, for theirs is the kingdom of Heaven. Blessed are those who hunger and thirst for righteousness, for they shall be filled. Blessed are the pure in heart, for they shall see God. Therefore you shall be perfect, just as [God] your Father in heaven is perfect. (Matthew 5:3,6,8,48)

> **Enter in by the narrow gate**; for the gate is wide and the way is broad that leads to destruction, and there are many who enter in by it. How narrow is the gate, and restricted is the way that leads to life! Few are those who find it. (Matthew 7:13-14)

This is how the Lord Jesus exhorted the people to choose the narrow way that leads to eternal life. Did you grasp what Jesus said about the way of salvation? It is extremely important. What must a person be like if he (or she)[97] is ever to see God and live in His holy presence forever? What did Jesus say about this? In short, He said: "You must have a pure and perfect heart."

---

97 The Wolof language does not have masculine and feminine pronouns

But how can a child of Adam who was conceived in sin have a pure and perfect heart? Is there something he can do to cause his polluted-by-sin heart to be transformed into the pure heart that God requires? No, he cannot. Man in himself has no means of purifying his heart. *Even if a log soaks a long time in water it will never be transformed into a crocodile.*[98] Similarly, we sinners cannot make ourselves pure before God. In the time left today though, we will see that what is impossible for man is possible for God.

Let's continue reading and meet a certain religious ruler from Jerusalem by the name of Nicodemus who, one night, came to talk with Jesus. The Lord Jesus told him how a sinner can receive a pure heart and God's gift of eternal life. We are reading in the Gospel of John, chapter 3. The Scripture says:

> [1]**Now there was a man of the Pharisees** named Nicodemus, a ruler of the Jews. [2]The same came to him by night, and said to him, "Rabbi, we know that you are a teacher come from God, for no one can do these signs that you do, unless God is with him." [3]Jesus answered him, "Most certainly, I tell you, unless one is born anew (born again[99]), he can't see God's kingdom." [4]Nicodemus said to him, "How can a man be born when he is old? Can he enter a second time into his mother's womb, and be born?" [5]Jesus answered, "Most certainly I tell you, unless one is born of water and spirit, he can't enter into God's kingdom. [6]That which is born of the flesh is flesh. That which is born of the Spirit is spirit. [7]Don't marvel that I said to you, 'You must be born anew.' [8]The wind blows where it wants to, and you hear its sound, but don't know where it comes from and where it is going. So is everyone who is born of the Spirit." [9]Nicodemus answered him, "How can these things be?" [10]Jesus answered him, "Are you the teacher of Israel, and don't understand these things? [11]Most certainly I tell you, we speak that which we know, and testify of that which we have seen, and you don't receive our witness. [12]If I told you earthly things and you don't

---

98 Familiar Wolof/African Proverb
99 In the original Greek this expression can be translated: born again, born anew, born from above, born from heaven, born from the source.

believe, how will you believe if I tell you heavenly things? [13]No one has ascended into heaven but he who descended out of heaven, the Son of Man, who is in heaven. [1]

[4]**As Moses lifted up the serpent in the wilderness**, even so must the Son of Man be lifted up, [15]that whoever believes in him should not perish, but have eternal life. [16]For God so loved the world, that he gave his one and only Son, that whoever believes in him should not perish, but have eternal life. (John 3:1-16)

Let us think a little about what the Lord Jesus told the religious ruler, Nicodemus. What did Jesus tell Nicodemus must happen before anyone could have eternal life and the right to live with God forever? He said, **"Most certainly, I tell you, unless one is born anew, he can't see God's kingdom. You must be born anew."** Did Nicodemus know what it meant to be *born anew*? He did not. That is why Jesus said to him, **"Are you the teacher of Israel, and don't understand these things? That which is born of the flesh is flesh. That which is born of the Spirit is spirit. Don't marvel that I said to you, 'You must be born anew.'"** (John 3:10,6-7)

In brief, Jesus was telling Nicodemus that anyone who wants to see God and live in His holy presence throughout eternity must be born twice. That does not mean that you must enter a second time into your mother's womb and be born again physically. Being born again means that the Spirit of God must remake you, washing your heart and renewing you by His power (Titus 3:5).

You must be born by the power that comes from heaven, which is completely different from the outward form of religion. You must be changed on the inside – in your heart. Whoever is born of Adam is stained with sin and cannot have a part in the kingdom of God. The children of Adam are powerless to remove the root of sin that grows in their hearts. Just as spending a long time in water does not transform a log into a crocodile, so also spending time performing religious rituals and doing good deeds can never make an evil heart pure. God Himself must work a miracle in your heart and renew it, because that which is mortal cannot possess

immortality; **neither does the perishable inherit imperishable.**
(See 1 Corinthians 15:50) In short, **"You must be born again."**

That is what Jesus taught the religious ruler, Nicodemus. But
Nicodemus had difficulty understanding this and he asked Jesus
how that could be, and how he himself could be born again and
receive a new and pure heart. Jesus answered him,

> [14]**As Moses lifted up the serpent in the wilderness,** even so
> must the Son of Man be lifted up, [15]that whoever believes in him
> should not perish, but have eternal life. [16]For God so loved the
> world, that he gave his one and only Son, that whoever believes
> in him should not perish, but have eternal life. (John 3:14-16)

To show Nicodemus how he could escape the judgment of hell and
receive eternal life, Jesus reminded him about what had happened
to his ancestors in the desert in the time of Moses. As we saw in the
Torah, once when the children of Israel complained against God
and Moses, God sent poisonous snakes among them to bite them
so that many died. But as soon as the children of Israel repented,
God commanded Moses to make a bronze snake and suspend it on
a pole. **Then when anyone was bitten by a snake and looked at
the bronze snake, they lived.** (Numbers 21:9 NIV)

That is how Jesus explained to Nicodemus that just as the children
of Israel had to look in faith at the bronze snake on the pole to
be saved from death, so the children of Adam must believe in
the remedy that God has provided to save them from eternal
punishment. We are all like the children of Israel who were bitten
by the snakes. Satan is like a poisonous snake, and sin is like
the poison which causes man to perish. Satan has bitten all the
children of Adam, and the poison of sin will cause us to perish
forever if God does not give us a remedy. We have no possible
means of saving ourselves from God's judgment, because the
wages of sin is death and hell. But praise be to the LORD God, for
just as He provided a remedy to save the children of Israel from
the poison of the snakes, so also He has provided a remedy to save
the children of Adam from the poison of sin.

Do you know God's plan to restore and renew the hearts of the children of Adam, which are polluted with sin? What did the Lord Jesus say about this to Nicodemus? He said that the holy Redeemer must be lifted up (on a pole; a cross) in order to endure the penalty of sin for sinners, **that whoever believes in him should not perish, but have eternal life.** (John 3:14-16)

Who is it that can be saved? What does the Scripture say? It says: **Whoever believes in Him… shall not perish.** In whom must we believe? We must believe in the Redeemer whom God has sent. Do you believe in Him? Do you believe in your heart that God, who does not want anyone to perish, sent Jesus the Savior down to earth for you, to bear for you the punishment your sin requires? God's righteous remedy for our problem of sin is Jesus' death on the cross. The Scripture says: **God made [Jesus the Messiah] who had no sin to be sin for us, so that in him we might become the righteousness of God.** (2 Corinthians 5:21 NIV)

Friends, God has not changed. What the Lord Jesus said to Nicodemus about two thousand years ago, He still says to you today: **"You must be born again."** God wants to cleanse and remake your heart and renew you by His power, but you must believe His Good News. You must believe in the Savior whom He sent. You must believe that Jesus, who never sinned, paid for your debt of sin, so that you can live in the holy presence of God forever. **"You must be born again…. Unless one is born anew, he can't see God's kingdom."** Amen.

Thank you for listening. In the next study, God willing, we will continue in the Gospel books and hear *what the Lord Jesus said to a woman who had had five husbands.*

God bless you as you think deeply about what Jesus the Messiah declared, saying,

> **You should not be surprised at my saying, "You must be born again."** (John 3:7 NIV) **Blessed are the pure in heart, for they shall see God.** (Matthew 5:8)

The Savior of the World

John 4; Luke 4

U p to now in our walk through the book of the Gospel
we have seen that Jesus the Messiah was unique in His
birth, in His character, in His works, and in His teachings.
Regarding His birth we saw that no one has ever been born as
Jesus was, because He, the Word of God, was born of a virgin, by
the power of the Holy Spirit of God. Jesus was also unique in His
character, because no one else has ever been born with a holy
nature like His. Jesus was also incomparable in His works since no
one has ever done miracles as He did. He would simply speak a
word, and the sick were healed, the blind could see, the lame could
walk, and the devil fled. We also discovered that Jesus was unique
in His teaching. In our last program we heard the conversation that
took place between Jesus and a religious ruler named Nicodemus.
Jesus showed Nicodemus that unless the Spirit of God renewed his
heart, he could never enter the presence of God. That is why the
Lord Jesus said to him, **"You must be born again."** (John 3:7)

Today we will hear how Jesus the Messiah spoke to someone
who was very different from Nicodemus. Nicodemus was a Jew,
but the person we will see in our lesson today was a Palestinian.
Nicodemus was a man; this person we will see today was a woman.
Nicodemus was a very religious person, but this woman was a
great sinner who had had five husbands. In the eyes of man, the
religious ruler, Nicodemus, was better than the immoral woman.
But that is not how God sees it, because all of Adam's offspring –
religious folk and great sinners alike – are under the dominion of
sin. That is why all of Adam's children must be born again by the
power that comes from above.

Now let us return to the Gospel and listen to the conversation Jesus had with the immoral woman from Samaria in Palestine. Samaria was the region between Judea and Galilee in the land of the Jews. Many Samaritans were foreigners; the Jews considered them pagans, which is why they did not get along with each other. However, Jesus the Messiah did not show favoritism because God does not show favoritism. Jesus came into the world to seek and to save every sinner who wants to have a new and pure heart. That is why Jesus was not ashamed to talk to the Samaritan woman who had had five husbands.

Now let us listen to what is written in the Gospel of John, chapter 4. The Scripture says:

> [5]**[Jesus] came to a city of Samaria**, called Sychar, near the parcel of ground that Jacob gave to his son, Joseph. [6]Jacob's well was there. Jesus therefore, being tired from his journey, sat down by the well. It was about the sixth hour.

> [7]**A woman of Samaria came to draw water.** Jesus said to her, "Give me a drink." [8]For his disciples had gone away into the city to buy food. [9]The Samaritan woman therefore said to him, "How is it that you, being a Jew, ask for a drink from me, a Samaritan woman?" (For Jews have no dealings with Samaritans.) [10]Jesus answered her, "If you knew the gift of God, and who it is who says to you, 'Give me a drink,' you would have asked him, and he would have given you living water." [11]The woman said to him, "Sir, you have nothing to draw with, and the well is deep. So where do you get that living water? [12]Are you greater than our father, Jacob, who gave us the well and drank from it himself, as did his children and his livestock?"

> [13]**Jesus answered her**, "Everyone who drinks of this water will thirst again, [14]but whoever drinks of the water that I will give him will never thirst again; but the water that I will give him will become in him a well of water springing up to eternal life." [15]The woman said to him, "Sir, give me this water, so that I don't get thirsty, neither come all the way here to draw."

¹⁶**Jesus said to her, "Go, call your husband**, and come here." ¹⁷The woman answered, "I have no husband." Jesus said to her, "You said well, 'I have no husband,' ¹⁸for you have had five husbands; and he whom you now have is not your husband. This you have said truly." ¹⁹The woman said to him, "Sir, I perceive that you are a prophet. ²⁰Our fathers worshiped in this mountain, and you Jews say that in Jerusalem is the place where people ought to worship." ²¹Jesus said to her, "Woman, believe me, the hour comes, when neither in this mountain, nor in Jerusalem, will you worship the Father. ²²You worship that which you don't know. We worship that which we know; for salvation is from the Jews. ²³But the hour comes, and now is, when the true worshipers will worship the Father in spirit and truth, for the Father seeks such to be his worshipers. ²⁴God is spirit, and those who worship him must worship in spirit and truth." ²⁵The woman said to him, "I know that Messiah is coming, he who is called Christ. When he has come, he will declare to us all things."

²⁶**Jesus said to her, "I am he, the one who speaks to you."** ²⁷At this, his disciples came. They marveled that he was speaking with a woman; yet no one said, "What are you looking for?" or, "Why do you speak with her?" ²⁸So the woman left her water pot, went away into the city, and said to the people, ²⁹"Come, see a man who told me everything that I did. Can this be the [Messiah]?" ³⁰They went out of the city, and were coming to him. ⁹From that city many of the Samaritans believed in him because of the word of the woman, who testified, "He told me everything that I did." ⁴⁰So when the Samaritans came to him, they begged him to stay with them. He stayed there two days. ⁴¹Many more believed because of his word. ⁴²They said to the woman, "Now we believe, not because of your speaking; for we have heard for ourselves, and know that this is indeed the Christ, the Savior of the world." (John 4:5-30,39-42)

This is where the story of the Samaritan woman ends. Truly it is an important story, because it shows how an immoral woman discovered that Jesus is the Savior whom God sent to earth.

And that discovery transformed her life. At the beginning of the conversation, the woman did not know who was speaking with her. She viewed Jesus as just another Jew among many Jews. However, during the conversation, Jesus told her some things that a mere man could not know, which was why she concluded that Jesus must be a prophet. But little by little she came to see that this Jesus who was talking with her was more than a prophet. He was the Messiah – the One about whom all the prophets had prophesied, the Savior of the world!

Once the woman recognized that this Man sitting on the edge of the well and speaking with her was the Messiah, she put down her water jar and ran into town, telling the people, **"Come, see a man who told me everything that I did. Can this be the [Messiah]?"**

The townspeople came out to Jesus and asked Him to stay. He stayed for two days, teaching them how they could have a new and pure heart and become true worshipers of God. The Gospel says: **Many more believed because of his word. They said to the woman, "Now we believe, not because of your speaking; for we have heard for ourselves, and know that this is indeed the Christ, the Savior of the world."** (John 4:41-42)

Now let us continue in the Gospel and see what happened a few days after Jesus' visit to Samaria. We will see that not everyone received Jesus as the Savior of the world. In the Gospel of Luke, chapter 4, the Scripture says:

> [14]**Jesus returned in the power of the Spirit** into Galilee, and news about him spread through all the surrounding area. [15]He taught in their synagogues, being glorified by all. [16]He came to Nazareth, where he had been brought up. He entered, as was his custom, into the synagogue on the Sabbath day, and stood up to read.

> [17]**The book of the prophet Isaiah was handed to him.** He opened the book, and found the place where it was written, [18]"The Spirit of the Lord is on me, because he has anointed me to preach good news to the poor. He has sent me to heal the broken

hearted, to proclaim release to the captives, recovering of sight to the blind, to deliver those who are crushed, [19]and to proclaim the acceptable year of the Lord." [20]He closed the book, gave it back to the attendant, and sat down. The eyes of all in the synagogue were fastened on him. [21]He began to tell them, "Today, this Scripture has been fulfilled in your hearing." (Luke 4:14-21)

With these words Jesus claimed that He was the Messiah and the Savior about whom the prophet Isaiah had written seven hundred years earlier. However, the Jews who lived in Nazareth could not accept that this Jesus, who had grown up among them, was the Savior of the world sent from heaven. That is why they scorned Him, saying, "Is he not the son of Joseph?" The Scripture goes on to say how Jesus warned the people of Nazareth not to despise the Messiah whom God had sent to them. But that only made them more angry. And so we read:

> [28]**They were all filled with wrath in the synagogue**, as they heard these things. [29]They rose up, threw [Jesus] out of the city, and led him to the brow of the hill that their city was built on, that they might throw him off the cliff. [30]But he, passing through the middle of them, went his way. (Luke 4:28-30)

Why did the people of Nazareth tried to kill Jesus? They tried to kill Him because He claimed to be the Messiah about whom all God's prophets had written. *Truth is a hot pepper.* Jesus' words of truth made the people of Nazareth so angry that they tried to throw Him off the cliff. But they could not do it because the time appointed by God for Jesus to die had not yet come.

Wolof wisdom says: *The woodcutter does not cut down the main tree in the village [under which folks meet].* Jesus the Messiah is God's "Meeting Place Tree." How foolish and wicked of men to want to "cut down" the One whom God appointed as the Savior and Judge of the world! Later, men would kill Him – but three days later He would rise from the grave, defeating the power of death. In a future lesson, we will learn more about this greatest event in history.

Today, then, we have heard about two groups of people. Both groups heard Jesus claim to be the Messiah, but their responses to His claim were very different. In the first narrative, we heard about the sinner woman at the well and the people of Samaria. They received the words of Jesus with great joy and believed that He is the Messiah, the Savior of the world. In our second narrative we saw the religious people of Nazareth. They despised the words of Jesus. They did not believe that Jesus, who had grown up in their town, was the Messiah, the Savior of the world.

How about you? Which of these two groups do you most closely resemble? Are you like the people of Samaria, who believed in Jesus as their Savior and Lord and received His gift of eternal life? Or are you like the people of Nazareth, who refused to believe that Jesus was the Messiah sent from heaven to save them from their sins? Do you recognize that Jesus is the Redeemer to whom all the prophets pointed? Have you received Him as *your* Savior?

Concerning Jesus the Messiah, the Holy Scripture says:

> ⁵**The light shines in the darkness**, and the darkness hasn't overcome it.…¹⁰He was in the world, and the world was made through him, and the world didn't recognize him. ¹¹He came to his own, and those who were his own didn't receive him. ¹²But as many as received him, to them he gave the right to become God's children, to those who believe in his name: ¹³who were born not of blood, nor of the will of the flesh, nor of the will of man, but of God. (John 1:5,10-13)

Listening friend, have you been born of God? Do you really believe in Jesus? Have you received Him as your Lord and Savior? We invite you to join us next time to see some of the signs Jesus showed so that all might know that He is the Savior of the world.

We leave you today with what the Samaritans said about Jesus:

> **[We] know that this is indeed the Christ, the Savior of the world.** (John 4:42)

Program 69

The Authority of Jesus

Matthew 12; John 5

I n the past few programs we have seen how Jesus traveled throughout the land of the Jews, teaching the multitudes as they followed Him, and healing their sick. Thus, a great crowd followed Him. But the religious rulers were jealous of Him because they could not refute the wisdom of the things He said, nor could they deny the wonders He performed.

Today we will continue in the Gospel and see how the Lord Jesus was confronted by the religious rulers regarding the day of rest, the Sabbath. This was the seventh day of the week, the day which God gave the Jews as a day of rest after they had worked six days. But the religious rulers of that time, the Pharisees, accused Jesus of violating the Sabbath because He did good works on that day. They were using this as a pretext to discredit Him because they could not find anything bad to accuse him of.

In the Gospel of Matthew, chapter 12, the Scripture says:

> ¹**At that time, Jesus went on the Sabbath day** through the grain fields. His disciples were hungry and began to pluck heads of grain and to eat. ²But the Pharisees, when they saw it, said to him, "Behold, your disciples do what is not lawful to do on the Sabbath." ³But he said to them, "Haven't you read what [the prophet] David did when he was hungry, and those who were with him: ⁴how he entered into God's house and ate the show bread, which was not lawful for him to eat, nor for those who were with him, but only for the priests? ⁵Or have you not read in the law that on the Sabbath day the priests in the temple profane the Sabbath and are guiltless? ⁶But I tell

you that one greater than the temple is here. [7]But if you had known what this means, 'I desire mercy, and not sacrifice,' you wouldn't have condemned the guiltless. [8]For the Son of Man is Lord of the Sabbath." (Matthew 12:1-8)

Did you notice what Jesus called Himself? He has hundreds of names and titles in the Holy Scriptures. One of those titles by which He often called Himself is *the Son of Man*. This title reminds us that the Messiah humbled Himself to take on the form of a son of Adam. It also reveals His glory, because this One who humbled Himself by becoming a man is the same One who possesses all authority over the children of Adam to save them or to judge them. Think of it: The Word and Spirit and the power and glory of God came to earth and took on a human body! Yes, Jesus Christ is the Son of Man, the Lord of the Sabbath and the Lord over all. But the Pharisees did not accept Him for who He really was.

Let us hear what happened next. The Scripture says:

> [9]**[Jesus] He departed from there** and went into their synagogue. [10]And behold, there was a man with a withered hand. They asked him, "Is it lawful to heal on the Sabbath day?" so that they might accuse him. [11]He said to them, "What man is there among you who has one sheep, and if this one falls into a pit on the Sabbath day, won't he grab on to it and lift it out? [12]Of how much more value then is a man than a sheep! Therefore it is lawful to do good on the Sabbath day." [13]Then he told the man, "Stretch out your hand." He stretched it out; and it was restored whole, just like the other. [14]But the Pharisees went out and conspired against him, how they might destroy him. [15]Jesus, perceiving that, withdrew from there. Great multitudes followed him; and he healed them all. (Matthew 12:9-15)

We see how the Pharisees accused Jesus of wrongdoing because He did not respect their traditions. What hypocrisy! These religious rulers had no compassion for the hungry or for the sick, yet they wanted to make people believe that their traditions, which prohibited good works on the Sabbath, came from God. But Jesus, who knew their hearts, reminded them of what God declares in the Scriptures, saying, **"But if you had known what this means, 'I desire mercy, and not sacrifice,' you wouldn't have condemned the guiltless. For the Son of Man is Lord of the Sabbath."**

Reading on in the Scripture we see:

> ²²**Then one possessed by a demon**, blind and mute, was brought to him; and he healed him, so that the blind and mute man both spoke and saw. ²³All the multitudes were amazed, and said, "Can this be the son of David?" ²⁴But when the Pharisees heard it, they said, "This man does not cast out demons except by Beelzebul, [that is Satan] the prince of the demons."

> ²⁵**Knowing their thoughts, Jesus said to them**, "Every kingdom divided against itself is brought to desolation, and every city or house divided against itself will not stand. ²⁶If Satan casts out Satan, he is divided against himself. How then will his kingdom stand? ²⁷If I by [Satan] cast out demons, by whom do your children cast them out? Therefore they will be your judges. ²⁸But if I by the Spirit of God cast out demons, then God's kingdom has come upon you. (Matthew 12:22-28)

> ¹**After these things, there was a feast of the Jews**, and Jesus went up to Jerusalem. ²Now in Jerusalem by the sheep gate, there is a pool, which is called in Hebrew, "Bethesda", having five porches. ³In these lay a great multitude of those who were sick, blind, lame, or paralyzed, waiting for the moving of the water;

> ⁵**A certain man was there who had been sick** for thirty-eight years. ⁶When Jesus saw him lying there, and knew that he had been sick for a long time, he asked him, "Do you want to be made well?" ⁷The sick man answered him, "Sir, I have no one to put me into the pool when the water is stirred up, but while I'm coming, another steps down before me." ⁸Jesus said to him, "Arise, take up your mat, and walk." ⁹Immediately, the man was made well, and took up his mat and walked.

Now it was the Sabbath on that day. [10]So the Jews said to him who was cured, "It is the Sabbath. It is not lawful for you to carry the mat." [11]He answered them, "He who made me well said to me, 'Take up your mat and walk.'" [12]Then they asked him, "Who is the man who said to you, 'Take up your mat and walk'?" [13]But he who was healed didn't know who it was, for Jesus had withdrawn, a crowd being in the place.

[14]**Afterward Jesus found him in the temple**, and said to him, "Behold, you are made well. Sin no more, so that nothing worse happens to you." [15]The man went away, and told the Jews that it was Jesus who had made him well. [16]For this cause the Jews persecuted Jesus, and sought to kill him, because he did these things on the Sabbath. [17]But Jesus answered them, "My Father is still working, so I am working, too." [18]For this cause therefore the Jews sought all the more to kill him, because he not only broke the Sabbath, but also called God his own Father, making himself equal with God. (John 5:1-3,5-18)

Let us pause here. Why did the religious rulers harass Jesus and seek to kill Him? Was it because Jesus healed the invalid on the Sabbath? That was not the whole reason. They were seeking to kill Jesus because He said that God was His Father. They could not accept that Jesus was the Messiah, who had come from the presence of God. For this they accused Him of blasphemy[100] and looked for a way to destroy Him. But the Scripture says:

[19]**Jesus therefore answered them**, "Most certainly, I tell you, the Son can do nothing of himself, but what he sees the Father doing. For whatever things he does, these the Son also does likewise. [20]For the Father has affection for the Son, and shows him all things that he himself does. He will show him greater works than these, that you may marvel. [21]For as the Father raises the dead and gives them life, even so the Son also gives life to whom he desires. [22]For the Father judges no one, but he has given all judgment to the Son, [23]that all may honor the

---

100 Literally in Wolof: *insulting God*

Son, even as they honor the Father. He who doesn't honor the Son doesn't honor the Father who sent him. [24]Most certainly I tell you, he who hears my word and believes him who sent me has eternal life, and doesn't come into judgment, but has passed out of death into life.

[31]**If I testify about myself**, my witness is not valid. [32]It is another who testifies about me. I know that the testimony which he testifies about me is true. [33]You have sent to John, and he has testified to the truth. [34]But the testimony which I receive is not from man. However, I say these things that you may be saved. [35]He was the burning and shining lamp, and you were willing to rejoice for a while in his light. [36]But the testimony which I have is greater than that of John, for the works which the Father gave me to accomplish, the very works that I do, testify about me, that the Father has sent me. [37]The Father himself, who sent me, has testified about me. You have neither heard his voice at any time, nor seen his form.

[38]**You don't have his word living in you**, because you don't believe him whom he sent. [39]You search the Scriptures, because you think that in them you have eternal life; and these are they which testify about me. [40]Yet you will not come to me, that you may have life. [41]I don't receive glory from men. [42]But I know you, that you don't have God's love in yourselves. [43]I have come in my Father's name, and you don't receive me. If another comes in his own name, you will receive him. [44]How can you believe, who receive glory from one another, and you don't seek the glory that comes from the only God? [45]Don't think that I will accuse you to the Father. There is one who accuses you, even Moses, on whom you have set your hope. [46]For if you believed Moses, you would believe me; for he wrote about me. [47]But if you don't believe his writings, how will you believe my words? (John 5:19-24,31-47)

Did you hear how the Lord Jesus reproved the Pharisees who wanted to kill Him? He told them that whoever rejects the Messiah whom God sent from heaven is rejecting the testimony of the Messiah's words and works; he is rejecting the testimony of the prophet John, the testimony of the prophet Moses, and the testimony of the Scriptures. In short, whoever rejects the Messiah is rejecting God Himself. He who dishonors the Son is dishonoring the Father who sent Him. To refuse the word and authority of Jesus is to refuse the word and authority of God – for Jesus is the Word of God and the One to whom God has entrusted all judgment and authority. Whoever truly believes God and His prophets will also believe that Jesus is the Messiah who came from heaven, because all of God's prophets testified of Him. Those who know and believe the writings of the prophets also know and believe that Jesus, the son of Mary, is the One whom God has chosen to be the Savior of the world. That is what Jesus told the religious rulers when He said,

> [39]**You search the Scriptures**, because you think that in them you have eternal life; and these are they which testify about me. [40]Yet you will not come to me, that you may have life. … [45]Don't think that I will accuse you to the Father. There is one who accuses you, even [the prophet] Moses, on whom you have set your hope. [46]For if you believed Moses, you would believe me; for he wrote about me. [47]But if you don't believe his writings, how will you believe my words? (John 5:39-40,45-47)

If we say that we believe the prophets, then we must believe the One about whom they testified, that is, Jesus the Messiah. Many are quick to believe the testimony of one man, but, strangely, few believe the confirmed testimony of God's many prophets who wrote the Holy Scriptures. How about you? **"Do you believe the prophets?"**[101] (Acts 26:27)

This is where we must bid you farewell today. We invite you to join us next time as we learn more of *Jesus and His matchless power*.

May God bless you as you think on what Jesus told the Pharisees:

> **But if you don't believe [the prophet Moses'] writings, how will you believe my words?** (John 5:47)

---

101 Emphasis on the "s", prophet**s**. (The question here is not: Do you believe *the prophe**t**.*)

Program 70

The Power of Jesus

Mark 4-6; Matthew 9-10

Last time we saw how the religious rulers of the Jews wanted to destroy Jesus because He said that God was His Father, thus claiming to be equal with God. A great crowd followed the Lord Jesus wherever He went. Among them were some who believed the words of Jesus and others who did not believe Him. Jesus chose twelve apostles (*messengers*) from among those who believed Him so that He might be with them, teach them and send them out to proclaim the Good News of salvation.

The twelve apostles whom Jesus chose were named Simon Peter, and Andrew his brother, James the son of Zebedee, and his younger brother John; those four were fishermen. The other apostles were Philip, Bartholomew, Thomas, Matthew the tax collector, James son of Alphaeus, Thaddaeus, Simon the Canaanite, and Judas Iscariot, who would betray Him. (Matthew 10:2-4) Those were the twelve disciples who accompanied Jesus. Several women also followed Jesus wherever He went: Mary Magdalene, from whom Jesus had driven out seven demons; Joanna, the wife of Cuza the manager of Herod's household; Susanna, and other women. These women helped to support Jesus out of their own means. (Luke 8:2-3)

As we have seen, the people were amazed at the teaching of Jesus, because He taught them with an authority which their religious teachers did not have. The authority of Jesus was not limited to mere words. His mighty works proved that His words were true. In today's program we will see how the Lord Jesus possessed power and authority over every creature and every force on earth.

We begin our reading in the Gospel of Mark, chapter 4:

³⁵**On that day, when evening had come**, [Jesus] said to them, "Let's go over to the other side." ³⁶Leaving the multitude, they took him with them, even as he was, in the boat. Other small boats were also with him. ³⁷A big wind storm arose, and the waves beat into the boat, so much that the boat was already filled. ³⁸He himself was in the stern, asleep on the cushion, and they woke him up, and told him, "Teacher, don't you care that we are dying?" ³⁹He awoke, and rebuked the wind, and said to the sea, "Peace! Be still!" The wind ceased, and there was a great calm. ⁴⁰He said to them, "Why are you so afraid? How is it that you have no faith?" ⁴¹They were greatly afraid, and said to one another, "Who then is this, that even the wind and the sea obey him?" (Mark 4:35-41)

¹**They came to the other side of the sea**, into the country of the Gadarenes. ²When he had come out of the boat, immediately a man with an unclean spirit met him out of the tombs. ³He lived in the tombs. Nobody could bind him any more, not even with chains, ⁴because he had been often bound with fetters and chains, and the chains had been torn apart by him, and the fetters broken in pieces. Nobody had the strength to tame him. ⁵Always, night and day, in the tombs and in the mountains, he was crying out, and cutting himself with stones. ⁶When he saw Jesus from afar, he ran and bowed down to him, ⁷and crying out with a loud voice, he said, "What have I to do with you, Jesus, you Son of the Most High God? I adjure you by God, don't torment me." ⁸For he said to him, "Come out of the man, you unclean spirit!" ⁹He asked him, "What is your name?" He said to him, "My name is Legion, for we are many." ¹⁰He begged him much that he would not send them away out of the country. ¹¹Now on the mountainside there was a great herd of pigs feeding. ¹²All the demons begged him, saying, "Send us into the pigs, that we may enter into them." ¹³At once Jesus gave them permission. The unclean spirits came out and entered into the pigs. The herd of about two thousand rushed down the steep bank into the sea, and they were drowned in the sea. ¹⁴Those who fed the pigs fled, and told it in the city and in the country. The people came to see what it was that had happened.

[15]They came to Jesus, and saw him who had been possessed by demons sitting, clothed, and in his right mind, even him who had the legion; and they were afraid. [16]Those who saw it declared to them what happened to him who was possessed by demons, and about the pigs. [17]They began to beg him to depart from their region. [18]As he was entering into the boat, he who had been possessed by demons begged him that he might be with him. [19]He didn't allow him, but said to him, "Go to your house, to your friends, and tell them what great things the Lord has done for you, and how he had mercy on you." [20]He went his way, and began to proclaim in Decapolis how Jesus had done great things for him, and everyone marveled. [21]When Jesus had crossed back over in the boat to the other side, a great multitude was gathered to him; and he was by the sea.

[22]**Behold, one of the rulers of the synagogue**, Jairus by name, came; and seeing him, he fell at his feet, [23]and begged him much, saying, "My little daughter is at the point of death. Please come and lay your hands on her, that she may be made healthy, and live." [24]He went with him, and a great multitude followed him, and they pressed upon him on all sides. [25]A certain woman, who had a discharge of blood for twelve years, [26]and had suffered many things by many physicians, and had spent all that she had, and was no better, but rather grew worse, [27]having heard the things concerning Jesus, came up behind him in the crowd, and touched his clothes. [28]For she said, "If I just touch his clothes, I will be made well." [29]Immediately the flow of her blood was dried up, and she felt in her body that she was healed of her affliction. [30]Immediately Jesus, perceiving in himself that the power had gone out from him, turned around in the crowd, and asked, "Who touched my clothes?" [31]His disciples said to him, "You see the multitude pressing against you, and you say, 'Who touched me?'" [32]He looked around to see her who had done this thing. [33]But the woman, fearing and trembling, knowing what had been done to her, came and fell down before him, and told him all the truth. [34]He said to her, "Daughter, your faith has made you well. Go in peace, and be cured of your disease."

³⁵**While he was still speaking**, people came from the synagogue ruler's house saying, "Your daughter is dead. Why bother the Teacher any more?" ³⁶But Jesus, when he heard the message spoken, immediately said to the ruler of the synagogue, "Don't be afraid, only believe." ³⁷He allowed no one to follow him, except Peter, James, and John the brother of James. ³⁸He came to the synagogue ruler's house, and he saw an uproar, weeping, and great wailing. ³⁹When he had entered in, he said to them, "Why do you make an uproar and weep? The child is not dead, but is asleep." ⁴⁰They ridiculed him. But he, having put them all out, took the father of the child, her mother, and those who were with him, and went in where the child was lying. ⁴¹Taking the child by the hand, he said to her, "Talitha cumi!" which means, being interpreted, "Girl, I tell you, get up!" ⁴²Immediately the girl rose up and walked, for she was twelve years old. They were amazed with great amazement. ⁴³He strictly ordered them that no one should know this, and commanded that something should be given to her to eat. (Mark 5:1-43)

²⁷**As Jesus passed by from there, two blind men** followed him, calling out and saying, "Have mercy on us, son of David!" ²⁸When he had come into the house, the blind men came to him. Jesus said to them, "Do you believe that I am able to do this?" They told him, "Yes, Lord." ²⁹Then he touched their eyes, saying, "According to your faith be it done to you." ³⁰Then their eyes were opened. Jesus strictly commanded them, saying, "See that no one knows about this." ³¹But they went out and spread abroad his fame in all that land.

³²**As they went out, behold, a mute man** who was demon possessed was brought to him. ³³When the demon was cast out, the mute man spoke. The multitudes marveled, saying, "Nothing like this has ever been seen in Israel!" ³⁴But the Pharisees said, "By the prince of the demons, he casts out demons." (Matthew 9:27-34)

¹**[Jesus] came into his own country**, and his disciples followed him. ²When the Sabbath had come, he began to teach in the

synagogue, and many hearing him were astonished, saying, "Where did this man get these things?" and, "What is the wisdom that is given to this man, that such mighty works come about by his hands? ³Isn't this the carpenter, the son of Mary, and brother of James, Joses, Judah, and Simon? Aren't his sisters here with us?" So they were offended at him. ⁴Jesus said to them, "A prophet is not without honor, except in his own country, and among his own relatives, and in his own house." ⁵He could do no mighty work there, except that he laid his hands on a few sick people, and healed them. ⁶He marveled because of their unbelief. He went around the villages teaching. ⁷He called to himself the twelve, and began to send them out two by two; and he gave them authority over the unclean spirits. ⁸He commanded them: (Mark 6:1-8) ¹⁶"Behold, I send you out as sheep among wolves. Therefore be wise as serpents and harmless as doves. ¹⁷But beware of men, for they will deliver you up to councils, and in their synagogues they will scourge you....

²⁸**Don't be afraid of those who kill the body**, but are not able to kill the soul. Rather, fear him who is able to destroy both soul and body in Gehenna. ... ³⁴Don't think that I came to send peace on the earth. I didn't come to send peace, but a sword. ³⁵For I came to set a man at odds against his father, and a daughter against her mother, and a daughter-in-law against her mother-in-law. ³⁶A man's foes will be those of his own household. ³⁷He who loves father or mother more than me is not worthy of me; and he who loves son or daughter more than me isn't worthy of me.... ³⁹He who seeks his life will lose it; and he who loses his life for my sake will find it. (Matthew 10:16-17,28,34-37,39)

Amen. Today we have seen the power of Jesus in His words and in His works, causing the multitudes that followed Him to ask:

"Where did this man get these things?" and, **"What is the wisdom that is given to this man, that such mighty works come about by his hands?"** (Mark 6:2)

From where did Jesus get His power and wisdom?

He didn't get it from anywhere, because He Himself is the Power and Wisdom of God. The Lord Jesus did the mighty works of God upon the earth to show people *where* He came from and *who* He was. He had authority over every created being and every kind of power because He was the *Kalimat Allah*; that is, He was and is *the very Voice and Word of God*. That is why Jesus could calm the storm and heal the demon-possessed man by simply speaking a word.

All of God's unlimited power resided in Him. That is why He could heal the woman who had suffered with bleeding for twelve years. This woman had wasted all her money on many doctors and their medicines, but the moment she touched Jesus' cloak she was healed. And when Jesus touched the eyes of the two blind men their sight was immediately restored. And Jesus' authority was not limited to those who were alive; He also had authority over the dead. That is why He could bring back to life the child who had died. Jesus was *the Word of God* in a human body.

Yes, the Scriptures tell us that all power and all authority have been given to the Lord Jesus Christ. That is why if you trust in Him, you will no longer need to fear anything: not death, not life, not evil spirits, not sorcerers, not the present, nor the future. You will no longer need to wear charms or pour out an offering to a personal protector spirit, because the Lord Jesus will protect you.

Dear friends, are you trusting in the One who is the head over every power and authority? Or are you trying to appease the lesser powers and authorities, the ones of this world?

Next time, we plan to hear *how Jesus taught with parables.*

May God bless you as you consider this amazing statement from Scripture for who have put their trust in Jesus:

> **For in Christ lives all the fullness of God in a human body. So you also are complete through your union with Christ, who is the head over every ruler and authority.** (Colossians 2:9-10 NLT)

Program 71

Two Parables

Luke 8; Matthew 13

I n our last program we discovered that Jesus the Messiah possessed authority which surpassed the authority of the prophets. Jesus was, in fact, the very Power of God in a human body. That is why He could calm the storm, cast out demons, heal the sick and the blind, and even raise the dead to life.

Today we will continue in the book of the Gospel (*Injil*) and hear how the Lord Jesus taught the crowd using parables (illustrations). Jesus often presented the truth in parables because most of the people who followed Him around did not really want to know the word of God. What they wanted was for Jesus to heal their bodies of sickness, but they did not want Him to heal their souls of sin. Also tagging along behind Jesus, like a pack of hyenas, were the religious rulers who listened to Him only to find an opportunity to accuse Him. When they were around, Jesus would speak to the crowd in parables, but He would wait until He was alone with His true followers to explain the meaning of the parables.

God wants everyone to know the truth and to be saved, but if our hearts are stubborn He will not reveal His truth to us. God wants us to seek after the truth as most people seek after riches. The prophet Solomon wrote, **If you seek her as silver, and search for her as for hidden treasures: then you will understand the fear of the LORD, and find the knowledge of God.** (Proverbs 2:4-5)

How about you? Do you cherish God's truth more than money or any other kind of wealth? Does the true word of God occupy the most important place in your mind and heart? Perhaps you do not know the true condition of your heart before God. Then listen carefully to the Lord Jesus' *Parable of the Sower*.

We are reading in the Gospel of Luke, chapter 8. The Scripture says:

> [4]**When a great multitude came together**, and people from every city were coming to him, he spoke by a parable. [5]"The farmer went out to sow his seed. As he sowed, some fell along the road, and it was trampled under foot, and the birds of the sky devoured it. [6]Other seed fell on the rock, and as soon as it grew, it withered away, because it had no moisture. [7]Other fell amid the thorns, and the thorns grew with it, and choked it. [8]Other fell into the good ground, and grew, and produced one hundred times as much fruit." As he said these things, he called out, "He who has ears to hear, let him hear!"
>
> [9]**Then his disciples asked him**, "What does this parable mean?" [10]He said,... [11]"Now the parable is this: The seed is the word of God. [12]Those along the road are those who hear, then the devil comes, and takes away the word from their heart, that they may not believe and be saved. [13]Those on the rock are they who, when they hear, receive the word with joy; but these have no root, who believe for a while, then fall away in time of temptation. [14]That which fell among the thorns, these are those who have heard, and as they go on their way they are choked with cares, riches, and pleasures of life, and bring no fruit to maturity. [15]Those in the good ground, these are those who with an honest and good heart, having heard the word, hold it tightly, and produce fruit with perseverance. (Luke 8:4-15)

Do you grasp the meaning of the parable of the sower? In this parable we see the seed and the soil. What does the seed illustrate? The Lord Jesus said that the seed illustrates *the true word of God*. How about the soil? What does it illustrate? The soil illustrates *the heart of man*.

Yes, the word of God is like good seed, because it is alive and has power to bring forth eternal life and true blessing in your heart, in

your life. But man's heart is like soil that can be very hard and dry.
Let us think a little about this. How many kinds of soil do we see in
the parable? We saw how the seed fell upon four kinds of soil.

1. There was the seed that fell upon *a hard path*.
2. There was the seed that fell on *soil with many rocks*.
3. There was the seed that fell *among thorns*.[102]
4. There was also the seed that fell into *good soil*.

First, Jesus taught that many in the world have a heart like *a hard
path* that people walk on. Some people's hearts are as hard as
concrete. If a seed falls onto a hard path, what will happen? Will it
spring to life and bear fruit? Of course not. It cannot even begin to
take root. People will walk on it and crush it, and the birds of the
air will eat it. This is what the hearts of many are like. People with
hearts like the hard soil are those who do not pay attention to the
writings of the prophets and consequently they do not believe
that Jesus is the Savior of the world. They only care about their
own ideas or the traditions of their ancestors. The true word of
God cannot produce life in their hearts, just as a seed which falls
on a hard path cannot produce life.

The second kind of soil had *many rocks and shallow soil*. The soil with
many rocks illustrates the heart of the one who listens to the word
of God and accepts it immediately with joy, but it does not last,
because the word of God did not take root in the person's heart.
This kind of person says he believes, but when some trial comes or
he is persecuted because of the word of truth, he turns away from
the truth. Many are like this. The word of God does not have deep
roots in their hearts, because they prefer the praise of man to the
praise of God. Consequently, the word of God is worthless to them,
just as the seed which fell in the rocky place is worthless.

The third kind of soil was *full of thorns*. What happens when seed
falls among thorns? Will it bear fruit? No, it will not. The thorns will
choke it before it can bear fruit. The soil with thorns illustrates the
heart of the one who listens to the word of God, but the cares of the

---

102 Literally in Wolof: *a kind of grass with burrs*

world and the deception of riches and greed overwhelm the hearer, choking the word so that it is unproductive. Many children of Adam have hearts like thorny soil. They think: "Yes, one day, I will begin to look into the writings of the prophets. When I have time, I will listen to the word of God, *'insha'a Allah!'*"[103] Satan, of course, knows very well that such people will never take time to understand the word of God. Everyday problems and needs will dominate their hearts and minds. They must work, make money, go to the market, buy, sell, study, sleep and so forth. Is this your experience? Is your life so full of needs and concerns that you have never yet taken time to seek after the Truth of God with your whole heart?

Remember that one day death will suddenly come and usher you into eternity. On that day you will know what was the truth and what was a lie, but knowing the truth which you neither sought nor obeyed during your life will be of no value to you, because the time of repentance will be gone and you will be eternally lost.

The fourth kind of soil was *good soil*. The seed that the farmer sowed in the good, well-cultivated soil took root, grew and produced an abundant crop so that the farmer reaped a hundred times more than he had sowed. The good soil that received the seed is like the one who hears the word of God, and retains it in an honest heart, leading to righteousness and eternal life. God's word is living and powerful and will produce eternal life and righteousness living in all who receive it with a humble and honest heart.

That, in brief, is what Jesus taught in the parable of the sower. The word of God is like the good seed and our hearts are like hard soil. What must happen before seed can be sown into hard soil? One must plough it, as any farmer knows. Similarly, the heart that pleases God is a broken and humble heart, prepared to accept the good seed of the word of God. The heart that pleases God is the heart that receives His word in humility and faith. That is what the Scripture declares when it says: **Let every man be swift to hear, slow to speak, ... Therefore, putting away all filthiness and**

---

103 Arabic: *If God wills it!*

overflowing of wickedness, receive with humility the implanted word, which is able to save your souls. (James 1:19,21)

What is the condition of your heart? Do you have a humble heart, prepared to accept what God says in the Holy Scriptures through His prophets? Is the word of God growing in your heart? Or do you have a heart like soil that is hard, rocky and thorny? God's word is good Seed, but it will produce life and blessing only in the hearts of those who truly believe it and obey it.

Now let us listen to another "farmer parable" which Jesus spoke to the crowd. It is the *Parable of the Weeds*. The Scripture says:

> [24]**He set another parable before them**, saying, "The kingdom of Heaven is like a man who sowed good seed in his field, [25]but while people slept, his enemy came and sowed darnel weeds also among the wheat, and went away. [26]But when the blade sprang up and produced grain, then the darnel weeds appeared also. [27]The servants of the householder came and said to him, 'Sir, didn't you sow good seed in your field? Where did these darnel weeds come from?' [28]He said to them, 'An enemy has done this.' The servants asked him, 'Do you want us to go and gather them up?' [29]But he said, 'No, lest perhaps while you gather up the darnel weeds, you root up the wheat with them. [30]Let both grow together until the harvest, and in the harvest time I will tell the reapers, "First, gather up the darnel weeds, and bind them in bundles to burn them; but gather the wheat into my barn."'

[36]**Then Jesus sent the multitudes away**, and went into the house. His disciples came to him, saying, "Explain to us the parable of the darnel weeds of the field." [37]He answered them, "He who sows the good seed is the Son of Man, [that is the Messiah, Himself]. [38]The field is the world, the good seeds are the children of the kingdom, and the darnel weeds are the children of the evil one. [39]The enemy who sowed them is the devil. The harvest is the end of the age, and the reapers are angels. [40]As therefore the darnel weeds are gathered up and burned with fire; so will it be at the end of this age. [41]The Son of Man will send out his angels, and they will

> gather out of his kingdom all things that cause stumbling and those who do iniquity, [42]and will cast them into the furnace of fire. There will be weeping and gnashing of teeth. [43]Then the righteous will shine like the sun in the kingdom of their Father. He who has ears to hear, let him hear." (Matthew 13:24-30,36-43)

Amen. In the parable of the weeds, the Lord Jesus compared the world to a field of wheat (grain). The Sower illustrates Jesus the Messiah. The wheat which grew in the field illustrates those who are children of God because of their faith in the good news of the Messiah. The enemy who sowed weeds among the wheat is the devil. The weeds are those who do not belong to God because they have not accepted God's good news. The harvest is the Day of Judgment. The wheat stored in the grain house illustrates those who have the right to live in the presence of God forever. As for the weeds which are gathered and burned, they illustrate those who will be cast into the eternal fire, the place God made to eternally quarantine all who choose to rebel against Him.

Listening friends, how about you? Are you like the wheat or are you like the weeds? Search your heart! The Day of Judgment is coming! The Judge is at the door! Do you have confidence to face the Judge in the Day of Judgment? You need not fear that day if you will believe in your heart the good news of the Savior who came to save you from eternal hell. Jesus is the Savior and will also be the Judge. Listen to what He said about the Day of Judgment. He said, **"Most certainly I tell you, he who hears my word and believes him who sent me has eternal life, and doesn't come into judgment, but has passed out of death into life."** (John 5:24)

Thank you for listening. Next time, God willing, we will continue in the Gospel and see *how Jesus miraculously fed more than five thousand people* with five loaves of bread and two fish.

May God give you insight into all that you have heard today as you remember these words of the Lord Jesus:

He who has ears to hear, let him hear. (Matthew 13:43)

Program 72
The Bread of Life

Mark 6; John 6

In our last lesson, we saw the Lord Jesus speaking to the crowds. He presented His teaching in parables which were packed with eternal truth. But most of the crowd did not grasp the meaning of the parables because their hearts were hardened. They did not appreciate the things of heaven, but only the things of earth. Most did not follow Jesus because they believed that He was the Savior of sinners but because of the physical benefits they received from Him.

Today we will listen to more words spoken by the Lord Jesus. We will also see how He confirmed His words by performing a miraculous sign. Our lesson today is called *The Bread of Life.*[104]

Now let us continue in the Gospel of Mark, chapter 6:

[30]**The apostles gathered themselves together to Jesus**…. [31]He said to them, "You come apart into a deserted place, and rest awhile." For there were many coming and going, and they had no leisure so much as to eat. [32]They went away in the boat to a deserted place by themselves. [33]They saw them going, and many recognized him and ran there on foot from all the cities. They arrived before them and came together to him. [34]Jesus came out, saw a great multitude, and he had compassion on them, because they were like sheep without a shepherd, and he began to teach them many things.

[35]**When it was late in the day, his disciples came to him**, and said, "This place is deserted, and it is late in the day. [36]Send

them away, that they may go into the surrounding country and villages, and buy themselves bread, for they have nothing to eat." [37]But he answered them, "You give them something to eat." They asked him, "Shall we go and buy two hundred denarii worth of bread, and give them something to eat?" [38]He said to them, "How many loaves do you have? Go see." When they knew, they said, "Five, and two fish." [39]He commanded them that everyone should sit down in groups on the green grass. [40]They sat down in ranks, by hundreds and by fifties.

[41]**He took the five loaves and the two fish**, and looking up to heaven, he blessed and broke the loaves, and he gave to his disciples to set before them, and he divided the two fish among them all. [42]They all ate, and were filled. [43]They took up twelve baskets full of broken pieces and also of the fish.

[44]**Those who ate the loaves were five thousand men.** [45]Immediately he made his disciples get into the boat, and go ahead to the other side, to Bethsaida, while he himself sent the multitude away. [46]After he had taken leave of them, he went up the mountain to pray. [47]When evening had come, the boat was in the middle of the sea, and he was alone on the land. [48]Seeing them distressed in rowing, for the wind was contrary to them, about the fourth watch of the night he came to them, walking on the sea, and he would have passed by them, [49]but they, when they saw him walking on the sea, supposed that it was a ghost, and cried out; [50]for they all saw him, and were troubled. But he immediately spoke with them, and said to them, "Cheer up! It is I! Don't be afraid." [51]He got into the boat with them; and the wind ceased, and they were very amazed among themselves, and marveled; [52]for they hadn't understood about the loaves, but their hearts were hardened. [53]When they had crossed over, they came to land at Gennesaret, and moored to the shore. (Mark 6:30-53)

[22]**On the next day**, the multitude that stood on the other side of the sea saw that there was no other boat there, except the one in which his disciples had embarked, and that Jesus hadn't entered with his disciples into the boat, but his disciples had gone away

alone…. [24]When the multitude therefore saw that Jesus wasn't there, nor his disciples, they themselves got into the boats, and came to Capernaum, seeking Jesus. [25]When they found him on the other side of the sea, they asked him, "Rabbi, when did you come here?" [26]Jesus answered them, "Most certainly I tell you, you seek me, not because you saw signs, but because you ate of the loaves, and were filled. [27]Don't work for the food which perishes, but for the food which remains to eternal life, which the Son of Man will give to you. For God the Father has sealed him." (John 6:22,24-27)

Let us pause here. Why did Jesus say to the crowd, **"Don't work for the food which perishes"**? Does that mean we should not work in order to have something to eat? No, it does not mean that, because the word of God also says: **If anyone is not willing to work, don't let him eat.** (2 Thessalonians 3:10) Why then did Jesus say, "Don't work for the food that perishes"? What Jesus was saying was this: If you work only for your stomach, and merely seek after the things of the world, you will end up losing everything, because your body is going to die and return to dust. However, there is something in your body that will never cease to exist. It is your soul. The human soul will exist forever – either in the glorious place called Heaven (Paradise) or in the dark place called hell. That is why Jesus said, "Do not work for food that spoils, but for food that endures to eternal life." That was how Jesus warned the crowd, so that they might not merely seek perishable food, but so that they might seek the word of God, which never passes away. Because **man shall not live by bread alone, but by every word that proceeds out of God's mouth.** (Matthew 4:4) That is what the Lord Jesus said.

Sadly, most of those who surrounded Jesus did not care about the word of God, nor did they believe in the One whom God had sent. Filling their stomachs with food was more important to them than filling their hearts with the truth that could save them from God's judgment. That is why Jesus said to them,

> [27]**"Don't work for the food which perishes**, but for the food which remains to eternal life…." [28]They said therefore to him, "What must we do, that we may work the works of God?"

> ²⁹Jesus answered them, "This is the work of God, that you believe in him whom he has sent." (John 6:27-29)

Did you hear Jesus' answer? How can a child of Adam, who is conceived in sin, please God? Can we work and accomplish deeds that please God? Can we somehow save ourselves from the power of Satan and sin and hell? Can we produce the perfect and pure heart that God requires? Never! *Even if a log soaks a long time in water it will never become a crocodile.* Nor does being religious make a person righteous. Praying and fasting and doing good deeds may make people appear righteous before men, but such efforts will never make them righteous before God. How then can a descendant of Adam please God? What did the Lord Jesus say about this? He said, **"This is the work of God, that you believe in him whom he has sent."** No person can ever begin to please God until he (or she)[105] believes in the Savior whom God has sent.

Sadly, most of the crowd did not believe that Jesus was the Savior whom God had sent. That is why they said to Him,

> ³⁰**They said therefore to him**, "What then do you do for a sign, that we may see and believe you? What work do you do? ³¹Our fathers ate the manna in the wilderness. As it is written, 'He gave them bread out of heaven to eat.'" ³²Jesus therefore said to them, "Most certainly, I tell you, it wasn't Moses who gave you the bread out of heaven, but my Father gives you the true bread out of heaven. ³³For the bread of God is that which comes down out of heaven, and gives life to the world." ³⁴They said therefore to him, "Lord, always give us this bread." ³⁵Jesus said to them, "I am the bread of life. Whoever comes to me will not be hungry, and whoever believes in me will never be thirsty." (John 6:30-35)

With those words, Jesus was teaching the crowd that even as God sent food down from heaven to feed the children of Israel so that they might live and not perish in the desert, so God has sent down "Food" from heaven to provide the children of Adam with eternal life so that they might not perish in their sin.

---

105 The Wolof language does not have masculine and feminine pronouns.

Where is this Food? Is there a physical food on earth which we can eat that will give us the right (power) to live in the presence of God forever? No, there is not. Then what is this Food that gives eternal life? Jesus answered that question when He said,

> ³⁵**"I am the bread of life.** Whoever comes to me will not be hungry, and whoever believes in me will never be thirsty. ³⁶But I told you that you have seen me, and yet you don't believe. ³⁷All those whom [God] the Father gives me will come to me. He who comes to me I will in no way throw out…. ⁴⁰This is the will of the one who sent me, that everyone who sees the Son, and believes in him, should have eternal life; and I will raise him up at the last day."

> ⁴¹**The Jews therefore murmured concerning him**, because he said, "I am the bread which came down out of heaven." ⁴²They said, "Isn't this Jesus, the son of Joseph, whose father and mother we know? How then does he say, 'I have come down out of heaven?'" ⁴³Therefore Jesus answered them, "Don't murmur among yourselves…. ⁴⁵Everyone who hears from the Father and has learned, comes to me. ⁴⁶Not that anyone has seen the Father, except he who is from God. He has seen the Father. ⁴⁷Most certainly, I tell you, he who believes in me has eternal life. ⁴⁸I am the bread of life. ⁴⁹Your fathers ate the manna in the wilderness and they died. ⁵⁰This is the bread which comes down out of heaven, that anyone may eat of it and not die. ⁵¹I am the living bread which came down out of heaven. If anyone eats of this bread, he will live forever…."

> ⁶⁰**Therefore many of his disciples**, when they heard this, said, "This is a hard saying! Who can listen to it?" ⁶¹But Jesus knowing in himself that his disciples murmured at this, said to them, "Does this cause you to stumble? ⁶²Then what if you would see the Son of Man ascending to where he was before? ⁶³It is the spirit who gives life. The flesh profits nothing. The words that I speak to you are spirit, and are life. ⁶⁴But there are some of you who don't believe." For Jesus knew from the beginning who they were who didn't believe, and who it was who would betray him.

⁶⁶**At this, many of his disciples went back,** and walked no more with him. ⁶⁷Jesus said therefore to the twelve, "You don't also want to go away, do you?" ⁶⁸Simon Peter answered him, "Lord, to whom would we go? You have the words of eternal life. ⁶⁹We have come to believe and know that you are the Christ, the Son of the living God." (John 6:35-37,40-43,45-51,60-64,66-69)

Many, many disciples turned away, choosing to no longer accompany Jesus because of His difficult teachings. But among those who followed Jesus there were some who would not leave Him, because they were convinced that He was the Savior from heaven, the Holy One from God – **the Bread of Life** – the True Food which gives eternal life.

Yes, that is it. Once you recognize who Jesus really is and what He is like and what He has done for you, you will never be satisfied with another master. Jesus is the only way to eternal life. And He alone can satisfy the heart that hungers for assurance of salvation and a close relationship with God.

How about you? Do you hunger and thirst for eternal life? Do you long to have total confidence before God here on earth and in the life to come? Then listen to this great invitation from the Lord Jesus Christ who says, **"Come to me, all you who labor and are heavily burdened, and I will give you rest.... I am the bread of life. Whoever comes to me will not be hungry, and whoever believes in me will never be thirsty."** (Matthew 11:28; John 6:35)

Friends, thank you for listening. Next time, God willing, we will continue in the Gospel and hear *how the crowd was divided because of Jesus.*

God bless you as you remember these life-giving words of Jesus the Messiah:

> **I am the bread of life. Whoever comes to me will not be hungry, and whoever believes in me will never be thirsty.**
> (John 6:35)

Jesus Causes Division

Matthew 15-16; John 7

I n our last program, we saw the Lord Jesus multiply five loaves of bread and two fish to feed a crowd of more than five thousand men. On the following day a great crowd surrounded Him, but Jesus, who knew their hearts, said to them,

> [26]"**Most certainly I tell you**, you seek me, not because you saw signs, but because you ate of the loaves, and were filled. [27]Don't work for the food which perishes, but for the food which remains to eternal life, which the Son of Man will give to you. For God the Father has sealed him. [35]...I am the bread of life. Whoever comes to me will not be hungry, and whoever believes in me will never be thirsty." (John 6:26-27,35)

Sadly, many people turned away and no longer followed Jesus because they valued the food that could nourish their bodies more than the food that could nourish their souls. But some continued to follow Jesus because they believed in their hearts that He was the Holy One from God and the only Source of eternal life.

Today we plan to continue in the holy Gospel and see how Jesus was confronted by the religious rulers of the Jews and how the Jews were divided because of Jesus. Before we begin, it is helpful to know that most of the Jews followed the customs that they and their ancestors had established. For example, when they returned from a public place, they would not eat until they had washed themselves in a certain way. They also had many other traditions, such as how they were to wash cups, water pots, and kettles so that they would be "clean." Let's listen to what is written in the Gospel of Matthew, chapter 15:

¹**Then Pharisees and scribes came to Jesus** from Jerusalem, saying, ²"Why do your disciples disobey the tradition of the elders? For they don't wash their hands when they eat bread." ³He answered them, "Why do you also disobey the commandment of God because of your tradition? ⁴For God commanded, 'Honor your father and your mother,' and, 'He who speaks evil of father or mother, let him be put to death. ⁵But you say, 'Whoever may tell his father or his mother, "Whatever help you might otherwise have gotten from me is a gift devoted to God," ⁶he shall not honor his father or mother.' You have made the commandment of God void because of your tradition. ⁷You hypocrites! Well did Isaiah prophesy of you, saying, ⁸'These people draw near to me with their mouth, and honor me with their lips; but their heart is far from me. ⁹And in vain do they worship me, teaching as doctrine rules made by men.'" (Matthew 15:1-9)

Did you notice how Jesus exposed the hypocrisy of the religious leaders? They were trying to be righteous before men, but Jesus knew what was in their hearts. Their hands, feet, and faces may have been clean, but their hearts were contaminated with sin. A clean heart is more important than clean hands. Ceremonial washings and ablutions do not purify your heart. If you have a cooking pot that is dirty on the inside, will merely washing the outside make the pot clean? No, it will not. Similarly, the religious ceremonies the Jews followed could not remove the sin that was in their hearts.

¹⁰[**Jesus**] **summoned the multitude**, and said to them, "Hear, and understand. ¹¹That which enters into the mouth doesn't defile the man; but that which proceeds out of the mouth, this defiles the man." ¹²Then the disciples came, and said to him, "Do you know that the Pharisees were offended when they heard this saying?" ¹³But he answered, "Every plant which my heavenly Father didn't plant will be uprooted. ¹⁴Leave them alone. They are blind guides of the blind. If the blind guide the blind, both will fall into a pit." ¹⁵Peter answered him, "Explain the parable to us." ¹⁶So Jesus said, "Do you also still not understand? ¹⁷Don't you understand that whatever goes into the mouth

passes into the belly and then out of the body? [18]But the things which proceed out of the mouth come out of the heart, and they defile the man. [19]For out of the heart come evil thoughts, murders, adulteries, sexual sins, thefts, false testimony, and blasphemies. [20]These are the things which defile the man; but to eat with unwashed hands doesn't defile the man."

[29]**Jesus departed from there** and came near to the sea of Galilee; and he went up into the mountain and sat there. [30]Great multitudes came to him, having with them the lame, blind, mute, maimed, and many others, and they put them down at his feet. He healed them, [31]so that the multitude wondered when they saw the mute speaking, the injured healed, the lame walking, and the blind seeing—and they glorified the God of Israel. (Matthew 15:10-20,29-31) [1][After that,] the Pharisees and Sadducees came, and testing him, asked him to show them a sign from heaven. [2]But he answered them, "When it is evening, you say, 'It will be fair weather, for the sky is red.' [3]In the morning, 'It will be foul weather today, for the sky is red and threatening.' Hypocrites! You know how to discern the appearance of the sky, but you can't discern the signs of the times! [4]An evil and adulterous generation seeks after a sign, and there will be no sign given to it, except the sign of the prophet Jonah. (Matthew 16:1-4)

[40]**"For as Jonah was three days and three nights** in the belly of the huge fish, so will the Son of Man be three days and three nights in the heart of the earth. [41]The men of Nineveh will stand up in the judgment with this generation and will condemn it, for they repented at the preaching of Jonah; and behold, someone greater than Jonah is here." (Matthew 12:40-41)

In this way, Jesus foretold that even as the prophet Jonah was in the belly of the great fish and came out on the third day,[106] so He,

---

106 The period of time Jonah was in the belly of the huge fish and the period of time Jesus was in the heart of the earth are both expressed in round numbers according to the Jewish way of speaking, which was to regard any part of a day, however small, as a full day. (Matthew 27:63-64; Genesis 42:17-18; 1 Samuel 30:12-13; Esther 4:16-5:1)

Jesus, would be buried and come out of the tomb on the third day, giving undeniable proof that He is the Messiah from heaven who came to save us from the power of sin and death and hell. But the religious experts persisted in their unbelief. In the Gospel of John, chapter 7, the Scripture says:

> [1]**After these things, Jesus was walking in Galilee,** for he wouldn't walk in Judea, because the Jews sought to kill him. [2]Now the feast of the Jews, the Feast of Booths, was at hand. [3]His brothers therefore said to him, "Depart from here and go into Judea, that your disciples also may see your works which you do. [4]For no one does anything in secret while he seeks to be known openly. If you do these things, reveal yourself to the world." [5]For even his brothers didn't believe in him. …

> [12][Also] **there was much murmuring** among the multitudes concerning him. Some said, "He is a good man." Others said, "Not so, but he leads the multitude astray." [13]Yet no one spoke openly of him for fear of the Jews. [14]But when it was now the middle of the feast, Jesus went up into the temple and taught. [15]The Jews therefore marveled, saying, "How does this man know letters, having never been educated?"

> [16]**Jesus therefore answered them,** "My teaching is not mine, but his who sent me. [17]If anyone desires to do his will, he will know about the teaching, whether it is from God, or if I am speaking from myself. … [19]Didn't Moses give you the law, and yet none of you keeps the law? Why do you seek to kill me?" [20]The multitude answered, "You have a demon! Who seeks to kill you?" [21]Jesus answered them, "I did one work and you all marvel because of it. [22]Moses has given you circumcision (not that it is of Moses, but of the fathers), and on the Sabbath you circumcise a boy. [23]If a boy receives circumcision on the Sabbath, that the law of Moses may not be broken, are you angry with me, because I made a man completely healthy on the Sabbath? [24]Don't judge according to appearance, but judge righteous judgment." … [30]They sought therefore to take him; but no one laid a hand on him, because his hour had not yet come. [31]But of the multitude, many believed in

him. They said, "When the Christ [or *Messiah*] comes, he won't do more signs than those which this man has done, will he?"

[37]**Now on the last and greatest day of the feast**, Jesus stood and cried out, "If anyone is thirsty, let him come to me and drink! [38]He who believes in me, as the Scripture has said, from within him will flow rivers of living water." ... [40]Many of the multitude therefore, when they heard these words, said, "This is truly the prophet." [41]Others said, "This is the [Messiah]." But some said, "What, does the [Messiah] come out of Galilee? [42]Hasn't the Scripture said that the [Messiah] comes of the offspring of David, and from Bethlehem, the village where David was?"

[43]**So a division arose in the multitude because of him.** [44]Some of them would have arrested him, but no one laid hands on him. [45]The officers therefore came to the chief priests and Pharisees, and they said to them, "Why didn't you bring him?" [46]The officers answered, "No man ever spoke like this man!" [47]The Pharisees therefore answered them, "You aren't also led astray, are you? [48]Have any of the rulers believed in him, or of the Pharisees? [49]But this multitude that doesn't know the law is cursed."

[50]**Nicodemus (he who came to him by night**, being one of them) said to them, [51]"Does our law judge a man, unless it first hears from him personally and knows what he does?" [52]They answered him, "Are you also from Galilee? Search, and see that no prophet has arisen out of Galilee." [53]Everyone went to his own house. (John 7:1-5,12-17,19-24,30-31,37-38,40-53)

This is where we must stop today. We have seen how the priests, the teachers of the law and the Pharisees harassed Jesus. They wanted to arrest Him and have Him put to death, but they could do nothing to Him, because the time which God appointed for Jesus to die as a sacrifice for sin had not yet come.

Sadly, most of the religious leaders had hard hearts. They despised Jesus and they threatened to expel from the synagogue anyone who said that Jesus was the Messiah. And so there was a division among the crowd because of Jesus. No one would say anything openly about Jesus because they were afraid of the religious leaders and the priests (marabouts). Secretly, among themselves, some whispered, "He is a good man." Others retorted, "No, he deceives the people!" The rest wondered, "When the Messiah comes will He do more miraculous signs than this man?"

Friends, what do *you* say about Jesus? What do *you* think about Him? Do you believe that Jesus is the Messiah about whom all the prophets wrote? Or do you think that He was just one of the prophets? Let no one mislead you in this matter. Your destiny in the hereafter depends on your response to this question. Do you know who Jesus really is? Do you know why He came into the world? Listen to what Jesus said about Himself:

> **I am the way, the truth, and the life.** No one comes to [God] the Father, except through me.… For this reason I have been born, and for this reason I have come into the world, that I should testify to the truth. Everyone who is of the truth listens to my voice. (John 14:6; 18:37)

Dear friend, whose side are you on? Are you willing to side with the Truth – even if means being rejected by your own family? Wolof wisdom says: *Whoever wants honey must brave the bees.* The Lord Jesus said,

> [34]**Don't think that I came to send peace on the earth**.… [35]For I came to set a man at odds against his father, and a daughter against her mother, and a daughter-in-law against her mother-in-law. [36]A man's foes will be those of his own household. [37]He who loves father or mother more than me is not worthy of me; and he who loves son or daughter more than me isn't worthy of me. (Matthew 10:34-37)

Thank you for listening. Join us next time to see how Jesus healed a man who was blind from birth.

God bless you as you consider these words of Jesus:

> **Everyone who is of the truth listens to my voice.** (John 18:37)

Program 74
The Light of the World

John 8-9

I n the last program we saw how the religious leaders harassed Jesus and attempted to arrest Him so that they could have Him put to death. But no one could take the Lord Jesus since God's time for Him to die as the perfect sacrifice for sin had not yet come. Today we will hear how Jesus rebuked those who opposed Him and how He healed a man who had been born blind.

The Gospel of John, chapter 8, tells us what happened early one morning when Jesus went into the temple in Jerusalem and people came to Him. He sat down and began to teach, saying,

> [12]**"I am the light of the world.** He who follows me will not walk in the darkness, but will have the light of life." [13]The Pharisees therefore said to him, "You testify about yourself. Your testimony is not valid." [14]Jesus answered them, "Even if I testify about myself, my testimony is true, for I know where I came from, and where I am going; but you don't know where I came from, or where I am going. … [23]He said to them, "You are from beneath. I am from above. You are of this world. I am not of this world. [24]I said therefore to you that you will die in your sins; for unless you believe that I am [the one I claim to be], you will die in your sins."

> [25]**They said therefore to him, "Who are you?"** Jesus said to them, "Just what I have been saying to you from the beginning." … [28]Jesus therefore said to them, "When you have lifted up the Son of Man, then you will know that I am [the one I claim to be], and I do nothing of myself, but as my Father taught me, I say these things. … [32]You will know the truth, and the truth will make you free."

³³They answered him, "We are Abraham's offspring, and have never been in bondage to anyone. How do you say, 'You will be made free'?" ³⁴Jesus answered them, "Most certainly I tell you, everyone who commits sin is the bondservant of sin. ³⁵A bondservant doesn't live in the house forever. A son remains forever. ³⁶If therefore the Son makes you free, you will be free indeed. ³⁷I know that you are Abraham's offspring, yet you seek to kill me, because my word finds no place in you. ³⁸I say the things which I have seen with my Father; and you also do the things which you have seen with your father." ³⁹They answered him, "Our father is Abraham." Jesus said to them, "If you were Abraham's children, you would do the works of Abraham. ⁴⁰But now you seek to kill me, a man who has told you the truth which I heard from God. Abraham didn't do this. ⁴¹You do the works of your father."

They said to him, "We were not born of sexual immorality. We have one Father, God." ⁴²Therefore Jesus said to them, "If God were your father, you would love me, for I came out and have come from God. For I haven't come of myself, but he sent me. ⁴³Why don't you understand my speech? Because you can't hear my word. ⁴⁴You are of your father, the devil, and you want to do the desires of your father. He was a murderer from the beginning, and doesn't stand in the truth, because there is no truth in him. When he speaks a lie, he speaks on his own; for he is a liar, and the father of lies. ⁴⁵But because I tell the truth, you don't believe me. ⁴⁶Which of you convicts me of sin? If I tell the truth, why do you not believe me? ⁴⁷He who is of God hears the words of God. For this cause you don't hear, because you are not of God."

⁴⁸Then the Jews answered him, "Don't we say well that you are a Samaritan, and have a demon?" ⁴⁹Jesus answered, "I don't have a demon, but I honor my Father and you dishonor me. ⁵⁰But I don't seek my own glory. There is one who seeks and judges. ⁵¹Most certainly, I tell you, if a person keeps my word, he will never see death." ⁵²Then the Jews said to him, "Now we know that you have a demon. Abraham died, as did the prophets; and you say, 'If a man keeps my word, he will never taste of death.' [53]Are you greater than our father, Abraham, who died? The prophets died. Who do you make yourself out to be?" [54]Jesus answered, "If I glorify myself, my glory is nothing. It is my Father who glorifies me, of whom you say that he is our God. [55]You have not known him, but I know him. If I said, 'I don't know him,' I would be like you, a liar. But I know him and keep his word. [56]Your father Abraham rejoiced to see my day. He saw it, and was glad." [57]The Jews therefore said to him, "You are not yet fifty years old! Have you seen Abraham?"

[58]**Jesus said to them**, "Most certainly, I tell you, before Abraham came into existence, I AM." [59]Therefore they took up stones to throw at him, but Jesus was hidden, and went out of the temple, having gone through the middle of them, and so passed by. (John 8:12-14,23-25,28,32-59)

[1]**As he passed by, he saw a man blind from birth.** [2]His disciples asked him, "Rabbi, who sinned, this man or his parents, that he was born blind?" [3]Jesus answered, "This man didn't sin, nor did his parents; but, that the works of God might be revealed in him. [4]I must work the works of him who sent me while it is day. The night is coming, when no one can work. [5]While I am in the world, I am the light of the world."

[6]**When he had said this, he spat on the ground**, made mud with the saliva, anointed the blind man's eyes with the mud, [7]and said to him, "Go, wash in the pool of Siloam" (which means "Sent"). So he went away, washed, and came back seeing. [8]The neighbors therefore, and those who saw that he was blind before, said, "Isn't this he who sat and begged?" [9]Others were saying, "It is he." Still others were saying, "He looks like him." He said, "I am he." [10]They therefore were asking him, "How were your eyes opened?" [11]He answered, "A man called Jesus made mud, anointed my eyes, and said to me, 'Go to the pool of Siloam and wash.' So I went away and washed, and I received sight." [12]Then they asked him, "Where is he?" He said, "I don't know." [13]They brought him who had been

blind to the Pharisees. [14]It was a Sabbath when Jesus made the mud and opened his eyes. [15]Again therefore the Pharisees also asked him how he received his sight. He said to them, "He put mud on my eyes, I washed, and I see." [16]Some therefore of the Pharisees said, "This man is not from God, because he doesn't keep the Sabbath." Others said, "How can a man who is a sinner do such signs?" So there was division among them.

[17]**Therefore they asked the blind man again**, "What do you say about him, because he opened your eyes?" He said, "He is a prophet." [18]The Jews therefore didn't believe concerning him, that he had been blind, and had received his sight, until they called the parents of him who had received his sight, [19]and asked them, "Is this your son, whom you say was born blind? How then does he now see?" [20]His parents answered them, "We know that this is our son, and that he was born blind; [21]but how he now sees, we don't know; or who opened his eyes, we don't know. He is of age. Ask him. He will speak for himself." [22]His parents said these things because they feared the Jews; for the Jews had already agreed that if any man would confess him as Christ, he would be put out of the synagogue. [23]Therefore his parents said, "He is of age. Ask him."

[24]**So they called the man who was blind a second time**, and said to him, "Give glory to God. We know that this man is a sinner." [25]He therefore answered, "I don't know if he is a sinner. One thing I do know: that though I was blind, now I see." [26]They said to him again, "What did he do to you? How did he open your eyes?" [27]He answered them, "I told you already, and you didn't listen. Why do you want to hear it again? You don't also want to become his disciples, do you?" [28]They insulted him and said, "You are his disciple, but we are disciples of Moses. [29]We know that God has spoken to Moses. But as for this man, we don't know where he comes from." [30]The man answered them, "How amazing! You don't know where he comes from, yet he opened my eyes. [31]We know that God doesn't listen to sinners, but if anyone is a worshiper of God,

and does his will, he listens to him. [32]Since the world began it has never been heard of that anyone opened the eyes of someone born blind. [33]If this man were not from God, he could do nothing." [34]They answered him, "You were altogether born in sins, and do you teach us?" Then they threw him out.

[35]**Jesus heard that they had thrown him out**, and finding him, he said, "Do you believe in the Son of God?" [36]He answered, "Who is he, Lord, that I may believe in him?" [37]Jesus said to him, "You have both seen him, and it is he who speaks with you." [38]He said, "Lord, I believe!" and he worshiped him. [39]Jesus said, "I came into this world for judgment, that those who don't see may see; and that those who see may become blind." [40]Those of the Pharisees who were with him heard these things, and said to him, "Are we also blind?" [41]Jesus said to them, "If you were blind, you would have no sin; but now you say, 'We see.' Therefore your sin remains." (John 9:1-41)

In this way the Lord Jesus healed the man who was born blind and rebuked the Pharisees for their blinded minds. These religious experts had a blindness that was worse than physical blindness. They could see, but they did not want to see, which is why they picked up rocks to throw at Jesus. These religious men had closed their minds to the truth about Jesus. They did not want to believe that He was the Messiah and the Light of the world. They did not want to believe that Jesus had existed before the prophet Abraham, that He was the Word that was with God in the beginning. *Truth is a hot pepper* and they did not want to receive it.

In today's story we have seen two kinds of blind people: those who are blind in the eyes and those who are blind in the mind. The darkness of a blinded mind is worse than the darkness of blind eyes. If your eyes are blind, you cannot see the things of the world, but if your mind and heart are blind, then you cannot see or understand the things of eternity.

The word of God teaches us that all of Adam's children are blind from birth – blind in their minds and hearts. Because of Adam's sin, we have all been born in the darkness of sin and ignorance. Like cockroaches that scatter when a light is turned on, we avoid the light of God's word, content to live our lives in the darkness. Sadly, most of Adam's offspring die in the darkness of sin and ignorance. Wolof wisdom says, *Before you know it, ignorance will kill you.* Similarly, the prophet Hosea wrote: **Hear the LORD's word. … "My people are destroyed for lack of knowledge. Because you have rejected knowledge, I will also reject you…."** (Hosea 4:1,6)

The good news is that God does not want any of us to perish in the darkness of sin and ignorance. That is why He visited planet earth by sending to us His Word, Jesus. The prophet Zacharias spoke of the Lord Jesus as "the Rising Sun" whom God would send from heaven **to shine on those who sit in darkness and the shadow of death; to guide our feet into the way of peace.** (Luke 1:79) The prophets were like the stars that illumine the night, but Jesus Christ is like the rising sun, bringing light and life to all who believe in Him. How many suns did God create to illuminate our world? Only one. How many Saviors has God sent from heaven to deliver sinners from the darkness of sin and eternal hell? Only one. However, most of Adam's children do not understand this, which is why they are still stumbling in the darkness of their sin and shame. That is what the Scripture declares about the Lord Jesus Christ, saying:

> 5**The light shines in the darkness**, and the darkness hasn't overcome it. … 10He was in the world, and the world was made through him, and the world didn't recognize him. (John 1:5,10)

Listening friends, has the Lord Jesus opened the eyes of your mind and heart? Or are you still stumbling in the darkness?

Thank you for listening. In our next study, God willing, we will see how *the glory of God shone out of Jesus like the sun.*

God bless you as you ponder this declaration by Jesus Himself:

> **I am the light of the world. He who follows me will not walk in the darkness, but will have the light of life.** (John 8:12)

The Lord of Glory

Matthew 16-17

In our study in the book of the Gospel, last time we heard how Jesus the Messiah opened the eyes of a man who was born blind. Nothing is impossible for Jesus because He is the Word of God who appeared on earth as a man. That is why He had power over every force upon earth – the wind and the sea, demons, disease, and death. Wherever Jesus went the crowds pressed in on Him, but few recognized who He really was. They considered Him a prophet but did not recognize that all the fullness of God dwelt in Him. They did not understand that Jesus was the Lord of Glory, who came from heaven. In today's program, God willing, we will see how the Lord Jesus displayed the glory of God. Now let us return to the holy Gospel. The Scripture says:

> [18]**As he was praying alone**, the disciples were with him, and he asked them, "Who do the multitudes say that I am?" [19]They answered, "'John the Baptizer,' but others say, 'Elijah,' and others, that one of the old prophets has risen again." (Luke 9:18-19)

> [15]**He said to them, "But who do you say that I am?"** [16]Simon Peter answered, "You are the Christ, [the Messiah] the Son of the living God." [17]Jesus answered him, "Blessed are you, Simon Bar Jonah, for flesh and blood has not revealed this to you, but my Father who is in heaven." (Matthew 16:15-17)

Truly, what Jesus asked His disciples is an important question which each of us must also answer. You who are listening today, who do you consider Jesus to be? What do you think about Him? Do you merely classify Him with the prophets? Or do you agree with Peter who declared that Jesus is "the Messiah, the Son of the Living God"?

Who do you think Jesus is? Do you believe that He is the Redeemer promised long ago by God on that day when our ancestors, Adam and Eve, sinned? Do you believe that Jesus is "the Son of the Living God" – the Word of God which came down from heaven?

As you know, to this very day, many people deny that Jesus is the Son of God because they think that this name means that God took a wife and had a child by her. But it does not mean that. God's glory is greater than that. God is Spirit and does not beget as a man begets, but that does not keep God from calling Jesus *His Son*. We have already illustrated it like this: If a Senegalese goes outside his country and folks call him "a son of Senegal," that does not mean that Senegal took a wife and had a son. No, he is called a son of Senegal because Senegal is where he comes from.

That is how it was with Jesus, the Messiah, who was born of a virgin. Even before He was born, He existed in heaven. He is the *Kalimat Allah* and the *Ruh Allah* – the very Word and Soul of God. Only Jesus is worthy to be called *the Son of the Most High*, because He alone is the Word that was with God in the beginning. This is a great mystery, but more than that, it is a great truth. God sent His Word-Son into the world not only to save us from our sins, but also to show us what God is like. Jesus displayed God's character on earth. Whoever sees the Son knows what the Father is like. Whoever sees Jesus knows what God is like. Jesus is called the Son of God, because He came from God, because He is like God, and because He is the very Word of God. Dear friends, whether we believe it or whether we refuse to believe it, the truth remains: Jesus is the Son of the Living God!

Let us now continue in the Gospel of Matthew and listen to what happened after Peter declared Jesus to be the Messiah, the Son of the Living God. The Scripture says:

> [21]**From that time, Jesus began to show his disciples** that he must go to Jerusalem and suffer many things from the elders, chief priests, and scribes, and be killed, and the third day be raised up. [22]Peter took him aside and began to rebuke him,

saying, "Far be it from you, Lord! This will never be done to you." [23]But he turned and said to Peter, "Get behind me, Satan! You are a stumbling block to me, for you are not setting your mind on the things of God, but on the things of men." (Matthew 16:21-23)

Did you hear what Jesus said to His disciples? He told them that He must go to Jerusalem and suffer many things at the hands of the elders, chief priests and teachers of the law, and that He must be killed and be raised to life again on the third day. In this way Jesus announced that He would pour out His blood to pay the debt for our sin.

But Peter could not accept that Jesus the Messiah, who possessed all power and all authority, would allow the evil religious rulers to arrest Him, torture Him, and kill Him. That was why Peter said to Jesus, "Never, Lord! This shall never happen to you!" But Jesus knew that He had come into the world to shed His blood as a sacrifice that takes away sin. That is the reason He said to Peter, **"Get behind me, Satan! You are a stumbling-block to me; you do not have in mind the things of God, but the things of men."**

Jesus knew why He had come into the world. He came to give His life by shedding His holy blood for sinners, just as God's prophets had predicted long beforehand. Jesus came so that the symbol of the sacrificial lamb might be fulfilled in Him.

Ah, fellow listeners, if we remember only one thing from the story today, let it be this: Jesus the Messiah came into the world to die as a sacrifice to pay for sin – my sin and yours. God willing, a few lessons from now, we will see how Jesus' prophecy about His own death was precisely fulfilled in Jerusalem. And so friends, even if some proclaim another message, a message which does not agree with what the prophets and the Messiah Himself foretold so long ago, the truth of Jesus' death and resurrection does not change. God Himself is the One who decreed the death of the Messiah on the cross, and no one can change the decrees of God. Jesus chose to die as the supreme Sacrifice. He did it because He loves you and me and does not want us to perish.

Now let us see what happened one week after Jesus informed His disciples that He would offer up His life in Jerusalem.

> [1]**After six days, Jesus took with him** Peter, James, and John his brother, and brought them up into a high mountain by themselves. [2]He was changed before them. His face shone like the sun, and his garments became as white as the light. (Matthew 17:1-2)

> [30]**Behold, two men were talking with him**, who were Moses and Elijah, [31]who appeared in glory, and spoke of his departure, which he was about to accomplish at Jerusalem. (Luke 9:30-31)

> [4]**Peter answered and said to Jesus**, "Lord, it is good for us to be here. If you want, let's make three tents here: one for you, one for Moses, and one for Elijah." [5]While he was still speaking, behold, a bright cloud overshadowed them. Behold, a voice came out of the cloud, saying, "This is my beloved Son, in whom I am well pleased. Listen to him." [6]When the disciples heard it, they fell on their faces, and were very afraid. [7]Jesus came and touched them and said, "Get up, and don't be afraid." [8]Lifting up their eyes, they saw no one, except Jesus alone. [9]As they were coming down from the mountain, Jesus commanded them, saying, "Don't tell anyone what you saw, until the Son of Man has risen from the dead." (Matthew 17:4-9)

Did you grasp what happened on that high mountain? It was an amazing and wonderful event. We read that Jesus' outward appearance was transformed – His face shone like the sun and His clothes radiated a dazzling white light. The same awesome, pure light that shines out of God and surrounds the throne of God in heaven was now shining out of Jesus! The glorious light that filled the Holiest Place in the Tent of the Meeting in the days when Moses and the Israelites were in the wilderness – that same glory was in Jesus, though men could not see it. But for a few brief moments, in the presence of Jesus' three disciples, God unveiled His awesome glory which was hidden in Jesus' body. And at the same moment, God sent down from heaven two prophets, Moses and Elijah, to talk with Jesus about His death in Jerusalem. We also read that a bright cloud covered the mountain, and the voice of the Almighty thundered from the cloud, saying, **"This is my Son, whom I love; with him I am well pleased. Listen to him!"**

What was the reason for all this? Why did God do all these glorious things in the presence of Peter, John and James? This is the reason. God wanted to give those three witnesses an unshakable proof that, in truth, Jesus is the Eternal Son of God from heaven, and that all must listen to Him. That is what the Scripture proclaims:

> **He who doesn't honor the Son** doesn't honor the Father who sent him. (John 5:23)

> [1]**God, having in the past spoken to the fathers** through the prophets at many times and in various ways, [2]has at the end of these days spoken to us by his Son, whom he appointed heir of all things, through whom also he made the worlds. [3]His Son is the radiance of his glory, the very image of his substance, and upholding all things by the word of his power, who, when he had by himself purified us of our sins, sat down on the right hand of the Majesty on high. (Hebrews 1:1-3)

You who are listening today, what do you think of Jesus? What do you say about Him? Do you believe that He is the Lord of Glory, who came from heaven? Or do you merely classify Him with the prophets? Before we bid you farewell today, let us listen to what Jesus' apostles, Peter and John, wrote about their experience in seeing the glory of God shining out of Jesus on the mountaintop.

The apostle Peter wrote:

> [16]**For we didn't follow cunningly devised fables** when we made known to you the power and coming of our Lord Jesus Christ, but we were eyewitnesses of his majesty. [17]For he received from God the Father honor and glory when the voice came to him from the Majestic Glory, "This is my beloved Son, in whom I am well pleased." [18]We heard this voice come out of heaven when we were with him on the holy mountain. (2 Peter 1:16-18)

The apostle John wrote:

> [1]**That which was from the beginning**, that which we have heard, that which we have seen with our eyes, that which we saw, and our hands touched, concerning the Word of life [2]and the life was revealed, and we have seen [it]....[14]We saw his glory, such glory as of the one and only Son of the Father, full of grace and truth. (1 John 1:1-2; John 1:14)

And in the end of the Gospel book, John wrote,

> [30]**Therefore Jesus did many other signs** in the presence of his disciples, which are not written in this book; [31]but these are written, that you may believe that Jesus is the Christ, the Son of God, and that believing you may have life in his name. (John 20:30-31)

Do you find all this hard to understand? God wants to give you insight into these marvelous truths. The Scripture says:

> [14]**Now the natural man doesn't receive** the things of God's Spirit, for they are foolishness to him, and he can't know them, because they are spiritually discerned.... [6]We speak wisdom, however, among those who are full grown, yet a wisdom not of this world nor of the rulers of this world who are coming to nothing. [7]But we speak God's wisdom in a mystery, the wisdom that has been hidden, which God foreordained before the worlds for our glory, [8]which none of the rulers of this world has known. For had they known it, they wouldn't have crucified the Lord of glory. (1 Corinthians 2:14, 6-8)

May God make clear all that we have read today.

Until next time, keep thinking about what the one true God declared on the mountaintop concerning Jesus the Messiah:

> **This is my beloved Son, in whom I am well pleased. Listen to him!** (Matthew 17:5)

Program 76

The Good Shepherd

John 10

I n the last program, we heard the Lord Jesus tell His disciples that He must die in Jerusalem and rise from the dead on the third day. Jesus knew that He had been born into the world to shed His blood as a sacrifice that takes away sin. Last time we also saw the Lord Jesus display His great glory when He was on the mountain with three of His disciples. The face of Jesus shone like the sun, and His clothes radiated a shining pure white light. That is how the glory of God residing in Jesus revealed itself.

Today we will continue in the Gospel (*Injil*) and hear how Jesus compared His people with *contented sheep*. We have already heard in the writings of the prophets how God compares the children of Adam to *lost sheep without a shepherd*. However, God who loves us does not want us to perish like sheep without a shepherd. That is why He sent from heaven the Messiah to guide us in the way of peace and to save us from our vicious enemies: Satan, sin, death, and hell. One day, Jesus said to the crowd gathered around Him:

> ¹**"Most certainly, I tell you**, one who doesn't enter by the door into the sheep fold, but climbs up some other way, is a thief and a robber. ²But one who enters in by the door is the shepherd of the sheep. … ⁶Jesus spoke this parable to them, but they didn't understand what he was telling them. ⁷Jesus therefore said to them again, "Most certainly, I tell you, I am the sheep's door. …

> ⁹**I am the door.** If anyone enters in by me, he will be saved, and will go in and go out, and will find pasture. ¹⁰The thief only comes to steal, kill, and destroy. I came that they may have life, and may have it abundantly.

¹¹**I am the good shepherd.** The good shepherd lays down his life for the sheep. ¹²He who is a hired hand, and not a shepherd, who doesn't own the sheep, sees the wolf coming, leaves the sheep, and flees. The wolf snatches the sheep, and scatters them. ¹³The hired hand flees because he is a hired hand, and doesn't care for the sheep. ¹⁴"I am the good shepherd. I know my own, and I'm known by my own; ¹⁵even as the Father knows me, and I know the Father. I lay down my life for the sheep. … ¹⁷Therefore the Father loves me, because I lay down my life, that I may take it again. ¹⁸No one takes it away from me, but I lay it down by myself. I have power to lay it down, and I have power to take it again. I received this commandment from my Father."

¹⁹**Therefore a division arose again** among the Jews because of these words. ²⁰Many of them said, "He has a demon, and is insane! Why do you listen to him?" ²¹Others said, "These are not the sayings of one possessed by a demon. It isn't possible for a demon to open the eyes of the blind, is it?"

²⁴**The Jews therefore came around him** and said to him, "How long will you hold us in suspense? If you are the Christ, tell us plainly." ²⁵Jesus answered them, "I told you, and you don't believe. The works that I do in my Father's name, these testify about me. ²⁶But you don't believe, because you are not of my sheep, as I told you. ²⁷My sheep hear my voice, and I know them, and they follow me. ²⁸I give eternal life to them. They will never perish, and no one will snatch them out of my hand. ²⁹My Father who has given them to me is greater than all. No one is able to snatch them out of my Father's hand. ³⁰I and the Father are one." ³¹Therefore the Jews took up stones again to stone him. ³²Jesus answered them, "I have shown you many good works from my Father. For which of those works do you stone me?"

³³**The Jews answered him,** "We don't stone you for a good work, but for blasphemy: because you, being a man, make yourself God." ³⁴Jesus answered them, "Isn't it written in your law, 'I said, you are gods?' If he called them gods, to whom the

word of God came (and the Scripture can't be broken), [36]do you say of him whom the Father sanctified and sent into the world, 'You blaspheme,' because I said, 'I am the Son of God?' [37]If I don't do the works of my Father, don't believe me. [38]But if I do them, though you don't believe me, believe the works, that you may know and believe that the Father is in me, and I in the Father." [39]They sought again to seize him, and he went out of their hand. (John 10:1-2,6-7,9-15,17-21,24-39)

Did you hear what Jesus said to the Jews? Since our time does not allow us to explain all the words of Jesus in detail, we will center our thoughts upon two of the names by which Jesus referred to Himself. Did you hear them? Those two names are: *The Door for the sheep* and *the Good Shepherd.*

First we heard that after Jesus compared people to sheep, He said to the crowd, **"I am the sheep's door.…If anyone enters in by me, he will be saved"** Why did Jesus call Himself **the Door for the sheep**? In those days, a shepherd would make an enclosure of thorny branches or rocks, constructed with a single doorway by which the flock could enter. When evening came and the sheep had entered, the shepherd himself would sleep in the doorway of the sheep pen to guard his flock. Thus, before any wild animal could enter the pen and kill a sheep, it would have to come through the doorway where the shepherd lay. The shepherd would then chase the wild animal away before it could harm the sheep. In this way the shepherd himself was **the door**.

The Lord Jesus called Himself **the Door for the sheep**. This means that Jesus cares for all those who belong to Him. This also means that before you can become a part of God's flock, you must come through Jesus. Whoever wants to be saved from the snares of Satan, from the penalty of sin, from the power of death, and the punishment of eternal hell must pass through Jesus. He alone is the door that can admit sinners into eternal life. That is why God's word says: **There is salvation in no one else, for there is no other name under heaven that is given among men, by which we must be saved.** (Acts 4:12) Jesus is the one and only door to Salvation.

Can you remember what we read some time ago about the prophet Noah and the flood? How many doors did God command Noah to make in the ark which would be a refuge to those who wanted to escape the judgment of the flood? Only one door. Anyone who wanted to escape the flood had to go through the one door of the ark. Whoever entered through the door was saved. Whoever did not enter through the door perished! Similarly, regarding the Day of Judgment, the Holy Scriptures confirm to us that God has opened only one door of salvation for the children of Adam. The Messiah Himself is the Door that can admit people into eternal life. That is why Jesus said:

> **"I am the door. If anyone enters in by me, he will be saved.** …[but the] one who doesn't enter by the door into the sheep fold, but climbs up some other way, is a thief and a robber."
> (John 10:9,1)

The second name by which Jesus referred to Himself is much like the first one. Jesus is not only **the Door for the sheep**, He is also **the Good Shepherd**. Jesus is the Good Shepherd because He is the One who loved us and gave His life for us. Oh, what a wonderful Shepherd He is! Concerning Him, the prophet David, wrote in the twenty-third Psalm (*Zabur*), saying:

> [1]**The LORD is my shepherd: I shall lack nothing.** [2]He makes me lie down in green pastures. He leads me beside still waters. [3]He restores my soul. He guides me in the paths of righteousness for his name's sake.

> [4]**Even though I walk through the valley** of the shadow of death, I will fear no evil, for you are with me. Your rod and your staff, they comfort me. [5]You prepare a table before me in the presence of my enemies. You anoint my head with oil. My cup runs over.

> [6]**Surely goodness and loving kindness shall follow me** all the days of my life, and I will dwell in The LORD's house forever.
> (Psalm 23:1-6)

What we need to realize is that the Messiah Himself is the Good Shepherd about whom David wrote. That is why Jesus could say, **"I am the good shepherd!"** and, **"I and [God] the Father are one!"** (John 10:11,30) But when Jesus declared that He was one with God, the Jews accused Him of blasphemy and picked up stones to throw at Him. They could not accept the idea that Jesus was God in a human body. To this very day, most of the children of Adam stumble over these words of Jesus. Some mistakenly think that to say Jesus is one with God must mean that there are two Gods. But that is not the way it is, for the scriptures of the prophets clearly declare the unity of God, saying: **"The Lord is our God. The LORD is One!"** (Deuteronomy 6:4) But the fact that *God is One* did not prevent God from revealing Himself on earth as a man.

Perhaps an illustration will help. Think about the sun which shines on the earth giving us light and heat. How many such suns do we have? Only one. Where is the sun? It is far out in space, yet it is also here on earth, penetrating our lives with its life-giving sunshine. The fiery sun with its light and heat are one. Similarly, God, His Word, and His Holy Spirit are one. That is why Jesus said, **"I and the Father are one!"** The Lord Jesus came into our world to communicate the light of God's love and salvation to us. Listen to what the Holy Scriptures declare about God and Jesus:

> **For our God is a consuming fire**… dwelling in unapproachable light! … No one has seen God at any time. The one and only Son, who is in the bosom of the Father, has declared him.… His Son is the radiance of his glory, the very image of his substance, and upholding all things by the word of his power, who, when he had by himself purified us of our sins, sat down on the right hand of the Majesty on high.…God was pleased to have all his fullness dwell in [Jesus Christ]! …For in [Christ] all the fullness of the Deity dwells bodily. (Hebrews 12:29; 1Timothy 6:16; John 1:18; Hebrews 1:3; Colossians 1:19 NIV; 2:9)

Yes, that is what the word of God declares. For **in [Christ] all the fullness of the Deity dwells bodily.** (Colossians 2:9) Thus, the Lord Jesus could say, **"I and [God] the Father are one!"**

Christ Jesus is the Good Shepherd who came from heaven, became a man, lived on earth, and laid down His holy life to redeem us from the curse which sin brought. He is also the One who rose from the dead and offers eternal life to all who hang their hope on Him. That is why Jesus could say:

> [14]**"I am the good shepherd**…[15]I lay down my life for the sheep…[17]that I may take it again. [18]No one takes it away from me, but I lay it down by myself. I have power to lay it down, and I have power to take it again. I received this commandment from my Father."** (John 10:14-15,17-18)

Beyond all question, Jesus is the Good Shepherd, because He is the One who loved us so much that He gave His life for us. Let's listen once more to the wonderful words of the Lord Jesus, who said:

> [9]**I am the door. If anyone enters in by me, he will be saved**. … [10]The thief only comes to steal, kill, and destroy. I came that they may have life, and may have it abundantly. [11]I am the good shepherd. The good shepherd lays down his life for the sheep. [12]He who is a hired hand, and not a shepherd, who doesn't own the sheep, sees the wolf coming, leaves the sheep, and flees.… [14]I am the good shepherd.… [27]My sheep hear my voice, and I know them, and they follow me. [28]I give eternal life to them. They will never perish, and no one will snatch them out of my hand. (John 10:9-12,14,27-28)

Listening friends, who are you following? The Good Shepherd? Or are you following someone else?

We thank you for listening and invite you to join us next time to hear what Jesus taught about the heart of God.

May God bless you and make Himself real to you as you remember what Jesus the Messiah said about Himself:

> **I am the door; If anyone enters in by me, he will be saved. …
> I am the good shepherd. The good shepherd lays down his
> life for the sheep!** (John 10:9,11)

Program 77

The Heart of God

Luke 18,15

Throughout our studies in the writings of the prophets, we have seen that God is holy and righteous and that He cannot tolerate sin. Yet we have also seen that He is also merciful and compassionate. That is wonderful news for us, because we desperately need His mercy, since we have all greatly offended God. Our trespasses and our sins are abhorrent to God, and they will condemn us forever unless He has mercy on us and provides for us a solution. Today we plan to read two parables which the Lord Jesus spoke to the crowds. Through these two interesting stories we will learn about the great mercy that fills God's heart, and how sinners can receive that mercy.

The first parable is about two men: one who did not receive God's mercy and one who received it. One belonged to the sect of the Pharisees and was very zealous in prayer, in fasting, and in giving alms. He was exceedingly religious in the eyes of people. The other man was a tax collector, and thus a great sinner in the eyes of people, because most tax collectors were dishonest.

Listen to the story of the Pharisee and the tax collector. We are reading in the Gospel of Luke, chapter 18. The Scripture says:

> ⁹**He also spoke this parable to certain people** who were convinced of their own righteousness, and who despised all others. ¹⁰"Two men went up into the temple to pray; one was a Pharisee, and the other was a tax collector. ¹¹The Pharisee stood and prayed to himself like this: 'God, I thank you that I am not like the rest of men, extortionists, unrighteous, adulterers, or even like this tax collector. ¹²I fast twice a week.

I give tithes of all that I get.' ¹³But the tax collector, standing far away, wouldn't even lift up his eyes to heaven, but beat his breast, saying, 'God, be merciful to me, a sinner!' ¹⁴I tell you, this man went down to his house justified rather than the other; for everyone who exalts himself will be humbled, but he who humbles himself will be exalted." (Luke 18:9-14)

What did Jesus want to teach the crowd through this short parable? In brief, Jesus taught that God shows mercy to those who acknowledge their unrighteousness before Him and that He condemns those who imagine themselves to be righteous before Him. That is what the Scripture declares when it says: **God resists the proud, but gives grace to the humble.** (1 Peter 5:5) What man esteems, God despises. Can God accept those who praise themselves, thinking, *"I am a righteous person! I repeat my prayers! I fast! I give alms! I go to the mosque! I go to church! I do this and that!"*? Are all these "I"s pleasing to God? Not at all! The heart of God cannot be happy with works that originate from pride.

God loathes the proud heart. Do you remember Cain, Adam's firstborn son, who tried to approach God by his own efforts? Did God accept his sacrifice? No, God did not accept it. Listening friends, God has not changed. To this day, the heart of God cannot be happy with the self-efforts of the children of Adam, because our efforts are not perfect before Him. What God wants is for us to recognize our sinful condition – like the tax collector who beat his breast saying, **"God, be merciful to me, a sinner!"** It is that kind of a broken heart that causes God to rejoice. But He abhors those who compare themselves with their fellowman – like the Pharisee who said to himself, **"God, I thank you that I am not like the rest of men, extortionists, unrighteous, adulterers, or even like this tax collector."**

What the Pharisee failed to realize was that on the Day of Judgment, God will not compare us with our sinful fellowman. Instead, He will compare us with His own holy and perfect law which declares: **For whoever keeps the whole law, and yet stumbles in one point, he has become guilty of all!** (James 2:10)

The God who said, "You shall not commit adultery" also said, "You shall not lie." If you have not committed adultery, but you have told a lie, then you have broken God's law. You cannot enter Paradise, the presence of God, because the Scripture says: **There will in no way enter into it anything profane, or one who causes an abomination or a lie.** (Revelation 21:27) That is why the children of Adam need the mercy of God. Dear friend, have you, like the tax collector in the parable, received God's mercy? Or are you, like the Pharisee, still trying to become righteous by your own efforts?

Now let us read the second parable which shows us that the heart of God is full of love and mercy, like a father who loves his children. In the Gospel of Luke, chapter 15, we read:

> [1]**Now all the tax collectors and sinners** were coming close to him to hear [Jesus]. [2]The Pharisees and the scribes murmured, saying, "This man welcomes sinners, and eats with them." [3]He told them this parable:

> [11]**"A certain man had two sons.** [12]The younger of them said to his father, 'Father, give me my share of your property.' So he divided his livelihood between them. [13]Not many days after, the younger son gathered all of this together and traveled into a far country. There he wasted his property with riotous living. [14]When he had spent all of it, there arose a severe famine in that country, and he began to be in need. [15]He went and joined himself to one of the citizens of that country, and he sent him into his fields to feed pigs. [16]He wanted to fill his belly with the husks that the pigs ate, but no one gave him any.

> [17]**"But when he came to himself he said**, 'How many hired servants of my father's have bread enough to spare, and I'm dying with hunger! [18]I will get up and go to my father, and will tell him, "Father, I have sinned against heaven, and in your sight. [19]I am no more worthy to be called your son. Make me as one of your hired servants."' [20]He arose, and came to his father. But while he was still far off, his father saw him, and was moved with compassion, and ran, and fell on his neck,

and kissed him. [21]The son said to him, 'Father, I have sinned against heaven and in your sight. I am no longer worthy to be called your son.' [22]But the father said to his servants, 'Bring out the best robe, and put it on him. Put a ring on his hand, and sandals on his feet. [23]Bring the fattened calf, kill it, and let's eat, and celebrate; [24]for this, my son, was dead, and is alive again. He was lost, and is found.' Then they began to celebrate.

[25]"**Now his elder son was in the field.** As he came near to the house, he heard music and dancing. [26]He called one of the servants to him, and asked what was going on. [27]He said to him, 'Your brother has come, and your father has killed the fattened calf, because he has received him back safe and healthy.' [28]But he was angry, and would not go in. Therefore his father came out, and begged him. [29]But he answered his father, 'Behold, these many years I have served you, and I never disobeyed a commandment of yours, but you never gave me a goat, that I might celebrate with my friends. [30]But when this your son came, who has devoured your living with prostitutes, you killed the fattened calf for him.' [31]He said to him, 'Son, you are always with me, and all that is mine is yours. [32]But it was appropriate to celebrate and be glad, for this, your brother, was dead, and is alive again. He was lost, and is found.'"
(Luke 15:1-3,11-32)

What does God want to teach us through this parable? In it, we saw three men: the father, the younger son and the older son.

The father in the story represents *God*. **The younger son** illustrates *sinners who repent* of and turn to God for mercy. **The elder son** illustrates *religious people who deceive themselves* by thinking they are righteous before God.

First, let us think a little about the younger son who followed his sinful nature in wild living in a faraway land. What became of him? We saw how he eventually recognized that he had offended God and man. He was grieved because of his sins and repented, saying, **"I will get up and go to my father, and will tell him, 'Father,**

I have sinned against heaven, and in your sight. I am no more worthy to be called your son. Make me as one of your hired servants." Thus, we saw how the younger son turned his back on the pig pen and headed for his father's house.

What about the father? What did he do? Was he angry with his son who had wasted his wealth and brought shame on the family name? Did he merely take him back as a slave? No! Jesus said,

> 20"But while [the son] was still far off, his father saw him, and was moved with compassion, and ran, and fell on his neck, and kissed him. … 22But the father said to his servants, 'Bring out the best robe, and put it on him. Put a ring on his hand, and sandals on his feet. 23Bring the fattened calf, kill it, and let's eat, and celebrate; 24for this, my son, was dead, and is alive again. He was lost, and is found.' Then they began to celebrate.'"
> (Luke 15:20,22-24)

What are we to learn from this? We learn that God is like that father who was full of mercy. God loves sinners, and wants to show them mercy, but He waits for each sinner to repent and submit to the way of righteousness that He has established.

Concerning the elder son, we saw an amazing thing. The elder son did not have a heart of compassion like his father. Instead, he became angry and refused to enter the house, saying to his father, **"Behold, these many years *I* have served you, and I never disobeyed a commandment of yours, but you never gave *me* a goat, that I might celebrate with *my* friends!"** Did you hear what the elder son said? He said, **"Behold, these many years I have served you!"** However, what the elder son did not understand was that the father did not want a son who worked for him like a slave. What he wanted was a son who would love him from the heart and take pleasure in doing his will.

To this day, many children of Adam are like that elder son. They consider themselves to be nothing more than "slaves of God." But God does not want us to be like mere slaves. He wants us to be like sons and daughters to Him. That is what the Holy Scripture declares concerning those who receive Jesus as their Lord and Savior, saying: **For you didn't receive the spirit of bondage again to fear, but you received the Spirit of adoption, by whom we cry, "Abba! (Papa) Father!"** (Romans 8:15)

Dear friend, do you view yourself as a slave of God or a son of God? How do you see yourself in the parable we just read? Are you like the younger son who recognized his sin and shame, and received his father's mercy? Or are you like the elder son who worked for his father like a slave?

God doesn't want you to be like a slave who fears his master. What God wants is for you to be like a son who loves his father, happy to do his will. God loves you and longs to show you mercy, but He is waiting for you to repent and turn to Him. That is what the prophet Isaiah wrote, saying: **Yet the LORD longs to be gracious to you; therefore he will rise up to show you compassion. For the LORD is a God of justice. Blessed are all who wait for him!** (Isaiah 30:18 NIV)

God, the Compassionate, the Merciful, waits for you to come to Him, just as the father in the parable waited for his younger son to come back home. God wants you to repent with a broken and humble heart. If you come in this way to God and seek Him with your whole heart, then you can be certain that you will meet the God who has a father's heart, full of compassion and mercy. But the one who is proud and scorns God's mercy can hope for nothing except God's judgment which will be without mercy!

Thank you for listening. In our next program, God willing, we will continue in the Gospel to see how Jesus restored to life a dead man who had been in the tomb for four days.

May God give you insight into what we have studied today. And may we all remember:

God resists the proud, but gives grace to the humble.

(1 Peter 5:5)

Program 78

The Resurrection and the Life

John 11-12

U p to this point in our study through the holy Gospel, we have learned that the Messiah, Jesus, has many names. These names help us to know who He is. We have already heard that Jesus was called: the Word which was with God in the beginning, the Son of the Most High, the Son of Man, the Lamb of God, the Savior, the Food that gives life, the Light of the World, the Lord of Glory, the Gate of the sheep pen, and the Good Shepherd. Today we will see two additional names of Jesus: they are: *the Resurrection* and *the Life.*

We have seen how Jesus traveled throughout the land of the Jews, preaching and teaching, doing good and healing the sick, the lame, the blind and the demon-possessed. A great crowd followed Him. But the religious "experts," known as the Pharisees, were extremely jealous of Jesus. They could not deny the wisdom with which He spoke, nor could they deny the miracles that He did.

Today we plan to continue in the Gospel. We will see how Jesus performed another supernatural wonder that revealed the glory of God in Him, so that people might believe in Him. Reading in the Gospel of John, chapter 11, the Scripture says:

> ¹**Now a certain man was sick**, Lazarus from Bethany, of the village of Mary and her sister, Martha. ²It was that Mary who had anointed the Lord with ointment and wiped his feet with her hair, whose brother, Lazarus, was sick. ³The sisters therefore sent to him, saying, "Lord, behold, he for whom you have great affection is sick." ⁴But when Jesus heard it, he said, "This sickness is not to death, but for the glory of God, that God's Son

may be glorified by it." ⁵Now Jesus loved Martha, and her sister, and Lazarus. ⁶When therefore he heard that he was sick, he stayed two days in the place where he was. (John 11:1-6)

Jesus knew that Lazarus would die. But Jesus planned to use the death of Lazarus to show the power of God which dwelt in Him, so that people would know who He was. So after staying for two more days where they were, Jesus said to His disciples:

⁷**"Let's go into Judea again."** ⁸The disciples asked him, "Rabbi, the Jews were just trying to stone you. Are you going there again?" ⁹Jesus answered, "Aren't there twelve hours of daylight?" … ¹¹He said these things, and after that, he said to them, "Our friend, Lazarus, has fallen asleep, but I am going so that I may awake him out of sleep." ¹²The disciples therefore said, "Lord, if he has fallen asleep, he will recover." ¹³Now Jesus had spoken of his death, but they thought that he spoke of taking rest in sleep. ¹⁴So Jesus said to them plainly then, "Lazarus is dead. ¹⁵I am glad for your sakes that I was not there, so that you may believe. Nevertheless, let's go to him."

¹⁷**So when Jesus came**, he found that he had been in the tomb four days already. ¹⁸Now Bethany was near Jerusalem, about fifteen stadia away. ¹⁹Many of the Jews had joined the women around Martha and Mary, to console them concerning their brother. ²⁰Then when Martha heard that Jesus was coming, she went and met him, but Mary stayed in the house. ²¹Therefore Martha said to Jesus, "Lord, if you would have been here, my brother wouldn't have died. ²²Even now I know that whatever you ask of God, God will give you." ²³Jesus said to her, "Your brother will rise again." ²⁴Martha said to him, "I know that he will rise again in the resurrection at the last day."

²⁵**Jesus said to her, "I am the resurrection and the life.** He who believes in me will still live, even if he dies. ²⁶Whoever lives and believes in me will never die. Do you believe this?" ²⁷She said to him, "Yes, Lord. I have come to believe that you are the Christ, God's Son, he who comes into the world."

²⁸When she had said this, she went away and called Mary, her sister, secretly, saying, "The Teacher is here and is calling you." ²⁹When she heard this, she arose quickly and went to him. ... ³²Therefore when Mary came to where Jesus was and saw him, she fell down at his feet, saying to him, "Lord, if you would have been here, my brother wouldn't have died."

³³**When Jesus therefore saw her weeping**, and the Jews weeping who came with her, he groaned in the spirit, and was troubled, ³⁴and said, "Where have you laid him?" They told him, "Lord, come and see." ³⁵Jesus wept. ³⁶The Jews therefore said, "See how much affection he had for him!" ³⁷Some of them said, "Couldn't this man, who opened the eyes of him who was blind, have also kept this man from dying?"

³⁸**Jesus therefore, again groaning in himself**, came to the tomb. Now it was a cave, and a stone lay against it. ³⁹Jesus said, "Take away the stone." Martha, the sister of him who was dead, said to him, "Lord, by this time there is a stench, for he has been dead four days." ⁴⁰Jesus said to her, "Didn't I tell you that if you believed, you would see God's glory?" ⁴¹So they took away the stone from the place where the dead man was lying.

Jesus lifted up his eyes, and said, "Father, I thank you that you listened to me. ⁴²I know that you always listen to me, but because of the multitude standing around I said this, that they may believe that you sent me." ⁴³When he had said this, he cried with a loud voice, "Lazarus, come out!" ⁴⁴He who was dead came out, bound hand and foot with wrappings, and his face was wrapped around with a cloth. Jesus said to them, "Free him, and let him go." (John 11:7-9,11-15,17-29,32-44)

Before finishing this amazing story, let's talk about the mighty miracle. From the creation of the world to today, no one ever heard of anyone who could give life to a corpse that had been four days in the tomb; a corpse that had begun to decay and stink. But that is what Jesus did when He raised Lazarus from the dead.

The power of death was not a problem for the Lord Jesus, because He is the word of God; the very Life of God, who came from heaven. As God has life in Himself, so the Messiah has life in Himself. And as God can resurrect dead bodies and give them life, so also the Messiah can give life to whomever He wants, because He Himself is the Source of Life. That is why, when Jesus called Lazarus to come forth, the corpse came back to life, sat up, and walked out of the tomb. That is also why Jesus could say to Lazarus' sister, **"I am the resurrection and the life. He who believes in me will still live, even if he dies!"**

Now let us finish the story and find out what the Jews did after they saw Jesus raise Lazarus from the grave. The Scripture says:

> [45]**Therefore many of the Jews who came to Mary** and saw what Jesus did believed in him. [46]But some of them went away to the Pharisees and told them the things which Jesus had done. [47]The chief priests therefore and the Pharisees gathered a council, and said, "What are we doing? For this man does many signs. [48]If we leave him alone like this, everyone will believe in him, and the Romans will come and take away both our place and our nation."

> [49]**But a certain one of them, Caiaphas**, being high priest that year, said to them, "You know nothing at all, [50]nor do you consider that it is advantageous for us that one man should die for the people, and that the whole nation not perish." [51]Now he didn't say this of himself, but being high priest that year, he prophesied that Jesus would die for the nation, [52]and not for the nation only, but that he might also gather together into one the children of God who are scattered abroad. [53]So from that day forward they took counsel that they might put him to death. [54]Jesus therefore walked no more openly among the Jews, but departed from there into the country near the wilderness, to a city called Ephraim. He stayed there with his disciples.

> [55]**Now the Passover of the Jews was at hand.** Many went up from the country to Jerusalem before the Passover, to purify themselves. [56]Then they sought for Jesus and spoke with one

another as they stood in the temple, "What do you think—that he isn't coming to the feast at all?" [57]Now the chief priests and the Pharisees had commanded that if anyone knew where he was, he should report it, that they might seize him. (John 11:45-57)

[1]**Then six days before the Passover**, Jesus came to Bethany, where Lazarus was, who had been dead, whom he raised from the dead. [2]So they made him a supper there. Martha served, but Lazarus was one of those who sat at the table with him. [3]Therefore Mary took a pound of ointment of pure nard, very precious, and anointed Jesus's feet and wiped his feet with her hair. The house was filled with the fragrance of the ointment. [4]Then Judas Iscariot, Simon's son, one of his disciples, who would betray him, said, [5]"Why wasn't this ointment sold for three hundred denarii, and given to the poor?" [6]Now he said this, not because he cared for the poor, but because he was a thief, and having the money box, used to steal what was put into it. [7]But Jesus said, "Leave her alone. She has kept this for the day of my burial. [8]For you always have the poor with you, but you don't always have me."

[9]**A large crowd therefore of the Jews** learned that he was there, and they came, not for Jesus' sake only, but that they might see Lazarus also, whom he had raised from the dead. [10]But the chief priests conspired to put Lazarus to death also, [11]because on account of him many of the Jews went away and believed in Jesus. (John 12:1-11)

Our time is about up, but before we say goodbye, there is something we must consider. Did you see how the religious rulers reacted to the miraculous sign (proof) Jesus gave them? None of them dared to deny the miracle Jesus did, because everyone could see for themselves the man who had been raised from the dead. But what did the High Priest and the other priests do? Did they repent and believe that Jesus was the Messiah who came from heaven? No, they did not. All the miraculous signs which Jesus performed did not cause the religious leaders and their disciples to repent and receive Jesus as their Lord and Savior.

So what did the High Priests do? They hated Jesus even more and conspired together to devise a plan to kill Him. They also planned to kill Lazarus whom Jesus had just raised from the dead, because he was the reason many Jews were turning away from the priests (marabouts) and following Jesus. How insincere and far from God were the hearts of those religious rulers! They did not love God or the truth. They ignored the obvious proofs– the many miracles – Jesus had done before their very eyes. But all they thought about was themselves and their own honor. They had been shamed again and again. So they conspired together to kill Jesus, because they were afraid that if they allowed Him to continue, all the Jews would turn away from them and follow Jesus.

What do you think about those religious rulers? Who put the idea in their minds to kill Jesus? Satan was guiding them, because he hates God and His Messiah. Satan thought that if the Jewish leaders put Jesus to death, God's plan to save the children of Adam from his power would fail. What Satan did not realize was that God planned to use the death of the Messiah to deliver the children of Adam from Satan's power! Also, Satan and those who went along with him did not realize that the power of death could not hold the Lord Jesus. The earth could not decompose[107] His body, because Jesus, who had no sin, is **the Resurrection and the Life**. That is why Jesus could say to the sister of Lazarus, **"I am the resurrection and the life. He who believes in me will still live, even if he dies. …Do you believe this?"** (John 11:25-26)

This is where we must leave you today. We invite you to join us in the coming study as we continue in the Gospel and see *how Jesus entered Jerusalem* and fulfilled what God's prophets had written about the Messiah 500 years beforehand.

May God Himself teach you the powerful meaning of these words from Jesus the Messiah:

> **I am the resurrection and the life. He who believes in me will still live, even if he dies. … Do you believe this?** (John 11:25-26)

---

107 Literally: *eat*

Jesus Enters Jerusalem

Luke 18-20, etc.

I n our last lesson, we saw how the Lord Jesus raised to life a corpse that had been in the grave for four days. The power of death was no problem for Jesus, because He Himself was (and is) *the Resurrection and the Life*. Today we plan to continue in the Gospel to see how Jesus entered Jerusalem where He was to be killed. Jesus knew what was going to happen to Him. He knew that the Jewish religious leaders would turn Him over to the Romans who would torture Him and nail Him to a cross. Still, that knowledge did not prevent Him from going to Jerusalem. The Gospel says: **It came to pass, when the days were near that he should be taken up, he intently set his face to go to Jerusalem.** (Luke 9:51)

Why did Jesus resolutely set out for Jerusalem? He did this to give Himself up to those who wanted to kill Him! This is amazing! If you knew that, in a certain city, men wanted to torture and kill you, would you resolutely set out for that city? That is exactly what Jesus did. Jesus knew that the reason He was born was to die as a sacrifice for the sins of the world. Jesus did not come into the world to seek His own pleasure, but to fulfill what the prophets had written long before about Him: that the Messiah would suffer and shed his blood outside Jerusalem on the same mountain range where Abraham offered the ram in place of his son. It was necessary that the symbolism of the sacrificial ram be fulfilled in Jesus. That was why the Messiah went to Jerusalem, the city which, for Him, was like a den of hungry lions awaiting their prey.

Now let us continue our study in the book of the Gospel. In Luke, chapter 18, the Scripture says:

³²**They were on the way, going up to Jerusalem**; and Jesus was going in front of them, and they were amazed; and those who followed were afraid. He again took the twelve, and began to tell them the things that were going to happen to him. (Mark 10:32) "Behold, we are going up to Jerusalem, and all the things that are written through the prophets concerning the Son of Man will be completed." (Luke 18:31) ³³"The Son of Man will be delivered to the chief priests and the scribes. They will condemn him to death, and will deliver him to the Gentiles. ³⁴They will mock him, spit on him, scourge him, and kill him. [But] on the third day he will rise again." (Mark 10:33-34)

³⁴**They understood none of these things.** This saying was hidden from them, and they didn't understand the things that were said. ³⁵As he came near Jericho, a certain blind man sat by the road, begging. ³⁶Hearing a multitude going by, he asked what this meant. ³⁷They told him that Jesus of Nazareth was passing by. ³⁸He cried out, "Jesus, you son of David, have mercy on me!" ³⁹Those who led the way rebuked him, that he should be quiet; but he cried out all the more, "You son of David, have mercy on me!" ⁴⁰Standing still, Jesus commanded him to be brought to him. When he had come near, he asked him, ⁴¹"What do you want me to do?" He said, "Lord, that I may see again." ⁴²Jesus said to him, "Receive your sight. Your faith has healed you." ⁴³Immediately he received his sight and followed him, glorifying God. All the people, when they saw it, praised God. (Luke 18:34-43)

¹**When they came near to Jerusalem** and came to Bethsphage, to the Mount of Olives, then Jesus sent two disciples, ²saying to them, "Go into the village that is opposite you, and immediately you will find a donkey tied, and a colt with her. Untie them and bring them to me. ³If anyone says anything to you, you shall say, 'The Lord needs them,' and immediately he will send them." ⁴All this was done that it might be fulfilled which was spoken through the prophet, saying, ⁵"Tell the daughter of Zion, behold, your King comes to you, humble, and riding on

a donkey, on a colt, the foal of a donkey." [6]The disciples went and did just as Jesus commanded them, [7]and brought the donkey and the colt and laid their clothes on them; and he sat on them. [8]A very great multitude spread their clothes on the road. Others cut branches from the trees and spread them on the road. [9]The multitudes who went in front of him, and those who followed, kept shouting, "Hosanna to the son of David! Blessed is he who comes in the name of the Lord! Hosanna in the highest!" (Matthew 21:1-9)

[39]**Some of the Pharisees** from the multitude said to him, "Teacher, rebuke your disciples!" [40]He answered them, "I tell you that if these were silent, the stones would cry out." [41]When he came near, he saw the city and wept over it, [42]saying, "If you, even you, had known today the things which belong to your peace! But now, they are hidden from your eyes [44]…because you didn't know the time of your visitation." (Luke 19:39-42,44)

[10]**When he had come into Jerusalem**, all the city was stirred up, saying, "Who is this?" [11]The multitudes said, "This is the prophet, Jesus, from Nazareth of Galilee." [12]Jesus entered into the temple of God and drove out all of those who sold and bought in the temple, and overthrew the money changers' tables and the seats of those who sold the doves. [13]He said to them, "It is written, 'My house shall be called a house of prayer,' but you have made it a den of robbers!"

[14]**The lame and the blind came to him** in the temple, and he healed them. [15]But when the chief priests and the scribes saw the wonderful things that he did, and the children who were crying in the temple and saying, "Hosanna to the son of David!" they were indignant, (They were angry because *Hosanna* means *God save us* – a word to be used for praising God alone) [16]and said to him, "Do you hear what these are saying?" Jesus said to [the religious leaders], "Yes. Did you never read, 'Out of the mouth of children and nursing babies, you have perfected praise'?" (Matthew 21:10-16)

[18]**The chief priests and the scribes heard it**, and sought how they might destroy him. For they feared him, because all the multitude was astonished at his teaching. (Mark 11:18)

[23]**Jesus answered [his disciples]**, "The time has come for the Son of Man to be glorified. [24]Most certainly I tell you, unless a grain of wheat falls into the earth and dies, it remains by itself alone. But if it dies, it bears much fruit."

[27]**"Now my soul is troubled. What shall I say?** 'Father, save me from this time?' But I came to this time for this cause. [28]Father, glorify your name!" Then a voice came out of the sky, saying, "I have both glorified it, and will glorify it again." [29]Therefore the multitude who stood by and heard it said that it had thundered. Others said, "An angel has spoken to him." [30]Jesus answered, "This voice hasn't come for my sake, but for your sakes. [31]Now is the judgment of this world. Now the prince of this world will be cast out. [32]And I, if I am lifted up from the earth, will draw all people to myself." [33]But he said this, signifying by what kind of death he should die. (John 12:23-24,27-33)

Let us pause here. We saw how Jesus entered Jerusalem, riding on a colt of a donkey, and how the crowd of Jews praised and applauded Him, wanting to make Him their king. However, the people did not understand why Jesus had entered Jerusalem. Even Jesus' disciples did not realize what was going to happen. They hoped that as the Messiah, Jesus would save the Jewish people from the dominion of their enemy, the Roman Empire. But that was not why God sent the Messiah into the world. Jesus did not come to destroy the empire of Rome, but to destroy the empire of Satan. He did not come down to change this corrupt world, but to change the hearts of people. Indeed, one day, Jesus Christ will return to judge the people of the world and to restore the created world. But when He came to earth the first time, He came to die as a sacrifice. He came to save the children of Adam from the penalty of their sin, just as God had promised through His prophets long beforehand.

Continuing the story, the Scripture says:

[47]**[Jesus] was teaching daily in the temple**, but the chief priests, the scribes, and the leading men among the people sought to destroy him. [48]They couldn't find what they might do, for all the people hung on to every word that he said. (Luke 19:47-48)

[1]**On one of those days, as [Jesus] was teaching the people** in the temple and preaching the Good News, thepriests and scribes came to him with the elders. [2]They asked him, "Tell us: by what authority do you do these things? Or who is giving you this authority?" [3]He answered them, "I also will ask you one question. Tell me: [4]the baptism of John, was it from heaven, or from men?" [5]They reasoned with themselves, saying, "If we say, 'From heaven,' he will say, 'Why didn't you believe him?' [6]But if we say, 'From men,' all the people will stone us, for they are persuaded that John was a prophet." [7]They answered that they didn't know where it was from. [8]Jesus said to them, "Neither will I tell you by what authority I do these things."

[9]**He began to tell the people this parable.** "A man planted a vineyard, and rented it out to some farmers, and went into another country for a long time. [10]At the proper season, he sent a servant to the farmers to collect his share of the fruit of the vineyard. But the farmers beat him, and sent him away empty. [11]He sent yet another servant, and they also beat him, and treated him shamefully, and sent him away empty. [12]He sent yet a third, and they also wounded him, and threw him out. [13]The lord of the vineyard said, 'What shall I do? I will send my beloved son. It may be that seeing him, they will respect him.' [14]But when the farmers saw him, they reasoned among themselves, saying, 'This is the heir. Come, let's kill him, that the inheritance may be ours.' [15]Then they threw him out of the vineyard and killed him. What therefore will the lord of the vineyard do to them? [16]He will come and destroy these farmers, and will give the vineyard to others." When they heard that, they said, "May that never be!" [17]But he looked at them and said, "Then what is this that is written, 'The stone which the builders rejected was made the

chief cornerstone?' ¹⁸Everyone who falls on that stone will be broken to pieces, but it will crush whomever it falls on to dust." ¹⁹The chief priests and the scribes sought to lay hands on him that very hour, but they feared the people—for they knew he had spoken this parable against them. (Luke 20:1-19)

Through the parable of the wicked farmers, Jesus warned those who were plotting to kill Him. Do you understand the meaning of this parable? It is easy to interpret. In it, the Lord Jesus compares God to the owner of the field. The field of grapes (vineyard) is the nation of Israel. The evil farmers illustrate the Jewish religious leaders. The servants (sent by the owner to collect the grapes) and mistreated by the farmers are the prophets. The son of the owner of the field, whom the farmers killed, represents the Messiah, Jesus.

We can understand why the priests and the teachers of the law became very angry. They knew very well that Jesus was speaking about them! They understood that Jesus was comparing them to the wicked farmers who had harassed the servants of the owner of the field, and, in the end, killed his son. Thus Jesus denounced them as those who ignored the words of the prophets, and as those who would kill the Messiah, the Son of the Most High. Not only did Jesus tell them the parable, but He also quoted that which is written about Himself in the Psalms, saying, **The stone which the builders rejected was made the chief cornerstone? Everyone who falls on that stone will be broken to pieces, but it will crush whomever it falls on to dust.** (Luke 20:17-18; Psalm 118:22) Thus Jesus warned the religious leaders that the Savior whom they planned to kill, would, in the end, become their Judge!

Friends, our time is up. God willing, in the next program, we will hear more about *Jesus and the angry religious rulers.*

God bless you as you think about what the Scripture declares concerning the Messiah:

> **He was in the world, and the world was made through him, and the world didn't recognize him.** (John 1:10)

Hard and True Words

Matthew 22-25

I n our last study, we saw how Jesus the Messiah entered Jerusalem, fully aware that Jerusalem was the city of the priests and the teachers of the law – the very ones who were conspiring together to murder Him. Jesus knew everything that was going to happen. He knew that He had been born to die as a sacrifice for the sins of the world. Only a few days were left before the priests would arrest Him and demand that He be nailed to a cross.

So, listening friends, wherever you may be today, we ask you to pay careful attention to the warnings Jesus the Messiah spoke to the religious rulers of the Jews. The words we will hear today are hard – and true. Sometimes it hurts to hear the truth. Indeed, *truth is a hot pepper.*

Now that Jesus was in Jerusalem, each day He went into the temple and taught the people. And each day the religious leaders tried to catch Him in something He said so that they might have an excuse to put Him to death. But they feared the people who were listening to Jesus attentively, not missing a word. In the Gospel of Luke, chapter 20, the Scripture says:

> [20][The chief priests] watched him and sent out spies, who pretended to be righteous, that they might trap him in something he said, so as to deliver him up to the power and authority of the governor. [21]They asked him, "Teacher, we know that you say and teach what is right, and aren't partial to anyone, but truly teach the way of God. [22]Is it lawful for us to pay taxes to Caesar, or not?" [23]But he perceived their craftiness, and [their hypocrisy, and said to them, "Why do you test me? Bring me a

denarius, that I may see it." ¹⁶They brought it. He said to them, (Mark 12:15-16)] ²⁴"Whose image and inscription are on it?" They answered, "Caesar's." ²⁵He said to them, "Then give to Caesar the things that are Caesar's, and to God the things that are God's." ²⁶They weren't able to trap him in his words before the people. They marveled at his answer and were silent. (Luke 20:20-26)

²³**On that day Sadducees** (who say there is no resurrection) came to him. They asked him, ²⁴saying, "Teacher, Moses said, 'If a man dies, having no children, his brother shall marry his wife and raise up offspring for his brother.' ²⁵Now there were with us seven brothers. The first married and died, and having no offspring left his wife to his brother. ²⁶In the same way, the second also, and the third, to the seventh. ²⁷After them all, the woman died. ²⁸In the resurrection therefore, whose wife will she be of the seven? For they all had her." ²⁹But Jesus answered them, "You are mistaken, not knowing the Scriptures, nor the power of God. (Matthew 22:23-29) ³⁴The children of this age marry, and are given in marriage. ³⁵But those who are considered worthy to attain to that age and the resurrection from the dead neither marry nor are given in marriage. ³⁶For they can't die any more, for they are like the angels, and are children of God, being children of the resurrection. ³⁷But that the dead are raised, even Moses showed at the bush, when he called the Lord 'The God of Abraham, the God of Isaac, and the God of Jacob.' ³⁸Now he is not the God of the dead, but of the living, for all are alive to him." (Luke 20:34-38)

³³**When the multitudes heard it**, they were astonished at his teaching. ³⁴But the Pharisees, when they heard that he had silenced the Sadducees, gathered themselves together. ³⁵One of them, a lawyer, asked him a question, testing him. ³⁶"Teacher, which is the greatest commandment in the law?"

³⁷**Jesus said to him, "'You shall love the Lord your God** with all your heart, with all your soul, and with all your mind.' ³⁸This is the first and great commandment. ³⁹A second likewise is this,

'You shall love your neighbor as yourself.' [40]The whole law and the prophets depend on these two commandments."

[41]**Now while the Pharisees were gathered together**, Jesus asked them a question, [42]saying, "What do you think of the Christ? Whose son is he?" They said to him, "Of David." [43]He said to them, "How then does David in the Spirit call him Lord, saying, [44]'The Lord said to my Lord, sit on my right hand, until I make your enemies a footstool for your feet'? [45]If then David calls him Lord, how is he his son?" [46]No one was able to answer him a word, neither did any man dare ask him any more questions from that day forward. (Matthew 22:33-46)

[1]**Then Jesus spoke to the multitudes and to his disciples**, [2]saying, "The scribes and the Pharisees sit on Moses' seat [3]…but don't do their works; for they say, and don't do. [4]For they bind heavy burdens that are grievous to be borne, and lay them on men's shoulders; but they themselves will not lift a finger to help them. [5]But they do all their works to be seen by men. They make their phylacteries broad and enlarge the fringes of their garments, [6]and love the place of honor at feasts, the best seats in the synagogues, [7]the salutations in the marketplaces, and to be called 'Rabbi, Rabbi by men. [8]But you are not to be called 'Rabbi', for one is your teacher, the Christ, and all of you are brothers. [9]Call no man on the earth your father, for one is your Father, he who is in heaven. [10]Neither be called masters, for one is your master, the Christ. [11]But he who is greatest among you will be your servant. [12]Whoever exalts himself will be humbled, and whoever humbles himself will be exalted.

[13]**"Woe to you, scribes and Pharisees, hypocrites!** For you devour widows' houses, and as a pretense you make long prayers. Therefore you will receive greater condemnation. [14]But woe to you, scribes and Pharisees, hypocrites! Because you shut up the kingdom of Heaven against men; for you don't enter in yourselves, neither do you allow those who are entering in to enter.

¹⁵"**Woe to you, scribes and Pharisees, hypocrites!** For you travel around by sea and land to make one proselyte; and when he becomes one, you make him twice as much a son of Gehenna as yourselves.

²³"**Woe to you, scribes and Pharisees, hypocrites!** For you tithe mint, dill, and cumin, and have left undone the weightier matters of the law: justice, mercy, and faith. But you ought to have done these, and not to have left the other undone. ²⁴You blind guides, who strain out a gnat, and swallow a camel!

²⁵"**Woe to you, scribes and Pharisees, hypocrites!** For you clean the outside of the cup and of the platter, but within they are full of extortion and unrighteousness. ²⁶You blind Pharisee, first clean the inside of the cup and of the platter, that its outside may become clean also.

²⁷"**Woe to you, scribes and Pharisees, hypocrites!** For you are like whitened tombs, which outwardly appear beautiful, but inwardly are full of dead men's bones and of all uncleanness. ²⁸Even so you also outwardly appear righteous to men, but inwardly you are full of hypocrisy and iniquity.

²⁹"**Woe to you, scribes and Pharisees, hypocrites!** For you build the tombs of the prophets and decorate the tombs of the righteous, ³⁰and say, 'If we had lived in the days of our fathers, we wouldn't have been partakers with them in the blood of the prophets.' ³¹Therefore you testify to yourselves that you are children of those who killed the prophets. ³²Fill up, then, the measure of your fathers. ³³You serpents, you offspring of vipers, how will you escape the judgment of Gehenna? … ³⁷Jerusalem, Jerusalem, who kills the prophets and stones those who are sent to her! How often I would have gathered your children together, even as a hen gathers her chicks under her wings, and you would not!" (Matthew 23:1-15,23-33,37)

¹**Jesus went out from the temple**, and was going on his way. His disciples came to him to show him the buildings of the

temple. [2]But he answered them, "You see all of these things, don't you? Most certainly I tell you, there will not be left here one stone on another, that will not be thrown down." [3]As he sat on the Mount of Olives, the disciples came to him privately, saying, "Tell us, when will these things be? What is the sign of your coming, and of the end of the age?"

[4]**Jesus answered them, "Be careful** that no one leads you astray. [5]For many will come in my name, saying, 'I am the Christ,' and will lead many astray. [6]You will hear of wars and rumors of wars. See that you aren't troubled, for all this must happen, but the end is not yet. [7]For nation will rise against nation, and kingdom against kingdom; and there will be famines, plagues, and earthquakes in various places. [8]But all these things are the beginning of birth pains. [9]Then they will deliver you up to oppression and will kill you. You will be hated by all of the nations for my name's sake.

[10]**"Then many will stumble**, and will deliver up one another, and will hate one another. [11]Many false prophets will arise and will lead many astray.... [23]Then if any man tells you, 'Behold, here is the Christ!' or, 'There!' don't believe it. [24]For there will arise false christs, and false prophets, and they will show great signs and wonders, so as to lead astray, if possible, even the chosen ones. [25]Behold, I have told you beforehand....

[27]**For as the lightning flashes from the east**, and is seen even to the west, so will the coming of the Son of Man be. ... [29]"But immediately after the suffering of those days, the sun will be darkened, the moon will not give its light, the stars will fall from the sky, and the powers of the heavens will be shaken; [30]and then the sign of the Son of Man will appear in the sky. Then all the tribes of the earth will mourn, and they will see the Son of Man coming on the clouds of the sky with power and great glory. [31]He will send out his angels with a great sound of a trumpet, and they will gather together his chosen ones from the four winds, from one end of the sky to the other. (Matthew 24:1-11,23-25,27,29-31)

³¹**"But when the Son of Man comes in his glory**, and all the holy angels with him, then he will sit on the throne of his glory. ³²Before him all the nations will be gathered, and he will separate them one from another, as a shepherd separates the sheep from the goats. ³³He will set the sheep on his right hand, but the goats on the left. ³⁴Then the King will tell those on his right hand, 'Come, blessed of my Father, inherit the kingdom prepared for you from the foundation of the world; … ⁴¹Then he will say also to those on the left hand, 'Depart from me, you cursed, into the eternal fire which is prepared for the devil and his angels.' ⁴⁶These will go away into eternal punishment, but the righteous into eternal life." (Matthew 25:31-34,41,46)

Listening friends, we must stop here today. Did you hear how the Lord Jesus admonished the religious rulers for their hypocrisy and hardness of heart? He also warned His disciples to watch out for those who would come after Him, pretending to be prophets and deceiving many people. Finally, we heard the Lord Jesus announce that He will one day return to earth, coming out of heaven with His mighty angels, to judge those who have refused to obey God's Good News about the Messiah, the Savior of sinners.

Yes, we have heard some hard words today, but they are also good words because they are true words – wonderful words of life for every man, woman, young person, and child who believes them. As Jesus the Messiah said, **"You will know the truth, and the truth will make you free!"** (John 8:32)

Friends, thank you for listening. We invite you to join us next time to hear Jesus' final words to His disciples before He laid down His life for them – and for you and me.

God bless you as you think on these words of the Lord Jesus:

> **You are mistaken, not knowing the Scriptures, nor the power of God.** (Matthew 22:29)
> **[But] the truth will make you free!** (John 8:32)

The Last Supper

Matthew 26

As most of you know, in our journey through the Holy Scriptures we are presently studying in the Gospel (*Injil*), the holy book which tells the Good News about Jesus the Messiah. Jesus is the holy Redeemer who came into the world to deliver the children of Adam from the dominion of Satan. The Redeemer was different from all other men; He was and is the Word which was with God in the beginning, who appeared upon earth as a man. The man Jesus was unique in His birth because He was born of a virgin by the power of the Spirit of God. Jesus was also unique in His character, because He was born with a holy nature; He never sinned. His works were also unique; no one ever did miracles as He did. The Lord Jesus had power over Satan and his demons, the wind and the waves, and sickness and death. His teaching was also unparalleled; even His enemies said, **"No man ever spoke like this man!"** (John 7:46)

Yes, Jesus Christ was unique in His birth, His character, His works and His words. Yet that did not cause everyone to recognize that He was the Savior who came from heaven. Most of the children of Adam did not understand who Jesus really was. Many considered Him to be a prophet, but they did not realize that God Himself had come to visit them. As for the Jewish religious rulers, they not only failed to believe who Jesus was, but they even conspired together to have Him put to death. In our last lesson, we heard how Jesus rebuked the religious leaders and the teachers of the Law because of their hypocrisy and wickedness. But Jesus' words to them did not cause them to repent. The religious rulers were obsessed with one thought: Jesus must be put to death!

The Lord Jesus knew that He was going to die in Jerusalem and that those religious rulers would be the ones who would put Him to death. And so we heard Jesus inform His disciples that the priests and the teachers of the Law would condemn Him to die. They would turn Him over to the Romans, so that they might mock Him, spit on Him, beat Him, and nail Him to a cross. But after three days He would rise again. Thus, Jesus announced not only *how* He would die and *where* He would die, but, as we will see in the chapter before us today, He even announced *when* He would die. Now let's continue in the Gospel of Matthew, chapter 26:

> ¹**When Jesus had finished all these words**, he said to his disciples, ²"You know that after two days the Passover is coming, and the Son of Man will be delivered up to be crucified." (Matthew 26:1-2)

Did you hear what Jesus said to His disciples? He told them that He would be nailed to a cross *on the day of the Passover feast*. In our study in the Torah of Moses we learned about the day of the Passover. This event took place in the first month of the Jewish calendar, which on our calendar is in March and April (Easter time). Each year on the day of the Passover, the Jews looked back to the time when their ancestors were slaves in Egypt. They recalled when God, in His righteous judgment, had condemned to death every first-born male in Egypt – and how God had also provided a way of deliverance for those who obeyed Him. God commanded every Israelite family to sacrifice a lamb without blemish and to stain the doorframes of their houses with the blood. God had promised them: **"When I see the blood, I will pass over you."** (Exodus 12:13) The people of Israel did as God had commanded and their firstborn sons were saved, redeemed by the blood of a lamb.

For 1500 years the Jews had been sacrificing lambs every year on the festival of the Passover in order to remember how God had saved them from the plague of death that fell on the land of Egypt. But God did not want them merely *to look back* and remember what had happened. By means of those sacrificial lambs, He wanted them *to look forward* and anticipate the day when the Messiah would shed His blood on the cross as **the Lamb of God, who takes away the sin of the world!** (John 1:29) Jesus the Lamb of God would provide deliverance from the plague that is worse than any other plague: the eternal fire of hell. The Redeemer's death on the cross would be the final and perfect sacrifice which would satisfy God's righteous law. God planned for the Redeemer to shed His blood on the day of the Passover feast and thus to fulfill the symbolism of the sacrificial lamb. This is how Jesus the Redeemer would finish God's plan to provide a way to punish sin without punishing the sinner who trusts in Him. Now let's continue reading, beginning with the verses we just read:

> [1]**When Jesus had finished all these words**, he said to his disciples, [2]"You know that after two days the Passover is coming, and the Son of Man will be delivered up to be crucified." [3]Then the chief priests, the scribes, and the elders of the people were gathered together in the court of the high priest, who was called Caiaphas. [4]They took counsel together that they might take Jesus by deceit and kill him. [5]But they said, "Not during the feast, lest a riot occur among the people." … [14]Then one of the twelve, who was called Judas Iscariot, went to the chief priests [15]and said, "What are you willing to give me if I deliver him to you?" So they weighed out for him thirty pieces of silver. [16]From that time he sought opportunity to betray him. (Matthew 26:1-5,14-16)

> [12]**On the first day of unleavened bread**, when they sacrificed the Passover, his disciples asked him, "Where do you want us to go and prepare that you may eat the Passover?" [13]He sent two of his disciples, and said to them, "Go into the city, and there a man carrying a pitcher of water will meet you. Follow him, [14]and wherever he enters in, tell the master of the house, 'The Teacher says, "Where is the guest room, where I may eat the Passover with my disciples?"' [15]He will himself show you a large upper room furnished and ready. Get ready for us there." [16]His disciples went out, and came into the city, and found things as he had said to them, and they prepared the Passover. (Mark 14:12-16)

¹⁴**When the hour had come**, he sat down with the twelve apostles. ¹⁵He said to them, "I have earnestly desired to eat this Passover with you before I suffer, ¹⁶for I tell you, I will no longer by any means eat of it until it is fulfilled in God's kingdom." (Luke 22:14-16) ¹⁸As they sat and were eating, Jesus said, "Most certainly I tell you, one of you will betray me—he who eats with me." ¹⁹They began to be sorrowful, and to ask him one by one, "Surely not I?" And another said, "Surely not I?" ²⁰He answered them, "It is one of the twelve, he who dips with me in the dish. ²¹For the Son of Man goes, even as it is written about him, but woe to that man by whom the Son of Man is betrayed! It would be better for that man if he had not been born." (Mark 14:18-21)

²⁵**Judas, who betrayed him, answered**, "It isn't me, is it, Rabbi?" He said to him, "You said it." (Matthew 26:25) ³⁰Therefore having received that morsel, he went out immediately. It was night. (John 13:30)

²⁶**As they were eating, Jesus took bread**, gave thanks for it, and broke it. He gave to the disciples and said, "Take, eat; this is my body." ²⁷[Next,] He took the cup, gave thanks, and gave it to them, saying, "All of you drink it, ²⁸for this is my blood of the new covenant, which is poured out for many for the remission of sins." (Matthew 26:26-28)

That is what is written in the Gospel about the last supper that Jesus had with His disciples before shedding His blood as the sacrifice that erases sin. Jesus made known to His twelve disciples that one of them would betray Him. It was Judas Iscariot. People thought that Judas was a faithful disciple of Jesus, but in his heart Judas cared only the things of the world. Also, Judas had expected a Messiah-King who would destroy the Roman occupiers and set up a new government in Jerusalem. He did not understand God's plan which required that, before the Messiah could reign over the earth, the sin debt of the world had to be paid and death had to be defeated. So Judas went to the chief priests and said to them, "What are you willing to give me if I hand him over to you?" The priests offered him thirty pieces of silver. This fulfilled what the prophet Zechariah had predicted hundreds of years earlier when he wrote that the Messiah would be betrayed for thirty pieces of silver. (See Zechariah 11:12-13) However, the most important thing in what we have just read is what Jesus told His disciples about **the new covenant**. Did you hear what He said and did? Let's read it again:

> [26]**As they were eating, Jesus took bread**, gave thanks for it, and broke it. He gave to the disciples and said, "Take, eat; this is my body." [27][Next,] He took the cup, gave thanks, and gave it to them, saying, "All of you drink it, [28]for this is my blood of the new covenant, which is poured out for many for the remission of sins." (Matthew 26:26-28)

How did Jesus announce **the new covenant** that would replace the old covenant which required the blood of animal sacrifices? Jesus placed two symbols before His disciples: the symbol of *the bread*, and the symbol of *the cup*. The bread which He broke and gave to His disciples illustrated His body, which He was going to offer up as a sacrifice. The cup with the juice of grapes illustrated the blood which Jesus the Redeemer would pour out to pay the debt of sin for people so that whoever trusts in Him and His sacrifice can enjoy a close relationship with the Lord God forever.

This is how Jesus taught His disciples that the reason He came into the world was to give His life – His body and His blood – as a sacrifice for sinners. Just as everyone on earth must take in food and water to stay alive, so also anyone who wants to live forever with God must believe that Jesus the Messiah sacrificed His body and blood to give us eternal life. The Lord Jesus Christ is the only One who can give eternal life, and the blood He shed is God's only remedy to redeem you and me from the curse that sin brought.

Oh, dear friends, if you remember only one thing from today's study, let it be this: **Christ Jesus came into the world to save sinners** (1 Timothy 1:15) – to save *you*. *That* is the message of God's prophets. *That* is the meaning of the ram which Abraham sacrificed in place of his son. The way of forgiveness is the way of the Perfect Sacrifice. God can forgive you of your sins through the sacrifice of the holy Redeemer, who poured out His blood *for you*.

For thousands of years God required animal sacrifices so that He could pass over (atone for, cover) the sins of the children of Adam. That is the Old Covenant, which God entrusted to His prophets; Jesus the Messiah is the One who brought in **the New Covenant**. He is the One who came to fulfill the symbolism of the animal sacrifices. Jesus Christ is the final Passover Lamb that was slain so that whoever believes in Him might be saved from God's righteous judgment. That is why the Holy Scripture says: **Christ, our Passover, has been sacrificed in our place.** (1 Corinthians 5:7) **God made him who had no sin to be sin for us, so that in him we might become the righteousness of God.** (2 Corinthians 5:21 NIV)

The blood of Jesus is of infinite value. Listen to what the Scriptures declare about the cleansing power of the blood of the Word of God who became human. The Scripture says:

> **The blood of Jesus Christ, his Son, cleanses us from all sin.**
> (1 John 1:7) [18]Knowing that you were redeemed, not with corruptible things, with silver or gold, from the useless way of life handed down from your fathers, [19]but with precious blood, as of a lamb without blemish or spot, the blood of Christ, [20]who was foreknown indeed before the foundation of the world, but was revealed in this last age for your sake, [21]who through him are believers in God, who raised him from the dead, and gave him glory, so that your faith and hope might be in God. (1 Peter 1:18-21)

May God grant you insight into these great truths. In the coming study we look forward to hearing some of *the amazing things Jesus told His disciples on the night when He was arrested.*

God bless you as you think deeply on what the prophet John had announced (more than three years earlier) about Jesus the Messiah:

> **"Behold, the Lamb of God, who takes away the sin of the world!"** (John 1:29)

Program 82

Jesus is Arrested

John 14; Matthew 26

L ast time, we learned about the Passover supper the Lord Jesus shared with His disciples before He suffered and died as the Lamb of God. We heard Him tell His twelve disciples that one of them would betray Him and turn Him over to the priests.[108] We also saw Jesus pass the bread and the cup to His disciples, announcing the long awaited new covenant, and explaining that the broken bread symbolized His body to be sacrificed, and the cup of the juice of grapes symbolized the blood to be poured out for the forgiveness of sins.

Today we plan to hear more of what Jesus told His disciples on the night of His arrest. We are reading in the Gospel of John, chapter 14. Knowing that it was time for Him to lay down His life, Jesus said,

> [1]**"Don't let your heart be troubled. Believe in God.** Believe also in me. [2]In my Father's house are many homes. If it weren't so, I would have told you. I am going to prepare a place for you. [3]If I go and prepare a place for you, I will come again, and will receive you to myself; that where I am, you may be there also. [4]You know where I go, and you know the way." [5]Thomas said to him, "Lord, we don't know where you are going. How can we know the way?"

> [6]**Jesus said to him, "I am the way, the truth, and the life.** No one comes to [God] the Father, except through me. [7]If you had known me, you would have known my Father also. From now on, you know him, and have seen him." [8]Philip said to him, "Lord, show us [God] the Father, and that will be enough for us."

[9]**Jesus said to him**, "Have I been with you such a long time, and do you not know me, Philip? He who has seen me has seen the Father. How do you say, 'Show us the Father?' [10]Don't you believe that I am in the Father, and the Father in me? The words that I tell you, I speak not from myself; but the Father who lives in me does his works. [11]Believe me that I am in the Father, and the Father in me; or else believe me for the very works' sake....

[15]**"If you love me, keep my commandments.** [16]I will pray to the Father, and he will give you another Counselor, that he may be with you forever: [17]the Spirit of truth, whom the world can't receive; for it doesn't see him and doesn't know him. You know him, for he lives with you, and will be in you. [18]I will not leave you orphans. I will come to you. [19]Yet a little while, and the world will see me no more; but you will see me. Because I live, you will live also. [20]In that day you will know that I am in my Father, and you in me, and I in you. [21]One who has my commandments and keeps them, that person is one who loves me. One who loves me will be loved by my Father, and I will love him, and will reveal myself to him....

[23]**If a man loves me, he will keep my word.** My Father will love him, and we will come to him, and make our home with him. [24]He who doesn't love me doesn't keep my words. The word which you hear isn't mine, but the Father's who sent me. [25]I have said these things to you while still living with you. [26]But the Counselor, the Holy Spirit, whom the Father will send in my name, will teach you all things, and will remind you of all that I said to you.

[27]**Peace I leave with you.** My peace I give to you; not as the world gives, I give to you. Don't let your heart be troubled, neither let it be fearful." (John 14:1-11,15-21,23-27)

In this way the Lord Jesus comforted the hearts of His disciples and prepared them for what was about to take place. Did you hear what Jesus announced to them about *the Counselor*?[109] It is

---

109 Literally: *Helper*

vital that we understand this, because some people today distort the words of Jesus and try to make people believe that He was announcing the coming of another prophet. But what Jesus said about the Counselor could not have referred to a prophet, nor to any man, because Jesus said that this Counselor was His invisible Spirit who would come to live inside of Jesus' true disciples.

Who is this Counselor? The Lord Jesus tells us plainly who the Counselor is. Listen again to what Jesus said,

> [16]**I will pray to the Father**, and he will give you another Counselor, that he may be with you forever: [17]the Spirit of truth... He... will be in you. [18]I will not leave you orphans. I will come to you.... [26]But the Counselor, the Holy Spirit, whom the Father will send in my name, will teach you all things, and will remind you of all that I said to you." (John 14:16-18,26)

Again, we ask the question: Who is the Counselor that Jesus promised to His disciples? He is the Holy Spirit, who comes from God and was in Jesus. He is the Spirit of God and Jesus. He is the Holy Spirit, whom God would place in the hearts of all who believe in Jesus as their Savior and Lord. Jesus promised His disciples that after He died, rose again, and returned to heaven, He would send His Holy Spirit into their hearts to regenerate them, cleanse them, strengthen them, and **guide you into all truth.** (John 16:13; see also Titus 3:4-7) A few studies from now, God willing, we will see how this is exactly what happened in Jerusalem, when, ten days after Jesus ascended to heaven, the Holy Spirit came down to live in the hearts of all of Jesus' disciples, just as He promised.

In a later program we will learn more about this Counselor, the Holy Spirit, who can transform a self-centered sinner into a person who loves God and wants to please Him. But now let us return to the Gospel to see what happened on that extraordinary night after Jesus ate the last supper with His disciples. The Scripture says:

> [30]**When they had sung a hymn**, they went out to the Mount of Olives. [31]Then Jesus said to them, "All of you will be made

to stumble because of me tonight, for [the prophets have] written, 'I will strike the shepherd, and the sheep of the flock will be scattered.' [32]But after I am raised up, I will go before you into Galilee." [33]But Peter answered him, "Even if all will be made to stumble because of you, I will never be made to stumble." [34]Jesus said to him, "Most certainly I tell you that tonight, before the rooster crows, you will deny me three times." [35]Peter said to him, "Even if I must die with you, I will not deny you." All of the disciples also said likewise.

[36]**Then Jesus came with them to a place called Gethsemane**, and said to his disciples, "Sit here, while I go there and pray." [37]He took with him Peter and the two sons of Zebedee, and began to be sorrowful and severely troubled. [38]Then he said to them, "My soul is exceedingly sorrowful, even to death. Stay here and watch with me." [39]He went forward a little, fell on his face, and prayed, saying, "My Father, if it is possible, let this cup pass away from me; nevertheless, not what I desire, but what you desire." (Matthew 26:30-39)

Let us pause here. What is the cup of suffering that Jesus dreaded to drink? Why was Jesus overwhelmed with sorrow to the point of death? He was in unimaginable distress because He knew that the time for Him to bear the punishment of sin for the children of Adam was at hand. The hour about which God's prophets had written had arrived. Men would torture the Redeemer and nail Him to a cross, but the most horrible thing for Jesus was knowing that God, His Father in heaven, who loved Him and whom He loved, was going to heap on Him the punishment for the sins of the whole world. That is the reason Jesus prayed saying, **"My Father, if it is possible, let this cup** (of unfathomable suffering) **pass away from me; nevertheless, not what I desire, but what you desire"** Next, the Scripture says:

[40]**[Jesus] came to the disciples and found them sleeping**, and said to Peter, "What, couldn't you watch with me for one hour? [41]Watch and pray, that you don't enter into temptation. The spirit indeed is willing, but the flesh is weak." [42]Again, a

second time he went away and prayed, saying, "My Father, if this cup can't pass away from me unless I drink it, your desire be done." ⁴³He came again and found them sleeping, for their eyes were heavy. ⁴⁴He left them again, went away, and prayed a third time, saying the same words. ⁴⁵Then he came to his disciples and said to them, "Are you still sleeping and resting? Behold, the hour is at hand, and the Son of Man is betrayed into the hands of sinners. ⁴⁶Arise, let's be going. Behold, he who betrays me is at hand."

⁴⁷**While he was still speaking**, behold, Judas [Iscariot], one of the twelve, came, and with him a great multitude with swords and clubs, from the chief priests and elders of the people. ⁴⁸Now he who betrayed him had given them a sign, saying, "Whoever I kiss, he is the one. Seize him." ⁴⁹Immediately he came to Jesus, and said, "Greetings, Rabbi!" and kissed him.

⁵⁰**Jesus said to him, "Friend, why are you here?"** Then they came and laid hands on Jesus, and took him. ⁵¹Behold, one of those who were with Jesus stretched out his hand and drew his sword, and struck the servant of the high priest, and cut off his ear. [But Jesus touched the man's ear and healed him, and said to the one who wanted to protect him, (Luke 22:51 NIV)] ⁵²"Put your sword back into its place, for all those who take the sword will die by the sword. ⁵³Or do you think that I couldn't ask my Father, and he would even now send me more than twelve legions of angels? ⁵⁴How then would the Scriptures be fulfilled that it must be so?"

⁵⁵**In that hour Jesus said to the multitudes,** "Have you come out as against a robber with swords and clubs to seize me? I sat daily in the temple teaching, and you didn't arrest me. ⁵⁶But all this has happened that the Scriptures of the prophets might be fulfilled." Then all the disciples left him and fled. ⁵⁷Those who had taken Jesus led him away to Caiaphas the high priest, where the scribes and the elders were gathered together. (Matthew 26:40-57)

And so we have seen today how Jesus delivered Himself into the hands of those who wanted to torture and kill Him. Perhaps someone would ask, "Why did Jesus allow Himself to fall into the hands of his enemies? He who calmed the storm, drove out demons, healed the blind, and raised the dead – why didn't He save Himself from His enemies?" Jesus Himself told us why. When one of His disciples attempted to protect Him, Jesus told him,

> ⁵²**"Put your sword back into its place**. … ⁵³Or do you think that I couldn't ask my Father, and he would even now send me more than twelve legions of angels? ⁵⁴How then would the Scriptures be fulfilled that it must be so?" (Matthew 26:52-54)

Why did Jesus allow Himself to be arrested by His enemies? He did so to fulfill the scriptures of the prophets who had prophesied repeatedly that the Messiah must suffer and shed His blood as a sacrifice which takes away sin. The Righteous Redeemer had to die for the unrighteous in order to bring us to God.

Jesus the Messiah came into the world to fulfill the words of the prophets. He came to fulfill the meaning of the millions of sheep that had been sacrificed on altars since the time of Adam. He came to save *you and me* from the eternal punishment that our sins require. That is why He allowed Himself to be arrested by those who hated Him. Jesus gave up His life for you and for me.

Have you ever thanked God for sending to earth this holy Savior, **"who loved [you] and gave himself up for [you]"**? (Galatians 2:20)

Friends, this is where we must stop today. We hope you will join us for the next study to see *how the religious leaders condemned Jesus to death*, thus fulfilling the words of the prophets.

God bless you as you remember what Jesus the Lamb of God told His disciples, when He said:

> **I lay down my life, that I may take it again.**
> **No one takes it away from me,**
> **but I lay it down by myself.** (John 10:17-18)

Jesus is Condemned

Matthew 26-27; John 18-19

I n our journey through the Holy Scriptures we have heard how God's prophets announced the plan of salvation which God arranged to save sinners from eternal punishment and bring them back into a close and holy relationship with Himself. Again and again, God's prophets had testified that the righteous Messiah would die, shed His blood for the unrighteous, and bear for us the punishment that our sins require, like an innocent sacrificial sheep. This was the only way God could forgive us of our sins and judge us as righteous without compromising His righteousness. In our chronological study through the Scriptures we are nearing the most important story of all, that is, the historical account of the death, burial, and resurrection of the Messiah. In the will of God, today and in the coming lessons we will see how the Messiah, Jesus, gave His life to pay off the sin-debt of the world.

In our last lesson, we witnessed how the chief priests paid a betrayer to lead them to the place where Jesus and His disciples were. We saw how they arrested Jesus, bound Him, and led Him away. Amazing! Why did Jesus, who was full of the power of God, allow His enemies to capture Him? He allowed them to capture Him so that He might fulfill the scriptures of the prophets which foretold that the Messiah must suffer and die and rise from the dead on the third day, so that everyone who has faith in Him will receive forgiveness of sins. Just as the prophets had prophesied, the Messiah would be **led like a lamb to the slaughter.** (Isaiah 53:7)

Now let us continue reading and see what happened on that dark night after the religious rulers had arrested Jesus. In the book of the Gospel, Mark, chapter 14, the Scripture says:

⁵³ **They led Jesus away to the high priest.** All the chief priests, the elders, and the scribes came together with him. ⁵⁴Peter had followed him from a distance, until he came into the court of the high priest. He was sitting with the officers, and warming himself in the light of the fire.

⁵⁵**Now the chief priests and the whole council** sought witnesses against Jesus to put him to death, and found none. ⁵⁶For many gave false testimony against him, and their testimony didn't agree with each other. ⁵⁷Some stood up, and gave false testimony against him, saying, ⁵⁸"We heard him say, 'I will destroy this temple that is made with hands, and in three days I will build another made without hands.'" ⁵⁹Even so, their testimony didn't agree. ⁶⁰The high priest stood up in the middle, and asked Jesus, "Have you no answer? What is it which these testify against you?" ⁶¹But he stayed quiet, and answered nothing. Again the high priest asked him, "Are you the Christ, the Son of the Blessed?"

⁶²**Jesus said, "I am.** You will see the Son of Man sitting at the right hand of Power, and coming with the clouds of the sky." ⁶³The high priest tore his clothes, and said, "What further need have we of witnesses? ⁶⁴You have heard the blasphemy! What do you think?" They all condemned him to be worthy of death. ⁶⁵Some began to spit on him, and to cover his face, and to beat him with fists, and to tell him, "Prophesy!" The officers struck him with the palms of their hands.

⁶⁶**As Peter was in the courtyard below**, one of the maids of the high priest came, ⁶⁷and seeing Peter warming himself, she looked at him, and said, "You were also with the Nazarene, Jesus!" ⁶⁸But he denied it, saying, "I neither know, nor understand what you are saying." He went out on the porch, and the rooster crowed. ⁶⁹The maid saw him, and began again to tell those who stood by, "This is one of them." ⁷⁰But he again denied it. After a little while again those who stood by said to Peter, "You truly are one of them, for you are a Galilean, and your speech shows it." ⁷¹But he began to curse, and to swear, "I don't know this man of whom you speak!" ⁷²The rooster crowed the second time. Peter

remembered the word, how that Jesus said to him, "Before the rooster crows twice, you will deny me three times." When he thought about that, he wept. (Mark 14:53-72)

¹**Now when morning had come**, all the chief priests and the elders of the people took counsel against Jesus to put him to death. ²They bound him, led him away, and delivered him up to Pontius Pilate, the governor. ³Then Judas, who betrayed him, when he saw that Jesus was condemned, felt remorse, and brought back the thirty pieces of silver to the chief priests and elders, ⁴saying, "I have sinned in that I betrayed innocent blood." But they said, "What is that to us? You see to it." ⁵He threw down the pieces of silver in the sanctuary and departed. Then he went away and hanged himself. (Matthew 27:1-5)

²⁸[Meanwhile,] **they led Jesus** therefore from Caiaphas [the High Priest] into the Praetorium. It was early, and they themselves didn't enter into the Praetorium, that they might not be defiled, but might eat the Passover. ²⁹Pilate therefore went out to them, and said, "What accusation do you bring against this man?" ³⁰They answered him, "If this man weren't an evildoer, we wouldn't have delivered him up to you." ³¹Pilate therefore said to them, "Take him yourselves, and judge him according to your law." Therefore the Jews said to him, "It is illegal for us to put anyone to death," ³²that the word of Jesus might be fulfilled, which he spoke, signifying by what kind of death he should die. ³³Pilate therefore entered again into the Praetorium, called Jesus, and said to him, "Are you the King of the Jews?" ³⁴Jesus answered him, "Do you say this by yourself, or did others tell you about me?" ³⁵Pilate answered, "I'm not a Jew, am I? Your own nation and the chief priests delivered you to me. What have you done?"

³⁶**Jesus answered, "My kingdom is not of this world.** If my kingdom were of this world, then my servants would fight, that I wouldn't be delivered to the Jews. But now my kingdom is not from here." ³⁷Pilate therefore said to him, "Are you a king then?" Jesus answered, "You say that I am a king. For this reason I have

been born, and for this reason I have come into the world, that I should testify to the truth. Everyone who is of the truth listens to my voice." [38]Pilate said to him, "What is truth?" When he had said this, he went out again to the Jews, and said to them, "I find no basis for a charge against him." (John 18:28-38) [5]But they insisted, saying, "He stirs up the people, teaching throughout all Judea, beginning from Galilee even to this place." [6]But when Pilate heard Galilee mentioned, he asked if the man was a Galilean. [7]When he found out that he was in Herod's jurisdiction, he sent him to Herod, who was also in Jerusalem during those days.

[8]**Now when Herod saw Jesus**, he was exceedingly glad, for he had wanted to see him for a long time, because he had heard many things about him. He hoped to see some miracle done by him. [9]He questioned him with many words, but he gave no answers. [10]The chief priests and the scribes stood, vehemently accusing him. [11]Herod with his soldiers humiliated him and mocked him. Dressing him in luxurious clothing, they sent him back to Pilate. [12]Herod and Pilate became friends with each other that very day, for before that they were enemies with each other.

[13]**Pilate called together the chief priests**, the rulers, and the people, [14]and said to them, "You brought this man to me as one that perverts the people, and behold, having examined him before you, I found no basis for a charge against this man concerning those things of which you accuse him. [15]Neither has Herod, for I sent you to him, and see, nothing worthy of death has been done by him. (Luke 23:5-15) [39]But you have a custom, that I should release someone to you at the Passover. Therefore, do you want me to release to you the King of the Jews?" [40]Then they all shouted again, saying, "Not this man, but Barabbas!" Now Barabbas was a robber. (John 18:39-40) [19][He was] one who was thrown into prison for a certain revolt in the city, and for murder. [20]Then Pilate spoke to them again, wanting to release Jesus, [21]but they shouted, saying, "Crucify! Crucify him!" [22]He said to them the third time, "Why? What evil has this man done? I have found no capital crime in him. I will therefore chastise him and release him." (Luke 23:19-22)

¹**So Pilate then took Jesus, and flogged him.** ²The soldiers twisted thorns into a crown, and put it on his head, and dressed him in a purple garment. ³They kept saying, "Hail, King of the Jews!" and they kept slapping him. [They spat on him, and took the reed and struck him on the head. (Matthew 27:30)] ⁴Then Pilate went out again, and said to them, "Behold, I bring him out to you, that you may know that I find no basis for a charge against him." ⁵Jesus therefore came out, wearing the crown of thorns and the purple garment. Pilate said to them, "Behold, the man!" ⁶When therefore the chief priests and the officers saw him, they shouted, saying, "Crucify! Crucify!" Pilate said to them, "Take him yourselves, and crucify him, for I find no basis for a charge against him." ⁷The Jews answered him, "We have a law, and by our law he ought to die, because he made himself the Son of God."

⁸**When therefore Pilate heard this saying**, he was more afraid. ⁹He entered into the Praetorium again, and said to Jesus, "Where are you from?" But Jesus gave him no answer. ¹⁰Pilate therefore said to him, "Aren't you speaking to me? Don't you know that I have power to release you and have power to crucify you?" ¹¹Jesus answered, "You would have no power at all against me, unless it were given to you from above. Therefore he who delivered me to you has greater sin." ¹²At this, Pilate was seeking to release him, but the Jews cried out, saying, "If you release this man, you aren't Caesar's friend! Everyone who makes himself a king speaks against Caesar!" (John 19:1-12)

²⁴**So when Pilate [heard this and] saw** that nothing was being gained, but rather that a disturbance was starting, he took water and washed his hands before the multitude, saying, "I am innocent of the blood of this righteous person. You see to it." ²⁵All the people answered, "May his blood be on us and on our children!" (Matthew 27:24-25) ¹⁵Pilate, wishing to please the multitude, released Barabbas to them, and handed over Jesus… to be crucified. (Mark 15:15)

Yes, everything took place precisely as the prophet Isaiah had foretold 700 years earlier, when he wrote this about the Messiah:

He was oppressed, yet when he was afflicted he didn't open his mouth. As a lamb that is led to the slaughter, and as a sheep that before its shearers is silent, so he didn't open his mouth. (Isaiah 53:7) I gave my back to those who beat me, and my cheeks to those who plucked off the hair. I didn't hide my face from shame and spitting. (Isaiah 50:6)

Today we have seen how the religious leaders of the Jews fulfilled the writings of the prophets. And why did the religious rulers condemn the Messiah to death? They condemned Him because they could not tolerate the light of the truth. As Jesus said, **"This is the judgment, that the light has come into the world, and men loved the darkness rather than the light; for their works were evil."** (John 3:19) And since the children of Adam could not tolerate the Light, their only solution was to extinguish it. So the Scriptures say:

The light shines in the darkness, and the darkness hasn't overcome it. (John 1:5) Which none of the rulers of this world has known. For had they known it, they wouldn't have crucified the Lord of glory. (1 Corinthians 2:8) He was in the world, and the world was made through him, and the world didn't recognize him. ¹¹He came to his own, and those who were his own didn't receive him. ¹²But as many as received him, to them he gave the right to become God's children, to those who believe in his name. (John 1:10-12)

Friends, thank you for listening. Be sure to join us next time to hear how Adam's descendants fulfilled the words of the Messiah, which the prophet David wrote in the Psalms, saying: **"They have pierced my hands and feet."** (Psalms 22:16)

God bless you as you ponder what the prophet Isaiah foretold about the Messiah 700 years earlier:

He was oppressed, yet when he was afflicted he didn't open his mouth. As a lamb that is led to the slaughter, and as a sheep that before its shearers is silent, so he didn't open his mouth. (Isaiah 53:7)

Program 84

It is Finished!

Matthew 27; Mark 15; Luke 23; John 19

In our last lesson we saw how the religious rulers arrested Jesus, led Him away to the house of the High Priest, tried Him at night, condemned Him, and led Him to Pilate, the governor of the land, so that they might have Him crucified. The soldiers savagely flogged Jesus, then twisted together a crown of thorns and put it on His head, mocking Him, striking Him on the face, spitting on Him, and striking Him on the head with a rod. This is how the children of Adam treated the King of glory who came from heaven. Those who tortured Jesus did not know that they were fulfilling the words of the prophets which announced that the Messiah would suffer in this way at the hands of sinners.

Today we will continue in the book of the Gospel (*Injil*) to see how Jesus the Messiah suffered and died on the cross, fulfilling God's great plan of salvation just as the prophets had predicted long beforehand. Before we begin today's study, you should know that when Jesus lived on earth, the Roman government executed certain criminals by nailing them to poles, or trees, or specially made crosses. Such a death is called *crucifixion*. To add public shame to excruciating pain, the Roman soldiers stripped victims naked before driving nails through their hands and feet. This painful and shameful death was reserved for the worst criminals.

Perhaps some of you are wondering why the LORD God required the Messiah to suffer such a painful and shameful death. It is because of the hideous nature of our sin. Sin is the problem of the world. We are all sinners and our sins are an offense to a holy and righteous God. If God is going to forgive you and me of our wrong-doings without compromising His righteous laws, then He must judge us with a perfect and just judgment. He cannot forgive our transgressions in just any sort of way. God is a righteous Judge and must punish every sin according to His law. The penalty for sin is death and eternal separation from God. This penalty must be paid in full. That is why God sent down His Word to became human, so that He could pay the penalty for our sins that God's wrath required.

Now, dear friends, we invite each of you to listen with your mind and heart as we continue reading from the Gospel:

> [16]**So then [Pilate] delivered him to them to be crucified.** So they took Jesus and led him away. [17]He went out, bearing his cross, to the place called "The Place of a Skull", which is called in Hebrew, "Golgotha". (John 19:16-17)

> [26]**When they led [Jesus] away**, they grabbed one Simon of Cyrene, coming from the country, and laid on him the cross, to carry it after Jesus. [27]A great multitude of the people followed him, including women who also mourned and lamented him. … [32]There were also others, two criminals, led with him to be put to death. [33]When they came to the place that is called "The Skull", they crucified him there with the criminals, one on the right and the other on the left. [34]Jesus said, "Father, forgive them, for they don't know what they are doing." … [35]The people stood watching. The rulers with them also scoffed at him, saying, "He saved others. Let him save himself, if this is the Christ of God, his chosen one!" [36]The soldiers also mocked him, coming to him and offering him vinegar, [37]and saying, "If you are the King of the Jews, save yourself!" (Luke 23:26-27,32-37)

> [19]**Pilate wrote a title also, and put it on the cross.** There was written, "JESUS OF NAZARETH, THE KING OF THE JEWS." [20]Therefore many of the Jews read this title, for the place where Jesus was crucified was near the city; and it was written in Hebrew, in Latin, and in Greek. [21]The chief priests of the Jews therefore said to Pilate, "Don't write, 'The King of the Jews,' but, 'he said, "I am King of the Jews."'" [22]Pilate answered, "What I have written, I have written." [23]Then the soldiers, when

they had crucified Jesus, took his garments and made four parts, to every soldier a part; and also the coat. Now the coat was without seam, woven from the top throughout. ²⁴Then they said to one another, "Let's not tear it, but cast lots for it to decide whose it will be," that the [word which the prophet David had written in the Psalms] might be fulfilled, which says, "They parted my garments among them. For my cloak they cast lots." Therefore the soldiers did these things. (John 19:19-24)

³⁹**One of the criminals who was hanged** insulted him, saying, "If you are the Christ, save yourself and us!" ⁴⁰But the other answered, and rebuking him said, "Don't you even fear God, seeing you are under the same condemnation? ⁴¹And we indeed justly, for we receive the due reward for our deeds, but this man has done nothing wrong." ⁴²He said to Jesus, "Lord, remember me when you come into your kingdom." ⁴³Jesus said to him, "Assuredly I tell you, today you will be with me in Paradise." (Luke 23:39-43)

³³**When the sixth hour had come, there was darkness** over the whole land until the ninth hour. ³⁴At the ninth hour Jesus cried with a loud voice, saying, "Eloi, Eloi, lama sabachthani?" which is, being interpreted, "My God, my God, why have you forsaken me?" (Mark 15:33-34)

The whole land became pitch-dark, beginning at noon. For three long hours God heaped His wrath-filled punishment for the sins of all the children of Adam upon the holy Redeemer. We cannot even begin to imagine the intensity of Jesus' sufferings for us. On the altar of the cross, the Lord Jesus felt the horror of being separated from God in heaven, which is why He cried out, **"My God, my God, why have you forsaken me?"** During those hours of darkness, hidden from the eyes of men, God took all our sins and put them on His holy Son. Jesus became the final sin offering.

²⁸**After this, Jesus, seeing that all things were now finished**, that the Scripture might be fulfilled, said, "I am thirsty." ²⁹Now a vessel full of vinegar was set there; so they put a sponge full of

the vinegar on hyssop, and held it at his mouth. [30]When Jesus therefore had received the vinegar, he said, "It is finished." (John 19:28-30) [46][Then] Jesus, crying with a loud voice, said, "Father, into your hands I commit my spirit!" Having said this, he breathed his last. (Luke 23:46)

[38][Then] **the veil of the temple was torn in two** from the top to the bottom. [39]When the centurion, who stood by opposite him, saw that he cried out like this and breathed his last, he said, "Truly this man was the Son of God!" [40]There were also women watching from afar, among whom were both Mary Magdalene, and Mary the mother of James the less and of Joses, and Salome; [41]who, when he was in Galilee, followed him and served him; and many other women who came up with him to Jerusalem. (Mark 15:38-41)

[31]**Therefore the Jews**, because it was the Preparation Day, so that the bodies wouldn't remain on the cross on the Sabbath (for that Sabbath was a special one), asked of Pilate that their legs might be broken, and that they might be taken away. [32]Therefore the soldiers came, and broke the legs of the first, and of the other who was crucified with him; [33]but when they came to Jesus, and saw that he was already dead, they didn't break his legs. [34]However one of the soldiers pierced his side with a spear, and immediately blood and water came out. [35]He who has seen has testified, and his testimony is true. He knows that he tells the truth, that you may believe. [36]For these things happened that the Scripture might be fulfilled, "A bone of him will not be broken. [37]Again another Scripture says, "They will look on him whom they pierced."

[38]**After these things, Joseph [a rich man from] Arimathaea,** being a disciple of Jesus, but secretly for fear of the Jews, asked of Pilate that he might take away Jesus' body. Pilate gave him permission. He came therefore and took away his body. [39]Nicodemus, who at first came to Jesus by night, also came bringing a mixture of myrrh and aloes, about a hundred Roman pounds. [40]So they took Jesus' body, and bound it in linen cloths

with the spices, as the custom of the Jews is to bury. ⁴¹Now in the place where he was crucified there was a garden. In the garden was a new tomb in which no man had ever yet been laid. ⁴²Then because of the Jews' Preparation Day (for the tomb was near at hand) they laid Jesus there. (John 19:31-42)

Friends, though the Messiah's story does not end in the tomb, this is where we must stop reading today. What we have heard is astounding. We have seen how the descendants of Adam despised the Messiah, the Lord of Life, and killed Him by nailing Him to a cross. But the death of the Messiah on that Roman cross was the fulfillment of God's plan of salvation. Do you remember what the Lord Jesus proclaimed from the cross before He died? He said:

"It is finished!" (John 19:30)

Why did He say that? He said, "It is finished!" because He had perfectly fulfilled God's plan of salvation. Do the religions of the world ever say *"It is finished."*? No, what they say is: *It is NOT finished. Try to save yourself by your own good efforts. Work to erase your own sins! Get with it! Try harder! Nothing is finished! If you want to enter Paradise then fulfill your religious duties, pray, fast, and hope for the best on Judgment Day!* That is the way of man's religion.

But the message of God's grace to you is: IT IS FINISHED. Believe what Jesus did on the cross and be saved! The Messiah has paid your debt of sin with His own blood. He can cleanse and transform your heart. That is what He did for the repentant criminal on the cross next to Him. Jesus told him, **"Assuredly I tell you, today you will be with me in Paradise."** (Luke 23:43)

Dear friends, the work that can save you from sin's penalty is DONE. God is completely satisfied with Jesus' sacrifice. God now tells us to STOP bringing sacrifices of sheep. The Lord Jesus Christ is God's perfect and final Sacrifice. Nothing remains for us except to believe what Jesus the Lamb of God declared from the cross: *"It is finished!"* Your sin debt is *paid in full!* Do you accept the payment Jesus made?

Seven hundred years before the Messiah came to earth, the prophet Isaiah wrote this about Him:

> **⁹They made his grave with the wicked**, and with a rich man in his death, although he had done no violence, nor was any deceit in his mouth. … ⁵But he was pierced for our transgressions. He was crushed for our iniquities. The punishment that brought our peace was on him; and by his wounds we are healed. ⁶All we like sheep have gone astray. Everyone has turned to his own way; and the LORD has laid on him the iniquity of us all. (Isaiah 53:9,5-6)

Listening friend, do you believe the message of the prophets? Do you believe that the Lord Jesus completed the work of salvation *for you*? Do you now understand the reason for His sufferings and death on the cross? You and I are the reason. It is because of our sins that He shed His blood, like a perfect sacrificial sheep. We deserve eternal punishment in hell, but God, out of His great love for us, sent His Word, the Lord Jesus to suffer our punishment and bear the penalty for our sins. The Scriptures say:

> ⁷**For one will hardly die for a righteous man.** Yet perhaps for a good person someone would even dare to die. ⁸But God commends his own love toward us, in that while we were yet sinners, Christ died for us. (Romans 5:7-8) God made him who had no sin to be [the sin offering] for us, so that in him we might become the righteousness of God. (2 Corinthians 5:21 NIV)

Glory to God the Merciful, the Compassionate: **It is finished!** Jesus is the final sacrifice! The meaning of the prophet Abraham's Sacrifice is now clear! In the same mountain range where Abraham sacrificed the innocent ram in his son's place, Jesus the sinless Messiah gave Himself to be sacrificed in our place so **that whoever believes in him should not perish, but have eternal life.** (John 3:16)

God bless you as you ponder the deep, liberating word which Jesus the Messiah announced from the cross just before He died:

> **It is finished!** (John 19:30)

Jesus is Risen!

Matthew 28; Luke 24; John 20

I n our last lesson, we saw how Jesus the Messiah shed His blood to pay for our sins and bring us back to God. Everything happened exactly as God's prophets had foretold it. The Messiah was mocked, scourged and nailed to a cross. Even as the innocent ram died in the place of Abraham's son, Jesus the sinless Redeemer died in our place. That is why just before Jesus died, He shouted, **"It is finished!"** (John 19:30) The death of the Messiah on the cross is the most important news in all the Scriptures, because that death is the reason God can forgive us our sins and still uphold justice.

After Jesus expired on the cross, a soldier took a spear and stabbed it into Jesus' side, bringing a sudden flow of blood and water which proved that He was dead. We saw also that a rich man took the body of Jesus and placed it in a new tomb that he had chiseled out of the rock for himself. A huge round stone was rolled over the tomb's entrance. Everything happened exactly as God's prophets had foretold it. Thus, in the Gospel, it is written:

> [62]**Now on the next day**, which was the day after the Preparation Day, the chief priests and the Pharisees were gathered together to Pilate, [63]saying, "Sir, we remember what that deceiver said while he was still alive: 'After three days I will rise again.' [64]Command therefore that the tomb be made secure until the third day, lest perhaps his disciples come at night and steal him away, and tell the people, 'He is risen from the dead;' and the last deception will be worse than the first." [65]Pilate said to them, "You have a guard. Go, make it as secure as you can." [66]So they went with the guard and made the tomb secure, sealing the stone. (Matthew 27:62-66)

¹**Now after the Sabbath, as it began to dawn** on the first day of the week, Mary Magdalene and the other Mary came to see the tomb. ²Behold, there was a great earthquake, for an angel of the Lord descended from the sky and came and rolled away the stone from the door and sat on it. ³His appearance was like lightning, and his clothing white as snow. ⁴For fear of him, the guards shook, and became like dead men. (Matthew 28:1-4)

¹**[When the women arrived at the cemetery]**, ²they found the stone rolled away from the tomb. ³They entered in, and didn't find the Lord Jesus' body. ⁴While they were greatly perplexed about this, behold, two men stood by them in dazzling clothing. ⁵Becoming terrified, they bowed their faces down to the earth. They said to them, "Why do you seek the living among the dead? ⁶He isn't here, but is risen. Remember what he told you when he was still in Galilee, ⁷saying that the Son of Man must be delivered up into the hands of sinful men and be crucified, and the third day rise again?" ⁸They remembered his words, ⁹returned from the tomb, and told all these things to the eleven and to all the rest. ¹⁰Now they were Mary Magdalene, Joanna, and Mary the mother of James. The other women with them told these things to the apostles. ¹¹These words seemed to them to be nonsense, and they didn't believe them. [For as yet they didn't know the Scripture, that he must rise from the dead. (John 20:9)] ¹²But Peter got up and ran to the tomb. Stooping and looking in, he saw the strips of linen lying by themselves, and he departed to his home, wondering what had happened.

¹³**Behold, two of them were going that very day** to a village named Emmaus, which was sixty stadia from Jerusalem. ¹⁴They talked with each other about all of these things which had happened. ¹⁵While they talked and questioned together, Jesus himself came near, and went with them. ¹⁶But their eyes were kept from recognizing him. ¹⁷He said to them, "What are you talking about as you walk, and are sad?" ¹⁸One of them, named Cleopas, answered him, "Are you the only stranger in Jerusalem who doesn't know the things which have happened

there in these days?" [19]He said to them, "What things?" They
said to him, "The things concerning Jesus, the Nazarene, who
was a prophet mighty in deed and word before God and all the
people; [20]and how the chief priests and our rulers delivered him
up to be condemned to death, and crucified him. [21]But we were
hoping that it was he who would redeem Israel. Yes, and besides
all this, it is now the third day since these things happened.
[22]Also, certain women of our company amazed us, having
arrived early at the tomb; [23]and when they didn't find his body,
they came saying that they had also seen a vision of angels,
who said that he was alive. [24]Some of us went to the tomb, and
found it just like the women had said, but they didn't see him."

[25]**He said to them, "Foolish men, and slow of heart** to believe
in all that the prophets have spoken! [26]Didn't the Christ have
to suffer these things and to enter into his glory?" [27]Beginning
from Moses and from all the prophets, he explained to them in
all the Scriptures the things concerning himself. [28]They came
near to the village where they were going, and he acted like he
would go further. [29]They urged him, saying, "Stay with us, for it
is almost evening, and the day is almost over." He went in to stay
with them. [30]When he had sat down at the table with them, he
took the bread and gave thanks. Breaking it, he gave it to them.

[31]**Their eyes were opened and they recognized him**, then he
vanished out of their sight. [32]They said to one another, "Weren't
our hearts burning within us, while he spoke to us along the
way, and while he opened the Scriptures to us?" [33]They rose up
that very hour, returned to Jerusalem, and found the eleven
gathered together, and those who were with them, [34]saying,
"The Lord is risen indeed, and has appeared to Simon!" [35]They
related the things that happened along the way, and how he
was recognized by them in the breaking of the bread.

[36]**As they said these things, Jesus himself stood among them**,
and said to them, "Peace be to you." [37]But they were terrified
and filled with fear, and supposed that they had seen a spirit.
[38]He said to them, "Why are you troubled? Why do doubts arise

in your hearts? ^{39}See my hands and my feet, that it is truly me. Touch me and see, for a spirit doesn't have flesh and bones, as you see that I have." ^{40}When he had said this, he showed them his hands and his feet.

^{44}**He said to them, "This is what I told you**, while I was still with you, that all things which are written in the law of Moses, the prophets, and the psalms, concerning me must be fulfilled." ^{45}Then he opened their minds, that they might understand the Scriptures. ^{46}He said to them, "Thus it is written, and thus it was necessary for the Christ to suffer and to rise from the dead the third day, ^{47}and that repentance and remission of sins should be preached in his name to all the nations, beginning at Jerusalem. ^{48}You are witnesses of these things." (Luke 24:1-40,44-48)

^{24}**But Thomas, one of the twelve**…wasn't with them when Jesus came. ^{25}The other disciples therefore said to him, "We have seen the Lord!" But he said to them, "Unless I see in his hands the print of the nails, put my finger into the print of the nails, and put my hand into his side, I will not believe."

^{26}**After eight days again his disciples were inside** and Thomas was with them. Jesus came, the doors being locked, and stood in the middle, and said, "Peace be to you." ^{27}Then he said to Thomas, "Reach here your finger, and see my hands. Reach here your hand, and put it into my side. Don't be unbelieving, but believing." ^{28}Thomas answered him, "My Lord and my God!" ^{29}Jesus said to him, "Because you have seen me, you have believed. Blessed are those who have not seen, and have believed." ^{30}Therefore Jesus did many other signs in the presence of his disciples, which are not written in this book; ^{31}but these are written, that you may believe that Jesus is the Christ, the Son of God, and that believing you may have life in his name. (John 20:24-31)

Yes, Jesus rose from the dead! Having paid the sin debt of the world, He then conquered man's most feared enemy: DEATH! The grave could not hold Him. On the third day, Jesus rose out of His grave clothes, like a butterfly leaving his chrysalis shell. Only the grave clothes remained where the body of Jesus had been. The Lord came back to life in a glorious body like the body which all who believes in Him will one day receive. The Scripture says:

> [20]**But now Christ has been raised from the dead.** He became the first fruit of those who are asleep. [21]For since death came by man, the resurrection of the dead also came by man. [22]For as in Adam all die, so also in Christ all will be made alive. (1 Corinthians 15:20-22)

The resurrection of Jesus proves that He is the One He claimed to be. Jesus said, "**I am the resurrection and the life. He who believes in me will still live, even if he dies.**" (John 11:25) Jesus promised to give eternal life to all those who believe in Him, but if He Himself had not conquered death, how could He save others from the power of death and sin and hell?

Perhaps an illustration will help. A child is playing in the waves along the seashore. Suddenly a strong current sweeps him out to sea. He desperately tries to get back to shore but cannot. The child will die unless someone rescues him. There is a man on the shore who sees the child and yells to him, "Don't be afraid. I will save you!" So the man swims out to where the child is, but, alas, the currents are too strong for him. Both he and the child drown. The man intended to rescue the child, but he lacked the power to carry out his intention. The ocean current was too strong for him.

Similarly, we hear those who claim to be saviors, telling people, "Follow me, trust me, and you'll get into Paradise." Those who make such promises may have good intentions, but they cannot accomplish what they promise. They cannot even save themselves, because they are unable to overcome the power of sin and death. The power of death is too strong for them, and when they die, they will be buried, their bodies will decay in the grave, and their souls will await the Day of Judgment. But it was not that way with the Lord. He is the One He claimed to be with the power to do what He promised. Everything took place just as He had predicted. Jesus died as a sacrifice to take away sin, was buried, and then on the third day He came out of the grave. Never has there been anyone among the prophets who died, was buried, and then came out of the tomb never to die again. But that is what Jesus the Messiah did. He defeated death and the grave. He overcame sin and Satan and death and hell. And the most wonderful thing in all of this is that whoever believes this good news about the death and resurrection of Jesus Christ will share in His glory forever! That is what the Lord Jesus proclaimed after He had risen from the dead, saying, **"Don't be afraid. I am the first and the last, and the Living one. I was dead, and behold, I am alive forever and ever. Amen. I have the keys of Death and of Hades."** (Revelation 1:17-18)

God raised Jesus to life so that you might know for sure that He is the Savior and Judge of the world, whom God appointed. That is what the Scriptures declare, when they say:

> **There is salvation in no one else,** for there is no other name under heaven that is given among men, by which we must be saved.

> **[God] has appointed a day in which he will judge the world** in righteousness by the man whom he has ordained; of which he has given assurance to all men, in that he has raised him from the dead.

> **If you will confess with your mouth** that Jesus is Lord, and believe in your heart that God raised him from the dead, you will be saved. …Whoever will call on the name of the Lord will be saved. (Acts 4:12; 17:31; Romans 10:9,13)

Friends, thank you for listening. God willing, in our next program we will continue in the Gospel to see how the Lord Jesus appeared to many witnesses after His resurrection and showed them many convincing proofs that He was alive.

May God grant you insight into all the implications of what the angel told the women who had come to the tomb:

> **He isn't here, but is risen!** (Luke 24:6)

Program 86

Jesus Ascends to Heaven

Matthew 28; Luke 24; Acts 1

For a long time we have been looking into the holy Gospel, the book that contains the story of the Savior, Jesus Christ. As we learned, *Jesus* means *God saves. Christ* is a Greek word for the Hebrew word *Messiah,* meaning *The One whom God appointed.* Jesus Christ is the One God sent to earth to save the children of Adam from the dominion of sin. But most people did not recognize who Jesus was. Some considered Him a prophet, but they did not grasp that He Himself was the Word of God (*Kalimat Allah*) in a human body. Some, like the chief priests and the rulers of the Jews, were jealous of Him and in the end they killed Him by having Him nailed to a cross. But none of these events took God by surprise. The Scripture says:

> [7]**But we speak God's wisdom in a mystery**, the wisdom that has been hidden, which God foreordained before the worlds for our glory, [8]which none of the rulers of this world has known. For had they known it, they wouldn't have crucified the Lord of glory. (1 Corinthians 2:7-8)

In our last program, we heard how God raised Jesus back to life on the third day after He was buried. The resurrection of Jesus proves that God accepted the blood which Jesus shed to redeem the children of Adam from the power of sin, the fear of death, and the punishment of hell. After Jesus came back to life, He appeared to His disciples, showing them the wounds where the soldiers had pounded nails through His hands and feet. The book of the Gospel relates how Jesus appeared to His disciples over a forty-day period and spoke with them about the kingdom of God. On one occasion, He appeared to more than five hundred of His disciples at the same time. (1 Corinthians 15:6) But the greatest proof that Jesus is alive today is in the fact that He lives by His Holy Spirit in the hearts of all who believe in Him and submit to His authority.

Today we will hear about the infinite authority God has given to the Lord Jesus, and we will see how Jesus parted from His disciples and ascended back to heaven. We begin today in the last chapter of the Gospel of Matthew. The Scripture says:

> [16]**But the eleven disciples went into Galilee**, to the mountain where Jesus had sent them. [17]When they saw him, they bowed down to him; but some doubted. [18]Jesus came to them and spoke to them, saying, "All authority has been given to me in heaven and on earth. [19]Go and make disciples of all nations, baptizing them in the name of the Father and of the Son and of the Holy Spirit, [20]teaching them to observe all things that I commanded you. Behold, I am with you always, even to the end of the age." (Matthew 28:16-20)

Did you hear what Jesus said to His disciples? He said, **"All authority has been given to me in heaven and on earth. Go and make disciples of all nations."** Why did Jesus say that He had all authority in heaven and on earth?

In the Torah of Moses we saw how God created the first man, Adam. We read that God gave Adam authority to rule over the earth. God wanted Adam to live with Him and rule with Him forever. But Adam forfeited that authority the day he disobeyed God's command and ate of the tree of the knowledge of good and evil. Since Adam is our forefather, and since *an epidemic does not confine itself to the one from whom it originates*,[110] we too have lost the privilege and authority of living and ruling with God. Like Adam, we are all sinners, born into the kingdom of sin, far from God and His majestic glory.

But God had a plan to get us back. The Scripture summarizes that plan like this: Jesus the Messiah **suffered for sins once, the righteous**

---

110 Wolof proverb used in previous programs

for the unrighteous, that he might bring you to God. (1 Peter 3:18) Like Adam, Jesus was tested, but Jesus never sinned. Jesus was perfect and holy even as God is perfect and holy. Like Father, like Son. And so, after the holy Son suffered and died for our sins, God raised Him back to life and gave Him authority, not just to rule on earth; God gave Jesus **all authority** on earth and **in heaven**.

Some might ask, "If Jesus has all authority, why is our world still so full of trouble and sin?" The Holy Scripture gives the answer:

> [22]**For as in Adam all die, so also in Christ all will be made alive.** [23]But each in his own order: Christ the first fruits, then those who are Christ's, at his coming. [24]Then the end comes, when he will deliver up the kingdom to God, even the Father, when he will have abolished all rule and all authority and power....[45]So also it is written, "The first man, Adam, became a living soul." The last Adam became a life-giving spirit. ... [47]The first man is of the earth, made of dust. The second man is the Lord from heaven. ... [49]As we have borne the image of those made of dust, let's also bear the image of the heavenly. (1 Corinthians 15:22-24,45,47,49)

> **He will wipe away every tear from their eyes.** Death will be no more; neither will there be mourning, nor crying, nor pain, any more. The first things have passed away. (Revelation 21:4)

Based on those verses and hundreds of others, we learn that God has committed all authority to Jesus, the heavenly man. The Scripture says that God **commands that all people everywhere should repent, because he has appointed a day in which he will judge the world in righteousness by the man whom he has ordained; of which he has given assurance to all men, in that he has raised him from the dead.** (Acts 17:30-31)

Jesus is the holy man appointed by God to judge the world. And so whoever you are and wherever you are, God is commanding you to turn to Him in faith. If you believe that the Lord Jesus Christ died for your sins, was buried, and rose again, God will forgive all your sins in Jesus' name, renew your heart by the power of the Holy

Spirit. If you believe in Christ, He will send His Spirit into your heart and establish His kingdom in you. Jesus Christ will not change the world until He returns in person to judge it. But He can change you today! Will you allow Him to establish His kingdom in your heart?

Dear friend, Jesus is the Savior *and* Judge of the world. He alone can save you from the condemnation of your sins. He alone can give you peace with God for time and for eternity. For all who refuse the risen Lord Jesus Christ as their righteous *Savior*, He will be their righteous *Judge*. The Scripture says:

> [7]**The Lord Jesus [will be] revealed from heaven** with his mighty angels in flaming fire, [8]punishing those who don't know God, and to those who don't obey the Good News of our Lord Jesus, [9]who will pay the penalty: eternal destruction from the face of the Lord and from the glory of his might, [10]when he comes in that day to be glorified in his saints and to be admired among all those who have believed, because our testimony to you was believed. (2 Thessalonians 1:7-10)

Friends, the word of God is clear. It tells us that whoever believes the Good News about Jesus Christ's death on the cross for your sins and His resurrection from the grave will be saved. But whoever does not believe it will be condemned. Jesus shed His blood as a sacrifice which can erase your debt of sin forever. But the blood which Jesus shed for you is of no value to you if you do not believe in it in your heart, because the Scripture says:

> [16]**For God so loved the world** that he gave his one and only Son, that whoever believes in him should not perish, but have eternal life. … [18]He who doesn't believe has been judged already, because he has not believed in the name of the one and only Son of God. (John 3:16,18)

Yes, if you believe the Good News of Jesus Christ, you will be saved, but if you do not believe it, you will perish in your sins. That is the word of salvation which God sent down to the children of Adam. That is the reason Jesus commanded His disciples, saying:

"All authority has been given to me in heaven and on earth. Go and make disciples of all nations." (Matthew 28:18-19)

Now let us continue the story. Jesus appeared to His disciples over a period of forty days after He had risen from the dead. One day while Jesus was eating with His disciples, He gave them this command:

> [4]**"Don't depart from Jerusalem, but wait** for the promise of the Father, which you heard from me. [5]For John indeed baptized in water, but you will be baptized in the Holy Spirit not many days from now." (Acts 1:4-5)

Did you hear what Jesus said? We have already read[111] how He promised His disciples that His Father in heaven would send to them the Counselor, the Holy Spirit, who would live in their hearts, cleanse them, renew them, strengthen them, and guide them in His truth. We also heard Jesus tell His disciples to wait in Jerusalem for His Holy Spirit, whom He would send down after He ascended back to heaven. In our next lesson, we will see how the Holy Spirit came down from heaven to live in the hearts of all who put their faith in Jesus Christ.

But now let's read how Jesus, forty days after His resurrection, met with His disciples on the Mount of Olives outside Jerusalem:

> [6]**Therefore when they had come together**, they asked him, "Lord, are you now restoring the kingdom to Israel?" [7]He said to them, "It isn't for you to know times or seasons which the Father has set within his own authority. [8]But you will receive power when the Holy Spirit has come upon you. You will be witnesses to me in Jerusalem, in all Judea and Samaria, and to the uttermost parts of the earth." [9]When he had said these things, as they were looking, he was taken up, and a cloud received him out of their sight. [10]While they were looking steadfastly into the sky as he went, behold, two men stood by them in white clothing, [11]who also said, "You men of Galilee, why do you stand looking into the sky? This Jesus, who was received up from you into the sky, will come back in the same way as you saw him going into the sky." (Acts 1:6-11)

---

111 Gospel of John, chapters 14-16

So Jesus ascended into heaven, returning to His Father's home from where He had come thirty-three years earlier. In His birth, life, death, burial, resurrection and ascension, Jesus of Nazareth had fulfilled all that the prophets wrote about Him.

Friend, do you know where the risen Lord is today? The Scripture says that He **is at the right hand of God, having gone into heaven, angels and authorities and powers being made subject to him.** (1 Peter 3:22) There in heaven, all created beings are in submission to Him. Meanwhile down here on earth, most people are not submitted to Him. How about you? Have you submitted yourself to the One chosen by God as the Savior and Judge of the world?

As we just read, after the Lord Jesus was taken back up to heaven, two angels appeared to His disciples and said to them, **"Why do you stand looking into the sky? This Jesus, who was received up from you into the sky, will come back in the same way as you saw him going into the sky."** (Acts 1:11) One day Jesus will return. Are you ready to meet Him? We leave you with this summary of the Messiah's life and mission:

> [5]**Christ Jesus,** [6]**who, existing in the form of God,** didn't consider equality with God a thing to be grasped, [7]but emptied himself, taking the form of a servant, being made in the likeness of men. [8]And being found in human form, he humbled himself, becoming obedient to the point of death, yes, the death of the cross. [9]Therefore God also highly exalted him, and gave to him the name which is above every name, [10]that at the name of Jesus every knee should bow, of those in heaven, those on earth, and those under the earth. (Philippians 2:5-10)

Friends, we hope you will join us next time to hear how God sent down His Holy Spirit to live in the hearts of all who trust in Jesus.

God bless you as you ponder this invitation from Him to you:

> **Believe in the Lord Jesus Christ, and you will be saved, you and your household.** (Acts 16:31)

The Holy Spirit Has Come!

Acts 1-2

In our last few studies in the Gospel, we have heard how the Lord Jesus fulfilled all that God's prophets had written long beforehand about the Messiah's death and resurrection. We read that Jesus shed His holy blood on the cross to pay the debt of sin for the children of Adam. We saw also that His body was taken down from the cross and laid in a tomb, but that on the third day, God raised Him back to life. After Jesus had risen, He appeared to His disciples over a period of forty days, proving to them that He truly was alive. Then in our last program, we watched as Jesus ascended into heaven while His disciples looked on.

Do you remember the last thing Jesus commanded His disciples, before He went up to heaven? Let us read again what He said:

> ⁴**Being assembled together with them**, [Jesus] commanded them, "Don't depart from Jerusalem, but wait for the promise of the Father, which you heard from me. ⁵For John indeed baptized in water, but you will be baptized in the Holy Spirit not many days from now. … ⁸You will receive power when the Holy Spirit has come upon you. You will be witnesses to me in Jerusalem, in all Judea and Samaria, and to the uttermost parts of the earth." ⁹When he had said these things, as they were looking, he was taken up, and a cloud received him out of their sight. (Acts 1:4-5,8-9)

Thus, Jesus parted with His disciples, returned to His heavenly home, and sat down at the right hand of the Majesty on high. Did you hear what Jesus commanded His disciples before He ascended to heaven? He told them to wait in Jerusalem until they were clothed with the Holy Spirit.

Who is this Holy Spirit? He is the Spirit of God and the Spirit that was in Jesus. He is One with God the Father and Jesus the Son, yet He is distinct from them. *The Holy Spirit* and *the Word* existed with God in the beginning when the world was created. The Holy Spirit is the Counselor whom Jesus promised to send upon His disciples, when He said:

> [16]**"I will pray to the Father**, and he will give you another Counselor, that he may be with you forever: [17]the Spirit of truth, whom the world can't receive; for it doesn't see him and doesn't know him. You know him, for he lives with you, and will be in you."** (John 14:16-17)

What Jesus told His disciples about the coming of this Counselor (Helper, Advocate) is important for us to understand, because some today want to make people believe that Jesus was announcing the coming of another prophet. But the Counselor whom the Lord Jesus promised cannot be a human being, because Jesus stated clearly that the Counselor was the pure Holy Spirit, and that no one could see Him, but that He would live inside Christ's disciples forever. So who is this Holy Spirit? He is the Spirit whom God places in the hearts of all who believe in Jesus the Messiah. He regenerates them, (causes them to be born again), cleanses them, strengthens them, marks them as God's own special people, and gives them the right to live in His holy presence forever.

Today we are going to see how God poured out His Holy Spirit on Jesus' disciples on the day of Pentecost. Pentecost was a festival God had established for the Israelites during the time of the prophet Moses. It took place each year, 50 days after the Passover. You can read about it in the Torah. Pentecost was a day for the Israelites to thank the LORD for the first harvest of grain. But it was also the day on which God planned to send His Holy Spirit to live inside all who believe in Jesus the Messiah. Just as the Pentecost festival took place 50 days after the Passover feast, so God planned to send the Holy Spirit 50 days after Jesus rose from the dead. All who believe in Him are part of God's great harvest.

Now let us hear what happened on the Day of Pentecost, ten days after Jesus went back up to heaven. The Scripture tells us that after the eleven disciples witnessed Jesus' ascension, they returned to Jerusalem where they met together with others who loved Jesus and had seen Him after He rose from the dead. This group of 120 believers included Mary the mother of Jesus, several other women, and the brothers of Jesus. (See Acts 1:12-15) The Scripture says:

> [1]**On the day of Pentecost** all the believers were meeting together in one place. [2]Suddenly, there was a sound from heaven like the roaring of a mighty windstorm, and it filled the house where they were sitting. [3]Then, what looked like flames or tongues of fire appeared and settled on each of them. [4]And everyone present was filled with the Holy Spirit and began speaking in other languages, as the Holy Spirit gave them this ability.

> [5]**At that time there were devout Jews from every nation** living in Jerusalem. [6]When they heard the loud noise, everyone came running, and they were bewildered to hear their own languages being spoken by the believers. [7]They were completely amazed. "How can this be?" they exclaimed. "These people are all from Galilee, [8]yet we hear them speaking in our own native languages! [9]Here we are – Parthians, Medes, Elamites, people from Mesopotamia, Judea, Cappadocia, Pontus, the province of Asia, [10]Phrygia, Pamphylia, Egypt, and the areas of Libya around Cyrene, visitors from Rome, [11](both Jews and converts to Judaism), Cretans, and Arabs. And we all hear these people speaking in our own languages about the wonderful things God has done!" [12]They stood there amazed and perplexed. "What can this mean?" they asked each other. [13]But others in the crowd ridiculed them, saying, "They're just drunk, that's all!"

> [14]**Then Peter stepped forward with the eleven other apostles** and shouted to the crowd, "Listen carefully, all of you, fellow Jews and residents of Jerusalem! Make no mistake about this. [15]These people are not drunk, as some of you are assuming. Nine o'clock in the morning is much too early for that. [16]No, what you see was predicted long ago by the prophet Joel: [17]'In the last days,' God

says, 'I will pour out my Spirit…. [21]And everyone who calls on the name of the LORD will be saved.'

[22]**"People of Israel, listen!** God publicly endorsed Jesus the Nazarene by doing powerful miracles, wonders, and signs through him, as you well know. [23]But God knew what would happen, and his prearranged plan was carried out when Jesus was betrayed. With the help of lawless Gentiles, you nailed him to a cross and killed him. [24]But God released him from the horrors of death and raised him back to life, for death could not keep him in its grip.

[25]**King David said this about him:** … [26]No wonder my heart is glad, and my tongue shouts his praises! My body rests in hope. [27]For you will not leave my soul among the dead or allow your Holy One to rot in the grave. [28]You have shown me the way of life, and you will fill me with the joy of your presence.'

[29]**"Dear brothers, think about this!** You can be sure that the patriarch David wasn't referring to himself, for he died and was buried, and his tomb is still here among us. [30]But he was a prophet, and he knew God had promised with an oath that one of David's own descendants would sit on his throne. [31]David was looking into the future and speaking of the Messiah's resurrection. He was saying that God would not leave him among the dead or allow his body to rot in the grave.

[32]**"God raised Jesus from the dead, and we are all witnesses** of this. [33]Now he is exalted to the place of highest honor in heaven, at God's right hand. And the Father, as he had promised, gave him the Holy Spirit to pour out upon us, just as you see and hear today….

[36]**"So let everyone in Israel know for certain** that God has made this Jesus, whom you crucified, to be both Lord and Messiah!"

[37]**Peter's words pierced their hearts**, and they said to him and to the other apostles, "Brothers, what should we do?" [38]Peter replied, "Each of you must repent of your sins and turn to God,

and be baptized in the name of Jesus Christ for the forgiveness of your sins. Then you will receive the gift of the Holy Spirit. [39]This promise is to you, to your children, and to those far away —all who have been called by the Lord our God." [40]Then Peter continued preaching for a long time, strongly urging all his listeners, "Save yourselves from this crooked generation!" (Acts 2:1-17,21-27,29-33,36-40 NLT)

Friends, did you understand Peter's sermon? He preached to the crowd in Jerusalem that God had sent the Messiah, Jesus, just as He had promised long ago through His prophets. Peter told them: You despised the Messiah whom God sent from heaven. You murdered Him by nailing him to a cross, but God raised Him from the dead. We are all witnesses of it. God has exalted Jesus to His right hand and has sent the Holy Spirit whom He promised. Repent and turn to Him! On another occasion, Peter preached: **All the prophets testify about HIM, that through HIS name everyone who believes in HIM will receive [forgiveness] of sins.** (Acts 10:43)

When the crowd heard Peter's words, they felt great pain in their hearts because they realized that Jesus of Nazareth, whom they had nailed to the cross, was the Messiah sent by God to be Savior and Judge of the world. That day many repented of their wrong thinking and put their faith in Him. These new disciples were baptized to give public testimony to the fact that they had been cleansed from their sin by faith in the death, burial, and resurrection of Jesus Christ. Being baptized in water did not wash away their sin – but it gave an outward sign of the cleansing that had taken place on the inside when they believed. And so the Scripture says:

[41]**Then those who gladly received his word were baptized.** There were added that day about three thousand souls. [42]They continued steadfastly in the apostles' teaching and fellowship, in the breaking of bread, and prayer. … [and] the disciples were filled with joy and with the Holy Spirit. (Acts 2:41-42; 13:52)

So on that very special Pentecost Day the church was born. The church is not a building or a religion. The word for *church* in Greek is *ekklesia* meaning *called out ones*. Listen to the apostle Peter's explanation of what it means to be one of God's *called out ones*:

> ⁹**But you are a chosen race, a royal priesthood**, a holy nation, a people for God's own possession, that you may proclaim the excellence of him who **called you out** of darkness into his marvelous light. ¹⁰In the past, you were not a people, but now are God's people. (1 Peter 2:9-10)

The moment you *stop trusting in your own works* and *transfer your faith to the Lord Jesus and His work*, you will become a part of the family God has called out of the nations to become part of His eternal family. Those who believe in Christ are called *Christians*. But not all who call themselves Christians are true followers of Christ. The true church of Jesus Christ is composed of all who, since that day of Pentecost, have been transferred from Adam's family to Christ's family by faith in Jesus and His perfect, finished sacrifice.

While the events of Pentecost we just heard about happened about 2000 years ago, to this day, the Holy Spirit still comes to live in the hearts of all who put their faith in Jesus. The Scripture says:

> ¹³**And you also were included in Christ** when you heard the message of truth, the gospel of your salvation. When you believed, you were marked in him with a seal, the promised Holy Spirit, ¹⁴who is a deposit guaranteeing our inheritance until the redemption of those who are God's possession—to the praise of his glory. (Ephesians 1:13-14 NIV)

Join us next time as we learn about *Jesus' return to earth*. God bless you as you think on what Jesus told His disciples:

> **You will receive power when the Holy Spirit has come upon you. You will be witnesses to me … to the uttermost parts of the earth.**" (Acts 1:8)

Jesus is Coming Back!

Revelation 19-22

We have come today to the 88th lesson in our chronological study of God's word. Over a period of several hundred years the Spirit of God inspired more than thirty prophets to write the first part of the Holy Scriptures, that is, the Torah, the Psalms, and the books of the prophets. That first part of God's Book is called the Old Testament, in which all the prophets pointed forward to the coming Messiah appointed by God to be the Savior and Judge of the world.

The second part of the Holy Scriptures, called the New Testament, tells the story of Jesus the Messiah – the only perfectly holy Person who ever lived. Jesus was full of the power of God, because He was the very Word of God in a human body. Of Him God declared, **"This is my beloved Son, with whom I am well pleased."** (Matthew. 3:17) Mankind murdered the holy One of God by nailing Him to a cross. But God raised Him to life on the third day. After Jesus was seen by many witnesses, He returned to heaven where God has exalted Him to the highest place. But the story doesn't end there.

This evil world has not seen the last of Jesus the Messiah. The word of God tells us that He will return to cast Satan and his evil angels into the lake of fire, judge the children of Adam, and make our planet perfect again. Your program today is called: *Jesus is coming back!*

We will be reading from the final section of the New Testament, from the book called *Revelation*. Revelation is a profound and powerful book, because it announces what will happen at the end of time. The book of Revelation has 22 chapters, which proclaim victory for all who believe in the Lord Jesus Christ. But these chapters also contain great terror for all who refuse Jesus as their Savior – it reveals how they will meet Him as their Judge. If you do not accept *the Lamb of God*, you will encounter *the Lion of God*, because the Lord Jesus, who shed His blood as the sacrificial lamb to take away sin, will return as a mighty lion to judge sin.

Now, let us listen carefully to some excerpts from the book of Revelation. After the Lord Jesus had returned to heaven, He sent His angel to the apostle John to reveal to him the events that will take place at the end of the world. In the first chapter, John wrote:

> ¹**This is the Revelation of Jesus Christ**, which God gave him to show to his servants the things which must happen soon, which he sent and made known by his angel to his servant, John, ²who testified to God's word and of the testimony of Jesus Christ, about everything that he saw. ³Blessed is he who reads and those who hear the words of the prophecy, and keep the things that are written in it, for the time is at hand. ⁴…Grace to you and peace from God, who is and who was and who is to come; and from the seven Spirits who are before his throne;… ⁵To him who loves us, and washed us from our sins by his blood—⁶and he made us to be a kingdom, priests to his God and Father—to him be the glory and the dominion forever and ever. Amen. ⁷Behold, he is coming with the clouds, and every eye will see him, including those who pierced him. All the tribes of the earth will mourn over him. Even so, Amen. ⁸"I am the Alpha and the Omega, " says the Lord God, "who is and who was and who is to come, the Almighty." (Revelation 1:1-8)

> ¹**After these things I heard something like a loud voice** of a great multitude in heaven, saying, "Hallelujah! Salvation, power, and glory belong to our God; ²for his judgments are true and righteous." … ⁶I heard something like the voice of a great multitude, and like the voice of many waters, and like the voice of mighty thunders, saying, "Hallelujah! For the Lord our God, the Almighty, reigns! (Revelation 19:1-2,6) The kingdom of the world has become the kingdom of our Lord, and of his Christ. He will reign forever and ever!" (Revelation 11:15)

¹¹**I saw the heaven opened, and behold,** a white horse, and he who sat on it is called Faithful and True. In righteousness he judges and makes war. ¹²His eyes are a flame of fire, and on his head are many crowns. He has names written and a name written which no one knows but he himself. ¹³He is clothed in a garment sprinkled with blood. His name is called "The Word of God." ¹⁴The armies which are in heaven followed him on white horses, clothed in white, pure, fine linen. ¹⁵Out of his mouth proceeds a sharp, double-edged sword, that with it he should strike the nations. He will rule them with an iron rod. He treads the wine press of the fierceness of the wrath of God, the Almighty. ¹⁶He has on his garment and on his thigh a name written, KING OF KINGS AND LORD OF LORDS. (Revelation 19:11-16)

¹**I saw an angel coming down out of heaven**, having the key of the abyss and a great chain in his hand. ²He seized the dragon, the old serpent, which is the devil and Satan, who deceives the whole inhabited earth, and bound him for a thousand years, ³and cast him into the abyss, and shut it, and sealed it over him, that he should deceive the nations no more, until the thousand years were finished. After this, he must be freed for a short time. ⁴I saw thrones, and they sat on them, and judgment was given to them. I saw the souls of those who had been beheaded for the testimony of Jesus, and for the word of God….They lived and reigned with Christ for a thousand years.

⁷**And after the thousand years**, Satan will be released from his prison, ⁸and he will come out to deceive the nations which are in the four corners of the earth… to gather them together to the war; the number of whom is as the sand of the sea. ⁹They went up over the width of the earth, and surrounded the camp of the saints, and the beloved city. Fire came down out of heaven from God and devoured them. ¹⁰The devil who deceived them was thrown into the lake of fire and sulfur, where the beast and the false prophet are also. They will be tormented day and night forever and ever.

[11]**I saw a great white throne, and him who sat on it**, from whose face the earth and the heaven fled away. There was found no place for them. [12]I saw the dead, the great and the small, standing before the throne, and they opened books. Another book was opened, which is the book of life. The dead were judged out of the things which were written in the books, according to their works. [13]The sea gave up the dead who were in it. Death and Hades gave up the dead who were in them. They were judged, each one according to his works. [14]Death and Hades were thrown into the lake of fire. This is the second death, the lake of fire. [15]If anyone was not found written in the book of life, he was cast into the lake of fire. (Revelation 20:1-4,7-15)

[1]**I saw a new heaven and a new earth:** for the first heaven and the first earth have passed away, and the sea is no more.… [3]I heard a loud voice out of heaven saying, "Behold, God's dwelling is with people, and he will dwell with them, and they will be his people, and God himself will be with them as their God. [4]He will wipe away every tear from their eyes. Death will be no more; neither will there be mourning, nor crying, nor pain, any more. The first things have passed away."

[5]**He who sits on the throne said**, "Behold, I am making all things new." He said, "Write, for these words of God are faithful and true." [6]He said to me, "I am the Alpha and the Omega, the Beginning and the End. I will give freely to him who is thirsty from the spring of the water of life. [7]He who overcomes, I will give him these things. I will be his God, and he will be my son. [8]But for the cowardly, unbelieving, sinners, abominable, murderers, sexually immoral, sorcerers, idolaters, and all liars, their part is in the lake that burns with fire and sulfur, which is the second death." (Revelation 21:1,3-8)

[1]**He showed me a river of water of life**, clear as crystal, proceeding out of the throne of God and of the Lamb, [2]in the middle of its street. On this side of the river and on that was the tree of life, bearing twelve kinds of fruits, yielding its fruit every month. … [3]There will be no curse any more. The throne of God

and of the Lamb will be in it, and his servants will serve him. [4]They will see his face, and his name will be on their foreheads. [5]There will be no night, and they need no lamp light or sun light; for the Lord God will illuminate them. They will reign forever and ever. [6]He said to me, "These words are faithful and true. The Lord God of the spirits of the prophets sent his angel to show to his bondservants the things which must happen soon."

[12]**"Behold, I [Jesus] come quickly.** My reward is with me, to repay to each man according to his work. [13]I am the Alpha and the Omega, the First and the Last, the Beginning and the End. [14]Blessed are those who do his commandments, that they may have the right to the tree of life, and may enter in by the gates into the city [15]Outside [is] … everyone who loves and practices falsehood. [16]I, Jesus, have sent my angel to testify these things to you for the assemblies. I am the root and the offspring of David, the Bright and Morning Star." [17]The Spirit and the bride say, "Come!" He who hears, let him say, "Come!" He who is thirsty, let him come. He who desires, let him take the water of life freely.

[18]**I testify to everyone who hears the words of the prophecy** of this book, if anyone adds to them, may God add to him the plagues which are written in this book. [19]If anyone takes away from the words of the book of this prophecy, may God take away his part from the tree of life, and out of the holy city, which are written in this book. [20]He who testifies these things says, "Yes, I come quickly." Amen! Yes, come, Lord Jesus. [21]The grace of the Lord Jesus Christ be with all the saints. Amen. (Revelation 22:1-6,12-21)

Thus ends God's book, the collection of writings that reveals the truth about God, man, sin, and salvation – from creation to Christ to new creation.

Dear friend, are you prepared for the day when you will stand before the One who loved you and gave Himself for you? Is your name written in the Lamb's Book of Life? The Scripture says:

> **If *you* will confess with your mouth that Jesus is Lord**, and
> believe in your heart that God raised him from the dead,
> you will be saved. (Romans 10:9)

Do *you* believe in your heart that on the cross the Lord Jesus Christ
suffered the penalty for your sins so that God can forgive you and
declare you righteous? Do *you* believe that He conquered death
and hell for you? Is your hope of salvation in Him alone? Then the
word of the Lord says that you **will be saved**!

What is your relationship with the Lord Jesus Christ? Is He your
Savior? Or will He be your Judge? The Scripture says:

> [8]**But don't forget this one thing, beloved**, that one day is with
> the Lord as a thousand years, and a thousand years as one day.
> [9]The Lord is not slow concerning his promise, as some count
> slowness; but he is patient with us, not wishing that anyone
> should perish, but that all should come to repentance. [10]But the
> day of the Lord will come as a thief in the night; in which the
> heavens will pass away with a great noise, and the elements
> will be dissolved with fervent heat, and the earth and the
> works that are in it will be burned up. (2 Peter 3:8-10)

> **Behold, now is the acceptable time.** Behold, now is the day of
> salvation. (2 Corinthians 6:2)

Dear friends, thank you for listening so attentively. Our prayer to
God is that what you hear on these *Way of Righteousness* programs
is a blessing springing up in your life, satisfying you and your
family and community with a clear understanding of God's gift of
salvation that He freely gives to all who put their trust in Him.

If you would like to receive a copy of the entire book of the Gospel
(*Injil*) from which we have read today, write to us.

God bless you as you think daily on Jesus' closing promise
found in the Holy Scriptures:

> **"Yes, I am coming soon." "** (Revelation 22:20 NIV)

The WAY of
RIGHTEOUSNESS

Summarized

"Come to me,
all you who are weary and burdened,
and I will give you rest."
– Jesus (Matthew 11:28)

Part 4

"How shall we escape if we ignore
such a great salvation?"
Hebrews 2:3

Program 89

The Good News

First draft of this program was written in Wolof
by Malick Fall, radio voice of *Yoonu Njub*[112]

I n our study in the book of the Injil (Gospel), we heard the Lord Jesus Christ, after He had risen, command His disciples: **"Go into all the world, and preach the Good News to the whole creation."** (Mark 16:15) And after Jesus was taken up into heaven, a man by the name of Paul (who was converted from being a brutal religious zealot to becoming a devout follower of Christ) wrote:

> [1]**Paul, a servant of Jesus Christ,** called to be an apostle, set apart for the Good News of God, [2]which he promised before through his prophets in the holy Scriptures.…[16]For I am not ashamed of the Good News of Christ, because it is the power of God for salvation for everyone who believes.… [17]For in [the good news] is revealed God's righteousness from faith to faith. As it is written, "But the righteous shall live by faith". (Romans 1:1-2,16-17)

The good news, the Good News! THE GOOD NEWS! What is this good news that the word of God tells us about again and again? Today, with the help of God, we would like to talk about this Good News proclaimed in the Holy Scriptures. But before we talk about *the Good News*, we need to remember *the bad news.*

What is the bad news? You may recall that in the beginning, after God created the heavens and the earth, He made Adam and Eve and placed them in the earthly garden of Paradise. God created them so that they might know Him, love Him, obey Him and glorify Him forever. Then, to test them, God said to Adam, **"You shall not eat of the tree of the knowledge of good and evil; for in the**

---

day that you eat of it, you will surely die." (Genesis 2:16-17) The bad
news is that Adam and Eve listened to the serpent, that is, the devil,
who tempted them to eat fruit from the forbidden tree. Adam and
Eve's sin brought trouble and death into the world, contaminating
them and all their offspring. As we often hear: *An epidemic is not
confined to the one from whom it originates.* God's word tells us the
bad news when it says:

> [27]**It is appointed for men to die once**, and after this, judgment.
> [14]The Lord is coming...[15]to judge everyone, and to convict
> all the ungodly of all the ungodly acts they have done in the
> ungodly way, and of all the harsh words ungodly sinners have
> spoken against him." (Hebrews 9:27; Jude 14-15 NIV)

The bad news is that we are all sinners facing God's judgment.

The Good News, though, began right there in the garden of
Paradise, where God, who is full of mercy, proclaimed that He would
one day send into the world a Person who would be unstained
by sin, born of a virgin. This holy Person, this righteous Redeemer,
would offer Himself to be killed as a sacrifice to pay for the sins
of Adam and all his descendants. The punishment we deserve for
our sin would fall on this sinless Redeemer. That is the Good News
which God announced on the day that Adam and Eve sinned.

God used many men to announce the coming of this Redeemer,
also called the Messiah. Each of God's prophets announced
something about the Messiah, so that when He came everyone
could recognize that He was the One whom God had appointed.
For example, the prophet Isaiah, who preceded the Messiah
by about 700 years, foretold how the Messiah would be born,
saying: **The virgin shall be with child, and shall give birth to a
son. They shall call his name Immanuel, which is, being interpreted, "God with us."** (Matthew 1:23; Isaiah 7:14) Another prophet,
Micah, prophesied that the Messiah would come from heaven and
be born in the village of Bethlehem. That is precisely where the
Messiah was born. Yet Micah prophesied this hundreds of years
before the Messiah's birth.

But the prophets did not merely announce the Savior's birth. They also prophesied that this Redeemer would suffer and die in the place of sinners. For example, the prophet David foretold that people would despise the Messiah, torture Him, pierce His hands and His feet, and kill Him. And David not only announced the death of the Messiah, he also predicted that God would raise the Messiah from the dead, thus proving that He was the one and only Savior whom God sent to save the children of Adam from the penalty of sin, which is death and eternal separation from God.

There is little argument over the birth of the Messiah, but many stumble over His death and resurrection. They do not understand how God could just stand by and watch as men humiliated the Messiah whom He had sent. What most people fail to grasp is that God, who loves us, is the very One who purposed that the Messiah should suffer like that for our sins. Yet that is what the prophets proclaimed, saying: **Yet it pleased the LORD to bruise him [as a sacrifice to pay for sin].** (Isaiah 53:10)

Do we believe the prophets? We say we believe them. But if we really believe the prophets then *we must believe what they wrote.* We must remember that the prophets did not proclaim their own ideas. It was God who planted in their spirits what they were to say. Therefore if we refuse to believe the message of the prophets, who are we really rejecting? Yes, we are rejecting God.

It is because God loves the world and does not want anyone to perish in sin that He planned the Messiah's death on the cross. It was necessary that a righteous Person die for unrighteous people to save them from God's judgment. That is what the offering of sacrifices of sheep and goats symbolized in earlier times. Jesus Christ, who was born of a virgin by the power of God is the final sacrifice from God. As it is said, *There is no need to draw a picture of a dwarf* (to depict what one is like) *if one is standing in front of you.*[113] Likewise, since we now have a perfect and permanent Sacrifice for sins, there is no need to weary ourselves

---

113 Wolof proverb; (Read Hebrews chapters 9 and 10)

by continuing to offer imperfect, symbolic sacrifices. Can you remember what the Lord Jesus declared on the cross just before He died? He said, **"It is finished."** (John 19:30) With His blood, He paid our debt of sin, once and for all time. The only thing that remains for us to do is to *believe it*. As we read: The Good News of Jesus Christ's death and resurrection **is the power of God for salvation for everyone who believes.** (Romans 1:16)

Sadly, many refuse to believe in Him, saying that this whole issue about the death and resurrection of Jesus is just a fable. Yet when we study the Gospel, we discover that everything the prophets foretold about the Messiah was fulfilled by Jesus the Messiah. Everything. Everything about His birth, His life, His death, His resurrection and His ascension. Thus, the Gospel declares **that Christ died for our sins according to the Scriptures [of the prophets], that he was buried, that he was raised on the third day according to the Scriptures [of the prophets].** (1 Corinthians 15:3-4) Everything happened just as the prophets predicted. Those who hated Jesus mocked Him, tortured Him and killed Him, and those who loved Him buried Him. But death could not keep Him in the grave. We saw that on the third day after His crucifixion some women got up at dawn and went to the tomb where Jesus was buried, and discovered that it was open and empty. After Jesus died and rose again, He showed Himself to His disciples over a period of forty days. More than five hundred people saw Him after His resurrection. It was true. The Messiah had conquered death, man's great enemy. Jesus' resurrection proved that God has accepted His sacrifice as a full payment for the sins of the children of Adam, so that everyone who believes in Him might share in His eternal life.

That is the Good News. Jesus Christ died to take away your sins, and He came out of the grave on the third day to give you and me eternal life. The purpose of this Good News is to save everyone who believes it. Therefore the question that you must answer is: Do I believe it? The Scripture says: **Now is the day of salvation.** (2 Corinthians 6:2) Do not harden your heart. Believe. Salvation is not a result of the works we do, because no one can do enough works to earn Paradise. God will never sell you His great salvation but He will give it to you! Good deeds, prayers and fasting may give you a good feeling inside, but they do not satisfy God's righteousness. There is only one way for you to enter God's Paradise. You must first recognize that *you are a sinner* and that you have no strength to please God. Then you must *believe that Jesus Christ is the Savior* that God sent to die on the cross to take away your sins and that God raised Him from the dead to give you eternal life. If you believe this Good News you can be sure that you will be taken to Paradise when you die, because God Himself has promised us in His word that we can know that we have eternal life, if we believe on the Name of the Lord Jesus Christ. (1 John 5:9-13

Let me pause here[114] to tell you how I became a believer in Jesus Christ. As a young man I was faithful to pray five times a day and to observe the yearly fast, but I did not know where I would go after I died. I asked all around, but didn't receive a clear answer. But when I studied the Gospel (*Injil*), I discovered that I could know where I would go after I died, because Jesus the Messiah Himself says in the Gospel: **"Most certainly I tell you, he who hears my word and believes him who sent me has eternal life, and doesn't come into judgment, but has passed out of death into life."** (John 5:24) He also said: **"I am the resurrection and the life. He who believes in me will still live, even if he dies!"** (John 11:25) Thus, I repented of my own efforts to save myself and believed in the Messiah about whom all the prophets prophesied, saying: **All the prophets testify about him that everyone who believes in him receives forgiveness of sins through his name.** (Acts 10:43 NIV) I took all my hope and hung it upon the Lord Jesus Christ. And from that time until now God has brought peace to my spirit. I no longer have a troubled conscience. My future is wonderfully bright because of the work of Jesus on the cross. In my life as a disciple of Christ, sometimes I face trouble and affliction because my faith differs from the opinions of my relatives and friends, but I have peace. The peace of God fills my heart and my mind. And Jesus who has given it to me says: **"If the world hates you, you**

---

114 What follows is Malick's personal testimony.

know that it has hated me before it hated you.… **Peace I leave with you. My peace I give to you; not as the world gives, I give to you. Don't let your heart be troubled, neither let it be fearful."** (John 15:18; 14:27) And friends, what the Lord has done for me and in me, He can do for each of you. He asks one thing from you: That you believe in Him from your heart. He will do the rest. For the Lord Jesus Himself has said, **"Come to me, all you who labor and are heavily burdened, and I will give you rest. Take my yoke upon you and learn from me, for I am gentle and humble in heart; and you will find rest for your souls."** (Matthew 11:28-29)

Are you weary and burdened because of your sins? Would you like to find rest for your soul? If you believe the Good News that Jesus the Lamb of God died for you and rose again for you, God will forgive you of your sins, judge you as righteous and write your name in the Lamb's Book of Life. If you believe this Good News, God will mark you as His own and send the Spirit of Jesus into your heart. The Holy Spirit, who lives in you, will change your heart, your life, and your way of living, because the Scripture says: **If anyone is in Christ, he is a new creation. The old things have passed away. Behold, all things have become new.** (2 Corinthians 5:17)

Friend, wherever you are, whatever your situation, whether you are a man or a woman, old or young, the Lord Jesus Christ can give you a new life – if you believe in Him. He died for you so that you might live with God forever. Do you believe this Good News?

May God bless you. We leave you with a verse of Scripture that expresses the peace and assurance God gives to all who place their hope in His Good News of salvation. God's word says:

> **For God saved us and called us to live a holy life. He did this, not because we deserved it, but because that was his plan from before the beginning of time—to show us his grace through Christ Jesus. And now he has made all of this plain to us by the appearing of Christ Jesus, our Savior. He broke the power of death and illuminated the way to life and immortality through the Good News.** (2 Timothy 1:9-10 NLT)

Program 90
Man's Questions and God's Answers

Part 1

Dear friends, we thank each of you who have written to us with questions about what the Holy Scriptures teach. We hope the letters, books and audio programs we have sent to you have been helpful. We also want to thank those of you who faithfully listen to *The Way of Righteousness* even if you have never written, called, or visited us. May God bless each of you with a clear understanding of His righteous way of salvation.

Today and in the next program, we plan to do something a little different. We would like to share with you some questions we have received from you, our listening friends. To answer each question, we will use the Holy Scriptures, since the word of God is the only sure light that can guide us through the darkness. As it is written in the Psalms: **Your word is a lamp to my feet and a light for my path.** (Psalm 119:105)

Now on to your questions. To help us today, a friend has joined us in the studio to read the questions.

1. Thank you. The first question, received in a letter, is:

> *What is the religion of those who produce The Way of Righteousness programs?*

Long ago God put it in our hearts to seek the truth – His Truth. We wanted to know for ourselves the word of the one true God. We wanted to know with absolute certainty that we would go to heaven when we die. We studied the Bible (which includes the Torah [*Tawrat*], the Psalms [*Zabur*], the Books of the Prophets, and the Gospel [*Injil*]). We recognized that Jesus the Messiah is the Savior all the prophets wrote about. God gave Jesus to be the perfect and final sacrifice to erase the debt of sin that weighs on all the children of Adam so that whoever believes in Him can live in the presence of God forever. Jesus Christ, who came from God, is the only one who can bring us to God. We have staked all our hope on Him.

Who are we then? We are disciples of Jesus Christ. The Qur'an calls us *Ahl al-kitab,* which means *the People of the Book.* Others call us *Christians*, meaning *Christ's people.* In telling you that we are Christians, we remind you that although many people call themselves Christians, not all of them are truly Christ's people. Just as *a log does not become a crocodile by soaking in water*, so a person does not become a Christian merely by doing the things that Christians do. Following a religion cannot give you a relationship with God. What gives us a relationship with God is when we believe and love the Lord Jesus Christ whom He sent into the world to die for our sins and to conquer death for us. How blessed we are to have Christ as our Savior, Lord, and Friend! He gives us a close relationship with God and confidence in the face of death. In the Gospel (*Injil*), one of Christ's followers put it like this: **"For to me to live is Christ, and to die is gain!"** (Philippians 1:21)

2. Thank you. The next question is important and deserves a clear answer. This person writes:

> Something really troubles me. I have read in the Qur'an where our prophet, Muhammad, commands all Muslims to believe certain books contained in the Bible such as the Torah and the Gospel. I respect the Bible and have started to read it. However, my father tells me that we cannot trust the Bible, because it has been corrupted and altered. They claim that the Bible today is different from the original Bible. What do you say about this?

Before answering this question, we have a few questions for those who claim that the ancient books of the prophets have been "corrupted and altered." *What is the source of the idea that the Bible has been falsified? What is the basis for such a serious accusation?* Tell us: *When was the Bible altered? Who altered it? Where was it altered? What changes have been made?* Can anyone give a single proof that the Holy Scriptures have been corrupted? If you honestly search out the facts about the Bible, you will discover that God has protected His holy word which He inspired His prophets to write. Those who claim that the Bible has been falsified are simply believing rumors. There is no evidence to support the accusation that the Bible has been altered. There is much evidence however to prove that the Bible has not been altered.

Today, in the great museums and universities of the world, scholars have preserved thousands of ancient scrolls of the Gospel Writings and the entire New Testament. Many of these scrolls existed hundreds of years before the time of the Qur'an, as did the scrolls of the Old Testament. If you compare those ancient books with the ones we have in our hands today, you will discover that God has preserved His word for us. The Bible we read today is the same Bible that existed long before the Qur'an.

The prophets wrote God's words on scrolls made from animal skin or plant fiber. Jewish scribes copied God's word onto new scrolls. These trained scribes were extremely careful to ensure that the copies were the same as the original text. The number of letters in a book was counted and its middle letter was compared to ensure that the copy was the same as the original. If there was an error, the entire scroll would be destroyed. These Jewish scribes believed that to tamper with God's word was to tamper with God Himself. Perhaps you have heard of the famous Dead Sea scrolls discovered in 1947. Did you know that these Old Testament scrolls were copied long before Jesus was born? Yet these ancient scrolls are consistent with scrolls copied one thousand years later. The Bible has not been altered.

No one can really alter the Bible. If someone wanted to change the Bible, he would have to change all the copies of the Bible, which, of course, would be impossible. In the period following the time of Christ, scholars began to translate the Bible from the original languages of Hebrew, Aramaic and Greek into many different languages. No one could change all the Bibles throughout the world. Today, the Bible (in part or in whole) is available in more than two thousand different languages. (Note: In English we are blessed with dozens of excellent translations.) God has preserved His holy word and His servants are translating it into the languages of the peoples of the world, because God wants everyone to hear it with their own ears, understand it in their own minds, receive it into their own hearts, and be saved.

Can the Lord God Almighty protect His word from Satan and those who want to alter and corrupt it? Indeed, He can preserve it and He has preserved it. *Allahu Akbar!* God is great! Of course, we are aware that from the beginning of the world until today Satan has attempted to alter the word of God in a more devious way: in the minds of people. For example, in the first book of the Bible, we heard God say to Adam, "The day you eat of this tree you will die." But Satan denied what God had said, telling Adam and Eve, "You will not die." Do you see how Satan attempted to alter the word of God? As you know, Adam and Eve chose to believe Satan and ate the forbidden fruit. As a result, their souls died and their bodies began to wither and die, just as God had said. Dear friends, God's word is sure. The devil is a liar and a deceiver. Satan wants to deceive people and make them believe that the Bible has been altered. But the Lord Jesus Christ says, **"The Scripture can't be broken."** (John 10:35) **"Heaven and earth will pass away, but my words will not pass away."** (Matthew 24:35)

3. Thank you for that clear answer. On to the third question.

> *Why do you call the prophet Jesus the Son of God? God does not beget and God was not begotten, therefore how can Jesus be His Son?*

We have answered this important question often, yet we will gladly answer it again; ignorance in such an important matter can be deadly. As the (Wolof) proverb says: *Before you know it, ignorance will kill you.* The questioner asks, "Why do you call Jesus the Son of God?" First, we must remind our listeners that *we* did not give Jesus the title *the Son of God*. God is the One who calls

Jesus His Son. Second, the name "Son of God" does not mean that God took a wife and begot a son. As we have seen, Jesus has hundreds of names and titles in the Bible. These names help us to understand better who He is. For example, He is called *the Door,* but that does not mean that Jesus is a door of wood or of sheet metal. He is also called *the Food which gives Life* (the Bread of Life) but that does not mean that Jesus is food like rice with fish which we take into our bodies. God's prophets called the Messiah *the Lamb of God,* but that does not mean He is a sheep. Similarly, when God calls Jesus His Son, you should know that this does not mean that God took a wife and had a child by her. That is blasphemy. If I leave the country, they call me "a son of Senegal" because I come from Senegal.[115] But that does not mean that Senegal took a wife and had a child. Similarly, God and the angels and the prophets called the Messiah "the Son of God" because He came from God's presence. Jesus was born of a virgin. He had no earthly father. Even before He was born, He was living in heaven, because He is the *Kalimat Allah;* that is, *the Word which was with God* in the beginning. That is what the Scripture declares:

> ¹**In the beginning was the Word**, and the Word was with God, and the Word was God. … ¹⁴The Word became flesh, and lived among us. We saw his glory, such glory as of the one and only Son of the Father, full of grace and truth. … ¹⁸No one has seen God at any time. The one and only Son, who is in the bosom of the Father, has declared him. (John 1:1,14,18)

Jesus is the eternal *Son of God – the Word of God* Who appeared on earth in a human body.

What is *the Word of God*? Perhaps you will answer that the word of God is the Holy Scriptures which God inspired the prophets to write. You are correct. The writings of God's prophets are God's word to us – like letters sent to us by God. But imagine you have a dear friend who lives in another town. Which would you prefer: that your friend merely write you some letters or emails or texts,

---

115 Reminder: the original *Way of Righteousness* radio series was produced in the Wolof language of Senegal, West Africa – and the radio voice is Senegalese.

or would you rather he come and visit you in person? Of course, you would prefer that he come in person, so that you can talk with him or her face to face. Similarly, since God is great and nothing is impossible for Him, and since He wants to make known to people what He is like and what His will is for us, do you think He would merely send us some letters or would He come in person to visit us? Friends, the good news which the prophets announced is that God Himself would come to visit sinful humanity.

In the Gospel, we discover that God has sent down His Word as a man to live among people so that He might save them from their sins. That Man from heaven is Jesus Christ. Jesus is worthy to be called the Son of God, because He is the Word which was with God in the beginning. Jesus is God's Eternal Son, God's perfect representative – the One who has revealed God's character to mankind. We often say of a young man, "He is just like his father." So it is with Jesus. Jesus bears the image of God. To know Jesus is to know God and what He is like. The Holy Scripture says:

> [1]**Long ago God spoke many times and in many ways** to our ancestors through the prophets. [2]And now in these final days, he has spoken to us through his Son. God promised everything to the Son as an inheritance, and through the Son he created the universe. [3]The Son radiates God's own glory and expresses the very character of God, and he sustains everything by the mighty power of his command. When he had cleansed us from our sins, he sat down in the place of honor at the right hand of the majestic God in heaven. (Hebrews 1:1-3 NLT)

One final word. God does not say that you must fully understand why He calls Jesus His Son – only that you must believe it. Remember that God is the One who inspired the prophet David to write in the Psalms:

> **Kiss the Son** (give Him homage and submission), lest He be angry and you be destroyed in your way, for His wrath can flare up in a moment. Blessed are all who take refuge in Him. (Psalm 2:12 NIV)

God is also the One who inspired the apostle John to write in the book of the Gospel:

> [30]**Therefore Jesus did many other signs** in the presence of his disciples, which are not written in this book; [31]but these are written, that you may believe that Jesus is the Christ, the Son of God, and that believing you may have life in his name. (John 20:30-31)

> **One who believes in the Son has eternal life**, but one who disobeys the Son won't see life, but the wrath of God remains on him. (John 3:36)

Thank you for listening. In the will of God, in the next broadcast, we will continue with more questions and answers.

God bless you as you consider this declaration from the Bible:

> **All flesh is like grass, and all of man's glory like the flower in the grass. The grass withers, and its flower falls; but the Lord's word endures forever.** (1 Peter 1:24-25)

Program 91

Man's Questions and God's Answers

Part 2

Today we will continue what we began in the last program: answering questions which we have received from you, our listeners. We thank each of you who have sent us letters. Before we begin, there is one thing that we need to make clear once again. In answering your questions, we dare not rely on our own knowledge or the knowledge of others. We rely on God's word alone. We do not have the answers to your questions, but God has the perfect answers and has given them to us in the Holy Scriptures. The Bible says: **The word of God is living and active, and sharper than any two-edged sword, piercing even to the dividing of soul and spirit… and is able to discern the thoughts and intentions of the heart.** (Hebrews 4:12 NIV) Now let us return to your questions. Again, we are glad to have a friend here to read them for us.

1. Thank you. In this letter a listener writes:

> *You said in one program: "That which is evil cannot come from God." I disagree with that, because I believe that God first created what is evil before He made what is good.*

We can answer this question with a question found in the Bible: **Does a spring send out from the same opening fresh and bitter water?** (James 3:11) Never! Just as a spring or a well does not give forth both fresh water and salt water, neither is God the source of both good and evil. The Holy Scriptures say:

God is light, and in him is no darkness at all. (1 John 1:5)

¹³**Let no man say when he is tempted,** "I am tempted by God," for God can't be tempted by evil, and he himself tempts no

one. ¹⁴But each one is tempted when he is drawn away by his own lust and enticed....¹⁶Don't be deceived, my beloved brothers. ¹⁷Every good gift and every perfect gift is from above, coming down from the Father of lights, with whom can be no variation, nor turning shadow. ¹⁸Of his own will he gave birth to us by the word of truth, that we should be a kind of first fruits of his creatures. (James 1:13-14,16-18)

God's prophet Habakkuk wrote: **"Your eyes are too pure to look on evil; you cannot tolerate wrongdoing.** (Habakkuk 1:13 NIV) Therefore since God cannot tolerate what is evil how can we believe that He can create what is evil? God created Lucifer as an angel, but Lucifer became the devil by choosing to rebel against his Creator. God created Adam, but Adam became a sinner by choosing to disobey God. The word of God teaches us that the devil and the unrighteous heart of man are the source of evil and that God and His word are the source of good.

2. The next question is:

If God is holy and full of mercy, then why does He stand by and watch the quarrels and wars and murders and wickedness of the world? Can't He do something to help people who are in trouble?

Indeed God is the Lord of Mercy, and what He should do to help people in trouble He has already done. He sent the Messiah to reconcile people to Himself and then to each other by dying for the sins of the world. However, before people can be truly reconciled among themselves, they must first believe in Jesus as the Savior whom God sent, and submit to Him. When our relationship with God is right, then our relationship with people can be right. Only then will there be true peace. Everything depends on our response to God. We must take the remedy God has provided. Also, remember that God will judge this world for its wickedness. The Lord Jesus Christ will return at the end of the age to judge all who refuse to accept and obey the truth. After the Lord Jesus has put down all of God's enemies, He will renew the entire creation. And then the Scripture will be fulfilled which says:

No longer will there be any curse. … He will wipe every tear from their eyes. There will be no more death or mourning or crying or pain, for the old order of things has passed away. (Revelation 22:3; 21:4 NIV)

3. The third question today is this:

Something troubles me. I've always believed that if I sin, that sin will affect me, but it will not affect my children because they did not commit it. But you say that the sin that our ancestor Adam committed in the Garden of Paradise spread to all of his descendants, and that God must punish them. How can this be?

The Wolofs say, *An epidemic is not confined to the one from whom it originates*; and: *The gazelle which jumps over (the underbrush) doesn't produce offspring that pierce through (it),* If you have a child, and you raise him in your own house, a lot of his character, good and bad, will come from you his parent. In many ways, he will reflect your way of speaking, your way of living, your way of thinking, and your way of doing things. All of us belong to the family of Adam and Eve. We have descended from those who disobeyed God's commandment. Are we not like our ancestors? Who among us can say that we have never departed from the way of God's commandments? We are all guilty. We were born with a nature that disobeys God's commandments. From whom did we inherit this disobedient nature? From Adam. Like an contagious disease, Adam's sin has spread to us all. Like it or not, that is the way it is. That is precisely what the word of God declares, when it says: **Therefore as sin entered into the world through one man, and death through sin; so death passed to all men, because all sinned.** (Romans 5:12) However, all hope is not lost, because the word of God also says: **So then as through one trespass [by Adam], all men were condemned; even so through one act of righteousness [by Jesus Christ], all men were justified to life.** (Romans 5:18)

4. The next question is:

Why is the Bible divided into two sections, an Old Testament and a New Testament?

In brief, everything that the prophets wrote in the *Old Testament*, that is, in the First Covenant, they wrote *before* the Messiah was born. Everything in the *New Testament,* the New Covenant, was written *after* the birth of the Messiah. The message of God's prophets who wrote the First Covenant was: *God will send the Messiah.* But the message of the New Covenant is: *God has sent the Messiah, just as He promised through His prophets.* We thank God that the Bible has two sections – a First Covenant and a New Covenant, since in those two sections, we can see that what God promised so long ago, He has accomplished. God sent a Savior, Jesus Christ, just as He promised our ancestors in the Torah, the Psalms and the other writings of the prophets. As the rivers flow into the sea, so the Scriptures of the prophets find their fulfillment in Christ.

5. Here's another question:

> *Many say that man cannot know whether he will go to heaven or to hell. God alone knows. But you say that you know that if you die today, you will go to heaven. On what do you base this claim?*

Again, let us respond with another question. Can God go back on His word? Is God faithful to keep His word? His word says:

> **All the prophets testify** about [the Lord Jesus Christ], that through his name everyone who believes in him will receive remission of sins. (Acts 10:43)

> **These things I have written to you who believe** in the name of the Son of God, that you may know that you have eternal life. (1 John 5:13)

Since God Himself has promised in His word **that you may know that you have eternal life**, who are we to say that no one can know where he is going to spend eternity? Yes dear friend, you can know where you will go after death. The question is: Do you truly believe in the Lord Jesus Christ and His perfect sacrifice? Or are you trusting in your own good works? Only those trusting in Christ can honestly say, "I know that I have eternal life."

6. Thank you. This listener asks:

Jesus announced that the Counselor, the "Parakletos," would come after Him. Of whom did Jesus speak?

Parakletos is a Greek word meaning *counselor, helper,* or *advocate.* In Scripture the name Parakletos is used both for Jesus (see 1 John 2:1) and for the Holy Spirit. (John 14:16,26; 15:26; 16:7) As we have read in the Gospel, before the Lord Jesus returned to heaven He promised His disciples, saying:

> [16]**I will pray to the Father**, and he will give you another Counselor, that he may be with you forever: [17]the Spirit of truth, whom the world can't receive; for it doesn't see him and doesn't know him. You know him, for he lives with you, and will be in you… [26]the Counselor, the Holy Spirit, whom the Father will send in my name, will teach you all things, and will remind you of all that I said to you.…[8]He will convict the world about sin…[9]because they don't believe in me… [4][Therefore] don't depart from Jerusalem, but wait for the promise of the Father, which you heard from me. [5]For John indeed baptized in water, but you will be baptized in the Holy Spirit not many days from now. (John 14:16-17,26; 16:8-9; Acts 1:4-5)

The Lord Jesus said that the Counselor was not a man, but a Spirit – God's Holy Spirit – whom no one can see. Jesus told His disciples that after He returned to heaven, God would send the Holy Spirit down to live in their hearts. A few programs ago we read how that is exactly what happened on the day of Pentecost, ten days after Jesus ascended to heaven.

In brief, the Counselor is the Spirit of Christ who comes to live in the hearts of all who accept the Good News. If you sincerely believe, the Holy Spirit will cleanse and renew your heart, mark you as God's own child, and give you a share in God's holy presence forever. That is what the Scripture declares, saying:

> [13]**You … having heard the word of the truth**, the Good News of your salvation—in whom, having also believed, you were

sealed with the promised Holy Spirit, [14]who is a pledge of our inheritance, to the redemption of God's own possession, to the praise of his glory. (Ephesians 1:13-14)

For those of us who believe, the Holy Spirit is our helper, our guide, our strength, our teacher, and so much more. He does so many things for us that we cannot begin to mention them all. One way He helps us is in our prayers. There is a big difference between reciting a prayer and truly praying to God. The Holy Spirit helps us to pray true prayers to God. As it is written: **The Spirit also helps our weaknesses, for we don't know how to pray as we ought. But the Spirit himself makes intercession for us with groanings which can't be uttered.** (Romans 8:26) All who truly believe the Gospel of Jesus Christ have this heavenly Guest, the Holy Spirit living inside them. The Scripture says: **But if any man doesn't have the Spirit of Christ, he is not his.** (Romans 8:9)

7. The final questioner writes:

I understand from your teaching that I will go to Paradise if I receive Jesus Christ as my Savior. Does this mean I can live just as I please and do evil things and still go to Paradise when I die?

The Scripture answers this question clearly in the book of Romans, chapter 6, where it says: **Shall we continue in sin, that grace may abound? May it never be! We who died to sin, how could we live in it any longer?** (Romans 6:1-2) The message of the death of Jesus the Messiah on the cross and His resurrection from the grave is God's righteous plan to deliver sinners not only from sin's penalty but also from sin's power. If you accept that Good News in your heart with a sincere faith, the word of God teaches that in the instant you believe God will accomplish two works in you:

First, God will forgive all your sins in the name of Christ, as He has promised. Second, He will renew your heart by the power of the Holy Spirit. You will begin to love righteousness and hate evil, because God has placed in you His holy nature. The Scripture says:

Therefore if anyone is in Christ, he is a new creation. The old things have passed away. Behold, all things have become new. (2 Corinthians 5:17)

[14]**[Christ] gave himself for us, that he might redeem us** from all iniquity, and purify for himself a people for his own possession, zealous for good works. (Titus 2:14)

When someone truly believes in the Lord Jesus Christ, he will no longer be able to enjoy a sinful lifestyle, because God has placed in him His Holy Spirit – and **the fruit of the Spirit [in the life of the disciple of Christ] is love, joy, peace, patience, kindness, goodness, faith, gentleness, and self-control.** (Galatians 5:22-23)

Our time is gone today, but, God willing, in the next program, we will look further into this important question of *how a follower of Christ should live.*

God bless you as you ponder this Psalm from the prophet David:

As for God, his way is perfect. The LORD's word is tried. He is a shield to all those who take refuge in him. (Psalms 18:30)

Program 92

How Should Christ's Disciples Live?

First draft of this program was written by Andreas Bode,
Paul's coworker in Senegal

As we promised in our last program, today we plan to look into how those who follow the Lord Jesus Christ should live in order to please God. The faith that disciples of Christ have in their hearts should affect the way they think, the way they talk, and the way they act – their whole way of living.

But before we consider the way a disciple of Christ should live, let us review what makes a person a true disciple. As we have seen, followers of Jesus are those who, first, admit that they are helpless sinners before God and that they have no hope of getting into Paradise by their own efforts. Second, they believe the plan announced by all of God's prophets, the plan by which God can forgive the sins of the children of Adam. That plan was the death of Jesus Christ on the cross. God delivered the sinless Redeemer over to death to pay the penalty for our sins and then raised Him to life so that He might judge us as righteous and give us eternal life.

In summary, the disciple of Jesus Christ is one who believes from the heart the Good News of Jesus the Messiah and knows for sure that the sins of all who believe in Him have been forgiven, as God has promised in His word. God adopts all such believers as His children. We find it written in the book of the Gospel that all who receive Jesus the Messiah and believe in His name are given **the right to become God's children,... who were born not of blood,... but of God.** (John 1:12-13) Dear friend, God wants you to know that if you become a child of God through faith in Christ and His sacrifice, you will never perish, and He will give you the right to live forever in His presence in Paradise.

Perhaps some would argue with this, saying: Ah, if entering Paradise is that easy for the disciple of Christ, then he[116] can live as he pleases and commit sin as he pleases, without any fear of judgment, because God has forgiven him of his sins already. Friends, this thought is absurd. Those who think like this do not yet know what sin is, nor do they know God the Holy One. Sin is a bad thing. Jesus Christ did not come to encourage us to continue in sin, but rather to deliver us from sin and its dominion. Whoever believes in Christ is no longer a slave of sin. Truly, only those who belong to the devil can thoroughly enjoy sin. The person God saves and forgives has a changed heart. God washes his heart and makes it clean. The person for whom God has done this will want to avoid all uncleanness. That is what the Scriptures declare, saying: **Therefore if anyone is in Christ, he is a new creation. The old things have passed away. Behold, all things have become new.** (2 Corinthians 5:17)

Tell us, if you are wearing a clean, white garment, will you sit in a filthy, dirty place? No, you will avoid anything that might stain your clothes. It is like that with everyone whom God has cleansed of his sins. You will no longer want to go along with anything that is not pleasing to God. You will want to please your Lord. If someone forgives you of a great debt of money, would you intentionally hurt him? No, you will do whatever you can to please him. So if the Lord God has forgiven you your great debt of sin and saved you from eternal punishment, should you not thank Him and honor Him in thought and word and deed your whole life long? The Scripture says:

> [3]**For we were also once foolish, disobedient**, deceived, serving various lusts and pleasures, living in malice and envy, hateful, and hating one another. [4]But when the kindness of God our Savior and his love toward mankind appeared, [5]not by works of righteousness which we did ourselves, but according to his mercy, he saved us through the washing of regeneration and renewing by the Holy Spirit, [6]whom he poured out on us richly, through Jesus Christ our Savior; [7]that being justified by his grace, we might be made heirs according to the hope of eternal life. (Titus 3:3-7)

---

116 The Wolof language does not have *he* and *she* pronouns.

¹⁴**As children of obedience**, not conforming yourselves according to your former lusts as in your ignorance, ¹⁵but just as he who called you is holy, you yourselves also be holy in all of your behavior; ¹⁶because it is written, "You shall be holy; for I am holy." (1 Peter 1:14-16)

How can we summarize the life of a disciple of Christ? Perhaps like this: God wants His children to show forth His character in their behavior here on earth. Simply put, God wants His children to be like Him. Well then, what is God like? In our studies in the Holy Scriptures we have seen two prominent characteristics of God. They are holiness and love. God is the Holy One. He is also the God of Love. So what is His will for each of us who belong to Him? He wants us to be holy as He is holy, and to love one another as He loves us. Holy lives and loving hearts distinguish those who belong to God from those who do not. God's word says:

¹⁰**In this the children of God are revealed**, and the children of the devil. Whoever doesn't do righteousness is not of God, neither is he who doesn't love his brother. (1 John 3:10) ¹¹For the grace of God has appeared, bringing salvation to all men, ¹²instructing us to the intent that, denying ungodliness and worldly lusts, we would live soberly, righteously, and godly in this present age; ¹³looking for the blessed hope and appearing of the glory of our great God and Savior, Jesus Christ, ¹⁴who gave himself for us, that he might redeem us from all iniquity, and purify for himself a people for his own possession, zealous for good works. (Titus 2:11-14)

²⁵**Therefore putting away falsehood**, speak truth each one with his neighbor. For we are members of one another. ²⁶"Be angry, and don't sin." Don't let the sun go down on your wrath, ²⁷and don't give place to the devil. ²⁸Let him who stole steal no more; but rather let him labor, producing with his hands something that is good, that he may have something to give to him who has need. ²⁹Let no corrupt speech proceed out of your mouth, but only what is good for building others up as the need may be, that it may give grace to those who hear.

[30]**Don't grieve the Holy Spirit of God**, in whom you were sealed for the day of redemption. [31]Let all bitterness, wrath, anger, outcry, and slander be put away from you, with all malice. [32]And be kind to one another, tender hearted, forgiving each other, just as God also in Christ forgave you. (Ephesians 4:25-32)

[1]**Be therefore imitators of God, as beloved children.** [2]Walk in love, even as Christ also loved us and gave himself up for us, an offering and a sacrifice to God for a sweet-smelling fragrance. [3]But sexual immorality, and all uncleanness or covetousness, let it not even be mentioned among you, as becomes saints; [4]nor filthiness, nor foolish talking, nor jesting, which are not appropriate, but rather giving of thanks. [5]Know this for sure, that no sexually immoral person, nor unclean person, nor covetous man, who is an idolater, has any inheritance in the kingdom of Christ and God.... [8]For you were once darkness, but are now light in the Lord. Walk as children of light. (Ephesians 5:1-5,8)

[7]**Beloved, let's love one another**, for love is of God; and everyone who loves has been born of God, and knows God. ... [20]If a man says, "I love God," and hates his brother, he is a liar; for he who doesn't love his brother whom he has seen, how can he love God whom he has not seen? [21]This commandment we have from him, that he who loves God should also love his brother. (1 John 4:7,20-21)

That is what the Scriptures teach about the way of life for all who follow Jesus Christ. Does all this mean that the disciple of Christ can no longer sin, or that he always loves his neighbor as he loves himself? No, he still commits sin, but he no longer lingers in it. When he sins, he can turn to the promise in the word of God that says:

[7]**The blood of Jesus… cleanses us from all sin.** [8]If we say that we have no sin, we deceive ourselves, and the truth is not in us. [9]If we confess our sins, he is faithful and righteous to forgive us the sins, and to cleanse us from all unrighteousness. (1 John 1:7-9)

Belonging to Jesus Christ is more than a religion; it is a relationship. When a person belongs to Christ, he is brought into fellowship with the holy God of love. That close relationship with God, which Adam and Eve lost because of their sin, is restored to us because Jesus paid our debt of sin. Through our relationship with Christ, God is our heavenly Father and we are His children.

Those who belong to Christ can enjoy a close relationship with God on earth and look forward to an eternal inheritance in heaven. But one might ask, how can the disciple of Christ enjoy this relationship which he has with God while he is still on earth? How can we grow in our relationship with God? God's word mentions *four responsibilities* (disciplines) which will help us know the will of God and live a life consistent with our position as children of God so that we might please Him in all things and increase in our knowledge of God.

1. The first responsibility of the disciple of Christ is to *feed on the word of God*, meditating on it daily and receiving it into our hearts with a desire to obey it. The Holy Scriptures reveal God's will for us. God talks to us through His word. God's word is the food that nourishes and strengthens our spirit. It is wonderful food. Whoever really loves God should not need to be urged to read or listen to the word of God, because we will hunger for it the way we hunger for food. The prophet Job said, **"I have treasured up [God's word] more than my necessary food."** (Job 23:12)

2. The second responsibility is to *pray to God*, our Father in heaven. Whoever wants to grow in their relationship with God will want to talk to Him often. For the disciple of Christ, prayer is talking to God, as you would talk to your best friend. There is no specific time that we must pray. We can speak in our heart language[117] to our heavenly Father at any time of the day or night. There should never be a moment when our minds are not conscious of God. He wants us to praise and thank Him continually for who He is and for all He has done for us. He also invites us to tell Him all our concerns. The

---

117 Literally in Wolof: the language we were nursed on

disciple of Christ knows that prayer is powerful. The Lord promised His disciples: **"If you will ask anything in my name, I will do it."** (John 14:14) and the scripture says: **In nothing be anxious, but in everything, by prayer and petition with thanksgiving, let your requests be made known to God [your Father].** (Philippians 4:6)

3. The third responsibility is to *fellowship with others* who love the Lord Jesus. As a lump of coal stays hot longer when left in the fire with the other coals, so our fellowship with other believers will help us to live for Christ and encourage others to do the same. God's word says: **Let's consider how to provoke one another to love and good works, not forsaking our own assembling together, as the custom of some is, but exhorting one another, and so much the more as you see the Day [of Christ's return] approaching.** (Hebrews 10:24-25)

4. The fourth responsibility of Christ's disciples is to *be His witnesses*. Before He ascended to heaven, Jesus commissioned His disciples: **"All authority has been given to me in heaven and on earth. Go and make disciples of all nations, baptizing them in the name of the Father and of the Son and of the Holy Spirit, teaching them to observe all things that I commanded you. Behold, I am with you always, even to the end of the age."** (Matthew 28:18-20) Amen. As disciples we are to tell others God's story and explain the Good News about His Son who died and rose again to give all who believe in Him a close relationship with God forever. Of course, our witness should not be limited to our words, but should be accompanied by lives of holiness and love. It is the change that Christ has made in our lives that will strengthen and confirm our message. As it is written: **For God's kingdom is not in word, but in power.** (1 Corinthians 4:20)

You who are listening, has there been a day in your life when you met the Savior, Jesus Christ, a day when He forgave your sins and renewed your heart? Do you love Him and people? Are you a true disciple of the Lord Jesus?

God bless you as you consider this word from God to His people:

You shall be holy; for I am holy. (1 Peter 1:16; Leviticus 11:44-45)

Program 93

Review 1: Adam:
The Problem of Sin

Genesis 1- 4

For a long time now we have been studying the scriptures of the prophets. We learned that God inspired more than forty men, over a span of more than fifteen hundred years, to write His word, the Book that reveals how sinners can be made righteous before God. We discovered that all the true prophets of God shared one idea and one message concerning that way of righteousness. What they wrote did not flow from their own minds but from the Spirit of God.

With the help of God, today and in the next three broadcasts, we plan to review and condense what we have studied in the Holy Scriptures. Our program today is called: *The Problem of Sin.*

So let us return to the foundation that God Himself laid, the first part of God's word, the Torah, which God put into the mind of His prophet Moses. Can you remember the first verse? It says: **In the beginning God created the heavens and the earth.** (Genesis 1:1) In this verse we saw that in the beginning, before the universe, angels and people were created, only God existed. God is the Lord of eternity, the eternal Spirit, the King of glory.[118] He has no beginning and no end. He is the All-powerful One who sees everything and knows everything. In the first chapter, we read how God, in six days, created the heavens, earth, oceans and all they contain. God prepared the earth for man, whom He planned to create. That is why, on the sixth day, God said:

---

118 To freely read, watch, and download the author's multi-language 70-scene picture book and the 15-episode movie *KING of GLORY* visit: **www.king-of-glory.com**

²⁶**God said, "Let's make man in our image,** after our likeness. Let them have dominion over the fish of the sea, and over the birds of the sky, and over the livestock, and over all the earth, and over every creeping thing that creeps on the earth." ²⁷God created man in his own image. In God's image he created him; male and female he created them. (Genesis 1:26-27)

Mankind is the most important of all the creatures that God created. God created man in His own image. God planned to have deep and wonderful fellowship with people. That is why He placed a spirit into the soul of the man and the woman so that they could know God, gave them a heart so that they could love Him, and entrusted them with a free will so that they could choose whether to obey God and to disobey Him.

In chapter 2 we read that God put the first man, Adam, into a vast, beautiful garden, full of trees bearing fruits beautiful to behold and delicious to eat. We also saw that God fashioned a woman out of a rib which He took from Adam and then presented her to him. Adam called her Eve. God blessed the man and woman and gave them everything they needed. Yet there was something God wanted to receive from them. What did God want from these two people He had created in His own image? He wanted them to love Him with all their mind, with all their heart, and with all their will, and thus to have a wonderful and increasingly deep relationship with Him forever. Consequently, we saw how God placed a test before them in order to reveal what was in their hearts.

God gave Adam this command: **"You may freely eat of every tree of the garden; but you shall not eat of the tree of the knowledge of good and evil; for in the day that you eat of it, you will surely die."** (Genesis 2:16-17) This is how God tested Adam, warning him that the consequence of straying from God's law would be death, that is, separation from God forever.

In chapter 3, the Scriptures recount that, one day, Satan, the angel who had rebelled against God, came to Adam and Eve as a cunning snake. He said to the woman:

[1]**"Has God really said,** 'You shall not eat of any tree of the garden'?" [2]The woman said to the serpent, "We may eat fruit from the trees of the garden, [3]but not the fruit of the tree which is in the middle of the garden. God has said, 'You shall not eat of it. You shall not touch it, lest you die.'" [4]The serpent said to the woman, "You won't really die, [5]for God knows that in the day you eat it, your eyes will be opened, and you will be like God, knowing good and evil." (Genesis 3:1-5)

What did God tell Adam and Eve would happen to them if they ate of the tree which He had prohibited? He said to them, "You will die." What did Satan say? He said, "You will not die." Whose word did Adam and Eve choose to believe and follow? Did they choose the word of God, or the word of Satan? They chose the word of Satan, God's enemy.

After that, what did God do? Did He just sit back and watch Adam and Eve? No. God did exactly what He had told them He would do. He summoned them, judged them, cursed them and the earth, and then put them outside the perfect garden He had created for them. On that sad day, Adam and Eve died in their souls. They became separated from God, the Source of life. The only thing they could expect now was physical death and eternal punishment, because the payment for sin is eternal death, just as God had warned them.

Truly, sin is a terrible calamity. Adam and all his descendants were separated from God by a single sin. Sin is somewhat like the virus called HIV and the disease called AIDS. As you know, AIDS is a sickness that people spread among themselves. It is a calamity that is all over the world. Once the AIDS virus enters a person's body, it will never leave him. Those who have AIDS can spread it to their children. AIDS is a killer, destroying all who have it. Sin is like that. Sin is everywhere, in everyone, and it causes people to perish forever. But thank God, there is a difference between the disease of sin and the disease of AIDS. With AIDS, there is no perfect cure for it, but there is a permanent and perfect cure for people contaminated by sin. God Himself has provided that remedy, which, if we use it, will cleanse us from sin forever.

Can you remember the wonderful promise which God made on the day that Adam and Eve sinned? Yes, on the same day sin entered the world, God promised that He would one day send to the earth a holy Redeemer who would make a way to get back the children of Adam from the destructive power of Satan and sin. We also heard God's announcement that this Redeemer would be born uniquely of a woman, because the Savior of sinners could not come from the descendants of Adam who were now contaminated by sin. He must come from the pure and holy Spirit of God.

Thus we saw in the Gospel [Injil] that thousands of years after God promised to send down that Savior, when God's appointed time had come, a perfectly righteous Man was born into the world; He had no earthly father; He was born of a virgin. His name was Jesus, which means *the LORD God saves*. Yes, Jesus Christ is the holy Redeemer whom God promised on the same day that Adam and Eve sinned. He is the one and only Savior.

Let us now return to our review of what happened on the day that sin entered the world. Can you remember what Adam and Eve did after they had eaten the fruit from the tree of the knowledge of good and evil? They wove together fig leaves, tying them to their waists in an attempt to hide their shame (because before they sinned they were naked and had felt no shame). Did God accept the clothes which they had made for themselves? No. Why did God not accept those clothes? He wanted to teach them that there was nothing that they could do to cover the shame of their sin before God. However, God did something for Adam and Eve. We saw how He selected some perfect, innocent animals, slaughtered them, skinned them, and made clothes for Adam and His wife. In this way God taught them that the payment for sin is death. God not only sacrificed the animals, but He also commanded Adam and his descendants to kill animals without blemish as a sacrifice to cover sin until the time when God would send the Redeemer down to earth.

That is how God showed them that there is only one way of salvation from sin: the way of the spotless sacrifice. The way of righteousness which God decreed required that sinners must choose animals without blemish and slaughter them as sacrifices which *cover sin*. These offerings illustrated the holy Redeemer who would come and shed His blood on a cross to pay the debt of sin for Adam's descendants. By such sin offerings God put before sinners a shadow of Jesus the Messiah, who would die as the perfect sacrifice to *take away sin*. In this way, God demonstrated that He is righteous, **that he might himself be just, and the justifier of him who has faith in Jesus.** (Romans 3:26)

In the chapter following the story of Adam's sin and God's promise to send a Redeemer, we read about Adam's first two children, Cain and Abel. We saw that Abel offered to God a lamb without blemish and slaughtered it as a sacrifice which covers sin, just as God had commanded. Cain tried to approach God by his own efforts, bringing to God fruits and vegetables that he had cultivated. But there was no blood. No death payment. That is why **the LORD respected Abel and his offering, but he didn't respect Cain and his offering.** (Genesis 4:4-5) Why did God not accept Cain's sacrifice? As we have seen, God's way of righteousness decreed that **apart from shedding of blood there is no [forgiveness of the sin debt].** (Hebrews 9:22)

Cain disregarded the way of sacrifice which God required. Cain pretended to believe God, but his deeds denied it, because he did not offer the blood sacrifice for his sins. That is why God rejected Cain and his sacrifice. But God accepted the sacrifice of Abel, forgiving him of all his sins, because Abel believed God's word and brought to Him the blood of a lamb. The lamb died in Abel's place.

Abel illustrates those whom God declares righteous because of their faith in Jesus the Messiah who shed His blood to pay for sin. Cain illustrates those who try to be righteous before God by their own efforts, refusing to accept the sacrifice of the Redeemer, whom God sent from heaven. To this day, there are only these two ways: *the way of Abel* and *the way of Cain*. Which way are you following? Have you accepted the way of Abel, that is, *the way of righteousness*, which is founded on the sacrifice of the holy

Messiah whom God sent from heaven to earth? Or are you still walking in the way of Cain, *the way of unrighteousness*, which is based on the works of man and the requirements of religion?

God wants us to know that He is righteous and cannot tolerate sin. God could not say to Adam and Eve, Cain and Abel, and all their descendants: "I know you've sinned, but that's O.K. It's no big deal, I'll simply forget that you ever sinned." Could God forgive sins in that way? Of course not. If God did that, how would sinners recognize His holiness? God is the Righteous Judge who must punish sin. The penalty for sin is DEATH. That is why the holy Redeemer had to die for our sins. When He died on the cross He paid the penalty for my sins and yours.

Listen to what is written in the Gospel about the way of righteousness planned and provided by God. The Scripture says:

> ²³**For everyone has sinned**; we all fall short of God's glorious standard. ²⁴Yet God, in his grace, freely makes us right in his sight. He did this through Christ Jesus when he freed us from the penalty for our sins. ²⁵For God presented Jesus as the sacrifice for sin. People are made right with God when they believe that Jesus sacrificed his life, shedding his blood. This sacrifice shows that God was being fair when he held back and did not punish those who sinned in times past, ²⁶for he was looking ahead and including them in what he would do in this present time. God did this to demonstrate his righteousness, for he himself is fair and just, and he makes sinners right in his sight when they believe in Jesus. (Romans 3:23-26 NLT)

Thank you for listening. Next time, God willing, we will continue to review the message of the prophets and recall how God called Abraham to be part of His plan to send the Savior into the world.

God bless you as you meditate on this statement from His word that can transform your life:

> **For the wages of sin is death, but the free gift of God is eternal life in Christ Jesus our Lord.** (Romans 6:23)

Review 2: Abraham:
Made Righteous by Faith

Genesis 6-22

Today we continue our review of the message of God's prophets. Their message is the True Story, God's story. It is the record of what the LORD God has done to seek and to save the children of Adam, who are lost in sin. In short, the message of God's prophets is the Good News about how unrighteous people can be made righteous before God. Our review lesson today is entitled: *Made Righteous by Faith*.

Like every story, the story contained in God's book has a beginning and an end. In our last study, we reviewed the beginning of the story and saw how the first person, Adam, chose to follow Satan, the enemy of God. Adam's one sin caused all of his descendants to be born in sin, on the path of eternal separation from God. Some try to deny this, saying: "Adam's sin was his own problem. It doesn't affect us." But those who say this ignore the scriptures of the prophets, which declare: **Therefore as sin entered into the world through one man, and death through sin; so death passed to all men, because all sinned.** (Romans 5:12)

Wolof wisdom says: *An epidemic's effects are not confined to the one who caused it*. Similarly, the curse of Adam's sin did not stop with him alone, but spread to us all, like a contagious disease. Adam's original sin is the reason that all men are born with a sinful nature. *A rat only begets that which digs*. Similarly, we have all inherited the nature of our forefather Adam. What is absolutely certain is that the sinful nature which is in us will condemn us forever – unless God provides for us a remedy. The good news is that the LORD

God has provided a remedy. As we read in the Torah, on the day Adam and Eve sinned, God, in His mercy, made a promise. He promised to send to earth a righteous Redeemer, who would be born of a virgin. This Redeemer would shed His blood as a sacrifice to pay the great debt for the sins of the children of Adam.

In our study in the book of the Gospel (*Injil*), we saw that when God's appointed time had come, He sent down the One whom He had promised. Who is this Savior promised and sent by God? He is the perfectly righteous man, Jesus Christ. Listen to how the word of God shows the difference between Adam, who sinned, and Christ, who did not sin. The Scripture says:

> [17]**For if by the trespass of the one**, death reigned through the one; so much more will those who receive the abundance of grace… reign in life through the one, Jesus Christ. [18]So then as through one trespass, all men were condemned; even so through one act of righteousness, all men were justified to life. [19]For as through the one man's disobedience many were made sinners, even so through the obedience of the one, many will be made righteous. (Romans 5:17-19)

That is what the Scripture says about those who are *in Adam* and those who are *in Christ*. We are all born in the likeness of Adam, but God is offering the children of Adam a way to be born again in their hearts, to put off the likeness of Adam, and to take on the likeness of Christ. How can this happen? It can only happen by **the obedience of faith.** (Romans 1:5) The Scripture says that if you repent of your wrong thinking and doings and believe in your heart that the Lord Jesus Christ paid for your sin, God will cause you to be born again by cleansing your heart and renewing you by the power of His Holy Spirit. You will become a new creation in Christ; you will no longer live for yourself, but for Him who died and rose again for you.

Now let us return to the Torah to continue our review by recalling how God advanced His plan to send the Redeemer into the world. In our chronological lessons we saw the first two sons of

Adam, Cain and Abel. Abel believed what God promised about the Savior who would come to shed His blood as the payment for sin, but Cain did not believe it. God called Cain to give account so that he might repent, but Cain only got angry and killed Abel, his younger brother.

After that, we saw that most of the children of Adam followed in the footsteps of Cain, reveling in sin, which is why when we come to the time of Noah, the Scripture says: **The LORD saw that the wickedness of man was great in the earth, and that every imagination of the thoughts of man's heart was continually only evil.** (Genesis 6:5) We saw how God purposed to destroy the children of Adam with a flood. In that corrupt and crooked time, Noah was the only one who believed and followed God's way of righteousness. Consequently, God commanded Noah to build a huge ship, one and a half times the length of a football field, which would be a refuge for his family and a pair of each animal kind. For a whole century God patiently endured sinners while Noah was building the ark. But no one repented and believed God's word except for Noah and his family. And so in the end, God, who is faithful to His word, did everything He promised, wiping out all those who refused to enter the ark of refuge which He had provided for them.

After that, we saw that Noah's descendants gradually forgot the word of God, because they too were children of Adam and sinners by nature. Then we read about the tower of Babel and how people tried to gather the peoples of the world to one place and to build a great city and a high tower in rebellion against God. However, God judged them by confusing their language and scattering them over the face of the earth.

Next, we came to the wonderful story of the prophet Abraham. Truly, Abraham had a very important role in God's plan to redeem the children of Adam from the dominion of sin. Abraham's father was an idol worshiper, and Abraham himself was a sinner like all of Adam's descendants. However, we saw that God, in His wonderful design, appeared to Abraham and ordered him to move out of his father's house and to leave his country. God planned to make of

Abraham a new nation, through which the holy Redeemer would enter the world. That is what we read in the Torah, in the book of Genesis, chapter 12, when God called Abraham, saying to him:

> [1]**"Leave your country, and your relatives**, and your father's house, and go to the land that I will show you. [2]I will make of you a great nation. I will bless you and make your name great. You will be a blessing. [3]I will bless those who bless you, and I will curse him who treats you with contempt. All the families of the earth will be blessed through you." (Genesis 12:1-3)

Why did God command Abraham to move to another land? God wanted to create from him a new nation. Why did He want to make of Abraham a new nation? Through that nation, God planned to raise up the prophets who would write the Scriptures. And through that same nation, He intended to bring into the world the Messiah. That is why God promised Abraham, **"I will bless those who bless you, and ... all the families of the earth will be blessed through you."**

Did God fulfill His promise to Abraham? Yes. When Abraham was one hundred years old, and Sarah, his wife, was ninety years old, God gave them a son, Isaac, just as He had promised. Isaac had a son, Jacob, who had the twelve sons who formed the new nation of Israel. Those of you who know the Holy Scriptures know that it was through the nation of Israel that the Redeemer came, because Mary (Jesus' mother) and Joseph (Jesus' adoptive father/guardian) were both descendants of Abraham. That is why the first verse in the Gospel says: **The book of the genealogy of Jesus Christ, the son of David, the son of Abraham.** (Matthew 1:1) As to His earthly life, Jesus Christ came through the descendants of Abraham, Isaac and Jacob. But as for His spirit and soul, He is the Son of the Most High, the eternal Word of God (*Kalimat Allah*) who came into our world.

Let us now return to the story of Abraham, because there is something else important to remember about him. We saw that Abraham was born in sin, like all the children of Adam. But the Holy Scriptures tell us that today Abraham is in heaven, in the presence of God the Holy One, where he will be forever. Now we must ask: What did Abraham do that moved God to forgive him of his sins, judge him as righteous, and welcome him into heaven? What does the Scripture say about this? It says that Abraham **believed in the LORD, who credited it to him for righteousness.** (Genesis 15:6)

Abraham believed the LORD God. Abraham believed God's words. That is why God credited him with righteousness, declaring Abraham to be forgiven and righteous! You who are listening today, do you believe the word of God as Abraham believed it? We are not asking if you believe that God exists, or whether God is One. The devil himself knows that God exists. What God requires is that you believe His way of salvation, as Abraham believed it. Abraham told us what we must believe. Do you remember what the prophet Abraham announced on that special mountain the day he offered the ram in place of his son? He said, **"God will provide himself the lamb for a burnt offering, my son."** (Genesis 22:8) And after he had slaughtered the sheep, he called that mountain **the LORD Will Provide.** (Genesis 22:14) Why did Abraham name that mountain *The LORD Will Provide,* when God had just provided the sacrificial sheep? Abraham, as a prophet, was announcing what was yet to happen. When Abraham said, "the LORD will provide," he was predicting what would happen on that mountain where the sheep had replaced his son on the altar. He was looking ahead to the day when, on that same mountain range, the Redeemer would shed His blood for all who believe in Him to save them from God's righteous judgment.

In our study in the Gospel we saw that the Messiah came into the world nearly 2000 years after the time of Abraham to fulfill Abraham's prophecy. Jesus told the Jewish religious leaders who wanted to kill Him, **"Your father Abraham rejoiced to see my day. He saw it, and was glad."** (John 8:56) Thus, it was outside the walls of Jerusalem, on the mountain range where Abraham sacrificed the sheep in place of his son, that the Redeemer, Jesus, shed His blood to ransom the children of Adam. That is why, after hours of indescribable agony on the cross, we heard Him shout,

"**It is finished!**" The word *finished* means *completed*. Why did Jesus say, "It is completed"? It was because His death on the cross completed the plan of salvation which God had announced long beforehand through His prophets. Jesus' death completed and fulfilled the symbolism of Abraham's sacrifice and of all animal sacrifices. It is finished.

You who are listening today, do you believe that Jesus Christ Himself is the perfect and final sacrifice sent by God from heaven to earth? Do you possess the faith of Abraham? Listen to what the Gospel says about Abraham's faith:

> [1]**What did [Abraham] discover about being made right** with God? [2]If his good deeds had made him acceptable to God, he would have had something to boast about. But that was not God's way. [3]For the Scriptures tell us, "Abraham believed God, and God counted him as righteous because of his faith."

> [21]**He was fully convinced that God is able** to do whatever he promises. [22]And because of Abraham's faith, God counted him as righteous. [23]And when God counted him as righteous, it wasn't just for Abraham's benefit. It was recorded [24]for our benefit, too, assuring us that God will also count us as righteous if we believe in him, the one who raised Jesus our Lord from the dead. [25]He was handed over to die because of our sins, and he was raised to life to make us right with God.
> (Romans 4:1-3,21-25 NLT)

Amen! We hope you will join us again for the next program as we continue our review of God's story and message, and learn from another well-known prophet whom God chose to prepare the way for the Savior of the world.

May God bless you as you think deeply on this wonderful statement from the Holy Scriptures:

> "**Abraham believed God, and it was credited to him as righteousness,**" and he was called God's friend.
> (James 2:23 NIV)

Program 95

Review 3: Moses: God's Holy Law

Exodus 1-20

T oday we plan to continue our review of the message of the prophets, the Good News which shows how sinners can be made right with God. We are still reviewing the Torah, the scriptures God placed in the mind of His prophet Moses. As we have seen, the Torah of Moses is of great value to all who desire to know the truth since it is the foundation which God laid so that we might verify everything we hear to know whether or not it comes from God.

In the beginning of the Torah we saw how our ancestor Adam sinned. His sin spread to all his descendants like a contagious disease, bringing sorrow, death and eternal punishment as God had forewarned. But the Scripture says: **But where sin abounded, [God's] grace abounded more exceedingly.** (Romans 5:20) Yes, on the very day that Adam and Eve sinned, God, in His justice, mercy, and grace, announced that He would one day send into the world a Redeemer to rescue Adam's race from the curse that sin brought.

In the last review lesson we saw that God called Abraham, promising to make of him a new nation through which the prophets and the Savior of the world would come. Abraham begat Isaac who begat Jacob, who begat twelve sons from whom came the twelve tribes of Israel. Let us now continue our review about how God used Abraham's descendants, the Israelites, as a way to teach mankind what the LORD God is like and which path sinners must take to escape His righteous judgment. Our program today is called: *God's Holy Law.*

In our study about the Torah, we saw that God allowed the children of Israel to become slaves in the land of Egypt for four hundred years, as He made known to Abraham beforehand. When the time appointed by God arrived, He sent Moses to the Israelites. Moses was an Israelite who had grown up in the house of Pharaoh, the wicked king of Egypt.

God sent Moses to Pharaoh to say to him, "The LORD God says: 'Let my people go that they may worship me.'" But Pharaoh refused and mocked, saying, "Who is the LORD? I will never let the people of Israel go." Then God made His power and glory known to Pharaoh and the Egyptians by means of nine terrible plagues which fell on all the people of the land except the Israelites. But the signs and wonders God did before Pharaoh did not cause him to repent and obey the word of Moses. God said to Moses, "I will bring one more plague on Pharaoh and on Egypt. After that, he will let you go." Do you remember what that plague was? Yes, it was the death of the firstborn in every household. And so we saw that the death angel killed the firstborn in the house of Pharaoh and in all the houses of Egypt. But the LORD delivered the firstborn of the Israelites because of the blood of the lamb which they, in obedience to God's command, had put on the doorframes of their houses. God Himself had promised: **"The blood shall be to you for a token on the houses where you are. When I see the blood, I will pass over you, and no plague will be on you."** (Exodus 12:13) Because of the blood of the lamb, God passed over the houses of the Israelites, protecting their firstborns.

As we have seen, the story of Passover has a deeper meaning than the deliverance of the Israelites from Pharaoh's dominion. The Scripture says: **These things happened to them by way of [illustrations for us].** (1 Corinthians 10:11) The story of the blood of the lamb which the Israelites stained on the doorframes of their houses so that God would spare their firstborns from death and deliver them from Pharaoh is an illustration. It illustrates the way of salvation established by God to save sinners from Satan, the taskmaster who is far more wicked than Pharaoh.

The word of God shows us that all the children of Adam are like slaves. Perhaps some of you are thinking, "Yes, we know that we are slaves of God." But that thought does not agree with what the Lord Jesus declared in the Gospel (*Injil*), saying, **"I tell you, everyone who commits sin is the bondservant of sin."** (John 8:34) And since all descendants of Adam are slaves of sin, they are also slaves of Satan because Satan is the master of sin. What is absolutely certain is that whoever is Satan's slave has no way to liberate himself. Can a slave free himself? Can he give something to his master so that he will allow him to go free? That might work with a good master, but it will not work with Satan. Like Pharaoh, Satan will never willingly allow his slaves to go free. Never! Oh, how we, the children of Adam, are cursed! Is there anyone who can deliver us from the dominion of Satan, who has made us his slaves? Yes! Praise be to God, there is a Deliverer! His name is Jesus. He is the One sent by God to liberate us. He is the powerful and righteous Savior who came from heaven, the One to whom all God's prophets point.

In the Torah, we read how God promised to crush the head of Satan through the holy Redeemer, who would be born of a virgin. In the Psalms, we heard how the prophet David wrote that this Redeemer, whom God calls His beloved Son, would be put to death in a terrible way – that He would be tortured and that His hands and His feet would be pierced. In the book of the Gospel we read great detail about this wonderful Redeemer. He is Jesus, the son of Mary, who lived a perfect life and then suffered and died on a Roman cross for our sins and rose again from the tomb. Yes, Jesus is the One who fulfilled what God's prophets had written long beforehand about this Savior of sinners.

God's word calls Jesus Christ **the Lamb of God.** (John 1:29) Like the lambs slaughtered on the day of the Passover, Jesus shed His blood to save us from judgment. About 1500 years after God delivered the Israelites by the blood of a lamb at the first Passover, God allowed the sons of Adam to put Jesus, the righteous Messiah, on a cross. And it was on the day of the Passover feast that He was nailed to that cross. Just as Jesus fulfilled the symbolism of

Abraham's sacrifice (*Id al-Adha*), so also He fulfilled the symbolism of the Passover lamb. The people who crucified Him that day did so in ignorance, but God had foreseen and planned that event before He created the world. (See Revelation 13:8; Acts 3:18)

Jesus is the perfect and final Sacrifice for sin. The blood of Jesus Christ is the legal price that God required to redeem the children of Adam from the dominion of sin. Accordingly the Scriptures declare:

> **Christ, our Passover, has been sacrificed in our place.**
> (1 Corinthians 5:7)

> [6]**For while we were yet weak**, at the right time Christ died for the ungodly. [7]For one will hardly die for a righteous man. Yet perhaps for a good person someone would even dare to die. [8]But God commends his own love toward us, in that while we were yet sinners, Christ died for us. (Romans 5:6-8)

Leaving the story of the Passover, let us now remember what we learned about the holy law, which God entrusted to the Israelites. In the Torah we saw how God revealed His holiness and glory to Moses and the Israelites in the wilderness, descending upon Mount Sinai in fire and thunder and lightning. That is where God gave the Israelites His Ten Commandments and many other commands, called *The Law of Moses*. God commanded the Israelites, saying: "You shall love the Lord your God with all your heart, with all your soul, and with all your mind: You shall have no other gods before me. You shall not make for yourself idols. You shall not misuse the name of the LORD your God. Remember the Sabbath day by keeping it holy. You shall love your neighbor as you love yourself. Honor your father and your mother. You shall not murder. You shall not commit adultery. You shall not steal. You shall not give false testimony against your neighbor. You shall not covet your neighbor's possessions." And to these commandments, God adds these words: **For whoever keeps the whole law, and yet stumbles in one point, he has become guilty of all.** (James 2:10) **Cursed is everyone who doesn't continue in all things that are**

written in the book of the law, to do them. (Galatians 3:10) The holy law that God transmitted to Moses condemns us all.

Listening friend, have you kept this holy law of God which requires you to be perfectly holy in thought and word and deed – from the day of your birth until the day of your death? Every day and every hour, night and day, you must love the Lord your God with all your heart, all your soul, and all your mind. Also, you must love your neighbor as you love yourself. Have you fulfilled this holy law? You and I know that we have not fulfilled it. The Scripture says: **There is no one righteous, no, not one.** (Romans 3:10) Not one of us has kept God's laws, because we were all born with a sin-bent nature.

Perhaps some would ask: If none of us can fulfill the law of Moses, why then did God give it to us? Does God want everyone to perish? No. God is Love, and does not want anyone to perish. Then why did God give sinners His holy commandments, when He knew that no one could keep them? What is the purpose of those commandments? God answers that question when He says:

> **Because by the works of the law,** no flesh will be justified in [God's] sight; for through the law comes the knowledge of sin. (Romans 3:20)

God gave His holy commandments to sinners to show us our sin and shame, and our need for the Savior who bore for us the curse and the shame that sin brought. Among all humanity, the Lord Jesus is the only One who kept the holy law God gave to Moses. Jesus was different from all other humans in that He did not share our sinful nature. Jesus is the Eternal Word who came from heaven to be born of a virgin. Jesus took on a body like ours, but did not take on our evil nature. That is why when He was on earth He could say, **"Don't think that I came to destroy the law or the prophets. I didn't come to destroy, but to fulfill."** (Matthew 5:17) Did you hear what Jesus said? It is a deep and wonderful truth. Jesus said that He came into the world to fulfill the holy law which God had entrusted to Moses. Do you understand what this means? Jesus did for us what we, the children of Adam, could never do for ourselves.

He kept God's holy law, and then He suffered and died on the cross to bear the curse of the law for lawbreakers like me and you – to save us from God's righteous judgment.

Jesus did not deserve to die, because He had never sinned. But to complete the plan of salvation which God had promised through the prophets, the Lord Jesus, of His own will freely gave His life for us. And after He shed His blood to pay our debt of sin, God raised Him from the dead on the third day. Listen to what the Holy Scripture declares about this:

> [1]**There is therefore now no condemnation** to those who are in Christ Jesus....[3]For what the law couldn't do, in that it was weak through the flesh, God did, sending his own Son in the likeness of sinful flesh and for sin, he condemned sin in the flesh. (Romans 8:1,3)

Listening friend, on what are you hanging your hope? Are you relying on the Good News of God about the righteous Redeemer who bore the punishment for your sins? Or are you still relying on your own good works? The word of God declares:

> [10]**For as many as are of the works of the law** are under a curse. For it is written, "Cursed is everyone who doesn't continue in all things that are written in the book of the law, to do them." ... [13][However, Jesus] Christ redeemed us from the curse of the law, having become a curse for us…that whoever believes in him should not perish, but have eternal life. (Galatians 3:10,13; John 3:16)

In the coming study, God willing, we will complete our review of the scriptures of the prophets and see how Jesus the Messiah fulfilled all that the prophets foretold about Him and opened a door of salvation and peace for the children of Adam.

May God give you insight into what we have studied today as you think on this promise from His word:

> **There is therefore now no condemnation to those who are in Christ Jesus.** (Romans 8:1)

Review 4: Jesus Christ: It Is Finished!

John 19, Hebrews 10

Three programs ago we began to review the message of the prophets of God. Today, we plan to conclude our review. This final part is called: *It is finished!*

As we have seen, God's book is in two sections, the Old Covenant, and the New Covenant. The Old (First) Covenant is the first section of God's wonderful Book. It contains the Torah (*Tawrat*), the Psalms (*Zabur*) and the other writings of the prophets. We saw in this first section of God's Book how our ancestor Adam disobeyed God, thus bringing all his descendants into the kingdom of Satan. However, we also learned that God promised to send down to the children of Adam a powerful Savior, to bring back into the kingdom of God all who believe in Him. This wonderful promise was an important part of the First Covenant (agreement).

To set in motion His plan to send down the Savior, God called Abraham in his old age and said to him, **"I will make of you a great nation. … All the families of the earth will be blessed through you."** (Genesis 12:2-3) Then we saw how God made Abraham the father of the nation of Israel. It was to that nation that God entrusted the writings of the prophets. For fifteen hundred years God sent to the Israelites His word, which He placed in the minds of many different men to write, from the prophet Moses to the prophet John. Through these prophets God reproved the unrighteousness of the children of Adam and revealed to them the coming of the holy Redeemer who would pour out His blood to pay their debt of sin.

As we have seen, the Old Covenant which God established with sinners required the sacrifice of animals. It declared that **without the shedding of blood there is no forgiveness of sin–because the payment of sin is death!** But the sacrifice of animals, which people carried out from the very first generation, could not really pay for sin, because the value of an animal and the value of a human are unequal. For example, if I have a toy car, can I go to the car dealer, and exchange it for a real car, let's say, a Mercedes? Of course not. Why not? Because the value of my toy car is not equal to the value of a real car. Similarly, the sacrifice of animals, which God required in early generations, could not remove sin because the value of an animal and the value of a human are not equal. As we have seen, animal sacrifices were only illustrations (symbols) awaiting the time when God would send down the actual sacrifice: the righteous Redeemer, who brought in the New Covenant. Animal sacrifices could only cover sins; they could not remove sins permanently.

The second part of God's Book is called the New Covenant or the Gospel (*Injil*). It tells us about the covenant (agreement) which God established with mankind through the blood of the Redeemer who came from heaven. The book of the Gospel is the story of Jesus the Redeemer, who fulfilled the symbolism of all the animal sacrifices when He shed his blood on the cross so that we might receive forgiveness of sins. Why did the Redeemer have to come from heaven? It was because every descendant of Adam bears the burden of sin. A sinner cannot redeem a sinner. To illustrate, can a woman who is carrying a basin of water on her head carry on her head a basin for someone else too? No. Likewise a sinner cannot bear sin's punishment for another sinner. But the Redeemer, Jesus Christ, whom God sent down, did not carry any burden of sin because He was the pure Son of God, the Word that was with God in the beginning. Because He was born of a virgin He had a body like ours but He did not have our evil nature. He did not have the burden of sin upon Him. That is why God could place on Him the sin burden of us all. Jesus the Holy One died for our transgressions and three days later, He rose from the dead to give us new life. He overcame the grave, death, sin, and Satan.

We were all born in the deep pit of sin and there is no one who can come to our rescue except the Messiah who came from above. If you hang your hope on Him, He will pull you out of that pit. He came from heaven to rescue the children of Adam from their sins, and now He has returned to heaven to mediate for those who believe in Him. That is what the Scripture says:

> [5]**For there is one God, and one mediator** between God and men, the man Christ Jesus, [6]who gave himself as a ransom for all, the testimony in its own times. (1 Timothy 2:5-6) [26]**For** such a high priest was fitting for us: holy, guiltless, undefiled, separated from sinners…. [3]When he had by himself purified us of our sins, sat down on the right hand of the Majesty on high. (Hebrews 7:26; 1:3)

As we saw in the Gospel, when Jesus the Messiah was on earth, some believed in Him. Those who recognized who Jesus was rejoiced greatly. They knew that for thousands of years God's prophets had been announcing the coming of the Messiah and now they were seeing Him with their own eyes. Among Jesus' disciples we heard those who sought out their relatives and friends and told them, **"We have found the Messiah! …We have found him, of whom Moses in the law, and the prophets, wrote!"** (John 1:41,45)

Tragically, most people living in Jesus' day did not recognize who He really was. Accordingly, the Scripture declares:

> [2]**The [Word who] was in the beginning with God** …[14]became flesh, and lived among us…. [5]The light shines in the darkness, and the darkness hasn't overcome it…. [10]He was in the world, and the world was made through him, and the world didn't recognize him. [11]He came to his own, and those who were his own didn't receive him." (John 1:2,14,5,10-11)

As we have seen, many people witnessed the signs and miracles which the Messiah did. Jesus had power over diseases, storms, demons, sin and death, yet most people did not recognize who

Jesus was because Satan had blinded their minds. The crowds touched Him and pressed in on Him but did not really know Him. They considered Him a prophet among the prophets, but they did not believe that all the fullness of God dwelt in Him.

As for the religious leaders of the Jews, we saw that they utterly rejected Jesus. They were extremely jealous of Him, and in the end they killed Him by having Him nailed to a cross. But that is how God planned it from the beginning; the death of the Messiah on the cross was according to His holy plan which He had announced long beforehand through His prophets. That is why, on the night when the priests arrested Jesus to have Him put to death, Jesus said to Peter, who wanted to protect Him, **"Or do you think that I couldn't ask my Father, and he would even now send me more than twelve legions of angels? How then would the Scriptures be fulfilled that it must be so?"** (Matthew 26:53-54)

Jesus knew why He had come into the world. He came to give His life, to shed His blood for sinners, as the prophets had foretold. Jesus came so that what was symbolized by Abraham's sacrificial ram and by all animal sacrifices might be fulfilled in Him. Can you remember what Jesus declared from the cross before He died? Yes, Jesus cried out with a loud voice, **"It is finished!"** (John 19:30) and then He died. The moment He died, the curtain hiding the Holiest Place of the temple was torn in two from top to bottom. The curtain of the Holiest Place in the temple, where they sprinkled the blood of the animal sacrifices each year to cover sin – why was it torn in two? Jesus declared, "It is finished!" and God tore that curtain in two so that everyone might know that it is by the blood of Jesus that God forgives the children of Adam their sins and gives them the authority to dwell in God's holy presence forever.

By His death, the Lord Jesus Christ fulfilled the words of the prophets and the symbolism of the animal sacrifices. And His resurrection on the third day gave proof that God accepted His sacrifice as the full price to pay for our sins forever. Jesus Christ is the perfect sacrifice which God provided for the world, so that whoever believes in Him will not perish, but have eternal life.

Now then, to finish our review of the message of the prophets, let's read some profound verses from God's word about the perfect and final sacrifice that Jesus the Messiah gave when He shed His blood on the cross to pay for sins. The Scripture says:

> [1]**For the law, having a shadow of the good to come**, not the very image of the things, can never with the same sacrifices year by year, which they offer continually, make perfect those who draw near. [2]Or else wouldn't they have ceased to be offered, because the worshipers, having been once cleansed, would have had no more consciousness of sins? [3]But in those sacrifices there is a yearly reminder of sins. [4]For it is impossible that the blood of bulls and goats should take away sins.

> [5]**Therefore when he comes into the world**, he says, "You didn't desire sacrifice and offering, but you prepared a body for me. [6]You had no pleasure in whole burnt offerings and sacrifices for sin. [7]Then I said, 'Behold, I have come …to do your will, O God.'" … [9]He takes away the first, that he may establish the second, [10]by which will we have been sanctified through the offering of the body of Jesus Christ once for all. [11]Every priest indeed stands day by day serving and offering often the same sacrifices which can never take away sins, [12]but he, when he had offered one sacrifice for sins forever, sat down on the right hand of God, [13]from that time waiting until his enemies are made the footstool of his feet. [14]For by one offering he has perfected forever those who are being sanctified. [15]The Holy Spirit also testifies to us, for after saying, [16]"This is the covenant that I will make with them: 'After those days,' says the Lord, 'I will put my laws on their heart, I will also write them on their mind;'" then he says, [17]"I will remember their sins and their iniquities no more." [18]Now where remission of these is, there is no more offering for sin.

> [19]**Having therefore, brothers,**[119] **boldness to enter** into the holy place by the blood of Jesus, [20]by the way which he

---

119 The word *"brothers"* here refers to all men, women, and children who are trusting in the Lord Jesus Christ as their personal Savior.

dedicated for us, a new and living way, through the veil, that is to say, his flesh, [21]and having a great priest over God's house, [22]let's draw near with a true heart in fullness of faith. ... [23]Let's hold fast the confession of our hope without wavering; for he who promised is faithful. ...

[26]**For if we sin willfully** after we have received the knowledge of the truth, there remains no more a sacrifice for sins, [27]but a certain fearful expectation of judgment, and a fierceness of fire which will devour the adversaries. [28]A man who disregards Moses' law dies without compassion on the word of two or three witnesses. [29]How much worse punishment do you think he will be judged worthy of who has trodden under foot the Son of God, and has counted the blood of the covenant with which he was sanctified an unholy thing, and has insulted the Spirit of grace? [30]For we know him who said, "Vengeance belongs to me. I will repay," says the Lord. Again, "The Lord will judge his people." [31]It is a fearful thing to fall into the hands of the living God. (Hebrews 10:1-7,9-23,26-31)

We who have heard this how shall we escape if we ignore such a great salvation? (Hebrews 2:3 NIV)

This is God's warning to the world not to ignore the One and Only Way of Salvation that He has provided. Whoever disdains the Sacrifice which God has provided by sending His Son, His Word the Messiah Jesus, needs to know that there is no other sacrifice for sins; there is nothing left except the judgment of God, which will be without mercy!

Friend, do you realize that Jesus has paid for your sins? Do you believe that He finished the work of salvation for you? Or are you still trying to save yourself by your own works that are polluted from their very source? How will you stand before a holy God?

Until next time, may God bless you as you consider the deep meaning of the Messiah's victorious cry from the cross:

"It is finished!" (John 19:30)

Program 97

Hell

Luke 16

The Holy Scripture says: **But for the cowardly, unbelieving, sinners…and all liars, their part is in the lake that burns with fire and sulfur.…** (Revelation 21:8) **[They] will be thrown out into the outer darkness. There will be weeping and gnashing of teeth. … Into the eternal fire which is prepared for the devil and his angels.** (Matthew 8:12; 25:41) **These will go away into eternal punishment, but the righteous into eternal life.** (Matthew 25:46)

Hell! No one likes to talk about it. We don't even want to think about it! But the topic of hell is what we plan to study today, because God has much to say about it. In the Holy Scriptures God has given hundreds of warnings so that people might not go there. Today and in the next lesson, we plan to learn what the Scriptures teach concerning hell and heaven (Paradise), and how we can be sure that we will go to heaven and not be sent to hell. Many people think that no one can know what will happen in the hereafter, or where they will spend eternity. They think that way because they do not know about the gift of salvation that God has provided for all who receive it by faith. Does the word of God tell us how we can know for sure that we will go to heaven and not to hell when we die? Absolutely. God's word says: **These things I have written to you who believe in the name of the Son of God, that you may KNOW that you have eternal life.** (1 John 5:13)

Listening friend, do you *know* that you have God's eternal life that His word offers? On the day that you die, do you know where your soul will go? Are you sure that you will enter Paradise and not be sent to Hell? If you do not have that assurance, our lesson today should be of great interest to you.

As we have seen in the Gospel, when Jesus the Savior was on earth, He often taught people about the place called Heaven and warned people about the place called Hell. Let us return to the Gospel to hear a true story Jesus told about two people who died, one who went to heaven and the other who went to hell. In the Gospel of Luke, chapter 16, Jesus spoke to the crowd, saying:

> [19]**"There was a rich man** who was dressed in purple and fine linen and lived in luxury every day. [20]At his gate was laid a beggar named Lazarus, covered with sores [21]and longing to eat what fell from the rich man's table. Even the dogs came and licked his sores.
>
> [22]**The time came when the beggar died** and the angels carried him to Abraham's side. The rich man also died and was buried. [23]In Hades,[120] where he was in torment, he looked up and saw Abraham far away, with Lazarus by his side. (Luke 16:19-23 NIV)

Let us pause here. Did you hear what happened to the rich man and to the beggar, Lazarus? Where did the beggar go when he died? Instantly his soul was in Paradise, in the presence of God, where the prophet of God Abraham also was. And the rich man, where did he go? Instantly, his soul was in hell, in torment.

Why did the beggar, Lazarus, go to Paradise and the rich man go to hell? First, know that being poor does not mean you will be saved, and having great riches does not mean that you will perish. Lazarus, the poor man, went to Paradise because he paid attention to the way of salvation which God announced in the writings of the prophets. As for the rich man, he ignored the word of God. That rich man was like many people today who are outwardly religious. They know that there is one God and that the writings of the prophets exist, but they are on the path to hell because they have never cared about the way of salvation presented in the Scriptures of the prophets. Like the rich man in our story, making money and having a good time is more important to them than listening to the word of truth, which can save their souls.

---

120 *Hades* is the Greek word for *"the unseen place,"* the present abode of departed spirits.

Let us continue with the story and hear how God allowed the rich man, who was in hell, to converse with the prophet Abraham, who was in Paradise. God wants us to learn from their conversation. Jesus said,

> [23]**"In Hades, where he was in torment**, he looked up and saw Abraham far away, with Lazarus by his side. [24]So he called to him, 'Father Abraham, have pity on me and send Lazarus to dip the tip of his finger in water and cool my tongue, because I am in agony in this fire.'

> [25]**"But Abraham replied**, 'Son, remember that in your lifetime you received your good things, while Lazarus received bad things, but now he is comforted here and you are in agony. [26]And besides all this, between us and you a great chasm has been set in place, so that those who want to go from here to you cannot, nor can anyone cross over from there to us.'

> [27]**"[The rich man] answered**, 'Then I beg you, father, send Lazarus to my family, [28]for I have five brothers. Let him warn them, so that they will not also come to this place of torment.'

> [29]**"Abraham replied, 'They have Moses and the Prophets**; let them listen to them.' [30]" 'No, father Abraham,' he said, 'but if someone from the dead goes to them, they will repent.' [31]"He said to him, 'If they do not listen to Moses and the Prophets, they will not be convinced even if someone rises from the dead.' " (Luke 16:23-31 NIV)

This is where the story of the rich man and Lazarus ends – and continues forever! Hell is a place where there is no mercy. No one could relieve the rich man's suffering, not even by giving him a drop of water. And this same rich man is still there today, awaiting the Day of Judgment when his soul and his body will be thrown into the place called *the lake of fire*. There he will be forever with all who died in their sins. The Scripture says: **If anyone was not found written in the book of life, he was cast into the lake of fire…[with] sulphur.…The smoke of their torment goes up forever and ever. They have no rest day and night.** (Revelation 20:15; 14:10-11)

Think of it! *Forever!* Everyone who has ignored God's righteous way of salvation and enters hell will *never* cease to exist, will *never* get out, and the fire will *never* be quenched. *Never!*

Some think that after sinners have suffered in hell for a time, they will get out and go to Paradise. But in hell and in heaven the element we call *"time"* does not exist. Both are places of an everlasting "now." As humans, we cannot grasp the concept of *eternity*. It is another dimension. Hell is a place of **eternal punishment** (Matthew 25:46) and the moment souls enter it, they will understand its solemn logic. There is no escape. That is why in the writings of the prophets there are no prayers for the dead. Praying for the dead comes purely from man's traditions. God's word says: **It is appointed for men to die once, and after this, judgment.** (Hebrews 9:27) Praying for the dead cannot relieve the sufferings of those in hell, nor can it save them in the Day of Judgment. Concerning those who are in heaven, they do not need our prayers, because they are in the presence of God and in perfect bliss.

Dear listeners, do not allow anyone to deceive you with empty words. Some people say, "Ah, God is good. He would not create his servants and then burn them. He will have mercy on us all and receive us into Paradise." Those who talk this way do not base their thoughts on God's word. They only say this to appease their consciences since they are willfully ignoring the way of salvation that God Himself has established. If they do not turn from their wrong ideas, and turn to God and believe His way of righteousness through Jesus Christ, one day they will know the reality of hell.

Did you hear what the rich man asked of Abraham? He asked him to send Lazarus to his father's house to warn his five brothers, who had not yet died, so that they would not also come to this place of torment. How did Abraham respond to him? He told him, "'**They have Moses and the Prophets; let them listen to them.' 'No, father Abraham,' he said, 'but if someone from the dead goes to them, they will repent.' "He said to him, 'If they do not listen to Moses and the Prophets, they will not be convinced even if someone rises from the dead.'"** (Luke 16:29-31 NIV)

Listening friends, do you know the Good News of God's prophets which can save you from hell? Seven hundred years before the Messiah came into the world, the prophet Isaiah put it like this: **All we like sheep have gone astray. Everyone has turned to his own way; and the LORD has laid on him the iniquity of us all.** (Isaiah 53:6) Yes, Jesus took your hell for you. Have you believed God's message? If you believe in your heart that He died for your sins, you will not go to hell. That is the Good News which can save you from God's righteous judgment.

As we discovered in our first lessons, God did not create hell for man, but for Satan and his evil angels. But then our forefather Adam chose to go the way of Satan. So the Scriptures tell us that **sin entered into the world through one man, and death through sin; so death passed to all men, because all sinned.** (Romans 5:12) If God had not provided a Savior for us, our sins would cause us to be forever separated from Him, since the payment for sin is death and hell. In our own strength we have no way of escape. But the Scripture says that **the wages of sin is death, but THE FREE GIFT OF GOD is eternal life in Christ Jesus our Lord.** (Romans 6:23) **Thanks be to God for his unspeakable gift!** (2 Corinthians 9:15) And what is His gift?

We have seen how men tortured Jesus, flogged Him, put a crown of thorns on His head, insulted Him, struck Him in the face, spit on Him, and nailed Him to a cross. God allowed people to mistreat the sinless Messiah. Jesus willingly took the punishment our sins deserved. And because of His great love for us, God laid the punishment for our sin on His Beloved, Eternal Son. And remember, the sufferings of Jesus on the cross were not limited to what men did to Him. While Jesus was on the cross, God Himself laid on Him a pain that our human minds cannot comprehend. God laid on Jesus the payment for our sin, that is, our hell. The prophet Job foretold the intense sufferings that the Messiah would endure from God when he wrote, **God delivers me to the ungodly, and casts me into the hands of the wicked....He has torn me in his wrath and persecuted me. He has gnashed on me with his teeth. My adversary sharpens his eyes on me.** (Job 16:11,9)

The payment for sin is to die and face God's wrath and enter the darkness of hell, where God consigns all who refuse to believe the gospel. But thank God, Jesus endured His wrath for us so that we might receive God's grace! As we have read, when Jesus was dying on the cross the whole land became pitch dark – like hell – from noon until three o'clock. During those hours, Jesus called out with a loud voice, **"My God, my God, why have you forsaken me?"** (Psalm 22:1; Matthew 27:46)

Why did God forsake the Messiah, His beloved, on the cross? You and I are the reason! Our sins are the reason! While Jesus was on the cross, God placed on Him the punishment for our sin; our hell. This is a profound truth which our minds cannot totally understand. However, what is absolutely certain is that if you, in your heart, believe in the Lord Jesus, you will be saved and you will never go to hell, because God will count you as righteous based on the sacrifice Jesus offered to rescue you from Satan, sin, death, and hell. Like the sacrificial sheep, which redeemed Abraham's son from death, Jesus the Messiah died to redeem you from the death which will never end, in the place called hell.

God put your hell on Jesus. Do you believe this? Do you believe that Jesus Christ, the Righteous One, paid your debt of sin for you? Or will you go to hell to go on paying your own debt of sin throughout eternity?

It is up to you. What do you choose? Heaven? Or Hell?

We invite you to join us next time to look into a subject drastically different from what we studied today, because, God willing, we will study about the wonderful place called Paradise.

God bless you as you contemplate these solemn words:

> **Enter in by the narrow gate; for the gate is wide and the way is broad that leads to destruction, and there are many who enter in by it. How narrow is the gate, and restricted is the way that leads to life! Few are those who find it.** (Matthew 7:13-14)

Paradise

Revelation 21-22

In the previous program, we contemplated hell, the place where punishment never ceases. Hell is a horrible place, created for Satan and his angels. It is where everyone who neglects the way of salvation which God has established must go, forever separated from God. That is what the Holy Scriptures declare, saying: **If anyone was not found written in the book of life, he was cast into the lake of fire.** (Revelation 20:15)

Surely hell is the most horrible subject that man can contemplate. But today we plan to look at one of the most wonderful subjects that the spirit of man can contemplate, the subject of heaven, also called *Paradise.*

People have many, many ideas about Paradise and what a person must do to qualify to enter it. For example, those who belong to eastern religions believe that there are many heavens (paradises) with varying degrees of pleasure and that where each person goes depends on his works. Others think that a person must first pass through hell and after he has paid his debt of sin, he will be transferred to Paradise. Still others think that Paradise is a place that God has reserved for those who are faithful in their religious duties and that it is a place where folks eat, drink, and pursue pleasure. Man certainly has many ideas about Paradise and how to get there. However, our concern today is not with what people think about Paradise, but with what God says about it in His holy word.

The place of Paradise has many names in the scriptures of the prophets. It is called *Heaven; the throne of God; the presence of God; the house of God; the dwelling place of God the Holy One; the Holy*

City; the City of the Living God; the heavenly Jerusalem; the home of the holy angels and the Lamb; the presence of the Lord Jesus and His great glory; and the home of God's people who have their names written in heaven. The Lord Jesus called Paradise *My Father's house,* because that was where He was before He was born on earth.

In summary, Paradise and or Heaven is the dwelling place of God. As we have seen, God is everywhere; nevertheless, there is a specific place that is holy, radiant, and beautiful, far beyond the stars, where God dwells in His glory. That place is where the Son of the Most High, Jesus, sits on His throne, at the right hand of the Almighty, waiting until He returns to the world to judge it and to renew it. Heaven is where thousands and thousands of angels surround the throne, together with the great multitude of people that God has redeemed for Himself through the blood of the Lamb, the Lord Jesus Christ.

At the end of the Holy Scriptures, in the last two chapters of the Revelation, God gave John His apostle a vision to show him the Holy City of Paradise, which the Lord made for those who have their names written in the book of eternal life. Listen to what the Scripture says about the City of Paradise. John wrote:

> [10]**[The angel] carried me away in the Spirit** to a great and high mountain, and showed me the holy city… [11]having the glory of God. Her light was like a most precious stone, as if it were a jasper stone, clear as crystal; [12]having a great and high wall; having twelve gates, and at the gates twelve angels.…[16]The city is square, and its length is as great as its width…. [19]The foundations of the city's wall were adorned with all kinds of precious stones…. [21]The twelve gates were twelve pearls. Each one of the gates was made of one pearl. The street of the city was pure gold, like transparent glass. [22]I saw no temple in it, for the Lord God, the Almighty, and the Lamb, are its temple. [23]The city has no need for the sun or moon to shine, for the very glory of God illuminated it, and its lamp is the Lamb. [24]The nations will walk in its light…. [25]Its gates will in no way be shut by day (for there will be no night there).… [27]There will in no way enter

into it anything profane, or one who causes an abomination or
a lie, but only those who are written in the Lamb's book of life.
(Revelation 21:10-12,16,19,21-25,27)

¹**He showed me a river of water of life**, clear as crystal,
proceeding out of the throne of God and of the Lamb, ²in the
middle of its street. On this side of the river and on that was
the tree of life, bearing twelve kinds of fruits, yielding its fruit
every month…. ³There will be no curse any more. [Death will be
no more; neither will there be mourning, nor crying, nor pain
(Revelation 21:4)]. The throne of God and of the Lamb will be in
it, and his servants will serve him. ⁴They will see his face, and
his name will be on their foreheads. ⁵There will be no night,
and they need no lamp light or sun light; for the Lord God will
illuminate them. They will reign forever and ever. (Revelation 22:1-5)

This is how God showed John the Holy City which He is preparing
for those who love Him. In the time we have left today let us think
about what God says in His word about the way that leads to
Paradise. How can we be sure that we will go to Heaven and not to
the Lake of Fire? Do you remember what Jesus said to His disciples
about His Father's house and the way that leads there? He said:

¹**Don't let your heart be troubled.** Believe in God. Believe also
in me. ²In my Father's house are many homes. If it weren't so,
I would have told you. I am going to prepare a place for you.
³If I go and prepare a place for you, I will come again, and will
receive you to myself; that where I am, you may be there also.
⁴You know where I go, and you know the way.…

⁶**I am the way and the truth and the life.** No one comes to the
Father, except through me. (John 14:1-4,6)

Jesus Himself is The Way. Whoever does not come by the holy
Redeemer sent by God, will never enter the holy presence of God.
No exceptions. That is what the Scriptures declare, saying:

There is salvation in no one else, for there is no other name
under heaven that is given among men, by which we must be

saved. (Acts 4:12) For there is one God, and one mediator between God and men, the man Christ Jesus, ⁶who gave himself as a ransom for all. (1 Timothy 2:5-6)

The Mediator, Jesus Christ, who came forth from God, is the way of salvation that leads to Paradise. In order to bring sinners to God, Christ was born into our world, lived a holy life on earth, shed His blood as the perfect sacrifice for sin, and then rose from the dead on the third day. No one comes to God except through Him. Do you believe that? Do you see that Jesus the Messiah is the only One who can bring sinners into the presence of God? Perhaps we can illustrate this reality with a little story.

A certain man lived in a small village far away in the bush. He belonged to a tribe of people who did not wear much clothes. They only wore something like a belt around their loins. This man had a piece of land which he farmed, but someone more powerful than he came and stole his land so that he had nowhere left to farm. No one would help him to reclaim his land because he had no means of paying them. One day he got the idea to go to the capital city to see the president, the ruler of the land, and ask him to help him, because he had heard that the ruler was a just and compassionate man. So he got up and walked and walked and walked until he came to the big city and to the presidential palace. Oh, what a big, beautiful house! When he arrived at the gate of the house, and tried to enter with his filthiness and nakedness, a guard said to him: "Hey you! What are you trying to do?" He replied, "I want to see the president." The guard said to him, "Ha! Do you suppose that anyone can just enter here as they please? Look at you! Don't you know that you can't come in here naked and dirty? Get away from here, man, or I'll throw you in prison!"

So the poor fellow turned and went away, but he did not give up. He went and begged from morning to afternoon until he had collected a few coins. Then he bought some used clothes, bathed himself, dressed and went back to the ruler's palace. Upon arriving back at the gate, the guard said to him, "You are wearing clothes, but the clothes are not good enough to allow you to come before the ruler of the land. And even if your clothes were good enough, you couldn't enter, because you must have special permission to enter the ruler's house. You have no right to enter. Now go!"

At this, the man became discouraged and said, "What's the use? After all the trouble I've gone through, I still can't get near the ruler of the land." His hope gone, he sat at the side of the road in great dismay. However, while all this was happening, the ruler of the land saw him. The ruler's eldest son saw him too. The ruler said to his son, "Go and find out what that fellow wants." When the ruler's son came up to the man, he squatted down beside him and said to him, "Sir, can I help you? What has brought you here and why are you so upset?" The man said to him, "I want to see the ruler of the land, but it is impossible. All my efforts have been for nothing."

The young man said to him, "I am the son of the ruler of the land, and my father sent me out here to help you. Follow me." Then he took him to the gate of the presidential palace. When they came up to the guard who had previously prevented the poor man from entering, the guard saluted them with great respect as they walked through the gate and into the court of the palace. The son gave the poor man one of his own beautiful robes to wear, and together they entered the presidential palace. Thus, the man was able to enter the palace and see the ruler of the land because of the help and authority of the ruler's son.

Friends, this is how it is with those who want to enter Paradise, the palace of the King of kings. God, the ruler of the universe is high and holy. We cannot just enter His glorious presence any way we please. Our own efforts can never gain us access into His presence. We are all like that poor man who attempted to enter the presence of the president by his own feeble efforts. The Scripture says: **For we have all become like one who is unclean, and all our right-eousness is like a polluted garment.** (Isaiah 64:6) Paradise is a holy place, and **there will in no way enter into it anything profane, or one who causes an abomination or a lie.** (Revelation 21:27) No one can get us into that holy place except the Holy One who came from there. That Person is the eternal Son of the Most High, the

Lamb of God, who came down to earth, became man, paid our sin debt, conquered death for us, and returned to heaven.

So then, who can enter Paradise? Only those who have been cleansed through faith in Jesus the Redeemer and in the blood that He shed. Only those will enter Paradise. That is what the Scripture declares when it says:

> **22For there is no distinction**, 23for all have sinned, and fall short of the glory of God; 24being justified freely by his grace through the redemption that is in Christ Jesus; 25whom God sent to be an atoning sacrifice, through faith in his blood. (Romans 3:22-25)

> **9If we receive the witness of men**, the witness of God is greater; for this is God's testimony which he has testified concerning his Son. 10He who believes in the Son of God has the testimony in himself. He who doesn't believe God has made him a liar, because he has not believed in the testimony that God has given concerning his Son. 11The testimony is this, that God gave to us eternal life, and this life is in his Son. 12He who has the Son has the life. He who doesn't have God's Son doesn't have the life. 13These things I have written to you who believe in the name of the Son of God, that you may know that you have eternal life, and that you may continue to believe in the name of the Son of God. (1 John 5:9-13)

You who are listening today, do you have eternal life? Are you sure that you will enter Paradise and rejoice in the presence of God forever? Have you believed on the name of the Son of God? Is your name written in the Lamb's book of life?

Think carefully about what you have heard today because God wants to give you insight into all of this.

God bless you as consider this thrilling verse from His holy word:

> **"No eye has seen, no ear has heard, and no mind has imagined what God has prepared for those who love him."**
> (1 Corinthians 2:9 NLT)

What Do You Think About Jesus?

Part 1
Adapted from a 10-question sermon by Charles R. Marsh
who for 37 years served the Kabyle people in Algeria.

For a long time now, we have been examining the scriptures of the prophets to see the righteous way established by God, by which sinners can become righteous before Him. We have seen how Jesus the Messiah fulfilled the words of God's prophets. Today and in the next lesson we intend to review with you the glory of the One about whom all the prophets spoke. We will call our final two lessons in this chronological study of the scriptures of the prophets: *What do you think about Jesus?*

In our study in the Gospel (*Injil*), we heard Jesus ask people, **"What do you think of the Christ? Whose son is he?"** (Matthew 22:42) This is the most important question in life that each of us must answer. Our destiny in the hereafter depends on our response to this question. Soon you will stand before Jesus the Messiah and when that happens, that is the one question that will matter, "How about you, what did you think of Me?"

Our goal is to make known to you who Jesus really is. Our greatest concern is that no one misleads you in this matter. We urge you not to assume that Jesus Christ was merely one of the prophets, or a good man among men. No, He is unique. He has no equal in this world or in the world to come. What do you think about Him? Who do you think He is? There are ten questions we would like to ask you about Jesus the Messiah, five in this program and five in the next.

1. First, *what do you think about His amazing birth?*

No one has ever been born like Him. He is Jesus *the Son of Mary*. You know that John was called *the son of Zacharias*, Solomon *the son of David*, Ishmael *the son of Abraham*. Everyone takes the surname of his father or adds his father's name to his own name. But in Jesus' case, why is the name of His mother attached to His name? It is because He did not have a father on earth. He was born of a young woman who was a virgin. He was born by the power of God. About seven hundred years before the Messiah was born, the prophet Isaiah predicted how He would be born, when he wrote: **Behold, the virgin will conceive, and bear a son, and shall call his name Immanuel.** (Isaiah 7:14) **Which is, being interpreted, "God with us".** (Matthew 1:23)

It was from the dust of the ground that God created our ancestor Adam. We all are descendants of Adam, as were the prophets. We are of the earth. But the Lord Jesus came from heaven. We are all like the dirty ground because of our sin, but Jesus was like the rain which comes from heaven. He was pure and holy, just as God is pure and holy. The Gospel record declares: **Jesus came into the world to save sinners.** (1 Timothy 1:15) Before Jesus came into the world, He was in the presence of God, because He is the Word of God and the Soul of God. He Himself chose to come and take on a human body to save us from our sins. He came from above.

The story is told of two men who fell into a deep well. One said to the other, "Hey man, save me from this wretched place! Get me out of this slimy mud!" But the other said to him, "How can I get you out when you and I both are in this pit?" They were both in it, and neither one could get the other out. Then they heard a voice from above telling them to grab hold of a rope that was being lowered into the well. Only someone who had not fallen into the well could help them.

The very best of the prophets could not save us from the deep, deep pit of sin, because they too were sinners. However, Jesus did not inherit the sinful nature that is in man. He came from above. He was born of a virgin. We also saw that God sent His angels and placed a great star in the sky to announce the birth of the holy

Messiah, the Savior of the world. How miraculous it all was. No man has ever been born like this Man. He is unique in His birth. He is incomparable. But the greatness of Jesus does not end with His birth. Jesus is also unique in His character. Our second question is:

2. *What do you think of His holy character?*

Jesus was perfect. He never committed a single sin. He never asked for forgiveness because He never did any wrong. Every person who fears God must repent and ask for forgiveness. All the prophets did this. However, you can search the word of God from beginning to end,[121] but you will not find a single verse which says that the Lord Jesus requested forgiveness. He did not need forgiveness since He never sinned. His friends and His enemies all testified that they could not find a single fault in Him. Friends, there is no one else who is without sin. The Lord Jesus is more than a prophet. He is the very Word of God that appeared upon earth as a man. Yes, Jesus is unique in His character. He is incomparable. But there is something else important to understand. Jesus is also unique in His words.

3. *What do you think about His wonderful words?*

One day His enemies sent soldiers to arrest Him. When they arrived and listened to His teachings they returned without arresting Him. They were amazed and said, **"No man ever spoke like this man."** (John 7:46)

Consider what Jesus said about Himself. **"I am the light of the world. He who follows me will not walk in the darkness, but will have the light of life."** (John 8:12) The prophets are like the moon and stars that provide a weak light at night. But Jesus is like the sun. Who needs the light of the moon and stars once the sun has risen? The prophets called the Messiah **the Sun of Righteousness.** (Malachi 4:2) The prophets are like the waning crescent moon. But Jesus Christ is the sun. Have you ever seen the sun wane? No, it never goes out. It lights all the continents. Jesus Christ is like the sun. He will never pass away. He is for every nation of the world.

---

121 Literally in Wolof: *go around until you meet up with where you started*

Jesus also said, **"I am the way, the truth and the life."** (John 14:6)
He is different from the religious leaders who give orders, saying,
"Do this, follow these rules. This is the way. Do these rituals…."
The Lord Jesus said, "I am the way. Believe in me, come to me, and
you will have the right to live in the presence of God forever." Jesus
Himself is *The Way*. Let us try to illustrate what this means.

A small boy was lost in a big city. The child asked a police officer
to explain to him the way back to his neighborhood. The officer
said to him, "Go straight ahead, turn left at the second corner, take
a right at the third corner, cross the bridge, take the traffic circle
and then follow the second main road …." The child burst into
tears. That police officer had explained the way, but the child was
too confused and afraid to follow what had been explained to
him. Just then an old friend from the same neighborhood came
along. He took the child by the hand and led him. When the child
was tired of walking, the man carried him until they arrived at the
child's house. The police officer explained the way, but the other
man *was the way*. Jesus said: **I AM the way.** I am the way that leads
to heaven, the house of God. **"I am the way, the truth, and the
life. No one comes to the Father, except through me."** (John 14:6)
No one ever spoke like the Lord Jesus Christ. He is incomparable.

But the glory of Jesus does not stop at His birth, His character and
His words. We can see it also in His works. The next question is:

4. *What do you think about the mighty works of Jesus?*

He can do anything. All power and all authority are given to Him.
Whatever works God has done, the Lord Jesus did on earth to
show people where He came from and who He was. Who can still
the wind but God? Jesus stilled the wind. Who can raise the dead
to life but God? Jesus raised the dead to life. Who can open the
eyes of the blind but God? Jesus did that too. He healed every
kind of disease. He spoke one word and the demons fled. He
changed the lives of many people and saved them from sin. God
gave some of the prophets the power to do certain miracles. But
the Lord Jesus did miracles by His own authority and power. He is

the One who could stand over a paralyzed man, look him in the eyes and say, **"I tell you, arise, take up your cot, and go to your house."** (Luke 5:24) The man stood up and went home praising God. Jesus didn't heal with medicine or magic. By the power and authority of His word alone He healed the sick.

A man named Lazarus died and was buried. When Jesus arrived Lazarus had already been buried for four days. Jesus went to the tomb and commanded, **"Lazarus, come out!"** (John 11:43) The corpse walked out of the tomb. Jesus has the authority to raise the dead, which is why He could say, **"I am the resurrection and the life."** (John 11:25) A day is coming when all who are in the tombs will hear His voice and arise to stand before Him. Listening friend, you too will come out of the tomb if you have died. Even now, the Lord Jesus can give you a new life and the authority to live forever in paradise, if you believe in Him as your Savior and Lord. Jesus is still transforming the lives of people around the world. He can transform your life too. What do you think about Jesus? What do you think about His works? He is unique. He is Almighty. There is none like Him.

Before we stop today, let us ask you one more question about Jesus:

5. *What do you think about His lofty names and titles?*

As we have seen in the writings of the prophets, Jesus has hundreds of names and titles. These names help us to better understand who He is. For example, He is called: *Immanuel... the Word... the Son of Man... the Lamb of God... the Redeemer... the Savior... the Bread of Life... the Good Shepherd... the Light of the World... the King of Glory... the Resurrection... the Alpha and Omega, the First and the Last, the Beginning and End... the Door... the Way, the Truth and the Life... the Lord of peace... and the Son of God.*

We saw that God's prophet, Moses, was called *the man of God.* The prophet Abraham was called *the friend of God.* But only one Person is called *The Son of God.* Tell us, who has the closest relationship to a man: his friend or his son? Speak the truth that is in your heart.

Yes, Jesus was called the Son of God. God called Jesus His Son to distinguish Him from all others. We read in the Gospel that God declared of Jesus, saying, **"This is my beloved Son, in whom I am well pleased. Listen to him."** (Matthew 17:5) What did God mean? We say that the Son is the shadow of the father. The son reflects the image of the father. Jesus shows us what God is like. That is what the Scripture declares when it says: **No one has ever seen God, but the one and only Son, who is himself God and is in closest relationship with the Father, has made him known.** (John 1:18 NIV) Do you want to know God, and have a close relationship with Him forever? Then come to the Lord Jesus, whom God calls His Son. A son can speak in the name of his father. That is what Jesus did when He was among men. That is why He was called *Immanuel*, meaning *God with us*.

Some assume that God cannot appear on earth in a human body. But anyone who thinks this way does not yet understand the plan God designed to save sinners. His plan required that the eternal Son of God appear upon earth in a human body, to make Himself known to the children of Adam, and ransom them from the hand of the devil.

God is great and He can do anything. God wants all people to know Him. That is why He became a man and lived on the earth.

What do you think about the names and titles of Jesus the Messiah? He is incomparable. What do you think about His birth, His character, His words and His works? Who do you consider Him to be? **What do you think of the Christ? Whose son is he?** (Matthew 22:42)

Our time is up today. God willing, next time we will ask and answer five more questions about Jesus and complete our journey through the Holy Scriptures of the prophets.

God bless you as you ponder this verse of Scripture:

> **In Christ all the fullness of the Deity lives in bodily form, and you [who believe] have been given fullness in Christ.**
> (Colossians 2:9-10 NIV)

Program 100

What Do You Think About Jesus?

Part 2
Adapted from a 10-question sermon by Charles R. Marsh
who for 37 years served the Kabyle people in Algeria.

P eace be with you. We greet you in the name of God, the
LORD of peace, who wants everyone to understand and
submit to the way of righteousness that He has established,
and have true peace with Him forever. We are happy to be able to
return today to present your program *The Way of Righteousness.*[122]

Today we will complete the talk we began last time, called: *What do
you think about Jesus?* This question is intensely important because
where we will spend eternity depends on how we respond to
Jesus the Messiah. In our last program, we asked what you thought
about His miraculous birth, His holy character, His wonderful
words, His mighty power and His lofty titles. Today we have five
more solemn questions we want to ask you about Jesus. The first
question today is:

6. *What do you think about His death?*

Do you know where you will die? Or how you will die? Do you
know when you will die? You and I must admit that we know
nothing about these things. But Jesus was not like us. He knew
where He would die and announced it. He would die in Jerusalem.
He also foretold how He would die. He told His disciples,

> [31]**Behold, we are going up to Jerusalem**, and all the things
> that are written through the prophets concerning the Son of
> Man will be completed. [32]For he will be delivered up to the

---

122 This is the typical greeting that each program begins with (see Programs 1 and 2).

Gentiles, will be mocked, treated shamefully, and spit on.
³³They will scourge and kill him. On the third day, he will rise again. (Luke 18:31-33)

He also told His disciples when He would die; that is, on the same day the Jews would be killing a lamb to celebrate the feast of the Passover. God planned for Him to die on that day as the Lamb of God to take away the sin debt of the world.

The death of Jesus was different from all other deaths. We heard Jesus say, **"No one takes [my life] away from me, but I lay it down by myself. I have power to lay it down, and I have power to take it again."** (John 10:18) Jesus never sinned; that is why He could have bypassed death. He could have simply ascended to heaven from where He came, without passing through death. But He chose to suffer and die because of His obedience to His Father's will and His love for sinners like you and me. He gave His life for us by allowing men to nail Him to a cross. He died to provide for us forgiveness of sins and guarantee a place for us in Paradise. About seven hundred years before the Messiah came into the world, God's prophet, Isaiah, declared why the Redeemer must die, when he said:

> ⁵**But he was pierced for our transgressions.** He was crushed for our iniquities. The punishment that brought our peace was on him; and by his wounds we are healed. ⁶All we like sheep have gone astray. Everyone has turned to his own way; and the LORD has laid on him the iniquity of us all. (Isaiah 53:5-6)

You and I are the reason Jesus the Messiah died. He is the Good Shepherd who willingly gave His life for His sheep. No man has ever died like Him. He is incomparable. He is unique among men.

Another important question to which everyone must respond is:

7. *What do you think about His victory over death, that is, His resurrection?*

Jesus died and was buried. His enemies did everything they could to guard the tomb. They rolled a huge stone to close door of the tomb, then sealed it tight. They placed soldiers there to guard the tomb. But all their efforts did not hinder Jesus from rising from the dead. Indeed, the Lord Jesus rose from the dead on the third day and appeared to His disciples. After that, He appeared to more than 500 witnesses at once. Those people saw Him, touched Him, and ate with Him after His resurrection. He showed them the wounds in His hands, His feet and His side. The tomb was empty. God raised Jesus from the dead, thus proving to the whole world that He is satisfied with the work of Jesus on the cross as the perfect and final Sacrifice which pays for sins.

Death is a great enemy. Our ancestors died. The prophets also died, and their corpses remain in their graves. We too will die some day. But praise be to God, Jesus Christ conquered death. He is a living Savior and can save all who come to God through Him, because He is alive and intercedes for all who believe in Him. Is any other prophet alive today after having died? No, not one. Jesus Christ is the only One who conquered the grave. He is alive today, which is why those of us who believe in Him are not afraid to die. To die is to go to be with our Lord above. Yes, Jesus is unique and incomparable. He has no equal on earth or in heaven. What do you think about His victory over death? Another question is:

8. *What do you think of His ascension to heaven?*

After the Lord Jesus arose from the dead, He appeared to His disciples for a period of forty days. Then we saw that He bid them farewell, ascended to heaven, and sat down at the right hand of God, the place of supreme honor, showing by this that He is greater than the angels, the prophets, and all humankind. That is what the Scripture declares, saying,

> [9]**Therefore God also highly exalted him**, and gave to him the name which is above every name, [10]that at the name of Jesus every knee should bow, of those in heaven, those on earth, and those under the earth, [11]and that every tongue should confess that Jesus Christ is Lord, to the glory of God the Father.
> (Philippians 2:9-11)

Yes, Jesus is unique. There has never been anyone like Him. In relation to this, another question you must answer is:

9. *What do you think about His return to the earth?*

Jesus Christ is going to come back. He declared it. The prophets announced it. The angels also said so. All true disciples of Christ are looking for Him to return. He will come and take His people to heaven. He will judge the world in righteousness and reign over all the earth. He will be the King of all the earth. He must reign for a thousand years until all His enemies bow at His feet. Yes, He is coming back soon. Everyone will confess that He is the King of kings, the Lord of lords. He is coming and you will stand before Him, the Great Judge. On the day when you will be face to face with Him, He will ask you, "What did you think of me?" What will you answer? If you answer, "I thought You were one of the prophets," then He will ask you why you did not sincerely believe Him and you will be condemned because you did not believe what He said about Himself, nor what the prophets wrote about Him: that He is the Son of God from heaven, the One and Only Savior.

Who is coming back to reign? Will Abraham, Moses, David or some other prophet return to reign? No. The Lord Jesus Christ is the One who is coming back. He will be the Judge. God has given proof of this fact by raising Him from the dead. He will return. Every eye will see Him. Every knee will bow. Every tongue will declare that Jesus Christ is LORD. Now we come to the final question:

10. *What do you think about what He wants you to do?*

The Lord Jesus says, **"Come to me, all you who labor and are heavily burdened, and I will give you rest. Take my yoke upon you and learn from me, for I am gentle and humble in heart; and you will find rest for your souls."** (Matthew 11:28-29) This very day He is calling you. When He called the first disciples to follow Him, they left everything: their homes, their families, and their work. He wants you to do the same. This does not necessarily mean that you must abandon your home and your job to follow Jesus, but you must surrender your whole life to Him and give Him first place in your heart. He wants you to trust Him, believe in Him, and receive Him as your Savior and Master. He wants all of you – your mind, heart, body and soul. If He is the One He claims to be, then everything He demands is logical.

As we have seen, Jesus Christ is unique and cannot be compared with anyone else. He is unique in His birth, in His character, in His teachings, in His works, in His names and titles, in His sufferings and death, in His resurrection, in His ascension, in His return, and in His power to change the hearts of the children of Adam. He is alive today. He is with those who believe in Him. Soon He will return. There is no one like Him in heaven or on earth. That is why He has the authority to be the King and the Lord of your life! The Lord Jesus Christ wants to be your Savior and your Lord. That is why He died on the cross and came back to life! He has the power to take away your sins and give you a deep and wonderful relationship with God forever. He can give you new life, wash your heart clean, and renew you in the power of the Holy Spirit, but you must hang your hope on (trust) Him and His sacrifice.

Tragically, so many consider Jesus Christ to be a great prophet but they have never received Him as their Lord and Savior. To believe that Jesus was a great prophet is not enough! You must agree with God that Jesus is the Lord of all and that when He died on the cross, He died in *your* place. All of us children of Adam have a serious problem: it is sin. God, in His great mercy, has provided a remedy for our problem, but we must take it. If I am sick and go to a medical clinic, the doctor writes me a medical prescription. So I go buy the medicine, return home, place it on my table. I look at the medicine and the medicine looks at me. Will that make me get well? Of course not. To get well, I must take the medicine and swallow it as prescribed. God's Medicine is the Lord Jesus Christ and what He did for us by His death on the cross and resurrection from the tomb.

Perhaps you are asking, "How can I take God's remedy for my sin?" Very simply, you must confess to God that you are a sinner, that your "good works" are like filthy rags before Him, and that you have no means of saving yourself from His righteous judgment. Then you must believe in your heart that the Lord Jesus Christ bore the punishment for your sins and conquered death for you. Jesus the Messiah satisfied completely God's every demand for judgment. If you believe that Christ died and rose again to save you, then God will forgive your sins, clothe you in the righteousness of Christ, send His Holy Spirit into your heart, and give you the right to live in His presence forever. Glory to God, you can be counted as righteous today – if you will believe.

Listening friends, have you taken God's medicine, which can heal you of the deadly disease of sin and save you from the eternal fire? Whoever despises God's medicine, that is, the blood that Jesus shed, must know that there is no other cure for your sin. None whatsoever. God has no other way to cleanse sinners and make them righteous before Him. There is no other way to Paradise.

Listen carefully to what the Holy Scripture declares concerning the one and only way of righteousness which God has provided for sinners to be made righteous before Him. The Scripture says:

> [20]**Because by the works of the law**, no flesh will be justified in his sight.… [21]But now apart from the law, a righteousness of God has been revealed, being testified by the law and the prophets; [22]even the righteousness of God through faith in Jesus Christ to all and on all those who believe. For there is no distinction, [23]for all have sinned, and fall short of the glory of God; [24]being justified freely by his grace through the redemption that is in Christ Jesus.… [27]Where then is the boasting? It is excluded. By what kind of law? Of works? No, but by a law of faith. (Romans 3:20-24,27)

> [8]**For it is by grace you have been saved, through faith** – and this is not from yourselves, it is the gift of God – [9]not by works, so that no one can boast. [10]For we are God's handiwork, created in Christ Jesus to do good works, which God prepared in advance for us to do. (Ephesians 2:8-9 NIV)

[9]**If you declare with your mouth, "Jesus is Lord,"** and believe in your heart that God raised him from the dead, you will be saved. ... [13]for, "Everyone who calls on the name of the Lord will be saved." (Romans 10:9,13 NIV)

Dear friend, have you called on the name of the Lord? Have you received His wonderful gift of salvation? He knows your heart. Admit to Him that you are a sinner, that you have broken His holy laws and deserve His righteous judgment. Then thank Him for suffering and dying for your sins and for rising from the grave to give you eternal life – with Him forever.

In His word, God makes this promise:

> **Believe in the Lord Jesus Christ, and you will be saved, you and your household.** (Acts 16:31)

Amen.

If you have put your trust in the Savior about whom all the prophets wrote, feel free to write to us[123] and tell us about what He has done for you.

Today is the one hundredth[124] program in our journey through the Holy Scriptures. Thank you for joining us. We bid you farewell with this prayer of blessing found in the word of God:

> **To him who is able to keep you from stumbling,**
> **and to present you before his glorious presence**
> **without fault and with great joy,**
> **To the only God our Savior**
> **be glory, majesty, power and authority,**
> **Through Jesus Christ our Lord,**
> **before all ages, now and forevermore!**
> **Amen.** (Jude 1: 24-25 NIV)

---

123 resources@rockintl.org
124 Once this 100th program has been aired, most radio stations go back to *Program #1* and begin to broadcast the entire series again. To listen to or download the series in many languages, visit: **www.rockintl.org/resources**

The WAY of
RIGHTEOUSNESS

Appendices

He said to them,
"How foolish you are, and how slow to believe
all that the prophets have spoken!
Did not the Messiah have to
suffer these things and then enter his glory?"
– The Risen Lord (Luke 24:25-26)

And beginning with Moses and all the Prophets,
He explained to them what was said
in all the Scriptures concerning himself.
(Luke 24:27)

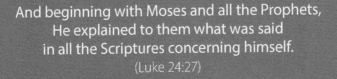

Appendix A

The Teaching Method

Line upon line

A preschool teacher does not start the children with $x^2 + 2x + 1 = (x + 1)^2$. She begins with *1 apple + 1 apple = 2 apples*. Her goal is to lay a foundation upon which her pupils can build. Similarly, God's revelation to the children of Adam is progressive, **precept on precept … line on line; here a little, there a little.** (Isaiah 28:10) God's Book begins with "**In the beginning God**" and goes on to reveal His complex Person and categorical plan by which He can declare sinners righteous.

The Way of Righteousness radio series presents the message of God's prophets in consecutive order. Through the narratives of the people, patriarchs, and prophets of the Holy Scriptures, listeners can discover for themselves God's uncompromising system of forgiveness: how He has provided a way by which the fallen children of Adam can be delivered from sin's curse and restored to happy fellowship with their Creator.

Considering a Muslim's understanding of God, mankind, sin, and salvation, this series employs a modified chronological approach, strategically drawing from the Holy Scriptures from Genesis to Revelation. The 100 lessons put a premium on repetition, especially since many listeners will not hear every program. Each lesson begins with a review of the previous one.

Why the Chronological Method?

The Lord Jesus Himself taught the Gospel chronologically. For example, on the day of His resurrection, He said to two of His incredulous followers, "**Foolish men and slow of heart to believe in all that the prophets have spoken!**" **… And beginning from**

Moses (Genesis, Exodus, etc.) **and from all the prophets, he explained to them in all the Scriptures the things concerning himself.** (Luke 24:25,27) Similarly, Muslims should be given the opportunity to hear and understand what the prophets (whom the Qur'an commands them to believe) have written so that they can give an honest answer to the question, **"Do you believe the prophets?"** (Acts 26:27) An unhurried journey through the Torah, the Psalms, the Prophets, and the Gospel affords them that opportunity.

Like all who are religious, Muslims need time to rethink much of what many have unquestioningly accepted as truth. Teaching from the whole of Scripture can help people to see that when we **preach Jesus Christ and him crucified** (1 Corinthians 2:2 NIV) **we are saying nothing but what the prophets and Moses said would happen, how the Christ must suffer, and how, by the resurrection of the dead, he would be first to proclaim light both to these people and to the Gentiles.** (Acts 26:22-23)

Presenting God's word chronologically exposes listeners both to the Old Testament stories about the unbelieving nation of Israel and to the New Testament stories about the hardhearted religious leaders of the Jews, causing some to examine themselves and ask: *Is my heart also hard? Will I, like the Israelites, also spurn the message of God's prophets and the Messiah sent down from heaven?*

The best of seed will not germinate in hard, unprepared soil. The good seed of God's word can produce eternal fruit only in prepared hearts. The Holy Torah is an effective plough. Remember the rich young ruler who came running to Jesus and asked, **"Good teacher, what good thing shall I do, that I may have eternal life?"** (Matthew 19:16; Mark 10:17) To the crowd, the young man's question seemed good, but not to the Lord. Jesus knew that this religious man had not yet grasped the foundational truths about God's infinite holiness and man's utter sinfulness. This self-righteous man imagined that he could earn his way into paradise. He was like a child holding out a grimy fistful of copper coins to the world's wealthiest man, and asking him, "How many shall I give to you so that I may inherit your estate?" How did Jesus answer the

man? He directed him back to the Torah and the Ten Commandments to show him that he could never in his own strength satisfy
God's perfect standard of righteousness. There is no eternal life for
those who think they can merit it by doing some "good thing."

Avoid Unnecessary Offense

In *The Way of Righteousness* series we strive to use familiar terms
and define misunderstood concepts whenever possible. For
instance, we refer to God's written word as the Holy Scriptures,
the writings of the prophets, the Torah, the Gospel, but rarely do
we call it *the Bible* (Latin for *the Book*). We do this because many
Muslims associate *the Bible* with the West or with Roman Catholi-
cism, a religion that erroneously bases salvation on human effort
rather than on divine accomplishment.

Being careful with terms does not mean toning down the truth.
We seek to avoid unnecessary offense, but never at the cost of
compromising the truth of the gospel. (Galatians 2:5,14; 1 Corinthians 9:22-23) The methods of presenting God's way of Salvation
will vary depending on the hearers, but the essential message
remains the same. The Lord Jesus' method of presenting the
message of salvation to a religious man like Nicodemus (John 3)
was quite different from the way He presented it to the immoral
woman of Samaria. (John 4) Like their risen Lord, the apostles were
sensitive to people's perceptions and prejudices, seeking to lead
their hearers from where they were to where they needed to be.
(Compare: Acts 2:14-39 with 10:34-43, and Acts 17:1-3 with 17:16-31)

Simple English

The Way of Righteousness is written in a simple, spoken style,
suitable for radio. While this English version is far from an exact
word-for-word translation from the Wolof series (this would make
for very uncomfortable reading), it maintains a similar simplicity
of structure and style. This makes for easier translation into other
languages. Obviously, the illustrations and Wolof proverbs used in
these lessons need to be adapted to express God's truth effective-
ly in the local culture and language.

Recyclable

These one hundred programs may be presented on a daily or weekly basis. We have been careful not to date the lessons in any way. Each program is approximately fifteen minutes in length when spoken at a normal conversational speed. As a weekly broadcast, the series lasts about two years (100 weeks). When broadcast five days a week, it takes under five months. These programs, which present the living, powerful, penetrating and never-outdated word of God, are intended to be broadcast over and over again. Program 1 follows Program 100.

God's Word, Not Ours

In each of these one hundred programs we present God's infallible word. Anyone who is offended by what is taught should talk to the true and living God about it, since it is His word, not ours. When handling the living word of the living God, the best defense is a good offense. To hear God's holy Book taught chronologically is to come face to face with the Almighty Himself.

When our Senegalese friends ask us, "Why do you not also teach the Qur'an?" our answer is simple. "In every town and village you have men teaching the Qur'an, but how many are teaching the Torah, the Psalms and the Gospel? Our unique purpose is to tell you the Good News of the prophets, which you seldom hear."

God's Theme, Not Ours

The theme of God's word and the theme of these one hundred lessons are identical: **The Good News (gospel) of God, which He promised before through His prophets in the holy Scriptures.** (Romans 1:1-2) That is what these lessons are about: **the gospel of God** – the righteous way of salvation established by God, the only system of forgiveness that satisfies both God and man. Man's efforts may give temporary feelings of satisfaction, but they can never satisfy the uncompromising righteousness of God. Only the gospel satisfies both man and God. **The Good News…is the power of God for salvation for everyone who believes…. For in it is revealed God's righteousness.** (Romans 1:16-17)

God's Power, Not Ours

The Scripture says: **the natural man doesn't receive the things of God's Spirit, for they are foolishness to him.** And: **the word of the cross is foolishness to those who are dying.** (1 Corinthians 2:14; 1:18) These programs by themselves will never reveal God's truth to a soul. Only the Spirit of God can do that. We count on Him to reveal His way of righteousness to those who listen to these programs. **For the weapons of our warfare are not of the flesh, but mighty before God to the throwing down of strongholds, throwing down imaginations and every high thing that is exalted against the knowledge of God....** (2 Corinthians 10:4-5)

Our Heartfelt Prayer

God is at work in Muslim minds and hearts around the globe. Muslim means *Submitted one.* Truth-seeking Muslims and others listening to these *Way of Righteousness* programs are for the first time in their lives hearing, considering, and submitting to God's way of righteousness – and experiencing what it means to be at peace with God. For those continuing in man's way of self-righteousness, we offer to God this prayer penned by the apostle Paul:

> **My heart's desire and my prayer to God is**...that they may be saved. For I testify about them that they have a zeal for God, but not according to knowledge. For being ignorant of God's righteousness, and seeking to establish their own righteousness, they have not submitted themselves to the righteousness of God. For Christ is the fulfillment of the law for righteousness to everyone who believes. (Romans 10:1-4)

Amen.

Appendix B
Wolof Proverbs

S torytelling is an important part of Wolof culture and tradition. The Wolofs use proverbs (*léebu*) to give a moral lesson to the story and to make it memorable. Some like to quote proverbs in everyday conversation and circumstances. In *The Way of Righteousness* we have used sixteen Wolof proverbs to illustrate and apply God's Eternal Truth. We have listed the proverbs below with their approximate English translation. The numbers in parentheses show the lessons in which the proverb has been used. The proverbs are listed according to their frequency of use in the lessons.

1. *Musiba du yem ci boppu boroom.*

    An epidemic is not confined to the one from whom it originates. (#7, 8, 9, 13, 28, 86, 89, 91, 94)

    Adam's sin with its consequences has spread to all his descendants. See Romans 5:12

2. *Nen du bëre ak doj.*

    An egg should not wrestle with a rock. (#1, 3, 16, 32, 33, 60)

    Man cannot oppose the word of God and win. 2 Peter 3:16

3. *Dëgg, kaani la.*

    Truth is a hot pepper. (#3, 9, 68, 74, 80, Appendix D)

    God's Truth is not always easy to accept nor is it appreciated by all. Romans 3:23

4. *Lu bant yàgg-yàgg ci ndox, du tax mu soppaliku mukk jasig.*

    Even if a log soaks a long time in water, it will never become a crocodile. (Preface, #67, 72)

    Man's religious rituals will never make a person righteous. John 3:6,7

5. *Ku bëgg lem, ñeme yamb.*

   Whoever wants honey must brave the bees. (#23, 45, 73, Appendix D)

   Whoever follows God's Way of Righteousness must be prepared to be misunderstood by family and friends. Hebrews 11:24-27

6. *Bala nga koy xam, xamadi dina la rey.*

   Before you know it, ignorance will kill you. (#50, 51, 74, 90)

   Ignorance regarding God's Way of salvation is deadly. Hebrews 2:3

7. *Janax du jur lu dul luy gas.*

   A rat (lit. *mouse*) **only begets that which digs.** (#8, 9, 16, 61, 94)

   We are born sinners. Psalm 51:5; Romans 5:12

8. *Kéwél du tëb doom ja bëtt.*

   The gazelle which jumps over (the underbrush) doesn't produce offspring that pierce through (it). (#7, 12, 91)

   We have inherited the sinful nature of our forefather Adam. Ephesians 2:1-3

9. *Ku yaag ci teen, baag fekk la fa.*

   A water pail will find the person who waits diligently at the well. (#1, 9)

   God rewards those who diligently seek Him. Hebrews 11:6

10. *Ndànk-ndànk, mooy jàpp golo ci Ñaay.*

    Slowly, slowly (and quietly) **one catches the monkey in the garden.** (#1)

    Be patient. Don't expect to grasp all of God's truth in one lesson. Isaiah 28:10

11. *Sa xaritu noon, sa noon la.*

    Your friend's enemy is your enemy. (#8)

    When Adam and Eve sided with the devil they forfeited their relationship with God. James 4:4-8

12. *Nag wéq na doomam, waaye bañu ko.*

    The cow may kick its calf but does not hate it. (#11)

    If God deals severely with you it's because He loves you and wants you to submit to His good plan for you. 2 Peter 3:9

13. *Fukki nit gas pax mu xoot, fukki nit suul ko, pënd mi bare na, waaye pax amul.*

   Ten men dig a deep hole, ten men fill it – there's lots of dust, but no hole. (#53)

   Religious rituals–no matter how zealously performed–do not produce the righteousness required by God. Romans 10:1-4

14. *Bala ngay fél gémmiñu sàmm, nga xam lu mu walis.*

   Before you slap the shepherd on the mouth, you should find out what he is whistling about. (#61)

   Before you criticize and condemn the teachings of the Bible, you should learn what they mean. Jude 10

15. *Garab gay doon pénc, lawbe du ko gis ba di ko gor.*

   The woodcutter does not cut down the main tree in the village (under which folks meet). (#68)

   Jesus the Messiah is God's main tree. How foolish and evil of men to scorn or ignore the One whom God has appointed as the Savior and Judge of the world. Acts 4:10-12

16. *Tungune du teew ñuy nataal.*

   No need to draw a picture of a dwarf (to depict what one is like), if one is standing before you. (#89)

   There is no need to waste your energy on making symbolic animal sacrifices when the Perfect and Final Sacrifice has been provided for you by God, once for all. Hebrews, chapters 9 & 10

Appendix C

Basic Truths Taught In Each Lesson

In 20 Groups

When this series was first written and recorded in the Wolof language between 1992 and 1994, in addition to airing it on the national radio station, believers began to distribute the recordings by the thousands on audio cassette tapes, a technology no longer used in today's digital world. The entire 100-lesson series fit nicely on 20 cassettes by using a combination of 60-minute tapes with 4 programs, and 90-minute tapes with 5 or 6 programs. Because the list contains some useful information, it is still included in this 2020 reprint of the 1998 book version of TWOR. Listed with the title is the primary Scripture reference on which each program is based – followed by a description of basic truths covered in the lesson.

#1 – THE BEGINNING

1. **God Has Spoken** – The Way of Righteousness.
    What is a prophet? God wants to speak to you.

2. **What Is God Like?** Genesis 1
    God's eternal greatness. He wants us to know Him.

3. **Satan and the Angels** Isaiah 14; Ezekiel 28
    Satan's origin. God's holiness.

4. **How God Made the World** Genesis 1
    God's wisdom, power, faithfulness, and goodness.

5. **Why God Created Man** Genesis 1-2
    Man: created in God's image. God's great purpose
    for people.

6. **Adam and Eve and the Garden of Paradise** Genesis 2
    God's command. Sin's penalty. Sin and death defined.

21. **Sodom's Ruin and Isaac's Birth**   Genesis 18-21
    God's judgment and faithfulness.

22. **Abraham's Sacrifice**   Genesis 22
    The Prophet Abraham pictures and predicts the Redeemer's
    greater Sacrifice. Jesus the Messiah fulfills it.

#5 – JACOB AND JOSEPH

23. **Esau and Jacob: The Temporal and the Eternal**   Genesis 25
    Eternal values.

24. **Jacob Becomes Israel**   Genesis 28-32
    The Ladder. Man's failure. God's faithfulness.

25. **Joseph's Humiliation**   Genesis 37-39
    Joseph: walked with God. No one can serve two masters.

26. **Joseph's Exaltation**   Genesis 40-42
    Joseph: a picture of the promised Redeemer.

27. **Joseph: The Rest of the Story**   Genesis 42-50
    God's sovereignty. Death's certainty.

28. **Review of the First Book of the Torah**   Genesis 1-50; Exodus 1
    God's perfect plan.

#6 – THE PROPHET MOSES

29. **The Prophet Moses**   Exodus 1-2
    Moses' birth. God's greatness, mercy, and faithfulness.

30. **Moses Meets God**   Exodus 3-4
    God reveals His awesome character (holy, faithful, merciful)
    and His unique Name.

31. **Pharaoh: Who Is the LORD?**   Exodus 4-7
    Religion v. relationship. Do not harden your heart.

32. **The Plagues**   Exodus 7-10
    Satan's imitations and limitations. The folly of fighting
    against God's word.

33. **The Passover Lamb**   Exodus 11-12
    The value of the blood of the sacrificial lamb. The Redeemer.

34. **A Path Through the Sea**   Exodus 13-15
    Man is helpless to save himself. God's salvation.

#7 – GOD'S HOLY LAW

35. **Food in the Desert** Exodus 16-17
Man's unbelief. God's goodness. The Bread of life.

36. **Fiery Mount Sinai** Exodus 19-20
Man's presumption. God's blazing holiness.

37. **Ten Holy Commandments** Exodus 20
The Ten Commandments interpreted: Guilty!

38. **Purpose of the Commandments** Exodus 20
God's X-Ray. Man's sin. Way of forgiveness.

39. **Broken Commandments** Exodus 32
The Golden Calf. Vain religion. True worship.

40. **The Tent of Meeting** Exodus 24-40; Leviticus 16
God's holiness and way of salvation portrayed.

#8 – ISRAEL'S UNFAITHFULNESS AND GOD'S FAITHFULNESS

41. **The Israelites' Unbelief** Numbers 13-14
Leviticus condensed. Sin of unbelief and its result.

42. **The Bronze Snake** Numbers 20-21
Sin's penalty. God's remedy: Look and live.

43. **Moses' Final Message** Deuteronomy
Brief review of the Torah. Moses' final exhortations.
The Greater Prophet.

44. **Joshua and the Land of Canaan** Joshua
God's faithfulness. Believing God and His word.

45. **Judges and Ruth** Judges; Ruth
The choice: God's Way or man's religion?

#9 – THE PROPHET DAVID

46. **Samuel, Saul, and David** 1 Samuel 1-16; Psalm 8, 23
God looks at the heart.

47. **David and Goliath** 1 Samuel 17; Psalm 27
The need to know God personally.

48. **King David and God's Promise** 1 Samuel 18–2 Samuel 7
David's Eternal Kingdom.

49. **David and Bathsheba**   2 Samuel 11-12; Psalm 51, 32
    David's sin and repentance. God's forgiveness.

50. **The Prophet David and the Messiah**   Psalms 1-2
    Prophesied: Messiah, King, Son of God.

51. **More from the Psalms**   Psalms 22,16
    Prophesied: Messiah's crucifixion and resurrection.

#10 – THE PROPHET SOLOMON TO THE PROPHET ISAIAH

52. **The Prophet Solomon**   1 Kings 2-10; Psalm 72
    Seeking the One who is greater than Solomon.

53. **The Prophet Elijah**   1 Kings 6-18
    The choice: Empty religion or the living God.

54. **The Prophet Jonah**   Jonah
    Salvation is from God. No favoritism with God. Man's choice.

55. **The Prophet Isaiah**   Isaiah
    Prophecies of Messiah's Person and Work.
    Bad news and Good News.

#11 – THE PROPHET JEREMIAH TO THE PROPHET MALACHI

56. **The Prophet Jeremiah**   Jeremiah
    God's prophet rejected. False prophets believed. Captivity.

57. **The Prophet Daniel**   Daniel 1,6
    Daniel's prophecies. Sincere faith. Fear God, not man.

58. **The Prophet Zechariah**   Ezra, Zechariah
    Messianic prophecies. Heed the prophets' message.

59. **The Message of the Prophets Summarized**   Malachi
    Review: God, Man, Messiah. The New Covenant foretold.

#12 – THE MESSIAH'S ARRIVAL

60. **The Prophet John**   Luke 1
    Why an Old & a New Testament? Why four Gospels?
    Introduction to the Injil.

61. **The Announcement**   Luke 1: Matthew 1
    His name: Jesus. Why is He called the Son of God?

62. **The Messiah's Birth**   Luke 2: Matthew 2
More than a prophet. No one born like Him.

63. **The Holy Son**   Luke 2, Matthew 3-4
His sinless nature. His distinction as the Son of God.

#13 – THE MESSIAH'S WORKS AND WORDS

64. **The Lamb of God**   John 1
John's testimony of Jesus. John's distinction as a great prophet.

65. **The Great Healer**   Mark 1-2
Jesus' power and authority. Sin, the worst disease.

66. **The Great Teacher**   Matthew 5-7
The unparalleled Sermon on the Mount.

67. **You Must Be Born Again**   John 3
God requires a pure heart. Mere religion will not suffice.

68. **The Savior of the World**   John 4; Luke 4
Accepting and rejecting the Messiah.

69. **Jesus' Authority**   Matthew 12; John 5
To believe Jesus is to believe the prophets.

#14 – THE MESSIAH'S POWER AND GLORY

70. **Jesus' Power**   Mark 4-6; Matthew 9-10
The Messiah's Deity. No need to fear the spirits.

71. **Two Important Parables**   Luke 8; Matthew 13
Man's heart condition. Coming Judgment.

72. **The Bread of Life**   Mark 6; John 6
Only Jesus can satisfy the hungry soul.

73. **Jesus Causes Division**   Matthew 15-16; John 7
Jesus v. religion. On whose side are you?

74. **The Light of the World**   John 8-9
The religious experts and the blind man.
The worst kind of blindness.

75. **The Lord of Glory**   Matthew 16-17
Who is Jesus? Son of God. Why did He come?

#15 – THE MESSIAH'S WISDOM AND MISSIONS

76. **The Good Shepherd** John 10
    Jesus: One with God; the Door and the Good Shepherd.

77. **The Heart of God** Luke 18, 15
    Two Parables: God's mercy is for the repentant. Slave or Son?

78. **The Resurrection and the Life** John 11-12
    Many believe. The religious leaders plot.

79. **Jesus Enters Jerusalem** Luke 18-20, etc.
    Jesus' approaching death. Warnings.

80. **Hard and True Words** Matthew 22-25
    Jesus' wisdom and warnings. End times.

81. **The Last Supper** Matthew 26
    The bread and the cup. The infinite value of Jesus' blood.

#16 – THE MESSIAH'S SACRIFICE AND CONQUEST

82. **Jesus is Arrested** John 14; Matthew 26
    Comforter promised. Why Jesus gave Himself up.

83. **Jesus is Condemned** Matthew 26-27; John 18-19
    Jesus tried and tortured.

84. **It is Finished!** Matthew 27; Mark 15; Luke 23; John 19
    "It is finished!"

85. **Jesus is Risen!** Matthew 28; Luke 24; John 20
    The tomb is empty: Jesus is who He claimed to be.

#17 – GOOD NEWS

86. **Jesus Ascends to Heaven** Matthew 28; Luke 24; Acts 1
    Christ's absolute authority.

87. **The Holy Spirit has Come!** Acts 1- 2
    Who is the Holy Spirit? The Gospel preached.

88. **Jesus is Coming Back!** Revelation 19-22
    Will Jesus Christ be your Savior or Judge?

89. **The Good News**
    The Gospel of God. You can know you are saved.
    Personal testimony.

Appendix D
Insights Into Islam

Muslims My Friends

With so much media attention given to radical, violent Muslim groups,[1] we need to remind ourselves that most Muslims are friendly, hospitable, peace-loving people. They are my neighbors and dear friends. In general, I feel more comfortable speaking with Muslims about the things of God than with secularized Americans. Unlike many in the West, most Muslims fear God, sense His impending judgment, and are willing to talk about God and the prophets. For those unfamiliar with a Muslim's beliefs and practices, the following observations may be helpful.

Islam, Muslims and Allah

Islam is the religion of Muslims. The Arabic word *Islam* means *submission*. *Muslim* means *one who submits*. *Allah* is the Arabic word for *God* (literally: *the God*). Before Islam, Arab Jews and Christians used it. To this day Arabic-speaking Christians use it. In Arabic Bibles, *Allah* is the generic term for "God." A transliteration of John 3:16 begins: *"Li-annhu haakadha ahabba **Allahu**…."*

Islam's fundamental concept of God is that God is one (*tawhid*). God is great, indescribable, almighty, and compassionate – especially to Muslims. Everything that happens in the world has been predetermined by God. Muslims believe that God has revealed His will but not Himself to humankind. Muslims view their relationship to God as a slave-master relationship, with no possibility of the more intimate son-father relationship.

---

1 Note: this article by the author was written in 1998, pre-9-11, 2001.

Five Pillars

Muslims around the world find themselves in widely differing socio-economic-cultural circumstances – ranging from the wealth of the Persian Gulf to the rural farmlands of West Africa. While local culture and perspectives affect Muslim beliefs (see note in the original preface under the subtitle *The Very Religious Wolofs*), all Muslims assent in one way or another to Islam's Five Pillars. Most Muslims believe that they must fulfill these five duties to atone for their sins and merit a place in paradise.

The Five Pillars of Islam are:
1.) The Witness (*Shahada*): *La illaha illa Allah, wa Mohammed Rasul Allah.* "There is no god but God, and Muhammad is the prophet of God."

2.) Ritual Prayers (*Salat*): Five times daily at hours specified, in the Arabic language, facing toward Mecca, preceded by a ceremonial washing of face, hands and feet.

3.) Alms (*Zakat*): Sharing 2.5% of one's wealth with those in need.

4.) Annual Fast (*Saum*): An obligatory, dawn-to-dusk, month-long fast which takes place during Ramadan, the ninth month on the Islamic lunar calendar.

5.) Pilgrimage to Mecca (*Hajj*): Required of all able-bodied Muslims who can afford it, at least once in a lifetime.

The Prophets and the Qur'an

Most Muslims profess belief in the prophets of the Bible. The Qur'an names more than twenty Bible prophets, including Abraham (*Ibrahim*), Moses (*Musa*), David (*Dawud*), John the Baptist (*Yahya*) and Jesus the Messiah (*Isa al Masih*). Muslims consider Muhammad (born in Mecca in AD 570 and buried in Medina in AD 632) to be the last and greatest prophet.

Muslims maintain that God revealed His will through four holy books: the Torah (*Tawrat*) of Moses, the Psalms (*Zabur*) of David, the Gospel (*Injil*) of Jesus, and the Qur'an (also spelled *Koran*) of Muhammad. Many Muslims assert that the Qur'anic revelation annuls the earlier revelations, but this assertion has no clear support from the Qur'an. They believe that Muhammad (who, it is said, never learned to read or write) received the Qur'anic verses over more than two decades from the angel Gabriel in a desert cave near Mecca. Muhammad recited the verses to his followers, who wrote them down. Years after Muhammad's death, these verses were collected into a single book known as *the Qur'an*, which means *recitation*.

The Qur'an has 114 chapters (*suras*) and is about two-thirds the length of the New Testament. Muslims venerate the Qur'an and are profoundly affected by its Arabic language and poetic style. Though most Muslims have never read the entire Qur'an, both it and the *Hadith* (records of the words and actions of Muhammad) are their point of reference for every area of life: religion, family, health, ethics, economics and politics. Like the Bible, the Qur'an affirms the reality of God and Satan, angels and evil spirits, a coming day of resurrection and judgment, a hell to shun and a paradise to gain. But the similarity ends there. The Qur'an's descriptions and definitions of these realities differ greatly from those recorded by the biblical prophets.

God

The Qur'an presents God as a single entity. *Say not, "Three." Forbear, it will be better for you. God is only one God! Far be it from His glory that He should have a son!* (4:172) [Note: "4:172" means chapter 4 and verse 172 of the Qur'an. However, the verse may be as many as five verses away in different versions and translations of the Qur'an.] This and other Qur'anic verses (e.g. 5:116), combined with the Roman Catholic Church's unscriptural practice of praying to Mary, have caused many Muslims to think that Christians believe in three gods: God, Mary, and Jesus. This is a serious misunderstanding of what a true follower of Jesus believes. The Bible says: **For there is one God, and one mediator between God and men, the man Christ Jesus.** (1 Timothy 2:5)

The Bible clearly condemns polytheism and idolatry, and consistently confirms the oneness of God, declaring: **"You shall worship the Lord your God, and you shall serve him only."** (Matthew 4:10)

The LORD is our God. The LORD is ONE.[2] (Deuteronomy 6:4,13; Mark 12:29) Oneness, however, does not preclude dimension and depth. The Qur'an presents God as unknowable and one-dimensional. The Bible reveals God as self-revealing and tri-dimensional-Eternal Father, Eternal Son and Eternal Holy Spirit.

Satan, Sin and Mankind

The Qur'an teaches that Satan became the Devil (*Iblis*) when he stubbornly refused to bow down to Adam at God's command. (7:11-18) Adam is said to have been in a heavenly Paradise before he ate the forbidden fruit. After Adam transgressed, God sent him down to earth. The Qur'an views Adam's disobedience as a minor slip rather than a major fall. According to many Qur'anic scholars, all Adam had to do to get back into God's favor was to learn and recite certain prayers. (7:18-30; 2:30-40) While the Bible portrays God as absolutely holy and man as totally depraved, the Qur'an portrays man as weak and misguided. In the Muslim view, man does not need redemption, he only needs some guidance so that he might develop the inherently pure nature with which the Creator has endowed him. If he will be faithful in his prayers, almsgiving and fasting, God is likely to overlook his sins and usher him into Paradise, a garden of sensual delights.

Jesus

Every Muslim professes to believe in *Isa* (Qur'anic name for Jesus). They believe that Jesus is one of 124,000 prophets, that he was sent uniquely to the Jews, that he denied the Trinity, that he predicted the coming of Muhammad, that he was not the Son of God and that he was not crucified. The Bible calls such a Jesus *another Jesus.* (2 Corinthians 11:4)

2 In the original language, the Hebrew word used for ONE is *echad,* meaning *a compound unity* (as in *one cluster of grapes*). In eternity, before creating angels or humans, God enjoyed a relationship of love and communication within Himself – with His Word and Holy Spirit. Even when He alone existed He was never alone. God is love. Love requires an object.

The Qur'anic profile of Jesus presents Muslims with a difficult paradox. While certain verses declare that Jesus was *no more than a prophet,* (4:171-173; 5:75; 2:136) others ascribe to him characteristics and titles never attributed to any other prophet. For example, the Qur'an affirms that Jesus was born of a virgin, that he was righteous and holy, and that he possessed the power to create life, open the eyes of the blind, cleanse the lepers, and raise the dead. (3:45-51; 5:110-112; 19:19) Furthermore, the Qur'an calls him the Messiah (*Al Masih*), the Word of God (*Kalimat Allah*) and the Spirit [Soul] of God (*Ruh Allah*). (4:171,172) These supernatural descriptions and titles have caused many Muslims to seek the truth about who Jesus really is.

One day, a devout Muslim man said to me, "The Qur'an calls Jesus *Ruh Allah.* If Jesus is the Soul of God, then He must be God!" This Muslim was beginning to grasp one of the most basic truths of Holy Scripture – not that a man became a god, but that God became a man in order to reveal Himself to the children of Adam and save them from their sins. Some time later, at the cost of being cast out by his family, this same Muslim boldly acknowledged Jesus as his Savior and Lord.

The Son of God

The ultimate sin in Islam is *"shirk"* (Arabic for *association*). *Shirk* is the sin of regarding anything or anyone as equal to God. The Qur'an rejects Jesus' title: *Son of God. They say: "Allah has begotten a son. God forbid!"* (2:116; 10:68) *Say: "If the Lord of Mercy had a son, I would be the first to worship him."* (43:81; 4:172; 5:72.73)

Unfortunately, most Muslims interpret Jesus title "Son of God" in a carnal sense. They understand the term to mean that God took a wife and had a son by her. In several *Way of Righteousness* lessons (including #50, 61, 63, 75, 90, and 99), we explain from the Bible why the prophets, the angels, and God Himself call Jesus *the Son of God*. These simple explanations have helped many Muslims so that they no longer say, *"Astaghferullah!"* ("God forgive you for this blasphemy!") when they hear Jesus called by His rightful title: *The Son of God.*

The Bible gives at least three reasons why Jesus is called *the Son of God*. Interestingly, the Qur'an contains verses that appear to affirm all three reasons.

1.) The Bible calls Jesus the Son of God because *He came from God*. (Isaiah 7:14; Luke 1:34,35) Similarly, the Qur'an teaches that Jesus came directly from God, that He was born of a virgin, that He had no earthly father. (3:47; 19:20) Also, the Qur'an sets Jesus apart from all other prophets by calling Him *the Messiah (the Anointed One)*. (4:157,171,172) Unlike Adam, who was formed from dust, the Messiah came from Heaven.

2.) The Bible calls Jesus the Son of God because *He is like God*. He has God's holy and sinless character and all of God's mighty attributes. Like Father, like Son. (Hebrews 1:1-9; Matthew 17:5) The Qur'an calls Jesus *a holy son*. (19:19; 3:46) While the Qur'an speaks of the other prophets' need of forgiveness, (38:24; 48:1) it never attributes a single sin to Jesus. Also, it ascribes to Jesus supernatural powers that God alone possesses. (3:45-51; 5:110-112)

3.) The Bible calls Jesus the Son of God because *He is One with God*. He is the Eternal Word who was in the beginning with God. (John 1:1-18; Philippians 2:5-11) Similarly, the Qur'an calls Jesus *the Word of God* and *the Soul/Spirit of God*. (4:171,172) Just as, in some mysterious way, a person is one with his words, spirit, and soul, so God and Christ are eternally One.

A question I like to ask my Muslim friends is, "I know that you have been taught that it is impossible for Almighty God to live on earth as a man, but just try to imagine for a moment that He actually wanted to be born into our world as a human in order to reveal His extravagant love to mankind. If God were to do so, how might that man be different from Jesus the Messiah, the Son of God?"

The Cross

All the prophets of the Bible, in one way or another, foretold the Messiah's sacrificial death. But the Qur'an says: *They denied the truth and uttered a monstrous falsehood against Mary. They declared:*

"We have put to death the Messiah, Jesus the son of Mary, the apostle of Allah." They did not kill him, nor did they crucify him, but it appeared so to them. (4:157) While Qur'anic scholars interpret this verse in various ways, most Muslims fervently deny the historical and Scriptural records concerning Jesus' death on the cross. They believe it inappropriate that a great prophet like Jesus should die such a shameful death. Thus Muslims dismiss the central message of the prophets of the Bible – that Jesus the Messiah *willingly* offered Himself as the final sacrifice to pay the sin-debt of the world **"that the Scriptures of the prophets might be fulfilled."** (Matthew 26:56)

The Qur'an omits the Good News of atonement through Jesus' shed blood by which God **might himself be just, and the justifier of him who has faith in Jesus.** (Romans 3:26) The Muslim sees no need for the sin-bearing death of the sinless Messiah. The Qur'an says: *No soul shall bear another's burden.* (6:164; 17:14-16; 39:7) Islam teaches that God excuses sin based on man's repentance and good works. (42:26,31; 39:54,55) The Qur'an bases salvation on what man can do for God. The Bible bases salvation on what God has done for man, saying, **not by works of righteousness which we did ourselves, but according to his mercy, he saved us.** (Titus 3:5)

Islam's Sacrifice

While Islam denies the Messiah's death on the cross, it faithfully commemorates an Old Testament sacrifice which prefigured the Messiah's sacrificial death. Every year, on the tenth day of the last month of the Islamic calendar, Muslims celebrate the Feast of Sacrifice (*Id al-Adha*). On this day Muslims around the world slay carefully selected rams (or lambs, male goats, cows or camels) in commemoration of the ram that God provided on the mountain to die in the place of the prophet Abraham's son. Tragically however, they overlook the fact that, about 2000 years after God provided the ram for Abraham, He fulfilled the symbolism of Abraham's sacrifice. For on the same mountain range (not far from where the Dome of the Rock is located today), Jesus the Messiah willingly shed His righteous blood as God's sufficient and final payment for sin. And three days later God raised Jesus from the dead – the triumphant Savior and Lord of all who believe.

Through Jesus' voluntary substitutionary sacrifice, God has revealed His great love and mercy to humankind. The Messiah's death and resurrection perfectly fulfilled God's plan of salvation about which the prophets had written, thus eliminating the need for continuing animal sacrifices. Yet millions persist in sacrificing animals while ignoring the purpose, meaning, and fulfilment of the animal sacrifice.

The Qur'an & the Bible

Many are surprised to learn that the Qur'an commands Muslims to believe the Torah, the Psalms and the Gospel. The Qur'an says:

> *If you are in doubt concerning what we revealed to you, then question those who read the Scripture that was before you.* (10:94)

> *We sent down the Torah in which there is guidance and light.* (5:44)

> *We have revealed to you as we revealed to Noah and the prophets after him, and as we revealed to Abraham, Ishmael, Isaac, Jacob, and the tribes; to Jesus, Job, Jonah, Aaron, Solomon and David, to whom we gave the Psalms.* (4:163)

> *We sent forth Jesus, the son of Mary, to follow in the footsteps of the prophets, confirming the Torah which was before him, and we gave him the Gospel with its guidance and light, confirmatory of the preceding Torah; a guidance and warning to those who fear God. Therefore let the people of the Gospel judge according to what God has sent down therein. Evildoers are those that do not judge according to God's revelations.* (5:46)

> *Those who treat the Book, and the message we have sent through our apostles, as a lie, will know the truth hereafter: when, with chains and collars around their necks, they shall be dragged through scalding water and burned in the fire of hell.* (40:71)

The Qur'an contains dozens of similar verses.

The Dilemma

Such Qur'anic verses confront sincere Muslims with a serious dilemma: How can one accept both the Bible and the Qur'an when they clearly contradict each other? Furthermore the Qur'an emphasizes the high risk involved: to treat any of the writings of the prophets as a lie is to be *burned in the fire of hell.* Many attempt to resolve their dilemma by contending that the original Bible has been lost or falsified and is no longer reliable. Yet this explanation does not satisfy those who know their Qur'an, which says: *The word of God shall never change. That is the supreme triumph.* (10:64) *None can change the decrees of God.* (6:34) The Qur'an claims that it was given to confirm and guard the preceding Scriptures. Muslims must ask themselves, "Would the Qur'an confirm a corrupted, unreliable book?"

Some suggest that Christians and Jews falsified the Bible after the time of Muhammad. This argument is disproved by the fact that today's Bibles are translated from ancient manuscripts which date to a time long before Muhammad. The Bible we are reading today is in harmony with the Bible of Muhammad's time. *Allahu Akbar!* God is great and has preserved His eternal word for every generation.

Those who read the Bible with a desire to understand it will discover that it defends itself. The best defense is a good offense. **The word of God which lives and remains forever** presents an awesome offense. **All flesh is like grass, and all of man's glory like the flower in the grass. The grass withers, and its flower falls; but the Lord's word endures forever.** (1 Peter 1:24-25)

The Way of Righteousness

Wolofs say: *Truth is a hot pepper* and *Whoever wants honey must brave the bees.* Similarly, the penetrating power of God's Truth and the everlasting sweetness of God's Way of righteousness make going after it worth every possible risk – even ostracism, persecution, and physical death.

The prophet Solomon wrote: **In the way of righteousness is life (a relationship with God); in its path there is no death (separation from God).** (Proverbs 12:28) Does this claim sound too good to be true? Friends, with God, nothing is too good to be true. *Allahu Akbar!* God is greater than anything you or I can imagine.

To all who submit to The LORD God's way of righteousness He promises to give freely that which religion can never provide: Salvation from the penalty and power of sin, a credited righteousness, assurance of sins forgiven, a cleansed conscience, a deep peace, an untouchable joy, a new nature, a personal relationship with God Himself, an eternal home with Him in Paradise, and infinitely more of the things which **God has prepared for those who love Him.** (1 Corinthians 2:9)

To all who have read or heard these one hundred lessons, we commit you to God, the Compassionate, the Merciful, the Righteous, who extends this life-giving and life-transforming promise to all who will claim it:

> **You shall seek me, and find me,**
> **when you search for me with all your heart.**
> (Jeremiah 29:13)

> **Blessed are those who hunger and thirst**
> **for righteousness, for they shall be filled.**
> (Matthew 5:6)

Appendix E
ROCK Resources

Some of the languages you'll find:

• English • Adyghe • Albanian • Arabic • Iraqi Arabic
• Lebanese Arabic • Moroccan Arabic • Bambara • Bengali
• Bengali • Borana • chiChewa • chiYao • Chinese • Dari • Dutch
• Farsi • French • Fulfulde • German • Haitian Creole
• Hassaniya • Hausa • Hindi • Indonesian • Kanuri Manga
• Karakalpak • Kashmiri • Kazakh • Korean • Kotokoli Tem
• Kurdish Sorani • Kyrgyz • Malayalam • Maninka
• Mongolian • Moore • Nahuatl • Nubian • Pashto • Pulaar
• Pular • Russian • Serer • Somali • Spanish • Swedish
• Swahili • Tajik • Tamajeq • Telugu • Turkish • Turkmen • Urdu
• Uyghur • Uzbek • Wolof • Yakan • Zarma • And many more

**For free downloads of all ROCK International
multi-language multi-media tools visit:**

www.rockintl.org/resources

[1] 70-SCENE PICTURE BOOK

With plain yet profound text alongside 70 beautiful and biblically accurate paintings, this panoramic journey through the Scriptures of the prophets tells and explains God's story and message in a way that makes sense. KING of GLORY helps people of all ages and cultures to connect the dots of Scripture, see the Bible as ONE BOOK and ONE STORY, and fall in love with the King.

"It has a way of explaining difficult concepts in elementary terms without talking down to people. It is such a gift!"
— Donna, Retired University Professor

[2] 15-EPISODE MOVIE

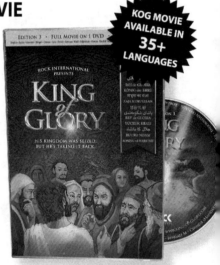

KOG MOVIE AVAILABLE IN 35+ LANGUAGES

Grouping the 70 scenes into 15 episodes, this animated, word-for-word, 222-minute rendition of the picture book lets you meet the King of the universe, experience His story, and understand His plan to rescue His rebel subjects from the kingdom of darkness and make them fit to live forever with Him in His kingdom of light, happily ever after. For real.

"I was able to dive in with all my emotions. I experienced the story like I was actually there!" — Lydia, College Student

www.KING-of-GLORY.com

[3] 15-LESSON STUDY GUIDE & ANSWER KEY

Filled with graphics from the movie and book, and a touch of geographical and archeological info, this Illustrated Study Guide reinforces the foundational truths about God, man, sin, and salvation embedded in the KING of GLORY story, from Genesis to Revelation, from creation to Christ to new creation.

"I learned so many things I never thought of before. I teared up a few times too!"
— Jodi, mature believer & mother of 3

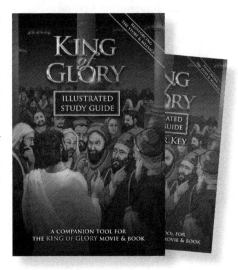

[4] 70-SCENE COLORING BOOK

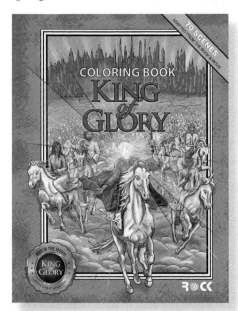

Rounding out the KING of GLORY curriculum, this is for all ages and skill levels. Each detailed line drawing is on a single-sided, perforated, 8.5 x 11 page. Great with colored pencils and felt-tip pens, but works with crayons too.

"The kids love the beautiful, detailed pictures. Today about twenty children were at my gate asking to color. Small groups of 4 or 5 are best for listening quietly to the Zarma KING of GLORY movie as they color."
—Ruth, Niger, West Africa

ONE GOD ONE MESSAGE

Weaving together real-life stories, e-mails from skeptics, and a cliché-free, mind-bending, three-stage chronological journey through history's best loved and most despised story, this 30-chapter (or 30-day) adventure of discovery helps truth-seekers over their obstacles and offers a framework for rethinking life's greatest questions.

"After reading this book, the logic in the Bible makes sense and clicks in my mind. It has created an interest in me to read the Bible."
— Muhammad, Middle East

YOUR STORY BOOKLET

This 40-minute read offers a panoramic view of the world's bestseller, and shows how your own story can be forever linked to your Creator's story. A powerful summary of the best story and message ever told.

"I am pleased that there is now a booklet that lays out a clear narrative presentation of the gospel from beginning to end."
— Ken, North Carolina

For free downloads of all of ROCK International multi-language multi-media visit:

www.KING-of-GLORY.com

THE WAY OF RIGHTEOUSNESS RADIO BROADCASTS

The Way of Righteousness is an English translation of one hundred 15-minute radio programs first written in the Wolof language of Senegal, West Africa. With Islam's worldview in mind, this chronological series presents the key stories and central message of God's prophets according to the biblical Scriptures.

All 100 programs are interconnected, yet each stands alone, challenging listeners to consider the only way of salvation that satisfies both the sinner's desperate need and the LORD God's uncompromising righteousness.

"I was impressed by the title of your program, THE WAY OF RIGHTEOUSNESS, and listened to it from beginning to end. It's a shame that the time is so short for something so important!" — Muslim School Teacher in Senegal, 1992

WHAT IF JESUS MEANT WHAT HE SAID?

What if Jesus' words were never intended to fit into your existing lifestyle? What if they were meant to change everything? What if Jesus never wanted to be a mere part of your life? What if He wants it all? Instead of offering easy answers, these pages ask difficult questions, with life-altering implications.

"Powerful. Challenging. You can't read this book and remain the same."
— Amazon Review

www.rockintl.org

NOTES

NOTES

NOTES

NOTES